Lecture Notes in Computer

Edited by G. Goos, J. Hartmanis, and

T0237768

Springer

Berlin
Heidelberg
New York
Barcelona
Hong Kong
London
Milan
Paris
Tokyo

Alberto Sangiovanni-Vincentelli
Joseph Sifakis (Eds.)

Embedded Software

Second International Conference, EMSOFT 2002
Grenoble, France, October 7-9, 2002
Proceedings

 Springer

Series Editors

Gerhard Goos, Karlsruhe University, Germany
Juris Hartmanis, Cornell University, NY, USA
Jan van Leeuwen, Utrecht University, The Netherlands

Volume Editors

Alberto Sangiovanni-Vincentelli
University of California at Berkeley, Department of EECS
Berkeley, CA 94720, USA
E-mail: alberto@eecs.berkeley.edu

Joseph Sifakis
Verimag, Centre Equation
2 rue de Vignate, 38610 Gieres, France
E-mail: Joseph.Sifakis@imag.fr

Cataloging-in-Publication Data applied for

Die Deutsche Bibliothek - CIP-Einheitsaufnahme

Embedded software : second international conference ; proceedings / EMSOFT
2002, Grenoble, France, October 7 - 9, 2002. Alberto Sangiovanni-Vincentelli ;
Joseph Sifakis (ed.). - Berlin ; Heidelberg ; New York ; Hong Kong ; London ;
Milan ; Paris ; Tokyo : Springer, 2002
   (Lecture notes in computer science ; Vol. 2491)
   ISBN 3-540-44307-X

CR Subject Classification (1998): C.3, D.1-4, F.3

ISSN 0302-9743
ISBN 3-540-44307-X Springer-Verlag Berlin Heidelberg New York

Springer-Verlag Berlin Heidelberg New York
a member of BertelsmannSpringer Science+Business Media GmbH

http://www.springer.de

© Springer-Verlag Berlin Heidelberg 2002
Printed in Germany

Typesetting: Camera-ready by author, data conversion by Olgun Computergrafik
Printed on acid-free paper   SPIN 10870669   06/3142   5 4 3 2 1 0

Preface

The purpose of the EMSOFT Workshop, inaugurated last year at Lake Tahoe, is to bring together researchers and practitioners interested in the foundations and methods of embedded software design with the goal of improving substantially the state of the art and stimulating the debate between researchers and designers. The scope of the EMSOFT Workshop spans all aspects of embedded software, including operating systems and middleware, programming languages and compilers, modeling and validation, software engineering and programming methodologies, scheduling and execution-time analysis, formal methods, communication protocols and fault tolerance.

While the first Workshop included only invited papers because of the need to establish a common framework and a basis for the scientific contributions, for this second EMSOFT, we attempted to strike a balance between invited and selected contributions. The program included 17 selected and 13 invited contributions. The invited speakers were: Giorgio Buttazzo (University of Pavia), Paolo Faraboschi (Hewlett-Packard Laboratories), Nicolas Halbwachs (Verimag), David Harel (Weizmann Institute), Christoph Kirsch (University of California at Berkeley), Luciano Lavagno (Politecnico di Torino and Cadence Research Labs), Nancy Leveson (MIT), Sharad Malik (Princeton), Al Mok (University of Texas at Austin), Amir Pnueli (Weizmann Institute), Lui Sha (University of Illinois at Urbana-Champaign), Douglas Schmidt (University of California at Irvine), and Bran Selic (Rational).

The program covers a wide variety of topics including requirements description and modeling, validation and analysis, synchronous languages, scheduling, real-time architectures and middleware, compilation and implementation, computerized control, and dependability. EMSOFT was colocated with CASES 2002 (International Conference on Compilers, Architectures and Synthesis for Embedded Systems), and to enhance interaction between the respective communities CASES and EMSOFT organized two joint invited sessions. The CASES invited speakers at the joint sessions were: John Rayfield (ARM Ltd.), Giovanni De Micheli (Stanford University), and Jens Palsberg (Purdue University).

The members of the EMSOFT Steering Committee were: Gerard Berry (Esterel Technologies), Tom Henzinger (Stanford University), Hermann Kopetz (TU Vienna), Edward Lee (UC Berkeley), Ragunathan Rajkumar (Carnegie Mellon University), Alberto Sangiovanni-Vincentelli (UC Berkeley), Douglas Schmidt (Washington University), Joseph Sifakis (Verimag), and John Stankovic (University of Virginia).

The EMSOFT 2002 Program Committee this year was: Rajeev Alur (University of Pennsylvania), Gerard Berry (Esterel Technologies), Manfred Broy (Technical University of Munich), Tom Henzinger (University of California at Berkeley),

Kevin Jeffay (University of North Carolina), Hermann Kopetz (Technical University of Vienna), Edward Lee (University of California at Berkeley), Sang Lyul Min (Seoul National University), Martin Rinard (MIT), John Rushby (SRI), Alberto Sangiovanni-Vincentelli (University of California at Berkeley), Shankar Sastry (University of California at Berkeley), Joseph Sifakis (Verimag), John Stankovic (University of Virginia), Lothar Thiele (ETH), Reinhard Wilhelm (Universität des Saarlandes), and Janos Sztipanovits (Vanderbilt University).

We would like to thank the following additional reviewers: Astrit Ademaj, Felice Balarin, Andrea Balluchi, Gunther Bauer, María Victoria Cengarle, Bertrand Delsart, Alberto Ferrari, Romain Guider, Wolfgang Haidinger, Ben Horowitz, Daniel Kaestner, Raimund Kirner, Orna Kupferman, Marc Langenbach, Thomas Losert, Heiko Lötzbeyer, Roman Obermaisser, Paritosh Pandya, Michael Paulitsch, Jan Philipps, Alexander Pretschner, Martin Rappl, Robert Sandner, Marco Sanvido, Joern Schneider, Bernhard Schtz, Katharina Spies, Stephan Thesing, Stavros Tripakis, Sebastian Winkel, and Sergio Yovine.

EMSOFT 2002 was organized by the Verimag laboratory. The Organizing Committee was composed of Joseph Sifakis, Stavros Tripakis, and Sergio Yovine who had the overall responsibility for coordination and helped with the assembly of the final camera-ready copy.

EMSOFT 2002 was held on the premises of the Institut National Polytechnique de Grenoble under the sponsorship of the European Network of Excellence ARTIST, on Advanced Real-Time Systems and received support from the Centre National de la Recherche Scientifique, the Institut National Polytechnique de Grenoble, and Université Joseph Fourier.

July 2002   Alberto Sangiovanni-Vincentelli
                                                                Joseph Sifakis

Table of Contents

Embedded Systems:
Challenges in Specification and Verification*
(An Extended Abstract)

Amir Pnueli

Weizmann Institute of Science
amir@wisdom.weizmann.ac.il

Abstract. In this position paper, we mention some of the challenges in specification and verification which are raised by the emerging discipline of embedded systems. The main proposition of the paper is that a feasible solution to the problem of effective, reliable, and dependable construction of embedded systems can be provided by a *seamless* development process based on a formal specification of the required system, which proceeds by the activities of verification and analysis of the specification at very early stages of the design, and then followed by automatic code generation, preceded if necessary by code distribution and allocation.

As a prototype example of such a development process, we quote some experiences from the *Sacres* project and its follow-up *Safeair*. Necessary extensions to these preliminary experiments are discussed and evaluated.

1 Introduction

Embedded systems are of vital economic importance and are literally becoming ubiquitous. They have already become an integral component of safety critical systems involving aviation, military, telecommunications, and process control applications. Interest in embedded systems is growing further due to the expectation that they will become a key component of many commonplace consumer appliances. Consumers will expect levels of reliability and predictability associated with the very best brands of cars, televisions, and refrigerators. Glitches, crashes, and general erratic behavior of the sort seen with prior generations of consumer PC software products will be unacceptable for these embedded applications. It thus becomes crucial that these embedded software systems satisfy correctness criteria not demanded from today's large software systems, which are often highly error-prone.

While embedded systems have been around for a long time, they were often treated as a second-class citizen. Typically, they were programmed in machine language, ignoring all the exciting developments in programming languages and programming methodology of the last 30 years. They were often implemented

---

* This research was supported in part by the John von Newman Minerva Center for the Verification of Reactive Systems.

A. Sangiovanni-Vincentelli and J. Sifakis (Eds.): EMSOFT 2002, LNCS 2491, pp. 1–14, 2002.

on inferior machines (called micro-controllers rather than top-of-the-line mirco-processors). In case they involved real-time, the very strict and constraining discipline of periodic scheduling was standardly used, as the only allowed mode of work. In fact, in the name of reliability, dependability, and predictability, many modern techniques of programming and optimizing compilation, as well as modern architectural ideas of parallelism and caching have been ruled out as unsuitable for embedded applications.

Many enhancements of diverse technologies are needed in order to make the development and maintenance of embedded systems achieve the required levels of dependability, reliability, and cost-effectiveness. Some of these enhancements involve improvements in hardware implementation and hardware design technologies, introducing new concerns of power consumption, memory size, and customization into the equation, and requiring new methods of optimizing designs across these multiple parameters. Others concentrate on software tools such as languages, specially designed operating systems, compilers, and their optimizing versions. Thus, the emerging field of embedded systems poses many new challenges to various scientific and engineering disciplines.

In this paper, we concentrate on the new challenges and possible impact of the emergence of embedded systems as a new focus of activity on the discipline of formal methods. The first and main question is whether embedded systems raise any new challenges in formal methods, which were not considered before. If we answer this question positively, we need to identify some of these new challenges and, hopefully, indicate directions for appropriate responses to these challenges.

Before answering the main question, we provide some background and examples of historical new challenges in the field of formal method. In the beginning of the 80's, formal verification diverged from the traditional task of verifying sequential programs, and started considering *reactive systems*. With the introduction of temporal logic [Pnu77,Lam83], model checking [CE81,QS83], various process algebras [Hoa78,Mil80], and verification of concurrent programs [OL82], the community of formal methods started specifying and verifying systems which interact with their environments, which is the essence of embedded systems, already quoted at that time as the main motivation for the study of reactive systems. The challenges at that time were to find good ways for specifying and verifying reactive systems, realizing that these must differ from the conventional methods of specifying and verifying sequential programs.

Other significant developments occurred in the beginning of the 90's, when researchers felt the need for extensions of the formal model to deal, first with real time [AH90,ACD90,AD94], and then with hybrid systems which include in the model also the continuous behavior of the environment [MMP92a,NSY92,CRH93] [ACH+95].

One can view these essential developments as building up the theoretical base upon which a viable approach to the formal specification, analysis, and systematic development of embedded systems can be constructed. Therefore, our answer to the question of what are the new theoretical challenges raised by the newly emerging field of embedded systems is that, what we need, is not a new theory of embedded systems. The formal models of reactive, real-time, and hybrid systems provide adequate theoretical support for most of our formal needs. What is required is the integration of the relevant theories and methods into a coherent development process and *making it work*.

The formal methods community has been preaching for a long time about the great advantages which can result from the deployment of formal specification and verification to the development of software systems. In particular, compared to the currently practiced informal methods which rely on testing and simulation for validating the correctness of design and implementation, formal methods have been promising a significant improvement in the quality of design and code and in the time and efforts which need to be spent on development and validation. Since these two factors: quality of product, and time to market, are among the top features which distinguish embedded software from all other run-of-the-mill software products, this is a great opportunity for the formal methods proponents to prove their long stated claims. It seems that this is one of the cases where the market is ready to pay the price if formal methods can deliver the goods.

Based on some of the preceding observations, the reader may falsely conclude that we did not identify any interesting challenges in the fields of specification and verification, resulting from the special needs of embedded systems. This is certainly not the case. In the rest of the paper, we will consider several such challenges.

Besides the requirement of a new standard of functional correctness, embedded systems pose additional challenges which were not fully addressed by previous validation and verification approaches. These include adequate guarantees of:

- Timeliness. It is very important to ensure that responses of an embedded system are properly timed. This includes not only the establishment of upper bounds (which explains the drive towards higher raw performance) but in many cases also proper lower bounds. Applications such as video transmission can perform very poorly if certain operations are executed too early, which may cause the undesired phenomena of jitter (i.e. uncontrolled deviations from precise periodicity) in the transmission.
- Low or controlled power consumption. Many embedded applications rely on battery power. For these, it becomes crucial to design and then validate for controlled power consumption. Modern micro-processors have the capability of shutting off parts of the system to decrease power consumption (and corresponding heat generation). It is essential that modern design and analysis methods address these needs and capabilities.
- Low or controlled memory utilization. In a similar way, many embedded applications are implemented on very small machines with random access memory of limited size. It is necessary to include memory considerations in the design, compilation, and analysis processes which will be applied for the construction of embedded systems.

Furthermore, embedded systems provide additional types of motivation for the application of formal methods. As previously mentioned, in typical applications of safety-critical and real-time systems (and many embedded systems belong to one or both categories), the element of predictability is of utmost importance. The common solution to this constraint has been to exclude from the implementation all elements which can potentially endanger absolute predictability. This usually leads to the employment of inferior architectures, e.g. no parallelism, no caching, no optimizing compilers, and inferior programming methods and languages, e.g., no use of pointers or linked lists. Since in modern embedded systems we would like to have it both ways, i.e., using most recent state-of-the-art architectures and programming methodologies, while still upholding the standard of predictability, it is up to formal verification and analysis to provides the absolute guarantees that a careful use of dynamic resources and programming, can still maintain the timing and memory (possibly also power) constraints required by the application. We strongly believe that this is possible and is one of the most exciting challenges raised by embedded systems. We refer the reader to [LPP01] as an example of an approach to the verification of real-time constraints which may ensure predictable execution of a C program, taking into account the underlying architecture which may contain instruction-level parallelism.

In the rest of the paper, we will talk about the importance of having a *seamless process* for the systematic development of embedded systems, what such a process may include, and which extensions to current technologies are needed. In particular, we will discuss methods for requirement specifications, and ways to extend the current capabilities of formal verification.

2   A Seamless Process for System Development

In order to guarantee the expected order-of-magnitude increase in reliability and dependability of embedded systems, we need an effective and reliable development process that will support a fast turn-around time as well as the ability to produce many customized variations of a product. To obtain the maximal benefits from a rigorous development process, it is essential that this process be *seamless*, starting from requirements and proceeding all the way down into software/hardware implementation, ensuring continuous preservation of the behavior and integrity of the design in each of the development steps.

A significant step towards achieving a similar goal was taken in the European project *Sacrecs* (*Safety Critical Embedded Systems*) [Con95,Ben98]. There, several industrial partners (British Aerospace, Siemens, and Snecma) and several tool vendors (I-Logix, SNI, and TNI) have collaborated with Inria, OFFIS, and the Weizmann Institute of Science, to develop a methodology and tool suite that supports the development of *safety-critical* embedded systems. The inputs to the Sacres system are formal specifications, expressed as a combination of the state-based specification formalism of Statecharts [Har88,HLN+90], or the data-flow specification language Sildex/Signal [BGJ91], and the output is a C or Ada code, that is formally proven to satisfy the specifications.

In Figure (1) we present the plan of the general architecture of the Sacres project.

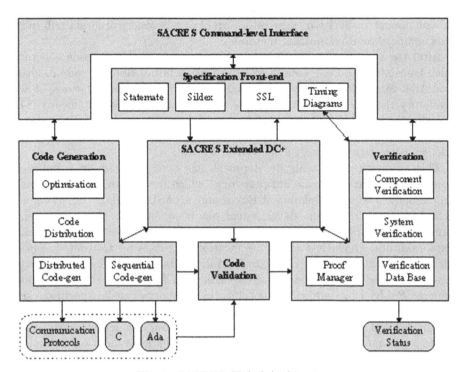

Fig. 1. SACRES Global Architecture

According to the Sacres methodology, development of an (embedded) system starts by the user submitting an (executable) specification written in a combination of the state-based specification language of Statecharts and the data-flow specification language *Sildex*. Typically, Statecharts are used to specify the main operational modes of the system and its response to external events, which may lead to changes in the internal state and generation of response signals and events. The data-flow language Sildex is used to represent computational tasks which manage a continuous control activity such as acquisition of data and signals and continuous outputs which drive external devices. The *System Specification Language* (SSL) is used to define the general system architecture and the association of components with their respective Statecharts/Sildex specification. This combined specification is then translated into a common format called DC+. Validation of the specification is performed by applying simulation and various testing procedures to each of the separate specification components, using the capabilities provided by the Statemate and Sildex tools. Then, we apply formal verification procedures to the combined DC+ specification.

   The formal verification capabilities are partitioned into *component verification* and *system verification*. Component verification analyzes a single unit, using the techniques of symbolic and bounded model checking. The properties to be verified are specified by the visual temporal-requirement language of *symbolic timing diagrams* [DJS94,FJ97]. System verification combines the results of several component verification tasks into a proof of a property of larger sub-units, using *compositional verification* methods.

After the specification is validated, the user may invoke the code generator which translates the DC+ combined specification into a running code in either C or Ada. Since this project was aimed at safety critical applications, it was mandatory that the code generation be validated by independent means. This is accomplished by the *Code Validation* module which reads the DC+ source program and the produced C/Ada code and validates formally that the target code is a correct translation of the source [PSS98].

This approach to systems development has been adopted by a follow-up project *Safeair* (http://www.safeair.org) which focuses on the development of an Avionic System Development Environment (ASDE) [BDL+02]. While the general approach to system development has been retained, there has been a change in the component languages used as specification inputs and for the common format into which the various specification languages are translated. *Safeair* still maintains *Statemate* as the state-(and mode-)based specification language. However, for the data-flow part of the specification ASDE uses the synchronous language *Scade*, while additional specification elements can be specified using the *Simulink* control-oriented package. The various specification languages are coordinated and integrated by the new tool *Model-Build* which translates them all into a common format based on *Scade*. The translation validation technology introduced in *Sacres* has been extended in *Safeair* to conduct also validation of the translation between the resulting C program and the compiled binary code.

The general tenet underlying our position is that the Sacres approach (including variations as illustrated by the *Safeair* follow-up) can be used as a foundation for the proposed seamless development process for embedded systems. With the appropriate adaptations from the domain of safety-critical systems where cost-effectiveness and performance is secondary to an extremely high level of predictability and reliability, into the domain of embedded systems where performance, and time-to-market become paramount while high level of reliability must be maintained, it may be possible to enhance and perfect the seamless development approach into a viable and useful tool for embedded systems. In order to do so, it is necessary to extend the Sacres approach in several significant directions and dimensions.

- The current process starts at the level of executable specifications. This is often too late and does not provide any help for formulating the *requirements* of the system and transforming them in a reliable way into an executable specification. It is necessary to add to the development process a requirement level with tools for validating a user-guided transformation into specification as well as for automatic derivation of such specifications from the requirements.

- An important element which should be added vertically to all phases of the development process is the specification and compliance validation of *real-time* constraints. This involves incorporating a real-time constraint to the requirement and specification languages, enhancing the verification and code-validation techniques to deal with real time, and exploring static analysis techniques to perform some of the task scheduling for real-time systems at compile (and analysis) time.

- Most embedded systems operate, sense, and manipulate continuous environments. In case the close interaction between the program and the environment is crucial for the success of the project, one has to shift to the more elaborate model of *hybrid systems* [MMP92b,KP92,ACH+95,HHWT97,KMP98], which incorporate into the development process elements of requirements, specification, verification, and validation of the continuous environment as well as of the designed system. The project *Safeair* recognized this need and provided a partial solution by adding *Simulink* to the specification inputs.

- Many embedded systems will be implemented on distributed platforms. The approach taken in our proposed development process is that the requirements and specification do not immediately address the issue of distribution. Rather, the system is first specified and validated in its entirety, following which the specification is transformed into a distributed specification while ensuring preservation of its properties. A component for this transformation of *code distribution* already appears in the Sacres plan but, due to budget cuts, was never fully developed. Part of this process will automatically synthesize the necessary communication and coordination protocols between the components.

- The current development process stops at the C level. For modern embedded systems, this has to be extended by a co-design phase in which some of the functionality will be relegated to custom-designed hardware, while the rest may be compiled into a highly optimizing reconfigurable architecture-driven compiler. The code validation tool must be extended to cover this part of the code-generation/compilation.

In Fig. 2 we present the grand view of a seamless development process for the reliable and effective construction of embedded systems. In this diagram, boxes represent processes which perform translation or verification tasks while oval nodes represent description of specification and systems at various level of details. Thus, every box process accepts some oval nodes as inputs and may produce some oval nodes as output.

At the highest level we start with a set of requirements. These may include behavioral requirements in the form of MSC-charts (possibly considering also their extensions into LSC's [DH99]) as well as temporal properties expressed in terms of an appropriate temporal logic. In addition, the requirements specification will include embedded-systems specific constraints such as real-time, power, and memory consumption. The process of *synthesis* will transform some of these requirements into an executable specification, as will be explained in Section 3. Even though the synthesis process is one of the important research topics in the field, we do not realistically expect it to be applicable to large systems in the near future. Therefore our methodology also allows an alternative entry level into the design process by which the user provides her own executable specifica-

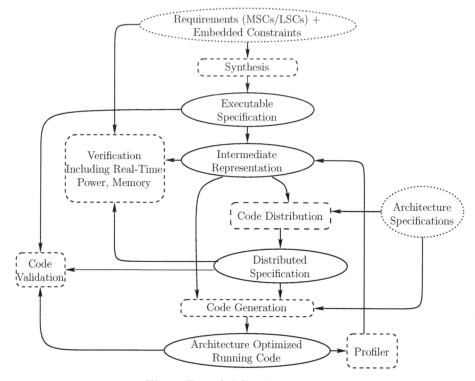

Fig. 2. Extended Seamless Process

tion directly, using the requirement level only for the formulation of properties (functional or quantitative) which will later be verified over the design.

For the representation of executable specification we propose to use a visual formalism such as Statecharts or an appropriate variant thereof. This form of user-friendly executable specification is then transformed into an internal representation which may also contain additional information such as allocation to hardware components, timing, and power/memory parameters associated with each of the modules of the system. In case the system is to be implemented on a distributed architecture, we may apply the processes of "code distribution" to obtain a more detailed "distributed specification". Finally, the process of code generation is applied to any of these executable specification to produce code which is specially optimized to specific architectures and takes into account the three types of embedded constraints (time, power, and memory consumption).

Two additional processes are employed to guarantee the integrity and correctness of the development. The process of verification verifies the executable specification against the high-level requirements which are either behavioral (e.g. temporal properties) or embedded constraints. Since the transformations from the executable specification downwards are all of the form of translations (or compilation), one may apply the technology of "code-validation" [PSS98] for validating the correctness of these translations.

In order to verify the embedded specifications (TPM - time/power/memory) already at the intermediate-representation level, it is necessary to associate the appropriate TPM parameters with code segments at this abstract level. A possible approach to this association is represented by the "Profiling" process which analyzes the machine level code for these architecture-dependent parameters and associates the resulting performance figures with their sources at the intermediate-representation level. To do so, it is necessary to ensure that all the translation processes maintain back-tracking links between code instructions and their sources.

A more detailed description of some of the mentioned extensions follows.

3   From Requirements to Specifications

Unlike specifications, requirements are not expected to provide a comprehensive and integrated description of a system. Rather, the process of *requirement elucidation* is a step-wise process, where each step may involve different formalism, and each *adds* a constraint on the system's behavior. There are several languages that can be used for formal requirements capture: Temporal logic [MP91], Symbolic Timing diagrams [DJS94], and Live Sequence Charts [DH99].

Among these mentioned options it appears that the *Live Sequence Charts* formalism can be adopted as the requirement language of choice. LSC's grew out of the *message sequence charts* language developed as part of the UML standard, when it was realized that MSC's have a too weak expressive power. Typically, an MSC specifies the *possibility* of a certain scenario to be manifested in a given system, but it cannot be used to specify that a certain scenario must never appear in the behavior of a system or that if a prefix of a scenario appears then the scenario must complete. Damm and Harel corrected these deficiencies in the language of Live Sequence Charts which has an expressive power equal to that of the most expressive temporal logics, and appears to enjoy the advantages of a visual specification language.

Following are some of the desired extensions to the requirement component:

3.1   Formulating a Requirement Language
with Real-Time and Hybrid Elements

The requirements language of LSC's should be enriched with annotations for real-time constraints, and hybrid elements. Typically, the hybrid annotation will identify that a certain node (object) is engaged in a particular continuous activity, according to given continuous-change laws, between two events observable in the chart. Starting, ending, and changing the mode of a continuous activity will be events observable in the live chart.

3.2   Extending the Specification Languages

In a corresponding way, the specification languages of Statecharts should be enriched by real-time and hybrid annotations. Even though Statecharts currently have some time-related components, they are mainly programming constructs which allows the specifier to schedule future events and actions based on preset future time triggers. It would be desirable to add time annotations which impose upper and lower bounds on the duration between two identified events in the spirit of [LPP98a] and [LPP98b], where such annotations were applied to C programs.

As to the extension of Statecharts with hybrid components, one may follow the suggestions of [KP92] which associates a continuous activity with every state (basic or compound) of a statechart. This approach generalizes the formalism of hybrid automata [ACHH93] to deal with hierarchical specifications and rich data structures.

With the introduction of the hybrid view into specification, it may also be useful to add *Simulink* as another specification language. Simulink is the language used by many embedded systems developers, in particular in the automotive and avionics industries to represent and simulate the behavior of the continuous components in the system (usually the environment, but also the controllers). One may integrate Simulink as an additional specification language with its code-generation capabilities into the general framework of the seamless development process.

3.3   Verification and Synthesis

Once the user captured the requirement of an embedded system, the process proceeds to derive an executable specification for the system, which can be simulated and validated. The main question is how to ensure the consistency between the requirements and specification. We propose two methods for ensuring this consistency.

1. A first possible approach is based on manual or computer-aided construction of the specification, followed by *formal verification* that the specification satisfies all the requirements. Here one may adopt the general methodology proposed in *Sacres* of partitioning the verification task into *unit verification* which will mainly employ automatic model checking methods (appropriately augmented to deal with the timing and hybrid elements), and *system verification* which will utilize the results of unit verification and combine them, using methods of composition, abstraction, and deduction, to derive properties of larger subsystems.

2. A second possible approach is based on *synthesis* where the requirements are automatically transformed into an executable specification. As basis for synthesis in the presence of real-time and hybridicity one may take the preliminary work done in [AMP95,AMPS98,AM99] and the general approach to synthesis from LSC's started at [HK00] and [HMKT00]. A most exciting recent development is the method of play-in/play-out proposed by Harel and Marelly [Har01,HM01] and described in greater details elsewhere in this volume.

3.4 Verifying for Power and Memory

One of the central challenges in the development of embedded systems is that power and memory consumption become important parameters over which the design has to be optimized. Faithful to the idea that analysis of the design should be carries out as early as possible, one needs ways to verify utilization of these resources already at a high level of the system description. This raises two questions: the first is what is the appropriate formal model by which one may verify continuous resource consumption, and the second is how can one associate basic consumption parameters with elements of a top level design. An example of the second question can be illustrated by asking how much power is consumed by a C assignment statement.

The answer to this question can be provided by a mechanism such as the profiler we included in Fig. 2. By using prototype translations of the high-level design and executing some experimental sample runs, we may be able to accumulate sufficient data that will enable us to back annotate the high-level elements by representative consumption figures. In the long run, it will be useful to develop special rule-based analyzers which can help us to associate consumption figures with high-level design.

As to the first question, i.e. what is an appropriate formal model on which one can base resource utilization verification, we do not have any definite answers yet. A promising direction is that such a model should be based on the formalism of hybrid systems, with which we already have some verification experience. Since the model need not be physically faithful, as long as it can provide good approximation to the accumulated consumption, we have the freedom of choosing a hybrid model which will be most amenable to analysis and verification.

Due to shortage of space, we cannot elaborate here on the other research topics mentioned in the preceding list, but hope to provide more information in a fuller version of this paper.

References

ACD90.   R. Alur, C. Courcoubetis, and D.L. Dill. Model checking for real-time systems. In *Proceedings of the Fifth Annual Symposium on Logic in Computer Science*, pages 414–425. IEEE Computer Society Press, 1990.

ACH+95.   R. Alur, C. Coucoubetis, N. Halbwachs, T.A. Henzinger, P.-H. Ho, A. Olivero, J. Sifakis, and S. Yovine. The algorithmic analysis of hybrid systems. *Theor. Comp. Sci.*, 138(1):3–34, 1995. Special issue on Hybrid Systems.

ACHH93.   R. Alur, C. Courcoubetis, T.A. Henzinger, and P.-H. Ho. Hybrid automata: an algorithmic approach to the specification and verification of hybrid systems. In R.L. Grossman, A. Nerode, A. Ravn, and H. Rischel, editors, *Hybrid Systems*, volume 736 of *Lect. Notes in Comp. Sci.*, pages 209–229. Springer-Verlag, 1993.

AD94.   R. Alur and D.L. Dill. A theory of timed automata. *Theor. Comp. Sci.*, 126:183–235, 1994.

AH90.   R. Alur and T.A. Henzinger. Real-time logics: Complexity and expressiveness. In *Proc. 5th IEEE Symp. Logic in Comp. Sci.*, pages 390–401, 1990. See [AlurHenzinger-LICS90] for Journal Version.

AM99.   E. Asarin and O. Maler. As soon as possible: Time optimal control for
           timed automata. In F. Vaandrager and J. van Schuppen, editors, *Hybrid
           Systems: Computation and Control*, volume 1569 of *Lect. Notes in Comp.
           Sci.*, pages 19–30. Springer-Verlag, 1999.
AMP95.   E. Asarin, O. Maler, and A. Pnueli. Symbolic controller synthesis for dis-
           crete and timed systems. In P. Antsaklis, W. Kohn, A. Nerode, and S. Sas-
           try, editors, *Hybrid System II*, volume 999 of *Lect. Notes in Comp. Sci.*
           Springer-Verlag, 1995.
AMPS98.   E. Asarin, O. Maler, A. Pnueli, and J. Sifakis. Controller synthesis for
           timed automata. In *IFAC Symposium on System Structure and Control*,
           pages 469–474. Elsevier, 1998.
BDL⁺02.   P. Bauferton, F. Dupont, R. Leviathan, M. Segleken, and K. Winkelman.
           Constructing correct systems in the safeair project. In *6th World Multi-
           conference on Systems, Cybernetics and Informatics (SCI'2002)*, Orlando,
           Florida, July 2002. To appear.
Ben98.   A. Benveniste. Safety critical embedded systems: the sacres approach. In
           A.P. Ravn and H. Rischel, editors, *FTRTFT 98: 5th International School
           and Symposium on Formal Techniques in Real-time and Fault-tolerant Sys-
           tems*, volume 1486 of *Lect. Notes in Comp. Sci.* Springer-Verlag, 1998.
BGJ91.   A. Benveniste, P. Le Guernic, and C. Jacquemot. Synchronous program-
           ming with events and relations: the SIGNAL languages and its semantics.
           Science of Computer Programming, 16:103–149, 1991.
CE81.   E.M. Clarke and E.A. Emerson. Design and synthesis of synchronization
           skeletons using branching time temporal logic. In *Proc. IBM Workshop on
           Logics of Programs*, volume 131 of *Lect. Notes in Comp. Sci.*, pages 52–71.
           Springer-Verlag, 1981.
Con95.   The Sacres Consortium. Safety critical embedded systems: from require-
           ments to system architecture, 1995. Esprit Project Description EP 20.897,
           URL http://www.tni.fr/sacres.
CRH93.   Z. Chaochen, A.P. Ravn, and M.R. Hansen. An extended duration calculus
           for hybrid real-time systems. In R.L. Grossman, A. Nerode, A. Ravn, and
           H. Rischel, editors, *Hybrid Systems*, volume 736 of *Lect. Notes in Comp.
           Sci.*, pages 36–59. Springer-Verlag, 1993.
DH99.   W. Damm and D. Harel. LSC's: Breathing life into message sequence
           charts. In P.Ciancarini, A. Fantechi, and R. Gorrieri, editors, *Proc. 3rd IFIP
           Int. Conf. on Formal Methods for Open Object-Based Distributed Systems
           (FMOODS'99)*. Kluwer Academic Publishers, 1999.
DJS94.   W. Damm, B. Josko, and R. Schlör. Specification and verification of VHDL-
           based system-level hardware design. In E. Börger, editor, *Specification and
           Validation Methods*, pages 331–410. Oxford University Press, 1994.
FJ97.   Konrad Feyerabend and Bernhard Josko. A visual formalism for real time
           requirement specifications. In Miquel Bertran and Teodor Rus, editors,
           *Transformation-Based Reactive Systems Development, Proceedings, 4th In-
           ternational AMAST Workshop on Real-Time Systems and Concurrent and
           Distributed Software, ARTS'97*, Lecture Notes in Computer Science 1231,
           pages 156–168. Springer-Verlag, 1997.
Har88.   D. Harel. On visual formalisms. *Comm. ACM*, 31:514–530, 1988.
Har01.   D. Harel. From play-in scenarios to code: An achievable dream. *IEEE Com-
           puter*, 34(1):53–60, 2001. Also, Proc. Fundamental Approaches to Software
           Engineering (FASE), Lecture Notes in Computer Science, Vol. 1783 (Tom
           Maibaum, ed.), Springer-Verlag.

HHWT97. T.A. Henzinger, P.-H. Ho, and H. Wong-Toi. HyTech: A model checker
         for hybrid systems. In *O. Grumberg, editor, Proc. 9th Intl. Conference
         on Computer Aided Verification, (CAV'97), volume 1254 of* Lect. Notes in
         Comp. Sci., *Springer-Verlag*, pages 460–463, 1997.

HK00.   D. Harel and H. Kugler. Synthesizing state-based object systems from LSC
         specifications. In *Proc. 5th Inf. Conf. on Implementation and Application
         of Automata (CIAA'00)*, Lect. Notes in Comp. Sci. Springer-Verlag, July
         2000. To appear.

HLN$^+$90. D. Harel, H. Lachover, A. Naamad, A. Pnueli, M. Politi, R. Sherman,
         A. Shtull-Trauring, and M. Trakhtenbrot. Statemate: A working envi-
         ronment for the development of complex reactive systems. *IEEE Trans.
         Software Engin.*, 16:403–414, 1990.

HM01.   D. Harel and R. Marelly. Specifying and Executing Behavioral Require-
         ments: The Play-In/Play-Out Approach. Tech. Report MCS01-15, The
         Weizmann Institute of Science, 2001. Submitted.

HMKT00. J.G. Henriksen, M. Mukund, K.N. Kumar, and P.S. Thiagarajan. On mes-
         sage sequence graphs and finitely generated regular MSC languages. In
         J.D.P. Rolim U. Montanari and E. Welzl, editors, *Proc. 27th Int. Colloq.
         Aut. Lang. Prog.*, volume 1853 of *Lect. Notes in Comp. Sci.*, pages 675–686.
         Springer-Verlag, 2000.

Hoa78.   C.A.R Hoare. Communicating sequential processes. *Comm. ACM*, 21:666–
         677, 1978.

KMP98.   Y. Kesten, Z. Manna, and A. Pnueli. Verification of clocked and hybrid sys-
         tems. In G. Rozenberg and F.W. Vaandrager, editors, *School on Embedded
         Systems*, volume 1494, pages 4 – 73. Springer-Verlag, 1998.

KP92.   Y. Kesten and A. Pnueli. Timed and hybrid statecharts and their textual
         representation. In J. Vytopil, editor, *Formal Techniques in Real-Time and
         Fault-Tolerant Systems*, volume 571 of *Lect. Notes in Comp. Sci.*, pages
         591–619. Springer-Verlag, 1992.

Lam83.   L. Lamport. What good is temporal logic. In R.E.A. Mason, editor, *Proc.
         IFIP 9th World Congress*, pages 657–668. North-Holland, 1983.

LPP98a. A. Leung, K.V. Palem, and A. Pnueli. A fast algorithm for scheduling
         time-constrained instructions on processors with ILP. In *The 1998 Inter-
         national Conference on Parallel Architectures and Compilation Techniques
         (PACT'98)*, Paris, October 1998.

LPP98b. A. Leung, K.V. Palem, and A. Pnueli. TimeC: A time constraint language
         for ILP processor compilation. In *The 5th Annual Australasian Confer-
         ence on Parallel And Real-Time Systems (PART'98)*, Adelaide, Australia,
         September 1998. Also available as Courant Institute Technical Report No.
         764, May 1998.

LPP01.   A. Leung, K. Palem, and A. Pnueli. Scheduling time-constrained instruc-
         tions on pipelined processors. *ACM Trans. Prog. Lang. Sys.*, 23(1):73–103,
         2001.

Mil80.   R. Milner. *A Calculus of Communicating Systems*. Lec. Notes in Comp.
         Sci. 94, Springer-Verlag, 1980.

MMP92a. O. Maler, Z. Manna, and A. Pnueli. From timed to hybrid systems. In J.W.
         de Bakker, C. Huizing, W.P. de Roever, and G. Rozenberg, editors, *Pro-
         ceedings of the REX Workshop "Real-Time: Theory in Practice"*, volume
         600 of *Lect. Notes in Comp. Sci.*, pages 447–484. Springer-Verlag, 1992.

MMP92b. O. Maler, Z. Manna, and A. Pnueli. From timed to hybrid systems. In J.W. de Bakker, C. Huizing, W.P. de Roever, and G. Rozenberg, editors, *Proceedings of the REX Workshop "Real-Time: Theory in Practice"*, volume 600 of *Lect. Notes in Comp. Sci.*, pages 447–484. Springer-Verlag, 1992.

MP91.   Z. Manna and A. Pnueli. *The Temporal Logic of Reactive and Concurrent Systems: Specification.* Springer-Verlag, New York, 1991.

NSY92.   X. Nicollin, J. Sifakis, and S. Yovine. From ATP to timed graphs and hybrid systems. In J.W. de Bakker, C. Huizing, W.P. de Roever, and G. Rozenberg, editors, *Proceedings of the REX Workshop "Real-Time: Theory in Practice"*, volume 600 of *Lect. Notes in Comp. Sci.*, pages 549–572. Springer-Verlag, 1992. See [atp:acta] for Journal Version.

OL82.   S. Owicki and L. Lamport. Proving liveness properties of concurrent programs. *ACM Trans. Prog. Lang. Sys.*, 4:455–495, 1982.

Pnu77.   A. Pnueli. The temporal logic of programs. In *Proc. 18th IEEE Symp. Found. of Comp. Sci.*, pages 46–57, 1977.

PSS98.   A. Pnueli, M. Siegel, and O. Shtrichman. The code validation tool (CVT)-automatic verification of a compilation process. *Software Tools for Technology Transfer*, 2(2):192–201, 1998.

QS83.   J.P. Queille and J. Sifakis. Fairness and related properties in transition systems — A temporal logic to deal with fairness. *Acta Informatica*, 19:195–220, 1983.

An Approach
to Designing Safe Embedded Software*

Nancy G. Leveson

Massachusetts Institute of Technology, Room 33-313, Cambridge MA 02139, USA
leveson@mit.edu
http://sunnyday.mit.edu

Abstract. The complexity of most embedded software limits our ability to assure safety after the fact, e.g., by testing or formal verification of code. Instead, to achieve high confidence in safety requires considering it from the start of system development and designing the software to reduce the potential for hazardous behavior. An approach to building safety into embedded software will be described that integrates system hazard analysis, user task analysis, traceability, and informal specifications combined with executable and analyzable models. The approach has been shown to be feasible and practical by applying it to complex systems experimentally and by its use on real projects.

1   Introduction

Embedded systems often involve control over processes that are potentially dangerous or could involve large losses (including loss of the system itself). Safety and human factors are often considered at too late a stage in embedded system development to have adequate impact on system design: It has been estimated that 70-90% of the decisions relevant to safety are made in the early conceptual design stages of a project [Joh80]. Relying on after-the-fact safety assessment emphasizes creating an assessment model that proves the completed design is safe rather than constructing a design that eliminates or mitigates hazards. Too often, after-the-fact safety assessment leads to adjusting the model until it provides the desired answer rather than to improving the design.

In the same way, when the human role in the system is considered after the basic automation is designed, the choices to ensure usability and safety in human–computer interaction are limited to interface design, training, and human adaptation to the newly constructed automation. This approach has been labeled *technology-centered design* and has been accused of leading to "clumsy" automation [WCK91] and to new types of accidents in high-tech systems, such as new fly-by-wire aircraft [SW95]. Most of these accidents have been blamed on pilot error but more accurately can be described as flaws in the overall system

---

* This work was partially supported by NSF ITR Grant xxx

A. Sangiovanni-Vincentelli and J. Sifakis (Eds.): EMSOFT 2002, LNCS 2491, pp. 15–29, 2002.
© Springer-Verlag Berlin Heidelberg 2002

and software design. Automation has the potential to overcome human perceptual and cognitive limits and to reduce or eliminate specific common human errors. At the same time, it also has the potential for leading to accidents if not designed correctly.

This paper describes an integrated safety and human-centered approach to developing software-intensive systems along with some specification, modeling and analysis tools for implementing it. SpecTRM (Specification Tools and Requirements Methodology) is both a methodology and supporting toolset for building embedded, software-intensive, safety-critical systems that focuses on the system engineering aspects of software and the development of safe and correct requirements. Most of the focus in computer science research has been on the implementation of requirements with much less work on the system-level aspects of embedded software development, i.e., how the software will interact with the other components in the system. Perhaps this lack of emphasis in research and tools is why so many problems seem to arise at this interface. To reduce communication problems, industry has developed Integrated Product Teams, where the software developers work closely with the system engineers. Simply putting people together on a team, however, is not adequate to solve the problem—common models and ways to communicate about system design issues are necessary for effective communication to take place.

SpecTRM is based on the principle that critical properties must be designed into a system from the start. As a result, it integrates safety analysis, functional decomposition and allocation, and human factors from the beginning of the system development process. Because neither formal or informal specifications alone are adequate to develop embedded software, SpecTRM uses both to accumulate the information needed to make tradeoff and design decisions and to ensure that desired system qualities are satisfied early in the design process when changes are easier and less costly. Because almost all accidents related to software have involved requirements errors and not coding or implementation errors, requirements specification and validation is emphasized.

The methodology is supported by a new specification structuring approach, called Intent Specifications, that supports traceability and documentation of design rationale as the development process proceeds. While most of the information specified is not written in a formal language (and does not need to be), some parts of the development process can benefit greatly from having formal, analyzable models. At the same time, most errors in requirements specifications will be found by application experts who understand the engineering and other requirements on the system. The formal modeling language, SpecTRM-RL (SpecTRM Requirements Language), was designed with readability as a primary criterion and therefore we believe the models that result can be used as an unambiguous communication medium among the system developers and software implementers.

The next section outlines the overall methodology and describes the general goals behind intent specifications. Then the types of information specified at each level of an intent specification is described along with associated analyses.

2   The SpecTRM Approach
to Designing Embedded Systems

The steps of the basic system engineering approach underlying SpecTRM are shown in Figure 1. The middle column represents the general engineering tasks. The right column shows special safety engineering activities and those in the left column represent human factors engineering. The separation is only shown to emphasize the safety and human factors activities; in any real project, they should be tightly integrated with the general engineering tasks but they are often separated—with unfortunate results. The process also involves more iteration and feedback than shown. While it may look like the process implies a pure waterfall model, the steps could be embedded in other lifecycle processes. Performing the later steps before the earlier ones, however, may result in a lot of backtracking and wasted effort or result in unsafe and difficult to use systems. The life cycle appropriate for embedded systems is very different than one appropriate for developing office software.

The steps of the process are supported by a new specification approach called Intent Specifications [Lev00a] and automated tools to assist with model construction, recording of design rationale, and traceability. The models are important in evaluating designs while design rationale and traceability are critical for certifiability and maintainability.

Embedded software will evolve and change continually throughout its life. Maintaining safety in such a changing environment requires high-quality specifications that include detailed descriptions of the externally visible behavior of the existing components as well as the rationale for the system design choices. The integration of new components must be based on the design and constraints of existing components and the surrounding environment, and any changes to the current system must be analyzed for their effect on system requirements, operator tasks and responsibilities, safety constraints, and human factors.

Determining whether a requirements, design, or implementation change has a potential effect on system safety also requires a level of traceability not normally found in specifications. Although such traceability implies more planning and specification effort at the beginning of a project, the effort will allow changes to be made much more quickly and easily. It could be prohibitively expensive, for example, to generate a new hazard and safety assessment for each system change that is proposed. Being able to trace a particular design feature or implementation item to the original hazard analysis will allows decisions to be made about whether and how that feature or code can be changed. The same is true for changes that affect operator activities and basic task allocation and usability principles. In some regulated industries, traceability is required by the certification authorities.

Intent Specifications organize system specifications not only in terms of the usual *what* and *how* (using refinement and part-whole abstractions), but also in terms of *why* (using intent abstraction) and integrate traceability and design rationale into the basic specification structure. They include both natural language and formal executable models. The design of Intent Specifications is

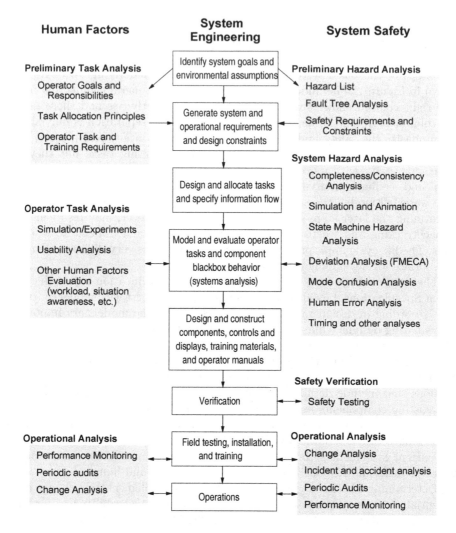

Fig. 1. A Safety and Human-Centered Approach to Building Embedded Systems

based on fundamental research on human problem-solving, systems theory, and basic system engineering. For a description of the systems theory and cognitive psychology research underlying Intent Specifications, see [Lev00a].

There are seven levels in an Intent Specification, each supporting a different type of reasoning about the system. A level does not represent refinement of the information at the level above, but instead contains a different view of the system. At the same time, the levels do not contain redundant information, but (as in basic system theory) instead higher levels represent constraints on the levels below. Each level also includes information about the verification and validation of the system model at that level. By organizing the specification in

	Environment	Operator	System and components	V&V
Level 0	Project management plans, status information, safety plan, etc.			
Level 1 System Purpose	Assumptions Constraints	Responsibilities Requirements I/F requirements	System goals, high-level requirements, design constraints, limitations	Preliminary Hazard Analysis Reviews
Level 2 System Principles	External interfaces	Task analyses Task allocation Controls, displays	Logic principles, control laws, functional decomposition and allocation	Validation plan and results, System Hazard Analysis
Level 3 Blackbox Models	Environment models	Operator Task models HCI models	Blackbox functional models Interface specifications	Analysis plans and results, Subsystem Hazard Analysis
Level 4 Design Rep.		HCI design	Software and hardware design specs	Test plans and results
Level 5 Physical Rep.		GUI design, physical controls design	Software code, hardware assembly instructions	Test plans and results
Level 6 Operations	Audit procedures	Operator manuals Maintenance Training materials	Error reports, change requests, etc.	Performance monitoring and audits

Fig. 2. The Structure of an Intent Specification

this way and linking the information at each level to the relevant information at the next higher and lower level, higher-level purpose or intent, i.e., the rationale for design decisoins, can be determined. In addition, by integrating and linking the system, software, human task, and interface design and development into one specification framework, intent specifications support an integrated rather than stovepiped approach to system design.

Curtis *et.al.* [CKI88] did a field study of the software requirements and design process for 17 large systems. One of the characteristics they found that appeared to set exceptional designers apart from their colleagues was the ability to map between the behavior required of the application system and the computational structures that implement this behavior. The most successful designers understood the application domain and were adept at identifying unstated requirements, constraints, or exception conditions and mapping between these and the computational structures. A goal of Intent Specifications is to support and foster this understanding.

The seven levels of an intent specifiation are shown in Figure 2. The top level represents the management view of the project and the second the customer view. The third level is the system engineering view while the fourth level represents the interaction between system and software engineers. The fifth and sixth levels contain the usual information developed and used during software development. The lowest level supports an operational view of the system. Note that the ordering of the levels does not imply an ordering of the activities. Most projects involve both top-down and bottom-up development, and the pieces of the Intent

Specifications will be filled in as the related activities are performed. The only requirement is that at the end of the development phase, the intent specification is complete enough to support system maintenance and evolution.

In the following description of the information at each level, parts of an example specification we produced for an Air Traffic Control Conflict Detection Tool (called Mid Term Conflict Detection or MTCD) are used. MTCD is currently being evaluated by Eurocontrol for possible use in the European airspace.

Level 0: Management Perspective

The top level of an intent specification contains management plans, system safety plans, and other planning documents. Links to lower levels allow management to maintain a view of the status and results of the process.

Level 1: Conceptual Design

One of the first steps in embedded software development is to identify high-level functional goals and the assumptions and constraints on the software design arising from the environment in which it will be used. For example, two high-level goals for MTCD are:

> **G1:** To provide a conflict detection capability to air traffic controllers for all flights in the area of operation.
> **G2:** To help keep the workload of the controllers within acceptable and safe limits despite an expected increase in traffic.

The success of any embedded software will rest on how well it fits within the larger system. For example, the ATC system within which MTCD fits consists of the conflict detection function itself, planning and tactical air traffic controllers for the sector, and the human–machine interface. MTCD interacts directly with the real-time flight data processing system, the environment data processing system, and a recording function, and indirectly with various automated decision aids, such as an arrival sequencing manager and monitoring aids. Two example assumptions about the interaction of MTCD with the real-time flight data processing system (FDPS) are:

> **Env-As-FDPS-01:** FDPS will provide MTCD with system trajectories for all eligible flights.
> **Env-AS-FCPS-03:** FDPS will inform MTCD when a flight leaves the area of operation.

Because we believe system design must consider human factors and system safety from the very beginning in order to achieve high levels of usability and safety, the first steps in the methodology involve a preliminary hazard analysis (PHA) and a preliminary controller task analysis (PTA). The PHA starts from agreed upon system hazards, such as violation of minimum separation between aircraft or entry of an aircraft into a restricted area, and identifies system behavior that could lead to those hazards.

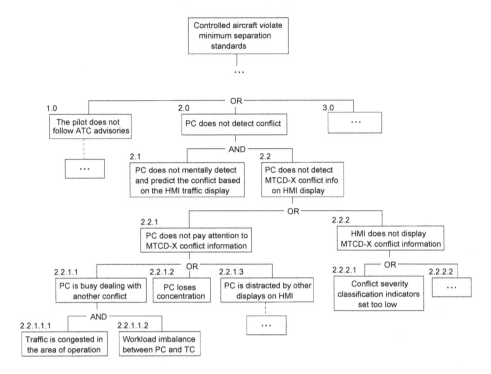

Fig. 3. A Piece of a Fault Tree for Violating Minimum Separation

Figure 3 shows a piece of the fault tree for the violation of minimum separation between controlled aircraft. The fault tree is used to derive requirements and design constraints related to safety. Each leaf node in the fault tree must either be traced to an operational or training requirement for the controller tasks or to an MTCD requirement or design constraint (and thence to the design feature used to eliminate or mitigate it). If a leaf node cannot be eliminated or mitigated, it must be accepted (and documented) as a necessary limitation of the system. Such limitations may in turn require changes in the operation or design of the overall air traffic management system. Information derived from the fault tree may also be used in the Preliminary Task Analysis (and vice versa).

The hazard analysis and system engineering processes are iterative and mutually reinforcing. In the beginning, when few system design decisions have been made, the hazard analysis may be very general. As the system design emerges, the hazard analysis will become more detailed and will impact additional design decisions. For example, the need for conflict severity categorization for MTCD was identified in the PHA and leads to a requirement:

MTCD-08: *MTCD shall support conflict severity categorization.*

The box labelled 2.2.2.1 (*Conflict severity classification indicators are set too low*) leads to requirements and design constraints related to conflict severity classification indicators, how they are set and how they can be changed, the conditions under which conflicts are displayed, and the need for feedback to the controller about the current value of the conflict severity categorization indicators. For example, the conflict detection function might include a requirement to allow the operators to change the conflict severity thresholds. At the same time, there may be a constraint on the controller tasks and interface design that requires permission before the conflict categorization indicators can be changed by the controller.

A Preliminary Task Analysis (PTA) is also performed at this early concept development stage and interacts closely with the concurrent PHA process. The PTA consists of cognitive engineers, human factors experts, and operators together specifying the goals and responsibilities of the users of a new tool or technology, the task allocation principles to be used, and operator task and training requirements.

For MTCD, we started by specifying all of the tactical controller (TC) and planning controller (PC) responsibilities, not just those directly affected by MTCD. All responsibilities were included because any safety or usability analysis will require showing that MTCD-X does not negatively impact any of the controller activities. For instance, the PC (Planning Controller) is responsible for detecting sector entry or exit conflicts and formulating resolution plans with the PC of the adjacent sector and the TC (Tactical Controller) of the current sector. The TC, on the other hand, is responsible for in-sector tactical conflict detection and for implementing the plans formulated by the PC for entry or exit conflicts.

The second step in the PTA is to define the task allocation principles to be used in allocating tasks between the human controllers and the automation. This process uses the results of the Preliminary Hazard Analysis, previous accidents and incidents, human factors considerations, controller preferences and inputs, etc. For example, some task allocation principles for conflict resolution might be:

> The human controller will have final authority as far as the use of the prediction tool, the need for intervention, and the criticality of the situation. The controller will be responsible for devising solutions to the conflict.

These principles, together with the PHA and high-level system goals, are used to write requirements for the controller tasks, the automated function, and the human-machine interface. For MTCD, the PHA, the controller responsibilities, and the task allocation principles may lead to the following operator requirements (among others):

MIT-OP-R02: The PC shall plan traffic using MTCD output, and where a problem persists shall notify its existence and nature to the TC.

MIT-OP-R03: If incorrect or inconvenient behavior (e.g. high rate of false alarms) is observed, the controller shall not use the MTCD function.

MIT-OP-R07: The controller shall address conflicts detected by MTCD in a criticality-based rather than time-based order.

The final step of the PTA is the generation of operator task and training requirements and constraints.

The system goals and environmental assumptions and constraints along with the results from the PHA and PTA are then used to generate a complete set of system requirements (including functionality, maintenance, management, and interface requirements), operational requirements, and design constraints.

Level 2: System Design

Using the system requirements and design constraints as well as the other information that has been generated to this point, a system design (or alternative system designs) is created and tasks are allocated to the system components (including the operators) to satisfy the requirements, task allocation principles, and operational goals. The specification at this level contains *system* design, not *software* design. Note that this process will involve much iteration as the results of analysis, experimentation, review, etc. become available. We have found that natural language is the most appropriate specification language at this level combined with standard engineering and mathematical notations, for example, differential equations or control block diagrams for documenting control laws.

Level 3: Allocating and Validating Requirements

The next step involves validating the system design and requirements and performing any tradeoff and evaluation studies that may be required to select from among a set of design alternatives. Various types of operator task analyses and system hazard analyses play a part in this process.

The methodology includes using formal models in SpecRLM-RL to assist in this evaluation and validation process. Designers construct formal, blackbox models of the required component behavior and operator tasks. The SpecTRM-RL modeling language was designed with readability and reviewability of the models by various domain experts as a major goal. The models act as a communication medium among everyone involved and therefore must be easily understandable and unambiguous.

An earlier version of the current modeling language (called RSML) was used to specify the official requirements for TCAS II [LHH94]. One requirement of that project was to provide a specification language that could be read and reviewed by any interested parties with minimal training (less than an hour). Our latest version of the formal modeling/specification language attempts to enhance readability and reviewability by reducing even further the semantic distance between the reviewer's mental model and the specification. We also elminated the features we found to be very error-prone, such as internal events. Our current research is focused on visualization techniques for complex, formal specifications and the use of domain-specific notations.

The blackbox component behavior models are built on an underlying state machine model [JLHM91]. SpecRLM-RL blackbox models combine a graphical notation with tabular descriptions of the legal state changes. Figures 4 and 5 show pieces of our SpecTRM-RL model for MTCD. The MTCD model could be combined with a model of the airspace and models of the other system components and executed or analyzed together in a system simulation environment.

The graphical part of the model (as shown in Figure 4), is drawn in the form of a control loop showing the direct interactions of MTCD with other system components (the environment data processing system, the flight data processing system, and the controller working position). A future planned interface with a new arrival manager tool (AMAN) is shown.

A SpecTRM-RL model of a component itself (in this case MTCD) usually has four parts:

- **Display modes:** the display mode will affect the information to be provided to the controller. A display mode specification is not needed for MTCD
- **Supervisory modes:** the supervisory mode specifies who is using the component at any time, which affects which operations are legal. In this case the supervisor may be the PC, the operations manager, or AMAN.
- **Component control modes:** the mode the automation is in. In the case of MTCD, these include unconfigured, configured, active, stopped, and failed.
- **Inferred system state:** a model of the inferred state of the controlled system, in this case, the airspace in the area of operation.

The controlled system (airspace) state at any time is inferred from the inputs received and may be incorrect if those inputs are incorrect or not timely. The airspace model within MTCD consists of a model of the assumed state of each of the aircraft being evaluated for conflicts. The model of MTCD shown has, for each aircraft, state variables representing the status of the flight data from that aircraft, the conflict detection status, the flight phase (needed because separation criteria will vary with flight phase), and the status of the current position information. Note that accidents occur when this inferred airspace state differs from the real state. The validation phase involves assuring that the model is correct and that the overall system is robust against errors in the information received about the current airspace state.

A complete model also needs to specify the conditions under which each of the MTCD control modes is used, the conditions under which the outputs are generated and their content, and how each of the inferred state variables is assigned a value. Figure 5 shows the logic for selecting the MTCD operating mode. The conditions under which each of the four values for operating mode become enabled are described using AND/OR tables. The operating mode takes a particular value when the *table* associated with that value evaluates to TRUE, which in turn happens when any *column* of the table evaluates to TRUE. A column is TRUE when each row satisfies the truth value shown (with a dot denoting "don't care"). In the example, the MTCD status becomes ACTIVE if either (1) the previous mode was CONFIGURED and an area of operation is received by MTCD *or* (2) the previous mode was STOPPED and a start command is received.

An executable human task modeling language has also been defined. In previous experimentation, we found that a different notation was more useful for modeling human tasks than that used for describing the automation behavior.

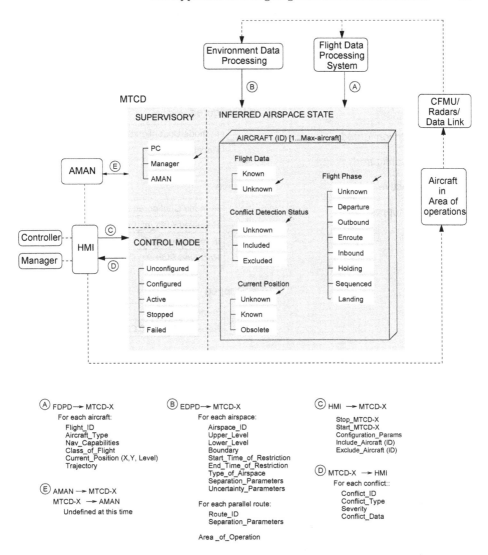

Fig. 4. Part of a SpecTRM-RL Model of MTCD

Both generate the same type of underlying formal model, which should allow integrated execution and analysis of the system as a whole, both the automation and the user tasks. An important aspect is the specification of the communication between the various controllers as well as between the controllers and the automation. We have shown how these task models can be used to find features of the combined automation and task design that can lead to mode confusion and other human errors [RZK00].

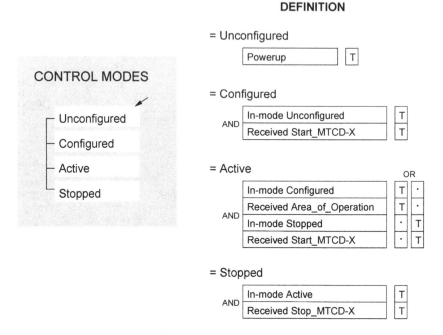

Fig. 5. The Logic for Selecting the Current Operating Mode

In addition to being reviewable by aviation and air traffic management experts, the formal models are executable and can be executed alone or integrated into an ATC simulation environment. Animation and visualization of the executing models assist in understanding and evaluating the proposed design of the automation and controller tasks. The executable specifications can also be used in experiments involving controllers to evaluate human factors. An advantage of executable specifications over prototypes or special simulation languages is that the specification can be changed as the evaluation proceeds. At the end of the evaluation stage, a final specification is ready for implementation without having to reverse engineer a specification from a prototype.

Because the modeling language is based on a formal mathematical model, various types of automated mathematical analysis can also be applied. We have developed techniques for analysis of consistency and completeness, robust operation in an imperfect environment, reachability of hazardous states, and potential mode confusion. A new hybrid (continuous and discrete) version of the basic modeling language (SpecTRM-H) allows safety analysis of the conflict detection algorithms themselves [Neo01].

Requirements errors and incompleteness account for most of the accidents in which digital automation has been involved. It is, therefore, particularly important that the requirements specification distinguish the desired behavior from that of any other, undesired behavior, that is, the specification must be precise (unambiguous), complete, and correct (consistent) with respect to the encompassing system requirements. We have built prototype tools to check our specifications for consistency and some aspects of mathematical completeness [HL96]. Other important completeness aspects are enforced by the design of SpecTRM-RL itself [Lev00b] or can be checked using inspection or simple tools.

Robustness can be evaluated using an automated technique called Software Deviation Analysis [RL87]. SDA determines how the software will operate in an imperfect environment by examining the effects of deviations of system parameters (inputs). The input to the SDA tool is an input deviation, for example, *"the altitude reported by the radar data processing function is lower than the actual altitude."* The output is a list of scenarios, where a scenario is defined as a set of deviations in the software inputs plus constraints on the software execution states that are sufficient to lead to a deviation in an identified safety-critical output. The deviation analysis procedure can optionally add further deviations as it constrains the software state, allowing for the analysis of the effects of multiple, independent failures.

Other tools can be used to assist in system and subsystem hazard analysis [LS87]. Information from these analyses is useful in eliminating hazards from the design or in designing controls and hazard mitigation. For example, one tool assists the designer in tracing back through the model from hazardous states to determine if and how they are reachable. Backward search can also reveal how the system can end up in a hazardous state if a failure occurs. Our backward reachability analysis on discrete state models has recently been augmented to include continuous states (a hybrid model) [Neo01], using some basic techniques from control theory. Neogi has experimentally applied this approach to evaluate the safety of the conflict detection algorithm used in MTCD.

Finally, the specification/model of the blackbox automation behavior can be evaluated for its potential to lead to mode confusion [LRK97]. We have identified six automation design categories have been identified as leading to mode confusion, based on accidents and simulator studies: (1) ambiguous interface modes, (2) inconsistent automation behavior, (3) indirect mode changes, (4) operator authority limits, (5) unintended side effects, and (6) lack of appropriate feedback. Analysis procedures are being developed to detect these features in SpecTRM-RL models. We have experimentally tested these ideas on real helicopter and aircraft flight management system software.

Once the engineers are happy with the operator task and logical system design, detailed design and construction of the system components, controls and displays, training materials, and operator manuals can begin.

Level 4 and 5: Component Design and Implementation

For some applications, the code can be automatically generated from the SpecTRM-RL models. For others, the real-time requirements require hand crafting of the code. In general, many of the software specification and design techniques currently popular do not afford the level of traceability and safety assurance necessary in safety-critical systems. We assume that reuse will start from the SpecTRM-RL specification because analysis at the system level will be necessary. Therefore, some of the design methodologies focused on reusing code components will be less important in this type of system. We are currently developing SpecTRM-RL macro components for spacecraft design, as well as a spacecraft-specific modeling language built on top of SpecTRM-RL, to evaluate the practicality and feasibility of this approach to reuse.

This level will contain most of the information about system and middleware design and hardware decisions. Many or most of the proposals for specifying and designing such computer system components will fit into the SpecTRM approach.

Level 6: Operations

Ensuring safety does not stop with development. Operations need to be monitored and periodically audited to ensure that the assumptions underlying the original hazard analysis and the safety-related design features hold in the current system. Operators change their behavior and the environment is very likely to change. The traceability and documentation of design rationale included in Intent Specifications should be useful in deriving auditing and performance monitoring procedures and metrics and in making any necessary changes to the software.

3   Status and Future Extensions

A methodology for building safety into embedded software has been described. The approach integrates system hazard analysis, operator task analysis, traceability, and documentation of design rationale as well as executable and analyzable models into the development process. A commercial toolset to support SpecTRM is in development and is currently being used to support industrial projects.

References

CKI88. B. Curtis, H. Krasner and N. Iscoe. A field study of the software design process for large systems. *Communications of the ACM*, 31(2): 1268–1287, 1988.

JLHM91. M.S. Jaffe, N.G. Leveson, M.P.E. Heimdahl, and B.Melhart. Software requirements analysis for real-time process-control systems . *IEEE Trans. on Soft. Eng.*, SE-17(3), Mar 1991.

HL96. Heimdahl, M.P.E. and Leveson, N.G. Completeness and Consistency in Hierarchical State-Based Requirements. *IEEE Trans. on Soft. Eng.*, SE-22, No. 6, June 1996.

Joh80. Johnson, W.G. *MORT Safety Assurance Systems*, Marcel Dekker, Inc., 1980.

Lev00a. Leveson, N.G. Intent Specifications. *IEEE Trans. on Soft. Eng.*, Jan. 2000.

Lev00b. Leveson, N.G. Completeness in Formal Specification Language Design for Process-Control Systems. *ACM Formal Methods in Software Practice*, Aug 2000

LHH94. Leveson, N.G., Heimdahl, M.P.E., Hildreth, H., and Reese, J.D. Requirements Specification for Process-Control Systems. *IEEE Trans. on Soft. Eng.*, SE-20, No. 9, Sept. 1994.

LRK97. Leveson, N.G., Reese, J.D., Koga, S., Pinnel, L.D., and Sandys, S.D. Analyzing Requirements Specifications for Mode Confusion Errors. *Int. Workshop on Human Error, Safety, and System Development*, Glasgow, March 1997.

LS87. Leveson, N.G. and Stolzy, J.L. Safety Analysis Using Petri Nets. *IEEE Trans. on Soft. Eng.*, Vol. SE-13, No. 3, March 1987, pp. 386-397.

Neo01. Neogi, N. Hazard Elimination Using Backward Reachability and Hybrid Modeling Techniques. Ph.D. Dissertation, Aeronautics and Astronautics, MIT, May 2002.

RL87. Reese, J.D. and Leveson, N.G. Software Deviation Analysis. *International Conference on Software Engineering*, Boston, May 1997.

RZK00. Rodriguez, M., Zimmerman, M., Katahira, M., de Villepin, M., Ingram, B., and Leveson, N.G. Identifying Mode Confusion Potential in Software Design. *Digital Aviation Systems Conference*, Philadelphia, October 2000 .

SW95. Sarter, N.D. and Woods, D. "How in the World did I Ever Get into That Mode?" *Human Factors 37*, 5–19.

WCK91. Wiener, E.L., Chidester, T.R., Kanki, B.G., Palmer E.A., Curry, R.E., and Gregorich, S.E. The Impact of Cockpit Automation on Crew Coordination and Communications. NASA Ames Research Center, 1991.

Can Behavioral Requirements Be Executed?
(And Why Would We Want to Do So?)

David Harel

The Weizmann Institute of Science

A novel approach to behavioral requirements for reactive systems is described, in which highly expressive scenario-based requirements are "played in" directly from the system's GUI, or some abstract version thereof [2], and behavior can then be "played out" freely, adhering to all the requirements [3]. The approach, which is joint with Rami Marelly, is supported and illustrated by a tool we have built – the *play-engine*.

As the requirements are played in, the play-engine automatically generates a formal version of them, in an extended version of the language of live sequence charts (LSCs) [1]. The extension includes symbolic instances [5] and time constraints [6]. As behavior is played out, the engine causes the application to react according to the universal ("must") parts of the specification; the existential ("may") parts can be monitored to check for successful completion. See Figure 1, which extends the series of figures appearing in [2], so that the current work is shown incorporated within the conventional framework for the development of reactive systems described in [2].

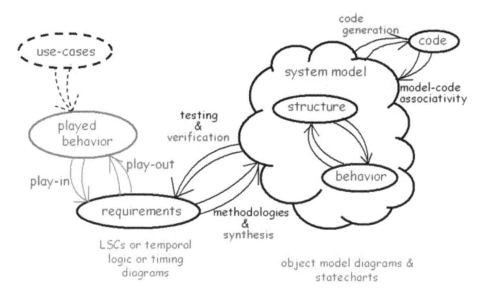

Fig. 1. Play-in/play-out within the development cycle; see Fig. 4 of [2]

A. Sangiovanni-Vincentelli and J. Sifakis (Eds.): EMSOFT 2002, LNCS 2491, pp. 30–31, 2002.
© Springer-Verlag Berlin Heidelberg 2002

We also describe our work on "smart" play-out, joint with Hillel Kugler and Amir Pnueli, whereby parts of the execution are driven by counterexamples produced using model-checking [4]. This makes it possible to avoid taking "bad" nondeterministic choices that may arise from the partial order within an LSC or the various interleavings of several LSCs. Thus, we employ formal verification techniques for driving the execution of the requirements, rather than for verifying the model's properties against those requirements later on. Smart play-out can also be used to find a way to satisfy an existential chart, i.e., to show how a scenario can be satisfied by the LSC specification, and is thus very useful for testing.

The entire play-in/out approach appears to be useful in many stages in the development of complex reactive systems, and could also pave the way to systems that are constructed directly from their requirements, without the need for intra-object or intra-component modeling or coding at all.

A particularly exciting application of the ideas is in the modeling of biological systems, where the information from experiments comes in the form of scenarios or scenario fragments. We are in the midst of a project involving modeling and analyzing parts of the development of the C. elegans worm using the play-engine, and will report on this effort separately.

References

1. W. Damm and D. Harel, "LSCs: Breathing Life into Message Sequence Charts", *Formal Methods in System Design* **19**:1 (2001).(Preliminary version in *Proc. 3rd IFIP Int. Conf. on Formal Methods for Open Object-Based Distributed Systems* (*FMOODS'99*), (P. Ciancarini, A. Fantechi and R. Gorrieri, eds.), Kluwer Academic Publishers, 1999, pp. 293–312.)
2. D. Harel, "From Play-In Scenarios To Code: An Achievable Dream", *IEEE Computer* **34**:1 (January 2001), 53–60. (Also, *Proc. Fundamental Approaches to Software Engineering* (*FASE*), Lecture Notes in Computer Science, Vol. 1783 (Tom Maibaum, ed.), Springer-Verlag, March 2000, pp. 22–34.)
3. D. Harel and R. Marelly, "Specifying and Executing Behavioral Requirements: The Play-In/Play-Out Approach", to appear.
4. D. Harel, H. Kugler, R. Marelly and A. Pnueli, "Smart Play-Out of Behavioral Requirements", *Proc. 4th Int. Conf. on Formal Methods in Computer-Aided Design* (FMCAD 2002), November 2002, to appear.
5. R. Marelly, D. Harel and H. Kugler, "Multiple Instances and Symbolic Variables in Executable Sequence Charts", *Proc. 17th Ann. AM Conf. on Object-Oriented Programming, Systems, Languages, and Applications* (OOPSLA '2002), November, 2002, to appear.
6. D. Harel and R. Marelly, "Time-Enriched LSCs: Specification and Execution", *Proc. 10th IEEE/ACM Int. Symp. on Modeling, Analysis and Simulation of Computer and Telecommunication Systems* (MASCOTS '02), October 2002, to appear.

Platform-Based Embedded Software Design for Multi-vehicle Multi-modal Systems

T. John Koo, Judith Liebman, Cedric Ma, Benjamin Horowitz,
Alberto Sangiovanni-Vincentelli, and Shankar Sastry

Department of Electrical Engineering and Computer Sciences
University of California at Berkeley
Berkeley, CA 94720

Abstract. In this paper, we present a methodology for the design of embedded controllers for multi-vehicle multi-modal systems. Our methodology is predicated upon the principles of platform-based design, which uses layers of abstraction to isolate applications from low-level system details and yet provides enough information about the important parameters of the lower layers of abstraction, to modularize the system design and to provide predictable system performance. An essential layer of abstraction in our methodology is the software platform provided by the programming language Giotto, which allows a clean implementation of a time-based controller application. Our methodology includes a hardware-in-the-loop simulation framework, in which system components can be replaced by actual implementation for high-fidelity simulation. To demonstrate the effectiveness of our design methodology, a helicopter-based unmanned aerial vehicle system is presented. We present simulation results which validate the quality of our embedded control system implementation.

1 Introduction

In the future, satellites will form a rigid structure to perform distributed observations. In automated highway systems (AHS), platoons of cars will be formed to enhance efficiency. Clusters of unmanned aerial vehicles (UAVs) will maintain formations to accomplish missions collectively in restricted areas. However, in order for distributed, network-centric, embedded systems to deliver high levels of mission reliability, they require *high-confidence* embedded software [8]: the embedded systems should ideally be correct by construction, fault-tolerant, and resistant to information attack. Therefore, the embedded software, which is used for the processing of information to and fro between the information and physical worlds, has to be designed in such a way that the embedded system can exhibit multi-modal behaviors for coping with different scenarios due to changes in the environment.

However, current design strategies for embedded software in control applications deal with system requirements and characteristics using ad hoc approaches. One of the most serious problems is the current disregard for the interaction of

A. Sangiovanni-Vincentelli and J. Sifakis (Eds.): EMSOFT 2002, LNCS 2491, pp. 32–45, 2002.

the control laws with their implementation. When a control law is designed, the computational power of the implementation platform is grossly estimated. This neglect leads to long re-design cycles when the timing requirements of the applications are not met. This situation has its origin in the difficulty of mixing implementation and functional design, and in the difficulty of evaluating quickly an alternative control law or implementation architecture. Another problem is the deficiency in component re-usability. Reusing components that are specific to function or implementation decreases time-to-market and validation time. Assuming a component is fully validated, the difficulty is in composing these objects to work properly.

This paper proposes a methodology where the dichotomy between functional design and implementation is bridged and the issues related to component re-use are addressed. One main goal of our design strategy is to build in modularity in order to make code reuse and substitutions of subsystems simple. The other main goal is to guarantee performance without exhaustive testing. To achieve these goals we draw on the principles of *platform-based design* [12]. A platform, in this context, is a layer of abstraction that hides the unnecessary details of the underlying implementation and yet carries enough information about the layers below to prevent design iterations. We achieve the latter goal by using a time-based controller. In particular, the choice of a specific software platform to guarantee correct timing performance for the control laws is of interest. Here we focus on the Giotto [4,5] software platform and we show how this software platform substantially aids the development of embedded software. Giotto consists of formal semantics [5] and a retargetable compiler. Giotto has already been used to redesign the helicopter control systems developed at UC Berkeley [6] and ETH Zürich [7]. There are related software platforms, such as the synchronous language Esterel [1] and Lustre [3], or the Open Control Platform (OCP) [15] being developed. A tool called Taxy [2] is especially developed to verify real-time properties of embedded systems in which Esterel is used to specify control flow of software components. OCP uses real-time CORBA (Common Object Request Broker Architecture) which is an object-oriented middleware to provide interoperability among heterogeneous software components. However, the major difference between the Giotto software platform and those software platforms is that the execution of control applications on the Giotto software platform are guaranteed to be correct since Giotto is designed to have well-defined semantics for executing periodical tasks and for performing deterministic mode switchings. There also exist computer architectures, such as the Time-triggered Architecture [10,9], which consider both hardware and software components for the construction of *high-confidence* embedded systems.

In order to validate the performance of embedded system implementation in the presence of faults and information attack, a hardware-in-the-loop simulation (HILS) framework is introduced. In a HILS, part of the simulated system is replaced by actual implementation in order to obtain a more useful simulation result. Any anticipated or unanticipated faults can be injected into the system during the hardware-in-the-loop simulation for testing the robustness of

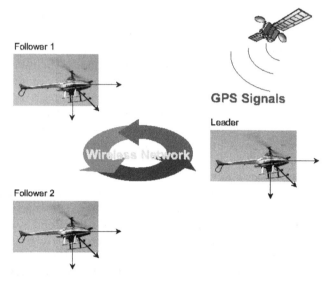

Fig. 1. A leading UAV and two following UAVs fly in a wedge formation. Each vehicle can localize itself by processing the received GPS signal and each follower can stay in a location relative to the leader by using the leader's information obtained from the wireless network.

the design. Another key feature of a HIL simulator is its ability to test the actual control implementation and embedded hardware instead of just the control laws. Due to the complexity of communication networks, it is difficult to obtain accurate network models for simulation. By using HILS, an actual communication network can be used and the system performance in the presence of the network can be examined.

The structure of this paper is as follows. In Section 2, we introduce the reader to the principles of platform-based design and we describe a software platform for programming time-based controller applications. We present the principles and construction of a HILS in Section 3. Finally, in Section 4, we present the embedded control system and HILS for a UAV. The difficulty and complexity of the application serve well the purpose of accentuating the features of the design method and demonstrating its power. The choices of design solutions are somewhat application-dependent but the overall idea is not, so that this example could provide a general guideline for the application of our method. We then extend the system design to multiple UAVs flying in formation (as depicted in Figure 1).

2   Platform-Based Design Methods

An embedded control system generally consists of three elements — sensors, actuators, and a computer. The control computer interacts with the continuous dynamics of the plant via the sensors and actuators. For each vehicle, we

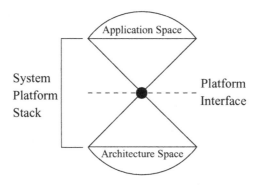

Fig. 2. The system platform stack

assume that there is only one computer system and its major function is to compute and generate control commands for the actuators that are based on sensor measurement.

A high-confidence embedded system should be designed so that its physical behavior can be easily analyzed and predicted. However, it is also important that the embedded system can be composed from a variety of heterogeneous components while satisfying the design specifications. Therefore, there is a demand for an approach to facilitate both time-based design and modular design:

A time-based design. The system should be time-based in order to allow easy analysis of its closed loop behavior. However, the system must maintain compatibility with existing devices such as the sensors, which are not necessarily time-based. A clear boundary between the system's synchronous and asynchronous elements must be drawn, and provisions must be made to bridge the gap.

A modular design. The new system must allow the designer to choose from a diverse mix of sensors, actuation schemes, and controllers. The new system must allow a configuration of the same software to run on different helicopters, which may have very different physical dynamics and devices.

To meet this design challenge, we draw on the principles of platform-based design. A platform is defined as a layer of abstraction which hides details of the underlying implementation, and through which only relevant information is allowed to pass. The main principle of platform-based design is that systems should employ precisely defined layers of abstractions. For example, a device driver provides a layer of abstraction between an operating system and a device. This layer hides most of the intricacies of the device, but still allows the operating system to configure, read from, and write to the device. Designs built on top of platforms are isolated from irrelevant subsystem details. A good platform provides enough useful information so that many applications can be built on top of it.

Typically, a system can be presented as the combination of a top level view, a bottom level view, and a set of tools and methods to map between the views. On the bottom, as depicted in Figure 2, is the architecture space. This space includes all of the options available for implementing the physical system. On the top is the application space, which includes high level applications for the system and leaves space for future applications. These two views of the system, the upper and the lower, should be decoupled. Instead of interacting directly, the two design spaces meet at a clearly defined interface, which is displayed as the shared vertex of the two triangles in Figure 2. The fact that the two spaces meet at one point conveys the key idea that the platform exposes only the necessary and relevant information to the space above. The entire figure, including the top view, the bottom view, and the vertex, is called the *system platform stack*.

2.1   A Time-Based Control Platform: Giotto

Control laws for autonomous vehicles are typically implemented on architectural platforms consisting of sensors, actuators, and computers which contain programmable components (e.g., micro-processors, DSPs) and memory (e.g., flash, RAM and ROM). The control laws are almost always implemented as software stored on ROM or flash memory running on the programmable components. There are often difficulties in mapping the control laws onto these kind of architectural platforms:

- In most cases, the controller must react in real-time. A software implementation is intrinsically slower than hardware. In addition, the computing part of the platform usually consists of a standard single microprocessor. Thus, the concurrency of the function to implement is lost: concurrent tasks have to be sequentialized. These platforms are equipped with a real-time operating system (RTOS), i.e., a light-weight, low-overhead, operating system that schedules tasks to be executed on the processor. There are many scheduling algorithms (e.g. rate monotonic, earliest deadline first, and their variants) available to optimize the processor utilization while maintaining deadlines for task execution. The most popular RTOSs support rate-monotonic scheduling algorithms.
- In the implementation of the control laws, the control designer must take into account the possibilities of inaccuracies and malfunctions in the sensors and actuators. However, if the software implementation directly uses information about the particular peripherals of the platform, then re-using the software on different platforms would be virtually impossible. An efficient solution for this problem is to use device-geared software processes to isolate the control software and the algorithms from the physical characteristic of the devices.

In order to ameliorate these problems, we introduce a new abstraction layer which will sit between the RTOS and the functional description of the control laws. This abstraction layer will provide the control designer with a more relevant and direct method for programming the control laws to meet real-time constraints. However, the control designer must adhere to the guidelines that this abstraction allows. In this way, the abstraction layer will restrict the design space available to develop the control laws, but will significantly shorten the design time and ensure the correctness of the design.

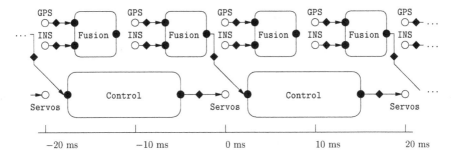

Fig. 3. An example Giotto program

To illustrate this idea using the hourglass figure of platform-based design, we place the possible control laws in the application space on top, and the RTOS in the architecture space on the bottom. The proposed abstraction layer makes up the interface between these two views. Ideally, this platform interface should pass the timing constraints of the application downwards, and should pass the performance capabilities of the architectural instance upwards. On the basis of these constraints, the platform's tools should be able to determine whether the timing requirements of the application can be fulfilled. In the next section, we discuss in detail an abstraction layer between the RTOS and the real-time control laws that is chosen for the helicopter embedded software. This abstraction layer is the Giotto programming language.

2.2 Giotto Program

Control applications often have periodic, concurrent tasks. For example, our UAV control application runs a measurement fusion task at a frequency of 100 Hz, and a control computation task at 50 Hz. These periodic tasks communicate with each other. The mechanisms used to implement such a communication pathway — whether they may be message queues, shared memory, or some other mechanisms — may vary depending on the operating system and the preference of the designer. Control applications also need a means to receive input from and send output data to the physical environment. Finally, control applications often have distinct *modes* of behavior; in two different modes, different sets of concurrent tasks may need to run, or the same set of tasks may need to run but at different rates. Giotto provides the control designer a way to specify applications with periodic, concurrent, and communicating tasks. Giotto also provides a means for I/O interaction with the physical environment, and for mode switching between different sets of tasks.

Consider the example program of Figure 3. The concurrent tasks — Fusion and Control — are shown in the figure as rounded rectangles. Each task has a logical execution interval. In our example, Fusion logically executes from 0 ms to 10 ms, from 10 ms to 20 ms, etc., whereas Control logically executes from 0 ms to 20 ms, from 20 ms to 40 ms, and so on. Each task has *input ports* and *output ports*, shown as black circles. A task's input ports are set at the beginning of its logical execution interval. During its execution, the task executes some computation, and the results are written to its output ports at end of its logical execution interval. For example, the input ports of Fusion are set at 0 ms; between 0 ms and 10 ms, Fusion computes its function; at 10 ms, the result of this function is written to Fusion's output ports.

A Giotto program may also contain *sensors* and *actuators*, both of which are depicted as white circles. Rather than being actual devices, sensors and actuators are programming language constructs which let the programmer define how to input data into and output data from a Giotto program. Logically, sensors and actuators are passive: they are *polled* at times specified in the Giotto program, and cannot push data into the program at their own times. Our example program has two sensors, GPS and INS, and one actuator, Servos. The sensors are read at 0 ms, 10 ms, 20 ms, etc., and the actuator is written at 0 ms, 20 ms, and so on.

Tasks communicate with each other, and with sensors and actuators, by means of *drivers*, which are shown as diamonds. In Figure 3, the drivers connect the GPS and INS sensors to the input ports of the Fusion task. They also connect the output port of Fusion to the input port of Control, and the output of Control to the Servos actuator. Thus, the Fusion task which executes between 0 and 10 ms receives its inputs from the GPS and INS readings at 0 ms. Similarly, the Control task which starts at 0 ms receives its inputs from the Fusion task which finishes at 0 ms, and writes its outputs to the Servos actuator at 20 ms.

3   Hardware-in-the-Loop Simulation

In this section, we discuss a hardware-in-the-loop simulation (HILS) system useful for the development of multi-vehicle multi-modal embedded systems. Embedded control systems can be viewed as two subsystems: a system under test (SUT), which is the embedded controller, and an environment. The environment contains all the elements that the SUT needs to interact with. HILS makes it possible to conduct comprehensive testing of an embedded system by replacing the real-world environment at the device's input-output interface with a simulated environment. HILS is particularly effective when normal testing is dangerous or costly since it facilitates *repeatable* testing. Though the HILS methodology provides an effective means for testing, its use requires care, especially if simulation results are to be accepted as assurance about real-world safety and performance.

A HILS methodology places stringent requirements on the implementation of the environment since the environment is usually modeled by sets of differential equations. Hence, the simulator which implements the environment needs to operate sufficiently fast in order to meet the hard deadlines. It therefore requires careful selection of underlying numerical methods[11] for solving differential equations. This constraint also greatly limits the choice of operating systems available to run the simulator.

Since accurate multi-vehicle simulation may be computationally intensive, a HILS should be able to scale to parallel execution on multiple interconnected computers.

4   Case Study: End to End Design of Helicopter Based UAV

In this section we discuss strategies for building a helicopter based UAV control system and HILS, with two main goals in mind.

1. The first goal is to incorporate both asynchronous input devices and a time-based controller. Conventionally, sensors are designed to send data at their own, possibly drifting, rates. However, a time-based controller reads from input devices at its own fixed times. Thus, combining these components gives rise to a mismatch in timing behavior which needs to be addressed.

2. The second goal is to build a system that is modular enough to allow one suite of devices (e.g., a sensor suite) to be replaced by another.

To achieve these two goals we will demonstrate the use of the principles of platform-based design. We will show how a layer of abstraction between the devices and the controller can be used to bridge the timing mismatch and to allow for the inclusion of different sensor suites.

4.1   Building Functional Description Using Platform-Based Design

In Section 2 we explained how to begin the platform-based design process by separating the system into two views: the application and the architecture. Here we apply this separation to our helicopter based UAV. From the top, a designer sees the time-based control application. From the bottom, a designer sees the available physical devices, such as the vehicle, the sensors, and the actuators. Following the *meet-in-the-middle* approach of platform-based design, we include an intermediate abstraction layer, the UAV platform, whose top view is suitable for time-based control and whose bottom view is implementable using the available devices.

We next describe the functionality of the UAV platform.

Interaction with devices. The UAV platform should be able to receive data from the sensors at their own rates and without loss of data. Similarly, the platform should be able to send commands to the actuators in the correct formats. It will also need to initialize the devices. Furthermore, the platform should be able to carry out these interactions with a variety of different sensor and actuator suites.

Interaction with control application. The UAV platform should provide measurement data to the control application in the format and at the frequency dictated by the controller. Similarly, the platform should receive the commands from the controller at the controller's rate, and immediately send them on to the actuators. The platform should also be able to support a variety of controllers.

One natural conclusion is that the platform should *buffer* incoming data from the sensors, *convert* sensor data into formats usable by controller applications, and convert control commands into formats usable by actuators. In Section 4.2 we describe in detail two ways to implement the functions of the platform.

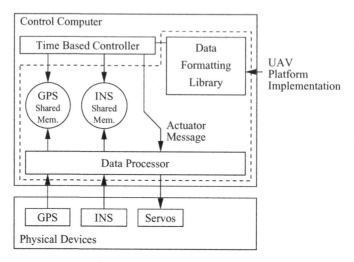

Fig. 4. First implementation of UAV platform

4.2 Implementing Functional Description Using Platform-Based Design

In this section we begin by discussing the realization of the controller application. This implementation, as discussed above in Section 4.1, places constraints on the platform. Platform implementations which meet these constraints are presented next.

Implementing the Controller Application. To attain the benefits of time-based control, the controller application is realized using the Giotto programming language. The two essential tasks for the controller are Fusion and Control. Fusion combines the INS and GPS data using a Kalman filter and is run at a frequency of 100 Hz. Control uses the output from Fusion to compute the control law shown in [6] at a frequency of 50 Hz. The frequencies of these two tasks are chosen based on the expectations of the control law and on the limitations of the devices. Each task is written as a separate C function. These C functions are referenced inside of the Giotto program, which schedules and runs them.

Implementing the UAV Platform. Having considered a realization of the time-based controller, we now turn to the UAV platform. In Section 4.1, we discussed the requirements that our UAV platform needs to fulfill. We now present a possible implementation of the UAV platform which fulfills these requirements. The implementation uses one computer, effectively implementing in software the buffer discussed in Section 4.1.

The single computer implementation has three main elements, which are depicted in Figure 4.

Data processor. The data processor is an independent process, similar to a standard interrupt handler. In the sensing case, it responds to the new sensor data sent by the devices, and saves this data to a shared memory space with the sensor specific data format intact. In the actuating case, the data processor passes on to the servos the messages sent by the controller application.

Shared memory. The shared memory contains recent sensor readings, and is implemented as circular buffers. Data are placed into the circular buffers by the data processor, and can be accessed by the controller application. In this way the controller application can grab the sensor data without worrying about the timing capabilities of each sensor.

Data formatting library. Within the controller application, the sensor specific data format must be converted to the format that the control computation expects. In the sensing case, the controller application uses the data formatting library to transform the buffered sensor readings. In the actuating case, the controller application uses the library to convert actuation commands into the format expected by the servos.

Recall from Section 2.2 that the controller application comes with guarantees about the deadlines of its own internal tasks. These guarantees, however, do not take into account the time that may be needed by other processes or interrupt handlers. If more than a *negligible* amount of time is spent in the other processes, then the timing guarantees of the controller application may cease to be valid. For this reason, the above design keeps the time needed by the data processor to a bare minimum. The data transformations necessary are instead written into the data formatting library and called from within the control tasks. The benefit of this approach is that the timing guarantees of the controller application are preserved, as much as possible. It may appear that the mixture of aperiodic tasks (reception of sensor data) and periodic tasks (Giotto tasks) makes it difficult to guarantee that Giotto tasks will meet their deadlines. However, one can use well-known server techniques, like the deferrable server[14] or the sporadic server [13], to provide fast response times for the reception of sensor data, while still guaranteeing that the deadlines of periodic tasks (in this case, Giotto tasks) will be met. To perform the direct testing of the entire control system discussed in this section, we propose the use of a HIL simulator with the properties outlined in Section 3. Instead of mounting the control system onto the helicopter, the embedded control system, or SUT, is connected to a simulation computer.

The proposed simulation framework, in combination with platform-based design, allow for the development of automation control systems that are modular and have guaranteed performance.

4.3 Hardware-in-the-Loop Simulations

In this project we have obtained results through the combination of the controller application running in Giotto and the platform implementation presented in the previous section, and a realization of a HIL simulator.

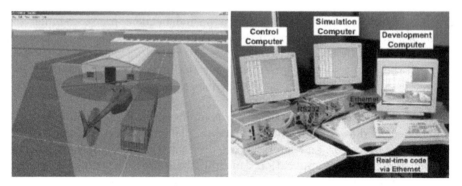

Fig. 5. a. Graphical flight display; b. Flight capable hardware with real-time operating systems.

The controller application, along with the realization of the platform currently runs on a flight capable computer running VxWorks. This control computer communicates with the HIL simulation computer using a high speed serial connection. The HIL simulator uses the dynamic model of the Yamaha R-50 whose origin is presented in [6]. The simulator generates the states of the model by using a numerical ODE solver. It also runs on the VxWorks real-time operating system. In order to visualize the performance of the overall system which consists of the Giotto controller, platform realization, and the HIL simulator, the current state of the simulated helicopter was sent via network to a 3-D visualization program where the helicopter is rendered on screen. Figure 5a is a screen shot of this program.

Experimental Results. Numerous test flights have been performed by 'flying' our Giotto and UAV platform embedded control system on the HIL simulator. In one series of test flights we configured the control task, which runs from within the Giotto program, to fly in a triangular flight pattern. The triangular pattern consisted of a repetition of the following modes of flight:

Takeoff: Flight in the forward and upwards directions at a 45 degree angle.
Flight: Flight in the backwards direction with no heading change.
Landing: Flight in the forwards and downwards directions at a 45 degree angle.

The desired velocities and heading references are displayed in Figure 6a. Figure 6b shows the actual velocities and heading output by the HIL simulator during a real-time test flight. By comparing the figures, one can conclude that the simulated helicopter follows very closely the desired references. This result attests to the accuracy of our embedded control system in implementing the control laws and to the usefulness of the hardware-in-the-loop simulator.

Figure 7a shows both the changing desired forward velocity, and the actual forward velocity output by the HIL simulator. Figure 7b shows the changing desired downwards velocity as compared to the actual downwards velocity. The two remaining figures, 7c and 7d, show the actual sideways velocity or heading with a desired velocity and a heading of zero.

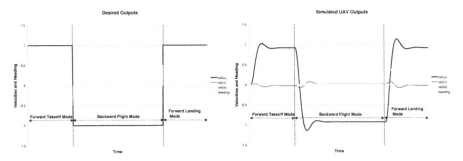

Fig. 6. a. Desired output setpoints; b. Simulated output trajectories.

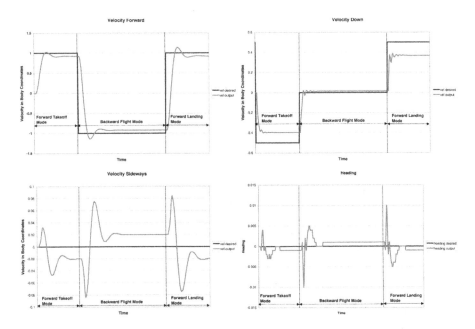

Fig. 7. a. Forward body velocity (top-left); b. Downward body velocity (top-right); c. Sideward body velocity (bottom-left); d. Heading angle (bottom-right).

These data only begin to illuminate the possible utility of the HILS. For example, flight mode switching anomalies can easily be compared between controllers. Furthermore, this simulation framework could be put to work simulating multiple helicopters flying in formation.

Multi-vehicle HIL System. A HIL system would be useful for testing networked embedded controllers due to the complexity of simulating a network and the safety concerns involved with multi-vehicle coordination testing. Here the physical network would be part of the system so it would not have to be simulated, and yet this realistic testing can be performed without using physical vehicles. In extending our HIL simulator for multiple vehicles we propose the

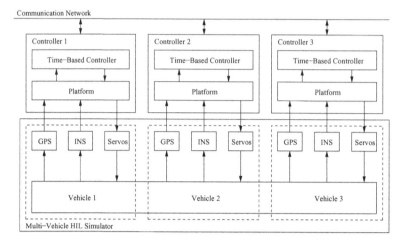

Fig. 8. Implementation of Hardware-In-The-Loop Simulation for three helicopter-based UAVs

use of a separate sensor suite for each simulated vehicle. However, the plant models could be concatenated so that the integration for all of the models can be performed simultaneously. This method will ease the software schedulability analysis necessary to determine how many vehicles each CPU can simulate. On the other hand, the timing of the inputs and outputs of each simulated vehicle can be individually determined by their separate sensors and servo processes. The implementation of HILS for multiple helicopters is shown in Figure 8.

5   Conclusion

In this paper, we presented a methodology for the design of embedded controllers for multi-vehicle multi-modal systems. Our methodology is predicated upon the principles of platform-based design. By providing the appropriate layers of abstraction, the methodology allows for the integration of both a time-based controller application and a non-time-based sensor suite. An essential layer of abstraction in our methodology is the software platform provided by the programming language Giotto, which allows a clean implementation of a time-based controller application. To demonstrate the effectiveness of our design methodology, a helicopter-based UAV design was presented that met our goals of a modular system with time guarantees. We also presented a HIL simulator for the UAV that was used to obtain controlled test flight results and can be expanded for multi-vehicle examinations.

Though our case study contains many details that are specific to our helicopter system, our methodology is widely applicable. We believe that the combination of time-based control and platform-based design can be generally applied to automatic control systems, for which legacy software, independently engineered subsystems, and strict reliability and timing requirements all play a crucial role.

Acknowledgments

The authors would like to thank the reviewers for their valuable comments. This work is supported by the DARPA SEC grant, F33615-98-C-3614.

References

1. G. Berry and G. Gonthier. The Esterel synchronous programming language: Design, semantics, implementation. *Information and Computation*, 163:172–202, 1992.
2. V. Bertin, E. Closse, M. Poize, J. Pulou, J. Sifakis, P. Venier, D. Weil, and S. Yovine. Taxys = Esterel + Kronos: A tool for verifying real-time properties of embedded systems. In *Proceedings of the 40th IEEE Conference on Decision and Control*, pages 2875–2880, December 2001.
3. N. Halbwachs, P. Caspi, P. Raymond, and D. Pilaud. The synchronous data flow programming language Lustre. *Proceedings of the IEEE*, 79(9):1305–1320, September 1991.
4. T.A. Henzinger, B. Horowitz, and C.M. Kirsch. Embedded control systems development with Giotto. In *Proc. of the Intl. Workshop on Languages, Compilers, and Tools for Embedded Systems (LCTES '01)*, pages 64–72, August 2001.
5. T.A. Henzinger, B. Horowitz, and C.M. Kirsch. Giotto: a time-triggered language for embedded programming. In *Proc. of the 1st Intl. Workshop on Embedded Software (EMSOFT '01)*, LNCS 2211, pages 166–184. Springer-Verlag, October 2001.
6. B. Horowitz, J. Liebman, C. Ma, T. J. Koo, A. Sangiovanni-Vincentelli, and S. Sastry. Platform-based embedded software design and system integration for autonomous vehicles. *submitted to IEEE Proceedings*, 2002.
7. C.M. Kirsch, M.A.A. Sanvido, T.A. Henzinger, and W. Pree. A Giotto-based helicopter control system (draft), 2002.
8. T. J. Koo, J. Liebman, C. Ma, and S. Sastry. Hierarchical approach for design of multi-vehicle multi-modal embedded software. In *Proc. of the 1st Intl. Workshop on Embedded Software (EMSOFT '01)*, LNCS 2211, pages 344–360. Springer-Verlag, October 2001.
9. H. Kopetz. *Real-time systems: design principles for distributed embedded applications*. Kluwer, 1997.
10. H. Kopetz and G. Grunsteidl. TTP – a protocol for fault-tolerant real-time systems. *Computer*, 27(1):14–23, January 1994.
11. J.A. Ledin. Hardware-in-the-loop simulation. *Embedded Systems Programming*, 12(2):42–60, February 1999.
12. A. Sangiovanni-Vincentelli. Defining platform-based design. *EEDesign of EE-Times*, February 2002.
13. B. Sprunt, S. Liu, and J. Lehoczky. Aperiodic task scheduling for hard-real-time systems. *Real-Time Systems*, 1(1):27–60, June 1989.
14. J. K. Strosnider, J. P. Lehoczky, and S. Lui. The deferrable server algorithm for enhanced aperiodic responsiveness in hard real-time environments. *IEEE Transactions on Computers*, 44(1):73–91, January 1995.
15. L. Wills, S. Kannan, M. Guler, B. Heck, J.V.R. Prasad, D. Schrage, and G. Vachtsevanos. An open platform for reconfigurable control. *IEEE Control Systems Magazine*, 21(3):49–64, June 2001.

A Giotto-Based Helicopter Control System[*]

Christoph M. Kirsch[1], Marco A.A. Sanvido[1],
Thomas A. Henzinger[1], and Wolfgang Pree[2]

[1] Department of Electrical Engineering and Computer Sciences
University of California, Berkeley, USA
{cm,msanvido,tah}@eecs.berkeley.edu
[2] Software Research Lab
University of Salzburg, Austria
pree@SoftwareResearch.net

Abstract. We demonstrate the feasibility and benefits of Giotto-based control software development by reimplementing the autopilot system of an autonomously flying model helicopter. Giotto offers a clean separation between the platform-independent concerns of software functionality and I/O timing, and the platform-dependent concerns of software scheduling and execution. Functionality code such as code computing control laws can be generated automatically from Simulink models or, as in the case of this project, inherited from a legacy system. I/O timing code is generated automatically from Giotto models that specify real-time requirements such as task frequencies and actuator update rates. We extend Simulink to support the design of Giotto models, and from these models, the automatic generation of Giotto code that supervises the interaction of the functionality code with the physical environment. The Giotto compiler performs a schedulability analysis on the Giotto code, and generates timing code for the helicopter platform. The Giotto methodology guarantees the stringent hard real-time requirements of the autopilot system, and at the same time supports the automation of the software development process in a way that produces a transparent software architecture with predictable behavior and reusable components.

1 Introduction

We present a methodology for control software development based on the embedded programming language Giotto [3], by implementing the controller for an autonomously flying model helicopter. A Giotto program specifies the real-time interaction of functional components with the physical world as well as among the components themselves. For the helicopter, we isolated the functional components from existing code, specified the timing of the component interaction using a Simulink model and automatically transformed it into a Giotto program. The actual timing code was then generated automatically by the Giotto compiler. The original helicopter system [1] was developed at the ETH Zürich as a customized system based on the programming language Oberon [9,10] and the real-time operating system HelyOS [7]. The reengineering in Giotto introduces a

---

[*] This research was supported in part by the DARPA SEC grant F33615-C-98-3614, the MARCO GSRC grant 98-DT-660, and the AFOSR MURI grant F49620-00-1-0327.

A. Sangiovanni-Vincentelli and J. Sifakis (Eds.): EMSOFT 2002, LNCS 2491, pp. 46–60, 2002.
© Springer-Verlag Berlin Heidelberg 2002

negligible overhead, and at the same time increases the reusability and reliability of the software. We started from a system that already met the desired objectives, i.e., a fully working system with a well-modularized software architecture. By reimplementing the system using Giotto we inductively proved that the Giotto concept is suited for complex control problems and automates the design and implementation of well-engineered control software. This shows that the implementation of difficult control tasks can be significantly simplified by adequate tools and programming languages.

This article begins with a conceptual overview of the Giotto methodology and discusses how Giotto helps to automate control software development. Then, a brief overview of the helicopter system is given. Next, the helicopter control software is presented in two steps. We first introduce Giotto's core constructs by means of Simulink's visual syntax, and then give their translation into Giotto's textual syntax. Finally, the paper discusses the compilation and execution of the resulting Giotto control system.

2   Overview of the Giotto Methodology

The goal of Giotto is to provide the high-level, domain-specific abstractions that allow control engineers and control software developers to focus on the control system aspects instead of the platform. By platform, we mean the specific hardware and operating system on which the control system runs. A Giotto program specifies the control system's *reactivity*, which is checked for its *schedulability* by the compiler. The term reactivity expresses what we mean by control system aspects: the system's functionality, in particular, the control laws, and the system's timing requirements. The term schedulability expresses what we mean by platform-dependent aspects, such as platform performance, platform utilization (scheduling), and fault tolerance. The Giotto programmer specifies reactivity; the Giotto compiler checks schedulability for a specific platform, and generates timing code for the platform. *Timing code* determines when a sensor is read or an actuator is updated as well as when a control law computation is invoked. *Functionality code* implements the actual sensor reading, actuator update, and control law computation. Functionality code must be written in a programming language such as C or Oberon. Timing and functionality code are executed on a runtime system that consists of a virtual machine called the *Embedded Machine* [4] and a real-time operating system. The timing code, also called *E code*, is interpreted by the Embedded Machine whereas the functionality code is scheduled for execution by the operating system's scheduler. The scheduling scheme of the operating system and the schedulability test of the Giotto compiler must be compatible.

The separation of reactivity and schedulability implies a shift in control software development away from low-level, platform-dependent implementation details towards high-level, domain-specific issues. This is analogous to high-level general-purpose programming languages, which abstract from the details of the underlying hardware. In this sense Giotto represents a high-level programming language for embedded control systems. Developers of such systems benefit from the separation of concerns in several ways. First, the development effort is significantly reduced, as the tedious programming of the timing code is handed over to the compiler. Also, the automation of the timing code implementation eliminates a common source of errors. Second, a Giotto program

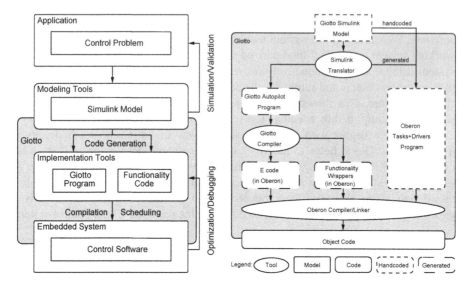

Fig. 1. The Giotto-based development process   **Fig. 2.** The Giotto tool chain

specifies reactivity in a modular fashion, which facilitates the exchange and addition of functionality. Also, functionality code can be packaged as software components and reused. Third, the system can easily be ported to other platforms for which an implementation of the Embedded Machine is available. Fourth, the reactive properties of a control system specified by a Giotto program (functionality and timing) can be subject to formal verification.

2.1   Giotto-Based Control-Systems Development

The traditional and the Giotto-based development of control systems is aided by *modeling tools* and *implementation tools* as shown in Figure 1. A modeling tool such as MathWorks' Simulink supports the development of a controller model that solves a given control problem. The controller model can be simulated and validated with respect to the requirements of the control problem. In this step the platform constraints such as CPU performance and code size are ignored. The design at this step is therefore *solution-oriented* and *platform-independent*. Once a controller model has been validated, a controller program that implements the model is generated. The functionality code of the controller program may be generated automatically by code generators for Simulink. The timing code, on the other hand, is typically hand-written. Then, implementation tools such as compilers and debuggers support the implementation and optimization of the controller program under platform-dependent constraints. Due to restricted platform performance, a controller program often needs to be optimized with respect to platform-dependent properties such as execution speed or size in order to implement the controller model correctly. Without Giotto the close correspondence between the controller model and program is typically lost in the optimization step, in particular, if it is done by hand: functionality code and timing code are often not reusable on a different platform or for a modified model. With Giotto the correspondence is maintained

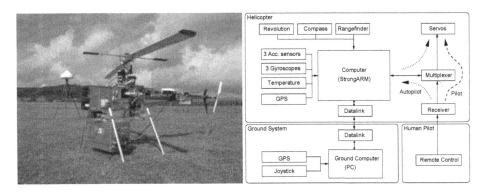

Fig. 3. The OLGA helicopter   **Fig. 4.** The OLGA ECS structure

because timing aspects such as the real-time frequencies of controller tasks are specified in a platform-independent way already in the controller model: Giotto decreases the gap between model and program. Then, a Giotto program is automatically generated from the model. In a final step, the Giotto compiler generates the timing code from the Giotto program for a given platform.

2.2 The Giotto Tool Chain

Figure 2 shows the Giotto tool chain used for the reengineering of the helicopter autopilot system. The developer starts by specifying a control model using the Giotto constructs made available in Simulink. The control model specifies the I/O timing and the timing of the interaction between functional units such as tasks, which perform computation, and drivers, which interface tasks with the hardware. Tasks and drivers are functionality code written in Oberon that we have reused from the original autopilot implementation. In principle, most of the functionality code could have been generated automatically by a Simulink code generator. From the control model in Simulink, we obtain executable code in two steps. First, a Giotto translator tool generates a Giotto program from the model. Second, the Giotto compiler checks the schedulability of the Giotto program on a given platform based on worst-case execution times for tasks and drivers, and then generates two Oberon programs: the E code (timing code), and so-called functionality wrappers that interface tasks and drivers with E code. Finally, the Oberon code is compiled and linked into an executable that is guaranteed to exhibit the same timing behavior as the original controller model. The same tool chain can be used if Oberon is replaced by another programming language and HelyOS by another RTOS. For example, the Giotto tools also support C and OSEKWorks [19].

3   The Helicopter System

The original helicopter system [1] was developed at ETH Zürich as part of an interdisciplinary project to build an autonomously flying model helicopter for research purposes.

The helicopter is a custom-crafted model with a single-CPU (StrongARM-based) control platform that was also developed at ETH Zürich [1]. All functional components are implemented in the programming language Oberon [9,10] on top of the custom-designed real-time operating system HelyOS [7].

The OLGA system (for *Oberon Language Goes Airborne*) consists of an aircraft, i.e., the model helicopter and a ground system. Figure 3 shows a picture of the helicopter; Figure 4 shows the system structure. The ground system (bottom of Figure 4) supports mission planning, flight command activation, and flight monitoring. As this part of the system is not relevant for the implementation of the autopilot system, it is not discussed here. All sensors for navigation purposes (except the GPS receiver used for the differential GPS) and the computational power needed for navigation and flight control are airborne. The sensors used on the helicopter are a GPS receiver, a compass, a revolution sensor, a laser altimeter (range finder), three accelerometers, three gyroscopes, and a temperature sensor. Note that the arrow on the right of Figure 4 labeled *Pilot*, which connects the boxes *Receiver* and *Servos*, represents the alternative control by a human pilot. It is required as a back-up for safety reasons. A human pilot is able to remotely switch to fully manual mode at any time during operation, short-cutting OLGA in case of any malfunctions.

The complexity of helicopter flight control results from the number of different sensors and actuators the system has to handle concurrently, the difficulty in flying the helicopter, and the limitations of the autopilot system (electrical consumption, limited computational power, vibrations, jitter, etc.). Moreover, the helicopter is a dangerous and expensive platform, where a trial-and-error approach cannot be used. The control and navigation algorithms are based on hard real-time assumptions that have to be guaranteed under all circumstances by the implementation. In our specific autopilot example, the controller and navigation frequency were chosen to run at 40 Hz. The computational power required for each step was in the worst case 12 ms, which gave a CPU utilization for control and navigation of more then 45%, leaving not much for the housekeeping activities such as background and monitoring. The complexity of the problem is evidenced by the fail/success rate, i.e., the number of research projects on autonomously flying helicopters, and the number of such projects that have not managed to implement a fully working system. In most cases the failure was not due to financial or human-resource constraints, but due to the complexity of the implementation itself. Simulating an autopilot system is relatively easy (look at the number of master's theses on this subject), but turning it into a working system is not. And turning it into a clean, structured, and well-engineered system (both hardware and software) is even harder. The references [11,12,13,14,15,16,17,18] are well-known ongoing academic helicopter projects. In [2] an overview of all major autonomous model helicopter projects is given.

4   The Autopilot Software

The autopilot system has six different modes of operation (see Figure 5). In each mode different tasks are active. The modes are Init, Idle, Motor, TakeOff, ControlOff, and ControlOn. The first three modes are needed in order to correctly handle the initialization procedure. The Motor and TakeOff modes handle the

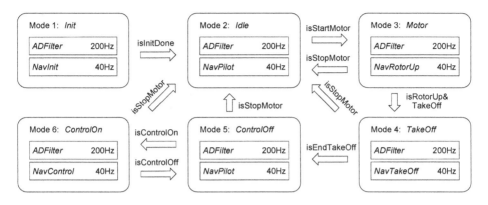

Fig. 5. The operating modes of the controller

transition from a 0 rpm rotor speed to a safe speed of 300 rpm. At this speed the helicopter is guaranteed not to take off, and only an active command from the ground station allows the transition to mode `TakeOff`. When the take-off procedure is finished, the helicopter is in mode `ControlOff`. In this mode, the rotor is at a nominal speed of 1200 rpm and the pilot has full control over the helicopter. At this point, the pilot is able to switch, at any time, to the `ControlOn` mode, activating the autopilot. For simplicity, we will henceforth focus only on the two modes `ControlOff` and `ControlOn`. In the `ControlOff` mode, a human pilot controls the helicopter, whereas in the `ControlOn` mode, the helicopter operates autonomously. The `ControlOff` mode consists of the 200 Hz task `ADFilter` and the 40 Hz task `NavPilot`. The `ADFilter` task decodes and preprocesses sensor values. The `NavPilot` task keeps track of the helicopter's position and velocity using the preprocessed data from the `ADFilter` task, and translates pilot commands received via the wireless link into servo commands. The `ControlOff` mode switches to the `ControlOn` mode if the pilot pushes a button on the remote control. Besides the 200 Hz task `ADFilter`, the `ControlOn` mode has the 40 Hz task `NavControl`, which replaces the `NavPilot` task. Besides keeping track of position and velocity this task implements the controller that stabilizes the helicopter autonomously. The `ControlOn` mode switches back to the `ControlOff` mode if the pilot pushes a take-over button on the remote control.

4.1 A Simulink Specification of the Giotto Model

We have extended Simulink with the capability of expressing Giotto models. A Giotto model in Simulink specifies the real-time interaction of its components with the physical world. All components of a Giotto model execute periodically. A Giotto model has a single parameter that specifies the hyper-period of the components. The hyper-period is the least common multiple period of all component periods. As an example consider Figure 6, which shows the Simulink specification of a Giotto model called `helicopter controller`, which is connected to a continuous-time model of the helicopter dynamics. The dynamics block contains only standard continuous-time Simulink blocks,

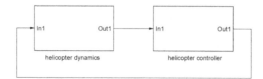

Fig. 6. The Giotto helicopter model in Simulink

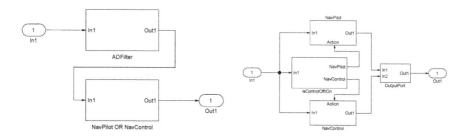

Fig. 7. The Giotto tasks in Simulink   **Fig. 8.** The Giotto case block in Simulink

whereas the controller block is a so-called *Giotto model block*, and exhibits Giotto semantics. The controller block contains a Giotto model that has two modes of operation: human control (`ControlOff`) and autonomous flight (`ControlOn`). The helicopter controller has a hyper-period of 25 ms.

Figure 7 shows the contents of the `helicopter controller` block. The block labeled `ADFilter` is a *Giotto task block*, which represents a single Giotto task — the basic functional unit in Giotto. A Giotto task is a periodically executed piece of Oberon code. In the example, the `ADFilter` block contains only standard discrete-time Simulink blocks that implement the decoding and preprocessing of sensor values. The second block in the Giotto model is an example of a *Giotto case block*, which may contain multiple Giotto tasks. Upon each invocation a case block picks exactly one of its tasks to execute. In the example, the case block contains the Giotto task blocks `NavPilot` and `NavControl`. The `NavPilot` task computes the helicopter position and velocity, and reads pilot commands from which it produces the correct servo values. Thus, every time the `NavPilot` task executes, the human pilot has full control of the helicopter. The `NavControl` task, by contrast, implements autonomous flight: it also computes position and velocity, but produces the servo values based on a control law computation. Each case block has a frequency given as an integer value relative to the hyper-period of the Giotto model. Here the case block has a frequency of 1, i.e., it executes with a period of 25ms. Both tasks in the case block inherit that frequency. Note that the `ADFilter` task block in the Giotto model is actually an abbreviation for a case block containing a single task. In fact, Giotto model blocks may contain case blocks only. The virtual case block around the `ADFilter` task has a frequency of 5, which means that the task runs five times per 25 ms, i.e., with a period of 5 ms.

Figure 8 shows the contents of the case block. Besides the two task blocks, there is a *Giotto switch block*, labeled `isControlOff/On`. A Giotto switch block may contain any standard discrete-time Simulink blocks in order to determine, based on its input port values, at least one task that gets to execute. If no task is chosen to execute all previous output port values are held. The isControlOff/On block reads a pilot command to switch from manual to autonomous mode and back. In our example, it always chooses between the NavPilot task and the NavControl task. The switch block is evaluated once for each invocation of the surrounding case block at the beginning of its period. Thus it is evaluated once every 25 ms. Note that the block labeled OutputPort is necessary only for connecting the outputs of the two tasks to a single output port. Moreover, the tasks and the switch block in a case block may only read from the input ports of the case block but not from any task output ports in that block. In order to do this one has to establish a link outside of the case block from an output port to an input port.

The time-triggered semantics of Giotto enables efficient reasoning about the timing behavior of a Giotto model, in particular, whether it conforms to the timing requirements of the control design. Moreover, Giotto models are compositional in the sense that any number of Giotto models may be added side by side without changing their individual semantics. For example, additional functionality can be added to the helicopter controller without changing the real-time behavior of the controller. This, of course, assumes the provision of sufficient computational resources, which is checked by the Giotto compiler for a specified platform. In order to simulate Giotto models in Simulink we have developed a translator that reads Simulink specifications of Giotto models and transforms them into standard discrete-time multi-rate Simulink models. The tool also generates the corresponding Giotto programs in textual form, which can then be processed by the Giotto compiler for schedulability analysis and to generate code.

4.2   The Giotto Program

Giotto defines the exact timing and communication between a Giotto program and its environment as well as among Giotto tasks. For this purpose, a Giotto program needs to make explicit semantical details that are left implicit or unspecified in the Simulink specification of a Giotto model. In order to transport values between ports, Giotto uses the concept of drivers. We distinguish *Giotto task*, *actuator*, and *mode drivers* from *Giotto device drivers*. The purpose of a Giotto task and actuator driver is to transport values from sensors and task output ports to task input ports and actuators, respectively; a Giotto mode driver evaluates a mode-switch condition and, if it evaluates to true, transports initial values to task output ports of the target mode; a Giotto device driver transports values from a hardware device or a non-Giotto task to a port or vice versa. In the Simulink specification of a Giotto model task and actuator drivers exist only implicitly as links, while Giotto device drivers are absent entirely. However, device drivers are required in a complete implementation of a Giotto program to link it to the hardware or non-Giotto tasks such as low-level event-triggered or non-time-critical tasks.

From a Giotto model block in Simulink, we generate a *Giotto program*, which is a collection of Giotto modes. Each *Giotto mode* has a hyper-period, a set of task invocations with specified frequencies, a set of actuator updates with specified frequencies, and a set of mode switches with specified frequencies. A task invocation executes the task driver followed by the task, an actuator update executes the actuator driver, and a mode switch evaluates a mode driver, possibly followed by a switch to the target mode. The following

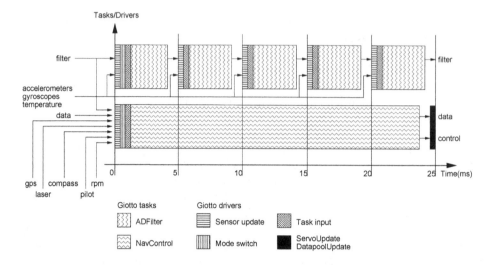

Fig. 9. The logical execution of the Giotto program in the `ControlOn` mode

example shows the Giotto program `helicopter controller`, which specifies the `ControlOff` and `ControlOn` modes:

```
mode ControlOff() period 25 {
   actfreq  1 do ServoUpdate;
   actfreq  1 do DataPoolUpdate;
   exitfreq 1 do ControlOn;
   taskfreq 5 do ADFilter;
   taskfreq 1 do NavPilot;}
mode ControlOn() period 25 {
   actfreq  1 do ServoUpdate;
   actfreq  1 do DataPoolUpdate;
   exitfreq 1 do ControlOff;
   taskfreq 5 do ADFilter;
   taskfreq 1 do NavControl;}
```

The hyper-period of both modes is 25 ms. The frequency of the tasks, mode switches, and actuator updates is specified relative to this period. For example, the `ADFilter` task runs in both modes five times per 25 ms, i.e., at 200 Hz. The helicopter `servos` and the `datapool`, which contains messages that are sent to the ground station, are updated once every 25 ms by invocations of the Giotto actuator drivers `ServoUpdate` and `DataPoolUpdate`, respectively. Figure 9 shows the logical execution of a single hyper-period of the `ControlOn` mode (the actual execution is shown in Figure 11 and will be discussed later). Logically, the `ADFilter` task runs five times exactly for 5 ms, while the `NavControl` task runs once exactly for 25 ms. Note that all Giotto drivers are executed in logical zero time. While a Giotto task represents *scheduled* computation on the application level and consumes logical time, a Giotto driver is *synchronous*, bounded code, which is executed logically instantaneously on the system level (since drivers cannot depend on each other, no issues of fixed-point semantics arise).

Intertask communication as well as communication from and to sensors and actuators works through *Giotto ports*. In the Giotto program we declare all sensor ports globally as follows:

```
sensor
  GPSPort      gps uses             GPSGet;
  LaserPort    laser uses           LaserGet;
  CompassPort  compass uses         CompassGet;
  RPMPort      rpm uses             RotorGet;
  ServoPort    pilot uses           ServoGet;
  AnalogPort   accelerometers uses  AccGet;
  AnalogPort   gyroscopes uses      GyrosGet;
  AnalogPort   temperature uses     TempGet;
  BoolPort     startswitch uses     StartSwitchGet;
  BoolPort     stopswitch uses      StopSwitchGet;
```

Besides a type name, we declare a Giotto device driver for each sensor port. For example, the sensor port gps has the type GPSPort and uses the Giotto device driver GPSGet to get new sensor values from the GPS device. Types and device drivers are implemented externally to Giotto. Here they are Oberon types and procedures. In Figure 9, at the 0 ms instant, the first action is to read the latest sensor values by calling the Giotto device drivers for all Giotto sensor ports. Subsequently, every 5 ms until the end of the hyper-period, the device drivers are called only for the sensor ports that are read by the ADFilter task. Giotto device drivers are always called in a time-triggered fashion. However, some devices require immediate attention using an event-triggered (interrupt-driven) driver. For example, the GPSGet device driver does not access directly the GPS device but a buffer in which an interrupt handler that is bound to the GPS device places the latest GPS readings. The interrupt handler is external to the Giotto program. The opposite direction for communication from a port to a device is done in a similar way and will be discussed below. At the 0 ms instant right after executing the Giotto device drivers for the sensor ports, the Giotto mode driver is called to determine whether to switch into the ControlOff mode or not. The driver is declared as follows:

```
driver ControlOff(stopswitch) output () {
  switch isControlOff(stopswitch)}
```

The driver has a single driver input port stopswitch, which is a globally declared sensor or task output port. In this case it is a sensor port whose Giotto device driver StopSwitchGet has just been called. The device driver reads the pilot switch AutopilotOn/Off from an FPGA, which decodes the pilot switch position transmitted via the wireless link from the remote control to the airborne system. Based on the value of the stopswitch port, the Oberon implementation of the isControlOff predicate returns true or false determining whether to switch to the ControlOff mode or not. Suppose that we stay in the ControlOn mode. The next step is to load the task input ports of the ADFilter and NavControl tasks with the latest values of the sensor and task output ports to which the tasks are connected as specified in the task declarations below. Before declaring the tasks all task output ports are declared globally as follows:

```
output
  AnalogPort    filter  := FilterInit;
  ServoPort     control := ServoInit;
  DataPoolPort  data    := DataPoolInit;
```

The filter port is the only task output port of the ADFilter task. The control and data ports are the task output ports of the NavControl task. For each task output port, in addition to the type, an initialization driver is specified, which is invoked once at start-up time to initialize the port. Here the initialization drivers are implemented by Oberon procedures. Initial values for all task output ports sufficiently describe a unique start configuration of a Giotto program. Then, for a given behavior of the sensors, a Giotto program computes a *deterministic* trace of actuator values, provided all tasks meet their deadlines [3]. The ADFilter and NavControl tasks are declared as follows:

```
task ADFilter(accelerometers, gyroscopes, temperature, filter)
  output (filter) {
  schedule ADFilterImplementation(accelerometers, gyroscopes,
                                  temperature, filter)}
task NavControl(gps, laser, compass, filter, rpm, pilot, data)
  output (control, data) {
  schedule NavControlImplementation(gps, laser, compass, filter,
                                    rpm, pilot, control, data)}
```

The ADFilter task reads from the accelerometers, gyroscopes, temperature, and filter ports. The filter port is also a task output port, which makes the port a state variable of the task. Prior to the invocation of the task, the values of all four ports are copied by a task driver to some local memory, which is only accessible to the task itself. The task driver does not have to be declared explicitly. The Oberon ADFilterImplementation corresponds to the functional part of the ADFilter implementation in the original OLGA system. The NavControl task is declared in a similar way. Now, the Giotto program is ready to invoke the ADFilter and NavControl tasks. The NavControl task runs logically for 25 ms, while the ADFilter task finishes after 5 ms. Then, new sensor values are read and the task input ports of the ADFilter task are loaded, before invoking the task again. This process repeats until the 25 ms time instant is reached. At that time instant new values in the control and data ports of the NavControl task are available. The new values are now transferred by the Giotto actuator drivers ServoUpdate and DataPoolUpdate to the servos and datapool actuator ports, respectively. In order to declare the actuator drivers we first need to declare the actuator ports globally as follows:

```
actuator
  ServoPort    servos   uses ServoPut;
  DataPoolPort datapool uses DataPoolPut;
```

Besides a type name, we declare a Giotto device driver for each actuator port. For example, the actuator port servos has the type ServoPort and uses the Giotto device driver ServoPut to transfer new actuator values to the helicopter servos. Again, types and device drivers are implemented externally to Giotto. Before the device drivers are called, the actuator drivers ServoUpdate and DataPoolUpdate are executed. The actuator drivers are declared as follows:

```
driver ServoUpdate(control) output (servos) {
  call ServoUpdateImplementation(control, servos)}
driver DataPoolUpdate(data) output (datapool) {
  call DataPoolUpdateImplementation(data, datapool)}
```

In Figure 9, at the 25 ms instant after the NavControl task finished, the helicopter servos and datapool are updated by first executing the Oberon ServoUpdateImplementation and DataPoolUpdateImplementation, which transport the values from the control and data ports to the servos and datapool ports, respectively. Then, the `ServoPut` device driver is called, which takes the new value from the `servos` port and then directly updates the servo devices. The `DataPoolPut` device driver is also called but instead of accessing a device it puts the value from the `datapool` port into a buffer, which gets transmitted over the wireless link as soon as the Giotto system becomes idle. The actual transmission is done by the asynchronous message handler task of the original OLGA system. This task is external to the Giotto program. The 25 ms hyper-period is now finished. In the next section, we will discuss the execution of the Giotto program and present the actual task schedule of the program.

5   The Giotto Compiler and Execution Environment

The Giotto-based implementation of the autopilot system has the same functionality as the original system but uses the Giotto programming language for the explicit specification of real-time requirements and inter-task communication. The autopilot functions, i.e., the navigation and control tasks, are released from any timing or scheduling code but otherwise correspond to their original OLGA implementations. The system architecture of the Giotto-based system is shown in Figure 10. The upper left portion shows the Giotto program, including the Oberon implementation of the Giotto device drivers as well as the Giotto tasks and drivers. The non-Giotto tasks shown in the upper right portion of Figure 10 implement event-triggered or non-time-critical tasks, which are interfaced to the Giotto system through Giotto device drivers. Event-triggered tasks must be taken into account by the schedulability analysis performed by the Giotto compiler; background tasks are performed only when the Giotto system is idle. In the middle of Figure 10, the original OLGA software system is shown extended by an implementation of the Embedded Machine [4] in the kernel of the HelyOS real-time operating system. The software system runs on the OLGA computer system.

A Giotto program does not specify where, how, and when tasks are scheduled. For example, the helicopter-control program can be compiled on platforms that have a single CPU (by time sharing the tasks) as well as on platforms with two CPUs (by parallelism); it can be compiled on platforms with preemptive priority scheduling (such as most real-time operating systems) as well as on truly time-triggered platforms. The mapping from the Giotto program to executable code for the helicopter platform is performed by the Giotto compiler. The Giotto compiler needs to ensure that the logical semantics of Giotto —functionality and timing— is preserved. The compiler targets the Embedded Machine, which interprets the generated E code in real-time. The E code instructions provide a portable API to the underlying RTOS. There are E code instructions to call or schedule the native implementation of tasks and drivers, respectively, as well as instructions to invoke the Embedded Machine at specific time instants or occurrences of events. The generated E code implements the logical semantics of the Giotto program provided the E code is *time-safe* [4], which intuitively means that all tasks meet their deadlines. The compiler performs a schedulability analysis by checking time safety of the given Giotto program [5] for given worst-case execution times of the tasks and drivers. Time-safe E code programs are *environment-determined* [4], which means that, for any given behavior of the physical world seen through the sensors, the E code computes a deterministic trace of actuator values at deterministic time instants. In other words, a

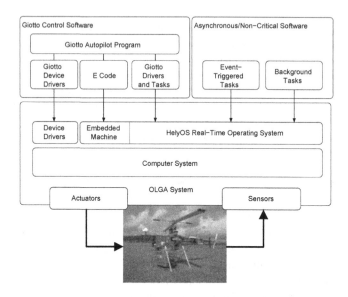

Fig. 10. The Giotto-based autopilot system

Giotto system exhibits no internal race conditions, which makes the behavior of Giotto systems predictable and verifiable.

Figure 11 shows the actual execution of the Giotto program from the previous section, as specified by the generated E code. The top row shows the execution of the ADFilter task and the drivers from the top row in Figure 9. The middle row shows the execution of the NavControl task and the drivers from the bottom row in Figure 9; note that the NavControl task is physically preempted. The bottom row shows the execution of background tasks. The Giotto compiler generates E code that accesses sensors and actuators as close as possible to the specified time instants in order to reduce I/O jitter. The existing I/O behavior of the system would not change if we were to add more Giotto tasks, provided the compiler succeeds in showing the resulting E code to be time-safe despite the additional load.

6   Conclusion

The successful reengineering of the OLGA system using Giotto shows the feasibility of the Giotto approach for high-performance, hard real-time embedded control systems. The Giotto compiler automatically generates timing code for a system with multiple modes of operation, multiple levels of task priorities, and time-triggered as well as event-triggered task activation. Giotto implies an overhead through predicate checks, calls of wrapper functions, and the copying of ports. Measurements have shown that this amounts to less than 2% of the 25 ms period, which is easily acceptable for helicopter flight control. The implementation of the Embedded Machine on top of HelyOS was accomplished in one week, and its source code is only 6 KB. Embedded control systems that are based on Giotto can expect a high degree of modularization. In particular, in

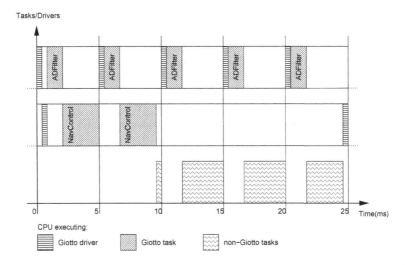

Fig. 11. The actual execution of the Giotto program in the `ControlOn` mode based on rate-monotonic scheduling

the helicopter control system, the timing concerns and the inter-process communication are decoupled from the navigation and control algorithms. The Giotto-based autopilot system is nonetheless functionally comparable to systems that use considerably more complex software architectures [8]. The functionality and reliability of the original ETH Zürich helicopter system has been proven by many flight tests. The Giotto-based reimplementation inherits the same functionality but with increased software reusability, flexibility, and transparency. The reimplementation was shown to be correct and working by means of on-the-ground tests. No actual on-flight tests have been done, not for technical reasons but for reasons outside our control. A similar reengineering approach has been used to assess the feasibility of other methodologies, for example, Meta-H has been applied to embedded missile control systems [6].

The case study has had substantial impact on the ongoing development of the Giotto concept. In particular, it has guided the refinement of Giotto from a theoretical to a practical language for embedded control software. For example, the precise interaction between Giotto ports (a concept of the formal Giotto semantics) and actual devices (such as sensors and actuators) needed much elaboration and is made concrete through the concept of Giotto device drivers. Second, while the formal Giotto semantics is purely time-triggered, the helicopter system shows how Giotto can, within its semantical requirements, interact with asynchronous events, such as communication from the ground station. On the other hand, the helicopter system has only a single CPU, and our future focus is therefore on extending the Giotto approach to distributed platforms.

Acknowledgments

We thank Niklaus Wirth and Walter Schaufelberger for their advice and support of the reengineering effort of the ETH Zürich helicopter system using Giotto.

References

1. J. Chapuis, C. Eck, M. Kottmann, M. Sanvido, and O. Tanner. Control of helicopters. In *Control of Complex Systems*, pages 359–392. Springer Verlag, 1999.
2. C. Eck. *Navigation Algorithms with Applications to Unmanned Helicopters*. PhD thesis 14402, ETH Zürich, 2001.
3. T.A. Henzinger, B. Horowitz, and C.M. Kirsch. Giotto: a time-triggered language for embedded programming. In *Proc. First International Workshop on Embedded Software (EMSOFT)*, LNCS 2211, pages 166–184. Springer Verlag, 2001.
4. T.A. Henzinger and C.M. Kirsch. The Embedded Machine: predictable, portable real-time code. In *Proc. ACM SIGPLAN Conference on Programming Language Design and Implementation (PLDI)*, pages 315–326. ACM Press, 2002.
5. T.A. Henzinger, C.M. Kirsch, R. Majumdar, and S. Matic. Time safety checking for embedded programs. In *Proc. Second International Workshop on Embedded Software (EMSOFT)*, LNCS. Springer Verlag, 2002.
6. D.J. McConnel, B. Lewis, and L. Gray. Reengineering a single-threaded embedded missile application onto a parallel processing platform using MetaH. *Real-Time Systems*, 14:7–20, 1998.
7. M. Sanvido. *A Computer System for Model Helicopter Flight Control; Technical Memo 3: The Software Core*. Technical Report 317, Institute for Computer Systems, ETH Zürich, 1999.
8. L. Wills, S. Kannan, S. Sander, M. Guler, B. Heck, V.D. Prasad, D. Schrage, and G. Vachtsevanos. An open platform for reconfigurable control. *IEEE Control Systems Magazine*, 21:49–64, 2001.
9. N. Wirth. *A Computer System for Model Helicopter Flight Control; Technical Memo 6: The Oberon Compiler for the StrongARM Processor*. Technical Report 314, Institute for Computer Systems, ETH Zürich, 1999.
10. N. Wirth and J. Gutknecht. *Projekt Oberon: The Design of an Operating System and Compiler*. ACM Press, 1992.
11. http://www.cs.cmu.edu/afs/cs/project/chopper/www/heli_project.html. The Robotics Institute, Carnegie Mellon University.
12. http://controls.ae.gatech.edu/labs/uavrf/. The UAV Lab, Georgia Institute of Technology.
13. *Aerial Robotics*. http://gewurtz.mit.edu/research/heli.htm. Laboratory for Information and Decision Systems, Massachusetts Institute of Technology.
14. *Autonomous Flying Vehicles*. http://www-robotics.usc.edu/~avatar. Robotics Research Laboratory, University of Southern California.
15. *Autonomous Helicopter Project*. http://www.heli.ethz.ch. Measurement and Control Laboratory, ETH Zürich.
16. *BEAR: Berkeley Aerobot*. http://robotics.eecs.berkeley.edu/bear. Electronic Research Laboratory, University of California at Berkeley.
17. *The Hummingbird Helicopter*. http://sun-valley.stanford.edu/~heli. Aerospace Robotics Laboratory, Stanford University.
18. *Marvin*. http://pdv.cs.tu-berlin.de/MARVIN. Institute for Technical Computer Science, Technische Universität Berlin.
19. *OSEKWorks Operating System*. http://www.windriver.com/products/html/osekworks.html WindRiver.

Principles of Real-Time Programming*

Christoph M. Kirsch

Department of Electrical Engineering and Computer Sciences
University of California, Berkeley
cm@eecs.berkeley.edu

Abstract. Real-time programming is a software engineering discipline
that has been around ever since the dawn of digital computing. The
dream of real-time programmers is to unlock the virtually unlimited potential of software for embedded computer systems – digital computers
that are supposed to behave like analog devices. The perfect embedded
computer system is invisibly hybrid, it works according to the largely
unidentified laws of embedded software but acts according to the laws of
physics. The critical interface between embedded software and physics is
real-time and yet, while physical processes evolve in real-time, software
processes do not. Only the embedded computer system as a whole – embedded software and hardware – determines a complex notion of so-called
soft-time to which the software processes adhere: mapping soft-time to
real-time is the art of real-time programming. We discuss various real-
time programming *models* that support the development of real-time
programs based on different abstractions of soft-time. We informally introduce a real-time process model to study (1) the *compositionality* of
the real-time programming models and (2) the *semantics* of real-time
programs developed in these models.

1 Introduction

Figure 1 shows an example of a (distributed) software process that interacts
with a physical process. At some real-time instant, the software process takes
some input from the physical process. Some time later, when the software process is finished processing the input it will return the result of its efforts to the
physical process. From the very beginning of taking the input until the very
end of returning the output, the software process evolves in soft-time. From
the perspective of the physical process, only *at* the real-time instants of input
and output, soft-time becomes real-time. In *between* input and output, soft-time
can be amazingly complex in relation to real-time when seen from the software
perspective. In the example, right after taking the input the software process
executes on some processor $\mathcal{A}$. After a while the process is granted a semaphore
that controls the access to some shared resource. Handling the semaphore briefly
delays the software process. Unavailable semaphores may result in longer and

---

* Supported in part by the DARPA SEC grant F33615-C-98-3614 and the MARCO
GSRC grant 98-DT-660.

A. Sangiovanni-Vincentelli and J. Sifakis (Eds.): EMSOFT 2002, LNCS 2491, pp. 61–75, 2002.

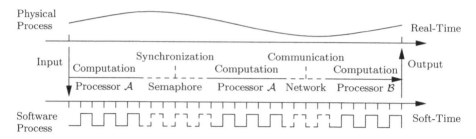

Fig. 1. Real-Time and Soft-Time

sometimes even unbounded delays: soft-time is *discontinuous*, unlike real-time. Then the software process continues to execute on processor $\mathcal{A}$ and computes an intermediate result that is transmitted across a network to some processor $\mathcal{B}$. Just like semaphores, network access also contributes to the discontinuity of soft-time. Before returning the output to the physical process, the software process now runs on processor $\mathcal{B}$. The real-time instant when it completes or, in other words, the relation between soft-time and real-time depends on a whole variety of factors: hardware performance and utilization, scheduling strategy and communication protocol, program and compiler optimizations. Improving any of these factors does not necessarily speed up soft-time. In fact, it can even slow soft-time down.

Software processes are not *composable* with respect to soft-time. For example, composing a software process $\mathcal{P}$ with a software process $\mathcal{Q}$ that shares some resources with $\mathcal{P}$ may result in a system with unbounded soft-time because of a *deadlock* although both processes run separately in bounded soft-time: the system behavior depends on their relative execution speed – a *race condition* on soft-time. An unrelated process $\mathcal{U}$, which may unintentionally yet non-deterministically delay $\mathcal{P}$ or $\mathcal{Q}$, can make the difference between good and bad. Programmers sometimes refer to $\mathcal{U}$ as "heavy load" under which the system exhibits unexpected behavior. In the presence of real-time constraints this scenario is known as the *priority inversion* phenomenon: a low-priority $\mathcal{Q}$ gains access to a shared resource before a high-priority $\mathcal{P}$ asks for it giving a medium priority $\mathcal{U}$ the chance to become the real winner by delaying $\mathcal{Q}$ and thus $\mathcal{P}$.

Yet real-time programming requires *compositional* models: the physical world is *concurrent*, so is embedded software; embedded hardware is *distributed*, so is embedded software. Section 2 discusses real-time programming models that address compositionality in different ways. Non-real-time, sequential programming models typically support a notion of procedural, functional, or logical composition of programs that are compatible in some sense, e.g., type-safe. Valid implementations are supposed to either compute reproducible results, or raise an exception – in case the compatibility check was wrong –, or may not even terminate. In Section 3, we follow this concept and introduce informally a real-time process model that lifts program composition to process composition: processes composed in that model compute, given a sequence of inputs, the same sequence of outputs (*value-determinism*) at the same time (*time-determinism*) provided

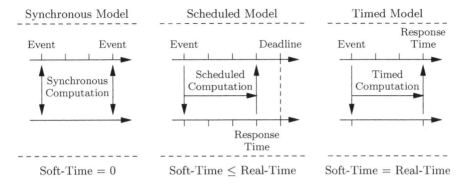

Fig. 2. Models for Real-Time Programming

the composition preserves the process timing (*time-invariant*) and is schedulable (*time-safe*), and the individual processes are value- and time-deterministic. In Section 4, we use this process model to study the semantics of real-time programs developed in the real-time programming models of Section 2.

2   Models for Real-Time Programming

This section presents three real-time programming models, compares their fundamental characteristics, and discusses typical application areas. We distinguish the *synchronous, scheduled*, and *timed* programming models shown in Figure 2. The selection is limited and by no means complete. Models for real-time programming have also been discussed elsewhere, e.g., in [10] or [14].

Synchronous Model. The principle of synchronous programming is based on the idea of zero time computation, see, e.g., [4]. The synchronous programmer assumes that any computational activity of a synchronous program including communication takes no time: soft-time in a synchronous program is always zero. A synchronous program is executed in the context of some physical or computational process that generates events as stimulus for the program. Figure 2 shows an example of an event timeline in the synchronous model. A synchronous program *reacts* to events in zero time by computing instantaneously some output (*reaction*) based on the input and control state of the program. A synchronous program is *deterministic* if it computes at most one reaction for any event and control state, and *reactive* if it computes at least one reaction for any event and control state, i.e., if it terminates. The *reactivity* of a synchronous program, i.e., the instantaneous and deterministic reactions to some stimulus, is what concerns the synchronous programmer. Synchronous programming is therefore often referred to as *synchronous reactive programming*. The problem of a compiler for synchronous programs is to implement reactivity. Since cyclic language constructs are present in many synchronous programming languages, the compiler typically needs to prove the existence of finite fixed-points or, in other words,

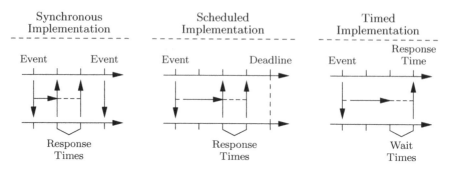

Fig. 3. Implementations of Synchronous, Scheduled, and Timed Programs

the absence of infinite cycles in a synchronous program. Depending on the representation of the control state of a synchronous program, proving reactivity is complex – in languages with explicit control flow such as Esterel [1] – or less difficult – in data-flow languages such as Lustre [5].

In the programmer's mind mapping soft-time in the synchronous model to real-time is simple. A synchronous and reactive program always runs at the speed of its context and, if the program is deterministic, even its output is determined by the behavior of its context. From the perspective of the (physical) context the behavior of a deterministic and reactive program in the synchronous model is perfect. Context and program are *synchronous*. An implementation of a synchronous program may approximate *synchrony* by computing any reaction to an event before the next event occurs while the exact time when a reaction is completed may vary as shown in Figure 3. Thus a compiler for synchronous programs ideally implements not only code generation but also a prover for reactivity and synchrony. A difficult part of showing synchrony is to estimate the (worst-case) execution times of program code [12].

Scheduled Model. The classical discipline of real-time programming [15] in languages such as Ada or, more recently, in Real-Time Java is based on the concept of scheduled computation. A scheduled program typically consists of processes, threads, or tasks. A scheduler determines which part of a scheduled program runs at what time. Soft-time in the scheduled model is the time it takes for some computational activity to complete. For example, the soft-time of a software task is the *response time* of the task. Thus soft-time is not abstract as in the synchronous model. Soft-time may vary depending on performance, utilization, and scheduling scheme and is not a priori determined in the scheduled model. Instead, soft-time in a scheduled program is constrained by real-time *deadlines*: soft-time must be less or equal than real-time. Figure 2 shows for the scheduled model an event that triggers some scheduled computation, which completes some time before its deadline. The exact time when it completes may vary in the implementation as shown in Figure 3. A compiler for a scheduled program typically implements only the functionality but not the scheduling, which is left to the runtime system, i.e., the scheduler of a real-time operating system. The *schedulability* of a scheduled program, i.e., the fact that all deadlines are met, must be shown according to the scheduling scheme used in the real-time operating system. A schedulability analysis also requires the analysis of (worst-case) execution times.

The deadlines in a scheduled program make the scheduled model a real-time programming model. *Hard* real-time deadlines must be met under any circumstances whereas *soft* real-time deadlines leave scheduled computation some time to complete after a deadline, which may result in degraded but still acceptable performance. There are many soft real-time applications such as video and audio processing. Application areas such as process control or embedded control systems require hard deadlines and are often mission- or even safety-critical. Hard and soft deadlines do not require different compilers but different schedulers. Much work has been devoted to scheduling theory and practice as well as, more recently, to the problem of hybrid schedulers for scheduled programs with hard and soft deadlines [3]. In practice, however, designers of hard real-time systems have mostly resisted to adopt complex schedulers and still rely on well-understood scheduling schemes such as rate-monotonic scheduling [11]. Mechanisms like semaphores that can cause blocking – unbounded soft-time – are often banned from hard real-time designs. Section 4 gives for more details.

Timed Model. The principle of *timed programming* is based on the idea of computation and communication that logically takes a fixed, non-zero amount of time no matter how much time it actually takes: soft-time in a timed program is equal to real-time. Figure 2 shows for the timed model an event that triggers some timed computation, which completes exactly at the specified time. The timed programmer specifies the real-time it takes for a timed program to compute some output assuming that enough soft-time is available, i.e., the timed program is *time-safe* [7]. Time safety depends on performance, utilization, and scheduling scheme. A compiler for timed programs checks time safety, i.e., if enough soft-time is available and rejects programs if not. Checking time safety is difficult [8] – it requires schedulability tests and execution time analyses – and may not always be feasible at compile-time. If the timed program is indeed late, a runtime exception may be thrown [7]. If the timed program finishes early, it delays its output until the specified real-time has elapsed as shown in Figure 3. The closer the implementation of the timed program outputs at the specified time, the better the implementation approximates the timed model. A timed program may run in the context of some physical or some other computational process. Similar to the synchronous model, the behavior of a deterministic and time-safe program in the timed model is perfect from the perspective of its context.

The timed model is well-suited for embedded control systems, which require timing predictability, e.g., for precise, low jitter input and output. The timed programming language Giotto [6] supports the development of embedded control systems [9], in particular, on distributed hardware. The key element in Giotto is a *timed task* that is *periodic* and *deterministic* with respect to its input and state. The logical execution time of a Giotto task is the period of the task. For example, a 10Hz Giotto task runs logically for 100ms before its output becomes available and its input is updated for the next invocation. As a consequence of the timed semantics, the behavior of a time-safe Giotto program is *determined* by its (physical) context, not by performance, utilization, or scheduling scheme. Since the parallel composition of timed programs does not change the timing behavior of the individual programs in the timed model, Giotto is *modular*: Giotto programs can be composed from smaller programs and Giotto programs can be compiled separately and even incrementally.

3   A Real-Time Process Model

We introduce a real-time process model that captures the semantics of the previously discussed real-time programming models. In Section 4 we use the process model to study the semantics of real-time programs developed in these models.

An *embedded process* $\mathcal{P}$ consists of program code and process variables X. The program code implements the *process actions* $A[\mathcal{P}]$ of the embedded process $\mathcal{P}$. Each process action $p \in A[\mathcal{P}]$ operates on a subset $X[p]$ of the process variables X. Process actions may share process variables but no control state: process actions compute or transport values of variables but do not invoke or control other process actions. Process actions are either *disabled*, or else *enabled* to be *scheduled* for execution. Process actions can be enabled at any time and then proceed according to any scheduling scheme. Enabling an already enabled process action leaves it enabled. Process actions complete voluntarily, they cannot be disabled. Thus the process activity of an embedded process evolves according to three orthogonal mechanisms: (1) a so-called *reactor* $\mathcal{R}$ that determines when a process action is enabled; (2) a *scheduler* $\mathcal{S}$ that determines which enabled process actions execute; and (3) the process actions themselves, which determine once enabled and scheduled when to complete and become disabled. Reactor and scheduler are part of an embedded process.

We define the semantics of embedded processes in terms of *process traces*: possibly infinite sequences $c_0, c_1, c_2, \ldots$ of process states c_i. The *process states* $C[\mathcal{P}]$ of an embedded process $\mathcal{P}$ consist of values for all process variables, an abstract *reactor* and *scheduler state*, and the *action states*: enabled or disabled. The sets of reactor and scheduler states are denoted by $R[\mathcal{P}]$ and $S[\mathcal{P}]$, respectively. A process trace starts with initial values for all process variables and initial action states in the process state c_0. The successor state c_{i+1} of a process state c_i is constructed in three steps: (1) the scheduler $\mathcal{S} \subseteq C[\mathcal{P}] \times A[\mathcal{P}] \times S[\mathcal{P}]$ chooses (non-deterministically) a process action p that is enabled in c_i to execute its next step and a new scheduler state s. We require that $\mathcal{S}$ always chooses well-defined actions and scheduler states. Let the intermediate process state c be equal to c_i except for the new scheduler state s; (2) the process action $p \subseteq X[p] \times X[p] \times \{enabled, disabled\}$ computes its next step, given the values of its action variables $X[p]$ in c_i, resulting in new values for $X[p]$ and its new action state, i.e., still enabled or now disabled. We require that p always computes well-defined values and action states. Let the intermediate process state c' be equal to c except for the new values of $X[p]$ and the new action state of p; and

(3) the reactor $\mathcal{R} : C[\mathcal{P}] \to 2^{A[\mathcal{P}]} \times R[\mathcal{P}]$ chooses, given the intermediate process state c', a subset E of all process actions to be enabled now and a new reactor state r. Let the successor state c_{i+1} be equal to c' except that the process actions in E are enabled in c_{i+1} in addition to the process actions that are already enabled in c and except for the new reactor state r. This completes the definition of the semantics of embedded processes. Note that the reactor is deterministic whereas the scheduler and the process actions, in particular, their duration can be non-deterministic. In order to model directly true concurrency in distributed systems, we could but, for simplicity, have not defined a scheduler $\mathcal{S}'$ to choose a subset of enabled process actions to execute simultaneously rather than a single enabled process action, cf., the definition of the reactor.

Process execution does not necessarily guarantee the *atomicity* of process actions: a process action p may execute in multiple steps interleaved with the execution of another process action that shares process variables with p. Guaranteeing atomicity is the problem of enabling process actions at the right time but not too rapidly and of scheduling process actions at the right time and not too late besides having process actions that complete fast enough. If we restrict the reactor to enable at most a single process action at the same time and not before any other process action completed, the scheduler disappears and we get atomicity and what valid implementations in the synchronous model do: a process trace is *event-safe* if in each state of the trace at most a single process action is enabled. An embedded process is *event-safe* if all its process traces are event-safe. Guaranteeing event safety requires the reactor not to enable process actions too rapidly while process actions must complete fast enough. This corresponds to proving reactivity and synchrony for implementations in the synchronous model. The following definition gives the reactor more freedom but requires a scheduler: a process trace is *time-safe* if a process action p never becomes enabled while another process action that shares process variables with p is enabled. An embedded process is *time-safe* if all its process traces are time-safe. Event safety implies time safety but not conversely. Implementations in the timed model require time safety. An equivalent definition of time safety, from the perspective of the scheduler and the process actions, is: a process trace is *time-safe* if each enabled process action p completes before another process action that shares process variables with p is enabled. In the following definition we put the burden onto the scheduler: a process trace is *space-safe* if in each state of the trace the scheduler never chooses an enabled process action to execute that shares process variables with another enabled process action that has previously been scheduled for execution but not yet completed. An embedded process is *space-safe* if all its process traces are space-safe. Time safety implies space safety but not conversely. Programmers in the scheduled model use synchronization mechanisms such as semaphores to ensure space safety.

Embedded processes can be composed to form an *embedded system* $\mathcal{E}$, which consists of the process actions of all processes, a reactor composed of the process reactors, and a scheduler composed of the process schedulers. The process actions of different processes may share process variables called *system variables* of $\mathcal{E}$ but no control state. In an embedded system $\mathcal{E}$, we distinguish *reactions* and *coactions* of a process $\mathcal{P}$: a reaction is a process action that operates on process variables of $\mathcal{P}$, including system variables; a coaction is a process action that operates exclusively on process variables of $\mathcal{P}$ that are not system variables. Coactions are a restricted form of reactions that can be enabled and scheduled independently of the reactions of other processes without violating space-safety. An embedded system is semantically a single embedded process composed of multiple embedded processes but with a namespace for process actions and variables that is syntactically structured according to the original embedded processes. Suppose that an embedded system $\mathcal{E}$ is composed of two embedded processes $\mathcal{P}$ and $\mathcal{Q}$ where $\mathcal{P}$ models a physical process and $\mathcal{Q}$ models a software process. $\mathcal{P}$ consists of a coaction p that models the physical process as well as a reaction s for sensing p and a reaction a for actuating p. Thus s and a can be seen as device drivers that transport data between process variables of p (physical world) and system variables (system memory). Similarly, $\mathcal{Q}$ consists of a coaction t (software task) as well as a reaction i (task input) and a reaction o (task output). i and o transport data between process variables of t (task memory) and system variables. A typical execution order of the process actions is $s, i, t, o, a, s, \ldots$ where p logically may run concurrently with i, t, and o.

The *output behavior* of $\mathcal{Q}$ is *value-deterministic* if the system variables of $\mathcal{E}$ carry deterministic values at the instants when reactions of other processes than $\mathcal{Q}$, e.g., the reaction a, become enabled. $\mathcal{Q}$ must compute deterministic values based on the values of its process variables and the system variables at the instants when reactions of other processes than $\mathcal{Q}$, e.g., the reaction s, complete. Value-determinism means that $\mathcal{Q}$ computes, given the same sequence of inputs, the same sequence of outputs but not necessarily at the same time. The *timing behavior* of $\mathcal{Q}$ is *time-deterministic* if the reactions of $\mathcal{Q}$ are enabled and complete at deterministic instants independently of the instants when reactions of other processes than $\mathcal{Q}$, e.g., the reaction s or a, are enabled or complete. A weaker property than time-determinism is that the reactions of $\mathcal{Q}$ such as i and o always eventually complete and thus enable the interaction of $\mathcal{P}$ with $\mathcal{Q}$: from the perspective of $\mathcal{P}$, $\mathcal{Q}$ is *time-live* if the reactions of $\mathcal{Q}$ always eventually complete. We also say that $\mathcal{Q}$ is *bounded time-live* if there is an upper bound on the time any reaction of $\mathcal{Q}$ is enabled. The composition of embedded processes is *order-preserving* if the reactor of the composed system enables the process actions deterministically in the same order as the reactors of the individual processes. The composition is *time-invariant* if the reactor of the composed system also enables the process actions at the same instants as the reactors of the individual processes. An embedded system composed of embedded processes is value-deterministic (and time-deterministic) provided the composition is order-preserving (and time-invariant) and event- or time-safe, and the individual processes are value-deterministic (and time-deterministic). This is not true for space-safety since the composed scheduler may have to change the order in which process actions that share variables are scheduled in the composed system.

4   Implementations of Real-Time Programs

In this section, we show how real-time programs developed in the synchronous, scheduled, and timed model can be implemented as embedded processes. The following table gives an overview of the model and process properties:

	Synchronous	Scheduled	Timed
Model Composition	value-deterministic	–	value-, time-deterministic
Model to Process	event-safe	space-safe	time-safe
Process Composition	order-preserving	–	order-preserving, time-invariant

Synchronous Implementation. A *synchronous system* is the implementation of a synchronous program based on synchronous processes. A *synchronous process* reacts to the stimulus and input from other processes. For example, a synchronous process Q is typically triggered by another process, e.g., a physical process P that generates the input for Q. As soon as the synchronous process is triggered, it takes the input and its internal state and computes some output and its next internal state. The output is returned to the physical process as soon as the synchronous computation is completed. Then the synchronous process waits for the next input. Synchronous processes can be modeled by *event-safe* embedded processes. Reactions model synchronous computation as well as input and output transfers from and to a synchronous process. Coactions are not required. Suppose that Q consists of a set R of reactions that implement Q, and suppose that P consists of a reaction s to transfer input from P to Q and a reaction a to transfer output from Q to P. The reactor enables s when P triggers Q. As soon as s completes, the reactor enables, given the input and internal state of Q, a reaction $r \in R$ to compute (part of) the output and next state of Q. When r completes, the reactor either enables another reaction in R, or else enables a to return the output to P. The reactor is typically implemented by some form of automaton. The job of the scheduler, on the other hand, is trivial since at any time in an event-safe execution of a synchronous process at most a single reaction is enabled. Non-trivial scheduling is only necessary if multiple synchronous processes are composed in parallel where some scheduling decisions are left open and not compiled into an automaton as, e.g., in *communicating reactive processes* with Esterel [2] or in the presence of *multiform time* with Lustre [13].

The design of a synchronous system requires a proof of event safety: before another input from P is available, the reactor must have stopped enabling reactions in R (reactivity) and all reactions must have completed (synchrony). Event safety implies time liveness if P always eventually generates new input for Q. Thus event safety ensures that P can progress. Q is value-deterministic with respect to P in an event-safe embedded system $\mathcal{E}$ if the reactor and all reactions implement functions. The value-determinism of synchronous systems is important and supports the development of mission- and safety-critical software in the synchronous model. The synchronous model is compositional with respect to value-determinism because an event-safe system composed of value-deterministic synchronous processes is again value-deterministic (provided the composition of the subsystem reactors is order-preserving). The composition of synchronous systems is an interesting research topic: if the subsystem reactors can be reused or even distributed onto multiple processors, modular and distributed synchronous programming as well as separate and incremental compilation may be possible.

Scheduled Implementation. A *scheduled system* is the implementation of a scheduled program based on scheduled processes. A *scheduled process* may run concurrently with other processes. Process communication is typically handled by semaphores that control the access to shared resources such as memory or I/O devices. A POSIX process is an example of a scheduled process. Program code that accesses a shared resource is called a *critical section* of a scheduled process. In order to preserve data consistency, a critical section must not be preempted by critical sections of other processes that access the same resource. Scheduled processes can be modeled by *space-safe* embedded processes. Coactions model non-critical program code whereas reactions correspond to critical sections. Thus taking or giving a semaphore requires two process actions and a transition from the process action that precedes the access to the semaphore to the process action that succeeds the access. The reactor handles the transitions by enabling succeeding process actions as soon as the preceding process actions complete. The scheduler can choose an enabled reaction r (critical section) for execution only if any other enabled reaction that shares system variables r has either completed or not yet started executing. The space-safe execution of the scheduled system is thus up to the scheduler, provided the original scheduled processes use the semaphores correctly.

The design of many scheduled systems is dominated by considerations on space safety through complex scheduling where neither the process actions nor the reactor have to worry about space safety. This is the strength and at the same time the weakness of the scheduled model. All the know-how and the tools for the development of complex but non-real-time systems is readily available in the scheduled model with deadlines because scheduled processes are not restricted in their control-flow and can be triggered to execute at any time. The scheduler, on the other hand, is responsible to guarantee space safety under as many circumstances as possible. This view has lead to an impressive amount of research in real-time scheduling, see, e.g., [3]. The downside of the scheduled model is that it is not compositional with respect to value- or time-determinism. In general, the composition of scheduled processes results in real-time behavior of the scheduled processes that is different from the real-time behavior of the processes when running individually. The problem is that the processes and the reactor can push the scheduler in situations such as *priority inversion* or *deadlock* that are hard or even impossible to handle. Traditionally, this problem has been addressed but not solved by making the scheduler smarter using so-called priority inheritance or priority ceiling protocols, see, e.g., [3].

An alternative approach is to shift the focus from space safety to time safety. Recall that the reactor in a time-safe embedded system never enables a process action p while another process action that shares variables with p is enabled. Thus the scheduler in a time-safe embedded system is only concerned with completing process actions before the reactor enables others but not with any particular ordering of the process actions: priority inversion and deadlock are not possible in a time-safe embedded system. Time safety requires the real-time programmer to keep in mind that the completion of a process action does not necessarily enable the next process action immediately. This means for a scheduled process that the process cannot simply *try to take* a semaphore but *has to accept* and *has to give up* a semaphore in a timely fashion. In particular, at the time when the process has to accept the semaphore the process must already be waiting for the semaphore: the process must be time-safe. We call a semaphore that must be accepted and released within some given time interval a *timed semaphore*. The semantics of a timed semaphore may be relaxed in applications where determinism is less important. For example, a scheduled process may be allowed to *anticipate* or even *reject* a timed semaphore. However, scheduled systems are not value- or time-deterministic even when using timed semaphores. Timed semaphores only prevent processes from delaying or blocking each other and thus avoid the problem of priority inversion and deadlock.

Timed Implementation. A *timed system* is the implementation of a timed program based on timed processes. A *timed process* consists of timed tasks that may run concurrently with other timed tasks or processes. A *timed task* is a sequential program with logically fixed execution time from invocation to completion. The invocation of timed tasks may be event- or time-triggered as well as task-triggered, i.e., triggered by the completion of a task. A Giotto task is an example of a timed process with a single timed task that is periodic and thus time-triggered. The logical execution time of the timed task is the period of the Giotto task. A timed task consists of a *task* for process computation and two *drivers* for process communication: an *input driver* that transports data from shared memory into task memory, the task that operates on task memory, and an *output driver* that transports data from task memory to shared memory. The execution of a timed task begins with the execution of the input driver followed by the execution of the task. The output driver executes after the task completes. The execution of a timed task ends with the completion of the output driver exactly at the time when the logical execution time of the timed task elapsed. Thus process communication with a timed task is only possible before and after but not during the execution of the timed task. Task memory may only be shared by multiple timed tasks of the same timed process. Since timed tasks have no means of synchronizing on task memory, timed tasks sharing task memory must be invoked and scheduled without preempting each other.

Timed processes can be modeled by *time-safe* embedded processes. Coactions model tasks whereas reactions correspond to drivers. The reaction that models the input driver of a timed task is enabled by the reactor as soon as the timed task is triggered. The coaction that models the task is enabled when the input driver completes. The reaction that models the output driver is enabled when the time is right to meet the specified completion time of the timed task. By then the task must have completed, i.e., the task must be time-safe. In a system with multiple timed processes, the reactor may enable multiple coactions (tasks)

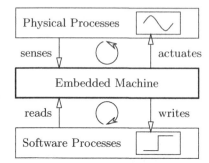

b: call(o)
       call(a)
       call(s)
       call(i)
       schedule(t)
       future(g, b)

Fig. 4. The Embedded Machine   **Fig. 5.** An E Code Program

but only a single reaction (driver) at the same time. For example, if a timed task T_1 is invoked (completes) at the same time when a timed task T_2 of a different process is invoked (completes), the reactor enables the reactions that model the input (output) drivers of T_1 and T_2 sequentially in some order. The coactions that model the tasks of T_1 and T_2 may be enabled at the same time. For a time-safe execution the scheduler is assumed to schedule reactions with higher priority than coactions. Since at most a single reaction is enabled at the same time, scheduling reactions is trivial. A coaction, on the other hand, must be scheduled such that it completes before the reactor enables a reaction that shares memory with the coaction. Thus the reactor is responsible for the precise timing of inter-process communication while the scheduler takes care of process computation.

The reactor for timed processes can be implemented by a virtual machine called the *Embedded Machine* [7] (*E machine* for short). The E machine mediates in real-time the interaction of physical processes and software processes as shown in Figure 4. The E machine has already been used as a target machine for the compilation of Giotto programs [8] to *E code*, the code interpreted by the E machine. Besides some auxiliary instructions, e.g., for control-flow, the E machine has three key instructions: (1) the call(d) instruction enables a driver d and blocks the E machine until d completes; (2) the schedule(t) instruction enables a task t without blocking the E machine. t will not be scheduled for execution before the E machine is finished executing E code; and (3) the future(g, b) instruction makes the E machine execute the E code at address b when the *trigger* g becomes true. Triggers control the invocation of the E machine such as event-, time- or task-triggered invocations. For example, g may be a *time trigger* that becomes true when, say, 10ms elapsed after the execution of a future instruction with g. Then we say that the E code block is *enabled*. The E machine uses a *trigger queue* to maintain the list of triggers that currently *guard* an E code block. As soon as a trigger in the queue becomes true it is removed from the queue and the guarded E code block is executed. The E code blocks that are enabled at the same instant are executed in the order of the triggers in the queue. New triggers are appended to the queue. When all enabled E code blocks have been executed, the E machine invokes a scheduler that takes care of scheduling the enabled tasks.

As an example of E code that requires only a singleton trigger queue, consider a timed process $\mathcal{Q}$ that invokes a timed task T periodically with a period of 10ms. The timed process $\mathcal{Q}$ is composed in parallel with a physical process $\mathcal{P}$. The E code program in Figure 5 implements the composition of $\mathcal{P}$ and $\mathcal{Q}$. The E machine begins executing the E code block at address b by calling the output driver o of the timed task T. Provided the task memory of T is initialized, o transports well-defined values from task memory to shared memory. The subsequent execution of the *actuator driver* a transports values from shared memory to the physical process $\mathcal{P}$. Thus o and a implement process communication from the timed to the physical process. The other direction is implemented by a *sensor driver* s of the physical process $\mathcal{P}$ and the input driver i of the timed task T. After calling the four drivers in the given order, the schedule(t) instruction enables the task t of the timed task T for execution. The future(g, b) instruction makes sure that the E machine wakes up after 10ms elapsed and executes the same E code block at address b again. In the programming model of the E machine, E code execution including driver execution is synchronous computation that takes no time. Since the actual execution of E code results in a delay of the driver execution, the above E code block implements the timed process $\mathcal{Q}$ correctly provided the E code execution is *time-safe*, i.e., task t always completes within 10ms minus the delay of the E code block. Then, from the perspective of the physical process $\mathcal{P}$, the behavior of the timed process $\mathcal{Q}$ is value-deterministic (provided the task and all drivers implement functions) and time-deterministic, up to the delay (jitter) caused by the output driver o but independent of the execution of task t. The E code can be further optimized such that the actuator and sensor drivers are executed independently of the E code for $\mathcal{Q}$. Optimizing E code for timed processes typically means more and smaller E code blocks with *more precise timing* rather than *faster execution*.

A sufficient criterion for value- and time-determinism with respect to the physical processes is to make sure that all drivers and tasks implement functions and all E code is event- or time-triggered. The composition of event- or time-triggered E code is time-invariant. Under these restrictions the timed model and thus Giotto is compositional with respect to value- and time-determinism. Notice that separate compilation of individual processes into E code is also possible. The following E code implements the same behavior as the E code of the previous example but can be generated separately for each process:

```
b1: call(o)          b2: call(a)          b3: call(i)          b4: future(g, b2)
    future(true, b3)      call(s)              schedule(t)
                         future(true, b4)      future(g, b1)
```

The E code blocks at $b1$ and $b3$ implement the timed process $\mathcal{Q}$. The E code blocks at $b2$ and $b4$ implement the interaction of the physical process $\mathcal{P}$ with $\mathcal{Q}$. Every 10ms the E code blocks will be executed in the order $b1$, $b2$, $b3$, and $b4$. The E machine starts executing with the initial trigger queue $\langle (0, b1), (0, b2) \rangle$ where, e.g., $(0, b1)$ means that the E code block at $b1$ must be executed now. After the E machine is finished executing the E code block at $b1$, the output driver o has executed and the trigger queue is $\langle(0, b2), (0, b3)\rangle$. The future(true, $b3$) instruction uses an already true trigger to make the E machine execute the E code block at $b3$ at the current instant but not before any other, already enabled E code blocks have been executed. The next step of the E machine is to execute the E code block at $b2$, which results in the trigger queue $\langle(0, b3), (0, b4)\rangle$. Then the E code block at $b3$ is executed, resulting in the trigger queue $\langle(0, b4), (10, b1)\rangle$ where $(10, b1)$ means that the E code block at $b1$ must be executed after 10ms from now have elapsed. The E machine finishes executing E code at the current instant with the trigger queue $\langle(10, b1), (10, b2)\rangle$ after executing the E code block at $b4$. Thus every 10ms the E machine will repeat the above behavior. Other timed and physical processes can now be added to the above system. For example, a second timed process could be compiled into E code, e.g., with a start address $b5$ and an entry $(0, b5)$ in the initial trigger queue. Similarly, partial Giotto programs can also be compiled separately into E code since Giotto programs are a special case of timed systems.

In general, the composition of timed and physical processes works in three steps: (1) *compilation* of each process into E code; (2) *linking* of E code; and (3) *validation* of E code with respect to time safety. In the previous example, E code is linked *online* through the trigger queue while executing the E code. Online linking of E code simplifies E code generation but suffers from runtime overhead for managing the trigger queue. On the other hand, E code could also be linked *offline*, which requires more complex E code generation with additional symbolic information but may result in linked E code that can be executed with less runtime overhead. Offline linking of E code does not necessarily mean that it has to be done at compile time. E code can be loaded and linked even dynamically while the E machine is running. Although E code is a static description of the timing behavior of real-time programs, linking E code has the potential to express dynamics that we know from traditional real-time operating systems while maintaining, e.g., time-determined system behavior. For example, changing the set of currently executing tasks in a real-time operating system corresponds to loading and linking appropriate E code in the E machine. Linking E code is therefore an interesting research topic. Validating E code with respect to time safety, in particular, in the context of dynamically changing E code is another interesting topic. The problem of checking time safety of embedded processes can be formulated as a three player game between the reactor, the scheduler, and the process actions. This approach has been demonstrated for the special case of the E machine as a two player game in which the E machine teams up with the *environment* (physical processes) against the scheduler [8].

5   Summary

The synchronous model supports the development of value-deterministic real-time programs for mission- and safety-critical applications. The scheduled model utilizes the experience and tools from the non-real-time world and is widely used in practice. The timed model supports the development of value- and time-deterministic real-time programs but has only been applied in the context of embedded control systems. The synchronous and scheduled model are in some sense more general than the timed model. In both models value- and time-deterministic real-time programs can also be developed. The restrictions of the timed model, however, can be exploited, e.g., in optimized code generation of value- and time-deterministic real-time programs even for distributed hardware.

Acknowledgments. We thank Jörn Janneck and Marco Sanvido for many valuable comments and suggestions.

References

1. G. Berry. The foundations of Esterel. In C. Stirling G. Plotkin and M. Tofte, editors, *Proof, Language and Interaction: Essays in Honour of Robin Milner*. MIT Press, 2000.
2. G. Berry, S. Ramesh, and R. K. Shyamasundar. Communicating reactive processes. In *Conference Record of the Twentieth Annual ACM SIGPLAN-SIGACT Symposium on Principles of Programming Languages*, pages 85–98, 1993.
3. G. Buttazzo. *Hard Real-Time Computing Systems: Predictable Scheduling Algorithms and Applications*. Kluwer, 1997.
4. N. Halbwachs. *Synchronous Programming of Reactive Systems*. Kluwer, 1993.
5. N. Halbwachs, P. Caspi, P. Raymond, and D. Pilaud. The synchronous dataflow programming language Lustre. *Proc. of the IEEE*, 79(9), 1991.
6. T.A. Henzinger, B. Horowitz, and C.M. Kirsch. Giotto: A time-triggered language for embedded programming. In *Proc. First International Workshop on Embedded Software (EMSOFT)*, LNCS 2211, pages 166–184. Springer Verlag, 2001.
7. T.A. Henzinger and C.M. Kirsch. The Embedded Machine: predictable, portable real-time code. In *Proc. ACM SIGPLAN Conference on Programming Language Design and Implementation (PLDI)*, pages 315–326, 2002.
8. T.A. Henzinger, C.M. Kirsch, R. Majumdar, and S. Matic. Time safety checking for embedded programs. In *Proc. Second International Workshop on Embedded Software (EMSOFT)*, LNCS. Springer Verlag, 2002.
9. C.M. Kirsch, M.A.A. Sanvido, T.A. Henzinger, and W. Pree. A Giotto-based helicopter control system. In *Proc. Second International Workshop on Embedded Software (EMSOFT)*, LNCS. Springer Verlag, 2002.
10. E.A. Lee. Embedded software. In M. Zelkowitz, editor, *Advances in Computers*, volume 56. Academic Press, 2002.
11. C. Liu and J. Layland. Scheduling algorithms for multiprogramming in a hard-real-time environment. *Journal of the ACM*, 20(1), 1973.
12. S. Malik and Y.-T. Li. *Performance Analysis of Real-Time Embedded Software*. Kluwer, 1999.
13. D. Pilaud and N. Halbwachs. From a synchronous declarative language to a temporal logic dealing with multiform time. In *Proc. of the Symposium on Formal Techniques in Real-Time and Fault-Tolerant Systems*, LNCS 331, pages 99–110. Springer Verlag, 1988.
14. J. Sifakis. Modeling real-time systems – challenges and work directions. In *Proc. First International Workshop on Embedded Software (EMSOFT)*, LNCS 2211, pages 373–389. Springer Verlag, 2001.
15. N. Wirth. Toward a discipline of real-time programming. *Communications of the ACM*, 20(8):577–583, 1977.

Time-Safety Checking for Embedded Programs*

Thomas A. Henzinger, Christoph M. Kirsch,
Rupak Majumdar, and Slobodan Matic

Department of Electrical Engineering and Computer Sciences
University of California, Berkeley, USA
{tah,cm,rupak,matic}@eecs.berkeley.edu

Abstract. Giotto is a platform-independent language for specifying
software for high-performance control applications. In this paper we
present a new approach to the compilation of Giotto. Following this approach, the Giotto compiler generates code for a virtual machine, called
the E machine, which can be ported to different platforms. The Giotto
compiler also checks if the generated E code is time safe for a given platform, that is, if the platform offers sufficient performance to ensure that
the E code is executed in a timely fashion that conforms with the Giotto
semantics. Time-safety checking requires a schedulability analysis. We
show that while for arbitrary E code, the analysis is exponential, for
E code generated from typical Giotto programs, the analysis is polynomial. This supports our claim that Giotto identifies a useful fragment of
embedded programs.

1 Introduction

We have advocated a *platform-independent* approach to embedded programming [4,5]: the programmer specifies the timing and functional aspects of the
program, and the compiler checks if the program can be executed as intended
on a particular platform in a particular environment. Besides providing the programmer with an application-level abstraction, and the obvious benefits of code
reuse, this approach offers maximal flexibility in the implementation: failure to
compile may be equally due to platform performance (CPUs too slow or too
few) and platform utilization (scheduling scheme inadequate) and environment
behavior (events too frequent), and therefore may be remedied by addressing
any one or more of these factors. Perhaps the most important benefit of the
platform-independent approach is that it permits a clean separation of timing
and function. An embedded program written in this way, called an *E program*,
consists of a timing part and a functional part. The *functional part* is a set of software processes, and the *timing part* is a control-flow skeleton that supervises the
invocation of the software processes relative to events. Platform independence
means that the programmer can think of each software process as an atomic

* Supported in part by the DARPA SEC grant F33615-C-98-3614, MARCO GSRC
grant 98-DT-660, AFOSR MURI grant F49620-00-1-0327, NSF grant CCR-9988172,
and a Microsoft Research Fellowship.

operation on a state; that is, as an infinitely fast, terminating program without internal synchronization points. The programmer's fiction of atomicity can be implemented by nonpreemption, as in the synchronous reactive languages [3]. We pursue maximal flexibility in the implementation and permit the system scheduler to preempt software processes as long as the compiler can ensure that the scheduler maintains logical atomicity. An execution of the program that maintains this fiction is called *time safe*. Thus a central task of the compiler is to check the time safety of all possible executions of a given E program on a given platform in a given environment. In other words, a compiler that checks time safety guarantees that the functional part of an E program can be executed as specified by the timing part.

Let us be more precise. The functional part of an E program consists of two kinds of software processes. Software processes with nonnegligible WCETs (worst-case execution times) need to be scheduled, and their execution can be preempted. These processes are called *tasks*. A typical example of a task is a control law computation. On the other hand, software processes with negligible WCETs —i.e., processes that can always be completed before the next environment event— can be executed synchronously. These processes are called *drivers*. A typical example of a driver is a sensor reading, or an actuator update. Both tasks (scheduled computation) and drivers (synchronous computation) are written in a conventional language, such as C. The timing part of an E program consists of a set of *E actions*. Each E action is triggered by an event, and may call a driver, which is executed immediately, or schedule a task, which is handed over to the scheduler of the operating system. It is important to note that the schedule action is independent of the scheduling scheme: between events that are separated in time, the OS allocates scheduled tasks to CPUs, but how this is done, is not specified by the E program. In this model, time safety —the logical atomicity of tasks— means that during an execution, the state of a scheduled task is not accessed (by a driver or another task) until the task completes. We have introduced two languages for specifying E actions. The *E machine* [5] is a virtual machine that executes *E code*, whose instructions can specify arbitrary sequences of E actions. *Giotto* [4] is a structured language for specifying limited combinations of E actions that occur in typical control applications, where a controller may switch between modes, and within each mode, periodically invoke a given set of tasks and drivers. From a Giotto source program we generate E code, similar to the way in which assembly code is generated from high-level programming languages. This offers portability, as Giotto programs can now be run on any implementation of the E machine.

Time safety is a property of an individual program execution. *Schedulability* is the existence of a scheduler that guarantees that all executions of a program are time safe. Here, we restrict ourselves to single-CPU platforms. Such a platform is specified by a WCET for each task. We solve two schedulability problems. First, we show that for arbitrary E code (defined in Section 2), schedulability checking is difficult: the problem corresponds to a game between the environment and the scheduler [1] on an exponential state space, and is therefore EXPTIME-complete (Section 3). Second, we show that for E code that is generated from a Giotto source program in a specific way (defined in Section 4), EDF (earliest-deadline-first) scheduling is well-defined and optimal. This fixes the strategy of the scheduler, and thus reduces schedulability checking to a reachability problem on an exponential state space, which is PSPACE-complete. Indeed, if we know that all modes of a Giotto program are reachable, then schedulability can be checked by solving a linear utilization equation for each mode independently, no matter how the program switches modes. This can be done in almost quadratic time (Section 5). These results give a technical justification for our intuition that Giotto captures a natural, widely applicable, and also easily schedulable fragment of E programs. They also provide the basis for the Giotto compiler we have implemented. The compiler generates E code following the algorithm of Section 4, and checks schedulability using the method of Section 5.

2   E Code

The E machine [5] is a virtual machine that mediates between the physical processes and the software processes of an embedded system through a control program written in *E code*. E code controls the execution of software processes in relation to physical events, such as clock ticks, and software events, such as task completion. E code is interpreted on the E machine in real time. In this paper, we restrict our attention to the *input-triggered* programs of [5]; they are *time-live*, that is, all synchronous computation is guaranteed to terminate.

Syntax. The E machine supervises the execution of *tasks* and *drivers* that communicate via *ports*. A task is application-level code that implements a computation activity. A driver is system-level code that facilitates a communication activity. A port is a typed variable. Given a set P of ports, a P *state* is a function that maps each port $p \in P$ to a value of the appropriate type. The set P is partitioned into three disjoint sets: a set P_E of *environment ports*, a set P_T of *task ports*, and a set P_D of *driver ports*, updated respectively by the physical environment, by tasks, and by drivers. The environment ports include p_c, a *discrete clock*. An *input event* is a change of value at an environment or task port, say, at a sensor p_s. An input event is observed by the E machine through an event interrupt that can be characterized by a predicate, namely, $p'_s \neq p_s$, where p'_s refers to the current sensor reading, and p_s refers to the most recent previous sensor reading.

All information between the environment and the tasks flows through drivers: environment ports cannot be read by tasks, and task ports cannot be read by the environment. Formally, a *driver* d consists of a set $P[d] \subseteq P_D$ of driver ports, a set $I[d] \subseteq P_E \cup P_T$ of read environment and task ports, and a function $f[d]$ from $P[d] \cup I[d]$ states to $P[d]$ states. A *task* t consists of a set $P[t] \subseteq P_T$ of task ports, a set $I[t] \subseteq P_D$ of read driver ports, and a function $f[t]$ from $P[t] \cup I[t]$ states to $P[t]$ states. The E machine handles event interrupts through triggers. A *trigger* g consists of a set $P[g] \subseteq P_E \cup P_T$ of monitored environment and task ports, and a predicate $f[g]$, which evaluates to true or false over each pair (s, s') of $P[g]$ states. We require that $f[g]$ evaluates to false if $s = s'$. The state s is the state of the ports at the time instant when the trigger is *activated*. The state s' is the state of the ports at the time instant when the trigger is *evaluated*. All active triggers are logically evaluated with each event interrupt. An active trigger that evaluates to true is *enabled*, and may cause the E machine to execute E code. The trigger g is a *time trigger* if $P[g] = \{p_c\}$ and $f[g]$ has the form $p'_c = p_c + \delta$, for some positive integer $\delta \in \mathbb{N}_{>0}$. A time trigger monitors only the clock and specifies an *enabling time* δ, which is the number of clock ticks after activation before the trigger is enabled.

The E machine has three non-control-flow instructions. An *E instruction* is either $\texttt{call}(d)$, for a driver d; or $\texttt{schedule}(t)$, for a task t; or $\texttt{future}(g, a)$, for a trigger g and an address a. The $\texttt{call}(d)$ instruction invokes the driver d. The $\texttt{schedule}(t)$ instruction schedules the task t for execution by inserting it into the ready queue of the OS. The $\texttt{future}(g, a)$ instruction marks the E code at address a for possible execution at a future time when the trigger g becomes enabled. The E machine also has two *control-flow instructions*: the conditional jump instruction $\texttt{if}(f, a)$, where f is a predicate over the driver ports P_D, and a is the target address of the jump if f is true; and the termination instruction $\texttt{return}$, which ends the execution of E code. Formally, an *E program* consists of a set P of ports, a set D of drivers, a set T of tasks, a set G of triggers, a set A of addresses, an initial address $a_0 \in A$, and for each address $a \in A$, an E or control-flow instruction $ins(a)$, and a successor address $next(a)$. All sets that are part of an E program are finite. We require that E code execution always terminates, i.e., for each address $a \in A$ and all branches of $\texttt{if}$ instructions, a $\texttt{return}$ instruction must be reached in a finite number of steps. The E program is *time-triggered* if all triggers $g \in G$ are time triggers.

Example. We illustrate the semantics of E code using a simple program with two tasks, t_1 and t_2. The task t_2 is executed every 10 ms; it reads sensor values using a driver d_s, processes them, and writes its result to an interconnect driver d_i. The task t_1 is executed every 20 ms; it obtains values from driver d_i (the result of t_2), computes actuator values, and writes to an actuator driver d_a. There are two environment ports (the discrete clock p_c and a sensor p_s), two task ports (for the results of the two tasks), and three driver ports (the destinations of the drivers). The following time-triggered E program implements the above behavior:

$$
\begin{array}{ll}
a_0\colon \texttt{call}(d_a) & a_1\colon \texttt{call}(d_s) \\
\quad \texttt{call}(d_s) & \quad \texttt{schedule}(t_2) \\
\quad \texttt{call}(d_i) & \quad \texttt{future}(p'_c = p_c + 10, a_0) \\
\quad \texttt{schedule}(t_1) & \quad \texttt{return} \\
\quad \texttt{schedule}(t_2) & \\
\quad \texttt{future}(p'_c = p_c + 10, a_1) & \\
\quad \texttt{return} &
\end{array}
$$

There are two blocks of E code; the block at a_0 is executed initially. The E machine processes each instruction in logical zero time. First, it calls the driver d_a

and waits until the execution of d_a is finished (in logical zero time), and then proceeds immediately to the next instruction. Once d_s and d_i have been called, all driver ports are updated. Then the E machine schedules the task t_1 by adding it to the ready queue of the operating system (which is initially empty). As we assume no particular scheduling scheme, we do not know the organization of the ready queue, and maintain the scheduled tasks as a set, called the *task set*. After inserting t_1 into the task set, the E machine immediately processes the next instruction and adds t_2 to the task set. Next, it proceeds to the **future** instruction, which creates a *trigger binding* $(p'_c = p_c + 10, a_1, s)$, where s is the current value of p_c, and appends it to a queue, called *trigger queue*, of active trigger bindings (initially empty). The trigger queue ensures that the E machine will execute the E code block at a_1 as soon as the trigger $p'_c = p_c + 10$ is enabled. For now the E machine proceeds to the **return** instruction. Since no active triggers are enabled, the E machine relinquishes control to the scheduler of the OS, which takes over to schedule the tasks t_1 and t_2 in the task set. The E machine wakes up again when an input event occurs that enables an active trigger. In particular, at 10 ms the trigger binding $(p'_c = p_c + 10, a_1, s)$ is removed from the trigger queue, and the E code at address a_1 is executed. The execution of block a_1 is similar to that of block a_0. The whole process repeats every 20 ms.

The above scenario assumes that the execution of a task has completed before it is scheduled again, in other words, we need that $w(t_1) + 2 \cdot w(t_2) \leq 20$, where $w(t)$ is the WCET of task t. This requirement must be checked by the compiler. We will see in the next section how this requirement can be derived automatically and checked statically.

Semantics. The execution of an E program yields an infinite sequence of program configurations, called *trace*. Each configuration tracks the values of all ports, the program counter, the task set, and the trigger queue. Formally, a (*program*) *configuration* $c = (s', a', Trigs, Tasks)$ consists of (1) a P state s', called *port state*; (2) an address $a' \in A \cup \{\bot\}$, called *program counter*, where the special symbol $\bot$ indicates termination; (3) a queue $Trigs$ of trigger bindings (g, a, s), called *trigger queue*, where g is a trigger, a is an address, and s is a $P[g]$ state; and (4) a set $Tasks$ of triples (t, s, Δ), called *task set*, where t is a task, s is a $P[t] \cup I[t]$ state, and $\Delta \in \mathbb{N}$ is the *CPU time*, i.e., the amount of time that the task has run. We assume that CPU time is given in discrete units of the clock p_c, which may represent CPU cycles. The *ready tasks* of configuration c are defined as $T_c = \{t \mid \exists s, \Delta. (t, s, \Delta) \in Tasks\}$. The configuration c is *initial* if the program counter is the initial address ($a' = a_0$), and the trigger queue and task set are empty ($Trigs = Tasks = \emptyset$). A trigger binding (g, a, s) is *enabled* at c if the trigger predicate $f[g]$ evaluates to true over the pair (s, s') of $P[g]$ states. The configuration c is *input-enabling* if $a' = \bot$ and $Trigs$ contains no enabled trigger bindings; otherwise, c is *input-disabling*.

The E machine runs as long as the program configuration is input-disabling. If the program counter a' is different from $\bot$, then the instruction $ins(a')$ is executed. This updates the current configuration $c = (s', a', Trigs, Tasks)$ to a new configuration $succ(c)$ as follows. We only specify the parts of the configuration $succ(c)$ that are different from c: if $ins(a') = \texttt{call}(d)$, then the new $P[d]$ state is $f[d](s'(P[d] \cup I[d]))$, and the new program counter is $next(a')$; if $ins(a') = \texttt{schedule}(t)$, then the new task set is $Tasks \cup \{(t, s'(P[t] \cup I[t]), 0)\}$, and the new program counter is $next(a')$; if $ins(a') = \texttt{future}(g, a)$, then the new trigger queue is $Enqueue(Trigs, (g, a, s'(P[g])))$, and the new program counter is $next(a')$; if $ins(a') = \texttt{if}(f, a)$ and f evaluates to true (respectively, false) over s', then the new program counter is a (respectively, $next(a')$); if $ins(a') = \texttt{return}$, then the new program counter is $\perp$. Note that the $\texttt{call}$ instruction updates the port state, the $\texttt{schedule}$ instruction updates the task set, and the $\texttt{future}$ instruction updates the trigger queue. When a $\texttt{return}$ instruction is reached, the program counter becomes $\perp$. Consider the configuration $c = (s', \perp, Trigs, Tasks)$. If some trigger binding in $Trigs$ is enabled at s', then let (g, a, s) be the first such binding, and define $succ(c)$ to be the configuration that differs from c in that the new program counter is a, and the new trigger queue results from $Trigs$ by removing (g, a, s). This leads to the execution of more instructions. If no trigger binding in $Trigs$ is enabled at s' (i.e., c is input-enabling), then event interrupts are enabled and the E machine relinquishes control of the CPU to the scheduler until a new input event enables an active trigger binding. While the E machine waits for an input event, scheduled computation can be performed.

A trace is a sequence of configurations such that from one configuration to the next, there is either an environment event, an elapse of one time unit possibly followed by a software event (i.e., the completion of a task), or the execution of an instruction of E code. An environment event causes a nondeterministic change in the values of some environment ports; the choice is up to the environment. A time elapse causes a nondeterministic change in the CPU time of some task; the choice of task is up to the scheduler. If the chosen task completes, it also causes a deterministic change in the value of the task ports according to the task function. The execution of E code causes a deterministic change as specified by the function $succ$ defined above. Formally, given an E program Π with task set T, a *WCET map* for Π is a map $w: T \to \mathbb{N}_{>0}$ that assigns to each task a positive integer. A *trace* of the pair (Π, w) is a finite or infinite sequence of program configurations such that (1) the first configuration is initial and (2) for any two adjacent configurations c and c', one of the following holds:

(*Environment event*) c is input-enabling, and c' differs from c at most in the values of environment ports other than p_c. In this case, we write $e\text{-}step(c, c')$.

(*Time elapse with idle CPU*) c is input-enabling, and c' results from c by incrementing the clock p_c. In this case, we write $t\text{-}step(c, \emptyset, c')$.

(*Time elapse with used CPU*) c is input-enabling, and c' results from c by incrementing the clock p_c. In addition, there is a task t such that the task set of c contains a triple of the form (t, s, Δ), and either $\Delta + 1 < w(t)$ and the task set of c' results from c by replacing (t, s, Δ) with $(t, s, \Delta + 1)$; or $\Delta + 1 = w(t)$ and the task set of c' results from c by removing (t, s, Δ), and the $P[t]$ state of c' is $f[t](s)$. In this case, we write $t\text{-}step(c, t, c')$.

(*E code instruction*) c is input-disabling, and $c' = succ(c)$.

Note that we consider only traces where all task invocations consume their full WCETs; this is a worst-case assumption necessary for schedulability analysis. A *trace with atomic task execution* of Π is a sequence of configurations such that (1) the first configuration is initial and (2) for any two adjacent configurations c and c', either (*Environment event*); or (*E code instruction*); or (*Time elapse*) c is input-enabling, the task set of c is empty, and c' results from c by incrementing the clock p_c; or (*Task completion*) c is input-enabling, the task set of c contains a triple of the form $(t, s, 0)$, the task set of c' results from c by removing $(t, s, 0)$, and the $P[t]$ state of c' is $f[t](s)$. In a trace with atomic task execution, all tasks are executed in zero time.

3   Time-Safety Checking for E Code

An E program executes as intended only if the platform offers sufficient performance so that the computation of a task t always finishes before drivers access task ports of t, and before another invocation of t is scheduled. A trace that satisfies these conditions is called time safe, because the outcomes of `if` instructions cannot be distinguished from a trace with atomic task execution. Formally, a configuration c with program counter a is *time safe* [5] if either $a = \perp$, or for every ready tast $t \in T_c$, the instruction $ins(a)$ that is executed at c obeys the following two conditions: if $ins(a) = \mathtt{call}(d)$, then $P[d] \cap I[t] = \emptyset$ and $I[d] \cap P[t] = \emptyset$; and if $ins(a) = \mathtt{schedule}(t')$, then $P[t'] \cap P[t] = \emptyset$. If one of these two conditions is violated, then we say that the configuration c *conflicts with* the task t. A trace is *time safe* if it contains only time-safe configurations.

Given a nonempty finite trace τ, let $last(\tau)$ be the final configuration of τ. A *scheduling strategy* is a function that maps every nonempty finite trace τ whose final configuration $last(\tau)$ is input-enabling, either to $\emptyset$ (meaning that no task is scheduled), or to some ready task $t \in T_{last(\tau)}$. An infinite trace $\tau = c_0 c_1 c_2 \ldots$ is an *outcome* of the scheduling strategy σ if for all nonempty finite prefixes $\tau' = c_0 \ldots c_j$ of τ, if c_j is input-enabling, then either $e\text{-}step(c_j, c_{j+1})$ or $t\text{-}step(c_j, \sigma(\tau'), c_{j+1})$. The E program Π is *schedulable* for the WCET map w if there exists a scheduling strategy σ such that all infinite traces of (Π, w) that are outcomes of σ are time safe. The *schedulability problem* for E code asks, given an E program Π and a WCET map w for Π, if Π is schedulable for w.

To solve the schedulability problem we need to eliminate some possible sources of infinity. An E program Π is *propositional* if it satisfies the following conditions: (1) all ports of Π except the clock p_c are boolean; (2) for all drivers d of Π, we have $p_c \notin I[d]$; and (3) for all triggers g of Π, either $p_c \notin P[g]$, or g is a time trigger. As time safety implies that a task must finish before it can be invoked again, along a time-safe trace, the size of the task set is always bounded by the number of tasks. However, the size of the trigger queue may grow unbounded [5]. A configuration c is *k-bounded*, for a positive integer $k \in \mathbb{N}_{>0}$, if the trigger queue of c contains at most k trigger bindings. A trace is *k-bounded* if it contains only k-bounded configurations. The *bounded schedulability* problem asks, given an E program Π, a WCET map w for Π, and a bound $k \in \mathbb{N}_{>0}$, if there is a scheduling strategy σ such that all infinite traces of (Π, w) that are outcomes of σ are both time safe and k-bounded.

Two-player safety games. Schedulability can be solved as a safety game on the configuration graph [1]. A *two-player safety game* [2] $\mathcal{G} = (V, E, V_0, U)$ consists of a finite set V of vertices, a relation $E \subseteq V \times V$ of edges, a set $V_0 \subseteq V$ of initial vertices, and a set $U \subseteq V$ of safe vertices. The vertices V are partitioned into V_1 and V_2. The game is turn-based and proceeds in rounds. For $i = 1, 2$, when the game is in $v \in V_i$, player i moves to v' such that $E(v, v')$. The goal of player 1 is to stay inside the safe set U. A *source-v_0 run* is an infinite sequence $v_0 v_1 v_2 \ldots$ of vertices in V such that $E(v_j, v_{j+1})$ for all $j \geq 0$. A *strategy* for player i, with $i = 1, 2$, is a function $f_i \colon V^* \times V_i \to V$ such that for every finite sequence $r \in V^*$ and vertex $v \in V_i$, we have $E(v, f_i(r, v))$. For a player-1 strategy f_1, a player-2 strategy f_2, and a state $v_0 \in V$, the *outcome* $\rho_{f_1, f_2}(v_0) = v_0 v_1 v_2 \ldots$ is a source-v_0 run such that for all $j \geq 0$, for $i = 1, 2$, if $v_j \in V_i$, then $E(v_j, f_i(v_0 \ldots v_{j-1}, v_j))$. The outcome $\rho_{f_1, f_2}(v_0)$ is *winning* for player 1 if $v_j \in U$ for all $j \geq 0$. The strategy f_1 is *winning* for player 1 if for all initial vertices $v_0 \in V_0$ and all player-2 strategies f_2, the outcome $\rho_{f_1, f_2}(v_0)$ is winning for player 1.

The schedulability game. Let Π be a propositional E program with ports P, tasks T, triggers G, and addresses A. Let w be a WCET map for Π, and let $k \in \mathbb{N}_{>0}$. We define the *schedulability game* $\mathcal{G}_{\Pi, w, k}$ as follows. Player 1 is the scheduler; it chooses during time elapses which task to run on the CPU. The environment is player 2; it chooses environment events. The actions of the E machine when executing E code are deterministic, so it does not matter to which player we attribute them; we choose player 2. From each configuration $c = (s', a', \mathit{Trigs}, \mathit{Tasks})$ of Π we obtain its *clock abstraction* $[c]$ as follows: remove the value of p_c from the port state s', and for each time trigger g, replace each trigger binding (g, a, s) in Trigs by $(g, a, s'(p_c) - s)$. Hence, for each active time trigger, the clock abstraction $[c]$ tracks only the number of clock ticks since the trigger was activated. A configuration c of Π *conforms with* w if $\Delta \leq w(t)$ for each triple (t, s, Δ) in the task set of c. Let $C_{\Pi, w, k}$ be the set of clock abstractions for all k-bounded configurations of Π that conform with w. As Π is propositional, the set $C_{\Pi, w, k}$ is finite. Specifically, the size of $C_{\Pi, w, k}$ is bounded by $2^{|P|} \cdot |A| \cdot (|T| \cdot 2^{|P|} \cdot \alpha) \cdot (|G| \cdot |A| \cdot 2^{|P|} \cdot \beta \cdot k)$, where $\alpha = \max \{ w(t) \mid t \in T \}$, and β is the greatest enabling time for all time triggers in G.

The vertices of the schedulability game $\mathcal{G}_{\Pi, w, k}$ are $V = C_{\Pi, w, k} \times \{1, 2\}$, where the second component indicates which player can choose the next move, that is, the second component defines the subsets V_1 and V_2. The initial vertices are those of the form $((\cdot, a_0, \emptyset, \emptyset), 2)$, where a_0 is the initial address of Π. There are three types of edges. The environment chooses new values for the environment ports (other than p_c): for all configurations c and c' with $e\text{-}step(c, c')$, there are two edges $(([c], 2), ([c'], 2))$ and $(([c], 2), ([c'], 1))$. The E machine executes E code in input-disabling configurations: if c is input-disabling, then there is an edge $(([c], 2), ([succ(c)], 2))$. The scheduler assigns the CPU to tasks: for all configurations c and c' with $t\text{-}step(c, \cdot, c')$, there is an edge $(([c], 1), ([c'], 2))$. A vertex $([c], i)$, for $i = 1, 2$, is in the safe set U if the configuration c is time safe. The objective of the scheduler is to ensure that the game always remains in U. A winning strategy of the scheduler prescribes a scheduling strategy for the program Π that guarantees time safety and k-boundedness under the WCET assumption w, no matter what the environment does. Conversely, if the scheduler does not win, then by the determinacy of the safety game $\mathcal{G}_{\Pi, w, k}$, there is an environment strategy that forces the game into a time-safety or k-boundedness violation, no matter what the scheduler does. Since safety games can be solved in linear time [7], this gives an exponential upper bound for checking bounded schedulability.

Hardness. The bounded schedulability problem is hard for EXPTIME by a reduction from alternating linear-space Turing machines. Let M be an alternating Turing machine that uses $\ell \cdot n$ tape cells for inputs of length n, and makes binary existential and universal choices. For an input x of length n, we construct a propositional E program $\Pi_{M,x}$ (with the WCETs of all tasks being 1) such that $\Pi_{M,x}$ is two-bounded schedulable iff M does not accept x. For each control state q of M, and each tape-head position $h \in \{1, \dots, \ell \cdot n\}$, the program has an address (q, h) that begins a block of E code. We have $\ell \cdot n$ task ports to keep the tape contents. The initial block of E code writes x followed by blanks to these ports, and jumps to $(q_0, 1)$, where q_0 is the initial control state of M. We encode the existential moves of M as choices made by the environment, that is, if q is an existential control state, then the E program reads an environment port and goes to one or the other successor configuration of M. For universal moves, the program schedules two tasks, each with WCET 1. Each task triggers an event upon completion. This event writes the identity of the task to a special port p_u. The scheduler chooses which task to run first, and this choice determines the order in which the tasks finish, and thus the value of p_u after 2 time units. The E program reads the new value of p_u and goes to the corresponding successor configuration of M. Every step of the simulation gives rise to a solvable scheduling problem. Finally, as soon as the Turing machine reaches an accepting state, the E program goes to an address that sets up an unsolvable scheduling problem. The trigger queue contains at any time at most two trigger bindings, and all numbers are bounded by a small constant.

Theorem 1. *Checking bounded schedulability for propositional E programs is complete for EXPTIME (even if all numbers are coded in unary).*

4   E Code Generation from Giotto

4.1   The Giotto Language

Giotto [4] is a programming language for time-triggered applications. Figure 1 shows an example of a Giotto program. The Giotto compiler generates time-triggered E code from a Giotto program. We demonstrate code generation based on the abstract syntax of a program, rather than its concrete syntax, and we use the program from Figure 1 as a running example.

```
sensor gps uses dev[gps]; toggle uses dev[toggle];
actuator servo uses dev[servo];
output
  ctrlOut := init[ctrlOut] uses copy[ctrlOut];
  filterOut := init[filterOut] uses copy[filterOut];

task control(ctrlIn) output (ctrlOut) private () {
  schedule task[control](ctrlIn, ctrlOut); }
task filter(filterIn) output (filterOut) private (filterState := init[filterState]) {
  schedule task[filter](filterIn, filterOut, filterState); }
task adaptiveFilter(filterIn) output (filterOut) private (adaptiveState := init[adaptiveState]) {
  schedule task[adaptiveFilter](filterIn, filterOut, adaptiveState); }

driver inputCtrl(filterOut) output (ctrlIn) {
  call driver[inputCtrl](filterOut, ctrlIn); }
driver inputFilter(gps) output (filterIn) { call driver[inputFilter](gps, filterIn); }
driver updateServo(ctrlOut) output (servo) { call driver[updateServo](ctrlOut, servo); }
driver switchFilter(toggle) output (ctrlOut, filterOut) {
  if condition[switchFilter](toggle) call driver[switchFilter](ctrlOut, filterOut); }

start normal {
  mode normal(ctrlOut, filterOut) period 6 {
    actfreq 1 do servo(updateServo);
    exitfreq 2 do adaptive(switchFilter);
    taskfreq 1 do control(inputCtrl);
    taskfreq 2 do filter(inputFilter); }
  mode adaptive(ctrlOut, filterOut) period 12 {
    actfreq 2 do servo(updateServo);
    exitfreq 3 do normal(switchFilter);
    taskfreq 2 do control(inputCtrl);
    taskfreq 3 do adaptiveFilter(inputFilter); }}
```

Fig. 1. A Giotto program with two modes

A *Giotto program* begins with declarations of a set *SensePorts* of sensor ports, a set *ActPorts* of actuator ports, and a set *OutPorts* of task output ports. The set *Ports* of all program ports also includes the set *InPorts* of task input ports and the set *PrivPorts* of task private ports, which are declared for each task separately. A sensor or actuator port p requires the declaration of a device driver $dev[p]$. For example, the sensor port *gps* uses the device driver $dev[gps]$ to read new sensor values. A task output port p requires the declaration of an initialization driver $init[p]$ and a copy driver $copy[p]$. Each task output port is double-buffered, that is, it is implemented by two copies, a *local* copy that is used by the task only, and a *global* copy that is accessible to the rest of the program. The initialization driver initializes the local copy; the copy driver copies data from the local copy to the global copy. The second part of a Giotto program are the task declarations. A *Giotto task* t has a set $In[t] \subseteq InPorts$ of input ports, a set $Out[t] \subseteq OutPorts$ of output ports, a set $Priv[t] \subseteq PrivPorts$ of private ports, and a task function $task[t]$ from the input and private ports to the private and output ports. In the example, the task *filter* has an input port *filterIn*, an output port *filterOut*, a private port *filterState*, and the task function $task[filter]$. Private ports have initialization drivers similar to task output ports. Each task function is implemented as an E machine task. The third part of a Giotto program are the driver declarations. Giotto drivers transport data between ports and initiate mode changes. A *Giotto driver* d has a set $Src[d] \subseteq Ports$ of source ports, an optional driver guard *condition*[d], which is evaluated on the source ports and returns a boolean, a set *Dst*[d] ⊆ *Ports* of destination ports, and a driver function *driver*[d] from the source to the destination ports. The driver guard is implemented as a branching condition of the E machine; the driver function, as an E machine driver. The driver *inputCtrl* is a *task driver* that transports data from the *filterOut* port to the input port *ctrlIn* of the *control* task. The driver *updateServo* is an *actuator driver* that updates the *servo* port with data from the *ctrlOut* port. The driver *switchFilter* is a *mode driver* that initiates a mode change whenever the driver guard *condition*[*switchFilter*] evaluates to true. Moreover, the driver function *driver*[*switchFilter*] may update the *ctrlOut* and *filterOut* ports when changing mode.

The final part of a Giotto program declares the set *Modes* of modes and the start mode *start* ∈ *Modes*. In the example, there are two modes, *normal* and *adaptive*, the former being the start mode. A *mode* m has a period $\pi[m] \in \mathbb{Q}$, a set *ModePorts*[m] ⊆ *OutPorts* of mode ports, a set *Invokes*[m] of task invocations, a set *Updates*[m] of actuator updates, and a set *Switches*[m] of mode switches. For example, the mode period $\pi[normal]$ of the *normal* mode is 6 ms, and its mode ports are *ctrlOut* and *filterOut*. For simplicity, we use milliseconds though another unit of time is possible. A *task invocation* $(\omega_{task}, t, d) \in$ *Invokes*[m] consists of a task frequency $\omega_{task} \in \mathbb{N}$ relative to the mode period, a task t, and a task driver d, which loads the task inputs. For example, the *normal* mode invokes the *control* task with the task driver *inputCtrl* and a period of 6 ms (i.e., once per mode period) as well as the *filter* task with the task driver *inputFilter* and a period of 3 ms. An *actuator update* $(\omega_{act}, d) \in$ *Updates*[m] consists of an actuator frequency $\omega_{act} \in \mathbb{N}$, and an actuator driver d. For example, the *normal* mode updates the *servo* port every 6 ms using the *updateServo* driver. A *mode switch* $(\omega_{switch}, m', d) \in$ *Switches*[m] consists of a mode-switch frequency $\omega_{switch} \in \mathbb{N}$, a target mode $m' \in$ *Modes*, and a mode driver d, which governs the mode change. For example, the *normal* mode may change to the *adaptive* mode every 3 ms using the *switchFilter* driver.

A Giotto program is *well-timed* [4] if for all modes $m \in$ *Modes*, all task invocations $(\omega_{task}, t, \cdot) \in$ *Invokes*[m], and all mode switches $(\omega_{switch}, m', \cdot) \in$ *Switches*[m], if $\omega_{task}/\omega_{switch} \notin \mathbb{N}$, then there exists a task invocation $(\omega'_{task}, t, \cdot) \in$ *Invokes*[m'] with $\pi[m]/\omega_{task} = \pi[m']/\omega'_{task}$. Well-timedness ensures that mode changes do not terminate tasks: if a mode change occurs when a task may not be completed, then the same task must be present also in the target mode. The Giotto program in Figure 1 is well-timed, because the *control* task, which may be preempted by a mode change, runs in both modes with the same period. All non-well-timed Giotto programs are rejected as ill-formed. A complete list of syntactic criteria for the well-formedness of a Giotto program, such as the condition that the ports of different tasks be disjoint, is given in [4].

For a mode m, the least common multiple of the task, actuator, and mode-switch frequencies of m is called the number of *units* of m, and is denoted $\omega_{max}[m]$. For example, $\omega_{max}[normal]$ is 2, and $\omega_{max}[adaptive]$ is 6. Thus a unit in the *normal* mode is equivalent to 3 ms, and a unit in the *adaptive* mode is equivalent to 2 ms. We use an integer $u \in \{0, \ldots, \omega_{max}[m] - 1\}$ as the *unit counter* for a mode m. Given a mode $m \in Modes$ and a unit u with $0 \le u < \omega_{max}[m]$, we need the following auxiliary operators for E code generation:

$$taskInvocations(m, u) := \{(\omega_{task}, t, d) \in Invokes[m] \mid u \cdot \omega_{task}/\omega_{max}[m] \in \mathbb{N}\}$$
$$tasks(m, u) := \{t \mid (\cdot, t, \cdot) \in taskInvocations(m, u)\}$$
$$taskDrivers(m, u) := \{d \mid (\cdot, \cdot, d) \in taskInvocations(m, u)\}$$
$$taskOutputPorts(m, u) := \{p \mid t \in tasks(m, u) \land p \in Out[t]\}$$
$$taskSensorPorts(m, u) := \{p \mid d \in taskDrivers(m, u) \land p \in Src[d] \cap SensePorts\}$$
$$preemptedTaskPeriods(m, u) :=$$
$$\{\omega_{max}[m]/\omega_{task} \mid (\omega_{task}, \cdot, \cdot) \in Invokes[m] \setminus taskInvocations(m, u)\}$$
$$actuatorDrivers(m, u) := \{d \mid (\omega_{act}, d) \in Updates[m] \land u \cdot \omega_{act}/\omega_{max}[m] \in \mathbb{N}\}$$
$$actuatorPorts(m, u) := \{p \mid d \in actuatorDrivers(m, u) \land p \in Dst[d]\}$$
$$modeSwitches(m, u) :=$$
$$\{(m', d) \mid (\omega_{switch}, m', d) \in Switches[m] \land u \cdot \omega_{switch}/\omega_{max}[m] \in \mathbb{N}\}$$
$$modeSensorPorts(m, u) :=$$
$$\{p \mid (\cdot, d) \in modeSwitches(m, u) \land p \in Src[d] \cap SensePorts\}$$

Consider the *taskInvocations* operator. For example, *taskInvocations(normal, 1)* returns $\{(2, \mathit{filter}, \mathit{inputFilter})\}$, because the *filter* task is the only task that is invoked at unit 1 in the *normal* mode. At unit 0 the operator returns the invocations of both the *control* and the *filter* task. All other operators work in a similar way, except the *preemptedTaskPeriods* operator, which returns the periods of the tasks that are preempted, not invoked, at the specified unit.

4.2 From Giotto to E Code

Algorithm 1 generates E code that implements the logical semantics of a well-timed Giotto program, as it is specified in [4]. The command *emit* generates E code instructions. The key programmer's abstraction in Giotto is that the computation of a task takes exactly as long as its period. Thus the outputs of a task are logically made available at the end of its period, not at the end of its computation. The compiler begins generating E code by emitting call instructions to the initialization drivers of all task output and private ports. Then an absolute jump is emitted to the first instruction of the start mode.[1] Since this instruction is unknown at this point, we use a symbolic reference *mode_address[m, u]*. The symbolic reference will be linked to the first instruction of the E code that implements mode m at unit u. Finally, Algorithm 2 is called to generate code for all modes and units. For the Giotto program from Figure 1, the following E code is generated by Algorithm 1:

$$\texttt{call}(\mathit{init}[\mathit{ctrlOut}])$$
$$\texttt{call}(\mathit{init}[\mathit{filterOut}])$$
$$\texttt{call}(\mathit{init}[\mathit{filterState}])$$
$$\texttt{call}(\mathit{init}[\mathit{adaptiveState}])$$
$$\texttt{jump}(\mathit{mode\_address}[\mathit{normal}, 0])$$

---

[1] The instruction jump(a) is shorthand for if$(true, a)$.

$\forall p \in OutPorts \cup PrivPorts$: $emit(\texttt{call}(init[p]))$;
$emit(\texttt{jump}(mode\_address[start, 0]))$;
$\forall m \in Modes$: invoke Algorithm 2 for mode m;

Algorithm 1: The Giotto program compiler

$u := 0$; $\gamma := \pi[m]/\omega_{max}[m]$;
while $u < \omega_{max}[m]$ **do**
    link $mode\_address[m, u]$ to the address of the next free instruction cell;
    $\forall p \in taskOutputPorts(m, u)$: $emit(\texttt{call}(copy[p]))$;
    $\forall d \in actuatorDrivers(m, u)$: $emit(\texttt{call}(driver[d]))$;
    $\forall p \in actuatorPorts(m, u)$: $emit(\texttt{call}(dev[p]))$;
    $\forall p \in modeSensorPorts(m, u)$: $emit(\texttt{call}(dev[p]))$;
    $\forall (m', d) \in modeSwitches(m, u)$: $emit(\texttt{if}(condition[d], switch\_address[m, u, m', d]))$;
    $emit(\texttt{jump}(task\_address[m, u]))$;

    $\forall (m', d) \in modeSwitches(m, u)$:
        link $switch\_address[m, u, m', d]$ to the address of the next free instruction cell;
        // compute the unit u' to which to jump in the target mode m' and
        // compute the time δ' before new tasks in the target mode m' can be scheduled
        if $preemptedTaskPeriods(m, u) = \emptyset$ **then**
            // jump to the beginning of m' if all tasks in mode m are completed
            $\delta' := 0$; $u' := 0$;
        else
            // compute the hyperperiod h of the preempted tasks in units of mode m
            $h := \text{lcm}(preemptedTaskPeriods(m, u))$;
            // compute the time δ to finish the hyperperiod h
            $\delta := (h - u \bmod h) * \pi[m]/\omega_{max}[m]$;
            // compute the time δ' to wait for the unit u' in the target mode m' to begin
            $\delta' := \delta \bmod (\pi[m']/\omega_{max}[m'])$;
            // compute the closest unit u' to the end of the mode period in m' after δ'
            $u' := (\omega_{max}[m'] - (\delta - \delta') * \omega_{max}[m']/\pi[m']) \bmod \omega_{max}[m']$;
        end if
        $emit(\texttt{call}(driver[d]))$;
        if $\delta' > 0$ **then**
            $emit(\texttt{future}(timer[\delta'], mode\_address[m', u']))$;
            $emit(\texttt{return})$;
        else
            $emit(\texttt{jump}(task\_address[m', u']))$;
        end if

    link $task\_address[m, u]$ to the address of the next free instruction cell;
    $\forall p \in taskSensorPorts(m, u)$: $emit(\texttt{call}(dev[p]))$;
    $\forall d \in taskDrivers(m, u)$: $emit(\texttt{call}(driver[d]))$;
    $\forall t \in tasks(m, u)$: $emit(\texttt{schedule}(task[t]))$;
    $emit(\texttt{future}(timer[\gamma], mode\_address[m, u + 1 \bmod \omega_{max}[m]]))$;
    $emit(\texttt{return})$;
    $u := u + 1$;
end while

Algorithm 2: The Giotto mode compiler

Algorithm 2 generates three types of E code blocks for each unit u of a mode m. The duration of a unit is denoted by γ. The first type of E code block, labeled *mode_address*$[m, u]$, takes care of updating task output ports, updating actuators, reading sensors, and checking mode switches. The compiler generates `call` instructions to the appropriate drivers and an `if` instruction for each mode switch. The block is terminated by a `jump` instruction to a block that deals with task invocations; see below. The `jump` is only reached if none of the mode switches is enabled. The second type of E code block implements the mode change to a target mode m' with a given mode driver d. We use the symbolic reference *switch_address*$[m, u, m', d]$ to label this type of E code block. Upon a mode change, the mode driver is called and then control is transfered to the appropriate E code block of the target mode. The compiler computes the destination unit u' as close as possible to the end of the target mode's period. We distinguish the two cases of whether the duration of either u or u' is a multiple of the other, or not. If so, then the compiler generates a `jump` instruction to the E code of the target mode for u'. If not, then the time δ' to wait for u' is computed and generated as part of a `future` instruction. The trigger *timer*$[\delta']$ is a time trigger with enabling time δ'; that is, it specifies the trigger predicate $p_c' = p_c + \delta'$, which evaluates to true after δ' ms elapse. The third type of E code blocks handles the invocation of tasks and the future invocation of the E machine for the next unit. The label for these blocks is *task_address*$[m, u]$. Before scheduling the tasks, the task drivers are called in order to load the task input ports with new data. The final `future` instruction makes the E machine wait for the duration γ of u and then execute the E code for the next unit. Note that the resulting E code is time-triggered. If, along a trace, the E code generated for m and u is executed consecutively without mode change for all units u with $0 \le u < \omega_{max}[m]$, then the trace contains a *full period* of mode m.

Figure 2 shows the E code generated for the *normal* mode of the Giotto program from Figure 1. The E code for the *adaptive* mode is not shown. The *normal* mode has a period of 6 ms and two units of 3 ms length each. At the 0 ms unit, the *control* and *filter* tasks are invoked; at the 3 ms unit, only the *filter* task is invoked. The mode switch to the *adaptive* mode is checked at both units. Consider the mode switch at unit 1 when the *control* task is preempted after 3 ms of logical computation time. In Algorithm 2 the number h of units in the *normal* mode until the task completes is 1. Thus the time δ to complete the task is 3 ms. The time δ' to wait for the next unit u' in the *adaptive* mode is 1 ms, because the duration of a unit in the *adaptive* mode is 2 ms. The closest unit u' to the end of the *adaptive* mode's period is 5. Within one more unit of 2 ms the end of the period will be reached. Thus the *control* task has exactly 3 ms time to complete even when the mode is changed to the *adaptive* mode.

5   Time-Safety Checking for Giotto

For special classes of E programs, schedulability can be checked efficiently. For example, a set T of *periodic* tasks can be scheduled iff it satisfies the utilization

$mode\_address[normal, 0]$:
call($copy[ctrlOut]$)
call($copy[filterOut]$)
call($driver[updateServo]$)
call($dev[servo]$)
call($dev[toggle]$)
if($condition[switchFilter]$, $switch\_address[$
    $normal, 0, adaptive, switchFilter]$)
jump($task\_address[normal, 0]$)

$mode\_address[normal, 1]$:
call($copy[filterOut]$)
call($dev[toggle]$)
if($condition[switchFilter]$, $switch\_address[$
    $normal, 1, adaptive, switchFilter]$)
jump($task\_address[normal, 1]$)

$switch\_address[normal, 0, adaptive, switchFilter]$:
call($driver[switchFilter]$)
jump($task\_address[adaptive, 0]$)

$switch\_address[normal, 1, adaptive, switchFilter]$:
call($driver[switchFilter]$)
future($timer[1]$, $mode\_address[adaptive, 5]$)
return

$task\_address[normal, 0]$:
call($dev[gps]$)
call($driver[inputCtrl]$)
call($driver[inputFilter]$)
schedule($task[control]$)
schedule($task[filter]$)
future($timer[3]$, $mode\_address[normal, 1]$)
return

$task\_address[normal, 1]$:
call($dev[gps]$)
call($driver[inputFilter]$)
schedule($task[filter]$)
future($timer[3]$, $mode\_address[normal, 0]$)
return

Fig. 2. E code generated for the *normal* mode of the Giotto program from Figure 1

test, i.e., the processor utilization $\sum_{t \in T} w(t)/\pi(t)$, where $w(t)$ is the WCET time and $\pi(t)$ is the period of task t, is less than or equal to 1 [6]. For E programs that are generated from typical Giotto source programs —namely, Giotto programs where each mode may be executed for a full period— we have a similarly simple schedulability test. More precisely, a mode m of a Giotto program G is *fully reachable* if there exists a trace with atomic task execution of Π_G that contains a full period of mode m. Note that the definition of full reachability does not depend on time safety, as it assumes atomic task execution. Given a (well-timed) Giotto program G, we write Π_G for the E program that is generated from G by Algorithm 1. The Giotto program G is *E schedulable* for the WCET map w if the E program Π_G is schedulable for w. The *E schedulability problem* for Giotto asks, given a Giotto program G and a WCET map w for Π_G, if G is E schedulable for w.

Theorem 2. *A Giotto program G is E schedulable for the WCET map w if for each mode m of G, the utilization equation $\sum_{(\omega_{task}, t, \cdot) \in Invokes[m]} w(t)/\pi(t) \leq 1$ holds, where $\pi(t) = \pi[m]/\omega_{task}$ is the period of task t. This condition is necessary if each mode of G is fully reachable.*

Assuming that all modes are fully reachable, Theorem 2 gives a polynomial-time algorithm for checking the E schedulability of a Giotto program: the utilization equation can be checked in time no more than $O(n^2 polylog(n))$, where n is the size of the Giotto program. This test shows, for example, that the Giotto program from Figure 1 is E schedulable for the WCETs $w(control) = 3$, $w(filter) = 1.5$, and $w(adaptiveFilter) = 2$. Note that E code schedulability is not the most general notion of schedulability for Giotto programs. While E code schedulability refers to the particular E code generation scheme specified by Algorithm 1, for any given Giotto program, there may be other, more flexible code generation strategies that are faithful to the Giotto semantics. For example, a task could be started as soon as all arguments are available, which may be before its logical release time.

Proof sketch. Suppose that each mode satisfies the utilization test. This means that each mode is schedulable by itself. We show that mode changes do not cause the system to become non-schedulable, by using the schedule that assigns to each ready task t a time slice equal to $w(t)/\pi(t)$ in every time unit. This is possible by the utilization equation. Now consider a mode change. By the semantics of a mode change in Giotto, in particular by the well-timedness condition, at the mode change, all tasks that are not present in the target mode have finished executing, and all tasks that are present in the target mode retain their deadline after the mode change. This implies that the common tasks have executed for exactly the same amount of time in the source mode up to the mode change as they would have, following the chosen schedule, in an execution that started in the target mode. Since the target mode can finish executing all tasks by their deadlines, it can do so even after the mode change. In fact, the only difference of an execution in the target mode after the mode change from an execution starting in the target mode is that some tasks in the target mode may not run in the former case. Since the target mode is individually schedulable, it remains schedulable after a mode change into it.

For the converse, suppose that the utilization test fails for a fully reachable mode m. Consider a trace τ with atomic task execution that contains a full period of m. Choose any scheduling strategy σ. If the environment plays against σ using the same behavior as used along τ in a game with WCET task execution, then either a time-safety violation occurs, or a full period of m is reached. In the latter case, time safety must be violated also, because of the failed utilization test. It follows that the program is not E schedulable.

EDF scheduling. For each configuration c and ready task $t \in T_c$, we define the *deadline* $D(c, t)$ as the weight of the shortest path in the (unbounded) game graph $\mathcal{G}_{\Pi,w,\infty}$ from $[c]$ to the clock abstraction of a configuration that conflicts with t, where each player 1 (scheduler) move has weight 1, and all other moves have weight 0; if no such path exists, then $D(c, t) = \infty$. An *EDF scheduling strategy* is a function that maps every nonempty finite trace τ to $\emptyset$ if the task set of the final configuration $last(\tau)$ is empty, and otherwise to a task $t \in T_{last(\tau)}$ such that for all ready tasks $t' \in T_{last(\tau)}$, we have $D(c, t) \leq D(c, t')$. The E programs that are generated from Giotto source programs using Algorithm 1 have the property that with the execution of a $\texttt{schedule}(t)$ instruction, the deadline of t is known and does not change in subsequent configurations until t completes. In particular, all deadlines are independent of the chosen scheduling strategy. It follows by a standard argument that EDF is optimal for Giotto.

Proposition 1. *Let σ be an EDF scheduling strategy. A Giotto program G is E schedulable for the WCET map w iff all infinite traces of (Π_G, w) that are outcomes of σ are time safe.*

The deadlines for an EDF scheduler can be computed directly on the Giotto source and may be passed to the scheduler as E code annotations [5]. The Giotto compiler we have implemented proceeds in two steps. First, it computes the relative deadline for each task in each mode and checks the E schedulability of the Giotto program by performing the utilization test of Theorem 2 for each mode. Second, it generates E code using Algorithm 1 and annotates each $\mathtt{schedule}(t)$ instruction with the deadline of t. Then, for an EDF scheduler that uses the deadlines, time safety is guaranteed for all possible environment behaviors.

Checking E schedulability. If there are modes that are not fully reachable, then the utilization test is only a sufficient condition for E schedulability. In general, however, it is PSPACE-hard to check if a mode is fully reachable, or if a Giotto program is E schedulable. We can reduce succinct boolean reachability to the reachability of a boolean port state, say s_f, in the start mode (using a driver to encode the transition relation). The start mode is schedulable, but if s_f is reached, the program switches to a non-schedulable mode. Then the Giotto program is E schedulable iff s_f is reachable. This gives half of the theorem below. For *propositional* Giotto programs, which have only boolean ports, inclusion in PSPACE follows from the following scheduling algorithm. First observe that if G is propositional, then so is Π_G. From Algorithm 1 it follows also that all traces of Π_G are one-bounded. Moreover, the number of E code instructions of Π_G is exponential in the size of the Giotto program G. By Proposition 1, we can fix an EDF scheduling strategy and check if a non-time-safe configuration can be reached on the game graph $\mathcal{G}_{\Pi_G,w,1}$. This is a reachability, rather than a game problem, on an exponential graph, and therefore in PSPACE.

Theorem 3. *Checking E schedulability for propositional Giotto programs is complete for PSPACE (even if all numbers are coded in unary).*

References

1. K. Altisen, G. Gössler, A. Pnueli, J. Sifakis, S. Tripakis, and S. Yovine. A framework for scheduler synthesis. In *Proc. Real-Time Systems Symp.*, pp. 154–163. IEEE Computer Society, 1999.
2. J.R. Büchi and L.H. Landweber. Solving sequential conditions by finite-state strategies. *Trans. AMS*, 138:295–311, 1969.
3. N. Halbwachs. *Synchronous Programming of Reactive Systems.* Kluwer, 1993.
4. T.A. Henzinger, B. Horowitz, and C.M. Kirsch. Giotto: a time-triggered language for embedded programming. In *Proc. Embedded Software*, LNCS 2211, pp. 166–184. Springer, 2001.
5. T.A. Henzinger and C.M. Kirsch. The embedded machine: predictable, portable real-time code. In *Proc. Conf. Programming Languages Design and Implementation*, pp. 315–326. ACM, 2002.
6. C. Liu and J. Layland. Scheduling algorithms for multiprogramming in a hard-real-time environment. *J. ACM*, 20:46–61, 1973.
7. J.W. Thatcher and J.B. Wright. Generalized finite-automata theory with an application to a decision problem in second-order logic. *Mathematical Systems Theory*, 2:57–81, 1968.

Compositional Modeling in Metropolis

Gregor Gössler and Alberto Sangiovanni-Vincentelli

University of California at Berkeley, Dept. of EECS
{gregor,alberto}@eecs.berkeley.edu

Abstract. METROPOLIS is an environment for the design of heterogeneous embedded systems. The framework is based on a general system representation called the METROPOLIS meta-model. This model forms the backbone of the software system and is used to integrate a variety of analysis and synthesis tools. Compositional modeling is a powerful method for assembling components so that their composition satisfies a set of given properties thus making the verification problem much simpler to solve. We use the meta-model to integrate the PROMETHEUS tool in METROPOLIS for supporting compositional modeling and verification of METROPOLIS specifications and present a first set of results on a nontrivial example, a micro-kernel real-time operating system, TinyOS.

1 Introduction

METROPOLIS [4] is a design environment for embedded systems. It supports a methodology that favors the reusability of components by explicitly decoupling the specification of orthogonal aspects over a set of abstraction levels. More precisely, computation, communication, and coordination are separated by having them described by different entities: processes, media, and schedulers. METROPOLIS proposes a formalism called *meta-model* that is designed so that various computation and communication semantics can be specified using common building blocks [8]. The meta-model supports progressive refinement of components, their communication and coordination. It allows executable code in a Java-like syntax as well as denotational formulas in temporal and predicate logic, so that the right level of details of the design can be defined at each abstraction. The METROPOLIS architecture encompasses a compiler front-end to translate a meta-model specification into an intermediate representation, and a set of back-end tools to support tasks such as synthesis, refinement, analysis, and verification of the model.

Building systems which satisfy given specifications is a central problem in systems engineering. Standard engineering practice consists in decomposing the system to be designed into a set of cooperating components. Sometimes this decomposition is dictated by the functionality of the system: for example, a network of sensors and actuators is naturally partitioned into components. We are interested in assessing whether the global behavior of the system satisfies given specifications. An essential problem to solve is how to compose the components. If indeed a rigorous design methodology is used when assembling the

A. Sangiovanni-Vincentelli and J. Sifakis (Eds.): EMSOFT 2002, LNCS 2491, pp. 93–107, 2002.

system from components, then the verification problem can be solved either by construction or using formal methods. Unfortunately, designers are used to ad hoc design methodologies that almost always lead to solutions that must be validated by simulation, rapid prototyping and testing. In some cases, it is possible to solve the composition problem by synthesizing a controller or supervisor that restricts the behavior of the components [16] so that the overall system behaves correctly by construction or is amenable to formal analysis. Both verification at the global system level and synthesis techniques have well-known limitations due to their inherent complexity or undecidability, and cannot be applied to complex systems. As an alternative to cope with complexity, *compositional* modeling techniques have been studied. By compositional modeling we understand that the components of a (real-time) system are modeled in such a way that important liveness and progress properties are preserved when a new component is added to the system.

We are interested in the design of complex systems such as an embedded system for automotive power-train control or a wireless network of sensors and actuators. We have experience in setting up a platform-based design methodology supported by METROPOLIS for these applications that uses extensively the principles of successive refinement as a way of simplifying substantially the verification problem. However, there is much room for compositional methods that, in addition to the successive refinement principle, can improve substantially the design process in an unobtrusive way [1].

In this respect, we are motivated by the analysis of a particular network of sensors and actuators being designed at the Berkeley Wireless Research Center. The components of this network are small, inexpensive embedded computers called nodes, which can be distributed over a building, measure parameters such as temperature, and communicate with each other over a low-power wireless device. TinyOS [10] is an operating system for these embedded systems that provides basic functionality, such as task scheduling, message passing, and interrupt handling, while being extremely small (less than a kilobyte) and supporting a modular structure of the application. Since, in this wireless network, direct communication is only possible over short distances, most nodes cannot communicate with each other directly. A sensing and routing application running under TinyOS on each node is in charge of periodically requesting data from a sensor, transmitting this data, and routing incoming messages towards their destination. The question we would like to answer in an environment like METROPOLIS is whether the nodes do not deadlock and operate in a safe mode. Applying standard verification techniques is a hard problem because of the complexity of their behavior. It is then essential to apply techniques such as compositional modeling to see whether these problems can be solved in a substantially better way.

---

[1] Let a component C satisfy a property P_C that guarantees the composition of C with the rest of the system to satisfy a property P. When C is refined into a set of components such that their composition satisfies P_C, then the entire system still satisfies P. This principle allows incremental verification of the system as it is refined.

2   Design Flow for Compositional Modeling in Metropolis

The basic question we address in this paper is how to link compositional modeling methodologies and tools with a general framework like METROPOLIS. For the verification of models given in an expressive modeling language like the meta-model of METROPOLIS, it is in general necessary to represent high-level constructs in a more basic formalism on which verification can be carried out. The choice of their representation is crucial for the applicability of compositional reasoning. Not all meta-model constructs can be modeled so that existing compositionality results can be applied. We therefore need to subset the language of the meta-model.

Sub-setting the language allows to leverage the compositional modeling tool PROMETHEUS [13]. In PROMETHEUS real-time processes, their synchronization, and scheduling policies can be specified in a high-level modeling language. For the interfacing with METROPOLIS, the parser front-end for processes has been replaced with a parser for the METROPOLIS meta-model.

PROMETHEUS constructs the real-time system incrementally by first analyzing the behavior of the processes, then taking into account their synchronization on shared resources, and finally applying the specified scheduling policy. The resulting model is compositionally checked for safety, liveness, and timing properties, by analyzing the properties of the processes and deriving properties of the system. Detailed diagnostics are given to accelerate debugging and help gaining confidence in the correctness of the specification.

The main limitation of the compositional modeling principles implemented in PROMETHEUS comes from its conservative character. In case a property cannot be guaranteed nor refuted by PROMETHEUS, help from "classical" verification techniques and tools is still needed. This help is provided by the validation platform IF [7] in which PROMETHEUS is integrated, allowing the user to export models towards a large range of existing tools in order to perform static analysis, simulation, model-checking, or generation of tests on the IF specification generated by PROMETHEUS.

In this paper, we are interested in assessing how compositional modeling can be adopted in the framework of METROPOLIS, as well as exploring and validating new methods for compositional design and verification. The design flow and interaction between the tools is sketched in fig. 1 and can be described as follows:

1. The system designer provides a restricted meta-model specification that is compatible with the PROMETHEUS formalism, and optionally a high-level description of a scheduling policy to be applied to the system.
2. The meta-model specifications are transformed in the PROMETHEUS formalism and the model is analyzed by PROMETHEUS. If a scheduler is specified, the behavior of the model is accordingly restricted. PROMETHEUS generates diagnostics about properties such as consistency of the requirements, safety, liveness, non-zenoness etc., and outputs dynamic priority rules describing the optional scheduling policy.

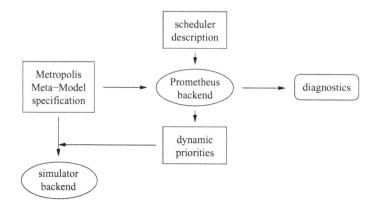

Fig. 1. Design flow and interaction between the tools.

3. The model can be executed using a simulator back-end. If desired, the model is equipped with a generic scheduler applying the priority rules generated by PROMETHEUS. The model can also be exported towards the validation platform IF, which is not shown in the figure.

The remainder of the paper is organized as follows. Section 3 gives an informal overview of the modeling formalism used by PROMETHEUS. In section 4 we show how some important constructs of the METROPOLIS meta-model are represented in the modeling formalism of PROMETHEUS such that compositional analysis techniques apply. Section 5 presents a case study, and section 6 discusses our approach and future work.

3   Modeling in Prometheus

In PROMETHEUS, real-time systems are modeled by timed systems with dynamic priorities. We give here a simplified presentation; a formal discussion can be found in [5,12].

3.1   Timed Systems

We model real-time processes as timed systems, a variant of timed automata [2]. Consider the timed system of fig. 2 modeling a process with period T and execution time E. Each transition is labeled by an action name, a guard, and possibly one or more clocks being reset. A *state* of a timed system is a tuple $(s, \mathbf{x})$, where s is a control state, and $\mathbf{x}$ is a *clock valuation*. The timed system can evolve in two different ways: by letting time pass (which means that the values of all clocks increase uniformly), or by taking some transition that is *enabled* — which means that its guard is verified for the current clock valuation — and resetting the specified clocks to zero. Taking a transition is instantaneous.

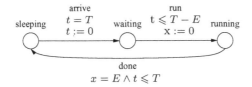

Fig. 2. Timed system modeling a simple process.

An enabled transition becomes *urgent* and must be taken before it gets disabled forever.

From control state *sleeping*, transition *arrive* leading to control state state *waiting* becomes enabled and urgent when the value of clock t reaches T. t is reset by *arrive*; it is used to measure the time elapsed since the last occurrence of *arrive*. Transition *run* leading from *waiting* to *running* must be taken by $t = T - E$ and resets another clock x measuring the time passed in state *running*. Finally, with transition *done*, the process returns to *sleeping* after having spent E time units in *running*.

We use a *flexible* parallel composition $\|$ of timed systems [6]. *Maximal progress* semantics ensures that synchronization transitions are taken whenever this is possible; a synchronizing transition may interleave only when no synchronization is possible. We refer to the parallel composition of timed systems as a *timed system of processes*.

3.2   Coordination

Priorities are widely used for scheduling [15,17], and for conflict resolution in modeling formalisms for concurrent systems, such as process algebras, see for example [3,9]. In most approaches, absolute priority levels are assigned to processes or transitions. This approach suffers from two problems that take away much of the potential strength of priorities as a modeling tool. First, absolute priority levels lead to models that are not *incremental*, in the sense that adding a process in general requires recomputing the priorities. Second, priority layers are not *composable*, in the sense that two priority assignments expressing two properties cannot be easily composed to a single priority assignment ensuring both properties. For these reasons, partial priority orders between the actions of processes are particularly interesting, since they allow to express *local* properties as priority relations that only apply between certain transitions, without side effect on other transitions.

We adopt the approach developed in [6,5,12], providing a general framework for dynamic priorities on the actions of a timed system of processes TS. The key to a modular description of different behavioral aspects by dynamic priorities is the composability principle studied in [1].

A *priority order* is a strict partial order $\prec$ on the set of actions of TS. A *priority function* associates priority orders with subsets of states of the system. More formally, a priority function pr is a set of priority rules $\{(C^j, \prec^j)\}_{j \in J}$, where J is a finite index set, and for any $j \in J$, C^j is a predicate on the control states and clock valuations of TS, specifying when the priority order $\prec^j$ applies. We require the C^j to be invariant under the progression of time. A *timed system with priorities* is a tuple (TS, pr).

In order to allow composition of priority functions, we first define a composition operator on priority orders. Given two priority orders $\prec^1$ and $\prec^2$, we represent by $\prec^1 \oplus \prec^2$ the least priority order, if it exists, that contains $\prec^1 \cup \prec^2$. $\prec^1 \oplus \prec^2$ is undefined if the relation $\prec^1 \cup \prec^2$ contains a circuit, indicating contradictory priority orders. We now extend the partially defined operator $\oplus$ to priority functions. Let pr_1 and pr_2 be two priority functions, and $(s, \mathbf{x})$ be a state of TS. If $\prec^i$ is the priority order associated by pr_i with the system state $(s, \mathbf{x})$, for $i \in \{1, 2\}$, then the priority function $pr_1 \oplus pr_2$ maps $(s, \mathbf{x})$ to $\prec^1 \oplus \prec^2$. A priority function that maps any system state to a priority order is called *well-defined*. Two priority functions are *consistent* if their composition is well-defined.

On the background of the growing complexity of real-time systems, it is a crucial, but more and more complex task to guarantee the absence of unwanted interference between the processes, which make the system behavior hard or impossible to predict. Priority functions are a natural and powerful means for modeling coordination between processes, including functional requirements such as mutual exclusion or atomicity, as well as non-functional aspects of process interaction like scheduling policies [5,12]. Modeling and composing different interactional aspects by priority functions helps detecting design flaws at an early stage. Inconsistencies can be backtracked up to a set of contradictory requirements. The diagnostic provided by the composition operation comprises the set of states for which the problem appears, and of the set of conflicting actions.

Scheduler modeling. A general modeling framework for scheduling policies based on priority functions has been discussed in [12,1] and implemented in PROMETHEUS. It has been shown how frequently used scheduling policies such as rate monotonic (RM) and earliest deadline first (EDF) scheduling [15], and the priority ceiling protocol [17], can be modeled in the scheduler description language of PROMETHEUS, and represented as priority functions.

Consider n instances TS_i, $i \in \{1, \ldots, n\}$ of the periodic process of fig. 2 with periods T_i and execution times E_i. We suppose that they use a shared CPU in the *running* states. Scheduling the processes according to the EDF policy means that the CPU is granted to the waiting process that is closest to its relative deadline. If we assume that the deadline of a process TS_i is equal to its period T_i, and the time elapsed since the beginning of its period is measured by a clock t_i, then the EDF policy is modeled by the priority function

$$pr_{\mathsf{pol}} = \bigoplus_{i \neq j} \{ (T_i - t_i < T_j - t_j, \{run_j \prec run_i\}) \}.$$

Intuitively, if TS_i is closer to its deadline than TS_j, then its action run_i is given priority over action run_j.

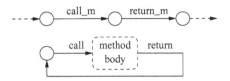

Fig. 3. Method call between process (top) and method (bottom). Transitions *call_m* and *call* synchronize, as well as *return_m* and *return*.

4 Translation of Some Meta-model Constructs

This section shows how a timed system of processes and a priority function, which can be analyzed by PROMETHEUS, are constructed from a meta-model specification. The current implementation of the PROMETHEUS back-end makes abstraction from data values, keeping only information about control, timing, and coordination. Translation of many meta-model constructs is simplified by the fact that in PROMETHEUS, as in METROPOLIS, computation and coordination are modeled separately. In the translation, components are represented by timed systems, whereas constraints on the coordination of components are modeled by priority functions that are then composed. As both the meta-model and timed systems with priorities have formal semantics, correctness of the translation can be formally proven, which is however beyond the scope of this paper. A back-end tool translating meta-model code into timed systems with priorities has been implemented.

Processes and Media. Each process or medium of a meta-model specification is represented by a timed system in PROMETHEUS, which is constructed bottom-up from the control structure of the process or medium: an atomic statement is represented by a single transition leading from an initial to an end state; a sequence of two statements is modeled by merging the end state of the first statement with the initial state of the second.

The meta-model enforces a strict separation between computation and communication. The only way for a process to communicate with another process is to call an interface method implemented by some medium. This is modeled under PROMETHEUS by decomposing each method call in two transitions, for the call and the return of control. They synchronize with corresponding transitions of the medium, as shown in fig. 3. This translation of method calls requires that any method of a given medium is executed by no more than one process at the same time, such that transition **return** synchronizes with transition **return_m** of a unique process.

Schedulers. The meta-model provides a class **Scheduler** whose instances can be connected to processes in order to coordinate their execution. Meta-model schedulers may contain executable code that is difficult to analyze, and more expressive than timed systems with priorities. In particular, it cannot exclude deadlocks. For this reason, PROMETHEUS currently does not support the full generality of the class but provides high-level language constructs to build dynamic priority schedulers.

Constraints. The meta-model allows the description of very general constraints including LTL (linear-time temporal logic) and first-order logic formulas. We focus on timing and synchronization requirements, for which the meta-model provides macro notations, and show how they can be modeled.

The maximal rate of an event, and the maximal latency between two events, can be specified by the statements

$$\textbf{maxrate } (block, d) \qquad \text{and} \qquad \textbf{maxlate } (block_1, block_2, d),$$

where *block*, $block_1$, and $block_2$ are labels referring to blocks of statements. The meaning of **maxrate** is that *block* may be entered at most every d time units. This is modeled in PROMETHEUS by having some clock x reset by all transitions entering *block*, and constraining the guards of all transitions entering *block* by $x \geqslant d$. The **maxlate** constraint signifies that $block_2$ must be left at most d time units after $block_1$ has been entered, which is modeled by resetting a clock x at all transitions entering $block_1$, and constraining all transitions leaving $block_2$ by $x \leqslant d$.

Mutual exclusion between two critical sections labeled by $block_1$ and $block_2$ belonging to two different processes P_1 and P_2 are specified in METROPOLIS by the primitive

$$\textbf{mutex } (P_1, block_1, P_2, block_2).$$

We adopt the Petri net notations $\bullet S$ to denote the set of actions entering a set of states S, and $S\circ$ for the set of actions internal to or leaving S. Using the shorthand notation $A \prec B$ with action sets A and B for the order $\{a \prec b \mid a \in A \land b \in B\}$, the mutual exclusion constraint is represented by the priority function $pr_{\mathsf{mutex}} = \big\{ \big(block_1, \bullet block_2 \prec block_1 \circ\big), \big(block_2, \bullet block_1 \prec block_2 \circ\big)\big\}$. By abuse of notation, $block_1$ and $block_2$ here denote the sets of control states in the timed system representation of the meta-model statements $block_1$ and $block_2$. Whenever P_1 is in $block_1$, and P_2 is ready to enter $block_2$, then P_1 must leave $block_1$ before P_2 can enter $block_2$, and vice versa. This order is expressed by the priority function pr_{mutex} disabling actions entering $block_2$ (resp. $block_1$) whenever some transition of a process in $block_1$ (resp. $block_2$) will eventually be enabled.

Await. The **await** statement of the meta-model is a powerful means to specify synchronization between processes. Its syntax is

> **await** {
>   ($guard_1$; $testList_1$; $setList_1$) $statements_1$;
>   ($guard_2$; $testList_2$; $setList_2$) $statements_2$;
>   ⋮
> }

where $guard_i$ are predicates, and $testList$ and $setList$ define a subset of the interface methods of media to which the object in which the **await** statement resides,

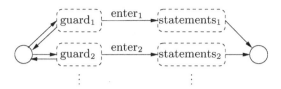

Fig. 4. Modeling the **await** statement.

is connected. *statements$_i$* is a block of statements. Intuitively, the semantics is as follows: if a process P comes to the **await** statement, then it can enter the critical section *statements$_i$* provided that *guard$_i$* is verified, and no other process is in one of the interface methods given in *testList$_i$*. As long as P is in *statements$_i$*, no other process can enter any of the interface methods specified in *setList$_i$*.

One possibility to represent **await** would be using explicit synchronization on semaphores. However, this solution would lead to a model that is difficult to analyze compositionally, especially if other requirements of coordination or timing constraints need to be taken into account. We have therefore chosen to represent the behavioral restriction imposed by **await** entirely by dynamic priorities. The control structure of the **await** statement is represented by the piece of automaton shown in fig. 4. The behavioral restriction is modeled by the priority function

$$pr_{\mathsf{await}} \;=\; \bigoplus_i \left(\left\{ guard_i, \quad enter_i \prec testList_i \circ \right\} \oplus \right. \\ \left. \left\{ statements_i, \quad \bullet setList_i \prec statements_i \circ \right\} \right)$$

saying that from the control states of the timed system modeling *guard$_i$*, internal and return transitions from one of the methods in *testList$_i$* have priority over the transition entering *statements$_i$*; similarly, in any state that is part of *statements$_i$*, transitions issued from there have priority over the transitions calling a method in *setList$_i$*. It can be shown that **mutex** and **await** statements do not introduce any deadly embrace between processes if the priority functions modeling the statements are consistent. Intuitively, a deadly embrace between processes comes from a cyclic waiting relation, which manifests as a circuit in the composition of the priority orders associated with the deadlocking process states.

Thus, a meta-model specification using the currently supported meta-model constructs is automatically translated into a timed system of processes with priorities, which can be analyzed by PROMETHEUS. The compositional modeling methodology discussed in [5,12] allows to combine parallel composition and dynamic priorities to build live systems from live components. To this end, we define three structural properties whose conjunction is a sufficient condition for liveness, and that are preserved under parallel composition and the restriction with a well-defined priority function. Informally, a timed system is

 - *structurally non-zeno* if in any circuit of the discrete transition graph at least one clock is reset, and it is tested against some positive lower bound. Structural non-zenoness implies that there is a positive lower bound to the execution time of any circuit;

- *locally timelock-free* if from any state, time can pass, or some transition is enabled. Local timelock-freedom excludes the physically unsound behavior where time progress is blocked, and is guaranteed by our model;
- *locally livelock-free* if for any control state, the post-condition of any entering transition implies that some outgoing transition will eventually become urgent.

These properties ensure common-sense requirements relying time progress and occurrence of events in the timed system: time must always diverge (local time-lock-freedom); only a finite number of events can occur within some finite amount of time (structural non-zenoness); the system will always progress (local livelock-freedom). *Structural liveness* is defined as the conjunction of the three properties. For example, the timed system of fig. 2 is structurally live if $0 \leqslant E \leqslant T \wedge T > 0$.

If the timed systems $TS_1, \ldots, TS_n$ obtained by the above translation satisfy one of the structural properties, then their parallel composition $TS = \|\{TS_1, \ldots, TS_n\}$ satisfies the same property. If the priority function $pr = pr_{\mathsf{mutex}} \oplus pr_{\mathsf{await}} \oplus pr_{\mathsf{pol}}$ modeling coordination is well-defined, then the same structural property is still verified by (TS, pr) [5,12]. The goal of compositional modeling in METROPOLIS is therefore to obtain a meta-model specification that is translated into a set of structurally live timed systems, such that liveness of the composed system is guaranteed by the compositionality results. If any of the properties is not verified by the PROMETHEUS model, this may indicate an unwanted behavior of the meta-model specification. PROMETHEUS checks the structural properties on each timed system, and outputs diagnostics. In case local livelock-freedom is not verified on some timed system, PROMETHEUS propagates the specified timing constraints over the transitions of this component, and checks again. For instance, when specifying a process as in fig. 2, it is possible to constrain only the period and execution time of a process, having the transition *run* automatically restricted by the constraint when execution must begin in order to keep the process live.

5   Case Study: TinyOS

TinyOS [10] is an extremely small (less than a kilobyte) foot-print operating system for embedded systems that provides basic functionality, such as task scheduling, message passing, and interrupt handling, and supports a modular structure of the application. TinyOS has been conceived to run on small, inexpensive embedded computers called nodes, which can be distributed over a building, measure parameters such as temperature, and communicate with each other over a low-power wireless device. Since direct communication is only possible over short distances, most nodes cannot communicate with each other directly. A sensing and routing application running under TinyOS on each node is in charge of periodically requesting data from a sensor, transmitting this data, and routing incoming messages towards their destination.

A TinyOS application consists of a set of modules that interact through two types of communication: commands, and signaling of events. Both are non-

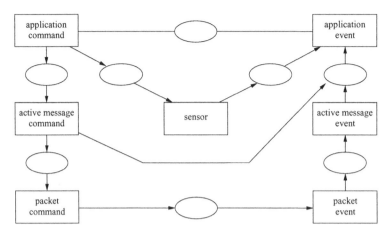

Fig. 5. Simplified METROPOLIS model of the TinyOS application.

blocking; command invocation only initiates the command execution and returns control to the caller. A TinyOS application therefore has a high degree of logical concurrency. Due to the boundedness of buffers, commands can be refused. In the application we consider, modules form a layered structure: higher-level modules call methods of lower-level modules, which in turn signal events to higher-level modules. In spite of the comparatively small size of the application, verifying its correctness with respect to properties such as liveness is non-trivial. Although TinyOS is not a real-time operating system, its modeling and verification under PROMETHEUS allows to check consistency of the safety constraints and structural liveness, and to generate dynamic priorities in order to simulate its behavior for different timing assumptions and scheduling policies.

We have modeled the sensing and routing application running on one node, in METROPOLIS by 7 processes and 8 media forming a protocol stack as shown in fig. 5. According to the METROPOLIS meta-model, processes (represented by rectangles) communicate by calling methods implemented by media (ovals). In TinyOS, commands and events are handled within the same module, with events preempting the execution of commands. Since the METROPOLIS meta-model assumes exactly one thread per process, and thus excludes intra-process preemption, we have chosen to render the TinyOS semantics by modeling each TinyOS module where command processing can be preempted by events, by two processes: one for executing commands, the other for processing events. Arrows in the figure indicate the direction of command invocation and event signaling of the TinyOS application: *application_command* periodically requests data from the *sensor* module that signals the sampled data to *application_event* as soon as the data are available. *application_command* then broadcasts these data through the protocol stack. Similarly, incoming messages are signaled through the stack to *application_event*, and forwarded by *application_command*. Our METROPOLIS model simplifies the actual TinyOS application in that the medium between *packet_command* and *packet_event* abstracts away lower levels of the protocol stack. The description consists of about 700 lines of meta-model code.

```
process Packet_event {                                ps.set_tx_bytes (true);
  port handles rx_byte_ready, tx_byte_ready;          tx_byte_ready.clear();
  port signals rx_packet_done, tx_packet_done;      }
  port p_shared ps;                                 (rx_byte_ready.event();;) {
                                                      block(d1) {}
  void thread() {                                     rx_byte_ready.clear();
    while(true) {                                   }
      block(arrival) {                              (rx_byte_ready.event();;) {
        await {                                       block(d2) {}
          (tx_byte_ready.event();;) {                 rx_packet_done.signal();
            tx_packet_done.signal();                  rx_byte_ready.clear();
            tx_byte_ready.clear();          } } } } } }
          }
          (tx_byte_ready.event() && !ps.tx_bytes();;) {
```

Fig. 6. Process packet_event.

Figure 6 shows the functional METROPOLIS model of process packet_event. The process declares five ports over which it can communicate with the media to which it is connected. The interfaces handles, signals, and p_shared provide methods for handling an incoming event, signaling an event to another process, and sharing information with packet_command, respectively; their specification is not shown here. The thread of the process repeats an **await** statement with empty *testList* and *setList* in a loop so as to react to incoming events. The **await** guards are not pairwise disjoint; this non-determinism comes from the fact that abstraction has been made from some TinyOS data variables in our model. For example, on a tx_byte_ready event signaling that the transmission of a byte has been completed, Packet_event reacts either by signaling the successful transmission of a packet (if it was the last byte of the packet) to the layer above, or — if no byte is currently being transmitted — it requests through the medium p_shared the transmission of the next byte (ps.set_tx_bytes(true)). In both cases, the event is then cleared (tx_byte_ready.clear()). The last two clauses of the **await** statement have a similar meaning for the reception of bytes. The blocks arrival, d1, and d2 are annotated with timing constraints in the sequel of the model. Such timing constraints, in terms of **maxrate** and **maxlate**, specify the minimal inter-arrival times of the processes, worst-case execution times of the blocks using the CPU, and latencies of the media.

The actual role of TinyOS, that is, scheduling the computation within different modules and their communication with each other, is modeled by a PROMETHEUS scheduler. It declares in which blocks of the model the CPU is used, and gives priority to event handling over command processing as to accessing the CPU.

The meta-model specification and the scheduler are then translated and analyzed by the PROMETHEUS back-end. The meta-model processes are represented by timed systems having between 13 and 34 control states, and up to 41 transitions each. Fig. 7 shows the timed system modeling the process *packet_event*; timing information has been omitted. Fat transitions indicate method calls, dashed transitions return from a method call. Boxes show the critical sections of the **await** statement. Its four clauses represent reactions depending on which event

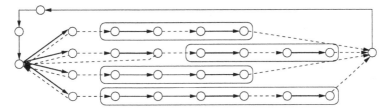

Fig. 7. Timed system modeling the process *packet_event*.

has occurred. The guards consist of method calls. Since data are not distinguished, the return transitions nondeterministically enter the critical section, and loop back to the initial state of the **await** statement. The meta-model does not specify how often the guards are evaluated; in our timed system model, an arbitrary lower bound on the delay between two evaluations of the same guard makes the loop structurally non-zeno.

The coordination constraints expressed by the **await** statements, mutual exclusion between the blocks using the CPU, and the scheduling policy are translated into 43 priority functions, and their consistency is verified. By applying the compositionality results, PROMETHEUS determines the model to be deadlock-free, non-zeno, and safe with respect to the mutual exclusion constraints on the CPU. However, there exist states in which a process can potentially stay forever since no timing constraints require it to eventually take a transition. Consequently, the model is not livelock-free. In fact, we have specified minimal, but no maximal inter-arrival times for the processes. After adding appropriate **maxlate** constraints in the METROPOLIS model, PROMETHEUS reports the processes to be structurally live. The timed systems modeling media are still not locally livelock-free: according to their role in METROPOLIS, media passively wait to be called. Applying compositional analysis, the composed system is reported to be deadlock-free, but structural liveness cannot be assured due to media not being locally livelock-free. This problem has been resolved in a later version of PROMETHEUS where methods are not modeled as timed systems of their own, but inlined by the calling process.

In spite of tight synchronization between processes and media, the product timed system would have more than half a billion control states, making non-compositional verification a hard problem. PROMETHEUS completes the verification above in less than 5 minutes. Verification of the structural liveness properties is done by verifying them on each component, and applying the compositionality results. The main source of complexity is the check for safety with respect to the **mutex** and **await** constraints. In contrast to formalisms where safety properties are ensured for example by using semaphores, modeling safety properties using priority functions relies on the fact that transitions violating the property, are disabled by dominating actions. *Structural safety* [12] is a sufficient condition for safety with respect to the invariance of a set of control states, which can be checked compositionally. In contrast to the check for structural liveness, its complexity grows polynomially with the number of transitions in the processes, and with the size of the priority function.

6   Discussion

We have presented a framework and tool support for compositional modeling and analysis of METROPOLIS models. The integration of PROMETHEUS in METROPOLIS constitutes a modeling and verification platform for the application of existing, and the development and experimentation of new methods for compositional modeling and analysis. The METROPOLIS meta-model is a particularly interesting case for compositional modeling and analysis: on the one hand, its expressiveness makes non-compositional verification difficult or infeasible, especially when a higher degree of refinement has been reached. Compositional verification seems a natural way to incrementally verify the model as it is progressively refined. On the other hand, the philosophy of *separation of concerns* encouraged and in part enforced by the meta-model helps making compositional modeling applicable.

PROMETHEUS translates a METROPOLIS model into a timed system of processes and a priority function, keeping descriptions about the components and their coordination separate. The obtained model allows to apply compositionality results in order to verify consistency, safety, and liveness properties of the model. The priority function helps to understand the modeled system and predict its behavior. Future effort is likely to aim at exploiting this rich source of information to verify more, also quantitative, properties of the model.

The TinyOS case study has shown the power of compositionally verifying the liveness and soundness of a non-trivial example, but also current limitations. Future work will explore two complementary directions to obtain stronger compositionality results for "difficult" properties such as schedulability or individual liveness of the processes in the system: first, to extend and generalize compositionality results, for example by applying assume-guarantee-reasoning [14], and by disposing of more information about the interaction between components, e.g. by typing their behavior using *interface automata* [11]. Second, to develop *modeling guide-lines* to enable compositional reasoning: in order for the results to fully apply, help in the form of an adapted programming style is needed. The meta-model has been designed so as to support a variety of design styles, allowing to adopt compositional modeling principles. Some guide-lines are already provided by existing compositionality results, for example, to model coordination in a declarative way (e.g., using **await**) rather than by an operational restriction such as semaphores.

Acknowledgment

The authors would like to thank the referees for their constructive comments.

References

1. K. Altisen, G. Gössler, and J. Sifakis. Scheduler modeling based on the controller synthesis paradigm. *Journal of Real-Time Systems, special issue on "control-theoretical approaches to real-time computing"*, 23(1/2):55–84, 2002.
2. R. Alur and D. Dill. A theory of timed automata. *Theoretical Computer Science*, 126:183–235, 1994.
3. J. Baeten, J. Bergstra, and J. Klop. Syntax and defining equations for an interrupt mechanism in process algebra. *Fundamenta Informaticae*, IX(2):127–168, 1986.
4. F. Balarin, L. Lavagno, C. Passerone, A. Sangiovanni-Vincentelli, Y. Watanabe, and G. Yang. Concurrent execution semantics and sequential simulation algorithms for the metropolis meta-model. In *Proc. CODES'02*, 2002.
5. S. Bornot, G. Gössler, and J. Sifakis. On the construction of live timed systems. In S. Graf and M. Schwartzbach, editors, *Proc. TACAS'00*, volume 1785 of *LNCS*, pages 109–126. Springer-Verlag, 2000.
6. S. Bornot and J. Sifakis. An algebraic framework for urgency. *Information and Computation*, 163:172–202, 2000.
7. M. Bozga, J.-C. Fernandez, L. Ghirvu, S. Graf, J.-P. Krimm, and L. Mounier. IF: A validation environment for timed asynchronous systems. In E. Emerson and A. Sistla, editors, *Proc. CAV'00*, volume 1855 of *LNCS*, pages 543–547. Springer-Verlag, 2000.
8. J. Burch, R. Passerone, and A. Sangiovanni-Vincentelli. Overcoming heterophobia: Modeling concurrency in heterogeneous systems. In *Proc. 2nd International Conference on Application of Concurrency to System Design*, 2001.
9. J. Camilleri and G. Winskel. CCS with priority choice. *Information and Computation*, 116(1):26–37, 1995.
10. D. Culler, J. Hill, P. Buonadonna, R. Szewczyk, and A. Woo. A network-centric approach to embedded software for tiny devices. In T. Henzinger and C. M. Kirsch, editors, *Proc. EMSOFT'01*, volume 2211 of *LNCS*, pages 114–130. Springer-Verlag, 2001.
11. L. de Alfaro and T. Henzinger. Interface theories for component-based design. In T. Henzinger and C. M. Kirsch, editors, *Proc. EMSOFT'01*, volume 2211 of *LNCS*, pages 148–165. Springer-Verlag, 2001.
12. G. Gössler. *Compositional Modelling of Real-Time Systems — Theory and Practice*. PhD thesis, Université Joseph Fourier, Grenoble, France, 2001.
13. G. Gössler. PROMETHEUS — a compositional modeling tool for real-time systems. In P. Pettersson and S. Yovine, editors, *Proc. Workshop RT-TOOLS'01*. Technical report 2001-014, Uppsala University, Department of Information Technology, 2001.
14. L. Lamport. Specifying concurrent program modules. *ACM Trans. on Programming Languages and Systems*, 5:190–222, 1983.
15. C. Liu and J. Layland. Scheduling algorithms for multiprogramming in a hard-real-time environment. *Journal of the ACM*, 20(1), 1973.
16. O. Maler, A. Pnueli, and J. Sifakis. On the synthesis of discrete controllers for timed systems. In E. Mayr and C. Puech, editors, *STACS'95*, volume 900 of *LNCS*, pages 229–242. Springer-Verlag, 1995.
17. L. Sha, R. Rajkumar, and J. Lehoczky. Priority inheritance protocols: An approach to real-time synchronization. *IEEE Transactions on Computers*, 39(9):1175–1185, 1990.

Timed Interfaces*

Luca de Alfaro[1], Thomas A. Henzinger[2], and Mariëlle Stoelinga[1]

[1] Computer Engineering, University of California, Santa Cruz
{luca,marielle}@soe.ucsc.edu
[2] EECS, University of California, Berkeley
tah@eecs.berkeley.edu

Abstract. We present a theory of *timed interfaces*, which is capable of specifying both the timing of the inputs a component expects from the environment, and the timing of the outputs it can produce. Two timed interfaces are *compatible* if there is a way to use them together such that their timing expectations are met. Our theory provides algorithms for checking the compatibility between two interfaces and for deriving the composite interface; the theory can thus be viewed as a type system for real-time interaction. Technically, a timed interface is encoded as a timed game between two players, representing the inputs and outputs of the component. The algorithms for compatibility checking and interface composition are thus derived from algorithms for solving timed games.

1 Introduction

A formal notion of component interfaces provides a way to describe the interaction between components, and to verify the compatibility between components automatically. Traditional type systems capture only the *data* dimension of interfaces ("what are the value constraints on data communicated between components?"). We have developed an approach, called *interface theories* [dAH01a,dAH01b], which can be viewed as a behavioral type system that also captures the *protocol* dimension of interfaces ("what are the temporal ordering constraints on communication events between components?"). This paper extends this formalism to capture, in addition, the *timing* dimension of interfaces ("what are the real-time constraints on communication events between components?"). This permits, for example, the specification and compatibility check of component interactions based on time-outs. *Timed interfaces* support the component-based design of real-time systems in the following ways:

Component interface specification. A component is an open system that expects inputs and provides outputs to the environment. An interface specifies how a component interacts with its environment, by describing both the assumptions made by the component on the inputs and the guarantees provided by the

---

* This research was supported in part by the NSF CAREER award CCR-0132780, the NSF grant CCR-9988172 the AFOSR MURI grant F49620-00-1-0327, the DARPA PCES grant F33615-00-C-1693, the MARCO GSRC grant 98-DT-660, and the ONR grant N00014-02-1-0671.

A. Sangiovanni-Vincentelli and J. Sifakis (Eds.): EMSOFT 2002, LNCS 2491, pp. 108–122, 2002.
© Springer-Verlag Berlin Heidelberg 2002

component on the outputs. Timed interfaces can refer to the timing of the input and output events. An interface is *well-formed* as long as there is *some* environment that satisfies the input assumptions made by the component; otherwise, the component would not be usable in any design.

Interface compatibility checking. When two components are composed, we can check that the components satisfy each other's assumptions. Since the result of composition is generally still an open system, it may depend on the environment whether or not this is the case. Two interfaces are *compatible* if their composition is well-formed, i.e., if there exists an environment that makes them work together. The composition yields a new interface for the composite system that specifies the derived input assumptions required to make the original components working together, as well as the resulting output guarantees.

An (untimed or timed) interface is naturally modeled as a *game* between two players, Output and Input. Player Output represents the component: the moves of Output represent the possible outputs that the component may generate (the output guarantees); player Input represents the environment: the moves of Input represent the the inputs that the system accepts from the environment (the input assumptions). For instance, a functional type $D \mapsto D'$ in a programming language is an interface that corresponds to a one-shot game. The Input player provides inputs that can be accepted (values in D) and the Output player provides outputs that can be generated (values in D'). If the sets of legal inputs and possible outputs can change dynamically over time, then the interface is naturally modeled as an iterative game played on a set of states [Abr96], where the moves —i.e., the acceptable inputs and possible outputs— may depend on the state of the system. Such an interface is *well-formed* if the Input player has a winning strategy in the game, i.e., the environment can meet all input assumptions. For *timed* interfaces, we need the additional well-formedness condition that a player must not achieve its goal by blocking time forever.

The game-theoretic view of interfaces becomes most apparent in their composition. When two interfaces are composed, the combined interface may contain *error states.* These occur when one component interface can generate an output that is not a legal input for the other component interface, showing that the first component violates an input assumption of the second. In addition, our timed games give rise to *time errors*, where one of the players cannot let time pass. Two interfaces are *compatible* if there is a way for the Input player, who chooses the inputs of the composite interface, to avoid all errors. If so, then there exists an environment of the combined system which makes both components satisfy each other's input assumptions.

Different theories of timed interfaces arise depending on the details of how timed games are defined. For example, communication can be through actions or shared variables, and composition can be synchronous or asynchronous. The main contribution of this paper does not lie in such details of the formalism (which may be changed), but in the notion of interface of a real-time component as a timed game. This notion sets our interfaces apart from the type systems for protocols of [RR01,CRR02], from message-sequence charts [RGG96], and from traditional models for timed systems such as timed automata [AD94,MMT91]. Many models are unable to express input assumptions and postulate that a component must work in all environments; this is the *input-enabled* approach of, e.g., [AH97,SGSAL98]. Models that can encode input assumptions, such as process algebras, often phrase the compatibility question as a *graph* (rather than *game*) question, in which input and output play the same role: two components are considered compatible if they cannot reach a deadlock [RR01]. In our game-based approach, input and ouput play dual roles: two components are compatible if there is *some* input behavior such that, for *all* output behaviors, no incompatibility arises. This notion captures the idea that an interface can be useful as long as it can be used in some design. In this, interfaces are close to types in programming languages, to trace theory [Dil88], and to the semantics of interaction [Abr96].

2   Timed Interfaces as Timed Games: Preview

In a timed interface, the Input and Output players have two kinds of moves: *immediate moves,* which represent events sent or received by the interface, and *timed moves,* that consist in an amount of time that the players propose to spend idle. We assume a time domain $\mathbb{T}$; suitable choices for $\mathbb{T}$ are the nonnegative reals $\mathbb{R}_{\geq 0}$, or the nonnegative integers $\mathbb{N}$. The successor state is determined as follows. When Input chooses $t_I \in \mathbb{T}$ and Output chooses $t_O \in \mathbb{T}$, the global time will advance by $\min\{t_I, t_O\}$; if a player chooses an immediate move and the other a timed move, the immediate move prevails; if both players choose immediate moves, one of them occurs nondeterministically [MPS95,AMPS98].

Only game outcomes along which global time diverges are physically meaningful. Obviously, each player is capable of blocking the progress of time by playing a sequence of timed moves whose summation converges (so-called Zeno behavior). To rule out such behavior, we require a *well-formedness* criterion, which states that at all reachable states, each player can ensure that time progresses unless the other player blocks its progress. The composition of timed interfaces may give rise to two kinds of error states: *immediate error states,* where one interface emits an output that cannot be accepted by the other, and *time error states,* where the well-formedness criterion is violated. Two interfaces are compatible if there is a strategy for Input in the combined interface that avoids all errors. The composite interface is obtained by restricting the input moves (i.e., the accepted environments) such that the error states are not entered.

We illustrate these concepts through a simple example from scheduling. The interfaces are modeled as *timed interface automata.* This is a syntax derived from timed automata [AD94]. However, the syntax is interpreted as a (timed) game, rather than as a (timed) transition system. In particular, timed automata use invariants for specifying an upper bound for the advancement of time at a location. Timed interface automata have two kinds of invariants: *input invariants,* which specify upper bounds for the timed moves played by Input, and *output invariants,* which specify upper bounds for the timed moves played by Output.

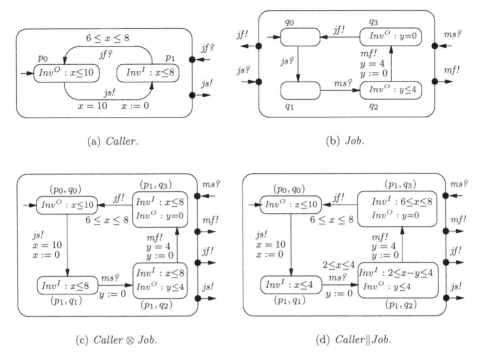

Fig. 1. Timed interface automata for periodic job scheduling.

Example: scheduling a periodic job. The timed interface automaton *Caller* shown in Figure 1(a) represents an application that activates a periodic job every 10 seconds. Each time the job is activated, it must terminate between 6 and 8 seconds. The clock x measures the time elapsed since the last activation of the job. At the initial location p_0, the Output player can play any timed move Δ such that $\Delta + x \leq 10$, that is, it can advance time only up to the point where $x = 10$. Once $x = 10$, in order not to block progress of time, Output must eventually play the move *js* (job start); i.e., the ouput invariant $x \leq 10$ expresses a deadline for the occurrence of the *js* action. Since the input invariant associated with p_0 is always true, the Input player can play any $\Delta \in \mathbb{T}$ (to reduce clutter, invariants that are always true are omitted from the figures). The move *js* resets x to 0, ensuring that x counts the time from the start of a periodic job activation.

At location p_1, Output can play arbitrary timed moves, since the output invariant is true. The input invariant $x \leq 8$ prevents the Input player from advancing time beyond $x = 8$. So, to let time progress, Input must play the move *jf* (job finished) somewhere between $6 \leq x \leq 8$. In particular, $x \leq 8$ is a deadline for the reception of action *jf*.

Composition. The timed interface automaton *Caller* can be composed with the timed interface automaton *Job*, which models the interface of the job to be executed. The job starts when the input move *js* (job start) is received; the job then waits for the input move *ms* (machine start) from a scheduler. Once *ms* is received, the job executes for 4 seconds (clock y keeps track of the execution time), after which it first indicates to the scheduler that the machine is no longer used (output move mf, machine finished), and then finishes (output move jf, job finished). Note how, at state q_2, the input invariant is true, indicating that Input can play any timed move, while the output invariant is $y \leq 4$, indicating that Output can let time progress only until $y = 4$. Again, to avoid blocking the progress of time, Output must eventually play the move mf. Similarly, Output is forced to play jf at state q_3.

To compute the composition $Caller \parallel Job$, we first compute their product $Caller \otimes Job$, shown in Figure 1(c), which represents the joint behavior arising from $Caller$ and Job. Moves synchronize in multi-way, broadcast fashion: the synchronization between corresponding input and output moves gives rise to an output move. To compute the composition $Caller \parallel Job$ from $Caller \otimes Job$, note that the product contains error states: at location (p_1, q_3), if $err_3 : \neg(6 \leq x \leq 8)$ holds, then interface Job can generate the output jf, which cannot be accepted by $Caller$. However, the Input player can avoid the error states by choosing the timing of the input ms. To see this, note that at location (p_2, q_1) the set of *uncontrollable states* from which Input cannot avoid reaching the error states is described by the predicate $uncontr_2 : \exists \Delta \in \mathbb{T}.(y + \Delta = 4 \wedge \neg(6 \leq x + \Delta \leq 8))$, or after simplification, $uncontr_2 : \neg(2 \leq x - y \leq 4)$. Hence, we conjoin $2 \leq x - y \leq 4$ to the input invariant of (p_2, q_1), which yields $2 \leq x - y \leq 4 \wedge x \leq 8$ as the input invariant in $Caller \parallel Job$ (see Figure 1(d)). We simpify this to $2 \leq x - y \leq 4$, because the states where $x > 8$ cannot be reached: from $y \leq 4$ (the output invariant) and $x - y \leq 4$ (a portion of the input invariant) follows $x \leq 8$.

Now, to avoid entering uncontrollable states at location (p_1, q_2) we have to restrict the time during which the input move ms can be received: the most liberal restriction consists in requiring $2 \leq x \leq 4$, which is added to enabling condition of ms. Finally, consider the location (p_1, q_1), whose input invariant is $x \leq 8$. To ensure progress of time beyond $x = 8$, Input must eventually play the move ms. However, this move is available only when $2 \leq x \leq 4$. Thus, if $x > 4$, the Input player does not have a strategy that ensures that time diverges unless blocked by the Output player. Therefore, $x > 4$ indicates time error states, which are ruled out by strenghtening the input invariant to $x \leq 4$. Notice how the composition of timed interfaces effects the composition of timing requirements: the requirement of $Caller$ that the job must be completed between 6 and 8 seconds gives rise to the requirement for the scheduler that the machine is started between 2 and 4 seconds after the job start.

3   Timed Interfaces as Timed Games: Definitions

We model interfaces as timed games between two players, Input and Output, abbreviated I and O.

Definition 1 (timed interfaces)   A *timed interface* is a tuple

$$\mathcal{P} = (S_\mathcal{P}, s_\mathcal{P}^{init}, Acts_\mathcal{P}^I, Acts_\mathcal{P}^O, \rho_\mathcal{P}^I, \rho_\mathcal{P}^O)$$

consisting of the following components.

- $S_{\mathcal{P}}$ is a set of *states*.
- $s_{\mathcal{P}}^{init} \in S_{\mathcal{P}}$ is the *initial state*.
- $Acts_{\mathcal{P}}^I$ and $Acts_{\mathcal{P}}^O$ are sets of *immediate input* and *output* actions, respectively. These sets must be disjoint from each other, and disjoint from the time domain $\mathbb{T}$. We denote by $Acts_{\mathcal{P}} = Acts_{\mathcal{P}}^I \cup Acts_{\mathcal{P}}^O$ the set of all immediate actions, by $\Gamma_{\mathcal{P}}^I = Acts_{\mathcal{P}}^I \cup \mathbb{T}$ the set of all input actions, and by $\Gamma_{\mathcal{P}}^O = Acts_{\mathcal{P}}^O \cup \mathbb{T}$ the set of all output actions. The elements in $\mathbb{T}$ are *timed actions*.
- $\rho_{\mathcal{P}}^I \subseteq S_{\mathcal{P}} \times \Gamma_{\mathcal{P}}^I \times S_{\mathcal{P}}$ is the *input transition relation*, and $\rho_{\mathcal{P}}^O \subseteq S_{\mathcal{P}} \times \Gamma_{\mathcal{P}}^O \times S_{\mathcal{P}}$ is the *output transition relation*. We often write an element (s, α, s') of a transition relation as $s \xrightarrow{\alpha} s'$, and call it a *step*. Given a state $s \in S_{\mathcal{P}}$ and a player $\gamma \in \{I, O\}$, the set of *moves* of player γ at s is $\Gamma_{\mathcal{P}}^{\gamma}(s) = \{\alpha \in \Gamma_{\mathcal{P}}^{\gamma} \mid \exists s' \in S_{\mathcal{P}}.(s \xrightarrow{\alpha} s') \in \rho_{\mathcal{P}}^{\gamma}\}$.

We require the transition relations to be deterministic: for $\gamma \in \{I, O\}$, if $(s, a, s') \in \rho_{\mathcal{P}}^{\gamma}$ and $(s, a, s'') \in \rho_{\mathcal{P}}^{\gamma}$, then $s' = s''$. Furthermore, we require time determinism for time steps over both relations: for all $\Delta \in \mathbb{T}$, if $(s, \Delta, s') \in \rho_{\mathcal{P}}^I$ and $(s, \Delta, s'') \in \rho_{\mathcal{P}}^O$, then $s' = s''$. Time steps of duration 0 do not leave the state: for $\gamma \in \{I, O\}$, if $(s, 0, s') \in \rho_{\mathcal{P}}^{\gamma}$, then $s = s'$. We also require Wang's Axiom [Yi90]: for all $\Delta, \Delta' \in \mathbb{T}$ with $\Delta' \leq \Delta$, we have $(s, \Delta, s'') \in \rho_{\mathcal{P}}^{\gamma}$ iff there is a state s' such that both $(s, \Delta', s') \in \rho_{\mathcal{P}}^{\gamma}$ and $(s', \Delta - \Delta', s'') \in \rho_{\mathcal{P}}^{\gamma}$. Finally, if there are any immediate actions available to a player in a state, then also the timed action 0 is available: for $\gamma \in \{I, O\}$, if $\Gamma_{\mathcal{P}}^{\gamma}(s) \neq \emptyset$, then $(s, 0, s) \in \rho_{\mathcal{P}}^{\gamma}$. ∎

The game proceeds as follows. At a state $s \in S_{\mathcal{P}}$, Input chooses a move from $\Gamma_{\mathcal{P}}^I(s)$, and Output chooses a move from $\Gamma_{\mathcal{P}}^O(s)$. If no moves are available for a player, that player will automatically lose the game. If two moves are played, then these determine both the successor state and the player bl that is *blamed* for having played first; assigning the blame is important in establishing whether a player is blocking the progress of time [AH97]. The following definition is asymmetric: when Input and Output play the same timed move, the Output player is blamed. As we will illustrate later, this asymmetry is necessary to capture the cause-effect relationship between outputs and inputs.

Definition 2 (move outcomes) For all states $s \in S_{\mathcal{P}}$ and moves $\alpha_I \in \Gamma_{\mathcal{P}}^I(s)$ and $\alpha_O \in \Gamma_{\mathcal{P}}^O(s)$, the *outcome* $\delta_{\mathcal{P}}(s, \alpha_I, \alpha_O)$ of α_I and α_O at s is the set of triples (α, s', bl) such that $(s \xrightarrow{\alpha} s') \in \rho_{\mathcal{P}}^I \cup \rho_{\mathcal{P}}^O$, and $\alpha \in \Gamma_{\mathcal{P}}^I \cup \Gamma_{\mathcal{P}}^O$ and $bl \in \{I, O\}$ are obtained as follows.

- If $\alpha_I, \alpha_O \in \mathbb{T}$, then $\alpha = \min\{\alpha_I, \alpha_O\}$. Moreover, $bl = I$ if $\alpha_I < \alpha_O$, and $bl = O$ otherwise.
- If $\alpha_I \in Acts_{\mathcal{P}}$ and $\alpha_O \in \mathbb{T}$, then $\alpha = \alpha_I$ and $bl = I$.
- If $\alpha_O \in Acts_{\mathcal{P}}$ and $\alpha_I \in \mathbb{T}$, then $\alpha = \alpha_O$ and $bl = O$.
- If $\alpha_I, \alpha_O \in Acts_{\mathcal{P}}$, then either $\alpha = \alpha_I$ and $bl = I$, or $\alpha = \alpha_O$ and $bl = O$. ∎

As usual, the players choose their moves according to strategies that may depend on the history of the game. Our strategies are partial functions, rather than total ones, because the sets of moves available to the players at a state can be empty. Furthermore, if both players choose immediate actions, then the outcome is nondeterministic. Consequently, the possible outcomes of two strategies form a set of finite and infinite sequences. A state is reachable in the game if it can be reached by some outcome of some input and output strategies.

Definition 3 (strategy outcomes)   A *strategy* for player $\gamma \in \{I, O\}$ is a partial function $\pi^\gamma \colon S_{\mathcal{P}}^* \rightharpoonup \Gamma_{\mathcal{P}}^\gamma$ that associates, with every finite sequence of states $\bar{s} \in S_{\mathcal{P}}^*$ whose final state is s, a move $\pi^\gamma(\bar{s}) \in \Gamma_{\mathcal{P}}^\gamma(s)$ provided that $\Gamma_{\mathcal{P}}^\gamma(s) \neq \emptyset$; otherwise $\pi^\gamma(\bar{s})$ is undefined. Let $\Pi_{\mathcal{P}}^I$ be the set of strategies for player I, and let $\Pi_{\mathcal{P}}^O$ be the set of strategies for player O. Given a state $s \in S_{\mathcal{P}}$, an input strategy $\pi^I \in \Pi_{\mathcal{P}}^I$, and an output strategy $\pi^O \in \Pi_{\mathcal{P}}^O$, the set of *outcomes* $\widehat{\delta}_{\mathcal{P}}(s, \pi^I, \pi^O)$ of π^I and π^O from s consists of all finite and infinite sequences $\sigma = (s_0, bl_0), \alpha_1, (s_1, bl_1), \alpha_2, (s_2, bl_2), \ldots$ such that (1) $s_0 = s$; (2) $bl_0 \in \{I, O\}$; (3) if $|\sigma| < \infty$, then σ ends in a pair (s_k, bl_k) such that $\Gamma_{\mathcal{P}}^I(s_k) = \emptyset$ or $\Gamma_{\mathcal{P}}^O(s_k) = \emptyset$; and (4) for all $n < |\sigma|$, we have $(\alpha_{n+1}, s_{n+1}, bl_{n+1}) \in \delta_{\mathcal{P}}(s_n, \pi^I(\sigma_{0:n}), \pi^O(\sigma_{0:n}))$, where $\sigma_{0:n}$ denotes the prefix $(s_0, bl_0), \alpha_1, \ldots, (s_n, bl_n)$ of σ with length n.

A state $s \in S_{\mathcal{P}}$ is *reachable* in $\mathcal{P}$ if there are two strategies $\pi^I \in \Pi_{\mathcal{P}}^I$ and $\pi^O \in \Pi_{\mathcal{P}}^O$, and $k \geq 0$, such that $s = s_k$ for some outcome $(s_0, bl_0), a_1, (s_1, bl_1), a_2, (s_2, bl_2), \ldots \in \widehat{\delta}_{\mathcal{P}}(s_{\mathcal{P}}^{init}, \pi^I, \pi^O)$. ∎

3.1   Well-Formedness of Timed Interfaces

A timed interface is well-formed if from every reachable state (i) Input has a strategy such that either time diverges, or Output is always to blame beyond some point; and (ii) symmetrically, Output has a strategy such that either time diverges, or Input is always to blame beyond some point. To give the precise definitions, let $time(\alpha) = \alpha$ for $\alpha \in \mathbb{T}$, and $time(\alpha) = 0$ otherwise.

Definition 4 (time divergence and time blocking)   Let $\sigma = (s_0, bl_0), \alpha_1, (s_1, bl_1), \alpha_2, (s_2, bl_2), \ldots$ be an outcome of a game in $\mathcal{P}$. We define $\sigma \models t\_div$ if the accumulated time in σ is infinite, that is, $\sum_{k=1}^{|\sigma|} time(\alpha_k) = \infty$. For $\gamma \in \{I, O\}$, we define $\sigma \models blame^\gamma$ if either σ is finite and $\Gamma_{\mathcal{P}}^\gamma(s) = \emptyset$ for σ's last state s, or σ is infinite and there is a $k \geq 0$ such that $bl_i = \gamma$ for all $i > k$. For a set $U \subseteq S_{\mathcal{P}}$ of states, we define $\sigma \models \square U$ if $s_k \in U$ for all $k \geq 0$. ∎

A state of a timed interface $\mathcal{P}$ is live in a set U of states if both players have strategies to stay forever in U and let time advance, unless the other player can be blamed for blocking the progress of time. Again, the game is not played symmetrically: Input can choose its strategy after Output, which shows that the game is turn-based (first Ouput chooses its move, then Input does).

Definition 5 (live states and well-formedness)   Let $U \subseteq S_{\mathcal{P}}$ be a set of states. A state $s \in S_{\mathcal{P}}$ is *I-live in* U if Input can win the game with goal $(t\_div \lor blame^O) \land \square U$; that is, if for all strategies $\pi^O \in \Pi_{\mathcal{P}}^O$ there is a strategy $\pi^I \in \Pi_{\mathcal{P}}^I$

such that $\sigma \models (t\_div \vee blame^O) \wedge \Box U$ for all outcomes $\sigma \in \widehat{\delta}_{\mathcal{P}}(s, \pi^I, \pi^O)$. A state $s \in S_{\mathcal{P}}$ is *O-live in* U if Output can win the game with goal $(t\_div \vee blame^I) \wedge \Box U$; that is, if there is a strategy $\pi^O \in \Pi_{\mathcal{P}}^O$ such that for all strategies $\pi^I \in \Pi_{\mathcal{P}}^I$ and outcomes $\sigma \in \widehat{\delta}_{\mathcal{P}}(s, \pi^I, \pi^O)$, we have $\sigma \models (t\_div \vee blame^I) \wedge \Box U$. A state $s \in S_{\mathcal{P}}$ is *live in* U if it is both *I*-live and *O*-live in U.

The timed interface $\mathcal{P}$ is *well-formed in* U if all reachable states of $\mathcal{P}$ are live in U. The timed interface $\mathcal{P}$ is *well-formed* if it is well-formed in $S_{\mathcal{P}}$. ∎

In particular, for all reachable states s of a well-formed timed interface $\mathcal{P}$, both $\Gamma_{\mathcal{P}}^I(s) \neq \emptyset$ and $\Gamma_{\mathcal{P}}^O(s) \neq \emptyset$. Only well-formed timed interfaces represent valid interface specifications. For this reason, we will only define the composition of well-formed timed interfaces.

3.2   Product and Composition of Timed Interfaces

Two timed interfaces $\mathcal{P}$ and $\mathcal{Q}$ are *composable* if $Acts_{\mathcal{P}}^O \cap Acts_{\mathcal{Q}}^O = \emptyset$. The *shared actions* of $\mathcal{P}$ and $\mathcal{Q}$ are given by $shared(\mathcal{P}, \mathcal{Q}) = Acts_{\mathcal{P}} \cap Acts_{\mathcal{Q}}$. For two composable timed interfaces $\mathcal{P}$ and $\mathcal{Q}$, their composition $\mathcal{P} \| \mathcal{Q}$ is computed in two steps: first, we form the *product* $\mathcal{P} \otimes \mathcal{Q}$ together with the set *i-errors*$(\mathcal{P}, \mathcal{Q})$ of immediate error states; then, $\mathcal{P} \| \mathcal{Q}$ is obtained by strengthening the input invariants of $\mathcal{P} \otimes \mathcal{Q}$ to make it well-formed in $S_{\mathcal{P} \otimes \mathcal{Q}} \setminus$ *i-errors*$(\mathcal{P}, \mathcal{Q})$. The product $\mathcal{P} \otimes \mathcal{Q}$ represents the joint behavior of $\mathcal{P}$ and $\mathcal{Q}$, in which $\mathcal{P}$ and $\mathcal{Q}$ synchronize on the input timed moves, on the output timed moves, and on the shared actions, and behave independently otherwise.

Definition 6 (product) Given two composable timed interfaces $\mathcal{P}_1$ and $\mathcal{P}_2$, the *product* $\mathcal{P}_1 \otimes \mathcal{P}_2$ is the timed interface that consists of the following components.

- $S_{\mathcal{P}_1 \otimes \mathcal{P}_2} = S_{\mathcal{P}_1} \times S_{\mathcal{P}_2}$, and $s_{\mathcal{P}_1 \otimes \mathcal{P}_2}^{init} = (s_{\mathcal{P}_1}^{init}, s_{\mathcal{P}_2}^{init})$.
- $Acts_{\mathcal{P}_1 \otimes \mathcal{P}_2}^I = Acts_{\mathcal{P}_1}^I \cup Acts_{\mathcal{P}_2}^I \setminus shared(\mathcal{P}_1, \mathcal{P}_2)$, and $Acts_{\mathcal{P}_1 \otimes \mathcal{P}_2}^O = Acts_{\mathcal{P}_1}^O \cup Acts_{\mathcal{P}_2}^O$.
- $\rho_{\mathcal{P}_1 \otimes \mathcal{P}_2}^I$ is the set of transitions $(s_1, s_2) \xrightarrow{\alpha} (s_1', s_2')$ such that for $i = 1, 2$: if $\alpha \in \Gamma_{\mathcal{P}_i}^I$, then $(s_i \xrightarrow{\alpha} s_i') \in \rho_{\mathcal{P}_i}^I$; otherwise $(s_i \xrightarrow{0} s_i') \in \rho_{\mathcal{P}_i}^I$.
- $\rho_{\mathcal{P}_1 \otimes \mathcal{P}_2}^O$ is the set of transitions $(s_1, s_2) \xrightarrow{\alpha} (s_1', s_2')$ such that for $i = 1, 2$: if $\alpha \in \Gamma_{\mathcal{P}_i}^O$, then $(s_i \xrightarrow{\alpha} s_i') \in \rho_{\mathcal{P}_i}^O$; if $\alpha \in Acts_{\mathcal{P}_i}^I$, then $(s_i \xrightarrow{\alpha} s_i') \in \rho_{\mathcal{P}_i}^I$; and otherwise $(s_i \xrightarrow{0} s_i') \in \rho_{\mathcal{P}_i}^I$. ∎

A state of the product is an *immediate error state* if one of the interfaces can produce an output that the other one cannot accept. A state of the product is a *time error state* if it is not live once we remove the immediate error states. The composition of two timed interfaces is obtained by pruning from the product all input transitions that start from or lead to a time error state.

Definition 7 (error states) Let $\mathcal{P}$ and $\mathcal{Q}$ be two well-formed and composable timed interfaces.

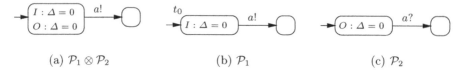

(a) $\mathcal{P}_1 \otimes \mathcal{P}_2$ (b) $\mathcal{P}_1$ (c) $\mathcal{P}_2$

Fig. 2. Timed interfaces illustrating why well-formedness is needed.

- *Immediate error states.* We say that a state $(s,t) \in S_{\mathcal{P} \otimes \mathcal{Q}}$ is an *immediate error state* if there is an action $\alpha \in shared(\mathcal{P}, \mathcal{Q})$ such that $(s \xrightarrow{\alpha} s') \in \rho_{\mathcal{P}}^{O}$ for some state s', but $(t \xrightarrow{\alpha} t') \notin \rho_{\mathcal{Q}}^{I}$ for all states t', or such that $(t \xrightarrow{\alpha} t') \in \rho_{\mathcal{Q}}^{O}$ for some t', but $(s \xrightarrow{\alpha} s') \notin \rho_{\mathcal{P}}^{I}$ for all s'. We denote by $i\text{-}errors(\mathcal{P}, \mathcal{Q}) \subseteq S_{\mathcal{P} \otimes \mathcal{Q}}$ the set of immediate error states.
- *Time error states.* We say that a state $(s,t) \in S_{\mathcal{P} \otimes \mathcal{Q}}$ is a *time error state* if (s,t) is reachable in $\mathcal{P} \otimes \mathcal{Q}$, but it is not I-live in $S_{\mathcal{P} \otimes \mathcal{Q}} \setminus i\text{-}errors(\mathcal{P}, \mathcal{Q})$. We denote by $t\text{-}errors(\mathcal{P}, \mathcal{Q}) \subseteq S_{\mathcal{P} \otimes \mathcal{Q}}$ the set of time error states. ∎

Note that the reachable immediate error states are a subset of the time error states. The composition $\mathcal{P} \| \mathcal{Q}$ is obtained by restricting the input behavior of $\mathcal{P} \otimes \mathcal{Q}$ to avoid all time error states. We restrict the input behavior only, leaving the output behavior unchanged, because when composing interfaces we can strengthen their input assumptions to ensure that no incompatibility arises, but we cannot modify their output behavior.

Definition 8 (compatibility and composition) Let $\mathcal{P}$ and $\mathcal{Q}$ be two well-formed and composable timed interfaces. The interfaces $\mathcal{P}$ and $\mathcal{Q}$ are *compatible* if $(s_{\mathcal{P}}^{init}, s_{\mathcal{Q}}^{init}) \notin t\text{-}errors(\mathcal{P}, \mathcal{Q})$. If $\mathcal{P}$ and $\mathcal{Q}$ are compatible, then the composition $\mathcal{P} \| \mathcal{Q}$ is defined by restricting the input transition relation, so that no error states are entered. Formally, abbreviating $U = S_{\mathcal{P} \otimes \mathcal{Q}} \setminus t\text{-}errors(\mathcal{P}, \mathcal{Q})$, we define $\rho_{\mathcal{P} \| \mathcal{Q}}^{I} = \rho_{\mathcal{P} \otimes \mathcal{Q}}^{I} \cap (U \times Acts_{\mathcal{P} \otimes \mathcal{Q}}^{I} \times U)$; all other components of $\mathcal{P} \| \mathcal{Q}$ are defined as in $\mathcal{P} \otimes \mathcal{Q}$. ∎

3.3 Discussion

Well-formedness. The composition of timed interfaces that are not well-formed may yield undesirable results, and hence is not defined in our theory. To illustrate this point, consider the interfaces in Figure 2. The time steps are represented as follows: for player $\gamma \in \{I, O\}$, if state s has label $\gamma : \Delta = 0$, then only the time step $(s, 0, s)$ is available for γ; if s has no γ-label, then all time steps (s, Δ, s) with $\Delta \in \mathbb{T}$ are available for γ at s. In interface $\mathcal{P}_1$, there is no deadline associated with the immediate move a: Output can play it at any time, or not at all. Similarly, $\mathcal{P}_2$ does not associate a deadline to a: Input can play it at any time, or not at all. Note that $\mathcal{P}_2$ is not well-formed. This is because Output can only play the timed move 0 at state t_0, so t_0 is not O-live: if Input also plays the timed move 0, Output can neither let time diverge, nor blame Input. Consider

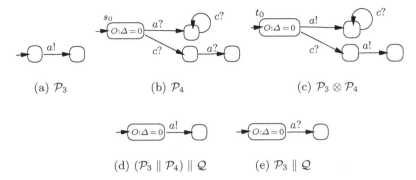

(a) $\mathcal{P}_3$ (b) $\mathcal{P}_4$ (c) $\mathcal{P}_3 \otimes \mathcal{P}_4$

(d) $(\mathcal{P}_3 \parallel \mathcal{P}_4) \parallel \mathcal{Q}$ (e) $\mathcal{P}_3 \parallel \mathcal{Q}$

Fig. 3. Timed interfaces illustrating why two transition relations are needed.

now the product $\mathcal{P}_1 \otimes \mathcal{P}_2$. The product specifies that the output move a *must* be played at time 0, even though no such deadline for a was present at $\mathcal{P}_1$ or $\mathcal{P}_2$. The problem, intuitively, is that the deadline of 0 for Output in $\mathcal{P}_2$ does not apply to any output move. When an unrelated output move becomes present, such as a in $\mathcal{P}_1 \otimes \mathcal{P}_2$, the deadline is improperly transferred to the move. The well-formness condition requires that a player has a deadline only if it also has an action that can satisfy the deadline, thus preventing such "deadline transfers."

Two transition relations. If we use a single transition relation, rather than one for Input and one for Output, then both players would share the same timed moves at a state. The following example shows that, if we do so, the composition of interfaces may again introduce timing requirements that are not present in the component interfaces. In particular, composition may not be associative. Consider the timed interfaces $\mathcal{P}_3$ and $\mathcal{P}_4$ in Figure 3, where the timing constraints apply to both Input and Output moves. The interfaces $\mathcal{P}_3$ and $\mathcal{P}_4$ are compatible. In state s_0, the interface $\mathcal{P}_4$ has to take an input action at time 0. This input need not be provided by $\mathcal{P}_3$, because $\mathcal{P}_3$ is not forced to take its $a!$ action. Nevertheless, $\mathcal{P}_3$ and $\mathcal{P}_4$ work together in an environment that provides a $c!$ action at time 0. Now consider the product $\mathcal{P}_3 \otimes \mathcal{P}_4$ in Figure 3(c); note that $\mathcal{P}_3 \otimes \mathcal{P}_4 = \mathcal{P}_3 \parallel \mathcal{P}_4$, because the product is well-formed. The composition $\mathcal{P}_3 \parallel \mathcal{P}_4$ specifies that, if c is not received at 0, then output a is produced at time 0. As a result, $\mathcal{P}_3 \parallel \mathcal{P}_4$ also works in environments that never provide a c input. More formally, let $\mathcal{Q}$ be the interface that has an output move c, which can never be taken. Then $(\mathcal{P}_3 \parallel \mathcal{P}_4)$ and $\mathcal{Q}$ are compatible. However, $\mathcal{P}_4 \parallel \mathcal{Q}$ (Figure 3(e)) and $\mathcal{P}_3$ are not compatible. Hence, the compatibility of $\mathcal{P}_3$, $\mathcal{P}_4$, and $\mathcal{Q}$ depends on the order in which they are composed.

Game asymmetry. This example uses the timed interface automata notation as in Section 2, to be introduced formally in the next section. Consider the automata $\mathcal{A}$, $\mathcal{A}_1$, and $\mathcal{A}_2$ in Figure 4, where $\prec \in \{<, \leq\}$. Note that $\mathcal{A} = \mathcal{A} \otimes \mathcal{A}_2$. Since $\mathcal{A}_1$ provides an output a within the deadline required by $\mathcal{A}_2$, the automata $\mathcal{A}_1$ and $\mathcal{A}_2$ should be compatible, and $\mathcal{A}$ should be well-formed. Consider first the case when $\prec$ is $\leq$. If Input is blamed when it plays the same time move

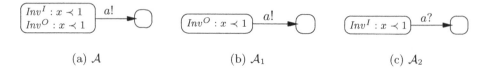

(a) $\mathcal{A}$ (b) $\mathcal{A}_1$ (c) $\mathcal{A}_2$

Fig. 4. Timed interfaces illustrating why O is blamed and why I plays second.

as Output, then $\mathcal{A}$ is not well-formed. In fact, Output can play the strategy of advancing time until $x = 1$, and thereafter always play timed move 0. Input cannot let time progress, nor can it blame Output. Hence, any state (s_0, x) with $x \leq 1$ is not I-live, and $\mathcal{A}$ is not well-formed. Consider now the case when $\prec$ is $<$. If Input cannot play second, then for each strategy π^I of Input, there is a strategy π^O for Output that plays later, i.e., a strategy π^O such that $\pi^I(\bar{s}) < \pi^O(\bar{s}) < 1$ for all histories $\bar{s}$. Then the outcome of this strategy neither is time divergent nor does it blame O. If, on the other hand, I plays second, then it can win the game by playing later than O.

4   Timed Interface Automata

Timed interfaces provide a finite representation for timed games and serve as a basis on which the algorithms for compatibility checking and composition operate. Their syntax recalls that of timed automata [AD94]. In particular, timed interface automata use *clock variables* in order to keep track of the amount of time elapsed. The value of these variables can be reset to 0 when immediate actions occur, and otherwise increase with unit rate. Let $\mathcal{X}$ be a set of variables over the time domain $\mathbb{T}$. A *clock condition* over $\mathcal{X}$ is a boolean combination of formulas of the form $x \prec c$ or $x - y \prec c$, where c is an integer, $x, y \in \mathcal{X}$, and $\prec$ is either of $<$ or $\leq$. We denote the set of all clock conditions over $\mathcal{X}$ by $\Xi[\mathcal{X}]$.

Definition 9 (timed interface automata)   A *timed interface automaton* (or TIA) is a tuple $\mathcal{A} = (Q_{\mathcal{A}}, q_{\mathcal{A}}^{init}, \mathcal{X}_{\mathcal{A}}, Acts_{\mathcal{A}}^I, Acts_{\mathcal{A}}^O, Inv_{\mathcal{A}}^I, Inv_{\mathcal{A}}^O, \rho_{\mathcal{A}})$ consisting of the following components.

- $Q_{\mathcal{A}}$ is a finite set of *locations*.
- $q_{\mathcal{A}}^{init} \in Q_{\mathcal{A}}$ is the *initial location*.
- $\mathcal{X}_{\mathcal{A}}$ is a finite set of *clocks*.
- $Acts_{\mathcal{A}}^I$ and $Acts_{\mathcal{A}}^O$ are finite and disjoint sets of *input* and *output actions*, respectively. Let $Acts_{\mathcal{A}} = Acts_{\mathcal{A}}^I \cup Acts_{\mathcal{A}}^O$ denote the set of all actions of $\mathcal{A}$.
- $Inv_{\mathcal{A}}^I: Q_{\mathcal{A}} \mapsto \Xi[\mathcal{X}_{\mathcal{A}}]$ maps each location of $\mathcal{A}$ to its *input invariant*.
- $Inv_{\mathcal{A}}^O: Q_{\mathcal{A}} \mapsto \Xi[\mathcal{X}_{\mathcal{A}}]$ maps each location of $\mathcal{A}$ to its *output invariant*.
- $\rho_{\mathcal{A}} \subseteq Q_{\mathcal{A}} \times \Xi[\mathcal{X}_{\mathcal{A}}] \times Acts_{\mathcal{A}} \times 2^{\mathcal{X}_{\mathcal{A}}} \times Q_{\mathcal{A}}$ is the *transition relation*. For $(q, g, a, r, q') \in \rho_{\mathcal{A}}$, the locations q and q' are the source and destination of the transition, $g \in \Xi[\mathcal{X}_{\mathcal{A}}]$ is a guard on the clock values that specifies when the transition can be taken, $a \in Acts_{\mathcal{A}}$ is an action labeling the transition, and $r \subseteq \mathcal{X}_{\mathcal{A}}$ is a set of clocks that are reset by the transition. We require the transition relation to be deterministic: for all $q \in Q_{\mathcal{A}}$ and $a \in Acts_{\mathcal{A}}$, there is at most one tuple of the form (q, g, a, r, q') with $(q, g, a, r, q') \in \rho_{\mathcal{A}}$. ∎

A *valuation* over a set $\mathcal{X}$ of clock variables is a function $v \colon \mathcal{X} \mapsto \mathbb{T}$. We write $\mathbf{0}_{\mathcal{X}}$ for the valuation that assigns 0 to all clocks in $\mathcal{X}$, and $\mathcal{V}(\mathcal{X})$ for the set of all valuations over $\mathcal{X}$. Given a valuation $v \in \mathcal{V}(\mathcal{X})$, we write $v + \Delta$ for the valuation defined by $(v + \Delta)(x) = v(x) + \Delta$ for all $x \in \mathcal{X}$. Given a set $r \subseteq \mathcal{X}$ of clocks, we write $v[r := 0]$ for the valuation that maps x to 0 if $x \in r$, and otherwise to $v(x)$. Given a clock condition $\varphi \in \Xi[\mathcal{X}]$, we write $v \models \varphi$ if φ is true under the valuation v. For $r \subseteq \mathcal{X}$, we write $\varphi[r := 0]$ for the condition obtained from φ by replacing every $x \in r$ by 0; obviously, $v[r := 0] \models \varphi$ iff $v \models \varphi[r := 0]$.

Definition 10 (timed interfaces induced by TIA)   The TIA $\mathcal{A}$ is *nonempty* if $\mathbf{0}_{\mathcal{X}_{\mathcal{A}}} \models Inv_{\mathcal{A}}^{I}(q_{\mathcal{A}}^{init}) \wedge Inv_{\mathcal{A}}^{O}(q_{\mathcal{A}}^{init})$. A nonempty TIA $\mathcal{A}$ induces a timed interface $\mathcal{P} = [\![\mathcal{A}]\!]$ that has the state set $S_{\mathcal{P}} = \{\langle p, v \rangle \mid p \in Q_{\mathcal{A}},\, v \in \mathcal{V}(\mathcal{X}_{\mathcal{A}})\}$ and the initial state $s_{\mathcal{P}}^{init} = \langle q_{\mathcal{A}}^{init}, \mathbf{0}_{\mathcal{X}_{\mathcal{A}}} \rangle$. The actions are $Acts_{\mathcal{P}}^{I} = Acts_{\mathcal{A}}^{I}$ and $Acts_{\mathcal{P}}^{O} = Acts_{\mathcal{A}}^{O}$. For $\gamma \in \{I, O\}$ the transition relations of $\mathcal{P}$ are defined by $(\langle p, v \rangle \xrightarrow{\alpha} \langle p', v' \rangle) \in \rho_{\mathcal{P}}^{\gamma}$ if either (1) $\alpha \in \mathbb{T}$, $p = p'$, $v' = v + \alpha$, and for all $0 \leq \Delta' \leq \alpha$, we have $v + \Delta' \models Inv_{\mathcal{A}}^{\gamma}(p)$; or (2) $\alpha \in Acts_{\mathcal{A}}^{\gamma}$, and there is a tuple $(p, g, \alpha, r, p') \in \rho_{\mathcal{A}}$ with $v \models Inv_{\mathcal{A}}^{\gamma}(p) \wedge g$, $v' = v[r := 0]$, and $v' \models Inv_{\mathcal{A}}^{\gamma}(p')$.

The TIA $\mathcal{A}$ is *well-formed* if it is nonempty and the corresponding timed interface $[\![\mathcal{A}]\!]$ is well-formed. ∎

4.1   Product and Composition of Timed Interface Automata

Two TIAs $\mathcal{A}$ and $\mathcal{B}$ are *composable* if $Acts_{\mathcal{A}}^{O} \cap Acts_{\mathcal{B}}^{O} = \emptyset$ and $\mathcal{X}_{\mathcal{A}} \cap \mathcal{X}_{\mathcal{B}} = \emptyset$; their *shared actions* are $shared(\mathcal{A}, \mathcal{B}) = Acts_{\mathcal{A}} \cap Acts_{\mathcal{B}}$.

Definition 11 (product)   For two composable TIAs $\mathcal{A}_1$ and $\mathcal{A}_2$, the *product* $\mathcal{A}_1 \otimes \mathcal{A}_2$ is the TIA that consists of the following components.

- $Q_{\mathcal{A}_1 \otimes \mathcal{A}_2} = Q_{\mathcal{A}_1} \times Q_{\mathcal{A}_2}$, and $q_{\mathcal{A}_1 \otimes \mathcal{A}_2}^{init} = (q_{\mathcal{A}_1}^{init}, q_{\mathcal{A}_2}^{init})$.
- $\mathcal{X}_{\mathcal{A}_1 \otimes \mathcal{A}_2} = \mathcal{X}_{\mathcal{A}_1} \cup \mathcal{X}_{\mathcal{A}_2}$.
- $Acts_{\mathcal{A}_1 \otimes \mathcal{A}_2}^{I} = Acts_{\mathcal{A}_1}^{I} \cup Acts_{\mathcal{A}_2}^{I} \setminus shared(\mathcal{A}_1, \mathcal{A}_2)$, and $Acts_{\mathcal{A}_1 \otimes \mathcal{A}_2}^{O} = Acts_{\mathcal{A}_1}^{O} \cup Acts_{\mathcal{A}_2}^{O}$.
- $Inv_{\mathcal{A}_1 \otimes \mathcal{A}_2}^{I}(p, q) = Inv_{\mathcal{A}_1}^{I}(p) \wedge Inv_{\mathcal{A}_2}^{I}(q)$ and $Inv_{\mathcal{A}_1 \otimes \mathcal{A}_2}^{O}(p, q) = Inv_{\mathcal{A}_1}^{O}(p) \wedge Inv_{\mathcal{A}_2}^{O}(q)$.
- $\rho_{\mathcal{A}_1 \otimes \mathcal{A}_2}$ is the set of transitions $((q_1, q_2), g_1 \wedge g_2, a, r_1 \cup r_2, (q_1', q_2'))$ such that, for $i = 1, 2$: if $a \in Acts_{\mathcal{A}_i}$, then (q_i, g_i, a, r_i, q_i') is a transition in $\rho_{\mathcal{A}_i}$; otherwise $q_i = q_i'$, $g_i = true$, and $r_i = \emptyset$. ∎

Theorem 1   *For nonempty and composable TIAs $\mathcal{A}$ and $\mathcal{B}$, we have $[\![\mathcal{A} \otimes \mathcal{B}]\!] = [\![\mathcal{A}]\!] \otimes [\![\mathcal{B}]\!]$.*

A *location labeling* for a TIA $\mathcal{A}$ is a function $\xi \colon Q_{\mathcal{A}} \mapsto \Xi[\mathcal{X}_{\mathcal{A}}]$ that associates with each location p of $\mathcal{A}$ a condition $\xi(p)$ over the clocks in $\mathcal{X}_{\mathcal{A}}$. The location labeling ξ defines the state set $[\![\xi]\!]_{\mathcal{A}} = \{\langle p, v \rangle \in S_{[\![\mathcal{A}]\!]} \mid v \models \xi(p)\}$ of the corresponding timed interface. We denote by $I\text{-}live_{\mathcal{A}}(\xi)$ the location labeling that defines the set

$[\![I\text{-}live_{\mathcal{A}}(\xi)]\!]_{\mathcal{A}}$ of I-live states in $[\![\xi]\!]_{\mathcal{A}}$. By computing $[\![I\text{-}live_{\mathcal{A}}(\xi)]\!]_{\mathcal{A}}$ as the solution of a game on the region graph (see Section 4.2), we will see that the I-live states are indeed definable by clock conditions. To define the composition on TIAs, we also need the following enabling conditions. For $\gamma \in \{I, O\}$, a location $q \in Q_{\mathcal{A}}$, and an action $a \in Acts_{\mathcal{A}}^{\gamma}$, let $enab_{\mathcal{A}}^{\gamma}(q, a)$ be $Inv_{\mathcal{A}}^{\gamma}(q) \wedge g \wedge Inv_{\mathcal{A}}^{\gamma}(q')[r := 0]$ if there is a transition $(q, g, a, r, q') \in \rho_{\mathcal{A}}$; otherwise let $enab_{\mathcal{A}}^{\gamma}(q, a)$ be *false*. Given two composable TIAs $\mathcal{A}$ and $\mathcal{B}$, the states of $[\![\mathcal{A} \otimes \mathcal{B}]\!]$ that are not immediate error states can be defined by the location labeling $ok_{\mathcal{A} \otimes \mathcal{B}}$ that associates with each product location $(p, q) \in Q_{\mathcal{A} \otimes \mathcal{B}}$ the clock condition

$$\bigwedge_{a \in Acts_{\mathcal{A}}^{O} \cap Acts_{\mathcal{B}}^{I}} (enab_{\mathcal{A}}^{O}(p, a) \rightarrow enab_{\mathcal{B}}^{I}(q, a)) \wedge \bigwedge_{a \in Acts_{\mathcal{B}}^{O} \cap Acts_{\mathcal{A}}^{I}} (enab_{\mathcal{B}}^{O}(q, a) \rightarrow enab_{\mathcal{A}}^{I}(p, a)).$$

Definition 12 (compatibility and composition) Two well-formed and composable TIAs $\mathcal{A}$ and $\mathcal{B}$ are *compatible* if the corresponding timed interface $[\![\mathcal{A}]\!]$ and $[\![\mathcal{B}]\!]$ are compatible. The *composition* $\mathcal{A} \| \mathcal{B}$ is obtained from the product $\mathcal{A} \otimes \mathcal{B}$ by replacing the input invariants $Inv_{\mathcal{A} \otimes \mathcal{B}}^{I}$ with the location labeling $I\text{-}live_{\mathcal{A} \otimes \mathcal{B}}(ok_{\mathcal{A} \otimes \mathcal{B}})$. ∎

Theorem 2 *Two well-formed and composable TIAs $\mathcal{A}$ and $\mathcal{B}$ are compatible iff the composition $\mathcal{A} \| \mathcal{B}$ is nonempty. Moreover, if $\mathcal{A}$ and $\mathcal{B}$ are compatible, then $[\![\mathcal{A} \| \mathcal{B}]\!] = [\![\mathcal{A}]\!] \| [\![\mathcal{B}]\!]$, and $\mathcal{A} \| \mathcal{B}$ is well-formed.*

The following theorem states that composition is associative up to the equivalence $\equiv$, which for TIAs $\mathcal{A}$ and $\mathcal{B}$ is defined by $\mathcal{A} \equiv \mathcal{B}$ if $\rho_{[\![\mathcal{A}]\!]}^{I} \cap (Reach([\![\mathcal{A}]\!]) \times Acts_{[\![\mathcal{A}]\!]}^{I} \times S_{[\![\mathcal{A}]\!]}) = \rho_{[\![\mathcal{B}]\!]}^{I} \cap (Reach([\![\mathcal{B}]\!]) \times Acts_{[\![\mathcal{B}]\!]}^{I} \times S_{[\![\mathcal{B}]\!]})$ and all other components of $[\![\mathcal{A}]\!]$ and $[\![\mathcal{B}]\!]$ are the same. Here, $Reach(\mathcal{P})$ denotes the set of reachable states of the timed interface $\mathcal{P}$.

Theorem 3 *If $\mathcal{A}$, $\mathcal{B}$, and $\mathcal{C}$ are well-formed and pairwise composable TIAs, then $(\mathcal{A} \| \mathcal{B}) \| \mathcal{C} \equiv \mathcal{A} \| (\mathcal{B} \| \mathcal{C})$.*

4.2   Algorithms for Composition and Well-Formedness Checking

Live states. Before presenting the algorithms for checking well-formedness and computing composition, we show that, given a location labeling ξ, we can compute the labeling $I\text{-}live_{\mathcal{A}}(\xi)$ that defines the set of states in $\mathcal{A}$ where I can win the game on $\mathcal{A}$ with goal $(t\_div \vee blame^{O}) \wedge \Box [\![\xi]\!]_{\mathcal{A}}$.

To use existing algorithms, we first transform this game into an equivalent one with an ω-regular goal [Tho90]. Consider the TIA $Tick^{O}$ shown on the right, where the action *tick* and the clock x are fresh. Thus, $Tick^{O}$ observes the progress of time, and visits location q_1 every time unit. In particular, time diverges iff q_1 is visited infinitely often. Hence, Input can win in

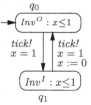

$[\![\mathcal{A}]\!]$ the game with goal $(t\text{-}div \vee blame^O) \wedge \Box[\![\xi]\!]_\mathcal{A}$ iff Input can win in $[\![\mathcal{A} \otimes Tick^O]\!]$ the game with goal $(blame^O \vee \Box\Diamond q_1) \wedge \Box[\![\xi]\!]_\mathcal{A}$. On the enlarged state space $S_{[\![\mathcal{A} \otimes Tick^O]\!]} \times \{I, O\}$, where the states record the blame, this latter goal can be rewritten as the ω-regular goal $\varphi_I \colon (\Diamond\Box(bl = O) \vee \Box\Diamond q_1) \wedge \Box[\![\xi]\!]_\mathcal{A}$. The game with goal φ_I can be solved using the algorithms of [EJ91,dAHM01], which use a *controllable predecessor operator IPre*. Given a timed interface $\mathcal{P}$ and a set U of states, $IPre_\mathcal{P}(U)$ yields all states in which Input can in one move force the game into U. Formally, $IPre_\mathcal{P}(U)$ contains all states $s \in S_\mathcal{P}$ such that $\forall\alpha_O \in \Gamma_\mathcal{P}^O(s). \exists\alpha_I \in \Gamma_\mathcal{P}^I(s). \delta_\mathcal{P}(s, \alpha_I, \alpha_O) \subseteq U$. The set win_I of states in $S_{[\![\mathcal{A} \otimes Tick^O]\!]} \times \{I, O\}$ where Input can win the game with goal φ_I can be characterized by [EJ91]

$$win_I = \nu Z.\mu Y.\nu X.\Big[\xi \wedge \big[(q_0 \wedge bl{=}O \wedge IPre_\mathcal{P}(X)) \vee$$

$$(q_0 \wedge bl{=}I \wedge IPre_\mathcal{P}(Y)) \vee (q_1 \wedge IPre_\mathcal{P}(Z))\big]\Big].$$

for $\mathcal{P} = [\![\mathcal{A} \otimes Tick^O]\!]$. One can define the *region graph* of a TIA as for timed automata [AD94]. Since the operation *IPre* is computable on the region graph [MPS95], the expression above suggests a symbolic fixpoint algorithm. The result win_I can be expressed as a location labeling ζ on $\mathcal{A}$. We then obtain the desired labeling $I\text{-}live_\mathcal{A}(\xi)$ by letting $I\text{-}live_\mathcal{A}(\xi)(p) = \exists x. \exists bl.(\zeta(p, q_0) \vee \zeta(p, q_1))$.

Well-formedness. The following theorem shows that, to check the well-formedness of a TIA $\mathcal{A}$, we need to compute the location labelings $Reach(\mathcal{A})$, $I\text{-}live_\mathcal{A}(True_\mathcal{A})$, and $O\text{-}live_\mathcal{A}(True_\mathcal{A})$. Here, $Reach(\mathcal{A})$ is the location labeling that defines the set $[\![Reach(\mathcal{A})]\!]_\mathcal{A}$ of reachable states of $[\![\mathcal{A}]\!]$, and $O\text{-}live_\mathcal{A}(\xi)$ is the labeling that defines the set of O-live states in $[\![\xi]\!]_\mathcal{A}$, and $True_\mathcal{A}$ denotes the labeling that assigns *true* to each location. The set $[\![Reach(\mathcal{A})]\!]_\mathcal{A}$ is definable from clock conditions, because it can be computed on the region graph in the same way as the reachable states of a timed automaton can be computed [AD94]. Since $[\![O\text{-}live_\mathcal{A}(\xi)]\!]_\mathcal{A}$, for a location labeling ξ, can be computed similarly to $[\![I\text{-}live_\mathcal{A}(\xi)]\!]_\mathcal{A}$, it is also definable by clock conditions.

Theorem 4   *A TIA $\mathcal{A}$ is well-formed iff for all locations $p \in Q_\mathcal{A}$ the implication $Reach(\mathcal{A})(p) \to (I\text{-}live_\mathcal{A}(True_\mathcal{A})(p) \wedge O\text{-}live_\mathcal{A}(True_\mathcal{A})(p))$ is valid.*

Composition. The composition of two well-formed and composable TIAs $\mathcal{A}$ and $\mathcal{B}$ can be obtained from their product by replacing the input invariants $Inv_{\mathcal{A}\otimes\mathcal{B}}^I$ with the location labeling $I\text{-}live_{\mathcal{A}\otimes\mathcal{B}}(ok_{\mathcal{A}\otimes\mathcal{B}})$ (Definition 12). Then their compatibility can be decided by checking whether their composition is empty (Theorem 2).

References

Abr96. S. Abramsky. Semantics of interaction. In *Trees in Algebra and Programming*, volume 1059 of *Lect. Notes in Comp. Sci.*, page 1. Springer, 1996.

AD94. R. Alur and D.L. Dill. A theory of timed automata. *Theoretical Computer Science*, 126:183–235, 1994.

AH97. R. Alur and T.A. Henzinger. Modularity for timed and hybrid systems. In *Concurrency Theory*, volume 1243 of *Lect. Notes in Comp. Sci.*, pages 74–88. Springer, 1997.

AMPS98. E. Asarin, O. Maler, A. Pnueli, and J. Sifakis. Controller synthesis for timed automata. In *Proc. IFAC Symp. System Structure and Control*, pages 469–474. Elsevier, 1998.

CRR02. S. Chaki, S.K. Rajamani, and J. Rehof. Types as models: Model checking message-passing programs. In *Proc. Symp. Principles of Programming Languages*, pages 45–57. ACM, 2002.

dAH01a. L. de Alfaro and T.A. Henzinger. Interface automata. In *Proc. Symp. Foundations of Software Engineering*, pages 109–120. ACM, 2001.

dAH01b. L. de Alfaro and T.A. Henzinger. Interface theories for component-based design. In *Embedded Software*, volume 2211 of *Lect. Notes in Comp. Sci.*, pages 148–165. Springer, 2001.

dAHM01. L. de Alfaro, T.A. Henzinger, and R. Majumdar. Symbolic algorithms for infinite-state games. In *Concurrency Theory*, volume 2154 of *Lect. Notes in Comp. Sci.*, pages 536–550. Springer, 2001.

Dil88. D.L. Dill. *Trace Theory for Automatic Hierarchical Verification of Speed-Independent Circuits*. MIT Press, 1988.

EJ91. E.A. Emerson and C.S. Jutla. Tree automata, mu-calculus, and determinacy. In *Proc. Symp. Foundations of Computer Science*, pages 368–377. IEEE Computer Society, 1991.

MMT91. M. Merritt, F. Modugno, and M. Tuttle. Time constrained automata. In *Concurrency Theory*, volume 527 of *Lect. Notes in Comp. Sci.*, pages 408–423. Springer, 1991.

MPS95. O. Maler, A. Pnueli, and J. Sifakis. On the synthesis of discrete controllers for timed systems. In *Theoretical Aspects of Computer Science*, volume 900 of *Lect. Notes in Comp. Sci.*, pages 229–242. Springer, 1995.

RGG96. E. Rudolph, P. Graubmann, and J. Gabowski. Tutorial on message sequence charts. *Computer Networks and ISDN Systems–SDL and MSC*, 28:1629–1641, 1996.

RR01. S.K. Rajamani and J. Rehof. A behavioral module system for the pi-calculus. In *Static Analysis Symposium*, volume 2126 of *Lect. Notes in Comp. Sci.*, pages 375–394. Springer, 2001.

SGSAL98. R. Segala, G. Gawlick, J. Søgaard-Andersen, and N. Lynch. Liveness in timed and untimed systems. *Information and Computation*, 141:119–171, 1998.

Tho90. W. Thomas. Automata on infinite objects. In J. van Leeuwen, ed., *Handbook of Theoretical Computer Science*, volume B, pages 135–191. Elsevier, 1990.

Yi90. Wang Yi. Real-time behaviour of asynchronous agents. In *Concurrency Theory*, volume 458 of *Lect. Notes in Comp. Sci.*, pages 502–520. Springer, 1990.

Description and Schedulability Analysis of the Software Architecture of an Automated Vehicle Control System

Stavros Tripakis

VERIMAG
Centre Equation, 2, avenue de Vignate, 38610 Gières, France
tripakis@imag.fr

Abstract. We describe the software architecture of an automated vehicle control system implemented in the PATH lab[1]. The system is responsible for automatic lateral and longitudinal control of a set of vehicles traveling in a *platoon* formation at close distance and at high speeds [15]. The software architecture consists of a set of processes running concurrently and communicating through a *publish/subscribe* database. Some processes are triggered periodically by external inputs (e.g., from sensors) while others are triggered by events from other (internal) processes. We model the architecture as a set of periodic *tasks* each consisting of a sequence of *sub-tasks* with varying priorities [3,4]. We perform a schedulability analysis to check whether a set of timing requirements expressed as *deadlines* are met.

1 Introduction

PATH's Advanced Vehicle Control and Safety Systems (AVCSS) project involves the design and implementation of automated vehicle control applications on a variety of vehicles, such as cars, trucks, or snow-plows. One such application aims to increase the capacity of highways, by having vehicles travel in *platoons*, that is, groups of up to 10 vehicles moving one behind the other, at a close distance (e.g., 10 feet), and at high speeds (e.g., 65 miles/hour).

There are obviously many challenges in designing and building such a system, from providing the supporting highway infrastructure (e.g., magnets placed on the center of a lane to keep the vehicle in track), to designing the autonomous *lateral* and coordinated *longitudinal* controllers that operate in each vehicle. The lateral control is responsible for keeping the car in the center of the lane, by reading magnet relative position information from the car's magnetometer and controlling the steering. The longitudinal control is responsible for maintaining a safe but short distance between the cars and for keeping the platoon stable. It does this by controlling braking and acceleration, using input information from

---

[1] PATH (Partners for Advanced Transit and Highways) is a research lab administered by the Institute of Transportation Studies (ITS), University of California, Berkeley, in collaboration with Caltrans. Web-site: www.path.berkeley.edu.

A. Sangiovanni-Vincentelli and J. Sifakis (Eds.): EMSOFT 2002, LNCS 2491, pp. 123–137, 2002.

the car's radar and other sensors, as well as information about the speed and acceleration of the car in front and the lead car of the platoon. This information is distributed among cars in the platoon using wireless communication.

In this document, we focus on the embedded software architecture, which implements the above control design. Designing such an architecture is a challenge by itself. The architecture must permit an easy implementation of the controllers (especially since this implementation is usually done by control engineers). It must also facilitate modularity and re-use of components: different hardware is used in different vehicles, each requiring different software components (e.g., device drivers); controller components are re-used as well, after being fine-tuned for each vehicle. Finally, the architecture must be amenable to analysis.

The objectives of this paper are two. First, to describe the software architecture of an existing and succesfully demonstrated automated vehicle control system; we believe this architecture is suitable for many similar real-time control applications. Second, to model this architecture and perform a schedulability analysis; for the analysis, we use existing results from real-time scheduling theory (in particular [3,4]); we believe the modeling and analysis methodology can also be re-used in other similar systems.

The AVCSS software architecture consists of a set of processes communicating through a *publish/subscribe* middleware (P/S). The latter is implemented in C on top of the operating system QNX [10]. P/S is essentially a database which allows processes to create, read and write variables, as well as to request notification whenever a given variable is updated. The P/S architecture has a number of important properties with respect to the requirements discussed above, namely, it is modular, generic and inherently asynchronous (producers and consumers need not know about each other and can work at different rates). The P/S architecture is described in Section 3.

Although a remarkable piece of engineering, the AVCSS software architecture has not been designed with a formal model in mind and it has only been informally tested by collecting execution traces. In Section 4 we develop a model for the particular AVCSS application of automated platoons, mentioned above. Our model includes, except from the *physical* QNX processes that implement the application, a set of real-time *logical tasks*, which represent the formal requirements of the system. For instance, a (logical) task might be: "every 5ms, sample the radar data and compute new throttle output". We identify such tasks by reverse-engineering the software. All tasks are time-triggered and periodic.

At the implementation level, each task is realized by a *chain* of QNX processes, each running at its own priority. For instance, the task above might involve a process A to do the sampling and store the data in the database, a process B to read the data and compute the control output, and a process C to write the output to the actuator. A (the head of the chain) is triggered periodically by the environment, then A triggers B, which in turn triggers C. As a minimal requirement, it has to be ensured that each activation of such a chain is completed before the next activation begins. We model this by setting for each task a *deadline* (in this case equal to the task period). Then, we use

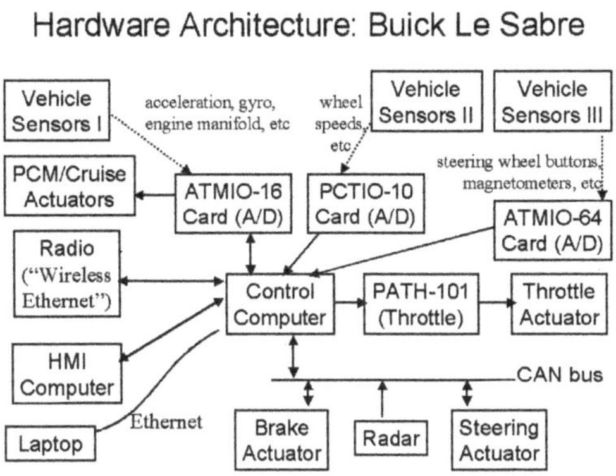

Hardware Architecture: Buick Le Sabre

Fig. 1. Automated vehicle control: hardware architecture

existing results from the real-time scheduling theory, in particular, the so-called *HKL analysis* [3,4,6], to check whether the deadlines are met. The analysis is presented in Section 5.

2 Hardware Architecture

For a better understanding of the software, we start by briefly presenting the hardware equipment (Figure 1) of the Buick Le Sabre vehicles, which are the ones used in the platoon application. The boxes in the figure represent different pieces of hardware. The arrows represent connections of these pieces, and the direction of the arrows represents data flow: for example, the control computer takes input from the radar but not vice-versa.

The control computer is a 166 MHz Pentium PC. The "sensors" boxes I, II, III, are analog circuits taking inputs from accelerometer, magnetometers, and so on. The ATMIO-16, ATMIO-64 and PCTIO-10 cards are essentially digital/analog converter boards, equipped also with timers. PATH-101 is a card developed at PATH to control the throttle actuator. The other two actuators (brake and steering) are connected to the control computer via a CAN bus, through which they receive control messages and send back status information. The radar (installed in the front of the vehicle) is also connected to the CAN bus. A Lucent Wavelan 2 Mbits/sec "wireless Ethernet" interface (compliant to the IEEE 802.11 protocol) is used for inter-vehicle communication. The laptop is used for initialization. The Human Machine Interface (HMI) computer provides status display to the passengers in the car.

3 The Publish/Subscribe Embedded Software Architecture

The software architecture consists of a set of processes running on the control computer of each vehicle (a PC), and communicating through the *Publish/Subscribe database*. All the software is written in C and runs on QNX [10].

We classify the processes (except the database process) into *device drivers*, *controllers*, and *data I/O processes*. The device drivers interact directly with the hardware. The data I/O processes transform data from the device drivers into high-level C structures to be read by the controllers, and also transform high-level output data written by the controllers into low-level data for the device drivers. The controllers read high-level sensor data and compute high-level actuator data.

Figure 2 shows the interaction between the different types of processes and the database. Notice that only the data I/O and controller processes interact via the database. Device drivers and data I/O processes interact with *synchronous message passing*, that is, the reader blocks waiting for a message from the writer (the message may be generated by another process or by the handler routine of a hardware interrupt).

The publish/subscribe middleware consists of a *database server* (implemented as a QNX process) and a C library that *client* processes use to communicate with the server. The library contains primitives for a process to register/deregister with the database, create/destroy a variable, read/update a variable, set/unset *triggers*. Setting a trigger for a variable means requesting notification whenever the variable is updated.

Regarding scheduling, the *static-priority scheduling* policy of QNX is used. Each process is assigned a priority, from 0 (lowest) to 31 (highest). At any time, a highest-priority process is chosen to run among the ready processes. The database server runs at the highest priority, so that client requests are served immediately.

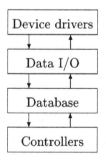

Fig. 2. The AVCSS Publish/Subscribe Software Architecture.

The main characteristics of the software architecture are the following:

(1) It is modular. Data I/O and controller processes are *loosely* coupled. They do not have to know about the existence of other processes, and only interact with the database. As long as the interface with the database is respected, one or more processes in the architecture can be replaced (e.g., when updating some piece of hardware) without changing the rest of the system. Also, processes can be developed by different groups, and then integrated in a straightforward manner.

(2) It permits the design of *asynchronous* controllers, e.g., having different sampling rates. Since the producers and consumers of data only interact via the database, the producer can be faster than the consumer (some values will be lost) or slower (some values will be read twice). Note that in many control applications, only "fresh" data are relevant. Because of its inherent asynchrony, the architecture is particularly suitable for applications where communications are used, and where variable delays can create problems, especially in synchronous designs. In cases where synchronization is required, it can be implemented through the use of triggers. For example, a process A may request to be "waken up" whenever a process B has updated a variable. Then B may do the same, and so on, which essentially allows the two processes to execute in *lock-step*.

(3) It is generic. The publish/subscribe library does not assume any fixed set of processes, or variables. It does not know the types of the variables (it only sees them as byte-strings). Therefore, it is also suitable in contexts where dynamic creation or destruction of processes is required. This is often the case in real-time control applications, where a change in the physical environment may require a change in the *control mode*. For example, failure of a sensor may require some processes to be stopped and others to be started.

(4) It is amenable to analysis. We perform such an analysis in Section 5.

For the above reasons, we believe that the software architecture is particularly suited for many real-time control applications.

In the full version of this paper (available from the home page of the author) we give more details on the semantics and implementation of the publish/subscribe middleware.

4   Embedded Software of the Platoon Application

We now present an instance of the embedded software architecture, for the platoon application mentioned in the introduction. In our description, we use the actual names of hardware components, software processes and variable names used in the application.

A diagram of the set of processes and their interactions appears in Figure 3. We omit the database from the figure. As mentioned before, interactions between device drivers and data I/O processes are direct, whereas interactions between data I/O processes and controllers are through the database (Figure 2).

Process types. In Figure 3, the device drivers are pctio10 (PCTIO-10 card), atmio16 (ATMIO-16 card), atmioe (ATMIO-64 card), path101 (PATH-101 card), and cani (CAN bus interface). The data I/O processes are veh_iols, canread, canbrake, cansteer, veh_lat, radio and hmi. The control processes are eng_spdl (longitudinal control) and hst (lateral control). The process buttons can also be seen as a control process, since it only interacts with the database. This process retrieves steering-wheel button activation data and current button status data from the database, computes new button status data and writes it back into the database.

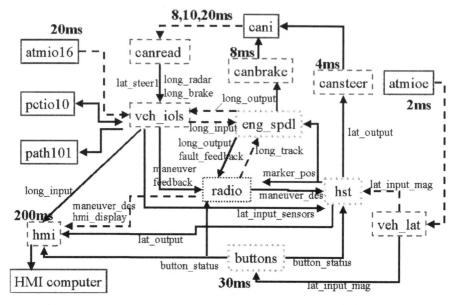

Fig. 3. Components of the platoon vehicle control system (in one car).

Dataflow. Figure 3 also shows the variables exchanged by data I/O and control processes. These variables are created and stored in the database. Each arrow labeled with a variable means that the origin of the arrow updates the variable in the database, and the target of the arrow reads the variable from the database. Notice that there is a *single producer* for each variable, that is, each variable is updated by only one process (though it can be read by many processes). The exact information contained in the variables is not important for this document. For example, **long_radar** contains the range (in meters) to the nearest object in the front of the vehicle (presumably car in front), **long_brake** contains requested and achieved brake pressure, **long_input** contains acceleration (in meters/sec²), engine speed (in rpm), and so on.

Time-driven and event-driven processes. All processes follow the same execution pattern, namely, an infinite loop which starts with a blocking `Receive()` call, waiting for a message. Once the message is received, the process wakes up, performs its function, and then goes back at the beginning of the loop waiting for the next message. Messages can arrive periodically or asynchronously. Accordingly, we say that a process is *time-driven* or *event-driven.*

Time-driven processes wake up and perform their function periodically. In Figure 3, time-driven processes are labeled with a period in milliseconds. The periodic message source can be either the operating system (e.g., `canbrake` sets an operating-system timer which expires every 8 ms and generates a software interrupt which sends a message and resets the timer), or an external device that raises a hardware interrupt (e.g., `atmio16` receives an interrupt generated by a timer on the ATMIO-16 card every 20 ms, and `cani` receives a message on the

CAN bus from the radar every 20 ms, from the steering actuator every 8 ms, and from the brake actuator every 10 ms).

Event-driven processes wait for triggers for one or more variables in the database. In Figure 3, each event-driven process has a dashed-arrow pointing to it, labeled with the name of the variable the process sets a trigger for. For example, eng_spdl sets triggers for long_input and long_track.

Notice that the hmi process is both time-driven and event-driven: it sets a trigger for hmi_display but also executes periodically every 200 ms.

Process priorities. The priorities of the processes have been assigned as follows. The database runs at priority 25 (highest). canbrake and cansteer run at priority 24. Device drivers run at priority 19 (hardware interrupt handlers are part of the device drivers, so they inherit their priority). hst and veh_lat run at priority 18. All other processes run at priority 10 (default).

Tasks. As mentioned in the introduction, we distinguish between the notions of *physical processes* and *logical tasks*. The former are the QNX processes shown in Figure 3. The latter represent the formal requirements of the system, including functional and timing requirements. For instance, a task of the platoon application is: "every 2ms, sample the magnetometer data and compute new steering control outputs".

Each task is realized at the implementation level by an "execution chain" of many processes. For instance, the chain for the task above is as follows. Every 2 ms, the ATMIO-64 card generates a hardware interrupt, which is handled by atmioe. The interrupt handler sends a message to veh_lat. This triggers execution of veh_lat, which reads data from the ATMIO-64 card and updates the lat_input_mag variable in the database. This update triggers a message to be sent from the database to hst. The latter reads variables lat_input_mag, lat_input_sensors, maneuver_des and button_status from the database, and computes and updates variables lat_output and marker_pos.

By reverse-engineering the software implementation of the platoon application (i.e., browsing the code) we identify eleven tasks in total. These are listed in Table 1 and summarized in the full version of this document.

It is worth noting that all tasks are time-driven and periodic[2]. Also notice that the same process might be invoked twice in a chain, e.g., veh_iols is invoked twice in the longitudinal chain, first by a message from atmio16, then by a trigger for long_output.

5 Analysis

Timing requirements of embedded software are typically described in the form of *deadlines*: a task must complete its execution at most x seconds after it becomes

---

[2] A wireless TDMA (*time division multiple access*) protocol ensures that vehicles in a platoon communicate without collisions, so that packets arrive deterministically every 20ms. There are no retransmissions. If a packet is corrupted it is discarded. If three consecutive packets are missed, the control goes into a fault mode.

Table 1. Tasks and chains in the platoon application.

Task	Chain
lateral input	atmioe, veh_lat, hst
steering output	cansteer, cani
brake output	canbrake, cani
steering input	cani, canread
brake input	cani, canread
radar input	cani, canread
longitudinal	atmio16, veh_iols, atmio16, pctio10, veh_iols, eng_spdl veh_iols, path101, pctio10
communication input	radio, eng_spdl, hmi
communication output	radio
buttons	buttons
HMI	hmi

ready. For the platoon application, we set the deadline of a task to be equal to its period. The fact that the deadline of, say, the lateral input task, is 2ms ensures that no hardware interrupt will be missed and that control outputs will be computed using "fresh" inputs[3].

It is not at all obvious that the software architecture meets its deadline requirements. In this section, we perform a formal analysis to check whether this is the case. We use results from real-time scheduling theory, in particular, fixed-priority scheduling theory (e.g., see [8,7,5,13,1,2,14]) and the so-called *HKL* model and analysis [3,4]. First, we cast the platoon application into the formal model. Then, we estimate the execution times and other latencies involved in the system, and compute the total CPU utilization. This is found to be about 74%, that is, less than 1, which is a necessary (but not sufficient) condition for schedulability. Finally, we apply HKL analysis to check whether the deadlines are met.

5.1   A Formal Model for the Platoon Application

We describe our application as a set of periodic tasks, each consisting of a sequence of sub-tasks with varying priorities. First we present our model, which is a special case of the one in [3,4].

We have a set of tasks $\tau_1, ..., \tau_n$. Each τ_i has a period $T_i > 0$ and a deadline $D_i = T_i$. Each τ_i is associated with a sequence $\tau_{i,1}, ..., \tau_{i,m(i)}$ of *sub-tasks*. Each sub-task $\tau_{i,j}$ has an execution time $C_{i,j}$ and a priority $P_{i,j}$. We define C_i to be

---

[3]   In general, stricter deadlines might be required: for example, it might be important for a controller to read inputs from sensors and output data to actuators immediately after the inputs become available, even if they become available not very often.

$\sum_{j=1}^{m(i)} C_{i,j}$, that is, the total execution time of τ_i. It is assumed that $C_i \leq T_i$, for all i [4].

Each τ_i becomes *ready* for execution at times $t_i^k = \phi_i + kT_i$, $k = 0, 1, 2, ...$, where ϕ_i is the initial *phase* of the task. At time t_i^k, the sub-task $\tau_{i,1}$ becomes *active* and remains active until it has executed for a total of $C_{i,1}$ time units, at which time it *finishes*. At that time, $\tau_{i,2}$ becomes active, and so on. When sub-task $\tau_{i,m(i)}$ finishes, the k-th *job* of τ_i finishes. At any time t the CPU executes one of the active sub-tasks that have the highest priority. If there are more than one such sub-tasks, ties are broken arbitrarily. We say that τ_i meets its deadline if for all $k = 0, 1, 2, ...$, the k-th job of τ_i finishes at time $t_i^k + D_i$ at the latest. We say that the set of tasks is *schedulable* if for all possible initial phases and all possible ways to break ties, all tasks meet their deadlines. The problem is, given a set of tasks, to check whether it is schedulable.

We now show how to cast the platoon application in the above model. In short, a task will be a logical task and its sub-tasks will be the processes involved in its execution chain. As an example, consider τ_1 (the lateral input task). We have $D_1 = T_1 = 2$ (assumed to be in milliseconds). The sub-tasks of τ_1 are extracted from the lateral input process chain. Recall that the latter involves the execution of `atmioe`, `veh_lat` and `hst`, in that order. However, we cannot consider only three sub-tasks, because `veh_lat` and `hst` interact with the database, which is implemented as a process itself. Indeed, each interaction of a process A with the database D includes A sending a request-message to D, D processing the request and replying to A with a response-message, and A receiving this message and continuing execution. Thus, such an interaction can be modeled as a sequence of three sub-tasks: $A_s, D_{r,s}, A_r$, where A_s models A sending the request, $D_{r,s}$ models D receiving the request, processing and replying, and A_r models A receiving the response. Now, if A executed two requests (say, a read and an update), we get a sequence of five sub-tasks: $A_s, D_{r,s}, A_{r,s}, D_{r,s}, A_r$, since we can combine receiving the first response and sending the second request in a single sub-task $A_{r,s}$.

Apart from interactions of data I/O processes with the database, we must also model the interaction of these processes with the device drivers. For example, when `veh_lat` reads data from `atmioe`, this comes down to `veh_lat` sending a request to `atmioe` and the latter replying back, which can be modeled by a sequence $A_s, B_{r,s}, A_r$.

Coming back to our lateral input task example, we combine the above remarks as follows. Given that `veh_lat` reads from `atmioe` and requests one database update, and `hst` requests four database reads and two updates, its sequence of sub-tasks is

$$A, V, A, V, D, V, H, D, H, D, H, D, H, D, H, D, H, D, H$$

---

[4]   The model of [4] is more general, in that each sub-task $\tau_{i,j}$ has its own deadline $D_{i,j}$, such that $D_{i,1} \leq D_{i,2} \leq \cdots \leq D_{i,m(i)} = D_i$, and also D_i can be smaller or greater than T_i. In our case, $D_{i,j} = D_i = T_i$.

Table 2. Task periods and their sub-tasks with their priorities.

i	T_i (ms)	$m(i)$	C_i (μs)	U_i (%)	$P_{i,j}$
1	2	19	740	37	19, 18, 19, 18, 25, 18, 18, (25, 18) repeated 5 times
2	4	5	250	6.25	24, 25, 24, 19, 24
3	8	5	250	3.12	24, 25, 24, 19, 24
4	8	6	270	3.38	19, 10, 19, 10, 25, 10
5	10	6	270	2.7	19, 10, 19, 10, 25, 10
6	20	6	270	1.35	19, 10, 19, 10, 25, 10
7	20	28	1060	5.3	19, 10, 19, 10, 19, 10, 25, 10, 25, 10, 25, 10, 25, 10, 25, 10, 10, 25, 10, 25, 10, 10, 25, 10, 19, 10, 19, 10
8	20	13	2080	10.4	19, 25, 19, 25, 19, 25, 19, 10, 25, 10, 10, 25, 10
9	20	11	620	3.1	19, 25, 19, 25, 19, 25, 19, 25, 19, 25, 19
10	30	7	270	0.9	10, 25, 10, 25, 10, 25, 10
11	200	11	340	0.17	10, 25, 10, 25, 10, 25, 10, 25, 10, 25, 10

(we use A for `atmioe`, V for `veh_lat` and H for `hst`). That is, τ_1 has $m(1) = 19$ sub-tasks in total.

Sub-task priorities are determined directly from the process priorities, given in Section 4. Thus, $P_{1,1} = P_{1,3} = 19$ since `atmioe` runs at priority 19, $P_{1,2} = P_{1,4} = 18$ since `veh_lat` runs at priority 18, $P_{1,5} = 25$ since the database runs at priority 25, and so on.

In a similar way, we can determine the parameters T_i, $m(i)$ and $P_{i,j}$ for all eleven tasks of the platoon application. The results are summarized in Table 2.

5.2   Estimation of Execution Times and Other Latencies

We estimate execution times by running many experiments and taking the average. Note that this is not necessarily a conservative approach: we do not compute worst-case times, but averages.

We first estimate the performance of the basic database primitives, namely, reads and updates, by spawning a number of processes, each executing a number of reads/updates, and measuring the total execution time. Then we average over the total number of reads/updates. The results are shown in Figure 4. We see that performance grows almost linearly with the number of processes, although the slope is larger than 1. The extra overhead is probably due to context switching. Based on such measurements, we estimate that a read (resp. update) call takes approximately 40μsecs (resp. 120μsecs). We denote these latencies r and w respectively.

Apart from r and w, we also consider the following latencies: h: latency to handle a hardware interrupt, p: latency to send a synchronous message between processes, t: latency to send an asynchronous trigger from the database to a client, c: context switching delay (includes scheduling). We use the following estimates for the above latencies, based on information from [10]: $h = 10\mu$s, $p = 40\mu$s, $t = 40\mu$s, $c = 30\mu$s.

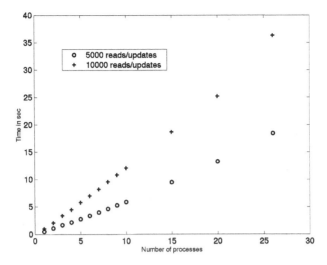

Fig. 4. Performance of the Publish/Subscribe library on a 166 MHz QNX PC.

We ignore floating point computation latencies, since they are extremely small. In experiments we conducted, 20 million floating point operations took approximately 0.12 seconds on the 166 MHz Pentium machine. This averages to approximately 1 microsecond for 166 floating point operations. A typical control computation involves fewer such operations.

We can now estimate the execution time $C_{i,j}$ for each sub-task $\tau_{i,j}$. For example, consider the steering input task τ_4, consisting of six sub-tasks. Sub-task $\tau_{4,1}$ models the interrupt handler of `cani` which sends a message to `canread`, thus, $C_{4,1} = h + p + c$ (we associate the context switch latency with the higher-priority process). Sub-tasks $\tau_{4,2}$ and $\tau_{4,3}$ model `canread` performing a hardware read operation, that is, the request message from `canread` to `cani` and the response message from `cani` to `canread`, thus, $C_{4,2} = C_{4,3} = p + c$. Sub-tasks $\tau_{4,4}$, $\tau_{4,5}$ and $\tau_{4,6}$ model `canread` performing a `clt_update`. Since we are interested in worst-case analysis, we estimate that the bulk of the latency in this operation is associated with $\tau_{4,5}$, i.e., the highest-priority database process. Therefore, we set $C_{4,4} = C_{4,6} \approx 0$ and $C_{4,5} = w$.

5.3 Total CPU Utilization

Based on the above estimates, we can compute the total execution time C_i of each task τ_i. For example, τ_1 involves one hardware interrupt handler, a message from `atmioe` to `veh_lat`, a context switch, a hardware read operation, a database update, a trigger, another context switch, four database reads and 2 updates. In total, we have $C_1 = h + p + c + p + c + w + t + c + 4r + 2w = 740\mu s$. Since τ_1 is invoked every 2000 μs, the partial CPU utilization induced by τ_1 is $U_1 = \frac{C_1}{T_1} = \frac{740}{2000} = 37\%$. Similarly, we can compute C_i and U_i for all i. The results are shown in Table 2.

Then, we can compute the total CPU utilization:

$$U = \sum_{i=1}^{11} \frac{C_i}{T_i} = \sum_{i=1}^{11} U_i = 73.67\%$$

We see that $U < 1$, which is a necessary condition for tasks to be schedulable.

5.4 Schedulability Analysis

A special case of our model, where each task consists of a single sub-task (i.e., $m(i) = 1$ for all i), is used by basic rate-monotonic analysis. In this simpler model, there are roughly two ways to check whether a set of tasks is schedulable.

- By computing the total CPU utilization U defined as above, and showing that $U \leq n(2^{1/n} - 1)$, where n is the number of tasks. This is only a sufficient condition for schedulability and assumes that priorities are assigned to the tasks according to the *rate-monotonic* policy, that is, priorities are inversely proportional to task periods. In fact this is an *optimal fixed-priority policy*, in the sense that if the tasks are schedulable with any other fixed-priority policy then they are also schedulable with the rate-monotonic policy [8].
- By performing the so-called *completion-time test* [7,5,6]. This is an exact test, that is, tasks are schedulable if and only if they pass the test.

We briefly describe the completion-time test for the simple model and then show how it is extended for the model of tasks with more than one sub-tasks. We try to make our description self-contained, although we obviously cannot give a thorough presentation. The reader is referred to [5,3,4,6].

Completion-time test for periodic tasks with uniform priority. Given a task i, let $H(i) = \{j | P_j \geq P_i\}$ be the set of indices of tasks of priority higher than or equal to i. Define $W_i(t) = \Sigma_{j \in H(i)} C_j \lceil \frac{t}{T_j} \rceil$. $W_i(t)$ represents the cumulative demand of all tasks of priority at least as i, in the time interval $[0, t]$. Also define the series $S_0^i = \Sigma_{j \in H(i)} C_j$, and $S_{k+1}^i = W_i(S_k^i)$. This series is monotonically increasing, so that eventually we will find a $k(i)$ such that either $S_{k(i)}^i = S_{k(i)+1}^i \leq T_i$, or $S_{k(i)}^i > T_i$. The completion-time theorem says that τ_i always meets its deadline iff $S_{k(i)}^i = S_{k(i)+1}^i \leq T_i$. In order to check whether a set of tasks is schedulable, we have to apply the completion-time test to each task individually.

HKL analysis for periodic tasks with sub-tasks of varying priority. We now return to the more general model which is applicable to our case. We first need some definitions.

The *canonical form* of a task τ_i is a new task τ_i' which consists of a sequence of sub-tasks $\tau_{i,1}', ..., \tau_{i,m(i)'}'$, such that their priorities are strictly increasing, and $\tau_{i,j}'$ has been obtained by "compressing" two or more consecutive sub-tasks of τ_i with equal or decreasing priorities. The priority of $\tau_{i,j}'$ is the smallest among the priorities of the merged sub-sequence. For example, the canonical form of τ_1 in the platoon application (see Table 2) is a task with a single sub-task of priority 18. The canonical form of τ_2 is a task with two sub-tasks with priorities $19, 24$.

The interest behind the canonical form of a task τ_i is as follows. Suppose sub-tasks $\tau_{i,j}$ and $\tau_{i,j+1}$ have priorities 10 and 9, respectively. The fact that $\tau_{i,j}$ has a higher priority than $\tau_{i,j+1}$ does not "help" task τ_i with respect to its total worst-case completion time (WCCT). Indeed, $\tau_{i,j+1}$ can be preempted or blocked by other sub-tasks of priority 9 or higher, and this will delay the entire task τ_i. Therefore, the WCCT of τ_i would be the same if the priority of $\tau_{i,j}$ was lowered to 9. This result allows one, instead of checking whether τ_i is schedulable, to check whether its canonical form is schedulable.

The latter can be checked with a modified version of the completion-time test, which uses an extra term, $B(i)$, called the *blocking time* of τ_i. $B(i)$ represents the amount of time τ_i can be blocked because of other tasks. We give a simplified description of how to compute $B(i)$ here. A more detailed example can be found in the full version of the paper.

To compute $B(i)$, tasks are classified according to their *relative priority levels* with respect to the minimum priority, $Pmin_i$, of τ_i. For example, $Pmin_1 = 18$ and the sequence of priorities of sub-tasks of τ_4 is $19, 10, 19, 10, 25, 10$, or, relative to 18, H, L, H, L, H, L (H stands for "higher or equal" and L for "strictly lower"). We say that τ_4 is a *type 2*, or $(H^+, L^+)^+$, task with respect to τ_1. There other other types of tasks relatively to τ_1. For example, a task of type 1 or H^+ can preempt τ_1 multiple times, since all sub-tasks have priority at least as the lowest priority of τ_1. A task of type 2 can preempt τ_1 at most once, since it must eventually execute a strictly lower priority segment L^+ and will therefore be preempted by τ_1. Each type of tasks j induces a blocking time $B_j(1)$ for τ_1. $B(1)$ equals the sum of $B_j(1)$ over all types j. For τ_1, we find $B(1) = 1220$.

We are now ready to generalize the completion-time test. Given a task τ_i, re-define $W_i(t) = \Sigma_{j \in H_1(i)} C_j \lceil \frac{t}{T_j} \rceil$. Also re-define the series $S_0^i = C_i + B(i) + \Sigma_{j \in H_1(i)} C_j$, and $S_{k+1}^i = C_i + B(i) + W_i(S_k^i)$. As in the simple model case, τ_i is schedulable iff there is a $k(i)$ such that $S_{k(i)}^i = S_{k(i)+1}^i \leq T_i$.

Applying the completion-time test to τ_1, we have:

$$S_0^1 = C_1 + B(1) + \Sigma_{j \in H_1(1)} C_j = C_1 + B(1) + C_2 + C_3 = 2460$$
$$S_1^1 = C_1 + B(1) + W_1(S_0^1) = C_1 + B(1) + C_2 \lceil \frac{2460}{4000} \rceil + C_3 \lceil \frac{2460}{8000} \rceil = 2460$$

We find that $S_0^1 = S_1^1 > T_1$, which means that the deadline of τ_1 may be violated.

6   Conclusions

We have described the embedded software architecture of a real automated vehicle control system and argued that the properties of the architecture make it attractive for other real-time control applications as well. We have also shown that the architecture is amenable to a formal schedulability analysis.

The idea of a publish/subscribe inter-process communication scheme is certainly not new. The scheme used in AVCSS has some differences with respect to other P/S architectures. For instance, it is not a "pure" P/S scheme as the one proposed in [12], where messages are sent only from publishers to subscribers. Instead, the P/S of AVCSS maintains the notion of a shared memory, where readers can access variables (atomically) at any time, while at the same time having the possibility to subscribe by setting triggers.

Performing the schedulability analysis manually has been both tedious and error-prone. Therefore, it is important that such analysis techniques be automated. This seems possible, once logical tasks have been identified and execution times of sub-tasks have been computed. It is also important to provide meaningful feedback to the user (e.g., in the form of a counter-example) in case some tasks miss their deadlines, as well as directives of which parameters to modify (e.g., priorities) in order to achieve schedulability.

Our estimation of execution times has been admittedly crude. However, our purpose was not to estimate execution times accurately but to show the applicability of the analysis in our architecture. In order for the analysis results to be valid, accurate *worst-case execution times* (WCET) of sub-tasks should be computed. This is an active area of research (e.g., see [11,9]), outside the scope of this paper.

The schedulability analysis has shown that the deadline of at least one logical task (the lateral input task) may be violated. If such a violation is indeed possible (and not the result of a too conservative estimation of execution times) its consequences on control are still unclear. The question is: does an infrequent violation of the deadline have grave consequences in the control of the vehicle? The answer may be no: if the deadline is violated, say, once every 10 seconds, then the control laws may be robust enough to compensate for the lateness in the outputs. Unfortunately, to answer this question, we need a reasoning methodology combining elements of both control and scheduling theory, but we lack such a methodology today.

Acknowledgments. I would like to thank Paul Kretz from PATH and Raj Rajkumar from CMU. I am also grateful to the anonymous reviewer who found an error in an earlier version of this paper.

References

1. N.C. Audsley, A. Burns, R.I. Davis, K.W. Tindell, and A.J. Wellings. Fixed priority pre-emptive scheduling: An historical perspective. *Real Time Systems*, 8(2-3), 1995.
2. A. Burns, K.W. Tindell, and A.J. Wellings. Effective analysis for engineering real-time fixed priority schedulers. *IEEE Trans. Software Engineering*, 21(5):475–480, 1995.
3. M. Harbour, M.H. Klein, and J. Lehoczky. Fixed priority scheduling of periodic tasks with varying execution priority. In *IEEE Real-Time Systems Symposium*, 1991.
4. M.G. Harbour, M.H. Klein, , and J.P. Lehoczky. Timing analysis for fixed-priority scheduling of hard real-time systems. *IEEE Transactions on Software Engineering*, 20(1):13–28, 1994.

5. M.G. Harbour, M.H. Klein, R. Obenza, B. Pollak, and T. Ralya. *A Practitioner's Handbook for Real-Time Analysis: Guide to Rate-Monotonic Analysis for Real-Time Systems*. Kluwer, 1993.
6. M.H. Klein, J. Lehoczky, and R. Rajkumar. Rate monotonic analysis for real-time industrial computing. *IEEE Computer*, January 1994.
7. J. Lehoczky, L. Sha, , and Y. Ding. The rate monotonic scheduling algorithm: Exact characterization and average case behavior. In *IEEE Real-Time Systems Symposium*, 1989.
8. C.L. Liu and J. Layland. Scheduling algorithms for multiprogramming in a hard real-time environment. *Journal of the ACM*, 20(1):46–61, January 1973.
9. Swedish WCET Network. Home page: www.docs.uu.se/artes/wcet/.
10. QNX overview.
    Link: `www.qnx.com/literature/whitepapers/archoverview.html`.
11. P. Puschner and A. Burns. A review of WCET analysis. *Real Time Systems: Special Issue on Worst-Case Execution-Time Analysis*, 18(2/3), 2000.
12. R. Rajkumar, M. Gagliardi, and L. Sha. The real-time publisher/subscriber inter-process communication model for distributed real-time systems: Design and implementation. In *IEEE Real-time Technology and Applications Symposium*, 1995.
13. L. Sha, R. Rajkumar, and S.S. Sathaye. Generalized rate-monotonic scheduling theory: A framework for developing real-time systems. *IEEE Proceedings*, January 1994.
14. J. Stankovic, M. Spuri, K. Ramamritham, , and G. Buttazzo. *Deadline Scheduling For Real-Time Systems: EDF and Related Algorithms*. Kluwer Academic Publishers, 1998.
15. P. Varaiya. Smart cars on smart roads: Problems of control. *IEEE Transactions on Automatic Control*, 38(2):195–207, February 1993.

Formal Modeling and Analysis
of Advanced Scheduling Features
in an Avionics RTOS*

Darren Cofer and Murali Rangarajan

Honeywell Laboratories, Minneapolis MN
{darren.cofer,murali.rangarajan}@honeywell.com

Abstract. Integrated modular avionics (IMA) architectures found in modern aircraft contain applications of different criticalities executing on the same CPU. The execution of these applications must be scheduled so that they do not inadvertently consume CPU time that has been budgeted for other applications. This scheduling function may be performed by a real-time operating system (RTOS) that provides time partitioning guarantees. The large number of variables affecting application execution interleavings makes it difficult and costly to verify time partitioning by traditional means.

This paper reports on our efforts to use model checking techniques to verify time partitioning properties in an avionics RTOS. Our modeling and analysis is based on the actual embedded software so as to capture the implementation details of the scheduler. We focus here on several advanced scheduling features of the RTOS that are particularly challenging to verify.

1 Introduction

The growing complexity and the safety-critical requirements of the embedded software in avionics systems present many challenges to current test-based verification technology. The use of formal verification methods can increase design assurance by exploring a larger range of execution interleavings than can feasibly be covered by testing. Furthermore, model checking can decrease development and testing costs by finding design errors early in the development cycle. Our experience in formally modeling and verifying key requirements of actual avionics software shows that realistic models can be produced and analyzed using state-of-the-art modeling checking tools.

Under a cooperative research agreement with NASA's Langley Research Center, Honeywell is developing and applying formal techniques to verify safety-critical properties in Integrated Modular Avionics (IMA) components such as the Deos^{TM} real-time operating system. We believe that the use of formal techniques to increase avionics software design assurance will be crucial to aviation safety over the next decade.

---

* This material is based upon work supported in part by NASA under cooperative agreement NCC-1-399.

A. Sangiovanni-Vincentelli and J. Sifakis (Eds.): EMSOFT 2002, LNCS 2491, pp. 138–152, 2002.

This work and the approach taken began with an earlier project undertaken with the Automated Software Engineering group at NASA Ames [9]. The model checker SPIN [5] was used to model and verify a portion of the original version of the Deos scheduler. In that project and the current work the model has been derived directly from the actual flight code so that the analysis results will be closely connected to the real system.

Our current work focuses on the modeling and analysis of advanced features of the latest version of Deos, such as slack scheduling and aperiodic interrupt servicing. These new features add considerably to the complexity of the software. Formal analysis of the system has allowed us to examine its behavior over a wider range of scenarios than is possible by testing alone and increased our confidence in the correct operation of the system.

1.1   The Deos RTOS

The Deos real-time operating system [1] was developed by Honeywell for use in our Primus Epic avionics suite for business, regional, and commuter jet aircraft. Deos hosts many safety-critical applications in these aircraft, including primary flight controls, autopilots, and displays.

Deos is a microkernel-based real-time operating system that supports flexible Integrated Modular Avionics applications by providing both space partitioning at the process level and time partitioning at the thread level. Space partitioning ensures that no process can modify the memory of another process without authorization, while time partitioning ensures that a thread's access to its CPU time budget cannot be impaired by the actions of any other thread.

The combination of space and time partitioning makes it possible for applications of different criticalities to run on the same platform at the same time, while ensuring that low-criticality applications do not interfere with the operation of high-criticality applications. This noninterference guarantee reduces system verification and maintenance costs by enabling an application to be changed and re-verified without re-verifying all of the other applications in the system. Deos itself is certified to DO-178B Level A [11], the highest level of safety-critical certification for avionics software.

The main components of a Deos-based system are illustrated in Figure 1. A given software application consists of one or more processes. Each process is executed as one or more threads. All threads in a process share the same virtual address space in memory. Each hardware platform in the system has a separate instance of the Deos kernel running on it. The kernel communicates with its underlying hardware via its hardware abstraction layer (HAL) and platform abstraction layer (PAL) interfaces. The HAL provides access to the CPU and its registers and is considered part of Deos itself. The PAL provides access to other platform hardware, such as I/O devices and interrupt signals. The application threads interact with the kernel and obtain the services it provides by means of a set of functions called the application program interface (API).

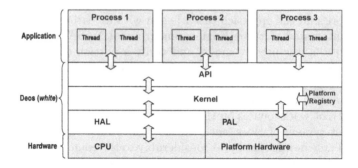

Fig. 1. Deos components (white boxes) and terminology.

1.2   Previous Work

Honeywell engineers and researchers at NASA Ames produced a model for use with the SPIN model checking tool developed at Bell Labs. The model was translated from a core "slice" of the Deos scheduler. This model was then checked for violations of a global time partitioning invariant, using SPIN's automated state space exploration techniques. We successfully verified the time partitioning invariant over a restricted range of thread types. We also introduced into the model a subtle scheduling error, originally discovered and fixed during the standard Deos review process; the model checker quickly detected that the error produced a violation of the time partitioning invariant. Results of this work are documented in [9].

Encouraged by the success of the early effort, we have continued to apply model-checking to Deos software, incorporating advanced scheduling features and improving the fidelity of model. This paper describes our current modeling work and the analysis results we have obtained.

2   Problem Description

Deos must ensure that every application gets its allotted amount of CPU time every period. This provision is called time partitioning, and is accomplished by the Deos scheduler. At system startup, each process is given a fraction of the total available CPU resource, called the process's CPU budget, for its use. The process then allocates its CPU budget to its threads. Deos ensures that each of the threads has access to its allocated CPU budget every period.

There are three types of threads managed by Deos: the idle thread, the main thread, and user threads. The idle thread does nothing and has the lowest priority in the system. It is executed whenever there is nothing else for the scheduler to run. Each Deos process has a main thread that is automatically created at startup and manages resources allocated to the process. The main thread may create any number of user threads to perform the work to be done by the application process. Resources for user threads (such as their time budgets) are provided by the main thread. User threads may be static and created at system startup, or dynamically created at run time. Both main and user threads may delete themselves.

The Deos scheduler enforces time partitioning using a Rate Monotonic Scheduling (RMS) policy [7]. RMS assigns thread priorities so that shorter period (high rate) threads are assigned a higher priority than long period (low rate) threads. Using this policy, threads run periodically at specified rates and they are given per-period CPU time budgets, which are constrained at thread creation so that the system cannot be overutilized.

In Deos, all periods are required to be harmonic. This means that the length of each period is an integer multiple of the length of the next shorter period. Harmonic periods allow Deos to achieve (near) 100% utilization of the available CPU time.

At the start of the thread's period the scheduler places it on a list of threads that are ready to execute in that period. When the thread is at the head of the list for its period, the scheduler starts it by switching the current execution context to that thread. The thread executes until one of three conditions occurs:

- The thread is preempted by the scheduler because a higher priority thread (with a faster rate) is ready to run. The thread is returned to the ready list for its period so that it can be resumed later in its period.
- The thread voluntarily waits for the start of its next period because it has completed its work for the current period.
- The thread uses all of its allotted time and must be stopped by the scheduler to preserve time partitioning. The thread will be run again in its next period and will receive a **threadBudgetExceeded** exception so that it can take any needed recovery actions.

2.1   Slack Recovery and Scheduling

The restriction of applications to the use of a fixed CPU time budget in each period is often suboptimal. Many applications (for example, network service applications) have highly variable demands on the CPU and have a desired level of performance considerably greater than the minimum required. Giving these applications only the minimum budget necessary will result in low performance; giving them a high enough budget to ensure the performance desired will result in severe underutilization of the CPU most of the time and may "crowd out" other applications that users want to have in the system.

For this reason, the Deos kernel provides a mechanism for *slack scheduling* which assigns unused system time ("slack") to threads on a first-come first-served basis. The classical view of slack scheduling is given in [6]. The version implemented in Deos incorporates several major modifications of this view necessitated by the special features of Deos (e.g. the capability to dynamically activate and deactivate threads, and the existence of aperiodic threads).

Honeywell's first real-time implementation of slack scheduling was in the MetaH architecture description and integration tool [4]. We later adapted slack algorithms to support incremental processing [3] and then dynamic threads and time partitioning [2] for use in Deos. The slack scheduling feature has been used to increase the throughput (3x) and dramatically reduce the reserved time budget of an FTP stack hosted on Deos. Slack scheduling is also being used in Primus Epic displays to improve the quality of non-critical display elements when additional computing time is available.

2.2 Servicing Aperiodic Interrupts

Deos permits applications to respond to hardware interrupts via the activation of an interrupt service routine (ISR) thread. An ISR thread has a period and budget associated with it, and like any other thread it is guaranteed access to its CPU budget in each of its periods. An ISR thread is activated by the arrival of its associated interrupt. Since the timing of the arrival of the interrupt can not be (in general) predicted, Deos does not guarantee that the ISR thread will complete in the same period that the interrupt arrived. This can happen, for example, if an interrupt arrives near the end of the thread's period when the time remaining is less than the thread's budget.

To prevent an unbounded overloading of the system by bursts of an interrupt, an ISR thread has a period and a budget just like other periodic threads. Deos guarantees that the ISR will not consume more than its allocated CPU budget in each period, but Deos does not restrict the rate or number of interrupts that arrive so long as the ISR thread's CPU budget is sufficient. System overhead (e.g., context switch time and cache effects) associated with preempting a running thread are all charged against the ISR thread's budget.

ISR threads have two properties that differentiate them from other periodic threads. First, they execute at a priority at least as high as any periodic threads, and may execute at strictly higher priorities. Second, they may be activated by the receipt of a specified interrupt instead of on a fixed and periodic basis. An ISR thread may also execute periodically, if desired.

If an ISR thread is preempted with a CPU `timeBudgetExceeded` exception, the interrupt remains masked. At the thread's next period, it is given a fresh budget and will execute with a raised `timeBudgetExceeded` exception.

3 Scheduler Modeling

We have limited the scope of our modeling effort to the Deos scheduler and those elements of the kernel that impact timing properties of the system. Our objectives are as follows:

- Formally demonstrate that the time partitioning guarantees of Deos hold under all executions of supported by the scheduler.
- Follow the actual Deos implementation as closely as possible in the model.

For the purposes of this paper and the models described here, scheduler overhead time has been assumed to be zero or, equivalently, accumulated with the execution of individual threads. However, there are many interesting issues associated with how the scheduler accounts for overhead time under various circumstances. Our work to explicitly model and verify overhead accounting in Deos will be reported separately.

3.1   Model Structure

The time partitioning properties of the Deos kernel cannot be analyzed independently since the kernel on its own doesn't actually do anything independent of its environment. The environment in this case consists of:

1. application software threads that invoke kernel services
2. platform hardware that provides timers and interrupts to the kernel.

Models in SPIN (or, more correctly, its modeling language PROMELA) are specified as collections of concurrently executing processes that communicate via message channels. There are three types of processes defined in our model: the Deos kernel, threads, and the platform environment. The processes and their interconnecting channels are illustrated in Figure 2. Channels represent vari-

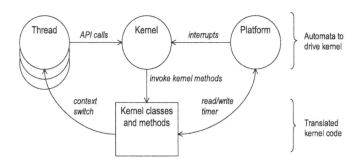

Fig. 2. Structure of kernel and environment model in SPIN.

ous synchronization mechanisms depending on the processes that they connect. Messages sent from threads to the kernel represent calls to services in the kernel API. Messages from the kernel to threads represent context switches to stop and resume thread execution. Messages from the platform to the kernel represent hardware interrupts, either from timers or physical I/O. Messages from the kernel to the platform are used to read and write timer registers. In all cases channels are defined to buffer zero messages, meaning that all process interactions are rendezvous synchronizations requiring the sender and receiver to be ready at the same time.

The Deos kernel process is by far the biggest and most complex process in the model. It consists of a simple state machine that represents a portion of the user API and the translated kernel code itself.

The kernel code that we are modeling consists of C++ classes and methods taken directly from the current Deos software. These structures have been translated into PROMELA by a very straightforward (though manual) procedure ensuring that the model remains in very close agreement with the actual software.

In the real system, the threads or the platform interface software would directly invoke functions in the kernel API, trapping to the desired service. Since we have modeled these interactions as PROMELA messages some mechanism is required to invoke the functions in the translated kernel code at the appropriate time. The top level state machine in the kernel model serves this purpose. It first calls all the initialization code in the kernel and then loops in an event handling structure. When it receives messages from the threads or the platform interface corresponding to function calls, it invokes the appropriate kernel function in response.

The kernel can respond to three types of interrupts from the platform environment:

1. System tick (`tickintrpt`). This is a periodic signal generated by the platform hardware that is used by the kernel to identify the start of all periods. Each period must be a multiple of the system tick rate. On receipt of a system tick, the `handleSystemTickInterrupt()` method is invoked in the kernel.
2. Timer (`timerintrpt`). This is the time-out signal from the thread timer. It indicates that a thread has reached the end of its budgeted time. On receipt of a timer interrupt the `handleTimerInterrupt()` method is invoked in the kernel.
3. Platform interrupt (`platformintrpt`). This is a user interrupt that may be generated by an I/O device in the system. If the interrupt is not masked, the `raisePlatformInterrupt()` method is invoked in the kernel.

The kernel can invoke the following services in the platform interface, again modeled as PROMELA messages:

1. Start timer (`start`). This sends a desired starting value computed by the kernel to the timer.
2. Read timer (`getTimeRemaining`). This reads the current value in the thread timer. The timer value is returned as a field in the `timeRemaining` message sent in reply by the platform process.

The kernel handles the following requests from the threads, each of which is analogous to a function in the kernel API:

1. Create thread (`create`). This indicates that a new thread is to be created by invoking the `createThread()` method in the kernel. The parameters associated with the thread to be created are supplied by reference to a template in the Deos registry. The desired thread template number is specified in the message and passed in as an argument to the API function.
2. Delete thread (`delete`). This indicates that a thread wishes to be deleted from the system by invoking the `deleteThread()` method in the kernel.

3. Wait for next period (`finishedforperiod`). This indicates that the calling thread has completed its work for this period and wishes to be suspended until the start of its next period. On receipt, the `waitUntilNextPeriod()` method is invoked in the kernel.
4. Wait for next interrupt (`waitforintrpt`). This message has been added to support the analysis of ISR threads. Similar to "wait for next period," this indicates that the caller has completed its work and wishes to be suspended until the arrival of its next triggering interrupt event. On receipt, the `waitUntilNextInterrupt()` method is invoked in the kernel.

The kernel can send the following two messages to the threads to perform a context switch:

1. Stop thread (`stop`). This signals the thread to suspend execution and wait to be resumed by the kernel. This may occur because the scheduler needs to run a higher priority thread or because the thread exceeded its time budget for the current period.
2. Resume thread (`resume`). This signals the thread to continue execution from the point at which it was previously suspended.

In reality, these are not actual requests sent to the threads. Via its hardware interface (HAL), the kernel triggers a context switch causing execution to transfer from one thread to another.

Most of the interesting time partitioning issues are associated with the scheduling interactions between threads. Therefore, our model has a single process consisting of its main thread and several dynamically created user threads. The threads in our model do not have to do any actual work. They provide part of the execution environment needed to analyze the Deos kernel and so they only need to exercise the kernel API in appropriate ways.

When the model starts, a SPIN process is created for each thread that we plan to model. The thread automaton starts in a 'not created' state and may non-deterministically choose to create itself at some time in the future. In reality, the thread would be created by the kernel during Deos initialization (for static threads) or by an API call issued by an existing thread (such as the main thread). We have taken the approach of having a thread create itself for simplicity, as it doesn't really matter who issues the thread creation API call – only that it can occur at some indeterminate point in time.

The idle thread does not participate in the create, delete, or finished for period services. It is created by default at startup and only stopped and resumed by the kernel.

3.2   Translation from Code

Our translation approach is based on the techniques developed by researchers at NASA Ames. The Deos kernel is written in an object-oriented style using C++. In contrast, PROMELA, the input language of the SPIN model checker, is a process-based imperative style language that uses shared memory and message passing for communication. In order to model objects within the framework of processes, and to make verification tractable, four basic techniques are used.

- Use data type abstractions for variables such as counters. For example, integers are modeled as bytes or even booleans, where possible.
- Model C++ objects as arrays and object pointers as indices into the arrays.
- Convert methods into inline macros and to replace recursion with distinct function calls.
- Flatten the inheritance hierarchy.

The details of these translations are described in [10].

3.3   Platform Environment

The purpose of the platform environment process in the model is to represent the hardware that the kernel interacts with during execution including timers, their associated interrupts, and other user-level interrupts such as those from physical I/O.

SPIN itself does not model time. One of the most important and challenging functions of the platform environment process is its responsibility for the elapsing of time in the model. This manifests itself in the way that the platform determines when to generate tick and timer events and the clock values reported to the kernel.

One approach documented in [8] to build an environment for the model uses progressive refinements to develop a correct model of the environment. In this work a universal environment which can generate all possible behaviors without any constraints was used as the starting point. When the kernel was verified in conjunction with this environment counterexamples were produced that were the result of illegal behaviors in the environment. The counterexamples were analyzed and eliminated by adding constraining expressions in linear temporal logic (LTL) that capture the illegal behaviors of the environment. This process would be repeated until a genuine counterexample (or completely correct behavior) was achieved.

The timing model we have used corresponds most closely to that used in discrete event simulations. At any step in the simulation, one or more events are eligible to occur next. The model selects one of these non-deterministically and processes that event. If there is any time associated with the occurrence of the event, the clock is advanced by that amount, and any newly eligible events are added as candidates for the next simulation step.

The automaton controlling the time-related activities of the environment is shown in Figure 3. The variable tick_time represents the time until the next system tick event while time remaining represents the time until the thread timer expires. If `tick_time` is less than `time_remaining`, the next event that can happen is a system tick, but if `time_remaining` is less than `tick_time` the time-out event must occur next. If they are equal either event may be chosen to occur non-deterministically. Platform interrupts produced by HW I/O (the

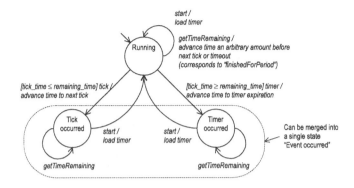

Fig. 3. New timer automaton from platform environment process.

`platformintrpt` message) can be sent to the kernel at any time. On the occurrence of a system tick, time is advanced to the point of the tick event by decrementing `time_remaining` by the value of `tick_time` and reloading `tick_time` with the length of a tick. On the expiration of the thread timer, time is advanced to the point of the time-out event by decrementing tick_time by the value of `time_remaining` and setting `time_remaining` to zero.

The selection of the amount of time that elapses on a finished for period event (the amount of time actually consumed by the thread) is important in determining what behaviors can be realized in the model. In the original timer environment this value was permitted to be either zero, half of the time remaining on the thread timer, or all of the time remaining. This is an approximation of the real behavior possible for a thread but was felt to be a reasonable simplification to keep the state space manageable.

However, there is a problem with this approach. If the time until the next system tick is less than half the time remaining on the thread timer then the only option actually available in the model (such that elapsed is less that the time of the next tick) is to have the thread consume zero time. This does not seem to permit a wide enough range of possibilities for executions in the system. To ensure that there are always three options available in the new timer environment, we compute min(`tick_time`, `time_remaining`) and allow the selection of zero, half, or all of this value for the elapsed time.

3.4 Slack

The introduction of slack scheduling greatly complicates the operation of time partitioning in Deos. Careful analysis is required to ensure that the use of slack will never imperil time partitioning; that is, the use of slack by one thread cannot prevent any other thread from having access to its fixed allocation of budget within its period. The addition of slack required a number of fundamental changes in the scheduler itself, our model of it, and the techniques we used to evaluate the time partitioning property.

Slack is CPU time made available from two sources:

1. If the system is not 100% utilized (i.e. the sum of all active thread utilizations is less than 100% of the CPU time), the unused utilization can be used as slack. This sort of slack is referred to as "periodic timeline slack." Deos calculates the amount of periodic timeline slack, adjusting it in response to (de)activations of threads, and at the beginning of each fastest period makes an increment available. For instance, if periodic timeline slack constitutes 20% of the total CPU time, and the length of the fastest period is 25000 microseconds, then Deos makes available 5000 microseconds at the beginning of each fastest period. Periodic timeline slack can be used by threads at any rate.
2. If a thread completes for period without using its entire allotted budget for the period, the leftover portion of the thread's budget can be used as slack. This sort of slack is referred to as *reclaimed slack*. Deos makes reclaimed slack available immediately upon the early completion of a thread. Reclaimed slack cannot be used by threads that run at a faster rate than the thread whose budget is reclaimed, but can be used by any thread at an equal or slower rate.

A thread may be a "slack requester," meaning it wishes to use system slack, or a "non-slack requester," meaning it does not wish to use slack. The slack requester attribute of each thread template is specified in the system registry.

The thread scheduling state diagram showing the effect of slack-enabled threads is shown in Figure 4. If a thread is a slack requester, and it exceeds its allocated CPU budget for a given period, Deos evaluates the amount of slack available to the thread. If that amount is sufficiently large, Deos grants the thread the ability to run on slack time, giving it a temporary budget equal to the amount of slack available. This slack is granted on a "best-effort" basis, meaning that there is no guarantee the thread will actually get to use all of the slack granted it; another thread may preempt the slack consumer and use the remaining slack itself.

If a thread exceeds its budget and sufficient slack is not available, Deos places the thread on a list of threads waiting for slack to become available. When more slack is made available by a period start or early thread completion, Deos selects a thread from this list and makes the thread ready to run so it can use that slack. If a thread never gets a chance to use slack for the remainder of its period, Deos makes it ready to run at the beginning of its next period so it can run again on its fixed budget.

3.5   Interrupt Handling

The only difference between a regular thread and an ISR thread as far as scheduling is concerned is the addition of the waiting for interrupt state and its associated transitions (dotted lines in Figure 4). Waiting for interrupt is the only state in which the thread's interrupt is unmasked. When the interrupt arrives,

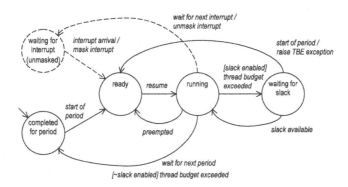

Fig. 4. Thread state in scheduler with slack recover. Additional operations for ISR threads are shown with dotted lines.

the associated interrupt event in the scheduler makes the associated thread ready to execute in the same way that the start of period event makes all associated threads ready to execute. The interrupt is also masked at the time of its arrival, inhibiting additional interrupts until service of the first occurrence is completed. When the ISR completes its service it calls `waitUntilNextInterrupt()`. This causes the scheduler to suspend the thread (as it would in response to a `waitUntilNextPeriod()` call) and unmask the associated interrupt.

Many changes to the model of the Deos kernel were necessary to incorporate interrupt handling. All the changes will support multiple interrupts and ISR threads, but currently only a single interrupt event is being exercised. A new channel was added between the platform environment and the kernel to represent the arrival of hardware interrupts from the platform. The platform environment was modified to add the ability to send a platformintrpt message to the kernel at any time. However, the kernel response is only enabled when the interrupt is unmasked. The arrival of an unmasked interrupt causes the `raisePlatformInterrupt()` method to be invoked in the scheduler.

Similarly, user thread processes have been given the ability to generate a `waitForNextInterrupt` message to the kernel. This message can only be sent if the thread has a valid interrupt number associated with it. The scheduler invokes the `waitUntilNextInterrupt()` method for the thread in response.

The principal data structure by which interrupts are described and handled is the `InterruptEvent` class. An interrupt event is created for each interrupt in the system in much the same way that a start of period event is associated with each period in the system. The interrupt event captures the mapping between interrupt numbers and ISR threads and stores state and configuration information such as the ISR execution priority and whether or not the ISR thread is waiting and ready to respond to the arrival of an interrupt.

In addition, the functions `raisePlatformInterrupt()`, `maskPlatform-Interrupt()`, and `unmaskPlatformInterrupt()` were included from the HAL code.

4   Analysis Results

The resulting model with slack scheduling and ISR handling incorporated has been used to analyze the time partitioning guarantees of Deos. As a result of these advanced features, a new means of checking the time partitioning property had to be devised. We have also analyzed the model to look for any non-progress cycles.

Our analysis has focused on a fairly generic configuration consisting of three thread rates (periods) and four threads (main thread, two user threads, and the idle thread). The threads have variously been configured to be slack consumers and/or ISR threads. Many combinations of thread budgets have been investigated.

4.1   Time Partitioning

In our original model we attempted to verify the following liveness property, which is necessary (but not sufficient) for time partitioning to hold: If the main thread does not have 100% CPU utilization, then the idle thread should run during every longest period. This condition is captured by the LTL property:

$$\Box(\texttt{beginperiod} \rightarrow (!\texttt{endperiod}\ U\texttt{idle}))$$

That is, it is always the case that when the longest period begins, it will not end until the idle thread runs.

When slack scheduling is added to the model a different timing property is needed. If the scheduler has allocated all available slack to other threads then the idle thread will not be given a chance to run in every period. The new property is captured as an assertion and is embedded in the existing control flow (i.e. no new looping structures introduced) of the model. It is invoked in the processing associated with the handling of the tick interrupts.

The time partitioning assertion consists of two parts: one referring to the currently running thread and the other referring to the threads in the runnable list that belong to the period that is just ending and all faster periods. It states that the thread under consideration is either the idle thread, or it received its full budgeted CPU time, or it gave up its unused budget voluntarily. In other words, this assertion ensures that all the threads other than the idle thread receive their full CPU budget.

The time partitioning property was analyzed for the baseline configuration with a main thread and two dynamic user threads. With all of the new structures for ISR handling added to the model but with neither thread designated as an ISR, the property was found to hold. However, when one of the threads is associated with a platform interrupt the property can no longer be verified. This is because once `waitUntilNextInterrupt()` is called, a thread has essentially given up its claim on its periodic time budget (similar to `waitUntilNextPeriod`) and no strict guarantees can be made about its later availability. A revised assertion is needed to accurately capture the guarantees made to both the ISR thread and the normal threads with respect to the impact of interrupt handling.

4.2   Non-progress Cycles

Most of our previous model checking work involved the use of assertions and
LTL properties, as well as checks for deadlock, for detecting errors. We have
augmented our regular verification techniques to include a check for livelock or
"non-progress cycles." Checking for non-progress cycles involves placing progress
labels in strategic locations in the model. If the model includes a cycle that does
not contain a progress label, it signifies the presence of a livelock. In our model
of Deos the particular livelock case in which we are interested is any cycle that
does not contain a system tick event, indicating that time is not elapsing as
expected.

This approach was used to find a livelock in the original non-slack version of
the code. In the non-slack version, the Idle thread runs in the fastest period, with
its priority artificially set to the lowest value. Its budget is equal to the length of
the fastest period. The assumption here is that Idle would use its entire budget
only if there is no other thread in the system, at which point, it doesn't matter
how long Idle runs. But when the user threads are either deleted or completed for
period, and the main thread also completes for period without using any time,
the Idle thread runs for a whole period. At the end of that period, its remaining
budget is zero. If the end of that period coincides with the end of the longest
period, the user and main threads get fresh quotas when they run in the next
(fastest) period, enabling them to run through to the end of that fastest period.
This means that Idle does not get a chance to run at all in this period and
causes the scheduler to think that Idle is not yet eligible for a refreshed budget.
Therefore, the scheduler starts the timer with the remaining time of the Idle
thread, which is zero since it ran for the whole period when it ran the previous
time. Therefore, the timer gets started with zero, and immediately interrupts
the Idle thread without advancing time at all, resulting in the livelock condition.

This live lock cannot occur in the real system. In our model the calls to the
timer consume zero time, whereas in the real system some small amount of time
would elapse. Therefore, even if the situation does arise, each call to the timer
consumes some finite amount of time, which means that at some point the tick
interrupt would occur causing scheduling to be performed again and ending the
livelock.

5   Conclusion

This paper has described recent work to model key portions of the Deos scheduler and verify its time partitioning features using the model checker SPIN. The
main elements included in the model to date are the core preemptive fixed priority scheduling mechanism, dynamic thread creation, slack time recovery, and
interrupt service routines. Future work will cover the following features:

1. The kernel overhead has been assumed to be negligible in the current model.
   However, its value is significant in certain scheduling operations (including
   ISR handling). In the case of an ISR, the thread must have sufficient budget

to compensate the thread it interrupts for both of the context switches (in and out) it causes. Including realistic values for overhead times and modeling the scheduler accounting mechanisms will enhance the fidelity of our model for these cases.

2. The process of translating software to produce a PROMELA model is very labor intensive. In principle, most of the translation steps can be automated and we are currently working on tools to do this. We are also working with researchers at KSU to apply their methods for automatic code slicing and abstraction to produce tractable models.

3. The abstraction which limits a thread's time consumption to 0/half/all of the available time covers the critical boundary cases that we are interested in but has not yet been demonstrated to be valid in the sense of providing complete coverage of all possible scheduler behaviors. We are investigating the use of theorem proving tools to establish the validity of this abstraction.

References

1. Design Description Document for the Digital Engine Operating System. Honeywell specification no. PS7022409.
2. Binns, Pam: A robust high-performance time partitioning algorithm: the Digital Engine Operating System (Deos) approach. 20th Digital Avionics System Conference (2001)
3. Binns, Pam: Incremental rate monotonic scheduling for improved control system performance. IEEE Real-Time Applications Symposium (1997)
4. Binns, Pam: Scheduling slack in MetaH. IEEE Real-Time Systems Symposium work-in-progress session (1996)
5. Holzmann, G: The model checker SPIN. IEEE Transactions on Software Engineering **23** (1997) 279–295
6. Lehoczky, J. P. and S. Ramos-Thuel: An optimal algorithm for scheduling aperiodic tasks in fixed-priority preemptive systems. IEEE Real-Time Systems Symposium (1992)
7. Liu, C. L. and J. W. Leyland: Scheduling Algorithms for Multiprogramming in a Hard Real Time Environment. Journal of the ACM **20** (1973) 46–61
8. Pasareanu, Corina S.: Deos Kernel: Environment Modeling using LTL Assumptions. NASA Ames Technical Report NASA-ARC-IC-2000-196 (2000)
9. Penix, J., W. Visser, E. Engstrom, A. Larson, and N. Weininger: Verification of Time Partitioning in the Deos Scheduler Kernel. International Conf. on Software Engineering (2000)
10. Penix, J., W. Visser, E. Engstrom, A. Larson, and N. Weininger: Translation and Verification of the Deos Scheduling Kernel. Technical report, NASA Ames Research Center/Honeywell Technology Center (1999)
11. RTCA/DO-178B: Software Considerations in Airborne Systems and Equipment Certification. RTCA, Inc., Washington DC (1992)

Scalable Applications
for Energy-Aware Processors

Giorgio C. Buttazzo

University of Pavia, Italy
buttazzo@unipv.it

Abstract. Next generation processors for battery operated computing
systems can work under different voltage levels to balance speed versus
power consumption. In such a way, the performance of a system can be
degraded to achieve a longer battery duration, or it can be increased
when the battery level is high. Unfortunately, however, in the presence
of timing and resource constraints, the performance of a real-time system does not always improve as the speed of the processor is increased.
Similarly, when reducing the processor speed, the quality of the delivered
service may not always degrade as expected.

This paper presents the potential problems that may arise in a voltage-
controlled real-time system and proposes an approach that allows to
develop real-time applications, whose performance can be scaled in a
controlled fashion as a function of the processor speed.

1 Introduction

Battery operated computing systems are very common today and will increase in
the future to include cell phones, wearable computers, portable televisions, GPS-
based systems, video games, and many other multimedia devices. Most of such
systems run under real-time constraints which determine the quality of service
delivered to the user. An important issue in these systems is the possibility to
control their energy consumption, which directly affects their lifetime, as well as
their performance.

In a computer system, the power consumption is related to the voltage at
which the circuits operate according to an increasing convex function, whose
precise form depends on the specific technology. For example, in CMOS circuits,
the power consumption due to dynamic switching dominates the power lost to
static leakage [11,18] and the dynamic portion P_d of power consumption is given
by

$$P_d = \alpha_T \cdot C_{load} \cdot f_C \cdot V_{dd}^2, \tag{1}$$

where α_T is the activity factor expressing the amount of switching, C_{load} is
the capacitance load, f_C is the clock frequency, and V_{dd}^2 is the supply voltage.
However, the voltage also affects the maximum frequency at which the processor
clock can run. In particular, circuit delay depends on the supply voltage as

$$D = k\frac{V_{dd}}{(V_{dd} - V_t)^2}, \tag{2}$$

A. Sangiovanni-Vincentelli and J. Sifakis (Eds.): EMSOFT 2002, LNCS 2491, pp. 153–165, 2002.

where k is a constant and V_t is the threshold voltage (i.e., the minimum voltage that can be supplied to the processor allowing full and correct functionality) [3].

Equation (1) and (2) express that supply voltage reduction can achieve a quadratic power saving at the expense of a roughly linear frequency reduction. Hence, the amount of energy (power x time) consumed by a portable system can be controlled through the speed and voltage at which the processor operates [13]: we could decide to have a high performace system for a short period, or a lower performance for a longer duration. To exploit such a possibility, next generation processors will be designed to work under different voltage levels, thus enabling applications to run at different speeds.

When increasing the speed, we would expect all the application tasks to finish earlier, in order to improve system's performance. Unfortunately this is not always the case. In [16], Graham showed that several scheduling anomalies may arise when running real-time applications on multiprocessor systems. When tasks share mutually exclusive resources, such anomalies may also arise in a uniprocessor system, as it will be shown in the next session.

Conversely, when voltage is decreased to save energy consumption, we would like the application to run slower in a controlled fashion, where all tasks increase their response times according to some predefined strategy (e.g., depending on their priority level). For reasons similar to the ones described above, this may not always be achieved in the presence of shared resources.

In addition, when the processor speed is decreased, all tasks increase their computation time, so the processor may experience an overload condition. If the overload is permanent, then the application behavior may be quite unpredictable.

The problem of achieving scalable applications in processors with variable speed has recently been addressed by some authors. Al Mok [23] illustrated the potential problems that can occur in a real-time system with variable speed when tasks are non preemptive, but no solution has been proposed to achieve scalability.

Yao et al. [28] described an optimal off-line scheduling algorithm to minimize the total energy consumption while meeting all timing constraints, but no on-line voltage change is assumed. Non-preemptive power-aware scheduling is investigated in [17].

The problem of minimizing the energy consumption in a set of periodic tasks with different power consumption characteristics has been solved by Aydin et al. [3], who proposed an algorithm to find the optimal processor speed for each task. However, tasks are assumed to be independent.

Aydin et al. [4] investigated the problem of scheduling hard real-time tasks using dynamic voltage scaling and proposed an algorithm to compute the optimal processor speed which allows to minimize energy consumption.

In [22], Melhem at al. proposed several scheduling techniques to reduce energy consumption of real-time applications in power-aware operating systems, but the scalability problem is not considered.

In this paper, we propose a computational model which allows to achieve scalability during voltage changes, in order to run real-time applications whose performace can be scaled as a function of the processor speed.

The rest of the paper is organized as follows: Section 2 introduces the problem to be solved and presents some scheduling anomalies that may arise when running real-time applications at different speeds. Section 3 states our terminology and assumptions. Section 4 presents a kernel communication mechanism that allows data sharing among periodic tasks while preserving scalability. Section 5 describes a technique to easily adjust task rates when the speed reduction causes a permanent overload condition. Finally, Section 6 states our conclusions and future work.

2   Problem Statement

This section illustrates the problems that may arise under specific circumstances when executing a set of real-time tasks in a processor with variable speed. Such problems prevent controlling the performance of a real-time application as a function of the voltage, since a task could even increase its response time when executed at a higher speed. Typically, such scheduling anomalies arise when tasks share mutually exclusive resources or are handled by non-preemptive scheduling policies.

Figure 1 illustrates a simple example, where two tasks, τ_1 and τ_2, share a common resource. Task τ_1 has a higher priority, arrives at time $t = 2$ and has a relative deadline $D_1 = 7$. Task τ_2, having lower priority, arrives at time $t = 0$ and has a relative deadline $D_2 = 23$. When the tasks are executed at the nominal speed S_n, τ_1 has a computation time $C_1 = 6$, (where 2 units of time are spent in the critical section), whereas τ_2 has a computation time $C_2 = 18$ (where 12 units of time are spent in the critical section). As shown in Figure 1a, if τ_1 arrives just before τ_2 enters its critical section, it is able to complete before its deadline, without experiencing any blocking. However, if the same task set is executed at a double speed $S = 2S_n$, τ_1 misses its deadline, as clearly illustrated in Figure 1b. This happens because, when τ_1 arrives, τ_2 already granted its resource, causing an extra blocking in the execution of τ_1, due to mutual exclusion.

Figure 2 illustrates another anomalous behavior occuring in a set of three real-time tasks, τ_1, τ_2 and τ_3, running in a non-preemptive mode. Tasks are assigned a fixed priority proportional to their relative deadline, thus τ_1 is the task with the highest priority and τ_3 is the task with the lowest priority. As shown in Figure 2a, when tasks are executed at the nominal speed S_n, τ_1 has a computation time $C_1 = 2$ and completes at time $t = 6$. Conversely, if the same task set is executed with double speed $S = 2S_n$, τ_1 misses its deadline, as clearly illustrated in Figure 2b. This happens because, when τ_1 arrives, τ_3 already started its execution and cannot be preempted (due to the non-preemptive mode).

It is worth observing that a set of non preemptive tasks can be considered as a special case of a set of tasks sharing a single resource (the processor) for their entire execution. In this view, each task executes as it was inside a big

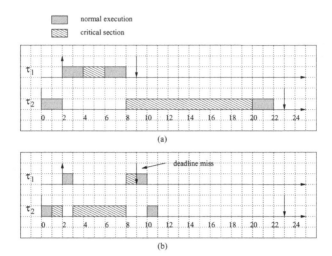

Fig. 1. Scheduling anomaly in the presence of resource constraints: task τ_1 meets its deadline when the processor is executing at its nominal speed S_n (a), but misses its deadline when the speed is doubled (b).

critical section with length equal to the task computation time. Once a task starts executing it locks the common semaphore, thus preventing other tasks from taking the processor.

The following example illustrates the negative effects of a permanent oveload condition caused by a speed reduction. In this case, decreasing the processor speed degrades the system's performance in an uncontrolled fashion.

Figure 3 illustrates an example with three tasks, τ_1, τ_2, and τ_3, in which the processor speed is decreased by a factor of 2. Figure 3a shows a feasible schedule produced by the Rate Monotonic (RM) algorithm [21] when the processor runs at its nominal speed S_n, so the tasks have computation times $C_1 = 2$, $C_2 = 2$, and $C_3 = 4$, respectively. Figure 3b shows the schedule obtained by RM when the processor speed is reduced by half, $S = S_n/2$, so that all computation times are doubled. In this case, a speed reduction generates a permanent overload, which causes τ_2 to miss its deadline and prevents τ_3 to execute at all.

3   Terminology and Assumptions

From the examples shown in Section 2, it is clear that, in order to achieve scalability as a function of speed, tasks have to be fully preemptive and cannot block on shared resources. In Section 4 we present a communication mechanism which allows tasks to exchange data asynchronously, without blocking on mutually exclusive buffers. Moreover, to avoid the negative effects of a permanent overload caused by a speed reduction, tasks periods need to be specified with some degree of flexibility, so that they can be resized to handle the overload condition.

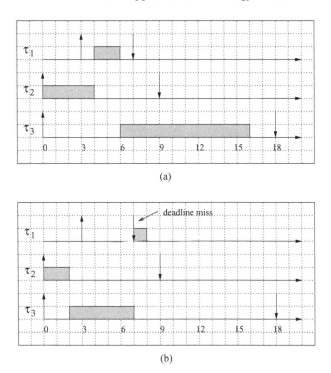

(a)

(b)

Fig. 2. Scheduling anomaly in the presence of non-preemptive tasks: task τ_1 meets its deadline when the processor is executing at its nominal speed S_n (a), but misses its deadline when the speed is doubled (b).

As an overload is detected, period adaptation can be performed using different methodologies.

In this paper, rate adaptation is performed using the elastic model [8,10], according to which task utilizations are treated like springs that can adapt to a given workload through period variations. The advantage of the elastic model with respect to the other methods proposed in the literature is that a new period configuration can easily be determined on line as a function of the elastic coefficients, which can be set to reflect tasks' importance. Once elastic coefficients are defined based on some design criterion, periods can be quickly computed on line depending on the current workload and the desired load level.

In summary, the computational model adopted in this work considers a uniprocessor system whose speed S can be controlled as a function of the supplied voltage. An application consists of a set of periodic tasks, each characterized by four parameters: a worst-case computation time $C_i(S)$ (which is a function of the speed) a nominal period T_{i_0} (considered as the desired minimum period), a maximum allowed period $T_{i_{max}}$, and an elastic coefficient E_i. The elastic coefficient specifies the flexibility of the task to vary its utilization for adapting the

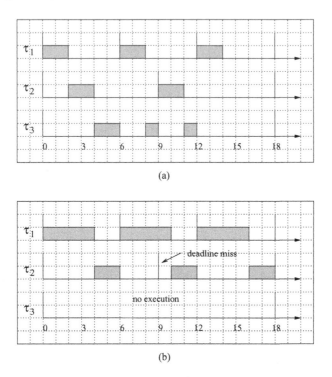

(a)

(b)

Fig. 3. Effects of a permanent overload due to a speed reduction. In case (b) the processor is running at half speed with respect to case (a).

system to a new feasible rate configuration: the greater E_i, the more elastic the task. Thus, an elastic task is denoted as:

$$\tau_i(C_i, T_{i_0}, T_{i_{max}}, E_i).$$

From a design perspective, elastic coefficients can be set equal to values which are inversely proportional to tasks' importance. In the following, T_i will denote the actual period of task τ_i, which is constrained to be in the range $[T_{i_0}, T_{i_{max}}]$. Any period variation is always subject to an *elastic* guarantee and is accepted only if there exists a feasible schedule in which all the other periods are within their range. In such a framework, tasks are scheduled by the Earliest Deadline First algorithm [21]. Hence, if $\sum \frac{C_i(S)}{T_{i_0}} \leq 1$, all tasks can be created at the minimum period T_{i_0}, otherwise the elastic algorithm is used to adapt the tasks' periods to T_i such that $\sum \frac{C_i(S)}{T_i} = U_d \leq 1$, where U_d is some desired utilization factor.

To simplify the analysis we assume that tasks have a relative deadline equal to their period ($D_i = T_i$).

In general, a set of periodic tasks is denoted by

$$\Gamma = \{\tau_i(C_i, T_i, D_i), i = 1, \ldots, n\}.$$

The release time $r_{i,k}$ and the absolute deadline $d_{i,k}$ of the generic kth instance $(k > 0)$ can then be computed as

$$r_{i,k} = \Phi_i + (k-1)T_i$$
$$d_{i,k} = r_{i,k} + D_i,$$

where Φ_i is the task phase, that is the activation time of the first task instance.

4   Avoiding Blocking through Asynchronous Buffers

This section describes how blocking on shared resources can be avoided through the use of Cyclical Asynchronous Buffers, or CABs, a kind of wait free mechanism which allows tasks to exchange data without forcing a synchronization. In a CAB, read and write operations can be performed simultaneously without causing any blocking. Hence, a task can write a new message in a CAB while another task is reading the previous message. Mutual exclusion between reader and writer is avoided by means of memory duplication. In other words, if a task τ_W wants to write a new message into a CAB while a task τ_R is reading the current message, a new buffer is created, so that τ_W can write its message without interfering with τ_R. As τ_W finishes writing, its message becomes the most recent one in the CAB. To avoid blocking, the number of buffers that a CAB must handled has to be equal to the number of tasks that use the CAB plus one.

CABs were purposely designed for the cooperation among periodic activities running at different rates, such as control loops and sensory acquisition tasks. This approach was first proposed by Clark [12] for implementing a robotic application based on hierarchical servo-loops, and it is used in the HARTIK kernel [7] and in the SHARK kernel [15] as a basic communication support among periodic hard tasks.

In general, a CAB provides a one-to-many communication channel, which at any instant contains the latest message or data inserted in it. A message is not consumed by a receiving process, but is maintained into the CAB structure until a new message is overwritten. As a consequence, once the first message has been put in a CAB, a task can never be blocked during a receive operation. Similarly, since a new message overwrites the old one, a sender can never be blocked.

Notice that, using such a semantics, a message can be read more than once if the receiver is faster than the sender, while messages can be lost if the sender is faster than the receiver. However, this is not a problem in many control applications, where tasks are interested only in fresh sensory data rather than in the complete message history produced by a sensory acquisition task.

To insert a message in a CAB, a task must first reserve a buffer from the CAB memory space, then copy the message into the buffer, and finally put the buffer into the CAB structure, where it becomes the most recent message. This is done according to the following scheme:

```
buf_pointer = reserve(cab_id);
<copy message in *buf_pointer>
putmes(buf_pointer, cab_id);
```

Similarly, to get a message from a CAB, a task has to get the pointer to the most recent message, use the data, and release the pointer. This is done according to the following scheme:

$$
\boxed{
\begin{aligned}
&\text{mes\_pointer} = \textbf{getmes}(\text{cab\_id}); \\
&<\text{use message}> \\
&\textbf{unget}(\text{mes\_pointer}, \text{cab\_id});
\end{aligned}
}
$$

4.1   An Example

To better illustrate the CAB mechanism, we describe an example in which a task τ_W writes messages in a CAB, and two tasks, τ_{R_1} and τ_{R_2}, read messages from the CAB. As it will be shown below, to avoid blocking and preserve data consistency, the CAB must contain 4 buffers. Consider the following sequence of events:

- At time t_1, task τ_W writes message M_1 in the CAB. When it finishes, it becomes the most recent data (*mrd*) in the CAB.
- At time t_2, task τ_{R_1} asks the system to read the most recent data in the CAB and receives a pointer to M_1.
- At time t_3, task τ_W asks the system to write another message M_2 in the CAB, while τ_{R_1} is still reading M_1. Hence, a new buffer is reserved to τ_W. When it finishes, M_2 becomes the most recent data in the CAB.
- At time t_4, while τ_{R_1} is still reading M_1, τ_{R_2} asks the system to read the most recent data in the CAB and receives a pointer to M_2.
- At time t_5, while τ_{R_1} and τ_{R_2} are still reading, τ_W asks the system to write a new message M_3 in the CAB. Hence, a third buffer is reserved to τ_W. When it finishes, M_3 becomes the most recent data in the CAB.
- At time t_6, while τ_{R_1} and τ_{R_2} are still reading, τ_W asks the system to write a new message M_4 in the CAB. Notice that, in this situation, M_3 cannot be overwritten (being the most recent data), hence a fourth buffer must be reserved to τ_W. In fact, if M_3 is overwritten, τ_{R_1} could ask reading the CAB while τ_W is writing, thus finding the most recent data in an inconsistent state. When τ_W finishes writing M_4 into the fourth buffer, the *mrd* pointer is updated and the third buffer can be recycled if no task is accessing it.
- At time t_7, τ_{R_1} finishes reading M_1 and releases the first buffer (which can then be recycled).
- At time t_8, τ_{R_1} asks the system to read the most recent data in the CAB and receives a pointer to M_4.

Figure 4 illustrates the situation in the example, at time t_5, when τ_W is writing M_3 in the third buffer. Notice that at this time, the most recent data (mrd) is still M_2. It will be updated to M_3 only at the end of the write operation.

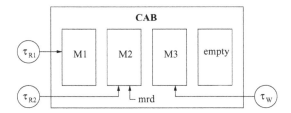

Fig. 4. Buffer configuration in the CAB, at time t_5.

5 Rate Adaptation under Permanent Overloads

Section 2 illustrated how the performance can be degraded when a permanent overload occurs due to a speed reduction. To avoid such a negative effect, tasks periods need to be adjusted to remove the overload condition. Rate adaptation can be performed by many ways. For example, Kuo and Mok [19] proposed a load scaling technique to degrade the workload of a system by adjusting the task periods. Tasks are assumed to be equally important and the objective is to minimize the number of fundamental frequencies to improve schedulability under static priority assignments. In [20], Lee, Rajkumar and Mercer proposed a number of policies to dynamically adjust tasks' rates in overload conditions. In [24], Nakajima showed how a multimedia activity can adapt its requirements during transient overloads by scaling down its rate or its computational demand. However, it is not clear how the QoS can be increased when the system is underloaded. In [6], Beccari et al. proposed several policies for handling overload through period adjustment. The authors, however, do not address the problem of increasing the task rates when the processor is not fully utilized.

In this paper, task rate adjustment is performed through the elastic task model [8,10], according to which task utilizations are treated like springs that can adapt to a given workload through period variations. The advantage of the elastic model with respect to the other methods proposed in the literature is that a new period configuration can easily be determined on line as a function of the elastic coefficients, which can be set to reflect tasks' importance. Once elastic coefficients are defined based on some design criterion, periods can be quickly computed on line depending on the current workload and the desired load level. Moreover, the elastic model can also be used in combination with a feedback mechanism, as done in [9], when system parameters are not known a priori.

5.1 The Elastic Approach

Whenever the total processor utilization $U_0 = \sum_{i=1}^{n} \frac{C_i}{T_{i_0}}$ is greater than one (i.e., there is a permanent overload in the system), the utilization of each task needs to be reduced so that the total utilization becomes $U_d = \sum_{i=1}^{n} \frac{C_i}{T_i} \leq 1$. This can be done as in a linear spring system, where springs are compressed by a force F (depending of their elasticity) up to a desired total length. The concept is illustrated in Figure 5.

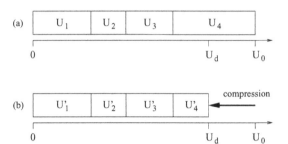

Fig. 5. Compressing the utilizations of a set of elastic tasks.

As shown in [10], in the absence of period constraints (i.e., if $T_{max} = \infty$), the utilization U_i of each compressed task can be computed as follows:

$$\forall i \quad U_i = U_{i_0} - (U_0 - U_d)\frac{E_i}{E_v}. \tag{3}$$

where

$$E_v = \sum_{i=1}^{n} E_i. \tag{4}$$

In the presence of period constraints $(T_i \leq T_{i_{max}})$, however, the problem of finding the values T_i requires an iterative solution. In fact, if during compression one or more tasks reach their maximum period, the additional compression has to affect only to the remaining periods. Thus, at each instant, the set Γ of tasks can be divided into two subsets: a set Γ_f of fixed tasks having maximum period, and a set Γ_v of variable tasks whose period can still be enlarged. Applying the equations to the set Γ_v of variable springs, we have

$$\forall \tau_i \in \Gamma_v \quad U_i = U_{i_0} - (U_{v_0} - U_d + U_f)\frac{E_i}{E_v} \tag{5}$$

where

$$U_{v_0} = \sum_{\tau_i \in \Gamma_v} U_{i_0} \tag{6}$$

$$U_f = \sum_{\tau_i \in \Gamma_f} U_{i_{min}} \tag{7}$$

$$E_v = \sum_{\tau_i \in \Gamma_v} E_i. \tag{8}$$

If there exist tasks for which $U_i < U_{i_{min}}$, then the period of those tasks has to be fixed at its maximum value $T_{i_{max}}$ (so that $U_i = U_{i_{min}}$), sets Γ_f and Γ_v must be updated (hence, U_f and E_v recomputed), and equation (5) applied again to the tasks in Γ_v. If there exists a feasible solution, that is, if the desired utilization U_d is greater than or equal to the minimum possible utilization $U_{min} = \sum_{i=1}^{n} \frac{C_i}{T_{i_{max}}}$, the iterative process ends when each value computed by equation (5) is greater than or equal to its corresponding minimum $U_{i_{min}}$. In [10] it is shown that, in the worst case, the compression algorithm converges to a solution (if there exists one) in $O(n^2)$ steps, where n is the number of tasks.

The same algorithm can be used to reduce the periods when the overload is over, so adapting task rates to the current load condition to better exploit the computational resources.

6   Conclusions

In this paper we presented the problems that can occur when running a real-time application in a processor with variable speed. It has been shown that, when tasks share mutually exclusive resources or execute in a non-preemptive fashion, response times could even increase when the processor runs at higher speeds. In addition, when the speed is decreased, a permanent overload could degrade the system's performance in an uncontrolled fashion. Such problems, if not properly handled, would prevent controlling the performance of a real-time system as a function of the voltage and would limit the use of algorithms for resource optimization (e.g., for minimizing energy consumption).

To address these problems, we proposed a set of mechanisms that can be implemented at the kernel level to develop scalable real-time applications, whose performance can be adjusted in a controlled fashion as a function of the processor speed. In particular, the use of non blocking communication buffers (like the CABs) has two main advantages: it avoids the scheduling anomalies that may arise due to speed variations and allows data exchange among periodic tasks with non harmonic period relations.

To cope with permanent overloads caused by a speed reduction, the elastic scheduling approach provides an efficient method for automatically adjusting the task rates based on a set of coefficients, that can be assigned during the design phase based on task importance. Both methods have been implemented on top of the HARTIK kernel [7] and have been experimented in a number of control applications.

In the future we plan to implement these techniques on top of other real-time kernels (e.g., RT-Linux and Linux-RK) as a middleware layer, to provide the basic building blocks for supporting for energy-aware real-time systems.

References

1. N. AbouGhazaleh, D. Mossé, B. Childers and R. Melhem, "Toward The Placement of Power Manegement Points in Real Time Applications", Proceedings of the Workshop on Compilers and Operating Systems for Low Power (COLP'01), Barcelona, Spain, 2001.
2. A. Allavena and D. Mossé, "Scheduling of Frame-based Embedded Systems with Rechargeable Batteries", Proceedings of the Workshop on Power Management for Real-Time and Embedded Systems, 2001.

3. H. Aydin, R. Melhem, D.Mossé and Pedro Mejia Alvarez, "Determining Optimal Processor Speeds for Periodic Real-Time Tasks with Different Power Characteristics", Proceedings of the Euromicro Conference on Real-Time Systems, Delft, Holland, June 2001.

4. H. Aydin, R. Melhem, D. Mossé, and Pedro Mejia Alvarez, "Dynamic and Aggressive Scheduling Techniques for Power-Aware Real-Time Systems", Proceedings of the IEEE Real-Time Systems Symposium, December 2001.

5. S. Baruah, G. Buttazzo, S. Gorinsky, and G. Lipari, "Scheduling Periodic Task Systems to Minimize Output Jitter," Proceedings of the 6th IEEE International Conference on Real-Time Computing Systems and Applications, Hong Kong, December 1999.

6. G. Beccari, S. Caselli, M. Reggiani, F. Zanichelli, "Rate Modulation of Soft Real-Time Tasks in Autonomous Robot Control Systems," IEEE Proceedings of the 11th Euromicro Conference on Real-Time Systems, York, June 1999.

7. G. C. Buttazzo, "HARTIK: A Real-Time Kernel for Robotics Applications", Proceedings of the 14th IEEE Real-Time Systems Symposium, Raleigh-Durham, December 1993.

8. G. Buttazzo, G. Lipari, and L. Abeni, "Elastic Task Model for Adaptive Rate Control," Proceedings of the IEEE Real-Time Systems Symposium, Madrid, Spain, pp. 286-295, December 1998.

9. G. Buttazzo and L. Abeni, "Adaptive Rate Control through Elastic Scheduling," Proceedings of the 39th IEEE Conference on Decision and Control, Sydney, Australia, December 2000.

10. G. Buttazzo, G. Lipari, M. Caccamo, L. Abeni, "Elastic Scheduling for Flexible Workload Management," IEEE Transactions on Computers, Vol. 51, No. 3, pp. 289-302, March 2002.

11. A. Chandrakasan and R. Brodersen, Low Power Digital CMOS Design, Kluwer Academic Publishers, 1995.

12. D. Clark, "HIC: An Operating System for Hierarchies of Servo Loops," Proceedings of IEEE International Conference on Robotics and Automation, 1989.

13. E. Chan, K. Govil, and H. Wasserman, "Comparing Algorithms for Dynamic Speed-setting of a Low-Power CPU", Proceedings of the First ACM International Conference on Mobile Computing and Networking (MOBICOM 95), November 1995.

14. M.L. Dertouzos, "Control Robotics: the Procedural Control of Physical Processes," Information Processing, 74, North-Holland, Publishing Company, 1974.

15. P. Gai, L. Abeni, M. Giorgi, G. Buttazzo, "A New Kernel Approach for Modular Real-Time Systems Development," IEEE Proceedings of the 13th Euromicro Conference on Real-Time Systems, Delft, The Netherlands, June 2001.

16. R. L. Graham: "Bounds on the Performance of Scheduling Algorithms," Chapter 5 in Computer and Job Scheduling Theory, John Wiley and Sons, pp. 165-227, 1976.

17. I. Hong, D. Kirovski, G. Qu, M. Potkonjak, and M. Srivastava, "Power Optimization of Variable Voltage Core-Based Systems", Proceedings of the 35th Design Automation Conference, 1998.

18. I. Hong, G. Qu, M. Potkonjak, and M.B. Srivastava, "Synthesis Techniques for Low-Power Hard Real-Time Systems on Variable Voltage Processors", Proceedings of the 19th IEEE Real-Time Systems Symposium, December 1998.

19. T.-W. Kuo and A. K, Mok, "Load Adjustment in Adaptive Real-Time Systems," Proceedings of the 12th IEEE Real-Time Systems Symposium, December 1991.

20. C. Lee, R. Rajkumar, and C. Mercer, "Experiences with Processor Reservation and Dynamic QOS in Real-Time Mach," *Proceedings of Multimedia Japan 96*, April 1996.
21. C.L. Liu and J.W. Layland, "Scheduling Algorithms for Multiprogramming in a Hard real-Time Environment," *Journal of the ACM* 20(1), 1973, pp. 40–61.
22. R. Melhem, N. AbouGhazaleh, H. Aydin and D. Mosse, "Power Management Points in Power-Aware Real-Time Systems", In Power Aware Computing, ed. by R. Graybill and R. Melhem, Plenum/Kluwer Publishers, 2002.
23. A. Mok, "Scalability of real-time applications," keynote address at the 7th International Conference on Real-Time Computing Systems and Applications, Cheju Island, South Korea, December 2000.
24. T. Nakajima, "Resource Reservation for Adaptive QOS Mapping in Real-Time Mach," *Sixth International Workshop on Parallel and Distributed Real-Time Systems*, April 1998.
25. M. Spuri, and G.C. Buttazzo, "Efficient Aperiodic Service under Earliest Deadline Scheduling", *Proceedings of IEEE Real-Time System Symposium*, San Juan, Portorico, December 1994.
26. M. Spuri, G.C. Buttazzo, and F. Sensini, "Robust Aperiodic Scheduling under Dynamic Priority Systems", *Proc. of the IEEE Real-Time Systems Symposium*, Pisa, Italy, December 1995.
27. M. Spuri and G.C. Buttazzo, "Scheduling Aperiodic Tasks in Dynamic Priority Systems," *Real-Time Systems*, 10(2), 1996.
28. F. Yao, A. Demers, and S. Shenker, "A Scheduling Model for Reduced CPU Energy," *IEEE Annual Foundations of Computer Science*, pp. 374-382, 1995.
29. D. Zhu, R. Melhem, and B. Childers, "Scheduling with Dynamic Voltage/Speed Adjustment Using Slack Reclamation in Multi-Processor Real-Time Systems", *Proceedings of the IEEE Real-Time Systems Symposium*, December 2001.

Upgrading Embedded Software in the Field: Dependability and Survivability

Lui Sha

University of Illinois at Urbana-Champaign
1304 West Springfield Ave., DCL 2125
Urbana, IL 61801, USA
lrs@cs.uiuc.edu

Abstract. The new millennium heralds the convergence between computing, communication and the intelligent control of our physical environments. Computers embedded in roads, bridges, buildings and vehicles tend to have a long life cycle. Application needs will change and computing, communication and control technologies willevolve rapidly. To keep systems modern, we need technologies to dependably and securely upgrade embedded software in the field. This paper provides a review of our work on how to upgrade embedded control systems without shutting them down, and how to protect the system from bugs and attacks that could be introduced by software upgrades.

1   Introduction

"The basic components of computing processors, memory, storage, and networking are becoming so small, powerful, and inexpensive that soon computing will be embedded in all kinds of everyday things that don't look at all like computing devices: cars, roads, machine tools, vending machines, houses. "[1] Embedded computers tend to have a long life cycle. Application needs will change; and computing, communication and control technologies willevolve rapidly. To keep systems up to date, we need to upgrade their software many times in the field. Since changes to existing software systems are known to be a potential source of errors, we need to find ways to ensure the integrity of the system in spite of errors that could be introduced by changes. Software upgrades to embedded system could also become a serious security hole; and we need to guard against attacks disguised as legitimate upgrades.

The demand for higher performance, reliability and security occurs at a time when the software for embedded systems is getting increasingly more complex. Complexity is a major contributor to software errors; and software errors can not only impair system operations but also create serious security holes. Thus, a critical task in embedded system software is to ensure its reliability. Indeed, comparing with desktop systems, the failure of embedded systems that control vital functions in roads, bridges, buildings and vehicles could be much more damaging.

---

[1] Lou Gerstner, 1998 IBM Annual Report.

A. Sangiovanni-Vincentelli and J. Sifakis (Eds.): EMSOFT 2002, LNCS 2491, pp. 166–181, 2002.

There are two basic approaches for software reliability. One is the fault avoidance method using formal specification-verification methods and a rigorous software development process such as DO 178B standard for flight control software certification. These are powerful methods that allow us to have computer controlled safety critical systems such as flight control. Unfortunately, they can only handle modestly complex software, and the high assurance development process is expensive. In addition, the trend towards using third party commercial-off-the-shelf (COTS) components also makes a direct application of fault avoidance methods much more difficult.

Another approach is software fault tolerance using diversity. It is a widely held belief that diversity entails robustness. However, is it really true? Would the system be more reliable if we devote all the efforts to developing a single version than dividing the efforts for diversity?

We will show that, depending upon the architecture, dividing the resource for diversity could lead to either improved or reduced reliability. The key to improving reliability is not the degree of diversity per se. Rather, it is the existence of a simple and reliable core component that can ensure the critical properties of the system, in spite of the failure of the complex software components that are useful but not essential. We call this approach "using simplicity to control complexity". In this paper, we show how to employ this approach in the domain of automatic control applications. We also give a brief review of our initial work on how to protect attacks disguised as upgrades, since the upgrades to deployed embedded system software could become a major security hole.

2   On Software Reliability

2.1   Diversity, Complexity and Software Reliability

Most of the existing software fault tolerance work builds on the assumption that diversity in software construction leads to improved reliability[2]. However, is it really true? To get some insights into this question, let's develop a simple model to analyze the relationship between reliability, development effort and the logical complexity of software.

Computational complexity is modeled as the number of steps to complete the computation. Likewise, logical complexity can be viewed as the number of steps that are needed to verify the correctness. A program can have different logical and computational complexities. For example, comparing with Heap Sort, Bubble Sort has lower logical complexity but higher computational complexity. This paper focuses on logical complexity.

Another important point we want to make is the distinction between logical complexity and residual logical complexity. A program could have high logical complexity initially. However, if it has been verified and can be used as is[2], then the residual

---

[2] It is important to point out that we cannot simply use a known reliable component in a new environment without verifying the assumptions made by the component.

complexity is zero. Unfortunately, software reuse is not easy. Most of the time, modification or extension is needed. Residual complexity models the effort that is needed to ensure the reliability of this modified software. Generally, residual complexity is low if the modification is expected by the original design. If the modification is incompatible with the architecture of the original design, it could be harder to verify than to write a new one.

In this paper, we focus on residual logical complexity because it is a dominant factor in software reliability. In the following, the term "complexity" refers to residual logical complexity unless stated otherwise. From a developer's perspective, the higher the complexity, and the harder it is to specify, to design, to develop, and to verify. From a management perspective, the higher the complexity, the harder it is to precisely understand the users' needs and to communicate them to developers, to find effective tools, to get qualified personnel and to keep the development process smooth without a lot of requirement changes. Based on what has been observed in software development, we make three postulates:

- *P1: Complexity Breeds Bugs:* Everything else being equal, the more complex the software project is, the harder it is to make it reliable.
- *P2: All Bugs Are Not Equal:* The obvious errors are spotted and corrected early during the development. As time passes by, the remaining errors are subtler and more difficult to detect and correct.
- *P3: All Budgets are Finite:* There is only a finite amount of effort (budget) that we can spend on any project.

P1 implies that for a given mission duration t, the reliability of software decreases as complexity increases. P2 implies that for a given degree of complexity, the reliability function has a monotonically decreasing rate of improvement with respect to development effort. P3 implies that diversity is not free. That is, if we go for diversity, we must divide the available effort.

We now develop a simple reliability model that satisfies these three postulates. For a normalized mission duration $t = 1$, the reliability function of a software system can be modeled as an exponential function of the software complexity, C, and available development effort, E, in the form of $R(E, C) = e^{-kC/E}$, where k is a scaling constant. For simplicity, we shall assume that $k = 1$ in the rest of this paper. $R(E,C)$ decreases as complexity C increases. This satisfies P1. It also has a monotonically decreasing rate of reliability improvement. This satisfies P2, which models the observation that as time passes by, the remaining bugs are subtler and more difficult to detect and correct.

Another way to arrive at the same formulation is to adopt the commonly used exponential reliability function $R(t) = e^{-\lambda t}$ and assume that the failure rate, λ, is proportional to the complexity of the software, C, and inversely proportional to the development effort, E. That is, $R(t) = e^{-kC.t/E}$. Again, for simplicity, we shall assume that the scaling constant $k = 1$. To focus on the interplay between complexity and development effort, we normalize the mission duration t to 1, and write the reliability function with a normalized mission duration in the form of $R(E, C) = e^{-C/E}$.

Using this model, the effect of diversity was analyzed by Sha in [5]. Figure 1 is a plot of the reliability as a function of available effort in three cases: (a) N-version programming with N = 3; (b) normal single version programming; and (c) using 2 versions where one of them implements only essential requirements for complexity reduction. As we can see, what really matters is not the degree of diversity per se. Rather, what leads to higher reliability is the existence of a simple and reliable core function that satisfies the critical requirements. This result is robust against the change of assumptions regarding the relationship between complexity, failure rates and available effort [5].

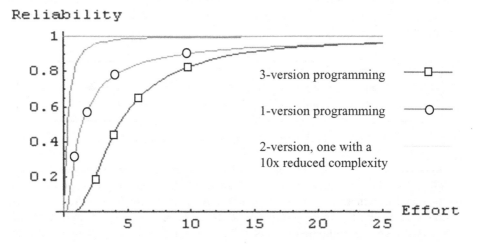

Fig. 1. Reliability as a function of complexity, diversity and available development effort

Thus, the principle of building robust software systems is to "use simplicity to control complexity". That is, using a simple and verifiable core to guarantee the critical properties of a complex software system, in spite the failures of complex components. This approach allows us to economically employ formal methods and high assurance development process for the core components, and then leverage it for the entire systems. Using simplicity to control complexity is the key idea of Simplex architecture [5,7].

2.2   Using Simplicity to Control Complexity: A Conceptual Framework

The wisdom of the reliability engineering commandment, "Keep it simple", is self-evident. It has been repeated by countless generations of engineers in all of the engineering disciplines. We all know that simplicity is the pathway to reliability. The importance of simplicity has also been well analyzed and documented by Leveson in [12]. Why is it so difficult to keep systems simple? One reason is the pursuit of features and performance. To gain a higher level of performance and functionality than the state of practice permits requires us to push the technology envelope, and to stretch the limits of our understanding. Given the keen competition on features, functionality and performance in the market places, the production and usage of complex software components, either in the form of custom components or COTS components, are unavoidable in most applications. Useful but not essential features cause most of the complexities.

From a software engineering perspective, the notion of using simplicity to control complexity allows us to separate critical properties from desirable properties. To illustrate this point, let's consider the following example. In sorting, the critical property is to sort items correctly. The desirable property is to sort them as fast as possible. Suppose that a new student Joe can formally verify Bubble Sort program but unable to verify his Heap Sort program. Can he safely use his unreliable Heap-Sort program?

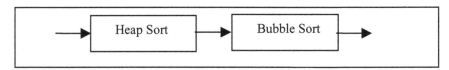

Fig. 2. Using Simplicity to control complexity

Intuitively, it seems that unreliable software components cannot contribute positively to a reliable system; and that we cannot use a slow component to "police" a fast component. Fortunately, none of these perceptions are unconditional truths. Indeed, gaining the ability to safely exploit the performance and features of unreliable software is the key to building practical robust software systems with many existing components whose reliability we do not have control.

In Figure 2, if Heap Sort works correctly, then the items are already sorted when Bubble Sort works on them. Hence, the computational complexity of the composite system is still *O(n log(n))*. If items were sorted incorrectly, Bubble Sort will resort them correctly, thus guaranteeing the critical property of sorting at a lower performance. Under this arrangement, we can not only guarantee the correctness of sorting but also gain a higher degree performance as long as Heap Sort works *most of the time*. It is worth to point out that most existing software components indeed work most of the time, but may fail under unusual conditions.

What if the Heap Sort program is so poorly written that it alters an item to be sorted? To ensure that the given collection of items are not altered, we can checksum them before sending them to Heap Sort. We then check the output from Heap Sort. If the checksum is wrong, the Bubble Sort uses the given collection of items directly. We note that the computational complex of this arrangement is still *O(n log(n))*, thanks to the low timing complexity of checksum operations. Similar arrangements could be made for many optimization applications, whenever there are logically simple greedy algorithms with lower performance, and logically complex algorithms with higher performance.

This simple example was designed to illustrate several concepts. First, all requirements are not equal. We should separate the critical ones with desirable ones, such as sorting correctness and sorting performance in this example. Second, it is possible to use the results of another software component without depending on it. The separation between the "use" relationship and "depend" relationship is a fundamental one in the composition of software systems using modules with different degree of reliability. In modern software systems, we can only develop and verify a small number of components. We have to use many third party components whose reliability is either unknown or we have no control. Third, for the software fault tolerance to work, we must ensure the precondition for the backup component during runtime. In this sorting example, the precondition is that the collection of items is not added, dropped or modified. As we will see later, in control systems such precondition can usually be represented as the largest "stability envelope" for the states of the plant under the backup controller. Fourth, it is possible to use slower/lower performance components as watchdogs for fast/high performance components.

In summary, the moral of this story is that we can exploit the features and performance of complex software even if we cannot verify them, as long as we can guarantee the critical properties by simple software. This is how we leverage the power of formal methods and high assurance development process.

2.3   Using Simplicity to Control Complexity: Control System Applications

In the operation of a plant (or a vehicle), there is a set of state constraints, called operation constraints, representing the safety, the device physical limitations, environmental and other operation requirements. The operation constraints can be represented as a normalized polytope in the N-dimensional state space of the system as shown in Figure 3. Each line represents a constraint. For example, the rotation of the engine must be no greater than k RPM. The states inside the polytope are called admissible states, because they obey the state constraints. To guard against failures of the device that can be caused by a faulty controller, we must ensure that the system states are always admissible. This means that we must be able to 1) take the control away from a faulty control subsystem and give it to the high assurance control subsystem before the system state becomes inadmissible, 2) the system is controllable by the high assurance control subsystem after the switch, and 3) the future trajectory of the system state after the switch will stay within the set of admissible states. Note that we cannot use the boundary of the polytope as the switching rule, just as we cannot stop the car without collision when the car is about to touch the wall. Physical systems have inertia.

A subset of the admissible states that satisfies these three conditions is called a recovery region. The recovery region is represented by a Lyapunov function inside the state constraint polytope. That is, the recovery region is a stability envelope within the state constraint polytope. Geometrically, a Lyapunov function defines a N-dimensional ellipsoid in the N-dimensional system state space as illustrated in Figure 3. A Lyapunov function has the following important property. If the system state is inside the ellipsoid associated with a controller, the system states will stay within the ellipsoid and converge to the equilibrium position. Thus, we can use the boundary of the ellipsoid associated with the high assurance controller as the switching rule.

Lyapunov function is not unique for a given system and controller combination. In order not to unduly restrict the state space that can be used by high performance controllers, we need to find the largest ellipsoid within the polytope that represents the operational constraints. Mathematically, finding the largest ellipsoid inside a polytope can now be solved by the Linear Matrix Inequality (LMI) method [11]. Thus, we can use Lyapunov theory and the LMI tools[3] to solve our recovery region problem. For example, given a dynamic system $X' = A^* X + B K X$, where X is the system state, A^* is the system equation and K represents a controller. We can first choose K by using well understood controller designs with a robust stability, i.e., the system stability should be insensitive to model uncertainty.

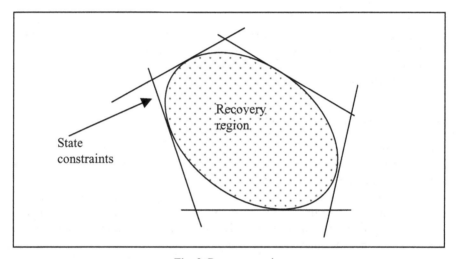

Fig. 3. Recovery region

The system under the control of this reliable controller is $X' = A X$, where $A = (A^*+B K)$, where the stability condition is represented by $A^T Q + Q A < 0$, and Q is the Lyapunov function. The operational constraints are represented by a normalized polytope. The largest ellipsoid inside the polytope can be found by minimizing *(log det Q^1)* [11], subject to stability condition. The resulting Q defines the largest normalized ellipsoid $X^T Q X = 1$, the recovery region, inside the polytope as shown in Figure 3.

In practice, we use a smaller ellipsoid, e.g., $X^T Q X = 0.7$, inside $X^T Q X = 1$. The distance between $X^T Q X = 1$ and $X^T Q X = 0.7$ is the margin reserved to guard against measurement errors during runtime and the approximation errors in the modeling of physical devices. During runtime, the plant is normally under the control of the high

---

[3] The software package that we used to find the largest ellipsoid was developed by Steven Boyd's group at Stanford.

performance control subsystem. The plant state X is being checked at every sampling period. If X is within the N-dimensional ellipsoid $X^TQX = c$, $0 < c < 1$, then the instantaneous error is considered acceptable. Otherwise, the high assurance control subsystem takes over the control. This ensures that the operation of the plant never violates the state constraints. Finally, we note the software that implements the decision rule, "if $(X^TQX > c)$, switch to high assurance controller", is logically simple.

Once we can ensure that the system will be kept in admissible states. Statistical performance evaluations of the high performance control subsystem can be conducted safely in the actual plant operations. The plant is also protected from latent faults that tests and evaluations fail to catch.

3   The Simplex Architecture

3.1   Analytically Redundant Units

Simplex architecture was designed to realize the concept of "using simplicity to control complexity". This concept is realized in the form of an analytically redundant unit of controllers with complementary properties as illustrated in Figure 4. Each unit consists of a high assurance control subsystem and a high performance control subsystem. In a large plant with my devices, it can be used whenever complex controllers are needed and its reliability cannot be assured. It is especially useful in the test of new experimental controllers in realistic settings.

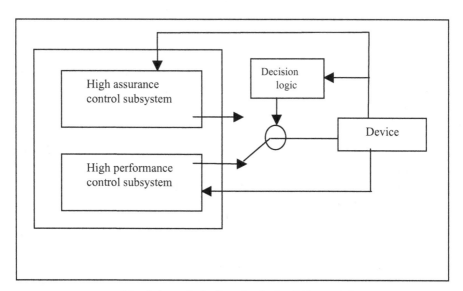

Fig. 4. An analytically redundant unit for control

The high assurance control subsystem

- Application level: using well-understood classical controllers designed to maximize the envelope of stability with a reduced level of control performance to keep the control software simple.
- System software level: using high assurance OS. For example, in safety critical applications such as flight control, certifiable Ada runtime originally developed for Boeing 777 is a good choice. This is a "no thrill" runtime that avoids complex data structure and dynamic resource allocation methods. It trades off usability for reliability.
- Hardware level: using hardware with well-established reliability records that meet the requirements. For fault tolerance systems, use well-established and simple fault tolerant hardware configurations, such as pair-pair or TMR.
- System development and maintenance process: using a suitable high assurance process appropriate for the applications, for example, DO 178B for flight control software.
- Requirement management: requirements here are limited to critical properties and essential services. Like the constitution of a nation, they should be stable and change very slowly.

This conservative high assurance control core is complemented by a high performance control subsystem. Depending on the nature of the applications, the high performance controller can be subject to different development processes. In safety critical applications, the high performance control system should also go through the same high assurance development process. The simple controller is used to guard against the potential imperfection of existing high assurance development process. For example, the backup controller (called secondary controller) in Boeing 777 reuses the much simpler control laws of 747[13].

On the other hand, many industrial control applications, e.g., semi-conductor manufacturing, are not safety critical but the downtime can be very costly. With a high assurance control in place to ensure the process remain to be operational, we can aggressively pursue advanced control technologies and cost reduction in the high performance subsystem.

The high performance control subsystem

- Application level: using advanced control technologies, including those that are difficult to verify, e.g., neural nets.
- System software level: using COTS real time operating systems and middleware that are designed to simplify the development of applications.
- Hardware level: using standard industrial hardware, such as industrial PCs.
- System development and maintenance process: using standard industrial software development processes.
- Requirement management: requirements for features and performance are handled here. With the protection offered by the high assurance subsystem, they can be changed relatively fast to embrace new technologies and to support new user needs.

Figure 4 is a block diagram that illustrates the basic structure of an analytically redundant unit for the control of a physical device. The high assurance and high performance subsystems are running in parallel. The high performance software is also
isolated from the high assurance control software logically or physically. Normally,
the device is under the control of the high performance controller.

For many common low-end embedded applications with modestly high availability
requirements, the high assurance and high performance controllers can be run in
different address spaces of a real time operating system on top of an industrial PC.

3.2   Supporting Upgrades in the Field

In addition to system reliability, Simplex architecture middleware was designed to
support dependable upgrades of embedded systems in the field. The upgrade of the
high performance controller described in the previous section can be done without
shutting the system operations. The following provides an overview of the dynamic
component binding service provided by Simplex architecture as illustrated in Figure
5, where a RPU represents an online replacement unit that encapsulates a high performance controller. We note that online upgrade of the safety controller is not permitted. The online upgrade middleware adds quite a bit of complexity and should be
isolated from the safety controller. The basic components of Simplex middleware
components for online upgrades are described below.

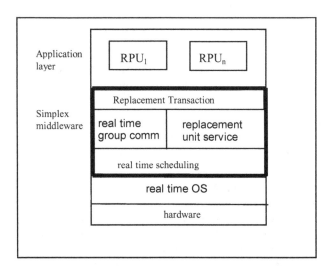

Fig. 5. Online software component replacement support

Real time scheduling service: In Simplex architecture, all the real time computation
and real time communication is explicitly scheduled by generalized rate monotonic
scheduling (GRMS) [6], which provides a simple analytic solution to many practical
real time scheduling problems including: scheduling periodic and aperiodic tasks,
task synchronization, transient overloads, bus and network scheduling.

Real time group communication service: This component provides a real time publication and subscription service to application software modules [9]. It decouples data producers and data consumers. Data producers will "publish" data at the service while applications that need the data will "subscribe" the data at the service. This way, we can change the data publisher transparently with respect to data subscribers.

Replacement units: Replacement units are virtual or physical computers that are used to encapsulate a set of computation activities that can be replaced online. It is typically implemented as a real time process together with a standardized communication interface. The communications are carried out via the real time publication and subscription service.

Replacement transaction facility: During a replacement transaction, state information (e.g. those relating to controllers or filters) may need to be transferred from the *old unit* to the *new unit*. Alternatively, the *new unit* may capture the dynamic state information of physical systems through plant input data. The replacement transaction of a single replacement unit is carried out in stages:

1. A *new unit* is created and its communication channels are connected using the lowest background priority. Once the creation is completed, its priority will be raised to what is assigned by GRMS.
2. Plant input data and other state information, if any, are provided to the *new unit*. The *new unit* begins computations. The output of the unit is monitored but not used.
3. The replacement transaction waits for the output of the *new unit* converges to a given criteria. Once the convergence is reached. The output of the *old unit* is turned off and the *new unit* is turned on. Alternatively, one can use application provided procedures to smooth out the transition from an old controller to a new controller.

A two-phase protocol is used when multiple replacement units are to be replaced simultaneously. The first phase is to wait for all the *new units* to reach a steady state (step 3 above). The second phase is a distributed action that simultaneously switches on all the *new units* and switches off all the *old units*. The granularity of "simultaneity" is modeled as finishing the work within a single sample period. The replacement transaction must finish with a prescribed duration or it will be aborted.

When the old replacement unit needs to be deleted, we first set its priority to the lowest background level. We then disconnect its communication channels and destroy the process used by the replacement unit at background priority. We use low background priority to create or destroy a replacement unit, because they are time-consuming operations and we don't want to interfere with the real time loops.

3.3   Protect Against Attacks

There are many aspects in system security. In this paper, we focus on system survivability in the context of application software upgrades. We assume that not all the application software submitted as upgrades can be trusted. The software may contain not only bugs but also deliberate attacks that could be the result of insider attacks or the use of compromised third party components. Since checking the properties of binaries are extremely difficult, we insist on the inspection of the safety of the source code via compiler time static analysis.

The unsafe nature of C is well known. There has been extensive research on software techniques for *code safety*, i.e., techniques that allow untrusted code to execute safely within the protection domain of a system [14], such as Java byte code within a Java virtual machine. In addition to efficiency issues, a practical limitation on the adoption of new languages is that there is a large body of legacy embedded software written in C. Backward compatibility with such code limits the acceptance of incompatible new languages. In addition, Java does not support low-level programming that is needed to manage hardware devices. As C++ to Small Talk, we would like to develop a safe C/C++ based programming environment that integrates some of the best ideas in Java while compatible to C/C++.

First, we note that separate address spaces are insufficient to protect against deliberate attacks. As illustrated in Figure 6, an attacker may put machine code of kill calls as data and later modify the return address and jump to execute it. This and many other forms of attacks are possible by exploiting the unsafe nature of C programming language. We now provide a summary of our initial research and implementations done in [1].

```
char killcode[] =

"\x55\x89\xe5\x89\xe5\xb9\x09\x00\x00\x00\xbb\xff\xff\xff\xff\xb8"
        "\x25\x00\x00\x00\xcd\x80\x89\xd3\xc3\x90";

main()
{
    int *ret;

    ret = (int *)&ret + 2;
    (*ret) = (int)killcode;
}
```

Fig. 6. An attack

We modified the gcc compiler to support the static analysis to examine if *every memory access performs only the permitted operations (i.e., read, write, and execution) to the area being accessed.* For example, we should not allow write/modify operations across the pre-allocated memory space boundaries such as arrays and the stack. A memory object is the unit where the permissions on the operations are assigned. The operations consist of read (**r**), write (**w**), and execution (**x**). A capability is a pair made up of a memory object identifier and a set of permitted operations on that memory object. For each process, a set of capabilities is associated according to the needed memory objects during the executing process. The rules of creating memory objects are as follows:

- Every static data variable creates a memory object. We call this kind of object *data object*. A data object has two attributes, the symbol name (i.e., start address) and the size of the variable.
- Every local variable creates a memory object. We call this kind of object *stack object*. A stack object has two attributes, the offset from the stack pointer and the size of the variable.
- Every code label creates a memory object. We call this kind of object *label object*. The size of a label object is not defined.
- Every function name creates a memory object. We call this object *function object*. We do not consider the size of the function object in this paper while the size of each function can be determined statically.

For each memory object created, a set of permissions is given to form a capability. A capability is created automatically by a compiler depending on the class of the corresponding memory object. The rules of the capability formation by the compiler are as follows:

- Each data object and stack object is given **r** and **w** permissions.
- Each label object and function object is given **r** and **x** permissions.

As an example, in Figure 6 a function object (i.e., `main` function), a data object (i.e., array `killcode`), and a stack object are created. Since the size of the stack object is determined as the size of an integer variable, the last statement of the main function is detected as an illegal operation and the compiler generates the security alarm. Moreover, since return address of the main function is modified to the address of the array `killcode`, another alarm can be generated due to the code execution from the data object.

The objective of our static code safety check is to detect all the capability violations before runtime. Each C source code is converted to a register transfer language (RTL) form or an assembly language. Symbolic execution is then performed to check if the code is memory safe. A number of optimization techniques such as path merging are used to speed up the symbolic execution[1].

This approach is useful for control and signal processing programs, since they have simple memory reference structures. This permits the efficient checking of code safety. The checking will classify a program as 1) safe, 2) unsafe, and 3) unknown due to highly complex memory reference structures. Only codes that are classified as safe will be executed. In the context of control and signal processing applications, memory reference structure so complex that it causes timeout in symbolic executions is either ill structured programs that should be rewritten or there are structures designed to hide attack codes from being detected by compiler static analysis.

Finally, from the perspective of small-embedded devices, code memory safety analysis has another payoffs. It allows us to use complier static analysis to replace the use of hardware supported address space protection. Once the memory safety of application code is assured, we can threads instead of processes. This allows us to implement analytically redundant units in a single address space and multi-threaded RTOS for small-embedded devices.

4   Summary

The new millennium heralds the convergence between computing, communication and the intelligent control of our physical environments. To keep systems modern, we need technologies to dependably and securely upgrade embedded software in the field.

In this paper, we have shown that the key to improving reliability is not the degree of diversity per se. Rather, it is the existence of a simple and reliable core component that can ensure the critical properties of the system, in spite of the failure of the complex software components that are useful but not essential. We call this approach "using simplicity to control complexity" and show how the Simplex architecture realizes this concept in the context in control systems. Simplex architecture allows operations to upgrade control system software without shutting them down, and protect the system from bugs and attacks that could be introduced by software upgrades. To demonstrate the feasibility of these ideas, we have developed a Web based testbed known as Telelab as illustrated in Figure 7. Telelab allows users anywhere on the Internet to experiment with a computer-controlled mechanical inverted pendulum (IP).

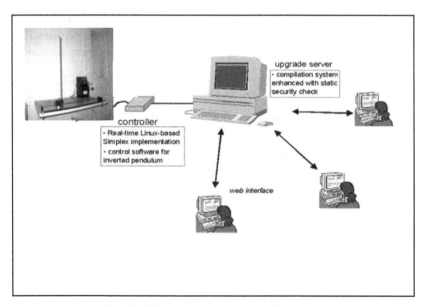

Fig. 7. Web based online upgrade of controllers

Telelab's embedded Simplex environment, called eSimplex, can safely run untrusted new control software sent to the system. Readers who are interested may download the interface by first going to http://pertsserver.cs.uiuc.edu/ and then select projects, drii, and finally select the link download Telelab.

During the experiment, a user can see the behavior of the computer controlled mechanical IP via streaming video. An user may open the file that contains the control code that is currently running, enhance the control logic, remotely compile it on our host, run it and test the control performance of the new controller. Alternatively, a user may attempt to launch attacks using resource depletion; faulty control logic; or attacks. If the control software submitted by a user is a stable controller, it will run for about 5 minutes[4]. If it is faulty or malicious, it will be rejected and our original (safety) controller will be used again.

In short, the Simplex system upgrade environment allows users to easily, quickly upgrade the control software without shutting the system down. If the new software performs similar to or better than the existing control software, it will be accepted. If the new software performs poorly or have bugs or attacks, it will be rejected while the Simplex system ensures the IP will always be under control without falling down.

Acknowledgement

This work is sponsored in part by the Office of Naval Research N0004-02-0102, and in part by DARPA's NEST program. Many has contributed to the success of Simplex architecture, in particular I want to thank Danbing Seto, Mark Spong and Karl Astrom for their inputs on the development of the stability controller; Michael Gagliardi, Raj Rajkumar and Kihwal Lee for their contributions to the original and the latest Simplex architecture research and demonstration; Sung-Soo Lim, Sumant Kowshik and Vikram Adve for their works on the compiler analysis for security upgrades.

References

1. Lim, S., Lee, K., and Sha, L., "Ensuring Integrity and Service Availability in a Web Based Control Laboratory," *Journal of Parallel and Distributed System*, Special Issue on Security in Mission Critical Real-time Systems, Accepted for publications.
2. Software Fault Tolerance, edited by Michael Lyu, John Willey & Sons, 1999.
3. Mareczek, J., Buss, M., and Spong, M.W., "Invariance Control for a Class of Cascade Nonlinear Systems," *IEEE Trans. Automatic Control*, to appear.
4. Mareczek, J., Buss, M., and Spong, M.W., "Invariance Control for Non-Cascade Nonlinear Systems," 2001 *American Control Conference*, Arlington, VA, May 2001.
5. Sha, L., "Using Simplicity to Control Complexity," *IEEE Software*, July/August, 2001.
6. Sha L., Rajkumar, R., Sathaye, S., "Generalized Rate Monotonic Scheduling Theory: A Framework for Developing Real-Time Systems", *Proceedings of the IEEE*, Vol. 82 No. 1, pp. 68-82, January 1994. (Invited paper)

---

[4] We keep it at 5 minutes so that others can use it. If you want to perform longer experiments, send emails to us and we will try to accommodate you.

7. Sha, L., "Dependable System Upgrades", *Proceedings of IEEE Real Time System Symposium*, 1998.
8. Spong, M.W., "Communication Delay and Control in Telerobotics," *Journal of the Japan Robotics*
9. Rajkumar, R., Gagliardi, M., Sha, L., "The Real-Time Publisher/Subscriber Inter-Process Communication Model for Distributed Real-Time Systems: Design and Implementation", *Proceedings of the First IEEE Real-time Technology and Applications Symposium*, pp. 66-75, May 1995.
10. Cliff Mercer, Ragunathan Rajkumar, and Jim Zelenka, "Temporal Protection in Real-Time Operating Systems". In *Proceedings of the 11th IEEE Workshop on Real-Time Operating Systems and Software,* May 1994.
11. Boyd, S., Ghaoul, L. E., Feron, E., and Balakrishnan, V., "Linear Matrix Inequality in Systems and Control Theory", *SIAM Studies in Applied Mathematics.* 1994.
12. Leveson, N. G., "Safeware: System Safety and Computers", Addison Wesley, Sept. 1994.
13. Yeh, Y. C. (Bob), "Dependability of the 777 Primary Flight Control System", *the Proceedings of DCCA Conference*, 1995.
14. Hashii, B., Lal, M., Pandey, R., and Samorodin, S., "Securing Systems Against External Programs," *IEEE Internet Computing,* 2(6):35-45, Nov-Dec 1998.

Real-Time Virtual Resource: A Timely Abstraction for Embedded Systems[*]

Aloysius K. Mok and Alex Xiang Feng

Department of Computer Sciences
University of Texas at Austin
Austin, TX 78712
{mok,xf}@cs.utexas.edu

Abstract. Embedded systems comprise of tasks that have a wide variety of timing requirements, from the lax to the very stringent. The mixing of such tasks has been handled by specialized real-time schedulers, from the traditional cyclic executive dispatcher to sophisticated dynamic-priority schedulers. A common assumption of these real-time schedulers is the availability of global knowledge of the entire task set, and this assumption is required to ensure the schedulability of the time-critical tasks notwithstanding the interference of the less time-critical tasks. In this paper, we discuss the notion of a real-time virtual resource which abstracts the sharing of a physical resource such as a CPU by multiple time-critical tasks. Each real-time virtual resource is a virtual resource in the traditional sense of operating systems but its rate of service provision varies with time and is bounded. The real-time virtual resource abstraction allows tasks with wide-ranging timing criticality to be programmed as if they run on dedicated but slower CPUs such that global knowledge of the tasks is not necessary for schedulability analysis. More importantly, events or signals that are timing sensitive may retain their timeliness properties to within a bound under the real-time virtual resource abstraction, thereby permitting the composition of real-time tasks to preserve global timeliness properties.

1 Introduction

As embedded systems become more complex, a typical embedded system will likely involve a mix of soft and hard real-time applications that share the same embedded run-time platform. In general, an application may consist of one or more tasks. For example, on a hand-held computer a user may want to read email and listen to synthesized music at the same time. The email application is a single task; the music synthesizer application may be made up of four tasks simulating the instruments of a quartet. While the email application has very loose if any real-time constraints, the music application has fairly stringent timing (quality of service) requirements. Ideally, an application developer should be able to write

---

[*] This research is supported partially by ONR grant N00014-99-1-0402 and NSF grant CCR-0207853.

A. Sangiovanni-Vincentelli and J. Sifakis (Eds.): EMSOFT 2002, LNCS 2491, pp. 182–196, 2002.

his application program as if it were running on a dedicated computer and not have to worry about interference from other applications. The music application must generate output at precise intervals independent of the progress of the email application; the music synthesizer's designer would have much better control of the timing of his quartet if he could assume that the synthesizer is the only application running. However, the operating system may not know about all the timing requirements of every application, and hence the email program might be allowed to intrude at undesirable moments. This poses two difficult problems for the real-time scheduling as well as the formal methods research communities: For the real-time scheduling community, the scheduling of soft and hard real-time applications without global knowledge poses new challenges in real-time resource allocation. For the formal methods community, the sharing of resources invalidates the assumption that the timing correctness of an application can be established by pretending that the application is running on a dedicated computer. A simplistic solution is to assign a high priority to timing-critical applications and let the non-real-time applications run only when the timing-critical ones are finished. This approach is viable only for the simplest embedded systems where there is only one real-time task and there is no interaction among the real-time and the non-real-time tasks. If all the applications are to various degrees timing-critical (hard or soft), then the distinction between real-time and non-real-time applications becomes blurry. We need new techniques and policies for managing complex embedded systems.

This paper serves as an introduction to the concept of *real-time virtual resource* and reviews some important technical properties pertaining to this concept[1]. A real-time virtual resource is an abstraction for separating the concerns of the real-time scheduling community and the formal methods community. From the programming point of view, the verification of logical correctness is made easier by the application of good modularity (decomposition) and information hiding (abstraction) principles. But the enforcement of modularity and information hiding implies that the detailed timing requirements of each application may not be accessible as global knowledge, and this eliminates real-time scheduling solutions that relies on global schedulability analysis. Inasmuch as application-specific resource scheduling policies might engender new timing interference among a mix of hard and soft real-time applications, the real-time scheduling community and the formal methods community will be working at cross purposes. This difficulty in separating the concerns is especially acute in the design for fault tolerance where a fault containment mechanism must be provided to prevent the propagation of a timing fault from one application to another.

Take for example the design of avionics systems. Traditionally, the control system of an aircraft is decomposed by functionality into distinct subsystems such as autopilot and auto throttle. A "federated" approach has been used to provide fault containment simply by dedicating a separate fault-tolerant computer

---

[1] This invited paper is a synthesis of and summarizes work reported in detail in the IEEE RTAS and RTSS conferences.

to implement each of the subsystems. The only interface between subsystems is through sensor or control data exchange. On its face, this federated approach perfectly solves the fault containment problem because of the narrow interface between subsystems so that a timing fault is unlikely to propagate. However, the subsystems are in fact tightly coupled because some control variables are affected directly by one another because of the flight dynamics. For example, whereas engine thrust is controlled by the auto throttle and pitch angle by the autopilot, a change in either of them may cause the other to change significantly. The coupling of control variables renders simple functionalities such as "cruise speed control" far from autonomous. A more recent development is a resource sharing scheme via partitioning known as Integrated Modular Avionics (IMA) [2,19]. IMA is to accomplish the same isolation requirement as the federated approach and also support higher level autonomous control and also maximize resource utilization. In IMA, a single computer system with internal replication is used as a common platform to run different subsystems. Inasmuch as they share the same platform, a single timing fault of a subsystem may cause other subsystems to miss their deadlines. Therefore, any implementation of IMA ensure fault isolation by *partitioning* in both time and space. The real-time virtual resource concept provides a way to resolve the temporal partitioning problem.

From an economic point of view, the notion of resource sharing via temporal partitioning is important in mass production. When we drive a car, say, a Volvo S80 to work, there are more than 50 embedded computers around us in the vehicle [1] and some of these embedded computers run highly timing-critical applications such as fuel injection while others are less timing-critical. Typically, there are dozens of embedded systems in one vehicle and each of them typically has its own processor and communication bus. If we could let some of them share resources like a more powerful processor or a communication bus with higher bandwidth and yet achieve the same fault tolerance requirements as before, the cost reduction could be substantial, given that in industries such as automobile manufacturing, a large volume, say, millions of cars of the same make are produced each year.

In the real-time scheduling community, the traditional focus has been primarily about allocating dedicated resources to service a set of real-time applications. Since the first real-time task scheduling model was introduced by Liu and Layland in 1973 [15], there have been many other task models proposed for various real-time application requirements, e.g., the sporadic model [18], the pinwheel model [9]. The schedulability analysis of these models always assumes that the resource to be allocated is made available at a uniform rate and accessible exclusively by the tasks of the application under consideration. Obviously, this assumption no longer holds when the resources are shared by two or more applications that may not be aware of the existence of one another. The operating environment is called an *open system* [6] by real-time system researchers when a physical resource may be shared by different classes of applications, some hard-real-time, others soft-real-time or even non-real-time; sharing is enforced by some kind of partitioning scheme that multiplexes the physical resource among the different application task groups with the proviso that each application task group may be programmed as if it had dedicated access to a physical resource, i.e., without interference from other task groups due to resource sharing.

The sharing of resources in open systems poses new difficulties not solved by traditional real-time scheduling algorithms. If the scheduling policy of each task group assumes exclusive access to a resource, the scheduling policies of the different task groups may conflict with one another. These conflicts may be resolved by a second-level scheduler which coordinates the access to the resource shared by the different task groups. One of the tenets of the open system approach is to avoid performing a global schedulability analysis that considers the timing requirements of all the tasks in all task groups together. Ideally, each task group should be analyzable by itself for schedulability. This may be possible if, for example, the shared resource can be time-shared by infinite time-slicing such that the net effect is as if each task group has exclusive access to the resource that is made available at a fraction of the actual rate. However, infinite time-slicing is impractical because of the context switching overhead costs and because of resource-specific constraints that may impose a lower bound on the time-slice size. For example, a communication bus cannot be infinitely time-sliced if a bus cycle must be at least as long as the signal propagation latency across the bus. Practical implementation of the open system approach may be accomplished by customizing the second-level scheduler to take advantage of the common real-time system model of the task groups so as to minimize context switching between task groups. This is the approach in recent work [6,10]. In the real-time virtual resource approach, we take a broader view. The general idea is to view each task group as accessing a virtual resource that operates at a fraction of the rate of physical resource shared by the group but the rate varies with time during execution. Ideally, a virtual resource should achieve a complete separation of concerns so that: (1) each application task group running on a virtual resource may be executed as if it had exclusive access to its own dedicated resource, and (2) there is minimal interaction between the resource-level scheduler and the application-task-level scheduler.

In the real-time virtual resource approach, we shall characterize the rate variation of each virtual resource by means of a delay bound D that specifies the maximum extra time the task group may have to wait in order to receive its fraction of the physical resource over any time interval starting from *any* point in time. This way, if we know that an event e will occur within x time units from another event e' assuming that the virtual resource operates at a uniform rate and event occurrence depends only on resource consumption (i.e., virtual time progresses uniformly), then e and e' will be apart by at most $x + D$ time units in real time. If infinite time-slicing is possible, the delay bound is zero. In general, the delay bound of a virtual resource will be task-group-specific. The characterization of virtual resource rate variation by means of the delay bound will allow us to better deal with more general types of timing constraints such as jitter. We call virtual resources whose rate of operation variation is bounded real-time virtual resources.

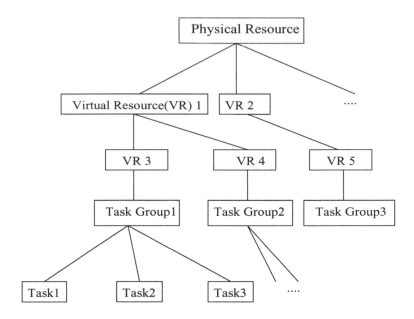

Fig. 1. Virtual Resource Structure Overview

The rate variation and therefore the delay bound of a real-time virtual resource is in general a function of the scheduling policy used to allocate the shared physical resource among the task groups. One approach to construct real-time virtual resources that are especially amenable to delay bound determination is through temporal resource partitioning. In this approach, the second-level scheduler is responsible only for assigning partitions (collection of time slices) to the task groups and does not require information on the timing parameters of the individual tasks within each task group. The schedulability analysis of tasks on a partition depends only on the partition parameters. This enforces the desired separation of concerns; scheduling at the resource partition (task group) level and at the task level are isolated at run time.

A structural overview of virtual resource provisioning is shown in Figure 1. At the top is a physical resource which is partitioned into several virtual resources; then, each virtual resource is partitioned recursively into several lower level virtual resources. Eventually, each virtual resource will be associated with one task group which consists of one or more tasks. The mapping relation between resource and partitions is 1-to-n; that between the partition and task group is 1-to-1 and the task group to tasks is 1-to-n again. Two classes of resource scheduling problems may be identified in this structure: one is how to schedule the tasks within a task group; the other is how to schedule virtual resources on a physical resource.

Throughout the paper it is assumed that time values have the domain the non-negative real numbers unless otherwise stated. Preemptive scheduling is assumed, i.e., a task executing on the shared resource can be interrupted at any instant in time, and its execution can be resumed later. Although a resource can be a processor, a communication bus, etc., we shall talk about a single processor as the resource to be shared.

Definition 1 *A task T is defined as a pair (c, p), where c is the (worst case) execution time requirement, p is the period of the task.*

Even though we do not specify a per-period deadline explicitly, we shall define deadlines when they are relevant to the results in this paper.

Definition 2 *A task group τ is a collection of n tasks that are to be scheduled on a real-time virtual processor (a partition), $\tau = \{T_i = (c_i, p_i)\}_{i=1}^{n}$.*

We use the term task group to emphasize its difference from the term task set in that a task set is to be scheduled on a dedicated resource while a task group is scheduled on a partition of the shared physical resource.

The rest of this paper is organized as follows. Section 2 defines Bounded Delay partition model and Section 3 investigates partition model on the integer domain. In Section 4 we discuss the partition scheduling problem. We end with a discussion of related work in Section 5 and finally the conclusion in Section 6.

2   Bounded-Delay Resource Partition Model

In this section we shall first start with a few preliminary definitions. Then we shall define the bounded-delay resource partition model and state a general schedulability theorem.

Definition 3 *A Resource Partition Π is a tuple (Γ, P), where Γ is an array of N time pairs $\{(S_1, E_1), (S_2, E_2), \ldots, (S_N, E_N)\}$ that satisfies $(0 \leq S_1 < E_1 < S_2 < E_2 < \ldots < S_N < E_N \leq P)$ for some $N \geq 1$, and P is the partition period. The physical resource is available to a task group executing on this partition only during time intervals $(S_i + j \times P, E_i + j \times P), 1 \leq i \leq N, j \geq 0$.*

The above definition enumerates every time interval that is assigned to a partition and is a general representation of periodic partitioning schemes, including those that are generated dynamically by an on-line partition scheduler. It provides a starting point upon which other approaches of defining partitions may be considered.

We shall refer to the intervals where the processor is unavailable to a partition *blocking time* of the partition. In traditional models where resources are dedicated to a task group, there is no blocking time and we may consider this as a special case corresponding to the partition $\Pi = (\{(0, P)\}, P)$.

Example 1 *As shown in Figure 2, $\Pi_1 = \{(1, 2), (4, 6)\}, 6)$ is a resource partition whose period is 6 with available resource time from time 1 to time 2 and from time 4 to time 6 every period.*

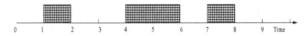

Fig. 2. Timing Diagram of Partition Π_1

Definition 4 *The Availability Factor (rate) of a resource partition Π is $\alpha(\Pi) = (\sum_{i=1}^{n}(E_i - S_i))/P$.*

The availability factor (rate) specifies what percentage of the total time of a resource is available to this particular partition. Obviously, the rate of service provision of a dedicated resource is 100%.

The availability factor of Π_1 in Example 1 is $\alpha(\Pi_1) = ((2-1)+(6-4))/6 = 0.5$.

Definition 5 *The Supply Function $S(t)$ of a partition Π is the total amount of time that is available in Π from time 0 to time t.*

Definition 6 *The Partition Delay Δ of Partition Π is the smallest d so that for any t_1 and t_2, $(t_2 - t_1 - d)\alpha(\Pi) \leq (S(t_2) - S(t_1)) \leq (t_2 - t_1 + d)\alpha(\Pi)$.*

Definition 7 *Let h denote the execution rate of the resource where partition Π is implemented. The Normalized Execution of partition Π is an allocation of resource time to Π at a uniform, uninterrupted rate of $(\alpha(\Pi) \times h)$.*

Partition delay measures the largest time deviation of a partition based on any time interval with regard to its normalized execution.

Definition 8 *A Bounded Delay Resource Partition Π is a tuple (α, Δ) where α is the availability factor of the partition and Δ is the partition delay.*

Note that the definition defines a set of partitions because there are many different partitions in the static partition model that may satisfy this requirement.

Theorem 1 *Given a task group τ and a bounded delay partition $\Pi = (\alpha, \lambda_n)$, let S_n denote a valid schedule of τ on the normalized execution of Π, S_p the schedule of τ on Partition Π according to the same execution order and amount as S_n. Also let λ denote the largest amount of time such that any job on S_n is completed at least λ time before its deadline. S_p is a valid schedule if $\lambda \geq \lambda_n$.*

In Theorem 1, λ defines the maximum allowable output jitter [5] for S_n. Therefore, informally, Theorem 1 could be written as: A task group is schedulable on a partition if the maximum allowable output jitter is no less than the partition delay.

Theorem 1 provides a practical way to schedule a task group on a partition. If we could find a schedule on the normalized execution and the smallest λ is no less than λ_n, we could use this schedule on the partition and be guaranteed that no deadline will be missed on the partition. The schedule on the normalized execution is the same as the traditional task schedule, for which there are many known techniques.

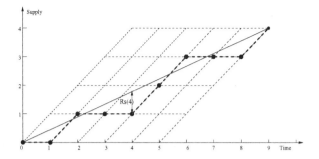

Fig. 3. Instant Regularity at Time 4 of Partition Π_1 in Example 1

3   Regularity Resource Partition Model

3.1   Regularity

In this section we shall introduce concepts that are useful for measuring the deviation of a partition from a resource with uniform provision rate. We first define *instant regularity* and later *temporal regularity* and *supply regularity*.

Definition 9 *The Instant Regularity $I(t)$ at time t on partition Π is given by* $S(t) - t\alpha(\Pi)$.

The notion of instant regularity is called dynamic regularity by Shigero et al. in [20]. We prefer the term instant regularity because it better captures the idea that it pertains to a particular time point and there are different types of regularity. The instant regularity measures at a particular time point the difference between the amount of supply that the partition has already gotten from the resource scheduler since time 0 and the amount that the partition would get if it were running on its normalized execution. As shown in Figure 3 the instant regularity at time t is equal to the distance from the supply function to the normalized function. Notice that it is a real number and could be negative as well.

Definition 10 *[20] Let a,b,e,k be non-negative integers, the Temporal Regularity $R_T(\Pi)$ of Partition Π is equal to the minimum value of k such that $\forall a, \forall b.\ a < b,$ $0 \le \exists e \le k,\ |I(b - e) - I(a)| < 1.$*

The temporal regularity measures the overall difference between the partition supply function and the normalized supply function from the time dimension. This measurement considers all possible time intervals no matter which time point is the start point.

Definition 11 *Let a,b,k be non-negative integers, the Supply Regularity $R_S(\Pi)$ of Partition Π is equal to the minimum value of k such that $\forall a, \forall b.\ a < b,\ 0 \le k,$ $|I(b) - I(a)| < k.$*

The supply regularity is the upper bound on the amount by which the actual supply during any time interval is more than or less than the amount of supply that the partition is supposed to obtain.

Definition 12 *[20] A Regular Partition is a partition with temporal regularity of 0.*

Definition 13 *A k-Temporal-Irregular Partition is a partition with temporal regularity of k where $k > 0$. A k Supply-Irregular Partition is a partition with supply regularity of k where $k > 1$.*

Given a partition, we now analyze the schedulability problem of a task group that may execute only during the available time slots of the partition. We shall first investigate the problem of regular partitions and later of irregular partitions.

3.2   Regular Partition

In this section, we shall show that regular partitions preserve the utilization bounds of both fixed priority scheduling (rate monotonic) and dynamic priority scheduling (earliest deadline first).

Theorem 2 *A task group G of m tasks is schedulable on a regular partition Π by Rate Monotonic if $U(G) \leq m(2^{\frac{1}{m}} - 1)\alpha(\Pi)$.*

This result is the analogue of the Liu and Layland's bound for m tasks on a dedicated resource which means the utilization bound is not affected by resource partitioning at all for regular partitions.

Just as the utilization bound of fixed-priority scheduling for regular partitions above, we can show that the utilization bound of dynamic-priority scheduling also remains the same for regular partitions.

Theorem 3 *[20] A task group G with n periodic tasks, $\tau_1, \tau_2, ..., \tau_n$ is schedulable on a regular partition Π by the earliest-deadline-first policy if and only if $U(G) \leq \alpha(\Pi)$.*

Intuitively, a task group is feasible when its least demand during any time interval t is always no greater than the supply during the same time interval. We shall visualize this on the supply graph. First, because the least demand is no greater than $U(G)t$ and $U(G) \leq \alpha(\Pi)$ the demand function is no greater than the normalized supply function. Second, because the demand is an integer the demand is at most the largest integer number below the normalized supply function, i.e., the supply function of the critical partition. Therefore, the least demand is no greater than the supply, thus guaranteeing the schedulability of the task group.

3.3   Irregular Partition

Definition 14 *The Virtual Time $V(t)$ of a partition Π is equal to $\lfloor S(t)/\alpha(\Pi)\rfloor$ where $S(t)$ is the supply function of Π.*

Definition 15 *Virtual Time Scheduling on a partition Π is the scheduling constraint such that a job is eligible to run only when it is released and its release time is no less than the current virtual time of Π.*

Virtual Time Scheduling may apply to all of the scheduling algorithms designed for dedicated resources. Therefore, we have Virtual Time Rate Monotonic Scheduling, Virtual Time Earliest-Deadline-First Scheduling, and other virtual time scheduling algorithms.

Theorem 4 *A task group G $\{T_i = (c_i, p_i)\}_{i=1}^n$ is schedulable on a k-temporal-irregular partition Π by virtual time rate monotonic scheduling according to its virtual time if $\sum_{i=1}^n \frac{c_i}{p_i - k} \leq \alpha(\Pi) n(2^{\frac{1}{n}} - 1)$.*

Similarly, we have

Theorem 5 *A task group G $\{T_i = (c_i, p_i)\}_{i=1}^n$ is schedulable on a k-temporal-irregular partition Π by virtual-time earliest-deadline-first if $\sum_{i=1}^n \frac{c_i}{p_i - k} \leq \alpha(\Pi)$.*

4   Partition Scheduling

Given the resource requirement of (α_k, Δ_k) for each partition S_k, a schedule must be constructed at the resource level. Note that the pair of parameters (α_k, Δ_k) requires only that the partition must receive an α_k amount of processor capacity with the partition delay no greater than Δ. It does not impose any restriction on the execution time and period. This property makes the construction of the schedule extremely flexible. In this section, we shall first discuss the partition scheduling problem on a single level, i.e. scheduling partitions directly on a dedicated resource; then we shall extend this problem to multi-level partitioning, i.e., scheduling partitions recursively on partitions.

4.1   Single Level Partition Scheduling

We suggest both static and dynamic scheduling algorithms for the single-level partition scheduling problem.

1. Static schedule:
In this approach, the resource schedules every partition cyclically with period equal to the minimum of $T_k = (\Delta_k/(1-\alpha_k))$ and each partition is allocated an amount of processor capacity that is proportional to α_k. If the T_k of the partitions are substantially different, we may adjust them conservatively to form a harmonic chain in which T_j is a multiple of T_i, if $T_i < T_j$ for all i and j. This way, the static resource schedule is repeated every major cycle which has length

equal to the maximum of T_k. Each major cycle is further divided into several minor cycles with a length equal to the minimum of T_k. This would reduce the number of context switches substantially[13,11].

2. Dynamic schedule:
In this approach, the resource schedules every partition using the Earliest Deadline Schedule with a period of $T_k/2$ and an execution time of $T_k \times \alpha_k/2$. The division of the period in the static schedule by 2 is because we need to guarantee the maximum separation of two executions in two contiguous periods to be less than the partition delay Δ so as to meet the requirement of partition delay.

Another way to achieve this is to separate the deadline and the period of the EDF scheduling. The period of a partition is assigned to be more than $T_k/2$ while its corresponding relative deadline is assigned to be less than $T_k/2$. However, the sum of the period and relative deadline is always equal to T_k.[24]

4.2   Multi-level Partition Scheduling

In the previous subsection, partitions are scheduled directly on top of a dedicated resource. In general, a partition may also reside directly inside another partition instead of a physical resource, and these partitions form a hierarchy. In this section, we shall first show a schedulability result on hierarchical partitioning. Then we shall discuss how to perform the actual scheduling.

Theorem 6 *A partition group $\{\Pi_i(\alpha_i, \Delta_i)\}$ $(1 < i \leq n)$ is schedulable on a partition $\Pi(\alpha, \Delta)$ if $\sum_{i=1}^{n} \alpha_i \leq \alpha$ and $\Delta_i > \Delta$ for all i, $(1 < i \leq n)$.*

Theorem 6 provides a method to determine the schedulability of scheduling partitions (a partition group) on another partition. However, it does not explain how to perform the actual scheduling since the infinite time slice scheme that is used in the proof is impractical. Therefore, the question remains how to schedule partitions using methods with finite context switch overhead.

Theorem 7 *Given a partition group $\{\Pi_i(\alpha_i, \Delta_i)\}$ $(1 < i \leq n)$ to be scheduled on a partition $\Pi(\alpha, \Delta)$. Let S_n denote a scheduler of scheduling $\Pi_i'(\alpha_i/\alpha, \Delta_i - \Delta)$ $(1 < i \leq n)$ on a dedicated resource with capacity of the same as the normalized execution of Π. Also let S_p denote the virtual time S_n scheduler of scheduling Π_i on Π. Then S_p is valid if S_n is valid.*

Theorem 7 justifies the observation that we may use essentially the same algorithms of scheduling partitions on dedicated resources for hierarchical partitioning by applying the virtual time scheduling scheme. This method is in two steps:

- Construct Scheduler S_n.
- For any interval (t_1, t_2) assigned to Π_i' in S_n assign $(P(t_1), P(t_2))$ to Π_i in S_p.

Example 2 *Consider scheduling Partitions Π_1 $(0.2, 5)$, Π_2 $(0.25, 6)$ and Π_3 $(0.05, 8)$ on Partition $\Pi(0.5, 4)$. Using this method, the scheduling problem is transformed into scheduling*

$$(0.2/0.5, 5 - 4), (0.25/0.5, 6 - 4), (0.05/0.5, 8 - 5)$$

i.e.

$$(0.4, 1), (0.5, 2), (0.1, 4)$$

on a dedicated resource. Suppose we use the simplest half-half algorithm describe in [17], this problem is further converted into an equivalent problem of scheduling three tasks with period and computation time of

$$(0.5, 0.2), (1, 0.5) and (2, 0.2),$$

respectively. Obviously, they are schedulable and the problem is trivial.

5   Related Work

The open system environment first proposed by Deng and Liu [6] allows real-time and non-real-time tasks not only to coexist but also to be able to join and leave the system dynamically. Therefore, the admission test on a real-time task needs to be independent of any other task in the system and a global schedulability analysis is out of the question. This concept was first discussed based on an EDF kernel scheduler and was later extended to the fixed priority scheduler as kernel scheduler[10]. We take a broader approach in that we do not base our kernel scheduler on any particular scheduling policy; we start out with descriptions of a partition and we investigate whether application-specific task models such as the Liu and Layland periodic task systems can be scheduled on a partition.

Because in an open real-time environment the parameters of real-time tasks are no longer required to be known *a priori*, efficient online scheduling algorithms are needed [3,22]. Also needed are practical mechanisms to provide isolation among tasks. One interesting approach is to assign each task a server with certain parameters [4,14]. However, the interaction between tasks and the higher-level scheduler may increase the unpredictability in task execution and hence make other requirements such as output jitter bound difficult to realize. We believe that a clean separation between the scheduling of tasks within partitions and scheduling partitions on resources is more consistent with the tenet of open system environment. To wit, even if the application task groups are not all specified in one common system model such as Liu and Layland periodic tasks, our partition models can still be used. We only need to figure out the schedulability conditions of the new system model on partitions. The effect of the partition scheduling on task group scheduling is captured by the partition parameter Δ in the bounded-delay model.

Our work also differentiates from Proportional Share in [21]. The lag in Proportional Share holds only for intervals starting from the same time point while in this paper the partition delay applies to any interval regardless of the starting point. This difference is crucial since the partition delays are most useful for bounding the separation between event pairs.

Compared with application architectural concepts such as IMA, the work in this paper provides the scheduling-theoretic foundation for those architectures. It has been pointed out that there are some significant issues that remain unsolved in the resource partition problem. First, IMA was found to have a large amount of output jitter [2]. Because the available time of a partition cannot in general be evenly distributed the completion time of a certain job of a task is affected not only by outstanding jobs of other tasks but also by the fluctuation of the partition. Second, IMA has been considered only for usage with STSPP [13]. In STSPP partitions have only one continuous time slot within each period and this need not be the case. The results in this paper provide answers to some of these issues.

Our work is also differentiated from Start-time Fair Queuing(SFQ) [8] and Fluctuation Constrained Server (FCS) [12,23]. Both SFQ and FCS have the similar notion of supply deviation for any time interval as our work. However, SFQ aims to minimize the delay to achieve near-optimal fairness while our work measures the delay as long as the delay could guarantee the schedulability of real-time tasks. Furthermore, SFQ depends on the number of threads (which are equivalent to partitions in our work) being scheduled; while the resource level delay in our work is specified by the partition request, thus providing stronger guarantee. On the other hand,FCS is intended to be on per stream basis while our work is on per task group basis. FCS does not provide any real-time schedulability analysis if a group of tasks instead of one single task (stream) are running on FCS, while task level scheduling is a major problem that real-time virtual resource addresses, as shown in [17] and [16].

6   Conclusion

In this paper, we explain the concept of real-time virtual resource and give a summary of the salient resource scheduling/partitioning results. The real-time virtual resource concept is especially useful in the open systems environment where the sharing of resources may not be visible to different application task groups and yet the execution of individual task groups must not cause timing failures in other task groups.

Our general idea is to view each task group as accessing a virtual resource that operates at a fraction of the rate of the physical resource but the rate varies with time during execution. We can characterize the service rate variation of each real-time virtual resource by means of a delay bound D that specifies the maximum extra time the task group may have to wait in order to receive its fraction of the physical resource over any time interval starting from *any* point in time. Suppose we know that an event e will occur within x time units from another event e' given that the virtual resource operates at a uniform rate and event occurrence depends only on resource consumption. Then e and e' will be apart by at most $x + D$ time units in real time. If the timing correctness of a task group needs to be established only to a certain precision, say, accurate to within D, then the application of formal methods to show that the task group meets its real-time requirements can be carried out as if the application runs on a dedicated processor without interference from other task groups.

Thus, the real-time virtual resource abstraction supports a universal paradigm for separating the concerns of proving the correctness of individual applications and ensuring that the aggregate resource requirements of the applications can be met, as follows: First, determine the timing precision of event occurrences that is required to establish the desired timing properties of individual applications. Second, use formal methods or otherwise to prove the correctness of each individual application by pretending that it has access to a dedicated resource which operates at a lower rate but has a delay bound that is adequate for the precision requirements. Third, show that the resource partition scheme used by the run-time system satisfies the delay bounds. In a nutshell, the real-time virtual resource abstraction gives us a handle on correctly composing applications with disparate timing requirements and shared resources.

References

1. Volvo technology report, no.1. Technical report, 1998.
2. N. Audsley and A. Wellings. Analysing apex applications. In *IEEE Real-Time Systems Symposium*, pages 39–44, December 1996.
3. S. Baruah. Overload tolerance for single-processor workloads. In *Real-Time Technology and Applications Symposium*, pages 2–11, 1998.
4. S. Baruah, G. Buttazzo, S. Gorinsky, and G. Lipari. Scheduling periodic task systems to minimize output jitter. In *The 6th International Conference on Real-Time Computing Systems and Applications*, 1999.
5. S. K. Baruah, D. Chen, and A. K. Mok. Jitter concerns in periodic task systems. In *IEEE Real-Time Systems Symposium*, 1997.
6. Z. Deng and J. Liu. Scheduling real-time applications in an open environment. In *IEEE Real-Time Systems Symposium*, pages 308–319, December 1997.
7. X. Feng and A. K. Mok. A model of hierarchical real-time virtual resources. Technical report, Dept. of Computer Sciences, Univ. of Texas at Austin (ftp://ftp.cs.utexas.edu/pub/amok/UTCS-RTS-2002-01.ps), 2001.
8. P. Goyal, H. M. Vin, and H. Cheng. Start-time fair queuing: A scheduling algorithm for integrated servicespacket switching networks. Technical report, Dept. of Computer Sciences, Univ. of Texas at Austin (ftp://ftp.cs.utexas.edu/pub/techreports/tr96-02.ps.Z), 1996.
9. R. Holte, A. Mok, L. Rosier, I. Tulchinsky, and D. Varvel. The pinwheel: A real-time scheduling problem. In *22th Hawaii International Conference on System Sciences*, January 1989.
10. T.-W. Kuo and C.-H. Li. A fixed-priority-driven open system architecture for real-time applications. In *IEEE Real-Time Systems Symposium*, pages 256–267, 1999.
11. T. W. Kuo and A. K. Mok. Load adjustment in adaptive real-time systems. In *IEEE Real-Time Systems Symposium*, pages 160–170, 1991.
12. K. Lee. Performance bounds in communication networks with variable-rate links. In *SIGCOMM*, pages 126–136, 1995.

13. Y. Lee, D. Kim, M. Younis, and J. Zhou. Partition scheduling in apex runtime environment for embedded avionics software. In *The 5th International Conference on Real-Time Computing Systems and Applications*, pages 103–109, 1998.
14. G. Lipari and S. Baruah. Efficient scheduling of real-time multi-task applications in dynamic systems. In *Real-Time Technology and Applications Symposium*, pages 166–175, December 2000.
15. C. L. Liu and J. W. Layland. Scheduling algorithms for multiprogramming in a hard-real-time environment. *Journal of ACM*, 20(1), January 1973.
16. A. Mok and X. Feng. Towards compositionality in real-time resource partitioning based on regularity bounds. In *IEEE Real-Time Systems Symposium*, pages 129–138, 2001.
17. A. Mok, X. Feng, and D. Chen. Resource partition for real-time systems. In *Real-Time Technology and Applications Symposium*, pages 75–84, 2001.
18. A. K. Mok. *Fundamental Design Problems of Distributed Systems for the Hard-Real-Time Environment*. PhD thesis, MIT, 1983.
19. J. Rushby. *Partitioning in Avionics Architectures: Requirements, Mechanisms, and Assurance*. NASA Contractor Report 209347. SRI International, Menlo Park, CA, 1999.
20. S. Shigero, M. Takashi, and H. Kei. On the schedulability conditions on partial time slots. In *Real-Time Computing Systems and Applications Conference*, pages 166–173, 1999.
21. I. Stoica, H. Abdel-Wahab, K. Jeffay, S. Baruah, J. Gehrke, and C. Plaxton. A proportional share resource allocation algorithm for real-time, time-shared systems. In *IEEE Real-Time Systems Symposium*, pages 288–299, 1996.
22. Y. L. T. Kuo and K. Lin. Efficient on-line schedulability tests for priority driven real-time systems. In *Real-Time Technology and Applications Symposium*, pages 4–13.
23. G. G. Xie and S. S. Lam. Delay guarantee of virtual clock server. *IEEE/ACM Transactions on Networking*, 3(6):683–689, 1995.
24. M. Xiong, R. Sivasankaran, J. Stankovic, K. Ramamritham, and D. Towsley. Scheduling transactions with temporal constraints: exploiting data semantics. In *IEEE Real-Time Systems Symposium*, pages 240–251, 1996.

JCOD: A Lightweight Modular Compilation Technology for Embedded Java

Bertrand Delsart, Vania Joloboff, and Eric Paire

Silicomp Research Institute
2, Avenue de Vignate
Gières, 38610, France

Abstract. JCOD[1] is a new compiler technology for appliances such as mobile phones or printers running embedded Java programs. Interpreted Java is sometimes too slow and one would like to compile bytecode into native code as this is achieved in JIT compilers on desktops. Our approach takes into account the memory and CPU constraints of the appliances. We have designed a distributed technology to efficiently detect "hot spots" of the application and compile them out of the appliance, on a network compile server that uses a lot of code size optimizations. This paper describes the different components and exhibits their flexibility. They can easily be upgraded independently or tailored for a specific kind of applications running on a given appliance.

1   Introduction

The development of the Java[2] bytecode as a universally portable execution format for software makes it attractive to manufacturers of appliances and embedded systems. However, to deliver its promises for embedded systems, Java must overcome two pitfalls: performance and footprint. Both issues can partly be addressed by the implementation of the Java Virtual Machine. However, no matter how smart an implementation of a bytecode interpreter is, performance of interpreted bytecode is still at least 10-20 times slower than corresponding compiled C, C++ or ADA code (some applications are reported 50 times slower). Although interpreted bytecode may be acceptable in some embedded applications (i.e. smart card applications where memory is very scarce but response time in seconds is OK), there are many cases where performance of interpreted bytecode is simply unacceptable. Then one has no choice but compiling Java bytecode to native code (or use a Java micro-processor).

   To obtain good performance on a Java embedded system, compiled native code can be stored in device ROM, using some Ahead-of-Time (AOT) compiling technique such as described in [1, 15, 19]. However, one major reason why vendors are adopting Java is the ability to install and to upgrade software into the device during its lifetime. For software downloaded after the device has been shipped to the customer, dynamic compilation appears to be more effective than AOT compilation.

---

[1] This work was accomplished with funding from Hewlett-Packard Corporation and a grant from the Japanese government, through its IPA agency.
[2] Java is a trademark from Sun Microsystems Inc.

A. Sangiovanni-Vincentelli and J. Sifakis (Eds.): EMSOFT 2002, LNCS 2491, pp. 197–212, 2002.

The idea of Just-In-Time (JIT) compilation has developed mostly with the advent of Java Virtual Machines. Although there are variants, we characterize JIT compilers by systematic compilation of code whenever the code is used the first time. JIT compilers provide very significant speed-up but also they introduce compile-time pauses and useless compilation for rarely executed code. In the server and desktop markets most Java vendors have added dynamic compiler technology to increase performance. Their Java Virtual Machine implementations often include JIT compilers that compile invoked methods on the fly. Although this approach has the great advantage to make the compilation process transparent to the users, it has the drawback to be unpractical for embedded systems, for two major reasons:

- the compiler requires CPU cycles that may not be available on the device, or would preclude to meet the response time constraints of the running application, as embedded systems processors are as not as powerful as workstation processors.
- the compiler also requires significant dynamic memory to store intermediate program representations (C or C++ compilers use temporary disk space but most of those appliances are diskless).
- the compiled version of all executed methods may also take some significant amount of writable memory, in addition to the static memory required for the compiler code itself.

A significant predecessor to our work is the idea of continuous compilation introduced by Plezbert and Cytron in [14]. This paper introduced the notion of starting execution of Java programs in interpreted mode and compiling on a separate processor on a multi-processor platform in order to avoid pauses due to compile time. The same paper also proposed the concept of "smart just-in-time", a threshold point for deciding when code should be compiled or remain interpreted. Our work is an extension of the continuous compiling system proposed by Plezbert and Cytron focused towards embedded systems driven by low cost or low power consumption requirements. We have extended the notion of continuous compilation on a separate network server instead of separate processor. Since there is no shared memory between the compiler and the appliance, we have defined a new object code format to perform dynamic code loading and linking on devices that may not support it [10]. The key ideas of these components are described in Section 4.

In addition, the Java bytecode is very dense. As the 'bytecode' name indicates, most JVM instructions fit on 1 byte or 2 bytes. Bytecodes are sophisticated instructions that can hardly be translated into a single native processor instruction as a rule. For example, if one bytecode instruction expands on average to two 32-bits machine instructions, the code size will expand by a factor of 8. Hence Java programs occupy less memory than actual machine code. Compiling the entire application may then become unacceptable (going from 128K to 1MB) for embedded systems where memory is scarce. Taking a rule of thumb that applications spend 80% of their time in 20% of the code, it is sufficient to compile these 20% to gain significant performance. Thus, the idea is to compile only the most frequently executed code, which Sun calls the "hot spots" [17]. Section 3 describes our profiling components and heuristics.

Section 5 gives some figures about the overhead and the efficiency of our solution.

2   JCOD Overview

A technology allowing for profiling of application, dynamic compilation and co-existence of interpreted code and compiled code makes the best trade-off between speed, device cost and manageability. We have developed such a dynamic compilation technology for embedded Java, named JCOD, which stands for "Java Compilation On Demand", with the following features:

- The Java Virtual Machine is augmented with a profiling component that does dynamic detection of performance critical code (i.e. "hot spots") and an agent that decides which of this critical code should be compiled. These components have a negligible performance and memory size overhead.
- Compilation is not achieved on the appliance, but on a separate network server. In addition, the compiler has a lot of code size optimizations and does not shoot for the best performance at any price. It attempts to generate the smallest code offering a significant performance increase in order to save memory.
- The design is modular and each component depends only on a few features. For instance, the compiler is VM independent and all the code installed on the appliance is compiler independent.

As a result, embedded Java applications could be run on a device with a small acceptable overhead, starting in interpreted mode. As the application runs, without visible pause or disruption, the most performance critical code is compiled, progressively replacing the interpreted code, showing significant performance improvement. At some point, dynamic compilation stops. It often happens when the compiled code has consumed a given amount of memory but our solution allows to take into account for instance the number of bytecodes interpreted per second. The application then reaches a "cruise mode" with a balance between interpreted code and compiled code.

In order to support this approach, in JCOD, the target embedded system runs a Java Virtual Machine augmented with new capabilities, mostly written in Java, that make it capable of supporting Compile-On-Demand. To increase the flexibility, most of this code is grouped into a JCOD service and can be dynamically downloaded. Our service initializer is controlled by Java properties and can talk to an administration server to override some configuration properties and download the specified JCOD service. As the application is running, the Java Virtual Machine on the device profiles the executed code, with an overhead and a granularity specified by the service (see section 3). Using this information, the service may decide which parts of the code need be compiled. Then, it sends a compilation request to the compile server. The compiler output is sent back to the service, which dynamically loads and links the resulting code (see section 4). On the next calls, the compiled code is executed instead of the bytecode. Figure 1 outlines system components activities as described above.

These tasks are performed by modular components. For instance, the compiler can be replaced, extended or upgraded. In addition, the downloaded service includes the profiling heuristic and the protocol used to discover and discuss with the compile server. Hence, our solution is dynamically configurable. Our prototype uses HTTP to initialize the service and a simple ASCII protocol over sockets for the compilations (with a reconnection mechanism to handle network failures and temporary connections). However, a more secure protocol and code signing could be used. In that case, the JCOD service should also be signed if it is not preinstalled on the device. Our protocol also includes the support for debug streams, remotely available on a JCOD console applet. All the components can write debug information on this console.

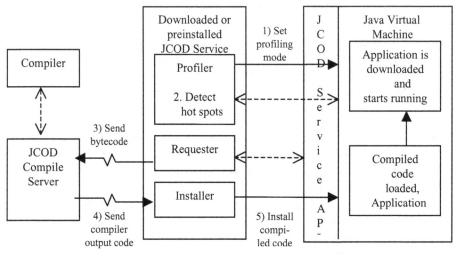

Fig. 1. JCOD Architecture

3   Dynamic Profiling

Our compiler technology does not allow for partial method compilation. In addition, feedback-directed optimizations, if available, should probably be performed only after the generation of simple compiled methods with instrumentation instructions [20]. Hence, our goal is only to dynamically detect which interpreted methods should be compiled. Depending on the type of program running, the profiling overhead must be balanced with the reactivity and the best time to select a method may vary. In addition, sophisticated profiling may not be a good idea for online profiling [6]. Thus, in this detection of "hot spots", we want to distinguish mechanism from policy. We want to allow multiple dynamically configurable policies based on a common generic profiling mechanism hard coded in the Java Virtual Machine. In our case, the mechanism consists in a flexible gathering of data. The policy, called the Decision Maker and programmed in Java, defines how often and how much CPU is devoted to examining the data and deciding which method should be compiled.

3.1   Mechanism: Interpreter Extensions and Profiler Runtime

Even if the mechanism is hard coded, we differentiate the modifications performed in the Java Virtual Machine and the runtime, consisting of a few methods than can be provided by a third party. The VM modifications collect the data described in this section and calls the C profiler runtime whenever entering or exiting a method. JCOD comes with a small runtime profiler that acts as a go-between the VM per se and the Decision Maker implemented in Java. The interface between the profiler and the Decision Maker consist of static fields and Java objects associated to profiled methods. Those **MethodData** objects are created by the Decision Maker and can be associated to one or several methods. Their fields reflect the data gathered by the VM.

The profiler's goal is to detect methods for which bytecode interpretation is expensive. A first idea would be to measure CPU time spent in each method, but this is complex and expensive to compute on the fly, as one need to exclude sub-calls and also to exclude CPU time for native calls, system calls, GC and alike services which cannot be improved by compilation. Since what one can optimize is the time spent in the interpreter itself for each method, we think better results are obtained by modifying the VM so that it just keeps track of the bytecodes executed and constructs for every targeted method a method cost, a number that reflects the cost of interpreting the method. The VM interpreter also measures other figures given later in this section. It gathers in its frame structure the information about the current run of a method.

When exiting a method, the profiling runtime is called and increments the **global_cost** static field. If the maximum value is reached, the static Java **global overflow notifier** of the Decision Maker is called. The Decision Maker can adapt the frequency of these calls by choosing its initial value.

In addition, if there is a MethodData object associated to the exited method, the profiling runtime updates its virtual fields. For each MethodData object, the Decision Maker can also decide how frequently its virtual Java **exit notifier** should be called. At one extreme, it can decide to be notified on every exit. This is fairly expensive and it is mainly used for debugging purpose, to track the current method or check the execution flow (together with an enter notification not described here). On the other hand, it can decide to work asynchronously without any notification... Basically, our interface allow to specify that every N calls, the runtime profiler performs the call only if the **NOTIFY_EXIT_ALL_METHODS** flag is set for this methodData or if something "interesting" has happened according to the statistics gathered. This is done by modifying a counter that, as a side effect, allows to asynchronously obtain the number of calls.

The interesting events and the gathered statistics has been defined by analyzing what are the relevant criteria for compilation policies. In a constrained environment, a MethodData object should not be allocated for each method. It would both increase the memory used and the time necessary to analyze the results. Typically, the Decision Maker temporarily associates the same object to all the compilation candidates, with N set to 1 and NOTIFY_EXIT_ALL_METHODS unset. Our definition of "interesting" event should ensure that a notifier is called if the method that exits should be associated to another MethodData object, which may then keep the history of this method (with a less expensive notification strategy).

One of the key factors is that the cost of a method call heavily depends upon whether the caller and callee methods are both compiled or not. The most efficient call is between two compiled methods. Two interpreted methods can also interact quite efficiently. When there is a switch from interpreted to compiled code and reciprocally, the cost is higher because one has to parse the arguments and do bookkeeping such as exception handling across the two [4]. In order to take this into account, the VM also reports the number C of interactions with compiled methods and the number I of interactions with interpreted methods, including the caller. In our profiler runtime, the exit notifier is called when C is not null and the NOTIFY_EXIT_ON_ CROSSCALL flag is set in the methodData associated to the exited method.

In addition, as the goal is to maximize performance for minimum code size expansion, the most interesting methods to compile are those that are called often or that contain loops executed several times. Without a per method history, the runtime profiler can only identify loops. However, since switching from interpreted mode to compiled mode is very expensive, methods called often should probably be compiled only if they are called from compiled code containing a loop. Hence, the loop detection is sufficient in most cases to detect the interesting methods (see section 5.1). Thus, the JCOD runtime calls the exit notifier when the interpreter has found a backward branch and the NOTIFY_EXIT_ON_LOOP flag is set for the methodData of the exited method.

The two previous events are sufficient to gradually allocate MethodData object to interesting compilation candidates and monitor them. In addition, like for the global overflow notifier, the exit notifier is also called when the cost field of a given methodData overflows to let the Decision Maker select methods only according to their interpretation cost.

In our VM implementation, the interpretation cost is an approximation of the number of bytecodes executed. The VM only needs to increment local variables at each branching instruction and method to compute the cost and the numbers of interpreted and compiled methods called. On each return instruction, it calls the runtime profiler, which only increases a few fields. Since the data need not be accurate, no synchronization is performed. If a notification policy is activated, a few values are compared but it often does not need to perform a Java call to the Decision Maker. The worst-case overhead of the runtime profiler (for a loop over a profiled empty static method not synchronized) is less than 5%. Hence, the global performance overhead of our profiling scheme is negligible. It is not perceptible for the applications that we have tested and does not even affect the EmbeddedCaffeine method score [13].

3.2   Policy: The Decision Maker

The goal of the Decision Maker is to find out for each interpreted method whether the trade-off between memory expansion and performance improvement obtained by compiling that method is valuable or not. To select the most valuable methods in the program, the idea is to attribute to each method a cost, and to compile only methods with the highest costs.

The Decision Maker critical role is therefore to define and compute the function that will associate a cost value to each method. There are many ways of doing that, as the cost of executing a method is compound by several factors. If the Decision Maker can for instance run when the system is idle and has freed a lot of memory, its heuristic can be more complex to obtain a better compilation set. This is why we wanted to have this function implemented in Java and made re-definable by system users. In this paragraph we consider possible techniques that can be implemented thanks to the mechanism described in section 3.1 and in particular the one we have used to measure the numbers used in section 5.1.

The Decision Maker can control the cost of the profiling mechanism, ranging from a very inexpensive update of a few fields up to a systematic call of a Java notifier. With this flexible profiler, the Decision Maker can implement different profiling policies. It can decide how often notifiers are called or decide to group methods to use a single profiling object. Here are some examples:

- *Systematic calls policy.* All the VM statistics are sent to the downloaded profiler on every method call. The cost of this policy is prohibitive. It should only be used for debug purposes.
- *Profiling delay.* Since it is often useless to profile the initialization phase of a program, the global_cost field can be initialized to a huge value and the real profiler can start only after the fist global overflow notification.
- *Interpretation cost lower bound.* Similarly, compilation is useless if the system is idle or spends most of its time in compiled methods or native code. Hence, profiling can be suspended as long as the interpretation cost is lower than a given value by milliseconds. This is done by comparing the elapsed time to variation of global_cost, either in an idle thread or in the global overflow notifier.
- *Asynchronous policy.* The profiler associates a MethodData object to each method and work without any notifications. It can link all the created profiler objects into a list and parse them at regular interval or when the virtual machine is idle. The regular interval can be specified either in terms of elapsed time or in terms of interpretation cost thanks to the global overflow notifier.
- *Asynchronous profiling of relevant methods.* Having a per method profiler object can be both expensive and inefficient. Hence, methods that cannot or should not be compiled, like the core classes or initialization methods, are never associated to a MethodData object. All the other methods can be associated to a default global object that activates a systematic notification. On the first notifier call, the Decision Maker can create a new object for profiling this method. If a profiled method has not been used for a long time, its profiling object can be freed.
- *Asynchronous focused profiling.* To further reduce the number of profiling objects, the previous policy can be extended by specifying that the global profiling object calls a notifier only when the method is an interesting compilation candidate. The mechanism described in the previous section allows the detection of methods that contain loops or that interact with compiled method.
- *Class statistics.* Another way to restrict the number of MethodData objects is to gather statistics at a class level. This may be particularly interesting for compilers that cannot compile methods individually. If the compiler supports method per method compilation, a profiling object can be associated to all the executed methods of the selected class by changing the notification policy associated to the class profiling object as described in the two previous algorithms.

- *Exit sampling.* If focused profiling fails to detect methods without loop but called often and big enough to compensate for the cross calls cost, a more expensive sampling technique can be used. For instance, every 100 exit for a shared method-Data, the exited method could be associated to a more important methodData. There can be several gradual methodData and if they are all reset when one reaches the 100 calls, the last ones should always have greater number of calls. If this is not the case, their methods are retrograded. Hence, with only a few methods datas, it should be possible to detect the methods called often with an overhead that should be approximatively 1% (for a frequency of 100 exits).

The particular policy we have implemented in our JCOD service to reach the performance results that are described in section 5.1 is based on asynchronous focused profiling. A java application launcher calls several times the real benchmark and interacts with the Decision Maker between two executions to compile the best method. The process stops when there is no interesting compilation candidate. For tests purposes, we have also used non focused asynchronous profiling on complex examples to show that the number of methods can be very huge and that the methods not found by focused profiling are not important.

For real application not controlled by an application launcher that calls the Decision Maker, the global overflow scheme can be used to decide how often compilation decision are taken. If the acceleration must happen faster, the cost field of each profiling object can be initialized to a huge value to ensure that the corresponding exit notifier is called as soon as one method has consumed a given amount of CPU. A simple profiler could memorize the global cost in the initialized method data and compare the method cost to the global cost on overflow.

Our flexible profiling mechanism has allowed us to test several different policies and to easily write the benchmark launcher. The performance drawback of Java does not really impact asynchronous Decision Makers since most of the work is done by the C profiler runtime without any call to their Java notifiers.

4   Compiler, Loader and Binder

Our compiler builds on traditional compiler technology, in particular a number of suggestions that have been made in the specific area of Java compilation such as [1, 2, 7, 11, 12, 19]. However, we have focused our research on code size and modularity. The compiler is still is prototype and does not yet compile all the floating-point instructions. However, it has a lot of interesting features:

- It factors commonly used code. It comes with compiled code library that for instance provides common code for 64 bits instructions, tableswitch and lookupswitch. It also shares the code required to restore registers and branch to the handler when an exception happens in code called from the compiled code. It even defines a few shared framings to replace the prelude and the postludes of the methods (to manage the execution context, update the stack pointer, check for overflow, handle the synchronization issues...). Complex framings can be used at a low cost.

For instance, it should be possible to move to another chained C stack in case of stack overflows if it agrees with both the threads library and the garbage collector. It should be particularly interesting for embedded systems.
- It favors code size over performance. As an example, constant propagation is a performance optimization that also results in code size gains. On the other hand, some typical performance optimization like code inlining or loop unrolling that expands code size may not be done. In other words, instead of always looking for the maximum performance at any price, our compiling technology seeks for the best performance for an affordable memory cost for code size. This is particularly effective with chips supporting 16 bits instruction sets such as the Hitachi SH, ARM Thumb Code, or the MIPS16 instruction set.
- In order to allow for a third-party market and fast deployment to many embedded chips, the compiler architecture include a processor independent front-end that interfaces with a processor dependent back-end. As the compile server consists of a single front-end and as many back-ends as there are device types, new back-ends can be added as new devices are added on the network. The back-end specifications are available to any third party that wants to develop their own back-end. The front-end also offers an API to plug in new optimizations.
- The object code generated by our compiler offers software platform independence. A compile server can serve simultaneously several devices, which may each operate with different operating systems and Java virtual machines.
- The generated code is totally compliant to the semantics of the Java bytecode.

The compiler is coded in Java. This facilitates our objective of supporting multiple back-ends for multiple devices. Because Java offers inherent dynamic loading, a back-end is a set of Java classes that gets loaded by the front-end part depending on arguments and configuration parameters.

4.1   Compiler Output Format

The standard Java Virtual Machine native code loader is designed to load native methods that have been implemented in another language than Java, typically in C, but that should be compliant with the Java Native Interface, JNI. Our compiler does not generate JNI compliant code, as we could not reach the same performance and code size with JNI. Moreover the compiler is operating on a remote compile server and it ignores which VM and which operating system is running on the target. We have designed the compiler so that its output code is only dependent upon Java semantics and the target processor. This code is dynamically loaded and linked on the target machine, which may be running any operating system or VM.

In order to reach that goal, we have designed a new object format. It is similar to traditional dynamically loadable formats such as ELF, widely used in the industry. It contains placeholders, called anchors, to support dynamic binding. To generate executable code, the installer part of the JCOD service must resolve the anchors and insert the corresponding code in the VM independent native code produced by the compiler.

There are two kinds of anchors, the JVM anchors and the compiler anchors. The most important one are the first ones, used to express JVM dependent behavior. For instance, the compilation of the 'getfield' bytecode for a double depends on the format of the java objects in a VM. Similarly, 'new' must generate a call to a VM dependent function. Compilation of these two bytecodes results in generation of JVM anchors, JVM_GETFIELD_D and JVM_NEWOBJECT. In addition, to reduce the code size, exceptions are not managed directly in the compiled code. If an exception can be launched, the compiled code must use a JVM anchor, like JVM_THROWNULLPOINTER. It will result in a call to a support function written in C and that implements this anchor semantic. The complete list of the JVM anchors is in [5].

As stated above, there is a compiled code library that factors commonly used code. This library is an array of native code downloaded from the compiler, which is not aware of its installation address. It may contain for example an entry called 'float_multiply'. The compilation of the 'fmul' bytecode puts the operands in the correct registers, followed by a COMPILER_LIBRARY compiler anchor that contains the index of the float_multiply entry. In addition, if a 'goto' jumps over a 'JVM' anchor, the compiler does yet not know the code size. Then, a COMPILER_UNCONDITIONAL anchor is used for the 'goto' statement and a COMPILER_DECLARATION anchor marks the jump destination. The full list of the compiler anchors can be found at [5]. In short, there are anchors for constant pool access, exception handlers, compact encoding of the tableswitch and lookupswitch bytecodes, trampolines (on systems where the CALL instruction cannot reach the whole address space), framings (at the beginning of the code to call one of the common prelude/postlude wrapper) and paddings.

4.2   Native Code Installer

The main task of the installer is to dynamically resolve anchors. Taking the fmul example again, the code binder looks at the anchor parameter when it encounters an anchor of type Library. As it knows where the entry point float_multiply is loaded in memory, it can replace the anchor with an effective call to the float_multiply subroutine. Thus, in the end, all 'fmul' bytecodes are translated into function calls to the effective floating point multiply software emulation routine for that specific processor.

To increase the modularity, the installer is processor independent. The compiler provides classes that define a pseudo assembler library written in Java. Instead of directly generating the machine code for the call to float_multiply, the installer uses the 'produce_call' method of this library, which generates the native code.

JVM anchors are harder to resolve. They may either be inlined or transformed into an external call to a C support function whose prototype is fixed by the JCOD specification. As stated above, they cannot be inlined if there is a potential exception.

Let's take for instance the JVM_PUTFIELD_L anchor, which corresponds to the putfield bytecode for a reference field. If the compiler cannot prove that the object is not null, the anchor cannot be inlined. In that case, the EXCEPTION_NULLPOINTER is set in the anchor flags. If the installer does not detect this flag, the behavior depends on the VM garbage collector. If there is a write barrier, the installer performs an external call to a support function that calls the write barrier API. In the other cases, the installer may use the pseudo assembler instructions to dereference the object, add a constant JVM dependent field offset and perform the write. It needs not be aware of the registers that contain the operands. The JVM anchor includes this information in a compiler dependent format, passed to the pseudo assembler when starting an inlined instructions sequence. If there is an external call, JCOD specifies that the prototype of the support function. For JVM_PUTFIELD_L, it is "void putfieldL(void **context, jobject object, jobject value, char *data)". The compiler prepares the first three arguments. The fourth, which identifies the accessed field, is a VM dependant data specified by the installer when it calls the pseudo assembler function that generates an external call.

When the binding task is terminated, all anchors have been substituted for real executable code. This process is quite complex. However, it only requires sufficient memory to store the compiler output and the generated code buffer. Hence, it can easily run on the appliance. In our prototype, it is indeed performed on the target because we wanted the compile server to be JVM independent in order to allow independent upgrades. However, if the compilation time is critical, it might be worth resolving the anchors on the compile server. In that case, another protocol should be defined between the compile server and the JVM. For instance, we could export to the server the address space of the appliance. It should be possible to resolve all the anchors remotely and to use the local installer only to allocate memory, send the address to the server, install the resolved code at this address and activate the compiled version of the method. Modularity can be preserved if the compile server downloads the JVM anchor resolver either from the appliance or from a JVM dependent server specified when the connection is established.

5   Preliminary Results

5.1   Efficiency

We have implemented this compiler architecture for the following systems:
- The compiler front-end and the JCOD services are coded in pure Java.
- We currently provide two code generator back-ends for the Intel ARM7 and the Hitachi SuperH processors.
- The extended virtual machine is Hewlett-Packard Chai VM (on any OS).

We have focused our work on the compiled code size, the portability, the remote aspects and the profiling. Hence, very few optimizations have been implemented in our compiler and the floating-point instructions are not completely supported. However, on a Hitachi SH3 processor, the embedded caffeine [13] score is nearly 6 times better (without even compiling the float test). It goes from a x0.8 loss on the strings test (because it spends most of its time interacting with non compiled core classes) up

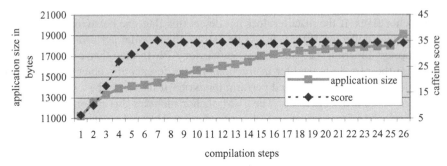

Fig 2. Gradual compilation of the Embedded Caffeine Benchmark

to a x30 gain for the loop test. If the float and the string tests are excluded from the score computation, the gain is x13. There is even a small gain on strings if the core classes are compiled (but we do not optimize the string allocations themselves). The final code size, including the compiled code, is only 1.7 times greater than the initial application code. If we do not take into account the FloatAtom class, which has not been compiled, the expansion factor only goes up to x1.8.

For a more realistic application, like Connect4 game solver implemented in the FhourStones benchmark [18] (named Search in JavaGrande [8]), the elapsed time has been divided by more than 4 while the code expansion is only x2.5. Unfortunately, more complex programs like the spec JVM 98 benchmarks [16] do not run on our small embedded platform.

However, the most striking fact is that figure 2 shows that thanks to our profiler, the score no longer evolves after a code size expansion of x1.3 although 40% of additional memory is consumed in the following steps. In fact, it is even better for realistic applications because the code is distributed over smaller methods and the well known rule stating that at least 80% (or 90%) of the execution time is spend in at most 20% (resp. 10%) of the code applies. With a worst-case average acceleration factor of x4 and average code expansion of x3, the gain is at x2.5 (100 / (20 + (80/4))) for a cost of x1.4 ((80 + (20 x3)) / 100) by compiling these 20% critical methods. With the 90/10 rule, the gain is x3 for a cost of x1.2. Of course, the gain could be improved with a better compiler.

We have profiled more complex benchmarks to check that our profiling policy identifies the interesting methods. As stated in section 3.2, it initially considers only methods than contain loop and gradually adds methods that call or are called from compiled methods. The only drawback of this policy is that it can miss a method that has no loop but is called very often from interpreted code. We have already stated that it might not be a good compilation candidate because of the overhead of switching between compiled and interpreted mode. In addition, we have also noted that such methods are very rare. The only counter example we have found is the Ray Tracer benchmark included in Java Grande. 80% of the CPU is spent on 3 methods that do not contain loops. However, two of them are not worth being compiled alone since they are very small. The last one calls them and is called very often by a method that contains a loop and that uses 14% of the CPU. Hence, focused profiling should immediately find this last method and propagate the compilation to the other three methods thanks to the huge number of interactions with compiled code. In the worst case, the Decision Maker could fall back to a sampling like profiling if it detects that the individually profiled methods do not cover most of the interpretation cost. On the other hand, the Jess benchmark [9] (included in the spec JVM 98 suite [16]), spends 80% of its time in methods that contain loops (including the core classes). Hence, even if the methods without loops are missed, they represent only 20% of the execution time (Fig. 3). In fact, we have checked that the methods that represent most of these 20% are indeed called by the methods that our Decision Maker immediately selects and that their interaction with compiled methods ensures that they are quickly identified. The JESS graph also shows that 80% of the time is spend in only 10% of the methods.

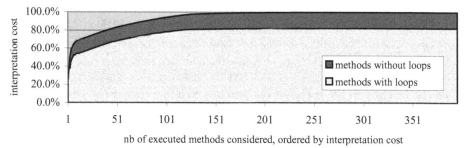

Fig 3. Global role of loops for Jess

5.2   Overhead

The time used to send a compilation request and resolve the anchors has not been optimized and depends on the CPU of the appliance. Hence, the delay between the selection of a method and the installation of its compiled code is not negligible (an average of 1 second per method for embedded caffeine on a SH3 at 60Mhz, with a peak at 2.5 seconds), even if the compiler itself is very efficient (more than 100000 bytes of class file per second with a Linux JDK 1.2-2 with JIT on a PIII at 733Mhz). However, very few methods should be compiled in an embedded system with huge memory constraints and the application can execute the interpreted version without waiting for the compiled version. Hence, the compilation delay is not an important factor in our case. In addition, we have checked that the CPU overhead of the asynchronous profiler, including the decision making, is negligible.

As regards the memory, a small Java object (8 bytes) is associated to each method for which individual statistics are gathered. It may be critical on system for which dynamic memory is very scarce. However, the simple focused profiling technique used above divides the cost by at least two since about half of the methods do not contain loops on the tested examples and others are never executed. It this is not sufficient, more complex focusing strategies can be used with our profiling mechanism. Several methods can share the same object and receive their own profiling object only if they globally represent the most expensive section.

Hence, the real overhead of our approach is the size of the code itself. There are different components, written either in C or in Java. We have used Java as often as possible to increase the portability and the deployment flexibility of our software. The Java components are:

- The local code, which contains the VM dependent anchor resolver and a mechanism to discover and download a remote service (6K)
- The service, which discovers the remote compiler, profiles the execution, selects methods and interact with the compiler (18K)
- The VM independent compiler output resolver, downloaded from the compiler (5K of generic code + 9K of SH3 specific code for the pseudo assembler)

The only parts in C are:

- The native methods for the Java local code (5K for SH3)
- The glue between the compiled code and the VM (10K for SH3)
- The requester, that calls the service to send a compilation request (5K for SH3)

The cost of the requester is heavy because the bytecode must be parsed to discover its size, which is not memorized in ChaiVM internal structures. In addition, both the C and the Java part of the requester can be removed if the compile server can obtain the downloaded classes for instance thanks to a proxy server. This should gain about 10K.

Moreover, the VM dependent anchor resolver could be installed on the compile server. In addition, our Java code has not been optimized and contains a lot of debug information, variants activated by configurable properties (profiling policy, systematic compilation, exclusion of methods ...) and complex mechanism like support of network failures or selection of different services. Hence, the overhead could probably be reduced to less than 20K if there is a huge ROM constraint. Since most of the code is written in Java, these kinds of changes can easily be performed. The modularity of our approach allows tailoring the solution for specific needs.

6 Conclusion

We have implemented a distributed modular compilation technology, well suited for embedded systems, which include the following features:

- First and above all, in order to avoid memory expansion, it supports mixed bytecode and native code, so that only the performance critical code may be compiled. It also makes it possible to start execution immediately without delay.
- It includes a profiling component that dynamically detects this performance critical code. This component can easily be adapted for particular targets
- Compilation is not necessarily achieved on the appliance if it is not powerful enough to run a JIT compiler.
- The compiler aims at the best trade-off between device cost (or battery consumption) and performance. It has a lot of memory optimizations and generates the smallest code as opposed to the fastest code. However, memory expensive optimization could be added or the compiler could be replaced by one that favors speed.

– The compiler is JVM independent. The VM and the compiler can be upgraded independently and the same compile server can be used by different kind of VMs.

The appliance need not be permanently connected to the compile server. A compile server could be plugged from time to time to an appliance to modify its compiled method set, depending on the usage since the last maintenance.

In addition to the dynamic mode, described in this paper, we have also deployed the technology in AOT mode, for the devices that do not have a low cost network access. A JCOD service including only an anchor resolver is installed on the appliance and the compiler output can be inserted in class file attributes. Since the code is VM independent, these attribute are valid for a lot of JCOD enhanced JVMs. The service recognizes the attributes corresponding to the appliance processor and installs their compiled code. It should even be possible to resolve all the anchors if there is a mechanism to resolve addresses not known at compile time (either with a new anchor or with an indirection table).

References

1. Bothner P. "Compiling Java for embedded systems", Embedded Systems Conference West, San Jose, 1997.
2. Budimlic and Kennedy K. "Optimizing Java: Theory and practice", Concurrency, Practice and Experience (UK), 9(11):445--63, November 1997. Java for Computational Science and Engineering - Simulation and Modeling II Las Vegas, NV, USA 21 June 1997.
3. Chambers C., Dean J. and Grove D. "Whole-program optimization of object oriented languages", Tech. Rep. 96-06-02, University of Washington, June 1996.
4. Colin de Verdiere & al. "Speedup Prediction for Selective Compilation of Embedded Java Programs", in Proceedings of EMSOFT02, Grenoble, France, October 2002.
5. Delsart B. and Paire E. "Description of JCOD anchors",
   http://www.ri.silicomp.com/~delsart/jcod/doc/anchors.html
6. Duesterwald E. and Bala V. "Software Profiling for Hot Path Prediction : Less is More", in 9th Conference on Architectural Support for Programming Languages and Operating Systems, Nov. 2000.
7. Hummel J., Azevedo A., Kolson D. and Nicolau A. "Annotating the Java byte codes in support of optimization", in Workshop on Java for Science and Engineering Computation, PPoPP97 (June 1997).
8. "The Java Grande Forum Benchmark Suite", http://www.epcc.ed.ac.uk/javagrande/
9. "Jess, the Java Expert Shell System", http://herzberg.ca.sandia.gov/jess
10. Levine J. R. "Linkers and Loaders", published by Morgan-Kauffman, October 1999, ISBN 1-55860-496-0.
11. Muller G., Moura B., Bellard F. and Consel C. "Harissa: a flexible and efficient Java environment mixing bytecode and compiled code", in Proceedings of COOTS97, 1997.
12. H. Ogawa H., K. Shumira K., Matsuoka S., Maruyama F., Sohda Y. and Kimura F. "OpenJIT : An open-ended, reflective JIT compiler framework for Java", in Proc. European Conference on Object-Oriented Programming, 2000
13. Pendragon, "Embedded caffeine benchmark",
    http://www.webfayre.com/pendragon/cm3/info.html

14. Plezbert M. and Cytron R. "Does "Just In Time" = "Better Late Than Never"?", in Proceedings of Symposium on Principles of Programming Languages, Paris, France, 1997.
15. Proebsting T. A., Townsend G., Bridges P., Hartman J.H., Newsham, T. and Watterson S. A. "Toba: Java for Applications: A Way Ahead of Time (WAT) Compiler", in Third Conference on Object Oriented Technologies, 1997
16. "Spec JVM98 benchmarks", http://www.spec.org/osg/jvm98/
17. Sun Microsystems Inc, "The Java Hotspot Performance Engine Architecture", http://java.sun.com/products/hotspot/whitepaper.html
18. Tromp J. "Fhourstones 2.0 benchmark", http://www.cwi.nl/~tromp/c4/fhour.html
19. Weiss M & al. "TurboJ, a Java Bytecode To Native Compiler", Proceedings of Languages Compilers and Tools for Embedded Systems (PLDI), Montreal, July 1998.
20. Whaley J. "Partial Method Compilation using Dynamic Profile Information", in ACM Conference on Object-Oriented Programming Systems, Languages and Applications, Oct. 2001

Decreasing Memory Overhead in Hard Real-Time Garbage Collection*

Tobias Ritzau and Peter Fritzson

Department of Computer and Information Science
Linköping University, SE-581 83 Linköping, Sweden
{tobri,petfr}@ida.liu.se

Abstract. Automatic memory management techniques eliminate many programming errors that are both hard to find and to correct. However, these techniques are not yet used in embedded systems with hard real-time applications. The reason is that current methods for automatic memory management have a number of drawbacks. The two major ones are: (1) not being able to always guarantee short real-time deadlines and (2) using large amounts of extra memory. Memory is usually a scarce resource in embedded applications.

In this paper we present a new technique, Real-Time Reference Counting (RTRC) that overcomes the current problems and makes automatic memory management attractive also for hard real-time applications. The main contribution of RTRC is that often all memory can be used to store live objects. This should be compared to a memory overhead of about 500% for garbage collectors based on copying techniques and about 50% for garbage collectors based on mark-and-sweep techniques.

1 Introduction

Memory related errors are often very hard to find and correct, since they may be located at places different from where they appear. For instance freeing the same memory region twice may not cause a problem until the region is reused. Automatic memory management, also referred to as garbage collection or GC, is used to reclaim memory that is no longer used by a computer program. This greatly reduces the risk of memory related errors in programs.

Tracing garbage collectors, e.g. copying, mark-sweep, and threadmill collectors, all share the problem that unreachable (garbage) objects are not reclaimed immediately when they become unreachable. This dramatically increases the memory overhead. Most tracing real-time GCs perform an increment of GC work when memory is allocated. The amount of work (W) performed is proportional to the amount of memory that is allocated (A). In short, the amount of work needed should be enough to complete a full GC cycle (to collect all unreachable objects) before all memory overhead (O) is used up by new objects.

---

* Supported by the EC funded IST project HIDOORS (High Integrity Distributed Object-Oriented Realtime Systems) and the ESA funded AERO project (Architecture for Enhanced Reprogrammability and Operability).

A. Sangiovanni-Vincentelli and J. Sifakis (Eds.): EMSOFT 2002, LNCS 2491, pp. 213–226, 2002.

The memory overhead is used as a buffer to store new objects while unreachable objects are collected. To calculate W, the total amount of GC work needed to complete a full cycle must be known (GCW). The work needed can be calculated as $W = GCW \times A/O$. Thus, the execution time is inversely proportional to the amount of memory overhead in the system. In a typical two-subheap copying collector 500% memory overhead is needed and in a typical mark-sweep collector 50% is needed. By using the technique presented in this paper no memory overhead is needed to store new objects. This is of extremely valuable in embedded systems with scarce memory resources.

Reference counting [9] has been known to have a number of disadvantages, causing many implementers to avoid its use. However, reference counting also has numerous advantages, especially for use in embedded systems.

The idea of reference counting is simple: count the number of references to every object and recycle the object if its reference count becomes zero. A reference counting memory handler contains two main operations: *increment* and *decrement* of reference counters. The decrement operation also frees objects when their reference counters become zero.

The advantages of reference counting are its *simplicity*, memory is *immediately reclaimed* when it becomes unreachable, *fine-grainedness* (only a few instructions need locking in multi-threaded systems), it *does not use separate garbage collection code to reclaim memory* (all work is done by the increment and decrement operations), and that data is *not moved* back and forth between different memory regions.

Simplicity makes reference counting more feasible in safety critical systems, since the method is easier to implement and to prove correct. Because of its fine-grainedness, reference counting is suitable for multi-threading, especially for uniprocessor systems where locking is cheap. Since all updates are performed by the increment and decrement operations, there is no need to execute garbage collection code when allocating memory or at any time other than when performing reference count updates. This simplifies worst-case execution time analysis. Reference counting keeps data in fixed memory locations, in contrast to copying garbage collection techniques. Keeping data at fixed locations simplifies interfacing to other systems and languages. Copying data also requires more memory, takes extra time, and makes synchronization between the garbage collector and the program harder.

However, there are also some disadvantages with standard reference counting. *Recursive freeing* occurs when the last reference to a large data structure is removed. This may cause long interruptions that may be hard to predict. Since memory is not compacted, *fragmentation* may also be an issue. In most applications fragmentation causes no problems, but it may in a safety critical system. Reference counting is often considered to be *slow*, and the basic technique is. The inability of reclaiming *cyclic* data structures is often considered the major drawback of reference counting.

Recursive freeing can be eliminated using a technique described by Weizenbaum [19]. The decrement operation is changed to put the object into a list instead of decrementing its children and freeing it (see Fig. 1). If the system runs out of memory when allocating an object, the list is processed and dead memory is reclaimed. This solves the problem of recursive freeing, but on the other hand garbage collection code needs to be executed when allocating objects. The technique is designed for applications where all objects are of the same size, but can easily be adapted to suit other systems as well.

Dividing objects into blocks of equal size can be used to handle external fragmentation. This approach is further discussed below.

Several techniques to reduce the execution time overhead of reference counting have been proposed. All of these aims to reduce the number of reference count updates either by not counting all references [10,2] or by statically finding redundant reference count updates [3].

Cyclic data structures can be reclaimed using several techniques. These include weak pointers [6], partial mark-sweep [8,1], reference counting cyclic data structures instead of their components [4] and using a backup real-time garbage collector. Partial mark-sweep algorithms require no manual administration, but the others do. This can cause problems since people are known to make mistakes, so they should be used with caution in safety critical systems. Partial mark-sweep techniques are feasible in interactive systems, but have not been proven to work in hard real-time systems.

This paper presents a technique that does not suffer from external fragmentation and is fully predictable in both memory usage and execution time. The main advantage is that the worst-case execution time of GC work is improved from $O(s + 1/f)$ to $O(s)$, where s is the size of the object and f is the minimum amount of free memory (the overhead) in many systems. Since the minimum amount of free memory is not a factor, all memory can be used for live objects. This is extremely valuable, especially in embedded systems, where memory usually is a scarce resource.

We classify real-time systems into three categories: interactive, soft real-time and hard real-time. *Interactive systems* are systems that interact on-line with the external world, e.g. X-Windows. There are not any deadlines on the response on these systems, but too long response times are annoying to the user. *Soft real-time systems* have deadlines but slightly missing one now and again does not cause any problems. Multimedia applications are examples of soft real-time. In *hard real-time systems* a deadline should never be missed. Missing a deadline could cause disaster. Medical equipment and on-board aircraft control systems are examples of hard real-time systems.

The term "real-time garbage collection" is often used even for interactive applications. However, this is not the target of our research. The technique presented in this paper targets the embedded hard real-time systems.

In this paper everything that is allocated on the heap is called an *object*. A *dead object* is an object that will not be used by the program anymore. The *children* of an object are the objects that are referred to by the object.

The remainder of this paper is organized as follows. Section 2 proposes a reference counting technique for hard real-time systems. In Section 3 a prototype implementation is presented. Section 4 presents an evaluation. Section 5 presents related work and Section 6 presents the conclusion and future work.

2   Real-Time Reference Counting

The following sections describe how the disadvantages of the standard reference counter can be eliminated.

2.1   Eliminating External Fragmentation

In most systems fragmentation causes no problem [13], but in hard real-time systems it must be guaranteed that fragmentation does not cause the system to run out of memory. Fragmentation can be eliminated by compacting memory, e.g. using copying [11] or mark-compact [15] garbage collection. However, these methods are often considered too expensive and/or unpredictable. Other solutions include prohibiting heap allocation or limiting allocation into arenas, large memory areas that are freed as a whole.

The technique proposed in this paper is based on dividing objects into equally sized blocks, as applied also in many file systems and virtual memory systems. This eliminates external fragmentation, but introduces internal fragmentation, i.e. the last block of an object will not always be fully used. An important difference between internal and external fragmentation is that internal fragmentation is predictable, but external is not.

There are several ways to connect blocks into an object, e.g. linked list [17] and index blocks. In the rest of this paper we assume that the blocks are kept in a linked list, but other techniques work as well. The requirements are that member access should be predictable, that taking a step in the iteration through the blocks of an object should take constant time, and that it must be possible to disconnect a block from the object in constant time.

2.2   Eliminating Recursive Freeing

The increment operation of reference counting just increments a variable, an operation with predictable worst-case execution time. However, the decrement operation is potentially recursive. In the worst case a decrement operation can free all objects on the heap, and even if the size of the heap is bounded, it is too long for essentially all real-time applications.

By using deferred reference counting [19] the decrement operation becomes constant in time. Using deferred reference counting, objects are added to a to-be-free list instead of decrementing its child references and freeing the object (see Fig. 1.) The child references still need to be decremented, which now is done by the allocator instead. When the allocator needs more memory, objects are taken from the to-be-free list. Before they are reused their child references are decremented.

```
algorithm decrrc(obj)
    if obj ≠ null then
        obj.rc ← obj.rc - 1
        if obj.rc = 0 then
            freelist.add(obj);
        end if
    end if
end
```

Fig. 1. Deferred reference counting

Deferred reference counting assumes that all objects are of equal size, but that is not case in most systems. The technique can be applied using RTRC since all blocks are of equal size, even though objects can contain multiple blocks. Using the deferred reference counting, all child references are decremented when an object is taken from the to-be-free list. This could cause problems when freeing large objects. However, if only the blocks that used by the new object are processed, the execution time becomes proportional to the size of the allocated object and does not depend on the objects in the to-be-free list. It must be possible to get a single block from the free list in constant time for this to work.

2.3   Reclaiming Cycles

Cyclic data structures are reclaimed using a real-time mark-sweep garbage collector. This increases the execution time overhead, but since the reference counter has loaded the objects into the cache, the overhead is small. No extra memory overhead is needed since the marks-sweep flags could be stored in the reference counter field (since the reference counter does not need all bits). The effect of combining these techniques is that all dead memory is reclaimed with drastically lower memory overhead (compared to real-time mark-sweep). The execution time of a real-time mark-sweep collector is proportional to $1/memory\ overhead$. Practically, this means that about 50% memory overhead is needed to get acceptable execution time. The execution time of the combination is decreased by the ratio of cyclic and non-cyclic garbage. This factor could by anything from 0 (no cycles) to 1 (all garbage belong to cycles). Many systems can be designed to produce little cyclic garbage.

If cycles can be guaranteed to be completely eliminated manually, e.g. using manual cycle breaking and/or weak pointers, no mark-sweep collector is needed. Thus, all memory could be used to store live blocks.

We now have achieved a system without external fragmentation and with predictable allocation and reference count update operations. It is also guaranteed that all dead blocks that do not belong in cycles are immediately available to new objects. Thus, memory overhead decreases or is even eliminated completely. If it is desirable to increase the speed of allocation in high-priority processes [12] this can be achieved by forcing the free list (which contains blocks which child references have already been decremented) to contain the number of blocks needed by the high priority process.

Dividing objects into blocks introduces an overhead in both memory usage and execution time. Using a linked list schema, each object needs a pointer to the next block. These pointers need to be traversed when accessing data in blocks other than the first. The number of pointers to traverse to get a field is known at compile time. Large objects such as arrays should not use a linked schema, because that would make the execution time of an indexing operation a linear function of the size of its argument. Arrays can be stored as trees that make the execution time a logarithmic function of the size of the array. To get the best performance, arrays can be allocated statically and contiguous.

The execution time overhead of object access is comparable to that of real-time copying garbage collectors, which always use one indirection [5] to find the current copy of the object. Thus, the block size should be selected to fit most objects in one or two blocks. Two other factors that are important when selecting block size is internal fragmentation and the cache memory. Experiments have shown that 32 or 64 byte blocks give good results in many applications.

The best block size depends on the application. To tune the application, the allocation function can be used to produce statistics about how many objects of different sizes are allocated.

The only disadvantage that remains in this proposal is the execution time overhead. The execution time overhead could be improved by static optimizations, such as removing redundant reference count updates and allocating objects on the stack.

3   Implementation

The RTRC technique has been implemented in the JOSES Java™ compiler, JoC [18,14]. During compilation the object types are divided into records smaller then a specified block size. Then all member accesses are updated to handle divided objects. Finally the run-time system was updated both to access members in divided objects and to create and handle such objects. The implementation only supports the linked list schema. Arrays are currently not divided, so they can cause external fragmentation. We are planning to implement arrays as trees of blocks in the near future. There is also no backup garbage collector in the system. RTRC has also been implemented as a set of CPP macros for use with C.

The data layout of objects had to be changed to eliminate external fragmentation. An object is constructed of blocks. Each block has a next pointer, pointing to the next block in the object. RTRC also need type information, a reference counter and a pointer that links the objects when they reside in one of the free lists (the to-be-free or free list). These fields are needed in the first block of all objects. Since the reference counter is not needed when the object reside in a free list, the pointer and the reference counter can share memory. The memory overhead per object is 4 bytes for reference counter/free list pointer plus 4 bytes per used block.

Two free lists are used by the run-time system. The to-be-free (tbf) list contains all objects that are dead, but their children have not been decremented, i.e. they have live references to the heap. The free list (freelist) keeps blocks that can be allocated immediately. A variable (available) keeps track of the number of blocks in the free list.

The run-time system is initiated by connecting all blocks on the heap into one free list. The worst case execution time of initialization is proportional to the number of blocks on the heap.

Allocating blocks from the free list is done by traversing the free list until the requested number of blocks has been found, terminating the list of blocks, and adjusting available and freelist. The worst case execution time of the function is proportional to the number of blocks being allocated.

Allocating from the to-be-free list is slightly more complicated. The function is shown in Fig. 2 and important data structures are shown in Fig. 3. First, one object is taken from the to-be-free list. The type information is stored in type; blockno is set to zero, and head points to the first block of the object that is allocated. For each block being allocated its child references are decremented using the decchildren function stored in the type information. If we run out of blocks in the current object, the next object in the to-be-free list is taken and its blocks are used. The execution time of function is proportional to the number of blocks being allocated.

The user function used to allocate objects allocates as many blocks from the free list as possible. The rest of the blocks are allocated from the to-be-free list. Finally, the lists of blocks are concatenated. The worst case execution time is proportional to the size of the object being allocated.

As stated earlier, it is sometimes beneficial to increase the execution speed of high-priority processes. In RTRC this can be accomplished by guaranteeing that all allocations of high-priority processes can be done from the free list. Thus, no time is spent decrementing child references. The run-time system contains a function (predec) which allocates blocks from the to-be-free list and put them directly into the free list. The allocation function must then always leave a specified number of blocks in the free list, except when allocating objects in high-priority processes. After the execution of high-priority code, the predec function must be called, so the free list is filled with blocks again. The number of blocks needed in the free list can be calculated using the technique presented in Henriksson's thesis [12]. The worst case execution time of predec is proportional to the number of blocks being pre-decremented.

The decrement and increment operations are implemented using deferred reference counting as presented in Fig. 1. The execution times of both operations are constant.

3.1   Complexity and Overhead

Initiating the memory manager is a matter of putting all blocks into a linked list. This could cause problems for virtual memory systems, but the embedded

```
tbf ← null     { The to-be-free-list }
block ← null   { The next block }
type ← null    { The type of the object containing block }
blockno ← 0    { The sequence number of the current block }

function tbf_alloc(size) returns object_ptr
    head ← block  { The first block of the new object }
    tail ← null      { The tail of the blocks in the new object }

    for n in 1 .. size do
        if block = null then
            block ← tbf
            if block = null then
                error("Out of memory")
            end if

            if head = null then
                head ← block
            end if

            type ← block.type
            tbf ← tbf.next_object
            blockno ← 0
        end if

        if tail ≠ null then
            tail.next ← block
        end if

        type.decchildren(block, blockno)
        tail ← block
        block ← block.next
        blockno ← blockno + 1
    end loop

    return head
end
```

Fig. 2. Allocating blocks from the to-be-free-list

systems we target do not have virtual memory. The worst-case execution time is linear with respect to the size of the heap.

Allocation (from the to-be-free-list or free-list) takes blocks from the respective list. When blocks are taken from the to-be-free-list their references must also be released. Since releasing references of a block takes constant time (the size of blocks is constant and thus the maximum number of references), the worst-case execution time of an allocation is linear with respect to the size of the allocated object. If the system can produce dead cycles, a backup mark-sweep collector is used. Then, some mark-sweep work is done here as well. The amount of work is proportional to the amount of memory allocated.

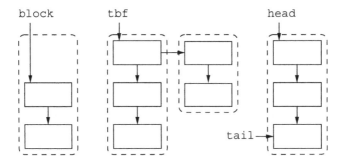

Fig. 3. Data structures used by **tbf_alloc**. The dashed boxes represent objects and the solid boxes represent blocks. To the left is the free object from which the blocks are currently taken. In the middle are the objects in the to-be-free list and to the right is the object being allocated.

In some systems it is desired that allocation in high-priority processes should be as fast as possible. This can be accomplished by pre-decrementing references of blocks in the to-be-free-list and moving these to the free-list. This is done by the **predec** function. The worst-case execution time of this function is proportional to the number of blocks that should be pre-decremented.

Finally, both the increment and decrement operations have a constant worst-case execution time.

4   Timing Benchmarks

All applications measured are compiled in various versions using RTRC, and without using any GC at all. The results presented are given as the execution time overhead in percent. Thus, a negative result is an improvement.

4.1   Java Grande Benchmarks

The RTRC technique has been evaluated using the Java Grande sequential benchmark [7]. These benchmarks were chosen by the JOSES project to evaluate the JoC compiler. Since the compiler is still unstable, we had to focus being able to compile one benchmark. The programs were compiled in four versions: without GC, with GC and contiguous, i.e. not divided, objects, with GC and 64-byte blocks, and with GC and 32-byte blocks.

Low Level Operations. The first section of the Java Grande sequential benchmarks contains tests of various low level operations, such as addition, multiplication, division and assignment. These where removed by the optimizer, except in one case that contained reference assignments. The test of reference assignments were optimized away when not using the reference counter, but not otherwise. However, such code should not appear in a real application.

Kernels. Section 2 of the Java Grande sequential benchmarks contains various computational heavy applications, such as IDEA-encryption, FFT and matrix multiplication. These applications make little use of objects and therefore cause only a small amount of garbage collection work. The tests are performed in three variations with different size of the input. The relative overhead is similar in all variations. The average overhead is 10%, 4%, and 11% for the contiguous, 64-byte, and 32-byte versions respectively. The results are presented in Fig. 4.

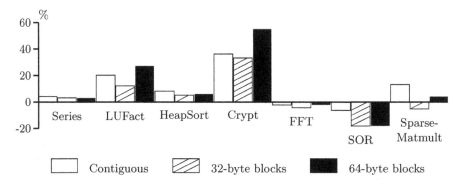

Fig. 4. Kernels benchmarks

Large Scale Applications. The JOSES compiler JoC had some difficulties compiling the applications in section 3 of the Java Grande Benchmarks. The applications are object-oriented and perform computational heavy calculations such as ray-tracing and alpha beta search. Only the alpha beta search binary could be executed with a valid result. The overhead in this test is significant, which can be explained by the amount of redundant reference count updates that is generated for all temporary reference variables that JoC generates. The overhead can be significantly reduced by static analysis. However, this is not yet implemented. The results show a 28%, 30% and 47% execution time overhead in the contiguous, 32-byte and 64-byte versions respectively.

4.2   Control System Application

To measure the impact of different memory usage profiles on a more realistic hard real-time application, RTRC was also tested on a small simulation of a control system application. This test was written in C to get more control of the generated code. The control system was tested in 12 variations with and without: dividing objects in two blocks of 32 bytes each (d), separating the blocks of an object by half the heap size (ds), reference counting (r), and running a thousand simultaneous simulations (t). The result of this evaluation is presented in Fig. 5.

The conclusion from these tests is that dividing objects is expensive when using more memory than can fit into the cache. However, it should be noted that no reference counting optimizations are performed. By comparing the reference counted variations to their non-reference counted counterparts, we get a

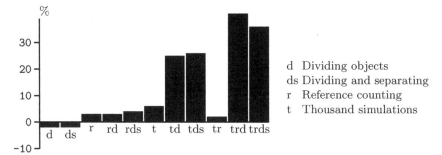

Fig. 5. Control system benchmarks

maximum overhead of 13%. The lowest overhead was achieved when comparing the test with a thousand simulations without dividing objects to its reference counted counterpart. The reference counted version was 4% faster. Over 24 million increment and decrement operations were performed in each run of the system (with reference counting enabled).

5   Related Work

5.1   Scheduling Garbage Collection

Henriksson proposes a scheduling strategy that can be implemented together with many different garbage collectors. An implementation using an incremental copying garbage collector based on Brook's algorithm [5] is presented in Henriksson's thesis [12]. The processes are divided into high and low priority processes. The high priority processes do a minimal amount of garbage collection work to increase their speed. The main garbage collection work is instead performed when entering the low priority processes and during their execution. To guarantee that high priority processes do not run out of memory, enough memory must be preallocated. Henriksson provides the analysis needed to calculate the amount of memory needed and the execution time of the garbage collector.

5.2   Real-Time GC in the Jamaica JVM

Siebert [16,17] proposes a combination of scheduling and dividing objects into equally sized blocks in an incremental mark-and-sweep collector. The blocks are garbage collected as separate entities. Arrays are stored either as contiguous memory blocks if such memory can be found fast enough, otherwise arrays are represented as trees.

Siebert also provides an analysis to guarantee non-disruptiveness of the application. The input to the analysis is an upper bound on the amount of reachable memory and the output is the number of GC increments needed per allocated block.

Table 1. Worst case execution time of operations in real-time garbage collectors (assuming no cyclic garbage.) The size of an object is denoted by s and the minimum amount of free memory (the overhead) by f.

Operation	RT-Copying	RT-Mark-Sweep	RTRC
Increment (or equivalent)	$O(1)$	$O(1)$	$O(1)$
Decrement (or equivalent)	$O(1)$	$O(1)$	$O(1)$
Allocation/Free	$O(s + \frac{1}{f})$	$O(s + \frac{1}{f})$	$O(s)$
Member access	$O(1)$	$O(s)$	$O(s)$
Array access	$O(1)$	$O(\log s)$	$O(\log s)$

5.3   Comparing to Other Techniques

As stated above, reference counting has some disadvantages compared to other garbage collection techniques. There do exist real-time copying and mark-sweep collectors, so the need for a real-time reference counting technique might be questioned. Table 1 compares the worst-case execution time of the operations of the real-time reference counter presented in this paper to the worst-case execution times of other real-time garbage collectors [12,17]. Neither the copying nor the mark-sweep algorithm use increment or decrement operations. However, both use read/write barriers that perform equivalent operations. In the table the worst-case execution time of the barriers are compared to the worst-case execution time of the increment/decrement operations. The size of an object is denoted by s and the minimum amount of free memory (the overhead) denoted by f.

In real-time systems, the amount of memory is often limited. The real-time reference counting technique enables the usage of all of the memory when no cyclic garbage is produced. If cyclic garbage is produced, the overhead of RTRC is calculated by multiplying the percentage of cyclic garbage with the overhead of a mark-sweep collector, i.e. if 10% of the garbage belongs to cycles, the overhead is 10% of the overhead using mark-sweep. Drastically decreasing the memory overhead is especially advantageous for embedded systems.

Copying garbage collectors have the advantage of compacting the memory during garbage collection, which gives fast allocation and eliminates external fragmentation. However, since objects move around, a handle is used to access the object. This cause an extra pointer dereference which could be compared to accessing data in the second block using RTRC. Thus, if most objects can be stored in one or two blocks, accessing members is as fast or faster in RTRC compared to using a copying garbage collector.

6   Conclusion and Future Work

This paper presents an automatic memory management technique (RTRC) for hard real-time systems. It does not suffer from external fragmentation and all operations are predictable in worst case memory usage and execution time. All (non-cyclic) dead blocks are immediately available for creation of new objects. Thus, the worst case execution time is the same if 10% or 100% of the memory is used (assuming no cycles). Even if cyclic garbage is produced, the overhead is drastically decreased for most systems. And finally, the high priority processes can be given the benefit of faster allocation if that is desired.

Previously presented real-time garbage collection techniques that take memory availability into account restricts memory usage. Garbage collectors based on a two sub-heap copying collector can only use half the heap for live objects. Practical experience indicates that often more than five times the live memory is needed to get an acceptable execution time overhead. The memory usage of the mark-sweep collector presented by Siebert [16] is better than that of copying collectors. The figures presented by Siebert suggest that a system need about 50% memory overhead to get acceptable execution time. The execution time overhead increases rapidly towards infinity when less memory is available.

A backup garbage collector is used to reclaim cyclic data. Having a backup garbage collector might not be a good solution if too much cyclic garbage is produced, but in most systems most cyclic garbage can be avoided. One could use weak pointers (that are not counted,) or one could break cycles manually before they become garbage. A good idea would be to run a backup garbage collector during development of the real-time application as a development aid to find and manually break cycles in the code.

The remaining disadvantage of RTRC is the execution time overhead. The execution time overhead can be greatly reduced using static optimizations. These optimizations can turn heap allocations into stack allocations and remove redundant reference count updates.

The continuation of this research will investigate in more detail topics such as how to optimize performance using static analysis, connect blocks into objects, choose block size, integrating a backup garbage collector, and what to do with large objects.

References

1. D. Bacon and V. Rajan. Concurrent cycle collection in reference counted systems. In *Proceedings of the Fifteenth European Conference on Object-Oriented Programming (ECOOP), Lecture Notes in Computer Science*, volume 2072. University Eötvös Loránd, Budapest, Hungary, Springer-Verlag, June 2001.

2. H. G. Baker. Minimising reference count updating with deferred and anchored pointers for functional data structures. *ACM SIGPLAN Notices*, 29(9), Sept. 1994.

3. J. M. Barth. Shifting garbage collection overhead to compile time. *Communications of the ACM*, 20(7):513–518, July 1977.

4. D. G. Bobrow. Managing re-entrant structures using reference counts. *ACM Transactions on Programming Languages and Systems*, 2(3):269–273, July 1980.

5. R. A. Brooks. Trading data space for reduced time and code space in real-time garbage collection on stock hardware. In G. L. Steele, editor, *Conference Record of the 1984 ACM Symposium on Lisp and Functional Programming*, pages 256–262, Austin, TX, Aug. 1984. ACM Press.

6. D. R. Brownbridge. Cyclic reference counting for combinator machines. In J.-P. Jouannaud, editor, *Record of the 1985 Conference on Functional Programming and Computer Architecture*, volume 201 of *Lecture Notes in Computer Science*, Nancy, France, Sept. 1985. Springer-Verlag.

7. J. M. Bull, L. A. Smith, M. D. Westhead, D. S. Henty, and R. A. Davey. A benchmark suite for high performance Java. *Concurrency: Practice and Experience*, (12):375–388, 2000.

8. T. W. Christopher. Reference count garbage collection. *Software Practice and Experience*, 14(6):503–507, June 1984.

9. G. E. Collins. A method for overlapping and erasure of lists. *Communications of the ACM*, 3(12):655–657, Dec. 1960.

10. L. P. Deutsch and D. G. Bobrow. An efficient incremental automatic garbage collector. *Communications of the ACM*, 19(9):522–526, Sept. 1976.

11. R. R. Fenichel and J. C. Yochelson. A Lisp garbage collector for virtual memory computer systems. *Communications of the ACM*, 12(11):611–612, Nov. 1969.

12. R. Henriksson. *Scheduling Garbage Collection in Embedded Systems*. PhD thesis, Lund Institute of Technology, July 1998.

13. M. S. Johnstone and P. R. Wilson. The memory fragmentation problem: Solved? In P. Dickman and P. R. Wilson, editors, *OOPSLA '97 Workshop on Garbage Collection and Memory Management*, Oct. 1997.

14. T. Ritzau, M. Beemster, F. Liekweg, and C. Probst. JoC — the JOSES compiler. Presented at the Java for Embedded Systems Workshop, London, May 2000.

15. R. A. Saunders. The LISP system for the Q–32 computer. In E. C. Berkeley and D. G. Bobrow, editors, *The Programming Language LISP: Its Operation and Applications*, pages 220–231, Cambridge, MA, 1974. Information International, Inc.

16. F. Siebert. Guaranteeing non-disruptiveness and real-time deadlines in an incremental garbage collector. In R. Jones, editor, *Proceedings of the First International Symposium on Memory Management*, volume 34(3) of *ACM SIGPLAN Notices*, pages 130–137, Vancouver, Oct. 1998. ACM Press. ISMM is the successor to the IWMM series of workshops.

17. F. Siebert. Eliminating external fragmentation in a non-moving garbage collector for Java. In *Proceedings of Compilers, Architectures and Synthesis for Embedded Systems (CASES'00)*, San Jose, November 2000.

18. A. Veen. The JOSES project - compiling Java for embedded systems. In D. U. Assmann, editor, *Java Optimization Strategies for Embedded Systems Workshop at ETAPS 2001*, Genova, Italy, Apr. 2001.

19. J. Weizenbaum. Symmetric list processor. *Communications of the ACM*, 6(9):524–544, Sept. 1963.

Speedup Prediction for Selective Compilation of Embedded Java Programs[*][**]

Vincent Colin de Verdière[1], Sébastien Cros[1], Christian Fabre[1],
Romain Guider[1], and Sergio Yovine[2]

[1] Silicomp Research Institute, 2 Ave de Vignate, F-38610, Gières, France
[2] Verimag, 2 Ave de Vignate, F-38610, Gières, France

Abstract. We propose a profile based code selection scheme for an AOT Java compiler. This scheme relies on a model that accurately predicts the speedup of a given selection. The model takes into account the cross-call patterns of the application. This approach allows us to reduce the size of compiled code significantly for several benchmarks.

1   Introduction

Java has been recognized as an attractive language and platform to program embedded systems. There are several reasons for this. Embedded systems use a large variety of processors. The portability of Java is very appealing in this context. Embedded systems have generally a limited memory size. Because Java has been designed to ease the communication of programs through the internet, one of it's design goals is the small size of executables (which is achieved by the use of a stack based bytecode). This feature is also beneficial to embedded systems.

However, in order to limit energy consumption, embedded systems are not built around high performance processors. So neither can they accommodate the low performance of purely interpreted Java nor the overhead of a JIT compiler [6,10]. One solution to the performance problem is the use of Ahead of Time compilers (AOT compilers)[11,12,13]. Because the compilation is done offline with such compilers, there is no runtime overhead imposed by compilation.

There still is a problem with AOT compilers: compilation increases the size of code. To address this problem, we have developed the TurboJ[13] compiler that partially compiles an application. The runtime, which is based on a Java Virtual Machine (JVM), allows a mixed execution mode where both compiled code and interpreted code are executed.

The TurboJ compiler allows code to be selected for compilation at the method level. The compiler is fed with the entry point of an application (from which it builds the list of classes that the application uses) and a list of methods that it must compile. Any other method remains interpreted. This feature is very

---

[*] Partially supported by French RNTL Project Expresso and FONGECIF.
[**] Contact authors: guider@ri.silicomp.fr, Sergio.Yovine@imag.fr.

A. Sangiovanni-Vincentelli and J. Sifakis (Eds.): EMSOFT 2002, LNCS 2491, pp. 227–239, 2002.

important and useful to solve the problem of code-size increase. However, in practice, it is not an easy task to select the methods to be compiled. In fact, it is not easy at all to figure out which methods are the most interesting to compile in order to get the best performance without expanding too much the size of the code.

The general problem that we deal with is as follows: given a memory size limit l what is the set of methods that when compiled produces the most efficient program whose size is lower than l? This corresponds to an optimization of programs for performance. The problem can also be seen the other way round: given a speedup s what is the method set that, when compiled produces the smallest program with the expected performance. This corresponds to an optimization of programs for size.

A first answer is to use a profiler and select the set of methods where the program spends most of its time[3]. This approach may give good results for some applications; however, experience proved that there are programs for which the result of such an approach is extremely poor: we encountered programs that were slower than their interpreted version.

Experience also shows that an important factor of performance degradation is the context-switching done when calling compiled code from interpreted code or when calling interpreted code from compiled code(cross-calls). In this paper we present a model of performance of compiled Java programs that take the impact of cross-calls into account. An algorithm to select compiled methods that uses this model to guide its choice has been implemented in the tool TurboJ.

Section 2 is devoted to the description of TurboJ, our AOT compiler and to the description of the profilers we developed. In Section 2.2 we describe a first, naive, approach for partitioning programs and show its limits. In Section 3 we propose a model of program performance that takes more elements into account to circumvent the limitations of the first approach. In Section 4 we present a method selection algorithm that exploits the model presented in the previous section. We discuss related work in Section 5. Then we conclude and discuss possible enhancements of our work in Section 6

2 Existing Framework

2.1 The TurboJ Compiler and Profiler

TurboJ[13] is a bytecode to native code compiler. It is an AOT compiler that supports mixed-mode execution (compiled/interpreted) of Java programs. Code can be selected for compilation at the method level. Mixed-mode execution is achieved by relying on a VM to execute interpreted code. The VM also serves as a runtime environment for the compiled code. Beside the possibility of mixed-mode execution, the advantage of this approach is that it makes it possible to cope with the full range of Java features such as reflection or dynamic loading.

---

[3] It is a well known rule of thumb that most programs spend 80% of the time in 20% of its code.

TurboJ is used along with a profiler that allows the extraction of information about Java programs that is useful to partition applications (e.g., number of bytecodes executed by a method, frequency of the call of a method at a call site, etc.). This profiler works by instrumenting the bytecode so that it is fully portable: it can be used with any VM and on any platform. Another advantage of our profiler is that the results reported are precise (no sampling is done) and are not influenced by the profiling because we count events instead of measuring time (i.e., no probe effect).

2.2   A Naive Model of Performance of Programs

The best possible selection is the set of methods that have the best speedup up to a given size of bytecode. Compiling in isolation each method of a program and measure the speedup it provides would not be tractable for obvious reasons. Instead we use a model of the speedup that allows to predict the speedup provided by a method without actually compiling it and running the program. It only requires an interpreted run of the instrumented program to extract execution profiles.

The first model that we tried is very simple: we consider a constant acceleration factor among all bytecodes. Under this model, the best selection of size l is the selection that maximizes the number of executed bytecodes.

We did not consider useful in practice to use an optimization package to solve this problem. Instead, we use a very simple heuristic: we present the methods sorted by decreasing number of executed bytecodes and select the first ones up to a given static size.

Our selection tool has a graphical interface that presents the results of the instrumented runs. Results are presented with sorted methods on the x-axis and their respective number of executed bytecodes on the y-axis.

2.3   Experiments (Limitations of the Approach)

Under the hypothesis that most of the execution time is spent in a small portion of the program, the speedup curves that result from the application of the above selection strategy should have a high slope at the beginning and become quickly almost horizontal. The initial high slope would also mean that, in most cases, the first sorted methods provide a good ratio of executed bytecode over size.

However, in practice the model of performance does not always predict the speedup of the partially compiled applications. In order to assess the problem, we ran experiments on several real-world applications. For lack of space we present here two of the most significant ones:

- compress, from the SpecJvm98 benchmark suite [5] and
- xalan, the Apache XSL processor [8].

Compress is a computation kernel code composed of 41 methods which is representative of code that can be found in embedded systems. Xalan is a large object-oriented application comprising 2372 methods.

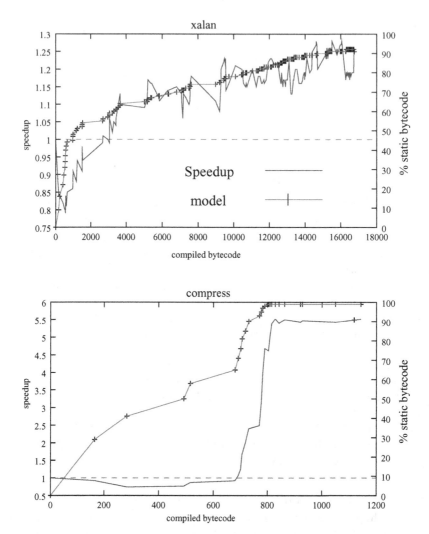

Fig. 1. Progression of the Speedup with the number of Compiled Bytecodes

Our model asserts that the more bytecodes are compiled (whatever bytecode they are) the faster the program is. To assess this, our experiment consists in the observation of the speedup progression in parallel with the progression of the number of compiled bytecodes. We generated, for each of our benchmarks, a suite of growing selections of methods - the methods being sorted by decreasing number of executed bytecodes. For each of these selections, we compiled the selected methods and ran the program. The reported results are the speedups of each of these runs as compared to the fully interpreted program. We ran our tests on a Intel 730MHz-Pentium III running Linux.

The results of our experiments (see Fig. 1) showed that the model is far from being accurate. The speedup obtained in the case of Compress for up to

Table 1. Speedups for the 4 kinds of calls.

Speedup	Int/Int	Int/Compl	Compl/Int	Compl/Compl
invokevirtual	1	0.3	0.6	5
invokeinterface	1	0.5	0.6	2.5
invokestatic	1	0.4	0.6	5
invokespecial	1	0.4	0.5	5

700 compiled bytecodes has an inverse progression as compared to the model. For Xalan, the speedup follows on average the model. However, it makes a lot of local oscillations that are not negligible. Moreover, there is a regression of performance when compiling up to 3000 bytecodes.

These results are not acceptable for mainly two reasons. First, the selection procedure would lead to selecting a set of methods which will slow down the application when compiled (e.g., Compress). Second, it shows unpredictable oscillations, that is, selecting one more method can dramatically reduce the speedup (e.g., Xalan). The major drawback of this approach is that it does not provide any convenient way to detect such problems. Therefore, it is unable to faithfully predict the speedup of a selection after compilation.

This raises some questions. First, how can we explain that compiling some bytecodes slows down the application? Second, are there bytecodes that provide more speedup than others when compiled? Or are there bytecodes that slow down the application when compiled until a small number of other bytecodes are compiled? In the next section we propose a model that solves the problems we observed on the benchmarks.

3   Taking Calls/Context-Switching into Account

Our investigations showed that cross-calls (calls from interpreted code to compiled code or from compiled code to interpreted code) are responsible for the slow down of applications by the compilation. Cross-calls are done through stubs that convert the argument passing convention and install exception handlers. These stubs imply costly (yet necessary) computations that are not done in case of direct calls. We made several experiments to assess the relative cost of the calls and its impact on the speedup provided by a selection.

3.1   The Cost and Impact of Cross-Calls

We ran micro-benchmarks that allowed us to isolate the speedup gained for each of the four kinds of call in various situations. The results of these measurements are summarized in the Table 1.

There is no relation between the lines of the table. For each line, the interpreted-interpreted cost is taken as reference. The other figures are the speedup of the call as compared to the performance of the interpreted-interpreted call. It is clear from these figures that the cross-calls can actually slow down an

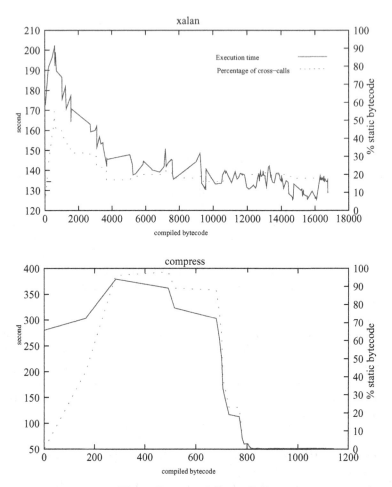

Fig. 2. Impact of Cross-Calls

application. For instance an interpreted `invokevirtual` is 70% slower when it calls compiled code than when it calls interpreted code.

To further convince the reader that the cross-calls are responsible for the slow down, we ran experiments on our 2 benchmarks. The experiment consists in measuring the number of cross-calls executed for each selection. We report (see Fig. 2), for each selection, its execution time and the amount of cross-calls in this number of compiled-bytecode executed. We observe that the amount of cross-calls and the execution time have related progressions. In particular, peaks of cross-calls coincide with peaks of execution time.

3.2   A New Model of Application Performance

From the experiments above, it is clear that the amount of cross-calls needs to be small enough for the compilation to provide some speedup. Moreover, compilation not only does not provide the same speedup for all the bytecodes but it may provide an anti-speedup when calls become cross-calls. This suggests that the speedup is inversely proportional to the number of cross-calls.

Given a set of methods M and a sub-set s of these methods, we note N_s the number of bytecodes executed by s on a run and C_s the number of cross-calls executed during a run when s is compiled. The model we propose to use is then

$$R_s = \frac{N_s}{C_s}$$

The intended use of this model is not to get an absolute measure of the speedup obtained when compiling a selection. Instead, we simply use it to compare selections so as to be able to select the best one with respect to our model.

3.3   Experiments

To assess our new model, we re-ran our benchmarks and for each selection we computed the value of R_s and measured the corresponding speedup. Results of these measurements are reported in Fig. 3. What we observe on these curves is that the model follows most of the progression of the speedup. That is most of the peaks of the speedup curves coincide with peaks of the model curve. This is particularly the case for Compress where the model and the speedup progression are very similar.

Thus, the model we propose is much better than the naive one that is commonly used in dynamic compilation systems. Moreover, this model has several important qualities:

- it is simple so that its evaluation can be done at low cost;
- its evaluation can be done in an incremental fashion as the selection evolves, there is no need to re-compute the model for the whole selection when a method is added;
- it does not contain any constant related to the platform.

The last point is quite important for us. In fact, our profilers instrument the bytecode so as to be independent of the JVM. With this model, the whole chain (instrumentation, profiling and method selection) remains independent of the platform.

4   A Partitioning Heuristics

4.1   A Greedy Algorithm to Select Methods

Having a model, we need an algorithm that finds good method selections using the model. While the naive model was linear, the model with cross-calls is not. Adding a method influences both N_s and C_s. Furthermore, it is not monotone with respect to N_s: adding a method to the selection can turn direct calls to cross-calls and so lower the model value. We propose a heuristic based on a greedy algorithm to find solutions.

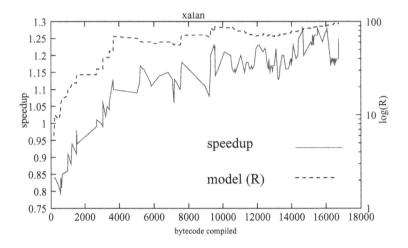

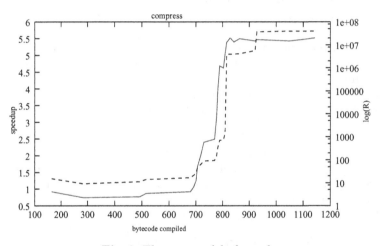

Fig. 3. The new model of speedup

Starting from an initial selection, our algorithm enhances the value of R_s by adding a method to the selection at each step. The algorithm selects the method that, if selected maximizes the increase of R_s. At each step, the search for a method is restricted to the set of methods that have an incident edge with some selected method. The values N_s and C_s are maintained at each step so that the value of R_s can be evaluated in an incremental fashion without looking at the entire selection.

4.2   Results

One first result is that our heuristic finds successive selections with a growing ratio R_s. We represent the evolution of the model and the corresponding speedup for our two examples Fig. 4. These are two representative results out of several

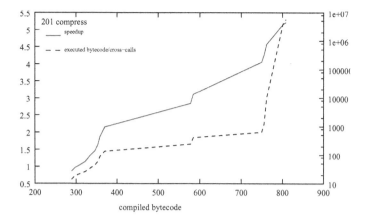

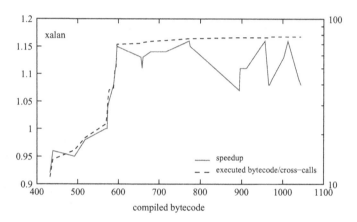

Fig. 4. Evolution of the speedup as compared to its model following the greedy heuristic

other experiments. The figure shows that these curves (the evolution of the model following the greedy algorithm) are useful tools in the search for a good selection. In the case of Compress, the progression of the ratio and of the real speedup are similar in that both are only growing.

Our model and heuristic provide a reliable tool to explore the tradeoff between application size and execution performance. The model does not reflect some oscillations in the case of Xalan, but the choice that the model leads to turns out to be the correct one with respect to the speedup curve. More generally, we observed in all our experiments (including some that are not reported in this paper) that when the model is growing then the real speedup is always growing, but when the value of the model is stable, there may be some oscillations of the real speedup. This makes our tool reliable because there is no reason to compile more methods if the model reports that they will not provide any additional speedup.

Table 2. Comparison of the results of the naive approach and the greedy algorithm

application	% Speedup	% Compiled bytecode	
		First method	Greedy
Xalan	89	35.6	4.0
	97	98.4	5.2
	100	100	7.8
	108		24.6
Compress	27	61.3	18.1
	39	62.4	32.1
	56	67.5	50.8
	82	69.8	66.1

To compare with the naive approach, we report in Table 2 the relative static quantities of bytecode that need to be compiled in both approaches to reach a given speedup. The figures for Compress and Xalan are drawn from the curve represented Fig. 4. We take, as a reference, the best solution found with the naive approach. Speedups are given as a percentage of the reference speedup (i.e., 100% of speedup corresponds to the maximum speedup achieved with the naive method). Static quantities of bytecodes are reported as a percentage of the reference static quantity of bytecodes (which corresponds to the reference speedup).

For Xalan, only 4% of the reference quantity of bytecode is selected to be compiled by the greedy algorithm to get 89% of the reference speedup. As compared to the 35% of bytecodes selected with the first approach to get the same speedup this is an improvement of 88%. To reach the reference speedup, only 7.8% of the reference quantity of bytecode needs to be compiled which yields 92% of improvement. Results are a bit less spectacular for Compress but we still observe that our new model significantly reduces the total amount of bytecode to be compiled.

The figures of Table 2 also show that we can improve the result both in terms of size and of performance: for Xalan, by compiling 24.6% of the bytecode needed to get 100% of the reference speedup we actually obtain 108% of this speedup. This means that we go beyond the best speedup observed with the naive approach while (at the same time) reducing by 75.4% the size of the compiled bytecode.

5   Related Work

Profiling information has been used for a long time to guide optimizers in static compilers. One trend of work [3,4] uses profiling information to detect frequently executed scenarios and transform the program so as to be able to optimize the frequently executed code. More recently, profiling information has been used in dynamic optimization systems. Some work only uses it to detect so-called hot spots [6,10] while others uses it to select the optimizations applied to the code [1,2]

There are many AOT compilers that mix interpreted and compiled Java code. Harissa [11] integrates an interpreter in its runtime environment to implement dynamic loading of code. TowerJ [12] also integrates an interpreter in its runtime environment and allows selective compilation but there is no mention of an assistance tool to partition applications. The company OTI developed a JVM called J9 and an AOT compiler that generates code that relies on the JVM as a runtime environment, much like TurboJ. They also have the possibility to selectively compile methods and they use profiling information to select methods that are worth compiling [7]. Their profiling approach is based on the Java interface for profiling [9] so that they implement a sampling profiler that records execution time and call frequency of each method. They select methods for compilation on the basis of their respective execution time. This is close to our naive approach. However, we see some limitations to this approach because they have no convenient way of identifying the kind of bytecodes executed in the methods that run for long times. As a consequence they cannot figure out the call patterns. Besides, our profiling method is less biased because we count events instead of measuring time (no probe effect). Moreover, the OTI approach is not portable since it requires writing JVMPI native code.

6 Conclusion

We propose a profile based code selection scheme for an AOT compiler that takes into account cross-call patterns of an application. We have shown that this approach allowed us to reduce the size of the compiled code significantly as compared to the algorithm that relies on the relative quantities of bytecode executed.

The greedy heuristic that we propose needs to be inseminated with an initial selection. On the one hand, a rich initial selection will offer the greedy algorithm more possibilities of selection at each step and, therefore, lead to better selections. On the other hand, a too large initial selection may contain a method that cannot be optimized by the greedy algorithm and compromise the results. Currently, we use the list of methods sorted by growing number of executed bytecode to build the initial selection. This strategy turned out to provide good results. Besides, if the prefixes of the list do not contain interesting an initial selection, the programmer can select methods individually through a graphical user interface that represents the classes of the program as well as the call graph.

One of the key features of our heuristic is that it is incremental and, therefore, fast. The greedy algorithm considers a sub-set of the methods of a program that depends on the size of the selection, not on the size of the program. Because the heuristic is fast, the programmer gets quickly feedback in the form of the curve of the evolution of the model. This allows testing several solutions for the initial selection in a short amount of time.

Due to the expected large size of the call graph (e.g., 2372 methods and 5008 edges in the case of Xalan), we do not envision the use of global and exact optimization algorithms. The greedy algorithm allows us to propose a suite of solutions that are built incrementally and that can be used by the programmer to explore the size/performance tradeoff. It is unclear whether a global approach would provide the same possibilities.

Our results are promising but can be enhanced in several ways.

One direction consists in taking recursion into account. Recursion corresponds to cycles in the call graph. A possible and simple approach would be to reduce the call graph to its strongly connected components and consider strongly connected components as compilation units in place of methods.

In our greedy algorithm, the choice of a method is restricted, at each step, to the set of methods that have an incident edge to a selected method. This allows us to reduce the size of the search space at each step. It would be actually possible to consider all the methods. A method that has no incident edge with a selected method, if selected, will only introduce cross-calls so that it is possible to evaluate the increase of the value of R_s for each of such methods independently of the selection and of other methods: it is simply the ratio of its quantity of executed bytecode and of the number of calls it makes. So if we maintain a list of non-candidate methods sorted by their local ratio, the head of the list (the method that has the maximum local ratio) is the best choice among all the non-candidate methods. This allows to open the choice of a candidate to all the methods at each step while increasing the size of the search space by only one. This approach would eventually lead to better selections where the ratio becomes flat (Fig. 4).

Finally, beside calls, we consider that all other bytecodes are accelerated in the same way. This is actually not true since, for instance, runtime type checks are not accelerated. We believe that we can still refine our model to take this into account.

References

1. M. Arnold, S. Fink, D. Grove, M. Hind, and P. F. Sweeney. Adaptive optimization in the jalapeno jvm. In *Proc. of ACM-SIGPLAN OOPSLA'00*, 2000.
2. Matthew Arnold, Michael Hind, and Barbara G. Ryder. An empirical study of selective optimization. In *Proc. International Workshop on Languages and Compilers for Parallel Computing*, 2000.
3. Pohua P. Chang, Scott A. Mahlke, and Wen-mei W. Hwu. Using profile information to assist classic code optimizations. *Software Practice and Experience*, 1991.
4. W. Chen, R. Bringmann, S. Mahlke, S. Anik, T. Kiyohara, N. Warter, D. Lavery, W.-M. Hwu, R. Hank, and J. Gyllenhaal. Using profile information to assist advanced compiler optimization and scheduling. In *Proc. of Advances in Languages and Compilers for Parallel Processing*. Pitman Publishing, 1993.
5. Standard Performance Evaluation Corporation. Spec jvm98 benchmarks. http://www.spec.org/osg/jvm98/.
6. B. Delsart, V. Joloboff, and Eric Paire. Jcod: A lightweight modular compilation technology for embedded java. In *Accepted for publication in EMSOFT'02*, 2002.
7. Aldo H. Eisma. Feedback directed ahead-of-time compilation for embedded java applications. In Uwe Assmann, editor, *JOSES Workshop at ETAPS'01*, Genova, 2001.

8. The Apache Software Foundation. Xalan-java version 2.
   http://xml.apache.org/xalan-j/index.html.
9. Sun Microsystems Inc. Java virtual machine profiling interface (jvmpi), java 2 sdk, standard edition documentation, version 1.2.2.
   java.sun.com/products/jdk/1.2/docs/index.html.
10. Sun Microsystems. The java hotspot performance engine architecture.
   http://java.sun.com/products/hotspot/whitepaper.html, april 1999.
11. Gilles Muller, Bárbara Moura, Fabrice Bellard, and Charles Consel. Harissa: A flexible and efficient Java environment mixing bytecode and compiled code. In *Proc. of Usenix COOTS'97*, Berkeley, 1997.
12. Tower Technology. Towerj 3.0. www.towerj.com.
13. Michael Weiss, François de Ferrière, Bertrand Delsart, Christian Fabre, Frederick Hirsch, E. Andrew Johnson, Vania Joloboff, Fred Roy, Fridtjof Siebert, and Xavier Spengler. Turboj, a java bytecode-to-native compiler. In *Proc. of LCTES'98*, volume 1474 of *LNCS*, 1998.

Synchronous Modelling
of Asynchronous Systems

Nicolas Halbwachs and Siwar Baghdadi

Vérimag, Grenoble – France

Abstract. We investigate the use of synchronous languages to model partially asynchronous systems. Through the use of intermittent activations and assertions, synchronous processes can be composed according to various asynchronous models. Common synchronization and communication mechanisms can be described. The resulting descriptions can be simulated and verified, using classical tools of synchronous programming.

1 Introduction

Synchronous programming [IEE91] is recognized as a very convenient paradigm for designing reactive systems. This success is due to several advantages: synchronous languages [LGLL91,HCRP91,BG92] enjoy clean formal semantics, synchronous parallel composition is an invaluable tool for structuring programs and reducing programming complexity, synchronous programs can be efficiently and safely implemented, usual verification methods [HLR92,LDBL93,JPV95,Bou98] work in general better on synchronous programs, etc.

Now, it is clear also that synchronous programming is not the panacea. There is a need for combining synchrony and asynchrony, from two opposite points of view: on one hand, to introduce synchrony in areas dominated by distributed systems, and on the other hand, in synchronous systems, to take into account the intrinsic asynchrony of interfaces and distributed implementations.

In the domain of distributed systems, and in particular, in telecommunications, people are naturally used with asynchronous languages (e.g., SDL [ITU94]). Now, they use the same languages for programming centralized parts (e.g., feature management), which would be obviously easier with synchronous languages. This shows an obvious need for programming this kind of systems as *"Globally Asynchronous, Locally Synchronous Systems"* (GALS), i.e., synchronous processes composed with each other in an asynchronous way.

On the other hand, asynchrony cannot be completely ignored in synchronous programming. First, the boundaries of a synchronous systems have to deal with asynchronous features, like sampling asynchronous signals [Cas01]. Also, reactive systems are often implemented on distributed architectures. When this implementation is done by hand, one needs some way of modelling the whole system, for early simulation and validation [CS00]. Even in case of automatic code distribution [CGP94,BCT99], there is a need for validating the resulting implementation, which cannot be strictly equivalent to the centralised one.

A. Sangiovanni-Vincentelli and J. Sifakis (Eds.): EMSOFT 2002, LNCS 2491, pp. 240–251, 2002.

Several formalisms have been proposed which combine synchronous and asynchronous primitives (e.g., [AH99]). More specifically, the concept of GALS has been investigated in several models and tools [BCG99,BS98,BCG+97]. In this paper, we investigate the use of synchronous languages as they are, to model asynchronous systems, allowing, thus, the modelling of GALS. This is nothing but a systematic presentation of what many people do (e.g., [BS01]) for simulating asynchronous systems with synchronous languages: synchronous processes are activated by more or less related conditions (or clocks), and non determinism is handled through additional inputs. After a formal definition of synchronous machines (Section 2), we formalise sporadic activation of synchronous processes (Section 3), and we investigate various synchronization and communication mechanisms (Section 4). Obvious advantages are that we get formal semantics of GALS for free, and that this synchronous modelling does not increase the size of the models.

2   Synchronous Machines

In this section, we give a general formalization of synchronous machines, independently of any synchronous language. The notion we have in mind is a straightforward generalization of synchronous circuits (Mealy machines) to work with arbitrary data-types: such a machine has a memory (a state), and a combinational part, computing the output and the next state as a function of the current input and state (Fig. 1.a). These machines can be composed in parallel, with possible "plugging" of one's outputs into the other's inputs (Fig. 1.b), as long as these wirings don't introduce any combinational loop.

Let *Var* be a set of variables, each variable $v \in Var$ taking its values in a domain D_v. If $X \subseteq Var$, a *valuation* of X is a function associating with each $v \in X$ its value $\in D_v$. We note $\mathcal{V}(X)$ the set of valuations of X.

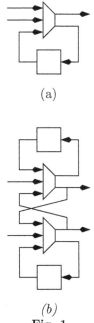

(a)

(b)

Fig. 1.
Synchronous machines
and their composition

Definition 1 (Synchronous machines) *Let $\mathcal{I}$, $\mathcal{O}$, $\mathcal{S}$, be three disjoint subsets of Var. A synchronous machine with input variables $\mathcal{I}$, output variables $\mathcal{O}$, and state variables $\mathcal{S}$, is given by an initial state $s_0 \in \mathcal{V}(\mathcal{S})$, an output function $\omega : \mathcal{V}(\mathcal{S}) \times \mathcal{V}(\mathcal{I}) \mapsto \mathcal{V}(\mathcal{O})$ and a next-state function $\sigma : \mathcal{V}(\mathcal{S}) \times \mathcal{V}(\mathcal{I}) \mapsto \mathcal{V}(\mathcal{S})$.*

The machine starts from the initial state s_0. In a given state s, it deterministically reacts to an input valuation i by returning the output valuation

$o = \omega(s, i)$ and moving to the state $\sigma(s, i)$. We will often consider the functions ω and σ as vectorial functions, $\omega_v(s, i)$ (resp. $\sigma_v(s, i)$) being the value $\omega(s, i)(v)$ (resp., $\sigma(s, i)(v)$) associated with v by the valuation $\omega(s, i)$ (resp., $\sigma(s, i)$).

Definition 2 (Dependence) *We will say that the output $v(\in \mathcal{O})$ of a machine depends on the input $w(\in \mathcal{I})$, if the function ω_v depends[1] on w.*

Definition 3 (Synchronous composition)
Let $M_p = (\mathcal{I}_p, \mathcal{O}_p, \mathcal{S}_p, s0_p, \omega_p, \sigma_p), (p = 1, 2)$, be two synchronous machines, satisfying:

- *$\mathcal{S}_p \cap (\mathcal{I}_q \cup \mathcal{O}_q \cup \mathcal{S}_q) = \emptyset, p = 1, 2, q = 2 - p$ (state variables are local)*
- *$\mathcal{O}_1 \cap \mathcal{O}_2 = \emptyset$ (disjoint outputs)*
- *for each $v_1 \in \mathcal{O}_1 \cap \mathcal{I}_2$ and each $v_2 \in \mathcal{O}_2 \cap \mathcal{I}_1$, either v_1 does not depend on v_2 (in M_1), or v_2 does not depend on v_1 (in M_2) (no combinational loop)*

Then, their synchronous composition $M_1 \times M_2$ is a synchronous machine, with

- *$\mathcal{I}_\times = \mathcal{I}_1 \setminus \mathcal{O}_2 \cup \mathcal{I}_2 \setminus \mathcal{O}_1$ as input variables*
- *$\mathcal{O}_\times = \mathcal{O}_1 \cup \mathcal{O}_2$ as output variables*
- *$\mathcal{S}_\times = \mathcal{S}_1 \cup \mathcal{S}_2$ as state variables*

and the output $\omega_\times$ and next-state $\sigma_\times$ functions are defined as follows: let i be a valuation of $\mathcal{I}_\times$, (s_1, s_2) be a valuation of $\mathcal{S}_\times$. Let us define conjointly[2] i_1, i_2, valuations of $\mathcal{I}_1, \mathcal{I}_2$, respectively, as follows

$$for\ p = 1, 2, q = 2 - p,\ i_p(v) = \begin{cases} \omega_q(s_q, i_q)(v) & if\ v \in \mathcal{O}_q \\ i(v) & otherwise \end{cases}$$

Then,

$$\omega_\times((s_1, s_2), i)(v) = \begin{cases} \omega_1(s_1, i_1)(v) & if\ v \in \mathcal{O}_1 \\ \omega_2(s_2, i_2)(v) & if\ v \in \mathcal{O}_2 \end{cases}$$

$$\sigma_\times((s_1, s_2), i)(v) = \begin{cases} \sigma_1(s_1, i_1)(v) & if\ v \in \mathcal{S}_1 \\ \sigma_2(s_2, i_2)(v) & if\ v \in \mathcal{S}_2 \end{cases}$$

3   Sporadic Activation and Nondeterminism

It is well-known, since [Mil81], that asynchrony can be simulated in a synchronous model, by letting processes non-deterministically "stutter", or "stay silent". As a matter of fact, most synchronous languages provide a way of "blocking" or "freezing" a process:

---

[1]   Here, we consider a syntactic notion of dependence. Of course, the whole problem of *causality* [Mal93,HM95,SBT96] is hidden here, but it will not be addressed in this paper.
[2]   Notice that this definition makes sense because of the absence of combinational loop.

- in Esterel, the "suspend" statement has been identified [Ber93] as a very basic primitive: "suspend P when S" prevents P from reacting when the signal S is present.
- in Lustre and Signal, the concept of clock is available to define when a process is triggered: according to the data-flow nature of these languages, an operator is only activated at the arrival rate of its operands. By "filtering" the input flows of a process according to a clock, one can rule out the activation rate of the process.
- in synchronous circuits also, this would be done by disabling the clock.

Let us formalize this notion in our model of synchronous machines: we define an operation consisting of adding a Boolean input to a machine, which freezes the state when it is 0. Now, we have to define the output when the machine is not activated. There are several solutions:

- In Esterel and Signal, the machine is "silent", meaning that the outputs take a special "absent" value.
- In Lustre, the outputs are frozen to their last taken values (through the use of the "current" operator). This may be expensive in memory (or in number of states, for verification).
- In circuits, the combinational part would keep computing the outputs, as a function of the frozen state and the current inputs. This is not a very intuitive behavior.

In fact, this point is not very important, since we will manage not to make use of the outputs of a process when it is not activated. Let us choose the Esterel and Signal solution, which is both clean and inexpensive:

Definition 4 (Activation) *Let $M = (\mathcal{I}, \mathcal{O}, \mathcal{S}, s0, \omega, \sigma)$ be a synchronous machine, and let $c \in Var \backslash (\mathcal{I} \cup \mathcal{O} \cup \mathcal{S})$ be a variable not involved in M, and such that $D_c = \{0, 1\}$. Then the activation of M according to c is a synchronous machine $c \triangleright M = (\mathcal{I} \cup \{c\}, \mathcal{O}, \mathcal{S}, s0, \omega^\triangleright, \sigma^\triangleright)$, where*

$$\sigma^\triangleright(s, (i, c)) = \begin{cases} \sigma(s, i) & \text{if } c = 1 \\ s & \text{otherwise} \end{cases} \qquad \omega^\triangleright(s, (i, c)) = \begin{cases} \omega(s, i) & \text{if } c = 1 \\ \bot & \text{otherwise} \end{cases}$$

c will be called the activation condition *of $c \triangleright M$.*

The second issue for modelling asynchrony, is non-determinism. Not only the non-deterministic scheduling of asynchronous processes must be modelled, but we will often have to model non-deterministic processes.

An obvious, and very convenient way of introducing non-determinism, is by using additional arbitrary inputs, with arbitrary values. For instance, non-deterministic scheduling will be modelled as follows: if each machine M_p has its own activation condition c_p, which is an input to the whole system, then the composition $(c_1 \triangleright M_1) \times (c_2 \triangleright M_2) \times \ldots$ will behave as the asynchronous product of the machines.

Now, we have to be careful about the communications in this asynchronous composition (since we decided that the outputs of a non-activated machine is the undefined value $\perp$). Moreover, in general, we want some synchronization between the machines. So, the issues of communication and synchronization must be addressed.

4   Communication and Synchronization

Many mechanisms have been proposed for the communication and synchronization in concurrent systems, and [Ber89] noticed that none of them can replace all the others. Here, we will show, on some examples, how these mechanisms can be modelled in our framework. Basically, we will use two ways for describing communication and synchronization:

- Communication and synchronization media will be modelled as synchronous processes. As far as activation is concerned, these processes need to be activated at least as often as the main processes they interact with. In general, we will consider that they are always active.
- Since non-deterministic scheduling is represented by means of auxiliary inputs, it can be restricted by means of constraints on these inputs. Once again, we can benefit of a feature which exists in most synchronous languages, which allows arbitrary *assumptions* to be expressed about the inputs of a program: "*relations*" in Esterel, "*assertions*" in Lustre, "*synchro*" in Signal.

4.1   Shared Memory

Let us start with a very simple model of time-sharing systems with shared memory. There is an assumption of *atomicity*: processes perform atomic actions in turn. In our setting, it means that the activation conditions are exclusive. Communication is by shared memory: a memory cell is a process, taking as inputs a "write" signal, and a "written" value, and continuously returning as output the last written "value", which is also its only state variable:

> value = state
> state' = if write then written else state

Example 1: Peterson mutual exclusion algorithm. As an example, Fig. 2 shows an Esterel program simulating the Peterson mutual exclusion algorithm. The program is written in pure Esterel (no values, only pure signals). Each process is an instance of the module "process", which implements the algorithm. Each atomic action is performed within a single step. An additional input "go" is used to control the non-deterministic arrival in and departure from the critical section. The three shared memory cells are instances of the module "cell", which implements a Boolean cell with pure signals. Finally, the main module "peterson" instanciates the two processes, activated by input signals "c0" and "c1" (assumed to be exclusive, by means of a "relation"), and the three memory

```
module process:                          module cell:
input d, dprime, x, go;                  input set, reset;
output sd, rd, cx, crit;                 output cell;
loop                                     loop
   await go;                                await set;
   emit sd; await tick;                      do sustain cell upto reset;
   emit cx; await tick;                   end.
   await [x or not dprime];
   do sustain crit upto go;
   emit rd; await tick;
end.
```

```
module peterson:
input c0, c1, go0, go1;
output crit0, crit1;
relation c0 # c1;
signal d0, d1, x0, x1,
       set0, reset0, set1, reset1, setx, resetx in
[
   suspend
      run process [ signal d0/d, d1/dprime, x1/x, go0/go,
                            set0/sd, reset0/rd, resetx/cx, crit0/crit ]
   when [not c0];
||
   suspend
      run process [ signal d1/d, d0/dprime, x0/x, go1/go,
                            set1/sd, reset1/rd, setx/cx, crit1/crit ]
   when [not c1];
||
   run cell [ signal set0/set, reset0/reset, d0/cell ]
||
   run cell [ signal set1/set, reset1/reset, d1/cell ]
||
   run cell [ signal setx/set, resetx/reset, x1/cell ]
||
   every [not x1] do emit x0 end
]
end.
```

Fig. 2. Peterson's algorithm in Esterel

cells (which are always active). If we generate the automaton of this program, we obtain exactly the classical one, meaning that our modelling does not introduce any extra complexity for verification. The mutual exclusion property is straightforwardly verified, using, e.g., Xeve [Bou98].

Notice that the exclusivity of the processes reactions could be weakenned, by assuming only that the "*write*" signals on the same memory (i.e., setx and resetx) are exclusive. This is not permitted by Esterel relations (which are restricted to input signals), but it would be possible with Lustre assertions.

4.2 Rendez-vous

Another popular mechanism is the synchronization and communication by rendez-vous. Here, both processes involved in a rendez-vous should share a step, so the activation conditions are not exclusive. We implement the rendez-vous as follows: both processes emit a Boolean variable (or maintain a pure signal) telling whether they are ready. A handler simultaneously returns them an acknowledgement when they are both ready and active. It's the responsibility of the processes to go through the rendez-vous when they receive the acknowledgement. Notice that this mechanism involves an "instantaneous dialogue" between the processes and the handler, and thus makes use of the full power of synchrony.

Example 2: Milner's cycler in Esterel
As a first example, we consider a very simplified version of the "cycler" proposed by R. Milner in [Mil80]: n processes, organized in a ring, have to be scheduled so that each of them makes a step in turn. For that, each process P_i first synchronizes with its predecessor in the ring, to get the grant, then perfoms its own step (emitting a signal a), and then synchronizes with its successor to transmit the grant. A special "starter" process first gives the grant to P_0.

Fig. 4 shows our solution, in Esterel, for two processes. Each process starts by a rendez-vous (with the other process) using a signal "read_g", and waiting for the acknowledgement "ack_g", then it emits its own signal "a" and starts a rendez-vous using the signals "send_G" and "ack_G". The starter is just a degenerate version of a process. A rendez-vous handler emits an aknowledgement whenever its "read" and "send" input signals occur simultaneously. Finally, the main program instanciates the starter and two processes — non deterministically activated by the input signals "c0", "c1", and "c2", respectively, on which there is no specified relation — and the two handlers.

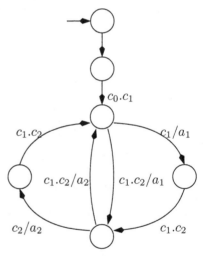

Fig. 3. The automaton of the cycler

Again, we get exactly the expected automaton (except for the spurious initial state, systematically introduced by the Esterel compiler), shown by Fig. 3.

Example 3: the alternating bit in Lustre Here we consider rendez-vous with communication. In Lustre, the writter process will make use of two variables: a Boolean variable signaling a request for communication, and another variable carrying the value to be passed. The reader process signals its readiness with a Boolean variable. The rendez-vous handler responds whenever both partners are active, and their Boolean variables (request, readiness) are true:

```
module proc:
input ack_g, ack_G;
output a, read_g, send_G;
loop
  weak abort sustain read_g when immediate ack_g;
  await tick; emit a;
  weak abort sustain send_G when immediate ack_G;
  await tick
end.

module handler:
input read, send;
output ack;
every [read and send] do emit ack end.

module starter:
input ack_G;
output send_G;
weak abort sustain send_G when ack_G .

module cycler:
input c0, c1, c2;
output a1, a2;
signal ack1, ack2, r1, r2, g1, g2 in
  suspend
    run proc [signal ack1/ack_g, ack2/ack_G, a1/a, r1/read_g, g2/send_G]
  when [not c1]
||
  suspend
    run proc [signal ack2/ack_g, ack1/ack_G, a2/a, r2/read_g, g1/send_G]
  when [not c2]
||
  suspend
    run starter [signal  ack1/ack_G, g1/send_G]
  when [not c0]
||
  run handler [signal r1/read,  g1/send, ack1/ack]
||
  run handler [signal r2/read, g2/send, ack2/ack]
end.
```

Fig. 4. Milner's cycler in Esterel

```
node Handler(act1, act2, ready1, ready2: bool)
  returns (rendez_vous: bool);
let
  rendez_vous = act1 and ready1 and act2 and ready2;
tel
```

In the considered version of the alternating bit, both the sender and the receiver process involved in the protocol have two states: in state N the sender acquires a new message (resp., the receiver transmits a new message), while in state S the sender tries to send the current message (resp., the receiver tries to receive a new message). We encode these automata by means of Boolean equations.

The sender elaborates the sequence of messages to be sent (here, for simplicity, the list of natural numbers!), it receives the grant for rendez-vous from the line to (SR) and from (RS) the receiver, together with the acknowledgement bit from the receiver (which it may only read when the rendez-vous RV_RS occurs). It outputs the current message and its associated bit, and the requests for rendez-vous with the line to and from the receiver. Its stays in state N only one step, in which it changes its bit and takes a new message (i.e., increment its value), then enters the state S, where it maintains requests for rendez-vous for sending the message and reading the acknowledgement, until it receives an acknowlegement bit equal to the bit sent.

```
node Sender (RV_SR, RV_RS: bool; bit_ack: bool)
returns (m_sent: int; bit_sent: bool; W_SR, R_RS: bool);
var N, S: bool (* the state *); mybit: bool;
let
    (m_sent,bit_sent) = (0,false) ->
                        if N then (pre(m_sent)+1,not pre(bit_sent))
                        else (pre(m_sent),pre(bit_sent));
            W_SR = S; R_RS = S;
            N = true -> pre(S and RV_RS and bit_ack=bit_sent);
    S = false -> pre(N or not RV_RS or bit_ack<>bit_sent);
tel
```

The receiver node is symmetrical. Each part of the line (from the sender to the receiver, and conversely) is modelled by a simple node, which has an additional input used to non-deterministically lose messages. Here is the line from the sender to the receiver:

```
node Line (RV_in, RV_out: bool; m_in: int; bit_in: bool;
          lose: bool)
returns (R_in, W_out: bool; m_out: int; bit_out: bool)
let
  R_in = true; W_out = true;
  (m_out,bit_out) = (m_in,bit_in) ->
                    if RV_in and not lose then (m_in,bit_in)
                    else (pre(m_out),pre(bit_out));
tel
```

It permanently asks for input (R_in) and output (W_out) rendez-vous, and changes the transmitted values of the message (m_out) and the bit (bit_out) whenever the input rendez_vous (RV_in) occurs and the transmission is not lost.

If we connect the four processes (Sender, Receiver, Line_SR, Line_RS), acti-vated with arbitrary activation condition, and connected through 4 rendez-vous handlers, we get the whole program, which behaves as expected, and can be verified with no extra cost.

4.3 Other Communication/Synchronization Mechanisms

Other classical communication mechanisms — like buffers, FIFO [dSB98],... — can be programmed in a similar way. Another game is to play with the con-trol we have on the activation conditions to express our knowledge about the processes speed: for instance, in [CS00], the authors introduce the concept of *quasi-synchrony*. In this model, processes are periodically activated, with almost the same periods. The only constraint is that, for any two processes in the sys-tem, there are at most two activations of each of them between two consecutive activations of the other. Since this is the only synchronization constraint between the processes, which otherwise communicate by shared memory, it must be taken into account in any simulation or validation of the system. This constraint can be easily modelled by assertions on the activation conditions (and this is exactly what is done in [CS00]).

5   Conclusion

In this paper we tried to systematize and popularize a way of modelling asyn-chronous systems by means of synchronous languages, for simulation and valida-tion purposes. This approach is not really new: for instance, it is eactly the way [BS01] simulates Multi-clock Esterel in basic Esterel. However, we think that it deserves better attention in the community of asynchronous system modelling and validation.

As a matter of fact, the approach has several advantages: it provides stan-dard semantics to various asynchronous composition mechanisms, it allows syn-chronous and asynchronous parts of a system to be simply, cleanly, and system-atically merged. Moreover, it allows a significant reduction of the validation cost: synchronous description of synchronous parts often involves a drastic reduction of the number of states, and experience shows that no extra cost is introduced by (careful) synchronous modelling of asynchronous composition.

This experience inspires also some conclusions about synchronous languages. While the sporadic activation exists in all languages, some care should be paid to the way it is defined: in Lustre, the fact that the outputs of a suspended process are frozen can result in many extra states, which can be expensive in verification. The use of a default value should be preferred. On the other hand, assertions appear to be a very important feature, for restricting asynchrony and non-determinism, and their full power is needed: we noticed that Esterel relations, in their current version, are too weak for some purposes.

The immediate perspectives of this work are twofold:

- A library of standard synchronization and communication modules should be defined, to help the user in describing GALs.
- The automatic translation of such description towards asynchronous or distributed implementation should be considered.

References

AH99.   R. Alur and T. A. Henzinger. Reactive modules. *Formal Methods in System Design*, 15:7–48, 1999.

BCG+97.   F. Balarin, M. Chiodo, P. Giusto, H. Hsieh, A. Jurecska, L. Lavagno, C. Passerone, A. Sangiovanni-Vincentelli, E. Sentovich, K. Suzuki, and B. Tabbara. *Hardware-Software Co-Design of Embedded Systems: The Polis Approach*. Kluwer Academic Publishers, 1997.

BCG99.   A. Benveniste, B. Caillaud, and P. Le Guernic. From synchrony to asynchrony. In J.C.M. Baeten and S. Mauw, editors, *CONCUR'99*. LNCS 1664, Springer Verlag, 1999.

BCT99.   A. Benveniste, P. Caspi, and Stavros Tripakis. Distributing synchronous programs on a loosely synchronous, distributed architecture. Research Report1289, Irisa, December 1999.

Ber89.   G. Berry. Real time programming: Special purpose or general purpose languages. In *IFIP World Computer Congress*, San Francisco, 1989.

Ber93.   G. Berry. Preemption and concurrency. In *Proc. FSTTCS 93*, Lecture Notes in Computer Science 761, pages 72–93. Springer-Verlag, 1993.

BG92.   G. Berry and G. Gonthier. The Esterel synchronous programming language: Design, semantics, implementation. *Science of Computer Programming*, 19(2):87–152, 1992.

Bou98.   A. Bouali. Xeve: an Esterel verification environment. In *Tenth International Conference on Computer-Aided Verification, CAV'98*, Vancouver (B.C.), June 1998. LNCS 1427, Springer Verlag.

BS98.   G. Berry and E. Sentovich. Embedding synchronous circuits in GALS-based systems. In *Sophia-Antipolis conference on Micro-Electronics (SAME 98)*, October 1998.

BS01.   G. Berry and E. Sentovich. Multiclock esterel. In *Correct Hardware Design and Verification Methods, CHARME'01*, Livingston (Scotland), September 2001. LNCS 2144, Springer Verlag.

Cas01.   P. Caspi. Embedded control: From asynchrony to synchrony and back. In *1st International Workshop on Embedded Software, EMSOFT2001*, Lake Tahoe, October 2001. LNCS 2211.

CGP94.   P. Caspi, A. Girault, and D. Pilaud. Distributing reactive systems. In *Seventh International Conference on Parallel and Distributed Computing Systems, PDCS'94*, Las Vegas, USA, October 1994. ISCA.

CS00.   P. Caspi and R. Salem. Threshold and bounded-delay voting in critical control systems. In *FTRTFT'2000*, Pune, India, September 2000. LNCS 1926.

dSB98.   R. de Simone and A. Bouali. A symbolic representation of asynchronous networks of synchronous processes. In *Tenth International Workshop on Logic Synthesis, IWLS'98*, Lake Tahoe, June 1998.

HCRP91.   N. Halbwachs, P. Caspi, P. Raymond, and D. Pilaud. The synchronous
           dataflow programming language LUSTRE. *Proceedings of the IEEE*,
           79(9):1305–1320, September 1991.
HLR92.   N. Halbwachs, F. Lagnier, and C. Ratel. Programming and verifying real-
           time systems by means of the synchronous data-flow programming lan-
           guage LUSTRE. *IEEE Transactions on Software Engineering, Special Issue
           on the Specification and Analysis of Real-Time Systems*, September 1992.
HM95.   N. Halbwachs and F. Maraninchi. On the symbolic analysis of combina-
           tional loops in circuits and synchronous programs. In *Euromicro'95*, Como
           (Italy), September 1995.
IEE91.   Another look at real-time programming. *Special Section of the Proceedings
           of the IEEE*, 79(9), September 1991.
ITU94.   ITU-T. *Recommendation Z-100. Specification and description language
           (SDL)*. 1994.
JPV95.   L. J. Jagadeesan, C. Puchol, and J. E. Von Olnhausen. Safety property
           verification of ESTEREL programs and applications to telecommunication
           software. In P. Wolper, editor, *7th International Conference on Com-
           puter Aided Verification, CAV'95*, Liege (Belgium), July 1995. LNCS 939,
           Springer Verlag.
LDBL93.   M. Le Borgne, Bruno Dutertre, Albert Benveniste, and Paul Le Guernic.
           Dynamical systems over Galois fields. In *European Control Conference*,
           pages 2191–2196, Groningen, 1993.
LGLL91.   P. LeGuernic, T. Gautier, M. LeBorgne, and C. LeMaire. Programming
           real time applications with SIGNAL. *Proceedings of the IEEE*, 79(9):1321–
           1336, September 1991.
Mal93.   S. Malik. Analysis of cyclic combinational circuits. In *ICCAD'93*, Santa
           Clara (Ca), 1993.
Mil80.   R. Milner. *A Calculus of Communicating Systems*. LNCS 92, Springer
           Verlag, 1980.
Mil81.   R. Milner. On relating synchrony and asynchrony. Technical Report CSR-
           75-80, Computer Science Dept., Edimburgh Univ., 1981.
SBT96.   T. R. Shiple, G. Berry, and H. Touati. Constructive analysis of cyclic
           circuits. In *International Design and Testing Conference IDTC'96*, Paris,
           France, 1996.

A Protocol
for Loosely Time-Triggered Architectures[*]

Albert Benveniste[1], Paul Caspi[2], Paul Le Guernic[1], Hervé Marchand[1],
Jean-Pierre Talpin[1], and Stavros Tripakis[2]

[1] Irisa/Inria, Campus de Beaulieu, 35042 Rennes cedex, France
firstname.lastname@irisa.fr, http://www.irisa.fr/sigma2/benveniste/
[2] Verimag, Centre Equation, 2, rue de Vignate, F-38610 Gieres
firstname.lastname@imag.fr, http://www.imag.fr/VERIMAG/PEOPLE/Paul.Caspi

Abstract. A distributed real-time control system has a time-triggered
nature, just because the physical system for control is bound to physics.
Loosely Time-Triggered Architectures (LTTA) are a weaker form of the
strictly synchronous Time-Triggered Architecture proposed by Kopetz,
in which the different periodic clocks are not synchronized, and thus may
suffer from relative offset or jitter.
We propose a protocol that ensures a coherent system of logical clocks
on the top of LTTA, and we provide several proofs for it, both manual
and automatic, based on synchronous languages and associated model
checkers. We briefly discuss how this can be used for correct deployment
of synchronous designs on an LTTA.

1 Loosely Time-Triggered Architectures (LTTA)

A distributed real-time control system has a time-triggered nature, just because
the physical system for control is bound to physics. Loosely Time-Triggered
Architectures are a weaker (and cheaper) form of the strictly synchronous Time-
Triggered Architecture (TTA) proposed by Kopetz [11].

An LTTA is an architecture in which: 1/ access to the bus occurs quasi-
periodically, in a non-blocking way, 2/ writings and readings are performed independently at each extremity of the bus in synchrony with each associated local
clock, and 3/ the bus behaves like a shared memory, i.e., values are sustained
by the bus and are periodically refreshed, based on a local clock. The term
"quasi-periodically" indicates that the different clocks involved, for writing in,
reading from, and updating the bus, are not synchronized. Still, this architecture
is time-triggered in the sense that these clocks are bound to *physical* time, and
deviate from each other in a certain "limited" way. LTTA are in use in several
major industries, they have been the subject of the CRISYS project [6], where
they are called *quasi-synchronous,* and of several investigations, by Caspi and
co-workers, of the fundamental issues raised when deploying control applications
on such architectures.

---

[*] This work is or has been supported in part by the following projects: Esprit LTR-
SYRF (Esprit EP 22703), and Esprit R&D CRISYS EP 25514.

A. Sangiovanni-Vincentelli and J. Sifakis (Eds.): EMSOFT 2002, LNCS 2491, pp. 252–265, 2002.

Our main result is presented in section 2. It consists in showing that, by adding some layer of protocol on the top of an LTTA, one can offer a platform ensuring a coherent distribution of *logical* clocks. We formally specify the protocol and prove that it satisfies the desired requirement. For the protocol to be correct, the clocks must be quasi-periodic (periods can vary within certain specified bounds), and must relate to each other within some specified bounds.

That one can offer, on the top of an LTTA, a platform ensuring a coherent distribution of *logical* clocks, has actual interests. Distributed sensor-to-actuators low level feedback control loops are in any case faced with the unavoidable uncertainty of sampling, whatever the actual considered bus architecture is. Hence, in any case, the robustness of the deployed application with respect to this type of "asynchrony" must be considered. This is the subject of [7] and is not considered here. However, complex distributed control applications also involve complex finite state machines, e.g., to govern modes of operation, and reconfigurate the application against degraded modes. The possibility to offer a coherent system of logical clocks is extremely useful to simplify the development and debugging of such finite state machines. Section 3 sketches a methodology for deploying, on an LTTA equiped with the proposed protocol, a finite state machine developed with any synchronous language.

Section 4 addresses the same problem as section 2, but using (nearly) automatic proof techniques. To this end, the protocol is specified using *synchronous languages*—we show the exercise with the languages Lustre and Signal [9]. It is interesting to note that synchronous languages can be used to model asynchronous systems—recall the three devices writer/bus/reader have independent and non synchronized clocks. Then the desired property for the protocol is expressed as an invariant, and proved.

Now, the assumptions ensuring correctness of the protocol, as stated in section 2, are quantitative in nature (tolerance bounds for the relative periods, and time variations, of the different clocks). Handling such type of quantitative assumption is beyond the scope of model checkers such as Lesar [10] or Sigali [14], the model checkers associated with Lustre and Signal, respectively. Hence the assumption is reformulated, by performing some abstraction and expressing it using booleans. While the two assumptions, strictly speaking, are not equivalent, they are good approximations to each other—but this claim cannot be proved by model checking!

Our protocol is presented and analysed in the case of two users: one writer and one reader. Section 5 discusses the case of multiple users. Then, a brief comparison with Kopetz'TTA is provided.

2   The Proposed Protocol and Its Robustness

2.1   Description of the protocol

See figure 1 for an illustration of this protocol (the three watches shown indicate a different time, *they are not synchronized*). We consider three devices, the *writer,* the *bus,* and the *reader,* indicated by the superscripts $(.)^w, (.)^b$, and

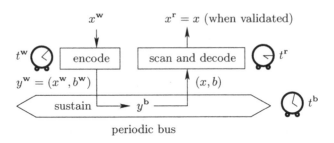

Fig. 1. *The protocol.* The map $y \mapsto y^{\mathbf{r}}$ is called a *virtual channel*.

$(.)^{\mathbf{r}}$, respectively. Each device is activated by its own, approximately periodic, clock. The different clocks are *not* synchronized. In the following specification, the different sequences written, fetched, or read, are indexed by the set $\mathbf{N} = \{1, 2, 3, \ldots, n, \ldots\}$ of natural integers, and we reserve the index 0 for the initial conditions, whenever needed.

The writer: At the time $t^{\mathbf{w}}(n)$ of the nth tick of his clock, the writer generates a new value $x^{\mathbf{w}}(n)$ it wants to communicate and a new alternating flag $b^{\mathbf{w}}(n)$ with:

$$b^{\mathbf{w}}(n) = \begin{cases} false & \text{if } n = 0 \\ not \ b^{\mathbf{w}}(n-1) & \text{otherwise} \end{cases}$$

and stores both in its private output buffer.

Thus at any time t, the writer's output buffer content $y^{\mathbf{w}}$ is the last value that was written into it, that is the one with the largest index whose tick occurred before t:

$$y^{\mathbf{w}}(t) = (x^{\mathbf{w}}(n), b^{\mathbf{w}}(n)), \text{ where } n = \sup\{n' \mid t^{\mathbf{w}}(n') < t\} \tag{1}$$

The bus: At the time $t^{\mathbf{b}}(n)$ of its nth clock tick, it fetches the value in the writer's output buffer and stores it, immediately after, in the reader's input buffer. Thus, at any time t, the reader's input buffer content offered by the bus, denote it by $y^{\mathbf{b}}$, is the last value that was written into it, i.e., the one written at the latest bus clock tick preceding t:

$$y^{\mathbf{b}}(t) = y^{\mathbf{w}}(t^{\mathbf{b}}(n)), \text{ where } n = \sup\{n' \mid t^{\mathbf{b}}(n') < t\} \tag{2}$$

The reader: At the time $t^{\mathbf{r}}(n)$ of its nth clock tick, it copies the value of its input buffer into auxiliary variables $x(n)$ and $b(n)$:

$$(x(n), b(n)) = y^{\mathbf{b}}(t^{\mathbf{r}}(n))$$

Then the reader extracts from the x sequence only the values corresponding to the indices for which b has alternated[1]. This can be modeled thanks to the

---

[1] This is the classical technique used in the Alternating Bit Protocol, to avoid the reader receiving the same message twice.

counter m, which counts the number of alternations that have taken place up to the current cycle. Then the value of the extracted sequence at index k is the value read at the earliest cycle when the counter m exceeded k:

$$m(0) = 0, \; m(n) = \inf\{k > m(n-1) \mid b(k) \neq b(k-1)\}$$
$$x^{\mathbf{r}}(k) = x(l), \text{ where } l = \inf\{n' \mid m(n') > k\} \tag{3}$$

Problem statement: The protocol is correct if the two sequences $x^{\mathbf{w}}, x^{\mathbf{r}}$ coincide, i.e.,

$$\forall n : x^{\mathbf{r}}(n) = x^{\mathbf{w}}(n) \tag{4}$$

2.2 Main Theorem about Robustness

Theorem 1 (sampling theorem). *Let the writing/bus/reading be systems with physically periodic clocks of respective periods $w/b/r$. Then, the protocol of subsection 2.1 satisfies the desired property:*

$$\forall n : x_n^{\mathbf{r}} = x_n^{\mathbf{w}}, \tag{5}$$

whatever the written input sequence is, iff the following conditions hold:

$$w \geq b \text{, and } \left\lfloor \frac{w}{b} \right\rfloor \geq \frac{r}{b}, \tag{6}$$

where, for x a real, $\lfloor x \rfloor$ denotes the largest integer $\leq x$.

Condition (5) means that the bus provides a coherent system of logical clocks. Note that, since $w \geq b$, then $w/2b < \lfloor w/b \rfloor$ follows. On the other hand, $\lfloor w/b \rfloor \leq w/b$, and $\lfloor w/b \rfloor \sim w/b$ for w/b large. Hence, for a fast bus, i.e. $b \sim 0$, the conditions (6) of theorem 1 reduce to:

$$w \gg b, \; w > r. \tag{7}$$

We illustrate the protocol on the figure 2, for two typical cases (shown in black and white arrows on the top of the diagram, respectively), depending on the relative position of the ticks of clocks $t^{\mathbf{b}}, t^{\mathbf{w}}, t^{\mathbf{r}}$. The two thick lines depict the sustained values of the two components, $(x^{\mathbf{w}}, b^{\mathbf{w}})$, of $y^{\mathbf{w}}$. Collect these two sustained values as the tuple $y^{\mathbf{b}}$. The dashed vertical lines depict the ticks of the bus clock $t^{\mathbf{b}}$. The vertical arrows sitting at the bottom depict the ticks of the writer clock. The vertical arrows sitting at the top depict the ticks of the reader clock. Note the role of the boolean flag for validation: even if the value of $x^{\mathbf{w}}$ was unchanged at two successive emissions, these would have been validated, thanks to the boolean flag. The role of this flag is also enlightened by the two cases for the relative position of the clocks (black and white arrows). The case of the black arrows is the "normal" one. Let us focus on the more tricky case of the white arrows. In this case, when the first instant of clock $t^{\mathbf{r}}$ (first white arrow), then the clock $t^{\mathbf{b}}$ has not yet seen the change in the sustained value of b,

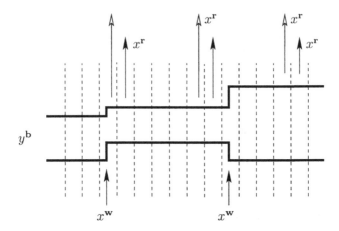

Fig. 2. *The sampling theorem.*

therefore the corresponding sustained value for x is not validated by the reader at this point. But a change in the sustained value of b is detected at the second occurrence of $t^{\mathbf{r}}$, and, then, the corresponding sustained value for x is validated. As seen from the diagram, changes in the boolean signals are detected at the receiver with a nondeterministic, but bounded delay. On the other hand, perfect physical synchrony is lost: reading occurs with a nondeterministic, but bounded, delay according to *physical* real time.

Proof. In the following, let $n, m, p \in \{0, 1, 2, \ldots\}$ denote integers. By properly renormalizing the three periods, we can assume, for the bus periodic clock, $b = 1$ and a zero phase. With this convention, let the writing/bus/reading sampling instants be:

$$
\begin{aligned}
t^{\mathbf{w}}(n) &= nw + \psi w, \ 0 \le \psi < 1 \\
t^{\mathbf{b}}(p) &= p \\
t^{\mathbf{r}}(m) &= mr + \varphi r, \ 0 \le \varphi < 1
\end{aligned}
\tag{8}
$$

where the writing/bus/reading periods are $w/1/r$, and ψ, φ denote the phases of the writer's and reader's clocks.

We first search for conditions ensuring that the bus does not miss any writing. Set:

$$
\tau^{\mathbf{b}}(n) = \min\{t^{\mathbf{b}}(p) \mid t^{\mathbf{b}}(p) > t^{\mathbf{w}}(n)\},
\tag{9}
$$

$\tau^{\mathbf{b}}(n)$ is the first instant where the bus can fetch the nth writing, and we have:

$$
\tau^{\mathbf{b}}(n) = \lfloor (n + \psi)w \rfloor + 1,
$$

whence:

$$
\delta\tau^{\mathbf{b}} \triangleq \min_{n \ge 0, \, 0 \le \psi < 1} \left(\tau^{\mathbf{b}}(n+1) - \tau^{\mathbf{b}}(n) \right) = \lfloor w \rfloor.
\tag{10}
$$

To ensure that the bus does not miss any writing whatever the phases of the different clocks are, it is necessary and sufficient that the map $n \longmapsto \tau^{\mathbf{b}}(n)$ is strictly increasing. Using (10), this holds iff:

$$\lfloor w \rfloor > 0 \text{ , i.e., } w \geq 1. \tag{11}$$

Next, we investigate conditions ensuring that the reader does not miss a writing, when the latter is fetched by the bus. Define:

$$\tau^{\mathbf{r}}(n) = \min\{t^{\mathbf{r}}(m) \mid t^{\mathbf{r}}(m) > \tau^{\mathbf{b}}(n)\}. \tag{12}$$

Thanks to the mechanism of the boolean alternating flag b, $\tau^{\mathbf{r}}(n)$ is the first instant where the reader sees the nth writing. Thus, using (10), our last duty is *not to miss a reading during any period of length $\delta\tau^{\mathbf{b}}$*, equivalently:

$$\lfloor w \rfloor \geq r \,. \tag{13}$$

Combining (11) and (13) yields the theorem.   ◇

We can generalize theorem 1 to time varying periods. Without loss of generality we can again assume that the bus clock is perfectly periodic, with period 1 and phase 0:

Theorem 2 (sampling theorem with quasi periodic clocks). *Assume that writing/bus/reading are only approximately periodic, i.e., they are related via the following equations—compare with (8):*

$$\begin{aligned}
t^{\mathbf{w}}(n) &= nw(1 + \delta^{\mathbf{w}}(n)) + \psi w \,, 0 \leq \psi < 1 \,, |\delta^{\mathbf{w}}(n)| \leq \delta^{\mathbf{w}} \\
t^{\mathbf{b}}(p) &= p \\
t^{\mathbf{r}}(m) &= mr(1 + \delta^{\mathbf{r}}(m)) + \varphi r \,\,, 0 \leq \varphi < 1 \,, |\delta^{\mathbf{r}}(m)| \leq \delta^{\mathbf{r}},
\end{aligned} \tag{14}$$

where $\delta^{\mathbf{w}}, \delta^{\mathbf{r}}$ are some given bounds. Then sufficient conditions, for the protocol formalized in section 2.1 to ensure condition (5), are the following:

$$w(1 - 2\delta^{\mathbf{w}}) \geq 1 \,, \text{ and } \lfloor w(1 - 2\delta^{\mathbf{w}}) \rfloor \geq r(1 + 2\delta^{\mathbf{r}}), \tag{15}$$

compare with conditions (11) and (13).

The proof of this theorem is a straightforward adaptation of that of theorem 1, and we leave it to the reader as an exercise. Of course, the interest of theorem 2 is that it guarantees a good degree of robustness of the protocol with respect to imperfect sampling clocks, since the relative *periods* of the clocks can vary with respect to each other, up to some maximal bound. Also, the jitter terms $\delta^{\mathbf{w}}(n)$ and $\delta^{\mathbf{r}}(m)$ can incorporate variable propagation delay in the bus.

3   Application to the Deployment of Synchronous Programs

Figure 3-left shows a synchronous design, with three components. In figure 3-right, additional synchronous modules are shown, they are depicted using the

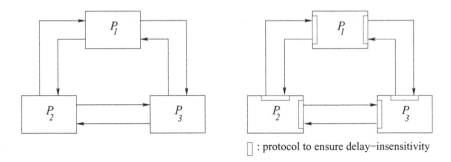

☐ : protocol to ensure delay−insensitivity

Fig. 3. *A synchronous design, securing delay-insensitivity.*

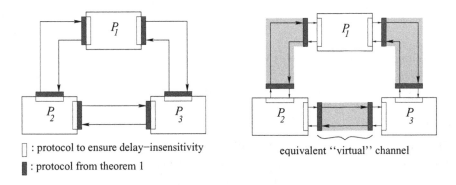

☐ : protocol to ensure delay−insensitivity

▮ : protocol from theorem 1

equivalent "virtual" channel

Fig. 4. *Encoding events as state changes. Introducing "virtual" channels.*

light grey rectangles and can be regarded as "protocols". Based on the theory developed in [3][4][5], these protocols aim at securing delay-insensitivity of the communications.

This means that the semantics of each individual synchronous component in the system is not modified if the perfectly synchronous communication channels are substituted with asynchronous channels of FIFO type, with unknown and unbounded delays, but no loss. This is formalized as the mathematical property (4). Of course the global timing of the program is lost. The automatic synthesis of such protocols is achieved by enforcing the so-called *endo/isochrony* of the synchronous commmunication network, see [3]. At this stage delay-insensitivity is achieved: each flow is individually preserved by the communication (but their global synchronisation is not).

Now we show in figure 4-left how to adapt this design for the case of an LTTA, i.e., with *loosely synchronised* channels. Note that loosely synchronised channels, if used directly, can duplicate data or can lose data. The idea is to include, on each port, the protocol proposed in section 2. These additional protocols are figured in figure 4-left by the dark rectangles. In figure 4-right, we have redrawn the figure 4-left in a different way. We combine the dark rectangles together with the "physical" channels, to obtain so-called "virtual" channels. The analysis performed in section 2 shows that each virtual channel satisfies the property (4). Therefore endo/isochrony guarantees a correct-by-construction deployment.

4   Automatic Proofs of the Protocol

In this section, we redo the section 2 by replacing human specifications and proofs, by computer ones. Synchonous languages with associated proof tools are used to this end. Some comments are in order.

The two theorems shown before involve both timing and logical aspects. The timing aspects can be modeled using parametric timed automata, since we want to prove the theorems using *symbolic* values for the periods and not instantiated ones. Unfortunately, the verification problem for parametric timed automata is undecidable [1], therefore, model checkers such as Kronos [8] or Uppaal [13], cannot be used. Semi-algorithmic methods for parametric timed automata exist (e.g., in Hytech), but they are not guaranteed to terminate. Instead we have decided to use standard model checking, and therefore abstractions are needed.

Two kinds of abstractions will be considered.

1. We want to show identity (5) irrespectively of the actual values for the input $x^{\mathbf{r}}$. Since we do not use theorem provers, we will actually prove (5) for finitely enumerated types. The proof with Lustre/Lesar assumes an input which is of type bit stream with a given concrete width.
2. Then, we need to propose boolean type of assumptions to replace the quantitative assumptions (6) or (15), from section 2. We ask the reader to have the proof of theorem 1 at hand. From (9,10,11), we get that the first condition, $w \geq b$, in (6) is abstracted as the following predicate:

$$(6) : w \geq b \leftrightarrow \text{never two } t^{\mathbf{w}} \text{ between two successive } t^{\mathbf{b}}. \tag{16}$$

Finding an abstraction for the second condition, $\lfloor w/b \rfloor \geq r/b$, in (6), is slightly less obvious. We just reexpress it by requiring that the sequence $\tau^{\mathbf{r}}(n)$ defined in (12) shall be strictly increasing, i.e., it shall never be the case that two or more $\tau^{\mathbf{b}}(n)$'s occur between two successive $t^{\mathbf{r}}(m)$'s:

$$(6) : \left\lfloor \frac{w}{b} \right\rfloor \geq \frac{r}{b} \leftrightarrow \text{never two } \tau^{\mathbf{b}}(.) \text{ between two successive } t^{\mathbf{r}}. \tag{17}$$

To complete the requirements, we must characterize $\tau^{\mathbf{b}}(.)$, this is provided by the formula (9).

Note that, since these abstractions have been performed *manually,* this is a (minimally) assisted proof, not a fully automated one.

The Lustre/Lesar proof. With these abstractions, the Lustre/Lesar proof is shown in Fig. 5 and Fig. 6. Note that these abstractions result in finite-state systems, which could be checked in principle with any model checker. As for the different delays involved in the reader/bus/writer (see formulas (1,2,3)), these are emulated by simply making the three clocks $t^{\mathbf{w}}, t^{\mathbf{b}}, t^{\mathbf{r}}$ pairwise exclusive: by doing so, instantaneous transfer can occur, neither from writer to bus, nor from bus to reader—this way is a bit of cheating, but it makes life a lot easier.

const n = 3;   – *the input is a bit stream of width 3*

node writer(x : bool^n) returns (xw: bool^n; bw: bool);
let
   bw = true → pre not bw;
   xw = x;
tel

const init = false^n;

node reader(x: bool^n; b: bool) returns (cro: bool; xr: bool^n);
let
   cro = not (b = (false → pre b));
   xr = if cro then x
        else (init → pre xr);
tel

node bus(xw: bool^n; bw: bool) returns (xr: bool^n; br: bool);
let
   xr, br = (xw, bw);
tel

node faster(cb, cw: bool) returns (prop: bool);
var w_before_b: bool;
let
   w_before_b = if cw then true
            else if cb then false
                else (false → pre w_before_b);
  – *tells that there is an unmatched cw*
   prop = not (cw and (false → pre w_before_b));
– *this node implements (17)*
tel

node firstafter(cb, cw: bool) returns (cbw: bool);
var waiting: bool;
let
   cbw = cb and (false → pre waiting) ;
   waiting = if cw then true
          else if cbw then false
             else (false → pre waiting);
– *this node implements (9)*
tel

Fig. 5. The Lustre/Lesar proof of theorem 1, part 1.

The Signal/Sigali proof. Signal has a small number of constructs, recalled in Fig. 9. Using the same abstractions as for Lustre, the proof in Signal/Sigali is shown in Fig. 7 and Fig. 8. There are some differences with the Lustre/Lesar proof. Firstly, unknown but short delays at ingress/egress of the bus are included (the shift processes). Also, the process fifo_2 is a cascade of 1-bounded fifos, so we

```
node vecteq(xw: bool^n; xr: bool^n) returns (prop: bool);
var aux: bool^(n+1);
let
    aux[0] = true;
    aux[1..n] = aux[0..n-1] and (xr = xw);
    prop = aux[n];
tel
```

```
node compare(cw: bool; xw: bool^n; xr: bool^n) returns (prop: bool);
var equal: bool; last: bool^n; unmatched: bool;
let
    last = if equal then xw else (init → pre last);
    − stores the value to be matched
    equal = vecteq(xr, (init → pre last));
    − tells whether the value to be matched is actually matched
    unmatched = if cw and not (true → pre equal) then true
                    else if equal then false
                        else false → pre unmatched;
    − tells that there are two values waiting for match
    prop = not(cw and (false → pre unmatched));
    − a new value should not arrive while two values are waiting for match
tel
```

```
node verif(cw, cb, cr: bool; (x: bool^n) when cw)
returns (prop: bool; xw, xr, xro: bool^n; bw, br: bool; cro: bool );
let
    xw, bw = if cw then current writer(x)
                else ((init, false) → pre(xw, bw));
    xr, br =   if cb then current bus((xw, bw) when cb)
                else ((init, false) → pre(xr, br));
    cro, xro =if cr then current reader((xr, br) when cr)
                else ((false, init) → pre(cro, xro));

    prop = compare(cw, xw, xro);

    assert faster(cb, cw) and faster(cr, firstafter(cb, cw));
    − these assertions implement (16) and (17)
    assert #(cw, cb, cr);
    − so as not to get bored by simultaneous clocks
tel
```

```
(*
moucherotte% lesar albert2.lus verif
−Pollux Version 2.0
TRUE PROPERTY
moucherotte%
)
```

Fig. 6. The Lustre/Lesar proof of theorem 1, part 2

```
process protocol = (? boolean xw; event cw, cb, cr ! boolean xr , inv)
    (| (xb, bb, sbw) := bus (xw, writer(xw,cw), cb)       % writer + bus %
     | (xr, br, sbb)  := reader (xb, bb, cr)              % reader %
     | cb ^= sbw default cb                               % condition (16) %
     | cr ^= (when switched(sbb)) default cr              % condition (17) %
     | xok := fifo_2 (xw)                                 % fifo_2 satisfies (4) %
     | inv := equal (xok, xr)                             % tests if xok=xr %
    |) where boolean bw, xb, bb, sbw, sbb, br, xok;

  process writer = (? boolean xw; event cw ! boolean bw)
      (| bw ^= xw ^= cw
       | bw := not (bw$1 init true)
      |);                                                 % bw: boolean flag %
  process bus = (? boolean xw, bw; event cb ! boolean xb, bb, sbw)
      (| (xb, bb, sbw) := buffer (xw, bw, cb) |);
  process reader = (? boolean xb, bb; event cr ! boolean xr, br, sbb)
      (| (yr, br, sbb) := buffer (xb, bb, cr) | xr := yr when switched (br) |)
      where boolean yr; end;                              % switched(br) validates xr %

  process switched = (? boolean b ! boolean c)
      (| zb := b$1 init true | c := (b and not zb) or (not b and zb) |)
      where boolean zb; end;                              % c=true when b alternates %

  process buffer = (? boolean x, b ; event c ! boolean bx, bb, sb)
      (| (sx, sb) := shift_2 (x, b) | (bx, bb) := current_2 (sx, sb, c) |)
      where boolean sx; end;                              % delays, sustains, filters %

  process shift_2 = (? boolean x, b ! boolean sx, sb)    % see shift_1 %
      (| (sx, sb) := current_2 (x, b, ^sb) | interleave (x, sx) |);
      process current_2 = (? boolean wx, wb; event c ! boolean rx, rb)
          (| rx := (wx cell c init false) when c
           | rb := (wb cell c init true) when c |);       % see current_1 %
      process interleave = (? boolean x, sx ! )
          (| x ^= when b | sx ^= when not b | b := not (b$1 init false) |)
          where boolean b; end;                           % x and sx interleave %

  process equal = (? boolean y, z ! boolean inv)
      (| i := (y and z) or (not y and not z) default inv
       | inv := i $1 init true
      |); where boolean i; end;                           % tests if y=z %

  process fifo_2 = (? boolean x ! boolean xok )
      (| xok := shift_1(shift_1(x)) |);
      process shift_1 = (? boolean x ! boolean sx)        % x,sx satisfy (4) %
          (| sx := current_1 (x, ^sx) | interleave (x, sx) |);
          process current_1 = (? boolean wx; event c ! boolean rx)
              (| rx := (wx cell c init false) when c |);   % current triggered by c %

end;
```

Fig. 7. The Signal/Sigali proof

Sigali:

---

set_reorder(1);
read("protocol.z3z");
read("Creat_SDP.z3z");
read("Verif_Determ.z3z");
POSSIBLE(B_False(S,inv)); → resultat False
Always(B_True(S,inv)); → resultat True

Fig. 8. The Sigali script.

$z := x$ op y	$z_\tau \neq \bot \Leftrightarrow x_\tau \neq \bot \Leftrightarrow y_\tau \neq \bot$, $\forall k : z_k = \mathrm{op}(x_k, y_k)$
$y \mathbin{\hat{=}} x$	$y_\tau \neq \bot \Leftrightarrow x_\tau \neq \bot$ (x and y possess identical clocks)
$\hat{x}$	the clock of $x : \hat{x} \in \{\mathrm{T}, \bot\}$, $\hat{x}_\tau \neq \bot \Leftrightarrow x_\tau \neq \bot$
$y := x\$1$ init x_0	$x_\tau \neq \bot \Leftrightarrow y_\tau \neq \bot$, $\forall k > 1 : y_k = x_{k-1}, y_1 = x_0$ (delay)
$x := u$ when b	$x_\tau = u_\tau$ when $b_\tau = \mathrm{T}$, otherwise $x_\tau = \bot$
$x := u$ default v	$x_\tau = u_\tau$ when $u_\tau \neq \bot$, otherwise $x_\tau = v$
$(\mid P \mid Q \mid)$	parallel composition
$y := x$ cell h init x_0	$(\mid y := x$ default $(y\$1$ init $x_0) \mid \hat{}y := \hat{}x$ default $h \mid)$

Fig. 9. Signal operators (left), and their meaning (right). In this table, x_τ denotes the status (absence, or actual value) of signal x in an arbitrary reaction τ, $\{\mathrm{T}, \mathrm{F}\}$ is the boolean domain, and the special value $\bot$ denotes absence in the considered reaction.

know that it satisfies the requirements of theorem 1. This fifo_2 has an unspecified delay, hence we can synchronize it with the output of the protocol, xr, and check whether they are both equal; this is performed in process **equal**. In fact, this proof says that the cascade of two 1-bounded fifos is a correct abstraction of the protocol, so the protocol satisfies the requirements of theorem 1. This style of proof deeply uses the capability, for Signal, of handling nondeterministic systems, and thus of emulating asynchrony.

5 Discussion

In this section, we discuss how our LTTA protocol can be extended to multiple users. Then we briefly compare LTTA with TTA.

Extension of the protocol to multiple users. Consider the case of several pairs {writer, reader}, transmitting several message sequences over the LTTA bus. Assume, for instance, that the bus scans periodically the output buffers of all writers.

Focus on one particular writer. For the analysis, we cluster together all readers into an overall "all_reader". Call $t^{\mathbf{b}}(n)$ the sequence of instants at which the bus fetches messages from the output buffer of *this* writer, to the input buffer of *some* reader. Equivalently, $t^{\mathbf{b}}(n)$ is the sequence of instants at which the bus fetches messages from the output buffer of *this* writer, to the (virtual) input buffer of *all_reader*.

Just apply Theorems 1 or 2, to the pair {this writer, all_reader}. If the (quasi) period b driving the $t^{\mathbf{b}}(n)$'s satisfies the assumptions of the theorems, then the protocol is correct for this pair. This implies that the protocol is also correct for {this writer, some_reader}, where some_reader denotes one particular reader. Assume that there are J users, and each user writes with period w and reads with period r, then it is enough that the actual bus period satisfies the conditions (6) of theorem 1 with b/J substituted for b.

Clearly, the choice of periodic scanning is the default choice. It can be adapted if the writing periods are different, for different users, in order to ensure proper balancing. Such quantitative issues are beyond the scope of this paper. But clearly, the theorem can be accomodated to such adaptation.

A brief comparison with Kopetz'TTA. We warn the reader that this brief discussion is by no means authoritative: closer investigations would be required for firm assessment and comparisons.

This being said, the first remark is that LTTA does not require implementing a clock synchronization algorithm, and our protocol is cheap. On the other hand, when designing the system based on LTTA, the engineer must consider issues of relative speed of writing/bus/reading. This difficulty does not appear with TTA, at a first glance. However, we think that the timing considerations when using LTTA, are quite natural for the designer. The bottom line is that, from the strict point of view of synchronization, LTTA seems an attractive approach.

The very question is that of fault tolerance. As extensively discussed by John Rushby [16], Kopetz'TTA takes advantage of the strict TTA, in order to provide fault tolerance and allow for a strict separation of different functions multiplexed over the same bus. The corresponding issue is certainly carefully considered by the industrial users of the LTTA approach, but we must say that we did not study it in detail.

6   Conclusion

We have presented a weakened form of time-triggered architecture, we called it *loosely* time-triggered. In contrast to Kopetz'TTA, clocks are periodic but are *not* synchronized. Strict synchronization may not be useful for continuous control, since modern control design is anyway robust against phase uncertainties—this justifies considering LTTA for real-time embedded control. We have proposed a protocol that offers, on the top of LTTA, a coherent system of logical clocks, and we have sketched how this can be used for correct deployment of controller designs based on synchronous languages. This protocol is of interest per se, as it accepts clocks with offset and jitter. But the way we have analysed the protocol is also of interest, it illustrates the use of synchronous languages for modeling asynchronous architectures. Still, a complete *automatic* proof of our theorems with their exact assumptions formulated in quantitative terms, is to be done.

This study was a first attempt toward designing distributed embedded systems that are robust against imperfect synchronization of the architecture. One important remaining question is the following: can LTTA offer lower cost fault-tolerance, as compared to TTA? This is not obvious, since Rushby [16], advocates that strict compliance with time is the key to fault-tolerance in TTA.

References

1. R. Alur, T.A. Henzinger, and M.Y. Vardi. Parametric Real-time Reasoning. In *Proc. of the 25th Annual Symposium on Theory of Computing (STOC)*, ACM Press, 1993, pp. 592-601.
2. R. Bannatyne. Time Triggered Protocol: TTP/C, *Embedded Systems Programming*, 9/98, pp. 52-54.
3. A. Benveniste, B. Caillaud, and P. Le Guernic. From synchrony to asynchrony. In J.C.M. Baeten and S. Mauw, editors, *CONCUR'99, Concurrency Theory, 10th International Conference*, volume 1664 of *Lecture Notes in Computer Science*, pages 162–177. Springer, August 1999.
4. A. Benveniste, B. Caillaud, and P. Le Guernic. Compositionality in dataflow synchronous languages: specification & distributed code generation. *Information and Computation*, 163, 125-171 (2000).
5. A. Benveniste. Some synchronization issues when designing embedded systems from components. In *Proc. of 1st Int. Workshop on Embedded Software, EMSOFT'01*, T.A. Henzinger and C.M. Kirsch Eds., LNCS 2211, 32–49, Springer Verlag, 2001.
6. P. Caspi, C. Mazuet, R. Salem, and D. Weber. Formal design of distributed control systems with lustre. In *Proc. Safecomp'99*, September 1999.
7. P. Caspi. Embedded control: from asynchrony to synchrony and back. In *Proc. of 1st Int. Workshop on Embedded Software, EMSOFT'01*, T.A. Henzinger and C.M. Kirsch Eds., LNCS 2211, 80–96, Springer Verlag, 2001.
8. C. Daws, A. Olivero, S. Tripakis, and S. Yovine. The tool Kronos. In *Proceedings of "Hybrid Systems III, Verification and Control"*, 1996. Lecture Notes in Computer Science 1066, Springer-Verlag.
9. P. Le Guernic, T. Gautier, M. Le Borgne, C. Le Maire. Programming Real-Time Applications with Signal. *Proceedings of the IEEE*, 79(9):1321-1336, September 1991.
10. N. Halbwachs, F. Lagnier and P. Raymond. Synchronous observers and the verification of reactive systems. In *Third Int. Conf. on Algebraic Methodology and Software Technology, AMAST'93*, Twente, M. Nivat and C. Rattray and T. Rus and G. Scollo, Eds., Workshops in Computing, Springer Verlag. Jun. 1993.
11. H. Kopetz, *Real-Time Systems: Design Principles for Distributed Embedded Applications*. Kluwer Academic Publishers. 1997. ISBN 0-7923-9894-7.
12. L. Lamport. Time, clocks and the ordering of events in a distributed system. *Communication of the ACM*, 21:558–565, 1978.
13. Kim G. Larsen, P. Pettersson, and Wang Yi. UPPAAL in a Nutshell. In *Springer International Journal of Software Tools for Technology Transfer*, 1(1-2), 134–152, Dec. 1997.
14. H. Marchand, E. Rutten, M. Le Borgne, M. Samaan. Formal Verification of SIGNAL programs: Application to a Power Transformer Station Controller. *Science of Computer Programming*, 41(1):85–104, Aug. 2001.
15. M. Pease, R.E. Shostak, and L. Lamport. Reaching agreement in the presence of faults. *Journal of the ACM*, 27(2):228–237, 1980.
16. J. Rushby. Bus architectures for safety-critical embedded systems. In *Proc. of 1st Int. Workshop on Embedded Software, EMSOFT'01*, T.A. Henzinger and C.M. Kirsch Eds., LNCS 2211, 306–323, Springer Verlag, 2001.

Automatic Production of Globally Asynchronous Locally Synchronous Systems*

Alain Girault[1] and Clément Ménier[2]

[1] INRIA Rhône-Alpes, BIP project, 655 avenue de l'Europe,
38334 Saint-Ismier Cedex, France, Tel: +33 476 61 53 51, Fax: +33 476 61 54 54
Alain.Girault@inrialpes.fr
[2] ENS Lyon, 46, Allée d'Italie, 69364 Lyon Cedex 07, France
Clement.Menier@ens-lyon.fr

Abstract. Globally Asynchronous Locally Synchronous (GALS) systems are popular both in software and hardware for specifying and producing embedded systems as well as electronic circuits. In this paper, we propose a method for obtaining automatically a GALS system from a centralised synchronous circuit. We focus on an algorithm that takes as input a program whose control structure is a synchronous sequential circuit and some distribution specifications given by the user, and gives as output the distributed program matching the distribution specifications. Since the obtained programs communicate with each other through asynchronous FIFO queues, the resulting distributed system is indeed a GALS system. We also sketch a correctness proof for our distribution algorithm, and we present how our method can be used to achieve hardware/software codesign.

Keywords: Globally synchronous-locally asynchronous (GALS), automatic distribution, distributed architectures, synchronous circuits, asynchronous communications, hardware/software codesign.

1 Introduction

1.1 Globally Asynchronous Locally Synchronous Systems

The globally asynchronous locally synchronous (GALS) paradigm [7] is used both in software and in hardware. In software, the GALS paradigm is used for composing blocks specified as finite state machines and making them communicate asynchronously [1]. This approach is particularly suited to embedded systems. In hardware, more and more circuits are designed as a set of synchronous blocks communicating asynchronously, instead of large synchronous circuits [13]. This method avoids the difficult and power consuming task of distributing the global clock to all parts of the circuits, therefore lowering the total consumption of the obtained GALS circuit [12].

---

* Many thanks to Stephen Edwards (Columbia University) and Tom Shiple (SYNOPSYS) for helpful discussions.

A. Sangiovanni-Vincentelli and J. Sifakis (Eds.): EMSOFT 2002, LNCS 2491, pp. 266–281, 2002.

We propose in this paper a method to obtain automatically GALS systems by first designing a centralised system with a high-level programming language, second compiling it into a centralised synchronous circuit, and third automatically distributing it into several synchronous circuits communicating harmoniously, according to distribution specifications given by the final user. We also give the sketch of a correctness proof for our method.

The main advantage of this approach is that it is always harder and error-prone to design directly a distributed system. This explains the recent success of automatic distribution methods. For instance, see [11] for a recent survey. The other advantage of this approach is the possibility to debug and formally verify the centralised program *before* its distribution, which is always easier and faster than debugging a distributed program.

1.2   Synchronous Circuits

The program model we address is a synchronous sequential circuit coupled with a table of actions for manipulating variables of infinite types (integers, reals...). This model represents finite state programs, where the control part is represented implicitly, instead of explicitly like a finite state automaton. The main advantage of such an implicit representation of the state space is its size. Indeed a sequential circuit with n registers is equivalent to a finite state automaton with 2^n states!

Synchronous circuits can be obtained from the ESTEREL compiler [2,3]. ESTEREL is used, for instance, for programming embedded software (e.g., in avionics, mobile phones, DSP chips...).

1.3   Related Work

Our distribution method is based on past work on the distribution of synchronous programs modelled as finite deterministic automata [6]. Here the problem is more complex since our programs have a *parallel, implicit, and dynamic* control structure, while automata have a *sequential, explicit, and static* control structure.

Besides that, the closest related work is an article from Berry and Sentovich [4]: they implement constructive synchronous circuits as a network of communicating Codesign Finite State Machines (CFMSs) inside POLIS [1], which are by definition GALS systems. There are a number of differences:

1. They consider *cyclic* synchronous circuits, with the restriction that these cyclic circuits must be *constructive* [14]. A constructive circuit is a "well-behaved" cyclic circuit, meaning that there exists an *acyclic* circuit computing the same outputs from the same inputs. However, their synchronous circuits only manipulate Booleans. In contrast, we only consider acyclic synchronous circuits, but they also manipulate *valued* variables such as integers, reals, and so on (see our program model in Section 2 below).
2. The CFSMs communicate with each other through *non-blocking 1-place* communication buffers, while we use *blocking n-places* FIFO queues.

3. Their method for obtaining a GALS system involves partitioning the set of gates into *clusters*, implementing each cluster as a CFSM, and finally connecting the clusters in a POLIS network. They therefore have the possibility to choose among several granularities, ranging from one gate per cluster to a single cluster for the whole synchronous circuit. On the other hand, they do not give a method to obtain such a clustering.

4. The CFSMs communicate with each other in order to implement the constructive semantics of ESTEREL (this is required because their circuits can be cyclic). This means that a CFSM communicates *facts* about the stabilisation of its *local* gates, so that the other CFSMs can react accordingly. The principle is that the network of CFSMs as a whole behaves exactly as the source centralised synchronous circuit. In contrast, each circuit of the GALS systems we obtain communicate *values* and the global coherency is ensured because each circuit implements the whole control structure (see Section 3 below).

1.4   Outline of the Paper

In Section 2, we present in details our program model, along with a running example. Then, in Section 3, we describe our algorithm for automatically distributing synchronous circuits. In Section 4, we sketch a correctness proof for our distribution algorithm, based on partial orders and semi-commutations. In Section 5, we describe a possible method for achieving hardware/software codesign with our distribution algorithm. Finally, in Section 6, we give some concluding remarks and present some possible directions for future research.

2   Program Model

We describe in this section our program model. It is composed of a *control part*, a synchronous sequential boolean circuit, and a *data part*, a table of external actions for manipulating the program variables.

A program has a set of input and output signals. Each of these can be *pure* or *valued*, in which case the signal is associated to a local variable of the corresponding type. Local variables are manipulated by actions of the table.

The sequential circuit is made of boolean gates, registers, and special nets that trigger actions of the table. These actions allow the manipulation of integer and real variables. Complex data type variables can also be defined and manipulated through external procedure calls. The program has a periodic behaviour and a central clock drives all the registers.

In the textual representation, a circuit is simply a list of numbered nets. Each net is connected in input to a simple boolean gate, represented by its *input boolean expression*: it is either a conjunction or a disjunction of nets or negated nets. Expressions cannot be nested, and two expressions are predefined: 0 and 1. The complete list of net kinds is:

- A **standard** net defines a net with an input boolean expression. It allows the building of complex boolean expressions.
- An **action** net drives an action defined in the action table. This action is triggered whenever the net bears the value 1. An action can be either a variable assignment with any expression at the right-hand side, or an external procedure call with possibly several variable parameters and with any expression at the value parameters.
- An **ift** net drives an expression test defined in the action table. This test action is triggered whenever the net takes the value 1. The **ift** net is assigned the result value of the test.
- An **input** net does two things: first it reads the input signal and sets the corresponding presence variable, and second it propagates 1 if the input signal is present, and 0 otherwise. So actually, this is represented by an **input** part and an **ift** part. The **ift** tests the presence Boolean of the input, and it behaves exactly like the **ift** net above. It also sets the variable associated to the input signal when this one is valued. It is the only net with no expression, since it is always executed at each clock tick.
- An **output** net corresponds to an output signal. It behaves like an **action** net by triggering the **emit** action whenever it bears the value 1. If the output signal is valued, then the **emit** action must have an expression of the output signal type as parameter.
- A **register** net is a register with a single fanin and an initial value (0 or 1).

We distinguish two classes of nets: the action triggering nets (**action**, **ift**, **input**, and **output**), and the non-triggering nets (**standard** and **register**).

The semantics of this program model is based on the *zero-delay* assumption: the circuit is viewed as a set of Boolean equations that communicate their results to each other in zero time. Since the circuit is acyclic, the equations can be totally ordered, such that any variable depends only on previously defined ones. Then, for any valuation of the registers and of the inputs, there exists a unique solution to the set of equations, meaning that the circuit has a unique behaviour [3].

Also we only consider *causal* programs, meaning that any given variable can only be modified in *one* parallel branch of the control structure. The purpose of this causality property, which has nothing to do with the control structure itself, is only to avoid non-deterministic programs.

Graphically, we represent our programs as synchronous circuits with the actions directly attached to their corresponding nets. A net having the identity as its input boolean expression will be represented by a simple buffer. Otherwise it will be represented by its boolean gate.

Figure 1 is an example of a synchronous circuit. It will serve as a running example for our distribution algorithm. Note that the presence variable associated to the input I1 (resp. I2) is noted PI1 (resp. PI2).

This program **foo** has two pure inputs, I1 and I2, and two valued outputs, O1 and O2, with two associated integer variables, respectively N1 and N2. Its table of actions is shown in Table 1. It contains all the actions triggered by the **action**, **ift**, **input**, and **output** nets.

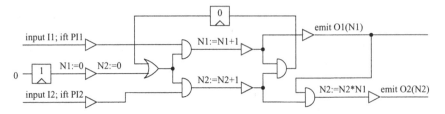

Fig. 1. An example of a synchronous circuit: the program `foo`

Table 1. Table of actions for the program `foo`

`input I1; ift PI1`	`N2 := N2 + 1`	`N2 := 0`
`input I2; ift PI2`	`N2 := N2 * N1`	`emit O2(N2)`
`N1 := 0`	`emit O1(N1)`	`N1 := N1 + 1`

3   Distribution Algorithm

3.1   Principle

The method we propose for obtaining automatically GALS systems involves first designing a centralised system with a high-level programming language, second compiling it into a centralised synchronous circuit, and third automatically distributing it into several synchronous circuits communicating harmoniously with asynchronous communication primitives. We focus in this paper on the third part, the automatic distribution of synchronous circuits.

When designing a GALS system, the user must specify the desired number of computing locations, and what will be the location of each of the system's inputs and outputs. Such a localisation will directly influence the localisation of the internal computations. In this paper, we do not address the problem of finding the best localisation of the computations w.r.t. the performances of the resulting distributed system. This problem is known to be NP-complete, and several heuristics have been proposed in the literature (see [11]–section 5 for references). Rather, we adopt the point of view that the localisation of the system's inputs and outputs is driven by the application, mainly by the *physical localisation* of the sensors and actuators.

For the program `foo` of Figure 1, the user wishes to distribute it over two locations L and M, according to the specifications of Table 2.

Table 2. Distribution specifications for the program `foo`

location L	location M
I1,O2	I2,O1

As said in introduction, our distribution method is based on past work on the distribution of synchronous programs modelled as finite deterministic automata [6]. The principle of our method is the following:

1. First, we assign a set of computing locations to each action of the circuit: each action will be executed by a *single* location, except all the `ifts` that will be computed by *all* locations. From this we can obtain one circuit for each computing location:
   - The data part will be obtained by removing all the non relevant actions.
   - The control part will be obtained by taking the original control part, changing each `action` and `output` net whose action is not assigned to the current computing location into a `standard` net, and changing each `input` net into what we call a simulation block (see below Step 4). In contrast, each `ift` net will be replicated on *all* the control parts.

   However, we will still work on a *single* circuit, until Step 3 when we will generate one circuit for each computing location. Until then, each computing location will thus have a *virtual* circuit.
2. After this first step, the virtual circuit of each computing location makes references to variables that are not computed locally and to inputs that are not received locally. Since the target architecture is a distributed memory one, each distributed program only modifies its local variables (owner computes rule), and therefore has to maintain its local copy of each distant variables and inputs, i.e., those belonging to another computing location. To achieve this, our algorithm adds communication instructions to each virtual circuit to solve the distant variables dependencies.
3. At this point, we generate one actual circuit for each computing location by copying each virtual circuit into a different file.
4. Finally, we add input simulation blocks to solve the distant inputs dependencies.

3.2 Communication Primitives

We need some form of communication and synchronisation between the distributed programs. Here, our goal is to be efficient, simple, and to maximise the actual parallelism. *Asynchronous* communications allow us to place the sending actions as soon as possible in the program, and the receiving actions as late as possible, therefore minimising the impact of the communication latency induced by the network [9].

Now, since the control structure of our program is *parallel*, the order between the concurrent communications may not be statically defined. Moreover, since the obtained circuit of each computing location will actually also run concurrently, one of them can send successively two values for the same variable before the receiving location performs the two corresponding receives. But, thanks to the causality property (see Section 2), any given variable can only be modified in one parallel branch of the control structure. Thus, the order of communication for a given variable can be statically determined. We therefore choose to have two FIFO queues for each pair of locations and for each variable, one in each direction. Hence, each queue is identified by a triplet $\langle \mathtt{src}, \mathtt{var}, \mathtt{dst} \rangle$, where `src` is the source location, `var` is the variable whose value is being transmitted, and `dst` is the destination location. Concretely, we use two communication primitives:

Table 3. Localisation of the actions for the program `foo`

loc.	action
L	input I1; ift PI1
M	input I2; ift PI2
M	N1 := 0

loc.	action
L	N2 := N2 + 1
L	N2 := N2 * N1
M	emit O1(N1)

loc.	action
L	N2 := 0
L	emit O2(N2)
M	N1 := N1 + 1

– On location `src`, the send primitive `send(dst,var)` sends the current value of variable `var` to location `dst` by inserting it into the queue $\langle src, var, dst \rangle$.
– On location `dst`, the receive primitive `var:=receive(src,var)` extracts the head value from the queue $\langle src, var, dst \rangle$ and assigns it to the variable `var`. Since the target architecture is a distributed memory one, `var` is the local copy of the distant variable maintained by the computing location `src`.

These primitives perform both the data-transfer and the synchronisation between the source and the destination locations. When the queue is empty, the `receive` is blocking. The only requirement on the network is that it must preserve the integrity and the ordering of messages. Provided that the `send` action nets are inserted on one location in the same order as the corresponding `receive` action nets in the other location, this will ensure that values are not mixed up.

3.3 Localisation of the Actions

As said in Section 3.1, we do not try to obtain the *best* distribution possible. We derive the localisation for all the actions and all the variables of the synchronous circuit directly from the localisation of the inputs and outputs and from the data-dependencies between the actions. For instance, if the output signal X must be computed by location L, then so does the action `emit X(Y)`. Then, the variable Y and the action `Y := 2` both become also located on L, unless they were already located elsewhere. Such a localisation is unique w.r.t. which inputs and outputs we start from.

The localisation of `foo`'s actions according to the distribution specifications given in Table 2 is shown in Table 3.

Remember that during the whole process, we actually work on a *single* synchronous circuit, and we will generate the distributed circuits only at the very end (see Section 3.1).

Once we have assigned to each action a unique computing location, we face two problems:

1. The **distant variables problem**: Some variables are not computed locally.
2. The **distant inputs problem**: Some inputs are not received locally.

We address the first problem by adding `send` and `receive` actions to the distributed program of each computing location (see Section 3.4).

The second problem cannot be solved with the same technique because input signals convey two informations (see Section 2): the presence of the input and, in the case of a valued signal, its value. Its value will be treated like a regular variable by our algorithm for inserting sends and receives. But, according to the program model, its presence is directly encoded in the control circuit: the input net propagates 1 if the signal is present and 0 otherwise. As a result, an input net relative to a distant input does not propagate the correct value. This prevents boolean tests related to the presence of certain input signals, called input-dependent tests, to be correctly executed. We address this second problem by modifying the circuits and adding *input simulation blocks* (see Section 3.5).

3.4   Solving the Distant Variables Problem

Traversal of the Control Structure. As said in Section 1.3, the control structure of our synchronous circuits is *parallel, implicit, and dynamic*:

- **Parallel** because at a given instant the control can be in more than one parallel branch. Hence, values can be sent from one computing location to another concurrently, so we must avoid conflicts. Remember that our programs are what we call causal (any given variable can only be modified in one parallel branch of the control structure), so such conflicts can only occur between *distinct* variables.
- **Implicit** because the internal state of the program is encoded in the values stored inside the registers of the circuit. Hence, we must initiate the traversal of the control structure at *each* of the circuit inputs and registers.
- **Dynamic** because the values stored inside the circuit registers are not known at compile time. Hence, for any net that is the output of an **or** gate, it is not possible to know *statically* from which of the fanin the control will arrive. Therefore we have to work *separately* on each buffered path of the circuit. A buffered path is a sequence of connected nets, each separated by a simple buffer, i.e., without any boolean gate.

In order to traverse the control structure of a given program, we therefore start at each of the circuit inputs plus each of the registers. We successively start for each of these inputs, and we traverse the control structure forward while marking each visited net. Whenever we reach a gate, we mark the outgoing net as root, and when we reach the next gate, we mark the last net as tail. We then apply our algorithm for inserting sends and receives in the buffered path starting at the root net and ending at the tail net. After which we proceed the traversal in each of the outgoing net of the tail gate, except on those nets that are already marked as visited.

Insertion of Sends. As said above, we insert **send** action nets on each buffered path of the control structure. Our algorithm for inserting **send** and **receive** action nets is derived from the one presented in [6]. It involves two traversals of each buffered path. The first traversal is done backward and inserts the **send** action nets by computing the distant variables needed by each action along the buffered path. The second traversal is done forward and inserts the **receive**

action nets matching the previously inserted **send** action nets. The goal here is to insert the sends as soon as possible and the receives as late as possible, in order minimise the impact of the communication latency, and maximise the actual parallelism between the computing locations.

For each action triggering net (**action**, **ift**, **input**, or **output**), we define two sets **varin** and **varout**:

- The action triggered by an **action** net can be either a variable assignment or an external procedure call. In both cases, the sets **varin** and **varout** contain respectively the variables used and modified by the action. For instance, to the assignment **x:=y*z** correspond the sets **varin**={y,z} and **varout**={x}.
- For an **ift** net, **varin** contains the variables used by the expression tested, while **varout** is empty.
- For an **input** net, **varin** is empty, while **varout** contains the presence variable of the signal, plus the associated variable if the **input** signal is valued.
- For an **output** net, **varout** is empty, while **varin** is empty if the **output** signal is pure, and contains the input variables of the associated expression otherwise.

To insert the **send** nets, we define for each location s the set Need_s of all the distant variables that location s will certainly need, provided that their value has not previously been sent by their respective owning location. The computation of the Need_s sets allows the insertion of **send** action nets so that any location that *needs* a variable for a given action net will receive it before the concerned action net. For each buffered path and location s, the algorithm consists in placing an empty set Need_s at its tail, and then propagating this set backward to its root in the following way:

- When reaching a triggering action net belonging to location s, for each $x \in$ **varin**, if x is a *distant* variable for s, then add x to Need_s. Also, for each $y \in$ **varout**, for each location s such that $y \in \text{Need}_s$, insert a **send(s,y)** action net just after this triggering action net. Finally, remove y from each concerned set Need_s.
- When reaching its root, for each location s, insert at the root of the path one **send(s,x)** action net for each variable x of the set Need_s.

Insertion of Receives. To insert the **receives**, we simulate at any time the content of the waiting queues. Since each queue corresponds to one variable, we only need to count the number of values present in the queue at any instant. Therefore, we define for each queue $\langle t, x, s \rangle$ an integer $\text{Queue}^x_{t \triangleright s}$ containing the number of values of x that have been sent by location t and not yet received by location s.

The algorithm consists in initialising each integer $\text{Queue}^x_{t \triangleright s}$ to zero, and propagating them forward from the root to the tail of each buffered path in the following way:

- When reaching an `action` net triggering a `send(s,x)` on location `t`, increment $Queue^x_{t\triangleright s}$.
- When reaching a triggering action net located on `s`, then for each $x \in$ `varin`, if `x` is a *distant* variable for `s`, check $Queue^x_{t\triangleright s}$. If it is > 0, decrement it, and insert the action net `x:=receive(t,x)` on location `s`. If it is $= 0$, then do nothing because the value is already known by location `s`.
- When reaching the tail of the buffered path, each $Queue^x_{t\triangleright s}$ is by construction equal to zero, so there is nothing else to do.

The result obtained for our program `foo` will be presented in Section 3.6, Figure 4.

3.5 Solving the Distant Inputs Problem

Principle. To solve the distant inputs problem, a first method would be to have each computing location sending, at each clock tick, the presence information of each of its local inputs to each other computing location. This way, all the input nets would always propagate the correct value.

But in the general case, there are a lot of inputs, so this is time consuming. Hence, our goal is to send the presence information only to those computing locations that *need* them. In order to do so, we propose to modify the circuit of the source program as described bellow. We distinguish *pure* input-dependent nets, which depend only on the inputs' presence, from *impure* input-dependent nets, which also depend on the control flow. Our method involves three successive steps, presented in the three following subsections:

1. detection of impure input-dependent nets and the inputs they require;
2. creation of the simulation blocks for the input nets;
3. connection of the detected nets to the required simulation blocks.

We perform these three steps *after* having solved the distant variables problem. At this point we still have a single program containing all the `action` nets located on all the computing locations. Then, we split this single program into n programs, one for each computing location, by transforming any `action` or `output` net not located on the current location into a `standard` net. And finally, we create and connect the simulation blocks.

Computation of the Inputs Required by Each Net. The first step is done by decorating each net with a set `Input` of inputs whose presence are needed to calculate the output value of the net. Initially, these sets are empty. Then, starting from each `input` net, we partially traverse the graph, marking the visited nets and propagating forward the sets `Input` in the following way:

- At the beginning of the traversal, the `input` net related to the input `s` propagates {`s`} to all its fanouts.

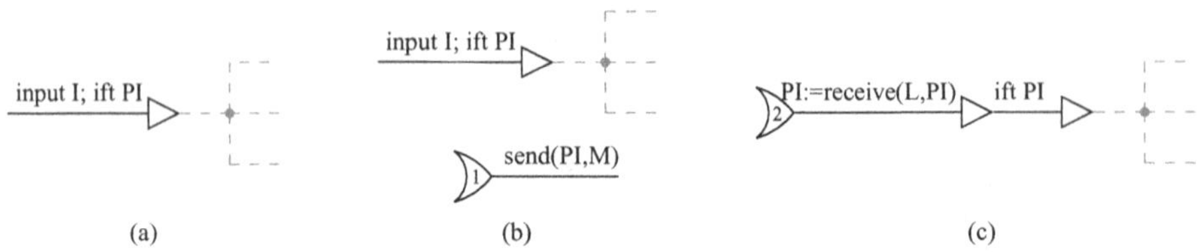

Fig. 2. Transformation of an input net (a) into a simulation block (b) on the location L owning the input; and (c) on location M not owning the input

- A net with only one fanin propagates its incoming set Input^{in} to all its fanouts, and it resets its own set since it is a pure input-dependent net: $\text{Input} := \emptyset$.
- If a net has more than one fanin, then:
  - it assigns $\text{Input} := \text{Input} \cup \text{Input}^{in}$;
  - if all its fanins are marked as visited, then it is a pure input-dependent net: it propagates Input^{in} to all its fanouts, and it resets its own set: $\text{Input} := \emptyset$.

After this partial traversal, the set Input of a given net is non-empty if and only if this net is impure input-dependent, in which case it contains the inputs needed to the computation of its value. In contrast, pure input-dependent nets are identified by their empty set Input and are marked as visited.

Creation of the Input Simulation Blocks. The second step consists in transforming each input net as described in Figure 2. The gates 1 and 2 will have their fanins connected during the third step. They will be connected to all the gates actually needing the presence variable of the input signal (see below).

Connection of the Input Simulation Blocks. The third step consists in connecting each impure input-dependent net to the required simulation blocks. If this net is an **and** then we duplicate it, suppress all its fanins that are connected to pure nets, and connect its fanout to the entry of the simulation block of each input in Input. It is quite similar if it is an **or**, except that the new net is an **and** whose fanins are inverted. Figures 3(a) and (b) represent the results of these connections, respectively for an **and** and an **or** net:

These connections are made so that simulation occurs only when they are really needed, thus avoiding useless communications between the computing locations.

In the case of the program **foo**, the result is shown in the final distributed circuit, in Figure 4.

3.6   Final Result

The Figure 4 shows the final distributed circuit obtained for our program **foo**. This is indeed a GALS system since it is a distributed program such that each

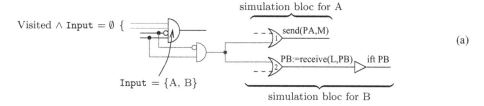

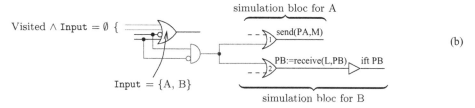

Fig. 3. (a) Connection of an impure **and** net to the required simulation blocks; (b) same with an **or** net.

Table 4. Tables of actions for the program **foo** on locations L and M

location L
input I1; ift PI1
ift PI2
N2 := 0
N2 := N2 + 1
N2 := N2 * N1
emit O2(N2)
send(M,PI1)
PI2 := receive(M,PI2)
N1 := receive(M,N1)

location M
input I2; ift PI2
ift PI1
N1 := 0
N1 := N1 + 1
emit O1(N1)
PI1 := receive(L,PI1)
send(L,PI2)
send(L,N1)

local program is a synchronous circuit, and such that these synchronous circuits communicate with each other through asynchronous communications.

Of course, some of the gates we have inserted when connecting our input-simulation blocks can be replaced by wires since they are **and** and **or** gates with a single fanin.

Finally, it should be noted that since our method distributes only the data part of the program (the control structure is replicated), we can only expect a performance increase if the source program has a large data part (i.e., not too control dominated).

4   Correction Proof of Our Distribution Algorithm

In this section, we present the sketch of a correction proof for our distribution algorithm. It is based on a former proof made for a distribution algorithm working on finite state automata [5]. In order to prove that our distribution algorithm

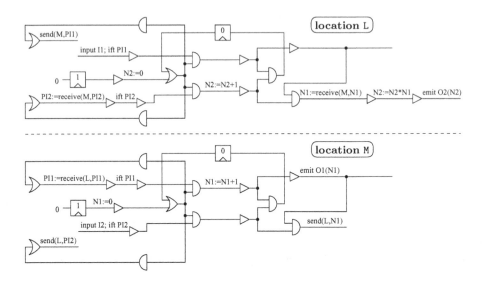

Fig. 4. The program `foo` distributed over the two locations L and M

is sound, we have to prove that the behaviour of the initial centralised program is equivalent to the behaviour of the final parallel program.

We first model the initial centralised program by a finite deterministic automaton labelled with actions. In order to do this, we build the 2^r possible valuations of the r registers of the program. For each such valuation, we simulate the behaviour of the control circuit, we sequentialise the triggered actions, and we compute the next valuation. The presence of `ift` nets can lead to the presence of deterministic binary branchings in the obtained sequential control structure. Of course, this translation gives a finite state automaton whose size is exponential w.r.t. the size of the control circuit. But we only need this translation for the proof purpose.

We define the behaviour of this automaton to be the set of finite and infinite traces of actions it generates (trace semantics). The distribution specifications are given as a partition of the set of actions into n subsets, n being the number of desired computing locations.

We then define a *commutation relation* between actions according to the data dependencies. This commutation relation is actually a semi-commutation [8], and it induces a *rewriting relation* over traces of actions. The set of all possible rewritings is the set of all admissible behaviours of the centralised program, with respect to the semi-commutation relation. The problem is that this set cannot, in general, be recognised by a finite deterministic automaton. The intuition behind our proof is that this set is identical to the set of *linear extensions* of some partial order. For this reason we introduce a new model based on partial orders.

– First, we build a centralised *order automaton* by turning each action labelling the initial automaton into a partial order capturing the data dependencies

between this action and the remaining ones. The behaviour of our order automaton is the set of finite and infinite traces of partial orders it generates (trace semantics). By defining a concatenation relation between partial orders, each trace is then itself a partial order. Thus the behaviour of our order automaton is a set of finite and infinite partial orders. Our key result is that the set of linear extensions of all these partial orders is identical to the set of all the admissible behaviours of the centralised program, with respect to the semi-commutation relation (as defined above).
- Second, we show that our order automaton can be transformed into a set of parallel automata, by turning the data dependencies between actions belonging to distinct locations into communication actions, and by projecting the resulting automaton onto each computing location. We prove that these transformations preserve the behaviour of our order automaton.

This formally establishes that the behaviour of the initial centralised program is equivalent to the behaviour of the final parallel program.

5   Hardware/Software Codesign

We propose a three-steps method to achieve hardware/software codesign, starting from our program model described in Section 2:

1. We identify all the variables that are *pure Booleans*. These are boolean variables that depend only on boolean variables for computing their value. For instance, a Boolean B that appears somewhere in the left-hand part of an assignment of the form B := X > 2 is not considered as a pure Boolean.
2. We generate distribution specifications such that all the pure Booleans are assigned to one computing location, the second computing location having all the remaining variables. Then we apply the algorithms described in Section 3 to distribute automatically the source program onto two computing locations.
3. We transform the program of the computing location that has been assigned only pure Booleans such that all the actions are transformed into circuit portions added to the control circuit of the program. In order to do this, is it necessary to build one datapath for each pure Boolean, as in [10] for instance. From this expanded program, it is then possible to obtain VHDL code and then to compile the program into silicon.

Applying these three steps allows us to obtain *automatically* two programs communicating harmoniously, one compiled into a silicon circuit, and the other one compiled into standard C code embedded in a micro-controller.

6   Conclusion and Future Research

In this article, we have presented a method to obtain *automatically* Globally Asynchronous Locally Synchronous (GALS) systems. We start from a source program compiled into a synchronous circuit coupled with a table of actions for manipulating variables of infinite types (integers, reals...). Then, if the user wants this program to run onto n computing locations, he has to provide distribution specifications in the form of a partition of the set of inputs and outputs into n subsets. Our method transforms automatically the centralised source program into a distributed program performing the same computations as the source program, and such that the program of each computing location communicates harmoniously with the other remaining programs. Our communication primitives are sends and receives, performed over a network of FIFO queues.

The first step of our method involves localising each action into *one* computing location, according to the distribution specifications. At this point, we face two problems: first variables are not computed locally, and second some inputs are not received locally. We have presented several algorithms that insert at the correct place communication actions in order to solve these two problems. As a result, we obtain automatically a distributed GALS program: the program of each computing location is a *synchronous* circuit, and these programs communicate with each other *asynchronously*.

In order to prove that this automatic distribution is sound, we have given the sketch of a correctness proof, based on partial orders and semi-commutations. We have also shown that, by coupling our method with Boolean datapath generation, it can be used for hardware/software codesign. Finally, our method has been implemented in the prototype tool `screp`. It can be used, for instance, to produce automatically a GALS system from an ESTEREL synchronous program.

Now, one promising direction for future research would be to combine our method with that of Berry and Sentovich [4]. This would involve starting from a *valued* synchronous circuit, partitioning it into clusters of gates, and then making them communicate, both facts for the constructive semantics, and values for the coherency of the data computations.

References

1. F. Balarin, M. Chiodo, P. Giusto, H. Hsieh, A. Jurecska, L. Lavagno, C. Passerone, A. Sangiovanni-Vincentelli, E. Sentovich, K. Suzuki, and B. Tabbara. *Hardware-Software Co-Design of Embedded Systems: The POLIS Approach*. Kluwer Academic, June 1997.
2. G. Berry. ESTEREL on hardware. *Philosophical Transaction Royal Society of London*, 339:87–104, 1992.
3. G. Berry. The foundations of ESTEREL. In G. Plotkin, C. Stirling, and M. Tofte, editors, *Proof, Language, and Interaction: Essays in Honour of Robin Milner*, pages 425–454. MIT Press, 2000.
4. G. Berry and E. Sentovich. An implementation of constructive synchronous constructive programs in POLIS. *Formal Methods in Systems Design*, 17(2):165–191, October 2000.
5. B. Caillaud, P. Caspi, A. Girault, and C. Jard. Distributing automata for asynchronous networks of processors. *European Journal of Automation (RAIRO-APII-JESA)*, 31(3):503–524, 1997. Research Report INRIA 2341.

6. P. Caspi, A. Girault, and D. Pilaud. Automatic distribution of reactive systems for asynchronous networks of processors. *IEEE Trans. on Software Engineering*, 25(3):416–427, May/June 1999.

7. D.M. Chapiro. *Globally Asynchronous Locally Synchronous Systems*. PhD Thesis, Stanford University, October 1984.

8. M. Clerbout and M. Latteux. Semi-commutations. *Information and Computation*, 73:59–74, 1987.

9. A. Dinning. A survey of synchronization methods for parallel computers. *IEEE Computer*, pages 66–76, July 1989.

10. A. Girault and G. Berry. Circuit generation and verification of ESTEREL programs. In *IEEE International Symposium on Signals, Circuits, and Systems, SCS'99*, pages 85–89, Iasi, Romania, July 1999. "Gh. Asachi" Publishing.

11. R. Gupta, S. Pande, K. Psarris, and V. Sarkar. Compilation techniques for parallel systems. *Parallel Computing*, 25(13):1741–1783, 1999.

12. A. Hemani, T. Meincke, S. Kumar, A. Postula, T. Olsson, P. Nilsson, J. Oberg, P. Ellervee, and D. Lundqvist. Lowering power consumption in clock by using globally asynchronous locally synchronous design style. In *36th ACM/IEEE Design Automation Conference, DAC'99*, pages 873–878, New Orleans, USA, June 1999.

13. J. Muttersbach, T. Villiger, and W. Fichtner. Practical design of globally asynchronous locally synchronous systems. In *Int. Symp. on Advanced Research in Asynchronous Circuits and Systems, ASYNC'00*, Eilat, Israel, April 2000. IEEE.

14. T. Shiple, G. Berry, and H. Touati. Constructive analysis of cyclic circuits. In *European Design and Test Conference*, pages 328–333, Paris, France, March 1996.

Adaptive and Reflective Middleware
for Distributed Real-Time and Embedded Systems

Douglas C. Schmidt

Electrical & Computer Engineering Dept.
University of California, Irvine
Irvine, CA 92697-2625, USA
schmidt@uci.edu

Abstract. Software has become strategic to developing effective distributed real-time and embedded (DRE) systems. Next-generation DRE systems, such as total ship computing environments, coordinated unmanned air vehicle systems, and national missile defense, will use many geographically dispersed sensors, provide on-demand situational awareness and actuation capabilities for human operators, and respond flexibly to unanticipated run-time conditions. These DRE systems will also increasingly run unobtrusively and autonomously, shielding operators from unnecessary details, while communicating and responding to mission-critical information at an accelerated operational tempo. In such environments, it's hard to predict system configurations or workloads in advance. This paper describes the need for adaptive and reflective middleware systems (ARMS) to bridge the gap between application programs and the underlying operating systems and network protocol stacks in order to provide reusable services whose qualities are critical to DRE systems. ARMS middleware can adapt in response to dynamically changing conditions for the purpose of utilizing the available computer and network infrastructure to the highest degree possible in support of mission needs.

Motivation

New and planned distributed real-time and embedded (DRE) systems are inherently network-centric "systems of systems." DRE systems have historically been developed via *multiple technology bases*, where each system brings its own networks, computers, displays, software, and people to maintain and operate it. Unfortunately, not only are these "stove-pipe" architectures proprietary, but they tightly couple many functional and non-functional DRE system aspects, which impedes their

1. *Assurability,* which is needed to guarantee efficient, predictable, scalable, and dependable quality of service (QoS) from sensors to shooters
2. *Adaptability*, which is needed to (re)configure DRE systems dynamically to support varying workloads or missions over their lifecycles and
3. *Affordability*, which is needed to reduce initial non-recurring DRE system acquisition costs and recurring upgrade and evolution costs.

The affordability of certain types of systems, such as logistics and mission planning, can often be enhanced by using commercial-off-the-shelf (COTS) technologies. However, today's efforts aimed at integrating COTS into mission-critical DRE sys-

A. Sangiovanni-Vincentelli and J. Sifakis (Eds.): EMSOFT 2002, LNCS 2491, pp. 282–293, 2002.

tems have largely failed to support affordability *and* assurability and adaptability effectively since they focus mainly on initial non-recurring acquisition costs and do not reduce recurring software lifecycle costs, such as "COTS refresh" and subsetting military systems for foreign military sales. Likewise, many COTS products lack support for controlling key QoS properties, such as predictable latency, jitter, and throughput; scalability; dependability; and security. The inability to control these QoS properties with sufficient confidence compromises DRE system adaptability and assurability, *e.g.,* minor perturbations in conventional COTS products can cause failures that lead to loss of life and property.

Historically, conventional COTS software has been particularly unsuitable for use in mission-critical DRE systems due to its either being:

1. Flexible and standard, but incapable of guaranteeing stringent QoS demands, which restricts assurability or
2. Partially QoS-enabled, but inflexible and non-standard, which restricts adaptability and affordability.

As a result, the rapid progress in COTS software for mainstream business information technology (IT) has not yet become as broadly applicable for mission-critical DRE systems. Until this problem is resolved effectively, DRE system integrators and warfighters will be unable to take advantage of future advances in COTS software in a dependable, timely, and cost effective manner. Thus, developing the new generation of assurable, adaptable, and affordable COTS software technologies is an important R&D goal.

Key Technical Challenges and Solutions

Some of the most challenging IT requirements for new and planned DRE systems can be characterized as follows:

* Multiple QoS properties must be satisfied in real-time
* Different levels of service are appropriate under different configurations, environmental conditions, and costs
* The levels of service in one dimension must be coordinated with and/or traded off against the levels of service in other dimensions to meet mission needs and
* The need for autonomous and time-critical application behavior necessitates a flexible distributed system substrate that can adapt robustly to dynamic changes in mission requirements and environmental conditions.

Standards-based COTS software available today cannot meet all of these requirements simultaneously for the reasons outlined in Section *Motivation*. However, contemporary economic and organizational constraints—along with increasingly complex requirements and competitive pressures—are also making it infeasible to built complex DRE system software entirely from scratch. Thus, there is a pressing need to develop, validate, and ultimately standardize a new generation of *adaptive and reflective middleware systems* (ARMS) technologies that can support stringent DRE system functionality and QoS requirements.

Middleware [Sch01a] is reusable service/protocol component and framework software that functionally bridges the gap between

1. the end-to-end functional requirements and mission doctrine of applications and
2. the lower-level underlying operating systems and network protocol stacks.

Middleware therefore provides capabilities whose quality and QoS are critical to DRE systems.

Adaptive middleware [Loy01] is software whose functional and QoS-related properties can be modified either

- *Statically*, *e.g.*, to reduce footprint, leverage capabilities that exist in specific platforms, enable functional subsetting, and minimize hardware and software infrastructure dependencies or
- *Dynamically*, *e.g.*, to optimize system responses to changing environments or requirements, such as changing component interconnections, power-levels, CPU/network bandwidth, latency/jitter, and dependability needs.

In DRE systems, adaptive middleware must make these modifications dependably, *i.e.*, while meeting stringent end-to-end QoS requirements.

Reflective middleware [Bla99] goes a step further to permit automated examination of the capabilities it offers, and to permit automated adjustment to optimize those capabilities. Thus, reflective middleware supports more advanced adaptive behavior, *i.e.*, the necessary adaptations can be performed autonomously based on conditions within the system, in the system's environment, or in DRE system doctrine defined by operators and administrators.

The Structure and Functionality of Middleware

Networking protocol stacks can be decomposed into multiple layers, such as the physical, data-link, network, transport, session, presentation, and application layers. Similarly, middleware can be decomposed into multiple layers, such as those shown in Figure 1.

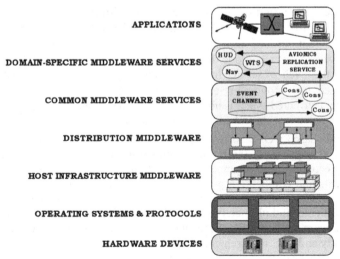

Fig. 1. Layers of Middleware and Their Surrounding Context

Below, we describe each of these middleware layers and outline some of the COTS technologies in each layer that are suitable (or are becoming suitable) to meet the stringent QoS demands of DRE systems.

Host infrastructure middleware encapsulates and enhances native OS communication and concurrency mechanisms to create portable and reusable network programming components, such as reactors, acceptor-connectors, monitor objects, active objects, and component configurators [Sch00b]. These components abstract away the accidental incompatibilities of individual operating systems, and help eliminate many tedious, error-prone, and non-portable aspects of developing and maintaining networked applications via low-level OS programming API, such as Sockets or POSIX Pthreads. Examples of COTS host infrastructure middleware that are relevant for DRE systems include:

- *The ADAPTIVE Communication Environment* (ACE) [Sch01], which is a highly portable and efficient toolkit written in C++ that encapsulates native operating system (OS) network programming capabilities, such as connection establishment, event demultiplexing, interprocess communication, (de)marshaling, static and dynamic configuration of application components, concurrency, and synchronization. ACE has been used in a wide range of commercial and military DRE systems, including hot rolling mill control software, surface mount technology for "pick and place" systems, missile control, avionics mission computing, software defined radios, and radar systems.

- *Real-time Java Virtual Machines* (RT-JVMs), which implement the Real-time Specification for Java (RTSJ) [Bol00]. The RTSJ is a set of extensions to Java that provide a largely platform-independent way of executing code by encapsulating the differences between real-time operating systems and CPU architectures. The key features of RTSJ include scoped and immortal memory, real-time threads with enhanced scheduling support, asynchronous event handlers, and asynchronous transfer of control between threads. Although RT-JVMs based on the RTSJ are in their infancy, they have generated tremendous interest in the R&D and integrator communities due to their potential for reducing software development and evolution costs.

Distribution middleware defines higher-level distributed programming models whose reusable APIs and mechanisms automate and extend the native OS network programming capabilities encapsulated by host infrastructure middleware. Distribution middleware enables developers to program distributed applications much like stand-alone applications, *i.e.*, by invoking operations on target objects without hard-coding dependencies on their location, programming language, OS platform, communication protocols and interconnects, and hardware characteristics.

At the heart of distribution middleware are QoS-enabled object request brokers, such as the Object Management Group's (OMG) *Common Object Request Broker Architecture* (CORBA) [Omg00]. CORBA is distribution middleware that allows objects to interoperate across networks regardless of the language in which they were written or the OS platform on which they are deployed. In 1998 the OMG adopted the Real-time CORBA (RT-CORBA) specification [Sch00a], which extends CORBA with features that allow DRE applications to reserve and manage CPU, memory, and networking resources. RT-CORBA implementations have been used in dozens of DRE systems, including telecom network management and call processing, online trading services, avionics mission computing, submarine DRE systems, signal intelligence and C4ISR systems, software defined radios, and radar systems.

Common middleware services augment distribution middleware by defining higher-level domain-independent components that allow application developers to concentrate on programming application logic, without the need to write the "plumbing" code needed to develop distributed applications by using lower level middleware features directly. Whereas distribution middleware focuses largely on managing end-system resources in support of an object-oriented distributed programming model, common middleware services focus on allocating, scheduling, and coordinating various end-to-end resources throughout a distributed system using a component programming and scripting model. Developers can reuse these services to manage global resources and perform recurring distribution tasks that would otherwise be implemented in an *ad hoc* manner by each application or integrator.

Examples of common middleware services include the OMG's CORBAServices [Omg98b] and the CORBA Component Model (CCM) [Omg99], which provide domain-independent interfaces and distribution capabilities that can be used by many distributed applications. The OMG CORBAServices and CCM specifications define a wide variety of these services, including event notification, logging, multimedia streaming, persistence, security, global time, real-time scheduling, fault tolerance, concurrency control, and transactions. Not all of these services are sufficiently refined today to be usable off-the-shelf for DRE systems. The form and content of these common middleware services will continue to mature and evolve, however, to meet the expanding requirements of DRE.

Domain-specific middleware services are tailored to the requirements of particular DRE system domains, such as avionics mission computing, radar processing, weapons targeting, or command and decision systems. Unlike the previous three middleware layers—which provide broadly reusable "horizontal" mechanisms and services—domain-specific middleware services are targeted at vertical markets. From a COTS perspective, domain-specific services are the least mature of the middleware layers today. This immaturity is due in part to the historical lack of distribution middleware and common middleware service *standards*, which are needed to provide a stable base upon which to create domain-specific middleware services. Since they embody knowledge of a domain, however, domain-specific middleware services have the most potential to increase the quality and decrease the cycle-time and effort that integrators require to develop particular classes of DRE systems.

A mature example of domain-specific middleware services is the Boeing Bold Stroke architecture [Sha98]. Bold Stroke uses COTS hardware, operating systems, and middleware to produce an open architecture for mission computing avionics capabilities, such as navigation, heads-up display management, weapons targeting and release, and airframe sensor processing. The domain-specific middleware services in Bold Stroke are layered upon COTS processors (PowerPC), network interconnects (VME), operating systems (VxWorks), infrastructure middleware (ACE), distribution middleware (Real-time CORBA), and common middleware services (the CORBA Event Service).

Recent Progress

Significant progress has occurred during the last five years in DRE middleware research, development, and deployment, stemming in large part from the following trends:

- *Years of research, iteration, refinement, and successful use* – The use of middleware and DOC middleware is not new [Sch86]. Middleware concepts emerged alongside experimentation with the early Internet (and even its predecessor ARPAnet), and DOC middleware systems have been continuously operational since the mid 1980's. Over that period of time, the ideas, designs, and most importantly, the software that incarnates those ideas have had a chance to be tried and refined (for those that worked), and discarded or redirected (for those that didn't). This iterative technology development process takes a good deal of time to get right and be accepted by user communities, and a good deal of patience to stay the course. When this process is successful, it often results in *standards* that codify the boundaries, and *patterns and frameworks* that reify the knowledge of how to apply these technologies, as described in the following bullets.

- *The maturation of standards* – Over the past decade, middleware standards have been established and have matured considerably with respect to DRE requirements. For instance, the OMG has adopted the following specifications in the past three years:

  o *Minimum CORBA*, which removes non-essential features from the full OMG CORBA specification to reduce footprint so that CORBA can be used in memory-constrained embedded systems.
  o *Real-time CORBA*, which includes features that allow applications to reserve and manage network, CPU, and memory resources predictably end-to-end.
  o *CORBA Messaging*, which exports additional QoS policies, such as timeouts, request priorities, and queueing disciplines, to applications.
  o *Fault-tolerant CORBA*, which uses entity redundancy of objects to support replication, fault detection, and failure recovery.Robust implementations of

these CORBA capabilities and services are now available from multiple vendors. Moreover, emerging standards such as Dynamic Scheduling Real-Time CORBA, the Real-Time Specification for Java, and the Distributed Real-Time Specification for Java are extending the scope of open standards for a wider range of DRE applications.

- *The dissemination of patterns and frameworks* – A substantial amount of R&D effort during the past decade has also focused on the following means of promoting the development and reuse of high quality middleware technology:

  o *Patterns* codify design expertise that provides time-proven solutions to commonly occurring software problems that arise in particular contexts [Gam95]. Patterns can simplify the design, construction, and performance tuning of DRE applications by codifying the accumulated expertise of developers who have successfully confronted similar problems before. Patterns also elevate the level of discourse in describing software development activities to focus on strategic architecture and design issues, rather than just the tactical programming and representation details.

o *Frameworks* are concrete realizations of groups of related patterns [John97]. Well-designed frameworks reify patterns in terms of functionality provided by the middleware itself, as well as functionality provided by an application. Frameworks also integrate various approaches to problems where there are no *a priori*, context-independent, optimal solutions. Middleware frameworks can include strategized selection and optimization patterns so that multiple independently-developed capabilities can be integrated and configured automatically to meet the functional and QoS requirements of particular DRE applications.

Historically, the knowledge required to develop predictable, scalable, efficient, and dependable mission-critical DRE systems has existed largely in programming folklore, the heads of experienced researchers and developers, or buried deep within millions of lines of complex source code. Moreover, documenting complex systems with today's popular software modeling methods and tools, such as the Unified Modeling Language (UML), only capture *how* a system is designed, but do not necessarily articulate *why* a system is designed in a particular way. This situation has several drawbacks:

- Re-discovering the rationale for complex DRE system design decisions from source code is expensive, time-consuming, and error-prone since it's hard to separate essential QoS-related knowledge from implementation details.
- If the insights and design rationale of expert system architects are not documented they will be lost over time, and thus cannot help guide future DRE system evolution.
- Without proper guidance, developers of mission-critical DRE software face the Herculean task of engineering and assuring the QoS of complex DRE systems from the ground up, rather than by leveraging proven solutions.

Middleware patterns and frameworks are therefore essential to help capture DRE system design expertise in a more readily accessible and reusable format.

Much of the pioneering R&D on middleware patterns and frameworks was conducted in the DARPA ITO Quorum program [DARPA99]. This program focused heavily on CORBA open systems middleware and yielded many results that transitioned into standardized service definitions and implementations for the Real-time [Sch98] and Fault-tolerant [Omg98a] CORBA specification and productization efforts. Quorum is an example of how a focused government R&D effort can leverage its results by exporting them into, and combining them with, other on-going public and private activities that also used a common open middleware substrate. Prior to the viability of standards-based COTS middleware platforms, these same R&D results would have been buried within custom or proprietary systems, serving only as an existence proof, rather than as the basis for realigning the R&D and integrator communities.

Looking Ahead

Due to advances in COTS technologies outlined earlier, host infrastructure middleware and distribution middleware have now been successfully demonstrated and deployed in a number of mission-critical DRE systems, such as avionics mission computing, software defined radios, and submarine information systems. Since COTS middleware technology has not yet matured to cover the realm of large-scale, dynamically changing systems, however, DRE middleware has been applied to relatively small-scale and statically configured embedded systems. To satisfy the highly application- and mission-specific QoS requirements in network-centric "system of system" environments, DRE middleware—particularly common middleware services and domain-specific services—must be enhanced to support the management of individual and aggregate resources used by multiple system components at multiple system levels in order to:

- *Manage communication bandwidth, e.g.,* network level resource capability and status information services, scalability to 10^2 subnets and 10^3 nodes, dynamic connections with reserved bandwidth, aggregate policy-controlled bandwidth reservation and sharing, incorporation of non-network resource status information, aggregate dynamic network resource management strategies, and managed bandwidth to enhance real-time predictability.

- *Manage distributed real-time scheduling and allocation of DRE system artifacts (such as CPUs, networks, UAVs, missiles, radar, illuminators, etc), e.g.,* fast and predictable queueing time properties, timeliness assurances for end-to-end activities based on priority/deadlines, admission controlled request insertion based on QoS parameters and global resource usage metrics, and predictable behavior over WANs using bandwidth reservations.

- *Manage distributed system dependability, e.g.,* group communication-based replica management, dependability manager maintaining aggregate levels of object replication, run-time switching among dependability strategies, policy-based selection of replication options, and understanding and tolerating timing faults in conjunction with real-time behavior.

- *Manage distributed security, e.g.,* object-level access control, layered access control for adaptive middleware, dynamically variable access control policies, and effective real-time, dependability, and security interactions.

Ironically, there is currently little or no scientific underpinning for QoS-enabled resource management, despite the demand for it in most distributed systems. Today's system designers and mission planners develop concrete plans for creating global, end-to-end functionality. These plans contain high-level abstractions and doctrine associated with resource management algorithms, relationships between these, and operations upon these. There are few techniques and tools, however that enable *users, i.e.,* commanders, administrators, and operators, *developers, i.e.,* systems engineers and application designers and/or *applications* to express such plans systematically, reason about and refine them, and have these plans enforced automatically to manage resources at multiple levels in network-centric DRE systems.

Systems today are built in a highly static manner, with allocation of processing tasks to resources assigned at design time. For systems that never change, this is an adequate approach. Large and complex military DRE combat systems change and evolve over their lifetime, however, in response to changing missions and operational environments. Allocation decisions made during initial design often become obsolete over time, necessitating expensive and time-consuming redesign. If the system's requisite end-to-end functionality becomes unavailable due to mission and environment changes, there are no standard tools or techniques to diagnose configuration or run-time errors automatically. Instead, designers and operators write down their plans on paper and perform such reasoning, refinement, configuration generation, and diagnosis manually. This *ad hoc* process is clearly inadequate to manage the accelerated operational tempo characteristic of network-centric DRE combat systems.

To address these challenges, the R&D community needs to discover and set the technical approach that can significantly improve the effective utilization of networks and endsystems that DRE systems depend upon by creating middleware technologies and tools that can automatically allocate, schedule, control, and optimize customizable—yet standards-compliant and verifiably correct—software-intensive systems. To promote a *common technology base*, the interfaces and (where appropriate) the protocols used by the middleware should be based on established or emerging industry or military standards that are relevant for DRE systems. However, the protocol and service *implementations* should be customizable—statically and dynamically—for specific DRE system requirements.

To achieve these goals, middleware technologies and tools need to be based upon some type of layered architecture, such as the one shown in Figure 2 [Loy01]. This architecture decouples DRE middleware and applications along the following two dimensions:

- *Functional paths,* which are flows of information between client and remote server applications. In distributed systems, middleware ensures that this information is exchanged efficiently, predictably, scalably, dependably, and securely between remote peers. The information itself is largely application-specific and determined by the functionality being provided (hence the term "functional path").
- *QoS paths,* which are responsible for determining how well the functional interactions behave end-to-end with respect to key DRE system QoS properties, such as

  1. How and when resources are committed to client/server interactions at multiple levels of distributed systems
  2. The proper application and system behavior if available resources do not satisfy the expected resources and
  3. The failure detection and recovery strategies necessary to meet end-to-end dependability requirements.

In next-generation DRE systems, the middleware—rather than operating systems or networks in isolation—will be responsible for separating non-functional DRE system QoS properties from the functional application properties. Middleware will also coordinate the QoS of various DRE system and application resources end-to-end. The architecture in Figure 2 enables these properties and resources to change independently, *e.g.,* over different distributed system configurations for the same applications.

The architecture in Figure 2 is based on the expectation that non-functional QoS paths will be developed, configured, monitored, managed, and controlled by a different set of specialists (such as systems engineers, administrators, operators, and perhaps someday automated agents) and tools than those customarily responsible for programming functional paths in DRE systems. The middleware is therefore responsible for collecting, organizing, and disseminating QoS-related meta-information needed to

1. Monitor and manage how well the functional interactions occur at multiple levels of DRE systems and
2. Enable the adaptive and reflective decision-making needed to support non-functional QoS properties robustly in the face of rapidly changing mission requirements and environmental conditions.

These middleware capabilities are crucial to ensure that the aggregate behavior of complex network-centric DRE systems is dependable, despite local failures, transient overloads, and dynamic functional or QoS reconfigurations.

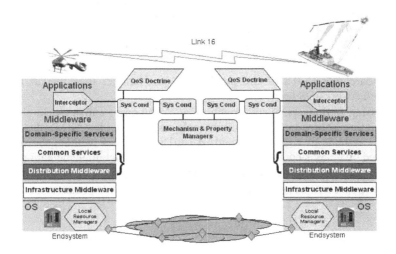

Fig. 2. Decoupling Functional and QoS Paths

To simultaneously enhance assurability, adaptability, *and* affordability, the middleware techniques and tools developed in future R&D programs increasingly need to be application-independent, yet customizable within the interfaces specified by a range of open standards, such as

- The OMG Real-time CORBA specifications and The Open Group's QoS Forum
- The Java Expert Group Real-time Specification for Java (RTSJ) and the Distributed RTSJ
- The DMSO/IEEE High-level Architecture Run-time Infrastructure (HLA/RTI) and
- The IEEE Real-time Portable Operating System (POSIX) specification.

Concluding Remarks

Advances in wireless networks and COTS hardware technologies are enabling the lower level aspects of network-centric DRE systems. The emerging middleware software technologies and tools are likewise enabling the higher level distributed real-time and embedded (DRE) aspects of network-centric DRE systems, making them tangible and affordable by controlling the hardware, network, and endsystem mechanisms that affect mission, system, and application QoS tradeoffs.

The economic benefits of middleware stem from moving standardization up several levels of abstraction by maturing DRE software technology artifacts, such as middleware frameworks, protocol/service components, and patterns, so that they are readily available for COTS acquisition and customization. This middleware focus is helping to lower the total ownership costs of DRE systems by leveraging common technology bases so that complex and DRE functionality need not be re-invented repeatedly or reworked from proprietary "stove-pipe" architectures that are inflexible and expensive to evolve and optimize.

Adaptive and reflective middleware systems (ARMS) are a key emerging theme that will help to simplify the development, optimization, validation, and integration of middleware in DRE systems. In particular, ARMS will allow researchers and system integrators to develop and evolve complex DRE systems assurably, adaptively, *and* affordably by:

- Standardizing COTS at the middleware level, rather than just at lower hardware/networks/OS levels and
- Devising optimizers, meta-programming techniques, and multi-level distributed dynamic resource management protocols and services for ARMS that will enable DRE systems to customize standard COTS interfaces, without the penalties incurred by today's conventional COTS software product implementations.

Many DRE systems require these middleware capabilities. Additional information on DRE middleware is available at www.ece.uci.edu/~schmidt.

References

[Bla99] Blair, G.S., F. Costa, G. Coulson, H. Duran, et al, "The Design of a Resource-Aware Reflective Middleware Architecture", *Proceedings of the 2nd International Conference on Meta-Level Architectures and Reflection*, St.-Malo, France, Springer-Verlag, LNCS, Vol. 1616, 1999.

[Bol00] Bollella, G., Gosling, J. "The Real-Time Specification for Java," *Computer*, June 2000.

[DARPA99] DARPA, *The Quorum Program*, http://www.darpa.mil/ito/research/ quorum/index.html, 1999.

[Gam95] Gamma E., Helm R., Johnson R., Vlissides J., *Design Patterns: Elements of Reusable Object-Oriented Software*, Addison-Wesley, 1995.

[John97] Johnson R., "Frameworks = Patterns + Components", *Communications of the ACM*, Volume 40, Number 10, October, 1997.

[Loy01] Loyall JL, Gossett JM, Gill CD, Schantz RE, Zinky JA, Pal P, Shapiro R, Rodrigues C, Atighetchi M, Karr D. "Comparing and Contrasting Adaptive Middleware Support in Wide-Area and Embedded Distributed Object Applications". *Proceedings of the 21st IEEE International Conference on Distributed Computing Systems (ICDCS-21)*, April 16-19, 2001, Phoenix, Arizona.

[Omg98a] Object Management Group, "Fault Tolerance CORBA Using Entity Redundancy RFP", OMG Docu-ment orbos/98-04-01 edition, 1998.

[Omg98b] Object Management Group, "CORBAServcies: Common Object Service Specification," OMG Technical Document formal/98-12-31.

[Omg99] Object Management Group, "CORBA Compon-ent Model Joint Revised Submission," OMG Document orbos/99-07-01.

[Omg00] Object Management Group, "The Common Object Request Broker: Architecture and Specification Revision 2.4, OMG Technical Document formal/00-11-07", October 2000.

[Sch86] Schantz, R., Thomas R., Bono G., "The Architecture of the Cronus Distributed Operating System", *Pro-ceedings of the 6th IEEE International Conference on Distributed Computing Systems (ICDCS-6)*, Cambridge, Massachusetts, May 1986.

[Sch98] Schmidt D., Levine D., Mungee S. "The Design and Performance of the TAO Real-Time Object Request Broker", *Computer Communications Special Issue on Building Quality of Service into Distributed Systems,* 21(4), 1998.

[Sch00a] Schmidt D., Kuhns F., "An Overview of the Real-time CORBA Specification," *IEEE Computer Magazine*, June, 2000.

[Sch00b] Schmidt D., Stal M., Rohnert H., Buschmann F., *Pattern-Oriented Software Architecture: Patterns for Concurrent and Networked Objects*, Wiley and Sons, 2000.

[Sch01] Schmidt D., Huston S., *C++ Network Programming: Resolving Complexity with ACE and Patterns*, Addison-Wesley, Reading, MA, 2001.

[Sch01a] Schantz R., Schmidt D., "Middleware for Distributed Systems: Evolving the Common Structure for Network-centric Applications," Encyclopedia of Software Engineering, Wiley & Sons, 2001.

[Sha98] Sharp, David C., "Reducing Avionics Software Cost Through Component Based Product Line Development", *Software Technology Conference*, April 1998.

Toward an Approximation Theory
for Computerised Control[*]

Paul Caspi[1] and Albert Benveniste[2]

[1] Verimag (CNRS), Centre Equation, 2, rue de Vignate, 38610 Gieres, France
caspi@imag.fr
http://www-verimag.imag.fr/VERIMAG/
[2] Irisa/Inria, Campus de Beaulieu, F-35042 Rennes cedex, France
benveniste@irisa.fr
http://www.irisa.fr/sigma2/

Abstract. This paper addresses the question of extending the usual approximation and sampling theory of continuous signals and systems to those encompassing discontinuities, such as found in modern complex control systems (mode switches for instance). We provide some evidence that the Skorokhod topology is a good candidate for dealing with those cases in a uniform manner by showing that, in the boolean case, Skorokhod uniformly continuous signals are exactly the signals with uniform bounded variability.

1 Introduction

1.1 Problem Statement

The question of how accurately a control system can be implemented on computers is clearly an important one. For instance, this question arises when a satisfactory control system has been obtained and has to be implemented: how the uncertainties arising from a computer implementation will impair the obtained results in terms of *e.g.,* stability? This question also arises when considering fault tolerance: in highly critical systems, fault tolerance is achieved by massive redundancy and voting. Though the computer science view of fault tolerance advocates the use of exact voting (two redundant units should agree bit-wise on their results)[11,8], in many systems, for instance in the Airbus "fly-by-wire" systems, a smoother approach is taken which can be seen as a "topological" approach. It consists of determining a "normal operation" neighbourhood into which signals should stay according to the several sources of uncertainty that can impair them. Then, the idea is that faults are detected if signals do not belong to the same neighbourhood [5].

This question is a classical one, as far as "continuous control" is considered and can be addressed by using classical distances. But modern control systems

---

[*] This work has been partially supported by Esprit R&D project CRISYS EP 25514 and by Airbus-Verimag contracts 2001-2002

A. Sangiovanni-Vincentelli and J. Sifakis (Eds.): EMSOFT 2002, LNCS 2491, pp. 294–304, 2002.

are more and more based on mixed (or "hybrid") techniques encompassing also non continuous computations: switches, modes, etc.

Our paper tries to extend the "classical approach" to these "hybrid systems". In a first section, we present this classical approach. We show here how approximation and sampling can be dealt with in terms of uniform continuity. In a second section, we consider the case of discontinuous signals and systems. Uniform bounded variability seems to appear here as the analogue of uniform continuity, in that it characterises "slow" varying signals that can be thoroughly sampled without loosing too much information. However, uniform bounded variability doesn't provide a nice topological framework. In the third section, we show that the Skorokhod distance gives us the missing topological framework as we can show that uniform bounded variability signals are exactly those which are Skorokhod uniformly continuous. Furthermore, it encompasses both cases, continuous and non continuous, and thus allows to deal with hybrid cases.

1.2   Related Works

Several approaches seem to have been followed for addressing the question:

- The topological approach initiated by Nerode [12,3] explicitly introduces the approximation and then tries to characterise it as a continuous mapping. This leads to equip the approximation space with an *ad-hoc* (small) topology.
- The equivalence or property preserving approaches followed for instance in [10,1,6,7] tries to construct an approximation of a given system and to check whether it is equivalent to or preserves some properties of the original system expressed in some logic.
- Finally, M. Broucke [9] mixes the two approaches and uses the Skorokhod distance in order to define an approximate bisimulation between several classes of hybrid systems. In this sense, her work is quite close from ours. However, the motivations are slightly different: it doesn't seem that uniformity is addressed and that a result similar to theorem 10 is obtained.

2   The Classical Continuous Framework

2.1   Basic Definitions

We consider systems that have to operate continuously for a long time for instance a nuclear plant control that is in operations for weeks or an aircraft control that flies for several hours. Thus, the horizon of our signals is not bounded. Hence, a *signal* x is for us simply a function from R^+ to R and a *system* is simply a function f causally transforming signals, that is to say, such that $f(x)(t)$ is only function of $x(t'), t' \leq t$.

The *delay operator* Δ^τ is such that $(\Delta^\tau x)(t) = x(t - \tau)$, and a system is *stationary* (or time invariant) if $\forall \tau, S(\Delta^\tau x) = \Delta^\tau(S x)$.

A signal x is *uniformly continuous (UC)* (figure 1) if there exists a positive function η_x from errors to delays, such that:

$$\forall \varepsilon > 0, \forall t, t', |t - t'| \leq \eta_x(\varepsilon) \Rightarrow |x(t) - x(t')| \leq \varepsilon$$

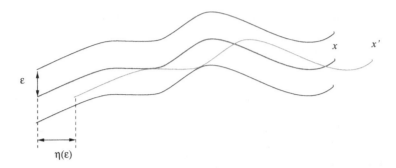

Fig. 1. A uniformly continuous signal

Such a definition can be rephrased in a functional way by introducing the $\| \ \|_\infty$ norm on signals, defined as

$$\|x\|_\infty = \inf_{x' \approx x} \sup_{t \in R^+} |x'(t)|$$

where $\approx$ denotes the equality "almost every where", that is to say such that isolated discontinuity points are not taken into account.

Then, a signal x is uniformly continuous if there exists a positive function η_x from errors to delays, such that:

$$\forall \varepsilon > 0, \forall \tau, |\tau| \le \eta_x(\varepsilon) \Rightarrow \|x - \Delta^\tau x)\|_\infty \le \varepsilon$$

2.2 Retiming and Sampling

A *retiming* function is a non decreasing function from R^+ to R^+. This is a very general definition which has many possibilities. For instance, a piece-wise constant retiming function can be seen as a sampler: if $x' = x \circ r$, and if r is piece-wise constant, then, at each jump of r, a new value of x is taken and maintained up to the next jump. This allows us to define a periodic sampler r, of period T_r by the piece-wise constant function:

$$r(t) = E(t/T_r)$$

where E is the integer part function (see figure 2).

Retiming allows us to restate the uniformly continuous signal definition, by saying that a signal x is uniformly continuous if there exists a positive function η_x from errors to delays, such that:

$$\forall \varepsilon > 0, \forall \ retiming \ r, \|r - id\|_\infty \le \eta_x(\varepsilon) \Rightarrow \|x - x \circ r\|_\infty \le \varepsilon$$

where *id* is the identity retiming function.

We can then define a *samplable* signal as a signal such that the sampling error can be controlled by tuning the sampling period:

$\cdots$

Fig. 2. A periodic sampling retiming

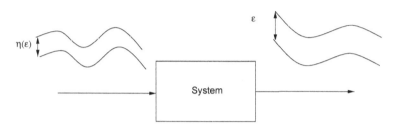

Fig. 3. A uniformly continuous system

Definition 1 (Samplable Signal). *A signal x is samplable if there exists a positive function η_x from errors to sampling periods, such that:*

$$\forall \varepsilon > 0, \forall\, periodic\ sampling\ r, T_r \leq \eta_x(\varepsilon) \Rightarrow ||x - x \circ r||_\infty \leq \varepsilon$$

Then the following theorem obviously holds:

Theorem 2. *A signal is samplable if and only if it is uniformly continuous.*

2.3   From Signals to Systems

This framework extends quite straightforwardly to systems by saying that a system S is uniformly continuous (figure 3) if there exists a positive function η_S from errors to errors such that:

$$\forall \varepsilon > 0, \forall x, x', ||x - x'||_\infty \leq \eta_S(\varepsilon) \Rightarrow ||(S\,x) - (S\,x')||_\infty \leq \varepsilon$$

and state the following theorem:

Theorem 3. *A uniformly continuous stationary system, fed with a uniformly continuous signal outputs a uniformly continuous signal.*

Proof. Given x UC, S UC, and $\varepsilon > 0$,

$$\forall x', ||x - x'||_\infty \leq \eta_S(\varepsilon) \Rightarrow ||(S\,x) - (S\,x')||_\infty \leq \varepsilon$$

and

$$\forall \tau, |\tau| \leq \eta_x(\eta_S(\varepsilon)) \Rightarrow ||x - (\Delta^\tau x)||_\infty \leq \eta_S(\varepsilon)$$

Thus,

$$\forall \tau, |\tau| \leq \eta_x(\eta_S(\varepsilon)) \Rightarrow ||(S\ x) - (S\ (\Delta^\tau x)||_\infty \leq \varepsilon$$

But $S(\Delta^\tau x) = \Delta^\tau(S\ x)$. We thus get

$$\eta_{Sx} = \eta_x \circ \eta_S$$

This theorem says that given an acyclic network of UC systems, one can compute maximum delays on system interconnection, sampling periods and maximum errors on input signals such that errors on output signals be lower than given bounds. This provides us thus with a nice approximation theory.

2.4   Generalisation

This extends to any distance between signals:

Definition 4 (Uniformly continuous signals). *A signal x is UC for the distance d if there exists a positive, error to delay function η_x such that:*

$$\forall \varepsilon > 0, \forall \tau, |\tau| \leq \eta_x(\varepsilon) \Rightarrow d(x, \Delta^\tau x) \leq \varepsilon$$

Definition 5 (Uniformly continuous systems). *A system is UC for the distance d if there exists a positive, error to error function η_S such that:*

$$\forall \varepsilon > 0, \forall x, x', d(x, x') \leq \eta_S(\varepsilon) \Rightarrow d((S\ x), (S\ x')) \leq \varepsilon$$

In this generalised background, the same theorem holds:

Theorem 6. *A uniformly continuous stationary system S, fed with a uniformly continuous signal x outputs a uniformly continuous signal:*

$$\eta_{Sx} = \eta_x \circ \eta_S$$

3   Uniform Bounded Variability Signals

We now consider boolean signals and we want to find some concept more or less equivalent to uniform continuity in the sense that it characterises "slowly" varying signals that can be sampled. For the sake of simplicity, we restrict ourselves in the remaining of the paper to *piece-wise continuous* signals, *i.e.*, signals for which there exists an increasing and either finite or diverging sequence of times $\{t_0, \dots t_n, \dots\}$ such that the signal is continuous in every open interval $]t_n, t_{n+1}[$. For this kind of signal we can introduce a *discontinuity count function*

Definition 7 (Discontinuity count function). *$dc_{t_1, t_2}(x)$ is the function counting the number of discontinuity points of a signal x in an interval $[t_1, t_2]$.*

$$dc_{t_1, t_2}(x) = card\{t \mid x(t^-) \neq x(t^+) \wedge t_1 \leq t \leq t_2\}$$

Fig. 4. Uniform bounded variability

where, as usual, $x(t^-), (x(t^+))$ is the left (right) limit of x at t.

When applied to boolean signals, this allows us to define these "slowly varying signals" as those signals which only have a bounded number of discontinuities in any time interval of given length:

Definition 8 (Uniform bounded variability signal (UBV)). *A boolean signal x has UBV (figure 4) if there exists a function from discontinuity counts to delays, η_x, such that:*

$$\forall n \in N^+, \forall t, t', |t - t'| \leq \eta_x(n) \Rightarrow dc_{t,t'}(x) \leq n$$

where N^+ denotes the set of positive integers. This definition "patches" the continuity one, but, in general the only interesting value for n is 1. Then $T_x = \eta_x(1)$ is the minimum stable time of the signal.

This definition could allow us to adapt the previous approximation theory to boolean signals. For instance we could define *samplable* boolean signal, as those signals for which a sampling period can be found such that a given minimum number of samples can be drawn at each constant valued interval. Then, clearly, samplable boolean signals correspond to uniform bounded variability ones.

However, this is not a topological definition and it lacks many of its appealing features, e.g., triangular inequality. For instance we cannot derive from it a convenient definition for systems. Furthermore, it is not clear how this definition combines with the classical one for mixed signals.

4   Skorokhod Distance

4.1   Definition

This distance [2] has been proposed as a generalisation of the usual distance so as to account for discontinuities.

Definition 9 (Skorokhod distance).

$$d_S(x, y) = \inf_{bijective\ retiming\ r} ||r - id||_\infty + ||x - y \circ r||_\infty$$

We see here the idea of this definition: instead of comparing the signals at the same times, we allow shifts in time before comparing points, provided the shifts are bijective, i.e., we don't miss any time. In this definition, the use of bijective retimings is fundamental. Otherwise, it could be easily shown that it would not be a distance: for instance symmetry and triangular inequality could be violated.

4.2   Skorokhod Distance and Uniform Bounded Variability

Let us show here that the Skorokhod distance can replace the non topological concept of uniform bounded variability. This is the main result of the paper and is summarised in the following theorem:

Theorem 10. *A boolean signal has uniform bounded variability if and only if it is Skorokhod uniformly continuous.*

Proof. The proof is based on the following lemmas:

Lemma 11. *A bijective retiming is both increasing and continuous and its inverse is continuous: it is an homeomorphism.*

This is a classical property whose proof is omitted.

Lemma 12. *If r is a bijective retiming with $||r - id||_\infty \leq \delta$, then*

$$dc_{0,t-\delta}(x) \leq dc_{0,t}(x \circ r) \leq dc_{0,t+\delta}(x)$$

In other words, a bounded bijective retiming preserves the number of discontinuities. This is due to the fact that is is an homeomorphism which preserves limits.

The proof then proceeds as follows:

Only if part: Let T_x be the minimum stable time associated with x. Let us show that x has $\eta_x(\varepsilon) = \inf\{\varepsilon, \frac{T_x}{3}\}$ as time to error function.

Let r be a retiming with $||r - id||_\infty \leq \eta_x(\varepsilon)$ and t a discontinuity point of x with, for instance $x(t^-) = 0, x(t^+) = 1$. We then have:

$$t' \in [t - \frac{T_x}{2}, t[\Rightarrow x(t') = 0$$

$$t' \in]t, t + \frac{T_x}{2}] \Rightarrow x(t') = 1$$

r being non decreasing, exists t_1 defined by

$$t_1 = \sup\{t' \mid r(t') < t\} = \inf\{t' \mid r(t') > t\}$$

with

$$|t - t_1| < \frac{T_x}{2}$$

Let us consider now the bijective retiming r' such that:

$$r'(t - \frac{T_x}{2}) = t - \frac{T_x}{2}$$

$$r'(t) = t_1$$

$$r'(t + \frac{T_x}{2}) = t + \frac{T_x}{2}$$

and defined by linear interpolation between these points:

$$t' \in [t - \frac{T_x}{2}, t] \Rightarrow r'(t') = t - \frac{T_x}{2} + \frac{t_1 - (t - \frac{T_x}{2})}{\frac{T_x}{2}}(t' - (t - \frac{T_x}{2}))$$

$$t' \in [t, t + \frac{T_x}{2}] \Rightarrow r'(t') = t_1 + \frac{t + \frac{T_x}{2} - t_1}{\frac{T_x}{2}}(t' - t)$$

Clearly $||r' - id|| \le \varepsilon$ holds over $[t - \frac{T_x}{2}, t + \frac{T_x}{2}]$, and $||x - x \circ r \circ r'||_\infty = 0$ holds on the same interval[1].

Then the proof can proceed by induction on the sequence of discontinuity points of x.

If part: Let us show that if x can have two discontinuity points arbitrarily close, it is not possible to find a value $\eta_x(0.5)$ such that, for any retiming r,

$$||r - id||_\infty \le \eta_x(0.5) \Rightarrow d_S(x, x \circ r) \le 0.5$$

Effectively, x must have an unbounded number of couples of discontinuity points closer than $\eta_x(0.5)/2$. There is thus a time t_1 for which this number n_1 of such discontinuity points is larger than $1/\eta_x(0.5)$.

On the other hand, it is easy to construct a retiming r with $||r - id||_\infty \le \eta_x(0.5)$ which "erases" every couple of discontinuity points closer than $\eta_x(0.5)/2$:

Let t, t' such a couple $t' - \eta_x(0.5)/2 < t < t'$. On can find two other points t'', t''' such that $t'' < t < t' < t''' < t'' + \eta_x(0.5)$ and take:

$$r(t'') = r(t''') = t''$$

Any bijective retiming $||r' - id||_\infty \le 0.5$ satisfies according to lemma 12

$$dc_{0,t_1}(x \circ r \circ r') \le dc_{0,t_1+0.5}(x \circ r)$$

But

$$dc_{0,t_1}(x \circ r) = dc_{0,t_1}(x) - n_1$$

as r erased n_1 discontinuities, and

$$dc_{0,t_1+0.5}(x \circ r) < dc_{0,t_1}(x)$$

as x cannot have n_1 non erasable discontinuities in $[t_1, t_1 + 0.5]$

Thus,

$$dc_{0,t_1}(x \circ r \circ r') < dc_{0,t_1}(x)$$

$$||x - x \circ r \circ r'||_\infty = 1$$

which contradicts the hypothesis

$$d_S(x, x \circ r) \le 0.5$$

---

[1] It may be the case that $x(t) \ne x \circ r \circ r'(t)$ because nothing has been assumed of the value of x at the discontinuity point t. It is here that the concept of equality "almost everywhere" is useful.

One clearly sees the idea of this theorem: if x has uniform bounded variability, one can find a continuous bounded retiming which has the same effect as a bounded but possibility discontinuous one. On the contrary, if variability is unbounded this is no more possible because a discontinuous retiming can erase discontinuity points which are too close from each other, while a continuous retiming cannot. Then the distance between signals that don't have the same number of discontinuities cannot get smaller than 1.

4.3   Skorokhod Distance and $|| \; ||_\infty$

As for continuous signals and systems, it is obvious that the Skorokhod distance encompasses the usual $|| \; ||_\infty$ one because for any x, y, $d_S(x, y) \leq ||x - y||_\infty$:

Theorem 13. *A uniformly continuous signal is Skorokhod uniformly continuous.*

This clearly shows that the Skorokhod distance can both deal with discontinuous signals, like booleans, and continuous ones. It is thus a good candidate for dealing with mixed cases *i.e.,* systems dealing with both continuous and, say, boolean signals as well as signals which are "piece-wise uniformly continuous".

5   Conclusion and Open Questions

This paper has thus addressed the question of extending the usual approximation and sampling theory of continuous signals and systems to those encompassing discontinuities, such as found in modern complex control systems (mode switches for instance). We have provided some evidence that the Skorokhod topology is a good candidate for dealing with those cases in a uniform manner.

Yet, much remains to do in order to achieve this goal. In particular, two important issues have to be raised here:

Multiple input-output systems: we only treated here the case of single input-output systems. The case of multiple ones is much more involved: what are the systems that are uniformly continuous in their several inputs? Some hints on the subject have been proposed in [5], but not linked with the topological approach followed here.

Links with stability: in fact, even the classical approach presented in section 2 is unsatisfactory, as it only applies to stable systems and it is well-known that many controllers are not stable. For instance the celebrated PID controller is not stable, since it contains an integral part, and hence, it is not uniformly continuous (figure 5). Thus controllers cannot be analysed in isolation of the systems they intend to stabilise and uniform continuity only applies to the closed loop system (figure 6).

This problem is likely to arise similarly in our framework and raises the question of stability characterisation and of feed-back stabilisation in the case

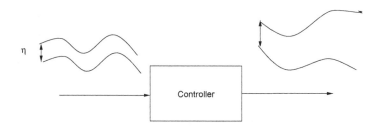

Fig. 5. An unstable system

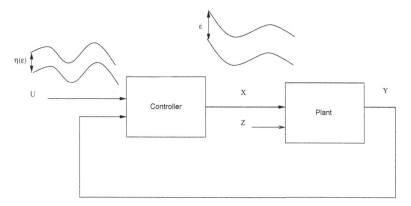

Fig. 6. Feed-back stabilisation

of mixed continuous-discontinuous signals and systems. In particular, it would be tempting to interpret critical race avoidance and protocols within this framework [4].

Acknowledgments

The authors kindly acknowledge Alberto San Giovanni-Vincentelli from Berkeley University for pointing us reference [9].

References

1. A.Chutinan and B.H.Krogh. Computing approximating automata for a class of hybrid systems. *Mathematical and Computer Modeling of Dynamical Systems*, 6:30–50, March 2000. Special Issue on Discrete Event Models of Continuous Systems.
2. P. Billingsley. *Convergence of probability measures*. John Wiley & Sons, 1999.
3. M.S. Branicky. Topology of hybrid systems. In *32nd Conference on Decision and Control*, pages 2309–2311. IEEE, 1993.
4. P. Caspi. Embedded control: from asynchrony to synchrony and back. In T. Henzinger and Ch. Kirsch, editors, *First International Wokshop on Embedded Software*, volume 2211 of *Lecture Notes in Computer Science*, 2001.

5. P. Caspi and R. Salem. Threshold and bounded-delay voting in critical control systems. In Mathai Joseph, editor, *Formal Techniques in Real-Time and Fault-Tolerant Systems*, volume 1926 of *Lecture Notes in Computer Science*, pages 68–81, September 2000.
6. E.Asarin, O.Maler, and A.Pnueli. On discretization of delays in timed automata and digital circuits. In R.de Simone and D.Sangiorgi, editors, *Concur'98*, volume 1466 of *Lecture Notes in Computer Science*, pages 470–484. Springer, 1998.
7. J.Ouaknine. Digitisation and full abstraction for dense-time model checking. In *TACAS 02*, volume 2280 of *Lecture Notes In Computer Science*, pages 37–51. Springer, 2002.
8. H. Kopetz. *Real-Time Systems Design Principles for Distributed Embedded Applications*. Kluwer, 1997.
9. M.Broucke. Regularity of solutions and homotopic equivalence for hybrid systems. In *Proceedings of the 37th IEEE Conference on Decision and Control*, volume 4, pages 4283–4288, 1998.
10. R.Alur, T.A.Henzinger, G.Lafferriere, and G.J.Pappas. Discrete abstractions of hybrid systems. *Proceedings of the IEEE*, 88:971–984, 2000.
11. J.H. Wensley, L. Lamport, J. Goldberg, M.W. Green, K.N. Lewitt, P.M. Melliar-Smith, R.E Shostak, and Ch.B. Weinstock. SIFT: Design and analysis of a fault-tolerant computer for aircraft control. *Proceedings of the IEEE*, 66(10):1240–1255, 1978.
12. W.Kohn and A.Nerode. Models for hybrid systems: automata, topologies, controllability and observability. In *Hybrid Systems*, volume 732 of *Lecture Notes in Computer Science*. Springer, 1993.

A New Facility for Dynamic Control
of Program Execution: DELI

Giuseppe Desoli, Nikolay Mateev, Evelyn Duesterwald,
Paolo Faraboschi, and Josh Fisher

Hewlett-Packard Laboratories
1 Main St., Cambridge, MA 02142, USA
{giuseppe_desoli,nikolay_mateev,paolo_Faraboschi,
josh_fisher}@hp.com duester@acm.org

Abstract. The DELI (Dynamic Execution Layer Interface) provides fine-grain control over the execution of programs, by allowing its clients to observe and optionally manipulate every single instruction at run time. It accomplishes this by opening up an interface to the layer between the execution of application software and hardware. To avoid the 100x implicit slowdown, DELI uses a technique typical of modern emulators: it caches fragments of the executable and always runs out of that cache. Unlike previous systems, DELI exposes the caching through a common interface, so that emulators themselves can take advantage of other DELI clients. This enables mixing emulation with already existing services and native code. In this paper, we describe the basic aspects of DELI: the underlying caching and linking mechanism, the Hardware Abstraction Mechanism (HAM), the Binary-Level Translation (BLT) infrastructure, and the Application Programming Interface (API). We also cover some uses, such as ISA emulation and software patching. Finally, we present emulation results of a PocketPC system on an embedded VLIW processor, where we achieve almost-native performance, and show how to mix-and-match native and emulated code.

1   Introduction

Most traditional program transformations terminate before the program binary runs, however several techniques continue manipulating code while the program is running, from dynamic loaders to Just-In-Time compilers. Most of these techniques share a fundamental property: they observe—and potentially transform—instructions of the target program immediately before they run.

System utilities that operate on *programs* as their targets have many different motivations. Sometimes the semantics of the target program are not meant to directly address the hardware on which it runs, and we use compilers and emulators for translation. Linkers and loaders process the target program in order for it to run correctly. Some tools check a target program for viruses or other properties, while others, such as profilers, measure performance-related properties of the target.

A. Sangiovanni-Vincentelli and J. Sifakis (Eds.): EMSOFT 2002, LNCS 2491, pp. 305–318, 2002.

- **Compile time vs. Run time**. Some programs process a target binary before it runs, and then get out of the way. We say that these transformations happen at *compile time* (or load time). Other approaches operate on a binary while it is running, and we sometimes say they operate at *run time*. Compilers are examples of the first type, as are most virus checkers. Interpreted emulators are examples of the second.

- **Persistent vs. Transient changes**. A similar consideration has to do with whether changes to the same part of the program have a long lifetime, or whether their effect only lasts briefly. For example, compile time techniques making a single long-lasting change to the program, and we call them *persistent*. Most run time techniques, however, change the same parts of the program repeatedly, and we thus refer to these as being *transient*.

- **Persistent changes at Run time**. It might be fair to refer to the actions of a run-time dynamic loader as persistent, since the effect of the changes is repeatedly used. Much more important is the *caching of translated code*, adopted by emulators to avoid repeating the translation of the same piece of code. When done well, this yields savings up to 100x. This type of mechanism combines the advantages of compile time and run time. We can amortize work over a long time, yet we take advantage of the near-perfect knowledge available at run time.

Effects of a New Control Point

Efficient emulation already gives a lot of power: even though code was produced for a stipulated ISA, code still runs correctly despite ISA changes. DELI extends this concept by providing a tool that gives clients ultimate fine-grain control over running programs by allowing the *observation and manipulation of every instruction at run time*. We do this by opening up an interface to the workings of a native-to-native binary emulator, which uses caching and linking to approximate native performance.

A capability like this can change some of our assumptions about computing. Just as superscalar hardware makes transient rearrangements of code at run time to match changing hardware, software can make persistent code changes at run time to match the hardware that is actually present when the code runs. This raises the level of processor compatibility above the hardware level, facilitates software migration, and allows us to design simpler hardware (that does not have to pay a price every cycle for compatibility). It also permits us to examine and manipulate code in many other ways, in the perfect light of run time, but with the cost of the necessary analysis and transformations amortized over the full period of the persistent use of the result.

1.1   Related Work

An important example of clients that manipulate running programs is *emulation*. Advanced emulation systems use varying degrees of code caching and optimization ranging from caching unoptimized translated code blocks [4] to sophisticated dynamic binary translation systems. Examples of the latter class are the *Daisy* binary translation system [7], Transmeta's *Code Morphing* software for the Crusoe processor [6] and Transitive's *Dynamite Software* [16]. These systems provide a complete software layer for dynamic binary translation between different ISA's, where the mechanisms for code caching, linking and optimization are integral part of the overall system. In contrast, in the DELI model, code cache related functionality is explicitly isolated in a separate software layer. The DELI is not an emulation system itself: it encapsulates the common code caching and linking functionality, which can then be leveraged across a number of different emulation systems. While optimization is tightly integrated in binary translation systems, the DELI offers it as a service. Thus, it frees emulation developers from designing and implementing target-specific optimizations.

We view dynamic optimizers [1,3,5,15,17] as native-to-native binary translation systems, where performance improvement is the sole desired effect of translation. As in dynamic optimizers, the DELI may employ code optimization transparently. However, it goes beyond that by specifically opening up the dynamic optimization functionality as a service to client applications. Under specific instructions from the client, the DELI enables dynamic code optimizations that are beyond the reach of a purely transparent dynamic optimizer, whose code knowledge is limited to the binary text.

Just-In-Time (JIT) Compilation [14] for the Java Virtual Machine (JVM) or the *Common Language Runtime* in the Microsoft's .NET environment [15] are advanced runtime systems for executing portable intermediate code (i.e., Java Bytecode or Microsoft IL). These emulation systems use dynamic caching of translations for performance. A JVM (or Common Language Runtime) provides a similar level of control over the execution of the intermediate code as the DELI achieves for the execution of binary code. However, the DELI is language independent, does not require a special code format and can therefore even handle legacy code.

2   Overview of the DELI System

The DELI is a software layer that operates between application software and the hardware (Fig. 1). Depending on the desired functionality, the DELI layer can be inserted above or underneath the O/S. If system code should execute under DELI control, the DELI would be inserted underneath the O/S.

A helpful analogy with DELI is the O/S. The DELI is to its clients what virtual memory is to an ordinary application. Strictly speaking, building an application does not require virtual memory or other O/S support, and embedded applications often embody significant portions of the O/S. However, the presence of an underlying operating system greatly simplifies application development. Similarly, while not strictly necessary, the DELI greatly facilitates dynamic code transformation clients.

The DELI layer (Fig. 1) includes three main components: the *Binary Level Translation* (BLT) layer, the *Hardware Abstraction Module* (HAM), and the *Application Programming Interface* (DELI API). The BLT provides the core code caching and linking functionality, and it includes several code caches and basic infrastructure elements for binary code transformation, such as optimization and instrumentation. HAM provides virtualization of the underlying hardware. The API makes the functionality accessible to client applications

2.1   The DELI API

Through its API, the DELI provides basic code caching and linking service, as well as the necessary infrastructure to support dynamic code transformation to the running client applications. For example, consider the scenario of a client emulation system that uses the DELI to cache and link translations of the emulated code. To avoid repeated emulation of the same code sequence, the emulation system produces a code fragment that contains a translation of the code sequence. The emulation system uses the DELI to emit the fragment for caching and linking via the API function:

```
deli_emit_fragment (tag, start, end, flags, user_data);
```

The next time the emulation system is about to emulate the code just translated, it can instruct the DELI to execute the fragment by invoking:

```
deli_exec_fragment(tag, context);
```

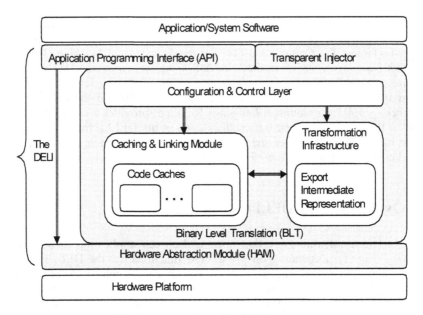

Fig. 1. An overview of the DELI system

Internally, the DELI directly interconnects all emitted fragment code whenever possible. Thus, invoking `deli_execute_fragment` may actually result in the execution of a sequence of fragments until we encounter a fragment exit that is not connected, in which case an exit tag will be returned to the client.

Besides implementing the API, the DELI is also capable of acting in a transparent mode with respect to the client application. In this mode, the DELI transparently takes control over the running client application, such that it operates like a native-to-native caching emulator similar to the HP Labs Dynamo dynamic optimizer [1]. The DELI intercepts the running applications and copies every piece of code that is about to execute into its code cache, so that execution only takes place out of the code cache. When placing code into the code cache, the DELI has the opportunity to optimize it, as in the Dynamo system. Unlike Dynamo, the DELI can be instructed (through the API) to perform other transformation or observation tasks (such as instrumentation or insertion of safety checks). Clients can explicitly turn on and off the transparent mode by invoking `deli_start()` and `deli_stop()`.

Table 1. A brief list of the most important functions in the DELI API.

DELI API Function	Description
`void deli_init();`	Initialize the DELI

`void deli_emit_fragment(`
`  tag, start, end, flags,`
`  user_data);`
	Emit a code fragment in the DELI code cache. Arguments include a client-level `tag` identifier, the location of the translation (`start` and `end` address), `flags` and `user_data`. The flags specify attributes of the emitted fragment, such as the optimization level to apply, or whether the fragment is instrumented for profiling.

`void deli_exec_fragment(` `  tag, context);`	Start executing code from the location identified by `tag` with the given `context`. Arguments include the fragment's tag identifier and a context that must be load before executing the fragment

`deli_handle`
`deli_lookup_fragment(`
`  tag);`
	Return a DELI internal handle for the fragment identified with tag, if it resides in the cache

`void`
`deli_invalidate_fragment(`
`  deli_handle);`
	Invalidate the fragments identified by the DELI internal handle.

`void`
`deli_install_callback(`
`  deli_event,`
`  callback);`
	Register a client-level callback function to be invoked upon a specific DELI event, such as fragment emission, cache exit, profile counter overflow, or out-of-space code cache condition. We can use the callback mechanism to implement a variety of tasks, such as enforcing client-level code assertion, controlling code cache flushes, or triggering optimization and reformation of fragment code once it becomes hot (when profile count exceeds a threshold).

`void deli_enum_fragment(` `  callback);`	Apply a client-level callback function to each fragment in the cache. Fragment enumeration is useful, for example, to enforce specific checks or instrumentation code on all fragments.

`cache_object_id`
`deli_setup_code_cache(`
`  cache_obj_description,`
`  flags, user_data);`
	Create a code cache object within DELI with given attributes (size, priority, policies) and properly links it in the DELI code cache stack.

`void`
`deli_code_cache_flush(`
`  cache_object_id,`
`  flags, timeout);`
	Initiate a DELI code cache flush on the given code cache, with a given `timeout`.

`int deli_gc(`
`  cache_object_id,`
`  flags, timeout);`
	Initiate an on-demand garbage collection step on a given code cache, with a given `timeout`

`void deli_start();`	Start DELI "transparent" mode, where DELI takes control of the running program
`void deli_stop();`	Stop DELI "transparent" mode

2.2   Binary Level Translation (BLT)

The BLT layer is the core component of the DELI that implements the API. It contains and manages a set of code caches and also provides the basic infrastructure for code transformations. The key to amortize the DELI overhead caused is to ensure that application code runs inside the code caches most of the time. The DELI's primary means for delivering performance are *fragment linking* and *dynamic optimization*.

Linking Fragments

Linking avoids unnecessary code cache exits by directly interconnecting the core fragments, and it requires matching the fragments' exit and entry tags. Fragment tags are unique identifiers created by the client when emitting code through the API. DELI also marks each fragment exit with a corresponding exit tag. Upon emission, the DELI inspects each fragment's exit tag to directly interconnect it to a corresponding entry. If no entry exists, DELI redirects the fragment exit to a special *trampoline*, which causes execution to exit the code cache and to return to the client with the missing exit tag.

The above strategy takes care of creating a fragment's outgoing links. To establish incoming links, the DELI uses a deferred strategy. Initially, a fragment is entered into the code cache without creating direct incoming connections. At each code cache exit a test is made to determine whether a fragment for the exiting target tag has been materialized in the meanwhile. If so, a direct link is established.

The Transformation Infrastructure

An important feature of DELI's BLT layer is the capability to dynamically optimize the emitted code. The BLT layer provides a complete dynamic optimization infrastructure to activate runtime code optimization, either explicitly through the API, or autonomously by setting the appropriate optimization policy.

The core of DELI's transformation infrastructure is the DELI *Intermediate Representation* (DELIR). DELIR is a low-level intermediate representation that maintains a close mapping to the underlying machine representation while providing sufficient abstraction for permitting code motion and code relocation. DELIR serves two purposes: to internally enable the transformation of fragment code, and to facilitate the construction of code fragments in the client. For the latter, DELIR is exported to the client through an extension of the DELI API. In addition to emitting a fragment in machine code representation, the client can construct a DELIR fragment and pass it to DELI for code emission. Table 2 shows a sample of the DELIR functionalities.

By instructing the DELI through the API, we can apply optimizations to a fragment either the first time the fragment is emitted, or when it becomes "hot" in the code cache. DELI considers a fragment "hot" when it exceeds an execution threshold that clients set through the API. When a fragment exceeds the threshold, DELI decodes the fragment to produce a DELIR fragment, which is then passed to the internal lightweight runtime optimizer and scheduler. Depending on the optimization level, the runtime optimizer performs a forward and a backward optimization pass, and. it collects data flow information *on the fly* as the pass proceeds. Our prototype (see section 4.1) targets the ST210 embedded VLIW architecture, so the current set of optimizations is targeted towards increasing ILP: *copy and constant propagation, dead code elimination* and *strength reduction*.

Table 2. The DELIR API

DELIR API Function	Description

`fragment* de-`
`lir_create_fragment(`
`    int id,`
`    unsigned flags);`
	Create a DELIR fragment, where `id` serves as a fragment identifier and the `flags` are used to specify various fragment properties. The function returns a handle to the created fragment.

`void delir_append_inst(`
`    fragment *frag_handle,`
`    inst *inst_handle);`
	Append an instruction (specified by the handle `inst_hande`) to the DELIR fragment specified by the handle `frag_handle`.

`inst* delir_make_opcode(`
`    int opcode,`
`    unsigned *arglist,`
`    unsigned flags);`
	Create a DELIR instruction with the specified `opcode`, the arguments that are passed in the `arglist` and the specified `flags`. The function returns a handle to the created instruction.

Our current prototype contains two lightweight scheduling algorithms. The **instruction scheduler** is a cycle-by-cycle scheduler with a fixed size look-ahead window, similarly to the way in which superscalar hardware operates. The **operation scheduler** traverses the code one operation at a time in an attempt to schedule each instruction in the earliest cycle, similar to the scheduling in the Daisy system [7].

2.3   Hardware Abstraction Module (HAM)

DELI clients may require low-level control of hardware events (such as exceptions) to do their job efficiently. In addition, we can make DELI itself more portable and resilient to changes in the underlying hardware platform if we adopt some form of abstraction from a specific platform. Modern O/Ss use a similar functionality, where a low level layer deals with the platform dependent ways of coping with hardware related features, such as enabling/disabling/dispatching interrupts, flushing the caches, and managing the TLBs. In the context of DELI (especially when it is below the OS), we need a similar piece of functionality, which needs to be separated from the equivalent OS layer. If we can extend or change the OS, then both the DELI and the OS could share the same layer.

From the point of view of DELI clients, it is useful to open up parts of this interface. For example, an emulator needs to efficiently emulate the virtual memory (VM) system of the original CPU, by mapping it onto the VM of the target system. To do this, the client needs access to the details of the hardware TLBs, to maintain a data structure (similar to a page table) for the emulated system, and to match it with the page table information of the native system. Only then it can service the TLB-related events. This method has many disadvantages: the hardware TLB may change from one implementation to another, even within the same CPU family; accessing the TLB though the OS interface that maps pages may not be expressive enough (for example, for security reasons); even when we can do this, it requires control over the OS to make the two VM systems properly overlap.

An alternative is to provide a 'virtualized view' of the hardware for both the OS and the DELI clients so that they can share the same representation, and that is what th HAM layer captures.

The HAM interface is quite extensive and a complete description is beyond the scope of this paper. The DELI's BLT uses part of HAM to manage hardware related needs, and, at the same time, HAM relies on the DELI API for some of his advanced functionality. For example, HAM uses the API for the emission of temporary fragments to materialize and execute transient trampolines, when clients require a specific exception behavior.

3   Using DELI as a Client

The DELI provides two types of services to client programs: an easy development of efficient emulators of different ISAs and OSs; and a control point to observe and potentially manipulate every single instruction of the target program. We find it useful to break down the many applications that benefit from DELI into three basic classes.

1. **Code manipulation**: clients that modify natively compiled programs at run-time. Examples include software patching, code decompression and decryption.
2. **Observation and control**: clients that observe the behavior of natively compiled programs at run-time and possibly enforce policies. Examples include sandboxing, dynamic virus detection, reporting program behavior, and profiling.
3. **Emulation**: clients that run an application compiled for a different virtual machine, a different ISA, or a different hardware configuration. Examples include ISA interpretation or emulation of virtual machine environments, such as Java or .NET.

Since code always runs out of the cache and nowhere else, these clients are guaranteed to be the last to see the code. DELI is a new concept, so not many applications have been written for it. In the rest of this section, we cover a few examples of each category, to show some of the DELI's capabilities.

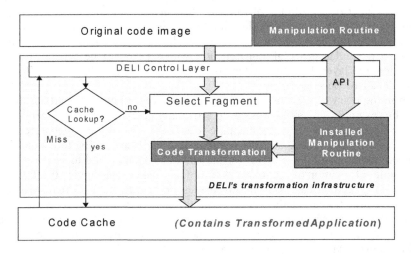

Fig. 2. Using DELI to dynamically manipulate code. The diagram expands the "DELI transformation infrastructure" component of Fig. 1 and shows how to install a manipulation routine.

3.1   Code Manipulation

Since DELI is the last piece of software that observes an instruction right before it runs, it can replace the observed instruction with another instruction sequence. All manipulation clients rely on DELI being a control point in the execution; DELI caches and optimizes the adjusted code, so it manages to keep the overhead to a minimum. Fig. 2 shows the common scheme for code transformations: clients provide a *manipulation routine* through the `deli_install_callback()` API call that DELI dynamically applies during fragment formation. The routine transforms the code that is then emitted to the DELI code cache for efficient execution or re-optimization.

In the following, we present two manipulation examples. In the first one—dynamically patching code—DELI replaces individual "broken" instructions with code that emulates them. In our second example—dynamic code decompression or decryption—every single instruction is adjusted at run-time.

- **Dynamically patching code.** Solving problems of faulty or missing hardware usually implies either replacing the faulty hardware, or replacing the software so that it never relies on the missing features. DELI gives us the opportunity to patch software dynamically and temporarily, while keeping the software untouched. DELI can detect which instructions are affected by the missing hardware functionality, and dynamically replace them with code that does not require it. The *manipulation routine* of Fig. 2 for this transformation maintains a patch table whose entries include an identifier of the missing hardware and a workaround code sequence.

- **Code decompression or decryption.** *Code compression* is a commonly used technique to improve the efficiency of program storage. DELI can be used to decompress fragments as they get executed, and still achieve good performance through caching. Referring to Fig. 2, the *manipulation routine* implements the decompression algorithm, and the transformed code is really the original program code before compression. In this way, the DELI only decompresses and caches smaller portions of the application, thereby reducing overhead and amount of dynamic decompression, and requiring less system memory. The same scheme can be used to *decrypt* code instead of decompressing it.

3.2   Program Observation and Control

The fine-grain control that DELI provides is also useful when we need to report program behavior, or enforce certain policies. Using a scheme similar to what we described in section 3.1, a client can install an *observation routine* through the API, cause DELI to examine the code at run time, and only emit it to the cache if it respects the policy to be enforced. This does not require transformations (beyond instrumentation), and the overhead is minimal.

For example, execution "sandboxes" are environments that support differentiated services for the different applications that share a computer system, and impose restrictions on resource usage. Resource restrictions can be qualitative (e.g., restricting application to only certain memory areas), and quantitative (e.g., limiting CPU usage). With DELI, we can install an observation routine that examines each code fragment before it is emitted into the code cache. That routine verifies the legality of the instructions, and instruments the code fragment to self-check other instructions that cannot be statically verified. Once the code is modified and cached, it self-checks its legality during execution without the need to interrupt the application. With profiling instrumentation, clients can also monitor and enforce quantitative policies.

4   Case Study: Emulating PocketPC

With DELI in place, we can imagine building the software infrastructure (and possibly efficient hardware) to implement a "universal core" for embedded applications. This system could pair emulation of an existing ISA with natively compiled high performance kernels.

This section presents an application of the DELI to the world of *mobile multimedia* devices. Mobile communication devices allow deployment of rich web and media enabled applications, thus demanding a significant increase in system complexity and performance requirements. Cost constraints of consumer-class devices have stifled architectural improvements for embedded system processors, in the otherwise very diversified embedded computing market. Therefore, the delivery of the necessary computational power often relies upon hardware solutions and multimedia accelerators. Embedded operating systems are consolidating to only a few, which are only going to support a restricted number of different ISAs. In this context, we can see *emulation* as a potential solution to some of these barriers to innovation, opening the way to new architectural features.

We can identify three main scenarios where efficient emulation of an embedded ISA would be beneficial.

- **Emulated platform with native media engines.** Emulation enables developer to leverage legacy applications and GUIs (such as *PocketPC*), while combining them with high-performance media engines natively compiled to a more powerful processor. This model requires an *emulated-to-native* interface like the one DELI provides.

- **Native platform with emulated plug-ins.** Even for entirely new platforms (such as embedded Linux devices), there may still be the need to support legacy applications, in the form of *plug-ins* (e.g., a media viewer). Similar considerations apply to the efficient execution for Java (or .NET) environments.

- **Incremental migration**. For families of binary incompatible processors (such as many VLIW embedded offerings), the problem of legacy code compatibility across different members of the same family could be efficiently tackled by the use of a lightweight dynamic translator. The DELI provides the building blocks that can be used to build such hybrid systems, so that we can guarantee a smooth migration between successive generations of processors.

All these scenarios require mixing emulated and native code at different levels; DELI efficiently tackles all of them, by exposing the desired level of granularity that best meets application needs at the programmer's level.

4.1   The DELIverX Prototype

DELIverX is a prototype emulation system that we built to help us better understand the details of the DELI. DELIverX is defined around a *Hitachi SH3* interpreted emulator, coupled with a just-in-time translator for the ST210 embedded VLIW core, which we use as a native target. DELIverX implements a platform emulator (i.e., ISA + system) that can be used as a target for a Microsoft WinCE operating system compiled for the SH processor. The SH-3 [2] is a simple load-store RISC processor with a 5-stage pipeline that executes most basic instructions in one clock cycle (although some contention between certain stages exists, such as instruction fetch and data memory accesses). The SH3 implements a 16-bit instruction set but fetches two instructions in a single access (subject to some alignment limitations). The target processor is the ST210 four-wide embedded VLIW engine (a member of the *Lx* family), jointly developed by Hewlett-Packard and STMicroelectronics [9,10].

DELIverX include a 'traditional' interpreted emulator for an SH3 ISA (the *"SH Emulator"* block), complemented by enough system components (timers, serial ports, display, etc.) to be able to support a (simple) configuration of the WinCE kernel. The other main component of the emulation system is the SH to VLIW Just-In-Time compiler, which translates SH instructions into sequences of native VLIW instructions.

We designed the JIT to be transparent to the SH3 emulator, so that we can turn it on or off. A common SH machine description feeds both the SH emulator and the JIT. The emulator invokes the JIT at every instruction fetch so that it can start, grow or stop translations for a new region of code, or release control to an already existing translation in the DELI code cache. At system bootstrap, the execution of emulated SH instructions takes place in the interpreted emulator. At the same time, the JIT produces new code fragments of translations and hands them to the DELI, occasionally releasing control to the few already translated fragments. After the initial warm-up phase, the DELI code cache is primed with the working set and most of the emulation time of the SH instructions is spent in the cache.

The JIT generates code for a run-time environment around which we built the SH virtual machine. In this world, the most difficult task is to efficiently handle a faithful emulation of the Virtual Memory (VM) system mapped onto the native VM. In general, the larger the distance between the VM parameters of the two systems, the greater the difficulties associated with it. In this particular case, we designed the Memory Management Unit (MMU) of the VLIW with a large degree of flexibility, exactly with the goal of simplifying the emulation task.

4.2   Performance Analysis

In this section, we report some experimental results of the DELIverX system. Table 4 lists the most significant parameters of the native and emulated systems.

For our experiments we use a cycle-accurate instruction set simulator (validated vs. the hardware), augmented with virtual memory support (the ST210 does not have an MMU), and also modeling the memory systems. For the SH3, we measure wall-clock time average of multiple runs on an *HP Jornada 548* palmtop with *PocketPC*.

Note that the ST210's performance is significantly higher than the SH3. While a comparison of the two might seem unfair, supporting legacy code is a burden that is likely to slow down the processor evolution curve. Preserve binary compatibility in hardware implies superscalar microarchitecture, with severe consequences on complexity, cost and power efficiency.

Table 3. Parameters of the emulated and native systems

	Emulated Processor	**Native Processor**
CPU	Hitachi SuperH SH3, 133 MHz	ST210 VLIW, 4 issue, 250MHz
L1 Cache	8 Kbytes unified L1 instruction and data cache	32KB direct mapped L1 I cache, and 32 KB 4-way set-associative L1 D cache
L2 Cache	None	None
MMU	4 entries instruction TLB fully associative; 32 entries, 4-way set associative unified (L2) TLB	32 entries 2-way set associative instruction TLB; 128 entries, 16-way set associative unified (L2) TLB
Memory	32 MB of DRAM	32 MB of DRAM

The benchmark suite is composed of a combination of micro-kernels and real applications from the *MiBench* suite [12], plus a few of the SPEC-2000 programs. We include audio (*adpcm, lame, mad*), and imaging (*jpeg*) algorithms to approximate a workload of a mobile computing appliance. DELIverX emulates exactly the Jornada system, including the PocketPC environment. To calibrate the reader on the difference between the two processors, the ST210 is on average about 7.0 times faster than the SH3 when running the benchmark suite in isolation (without OS overhead).

In Fig. 3 we show the results of the DELIverX system running on the VLIW processor that emulates the SH3. As we can see, we often achieve near-native performance (the average is 99%), and in some cases, we even exceed it (SHA emulated is 83% faster than the SH3). The chart also shows the substantial benefits of the DELI's dynamic code optimizer (on average, a 61% improvement over non-optimized code).

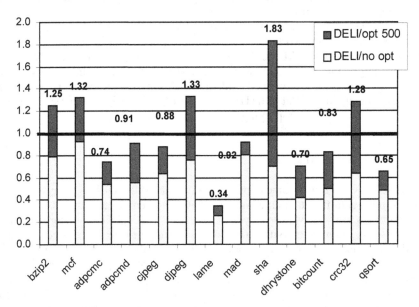

Fig. 3. Performance of the DELIverX system. The *y*-axis shows relative speedup (>1.0) or slowdown (<1.0) factors vs. SH3 (y=1.0). The bars represent performance of unoptimized and optimized emulation on the ST210 The average is 0.62 (unoptimized) and 0.99 (optimized)

Mixing Native and Emulated Code

The last set of evaluations that we present deals with the mixing of native and emulated code. We consider the case where we introduce a natively compiled function within a fully emulated platform. In this example, we use DELIverX running the PocketPC environment to invoke a cryptography kernel that executes the Secure Hashing Algorithm (SHA). SHA is a good example of code that benefits from instruction-level parallelism, and—as such—is an ideal target for a VLIW engine. In Fig. 4 we can see that by mixing native and emulated code we can get to about 50% of the speed of a native-only VLIW execution, but still more than five times faster than running the wcode on the SH3.

This example illustrates one of the major benefits of using DELI: in a practical environment it enables developers to scale performance by selectively porting the compute-intensive kernels of applications, without giving up the benefits of a legacy operating system and GUI. In a rich-media world, performance is likely to be dominated by kernels (like SHA) that we can easily encapsulate to get the benefits of a VLIW engine. In this environment, the effect of a modest slowdown for GUI emulation is likely to disappear in light of the performance improvements in the computational kernels.

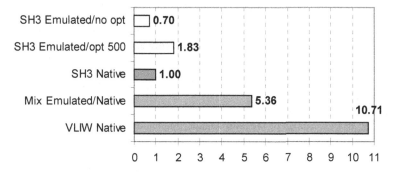

Fig. 4. Mixing native and emulated code in cryptography (SHA running for 4.18s). The x-axis represents speedup factors vs. the base case of a native SH3 execution (1.0). The "VLIW native" performance comes from running the code in isolation (without OS); all others include the overhead of running the PocketPC environment to access data and invoke the program. The "Mix" case runs emulated PocketPC, with the SHA routine compiled natively for the ST210.

5   Summary and Conclusions

The DELI is a new run-time control point that lets its clients manipulate unmodified binaries in novel ways. The DELI unifies many techniques that make persistent changes at run time, but is not itself an emulator. Rather, it is a way of giving clients (including emulators) access to a caching and linking mechanism that operates at the lowest software level of the system.

This paper describes the DELI, how it works, and what its interface looks like. It presents some of the clients that DELI supports, including code manipulation, observation and emulation. The emulation prototype often achieves native performance, and the dynamic code optimizer adds substantial benefits (a 61% improvement over non-optimized code). Finally, we show that we can transparently mix native and emulated code within the DELI, yielding tremendous performance increases.

The DELI is a new facility, and we know of no other such system that supports an interface in this way. We have done a significant amount of development on it, have learned a lot, have convinced ourselves that it has many practical applications, and have been able to demonstrate some of its vast power. That said, we believe have only scratched the surface of what can be done with it. At HP Labs Cambridge, we are continuing to build and refine the DELI infrastructure for different platforms and clients, and we are continuing to understand new ways in which we can use it.

References

1. V. Bala, E. Duesterwald, S. Banerjia. Dynamo: a transparent dynamic optimization system. In SIGPLAN Conf. on Programming Language Design and Implementation, pp1-12, 2000.
2. T.Baji, N. Kawashimo, I. Kawasaki, and K. Noguchi. SuperH and SuperH-DSP Microprocessors for the Mobile Computing Age. Hitachi Review, Volume 46 No 1. Feb 1997.
3. W. Chen, S. Lerner, R. Chaiken, and D. Gillies. Mojo: A dynamic optimization system. In Proc. of the 3rd Workshop on Feedback-Directed and Dynamic Optimization, Dec. 2000.
4. R.F. Cmelik and D. Keppel. Shade: a fast instruction set simulator for execution profiling. Tech. Report UWCSE-93-06-06, Dept. Comp.Science and Eng., Univ. Washington. 1993
5. D. Deaver, R. Gorton, and N. Rubin. Wiggins/Redstone: An on-line program specializer. In Hot Chips 11, Palo Alto, CA, Aug. 1999.
6. D. Ditzel. Transmeta's Crusoe: Cool chips for mobile computing. In Hot Chips 12: Stanford University. Aug. 2000.
7. K. Ebcioglu and E. Altman. DAISY: Dynamic compilation for 100% architectural compatibility. In Proceedings of the 24th Annual International Symposium on Computer Architecture. Pages 26-37, 1997.
8. K. Ebcioglu, E.R. Altman, E. Hokenek. A JAVA ILP Machine Based on Fast Dynamic Compilation. IEEE MASCOTS International Workshop on Security and Efficiency Aspects of Java. Eilat, Israel, January 9-10, 1997.
9. P. Faraboschi, G. Brown., J. Fisher., G. Desoli, F. Homewood. Lx: A Technology Platform for Customizable VLIW Embedded Processing. *Proc. 27ᵗʰ International Symposium on Computer Architecture (ISCA27)*. Vancouver, June 2000
10. P. Faraboschi, F. Homewood, ST200: A VLIW Architecture for Media-Oriented Applications, *Microprocessor Forum 2000*, October 9-13 2000, San Jose, CA
11. J.A. Fisher. Walk-time techniques: Catalyst for architectural change. Computer, 30(9):40-42, September 1997.
12. M.R. Guthaus, J.S. Ringenberg, D. Ernst, T.M. Austin, T. Mudge and R.B. Brown. MiBench: A Free, Commercially Representative Embedded Benchmark Suite. IEEE 4th Annual Workshop on Workload Characterization, December 2, 2001, Austin, TX
13. Klaiber. The Technology Behind Crusoe Processors. © 2000 Transmeta Corporation. Available as: http://www.transmeta.com/pdf/white_papers/paper_aklaiber_19jan00.pdf.
14. T. Lindholm, Frank Yellin. The Java Virtual Machine Specification, Second Edition.
15. Microsoft Corp. .NET specifications. Available at http://www.microsoft.com/net/
16. Robinson. Why Dynamic Translation? © 2x001 Transitive Technologies. Available as: http://www.transitives.com/downloads/Why Dynamic Translation1.pdf.
17. Srivastava H. Edwards, H. Vo. Vulcan: Binary translation in a distributed environment. Technical Report MSR-TR-2001-50, Microsoft Research, 2001.

Design Tools
for Application Specific Embedded Processors

Wei Qin[1], Subramanian Rajagopalan[1], Manish Vachharajani[1],
Hangsheng Wang[1], Xinping Zhu[1], David August[1], Kurt Keutzer[2],
Sharad Malik[1], and Li-Shiuan Peh[1]

[1] Princeton University, Princeton NJ 08544, USA
[2] UC Berkeley, Berkeley, CA 94720, USA

Abstract. A variety of factors make it increasingly difficult and expensive to design and manufacture traditional Application Specific Integrated Circuits (ASICs). Consequently, programmable alternatives are more attractive than ever. The flexibility provided by programmability comes with a performance and power overhead. This can be significantly mitigated by using application specific platforms, also referred to as Application Specific Embedded Processors, or Application Specific Instruction Set Processors (ASIPs).
ASIPs and the embedded software applications running on them, require specialized design tools - both during architectural evaluation to provide feedback on the suitability of the architecture for the application; as well as during system implementation to ensure efficient mapping and validation of design constraints. These functions result in requirements different from those of traditional software development environments. The first requirement is retargetability, especially during the early architectural evaluation stage where a rapid examination of design alternatives is essential. The second requirement is for additional metrics such as power consumption, real-time constraints and code size.
This paper describes a set of design tools and associated methodology designed to meet the challenges posed by architectural evaluation and software synthesis. This work is part of the MESCAL (Modern Embedded Systems, Compilers, Architectures, and Languages) project[1].

1 Introduction

Designing an ASIC in today's deep sub-micron geometries is harder than ever, and the problems continue to worsen with shrinking geometries. Design tools are finding it difficult to handle the complexity and electrical design challenges posed by each new technology generation. The net consequence is increasingly lowered design productivity despite increasingly expensive design tools. ASIC manufacturing costs are also rising - multi-million dollar mask sets are projected for sub-100nm designs. These high non-recurring design and manufacturing costs

---

[1] MESCAL is part of the Gigascale Silicon Research Center (GSRC), funded by DARPA and MARCO.

A. Sangiovanni-Vincentelli and J. Sifakis (Eds.): EMSOFT 2002, LNCS 2491, pp. 319–333, 2002.

imply either larger break even volumes at fixed per-unit costs, or prohibitive per-unit costs at fixed volumes. An alternative implementation style to ASICs that is rapidly emerging is the use of programmable solutions - alternatively referred to as programmable platforms, Application Specific Embedded Processors, or Application Specific Instruction Set Processors (ASIPs). For the hardware developer the programmability of these devices enables a larger volume, as multiple related applications, as well as different generations of an application can be mapped onto the same ASIP. For the application developer, a programmable solution provides a much lower risk as well as a predictable and shorter time-to-market solution - writing and debugging software is cheaper than designing, debugging and manufacturing working hardware. However, for the class of applications of interest here, the power/delay overhead of general purpose programmable solutions is unacceptable. ASIPs attempt to match application characteristics with hardware support to minimize the power and performance overhead of programmable solutions to the point where they are an attractive alternative to ASICs. There are a number of application domains where this class of highly specialized embedded processors is catching on as a replacement for ASICs - notably network and communication processing. In fact, there are signs of a revolution afoot, with an increasing trend of engineers from hardware application groups going off and rapidly deploying the application in software on available domain specialized processors [1].

Historically, designers adopting manageable alternatives have heralded a significant change in design methodology, typically much before the change in design methodology has stabilized and acceptable tool flows become widely available. The move from schematic capture to logic synthesis and simulation in the mid-80s was led by designers unwilling to deal with increasing complexity in a non-scalable methodology. Home-grown rudimentary simulation and synthesis tools were enough to deliver enough increased productivity for them to abandon the old tools and also some design optimality. It did not take mature stable tools for them to make the change - those tools followed to convert the trend to accepted design practice on a larger scale. We believe that we are at a similar watershed in design implementation practice today. The individual ASIC designers that today are abandoning hardware design for the productivity benefit of software solutions on an ASIP, even at some loss of design quality (measured in area, delay, power), portend the acceptable design practice of tomorrow. This paper describes tools that will get us rapidly to that tomorrow by targeting the development and deployment of these ASIPs.

This paper is organized to highlight key components of the MESCAL Design Environment shown in Figure 1. First, in Section 2, we describe the Liberty Simulation Environment (LSE), a simulator construction infrastructure used for all system simulation. In addition to a simulator construction engine, LSE provides a library for processing elements (PEs) and specialized hardware. To model on-chip communication architectures (OCAs), Section 3 presents a modeling methodology that distinguishes functional and architectural views. Section 4 describes the methodologies used to model the power consumed by both PEs and OCAs.

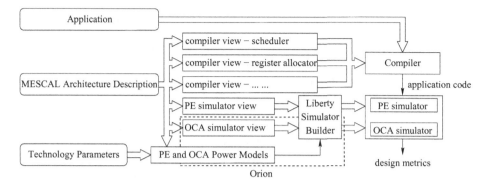

Fig. 1. The MESCAL Design Environment

Section 5 discusses the use of these methodologies in building Orion, a power-performance simulator for networks including OCAs. The MESCAL Architectural Description, described in Section 6, serves as the common specification used to generate appropriate views for use in modeling and compilation. The compiler is responsible for efficient mapping of applications onto these highly specialized architectures. Section 7 describes the philosophy and nature of algorithms of this compiler. We conclude with some final thoughts in Section 8.

2   The Liberty Simulation Environment

Traditionally, architects evaluate microarchitectures by running applications on a simulator written in a sequential programming language such as C or C++. Unfortunately, this and other simulator construction methods are not well suited for design-space exploration for ASIPs. To approach ASIC performance, ASIPs often contain elements that operate independently of the main execution pipeline, thus the timing is difficult to model in conventional sequential simulators. Furthermore, traditional techniques result in that simulators offer little to assure the architect of the accuracy of the simulation and do little to facilitate an understanding of the model from the simulator description. To make matters worse, many ASIPs contain multiple processing elements, that also have complex timing and memory interactions that are also difficult to model and lead to simulation inaccuracies [2].

These difficulties arise because the architect must map the microarchitecture, which is inherently structural and concurrent, to a sequential programming language. Correctly modeling small modifications to the structure of the microarchitecture can require large changes to the sequential simulator code, especially if the changes affect the relative timing of loosely coupled concurrently executing hardware elements. To avoid the laborious and error prone task of re-mapping for every candidate microarchitecture, designers may be tempted to make small changes to the simulator that approximate the changes in the microarchitecture. Unfortunately, these small changes in the simulator will often correspond to large, unanticipated, changes in the microarchitecture leading to an inaccurate evaluation of the change.

The Liberty Simulation Environment [3,4] (LSE) is a deliberate effort to address the mapping problem. LSE is a tool that can automatically map a concurrent and structural microarchitecture specification to an efficient simulator. Since LSE automatically maps microarchitectural specifications to a sequential program, an LSE microarchitecture specification resembles the hardware it models, thus only small changes in the specification are necessary to model small changes in a microarchitecture. Furthermore, LSE has been designed to allow modeling of specialized hardware common in ASIPs, but less frequently used in general purpose processors. The benefits of LSE allow architects to devote their full effort to exploring microarchitectures, instead of having them commit time, energy, and patience to manage an inherently complex and opaque sequential simulator.

In LSE, a user specifies the microarchitecture by describing the instantiation of architectural components, called *modules*, and their port to port interconnections. Each module roughly corresponds to a hardware block and has concurrent execution semantics, like actual hardware blocks, making specification easier and more accurate. The LSE specification allows a user to customize and extend modules using a *module extension* mechanism. Users can utilize pre-existing modules from the LSE library or create their own.

The ASIP design process is often incremental. Key parts of the system are initially modeled, and additional parts and details of the system are added as the application domain and design goals require. Furthermore, describing the complete microarchitecture for simulation is often a daunting task and development of novel microarchitectures for an application domain often involves simulating pieces of a microarchitecture without paying attention to unimportant details of the machine. LSE provides for this type of partial specification by assigning default semantics to unconnected ports; modules are required to behave in reasonable fashion if some ports are left unconnected. In this way, complete architecture descriptions can be developed incrementally, one piece at a time.

For rapid specification of ASIP design variants for architectural exploration, LSE provides a rich parameter system that allows the user to specify not only simple parameters such as sizes of hardware arrays, but also parameters that are algorithms. As a result, the user can override or augment the functionality of a module to incorporate new computation and form new hardware blocks from pre-existing ones. LSE also has special algorithmic parameters called *control points*. At each module port there is a control point in which the user may specify how data flows through the datapath, how signals are arbitrated, and how hardware blocks are activated. Since it would be quite tedious to have to write a control specification for each port on each module, or specify every parameter value, parameters have default values with reasonable defaults defined by the module author. Typically, for control points, this default control corresponds to back pressure control in a pipeline. Since computation in a microprocessor component often requires state from other portions of the machine, algorithmic parameters may reference another module's explicitly exported state to perform their computation.

During different parts of the design cycle, designers require different information from the simulator. Furthermore, different members of the design team will want different information. Hardware designers may be interested in monitoring hardware bottlenecks, and software developers may be interested in collecting profile data for the compiler. As a result, LSE has *data collectors* and *events* to facilitate data collection that is orthogonal to the simulator specification. Each time something "interesting" occurs in a module, the module will emit an event. The event notification will be tagged with the module that produced it, the time it was produced, and any associated data that the module wishes to emit. Data collectors, which are specified independently of the described architecture, get notified when events occur and aggregate the data contained in the event. Since certain collectors may be interested in only certain events, a mechanism is provided for collectors to filter the events they receive. These events and data collectors are similar to *aspects* in aspect-oriented programming [5].

Other systems can be used to specify ASIP designs, however, they are all less then ideal. HDLs, for example, typically require the user to specify every last detail of a complete machine. By employing default semantics, LSE allows the user to produce a working simulator from a partial machine description. LSE also allows for module communication through abstract data types, so that the user need not manage wires and bus widths and data encoding manually. Other concurrent languages, such as SystemC [6], partially address shortcomings of sequential languages and HDLs, but the user must still resolve, by hand, all issues related to partial specification and interoperability of the specified components.

3   On-Chip Communication Architecture Modeling

3.1   Motivation

The distributed computation architecture of the ASIPs being considered here can be generally decomposed into two inter-related parts: The Processing Elements (PEs) and the On-Chip Communication Architecture (OCA). The PEs are responsible for the computation of the desired functions and the OCA provides the communication mechanisms. Just as the computational capabilities of the PEs must provide a match for the computational requirements of the application domain, the communication capabilities of the OCA must be well matched to the communication requirements of the concurrent computation. This match significantly impacts the timing as well as power characteristics of the implementation.

Technology advances have provided designers greater freedom in selecting from different types of communication schemes. The traditional way of interconnecting on-chip modules is via on-chip buses, such as the IBM CoreConnect Bus Architecture [7] and the ARM AMBA bus system [8]. An emerging option for integrating a large number of processors is to use on-chip networks [9,10,11]. A design environment that can potentially select any one of these OCAs must be able to model and support these choices with their variants. This decision process must be guided through a design space exploration framework where these different OCA (and PE) design choices can be tried, simulated and evaluated within an execution-driven virtual prototyping environment in a "plug and play" fashion.

3.2 Methodology

The discipline of computer architecture clearly distinguishes between the Instruction Set Architecture (ISA), which is the programming/functional view of the processor, and the micro-architecture, which comprises implementation details such as the number of pipeline stages, size and organization of cache memories, the number and type of function units (FUs) etc. OCAs can also be viewed in the same fashion. On the functional side, there exist different ways of sending and receiving data from the OCA, e.g. read/write data through shared memory, send/receive data through a message-passing network. On the implementation side, the OCA contains various details such as input/output controllers, buffers, arbiters, crossbars, etc. While the elements of ISAs and a micro-architectures for PEs are well-understood and defined - even across a broad range of PEs, this is not the case for OCAs. This work attempts to fill this gap.

As our first step, we define the following atomic constructs as the functional primitives of the OCA in the shared memory and message passing models (each PE is denoted by its address $i \in N$):

OCA read (x, u) moves data x in the shared memory into local variable u
OCA write (y, v) writes value of local variable y into shared variable v
OCA send (x, i) sends the value of x to PE i asynchronously
OCA receive (y, j) receives the value of x from PE j synchronously

This generic OCA "ISA" provides a basis for the communication primitives needed. For a specific OCA, the actual functional primitives may vary, but they are likely to be variants of the above (e.g. blocking reads and writes).

The above separation of the functional primitives and their actual implementation is useful in both system simulation and compilation. Functional simulation needs to understand only the semantics of the primitives and thus can be fast. Detailed timing simulation will naturally require the micro-architectural implementation models. Compilation can use these primitives, with additional latency information provided for them, for the distributed mapping of the application. They can also be mapped to lower level operations using library routine calls.

On the structural side, after detailed object-oriented analysis (OOA) [12], we have derived a set of abstract object classes which are sufficient to compose a wide range of OCAs. As shown in Figure 2, a relatively small set of object classes is sufficient here. The key observation here is that the OCA micro-architectural primitives belong to one of the following small set: links, buffers, resource schedulers, and interfaces. Within each element of this set, there are variations which over time get added to the class hierarchy.

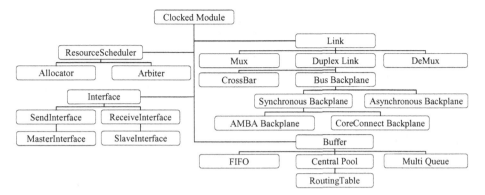

Fig. 2. Class Inheritance Hierarchy of OCAs

3.3 Use of Methodology

We have used this methodology to model OCAs as part of Orion in LSE (see Section 5), as well as Ptolemy II [13], an object-oriented, heterogeneous design and modeling framework. Both environments support construction of executable models in a modular fashion. For a specific OCA model, the designer needs to examine and implement individual building blocks by either instantiating or extending available modules in the class hierarchy. Thus, OCA design is simplified as a process of integration of these "plug and play" modules. Within these two environments, we implemented cycle-accurate models of two on-chip bus systems, AMBA [8] and CoreConnect [7], and an on-chip packet-switching network, the RAW [11] network [14]. Our experience finds that adopting the reusable hierarchical class diagram greatly reduces development time.

4   Power Modeling

As highlighted in Section 1, power has become a design metric that is as important, if not more important than timing. Thus, power modeling and simulation is an essential part of the design environment. In this section, we detail how power models are derived for the different hardware modules of both PEs and OCAs.

To facilitate retargetable simulation and design space exploration, several requirements are imposed on power models: flexibility, re-usability, and fidelity. These requirements are met by the following modeling hierarchy that enables easy model composition.

4.1   Model Hierarchy

The model hierarchy consists of 4 layers: atomic layer, structure layer, prototype layer and physical layer, from bottom to top as illustrated in Figure 3. Each layer plays a different role and layers are relatively independent of each other so that they can be modified without affecting other layers. The layers cooperate in computing the switching energy $E = \frac{1}{2}\alpha C V_{dd}^2$.

- The prototype and physical layers collect information needed by the lower layers and assemble results reported by lower layers.
- The structure layer computes switching activity factor α, and the atomic layer computes switching capacitance C.

Atomic Layer. This is the lowest layer. An atomic component consists of several capacitance elements which always switch simultaneously. For example, if gate A drives one input of gate B, then the output capacitance of gate A, the connection wire capacitance, and the input capacitance of gate B are in the same atomic component.

$$E_{atomic} = \frac{1}{2}V_{dd}^2 C_{atomic} \tag{1}$$

Structure Layer. This layer corresponds to circuit building blocks that perform some basic functions, e.g. decoder, comparator, etc. One structure layer component consists of several atomic components.

$$E_{structure} = \sum_i (\alpha_i E_{atomic}^i) \tag{2}$$

where α_i is the switching activity factor of the ith atomic component.

Prototype Layer. This layer models "virtual" function units, i.e. abstract function units with complete structure, but no specified functionality. A prototype model is a collection of structure models, with parameter definitions to specify structure model types, properties and connections. For example, the most widely used prototype model is the uniform array model, which essentially models generic SRAM array. The model has a complete list of structure components and parameters specifying whether these components are present and their model types.

$$E_{prototype} = \sum_i E_{structure}^i (input_i, state_i) \tag{3}$$

where $input_i$ and $state_i$ are information needed by structure models to compute switching activities.

Physical Layer. This layer models real function units. A physical layer model is just a prototype model with concrete parameters specifying functionality of the function unit. For example, the aforementioned uniform array model can model a data cache if configured with tag array, tag comparators and certain hit/miss policies, or a shared central buffer [15] if configured without tag array but with pipelined banks.

$$E_{physical} = E_{prototype} \tag{4}$$

Table 1. Parameter mapping between prototype layer and physical layer models

Prototype layer parameters of uniform array model	Physical layer parameters of	
	data cache	shared central buffer
rows	number of sets	number of chunks
cols	cache line size	pipeline depth $\times$ flit width
number of comparators	associativity	0
data width	integer width	flit width
...	...	...

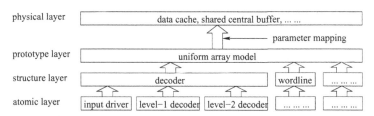

Fig. 3. Model hierarchy of data cache and central buffer power models

Advantages of Model Hierarchy.

1. Separation of micro-architecture dependency and technology dependency: Only atomic layer power models depend on fabrication technologies, while other layers are technology independent. Technology dependency is resolved by maintaining a minimal set of low level capacitance constants and scaling them according to technologies.
2. Fine-grained modeling granularity: This enables the tracking of dynamic switching activity at a level low enough to reflect physical reality. This scheme can achieve higher accuracy than using average switching activity or operation activity, which is unable to capture the effects of some low power techniques aiming at reducing switching activities.
3. Reusable prototype layer power models (templates) and structure layer power models (building blocks) to ease developing new models: For instance, when adding the crossbar power model, we re-use the structure layer tri-state output buffer model which is a component of cache model. In Table 1 and Figure 3, we show how the uniform array model can be re-used to model different function units through parameter mapping.
4. Easy maintenance: Modifying lower layer models or adding new model types will not affect higher layers.

4.2   Use of Methodology

Our methodology guided our development of power models for PEs as well as OCAs. Our PE power models have been integrated into LSE (see Section 2) using LSE's module extension mechanism and our network power models into Orion (see Section 5). For PEs, we have built a variety of power models: cache, branch predictors, register files, ALUs, and even some highly specialized function units such as the OMFLIP unit [16]. For networks, we have modeled input/output buffers, shared central buffers, crossbars, arbiters and links. Our models have been validated through comparisons with other simulators and low-level power estimates. Existing work focuses on further validation of the models, development of new models and support for static power in the modeling.

5   Orion – OCA Power Modeling and Simulation

As the use of multiple interconnected PEs becomes increasingly prevalent in application-specific embedded systems, the need to consider both power and performance of networks becomes pressing. Orion [17] provides this critical capability, with a dynamic power simulation environment for a wide range of interconnection networks, including OCAs. Orion extends LSE, building a library of router and link modules, each instantiated with functional, timing and power models. A user first *picks* modules to assemble the network he/she wishes to simulate, the modules are then *plugged* into LSE that builds a network simulator automatically, and a communication workload *played* on the network to evaluate its power and performance. This "pick, plug-and-play" environment allows users to rapidly explore the design space of interconnection networks.

MESCAL's methodology for OCAs (see Section 3) guided the selection of the building blocks of Orion. For each building block, the functional and timing behavior follows that characterized in [18] closely, while power modeling is carried out as outlined in Section 4. Orion has since been used to model a variety of network architectures and workloads, ranging from networks connecting PEs on a single chip to microprocessors with integrated routers and complex InfiniBand switches, providing valuable insights [19].

Orion forms a key piece in MESCAL's development of a complete tool suite for exploring application-specific embedded processors. While Orion is currently a stand-alone platform for investigating networks, we are in the process of tying it with PE power simulation within the LSE framework, so designers can explore interconnected processors in tandem with the network, in a single coherent environment.

6   Architectural Description

The MESCAL Architecture Description [20] (MAD) is designed as a unified architecture representation for MESCAL's retargetable software tool-chain including the optimizing C compiler and the simulators at various abstraction levels. The unified scheme eases the work for the description writers and ensures that all parts of the tool-chain share a consistent view of the architecture. To transform the single description to naturally-fit data models for individual components of the tool-chain, the MAD compiler analyzes the description and generates optimized view files, as shown in Figure 1. The current focus of MAD is the specification of individual PEs, future work will include OCAs in the same specification.

Architecture description languages (ADLs) have been the research focus of several past and ongoing projects [21,22,23,24,25]. However, we see no sign of convergence of the field for two main reasons. First, the extensive space of computer architectures and microarchitectures is difficult to capture accurately and efficiently with a single model. Second, the diverse requirements imposed by different software tools are hard to satisfy effectively with a single description scheme. Bearing in mind the difficulties, we currently confine MAD to a limited architecture scope including in-order RISC processors and statically scheduled VLIW processors. Within this restriction though, MAD can handle a wide range of application specific customizations - specialized functional units, memories, restrictions on Instruction Level Parallelism (ILP) etc. This enables it to model a fairly wide range of PEs. We also try to balance MAD between support for the retargetable compiler and support for the retargetable simulators.

For computer architectures, two abstraction levels are well understood: the instruction set architecture (ISA) and the micro-architecture. Since both provide useful knowledge to the optimizing compiler and the simulators, MAD includes the two in its behavioral part and its structural part, respectively. To bridge the gap between the two abstraction levels, MAD also provides a mapping part.

The Behavioral Part: The ISA is modeled in three sections: operand, operation and instruction. Similar to nML [22] and ISDL [23], MAD utilizes attribute grammar [26] to organize the semantics, binary encoding and assembly format across the layers.

The operand section describes the addressing modes. Two types of primitive operands can be defined: immediate and register. The immediate operand describes the constant values encoded in instruction words. The register operand describes the logical registers exposed to the ISA. Most PEs have complex addressing modes as the combinations of two or more primitive operands. One example is the shifting operand of the ARM [27] architecture. Since such complex addressing modes are often shared by many operations, a flat operation description scheme based purely on primitive operands will result in lengthy descriptions with much redundancy. To avoid this, we introduce an intermediate level "composite" operand to capture the complex addressing modes. A composite bases its semantics, encoding and syntax on those of its children primitive operands. Similar hierarchical schemes can also be found in nML and ISDL.

The operation section describes operations based on the operands. Besides encoding, assembly syntax and semantics, operations have two optional attributes: predicate and side_effects. The former specifies the predicate operand and the latter defines side effects like the altering of machine flags.

The instruction section describes possible bundling schemes of the operations for VLIW architectures. Irregular operation packing rules which often appear in low cost DSP designs can be described in the section and will be converted into resource constraints [28] for use in the optimizing compiler. For RISC processors, an instruction simply contains one operation.

The Structural Part: This part models the micro-architecture in the form of a coarse-grained netlist. MAD distinguishes between two categories of hardware units: pipeline stages and special function units. Pipeline stages are regular building fabrics of a PE as simple place-holders for operations. Their actual semantics as an ALU or a multiplier is ignored here since operation semantics are covered in the behavioral part. Special function units have heterogeneous semantics. Units like registers, memories, branch predictors are all treated as special function units. A library of basic special function units is built into MAD.

Each MAD hardware unit has input and output ports. Connections can be specified between ports. Essential connections such as those connecting pipeline stages and register files or memories are important for the MAD compiler to understand important architecture properties such as data path organization and memory banking.

The Mapping Part: Two types of mappings are described in this part: operand mapping and operation mapping. The operand mapping specifies the port through which an operand is accessed and the time of the access. The port information allows the compiler to schedule the operations properly to avoid port resource contentions. It also enables the simulator to interlock operations properly when such contentions occur. The operation mapping specifies the pipeline stages that an operation will flow through from its issue to completion. The description style in this section is similar to that of Maril [29] or EXPRESSION [25]. It describes the paths of an operation.

7   Retargetable Compiler

The compiler is a critical tool when designing systems with ASIPs. Along with tools such as execution-time estimators [30] and good input sets for performance evaluation, a high quality compiler allows designers to meet tight real-time deadlines and price/performance constraints without writing large amounts of assembly code. The compiler is also essential in properly evaluating the effectiveness of the hardware early in the design of the ASIP itself, since a microarchitecture cannot be properly evaluated without high quality benchmark code. Thus, the requirements for a compiler in the MESCAL environment are three-fold, *viz.* it must be highly retargetable to cover a wide range of architectures; it must have a wide variety of optimizations to produce good quality code; and it must be highly configurable to allow for different compile time vs. efficiency trade-offs during various stages of design. These requirements often conflict with each other, thus providing challenges that differentiate this compiler work from others.

The basic structure of the compiler is fairly standard. The front end is based on *lcc* [31] which is light-weight, documented and publicly available. The back-end, based on the Liberty-IR infrastructure [32], consists of three phases, namely, the code generation phase; the optimization phase including register allocation and instruction scheduling; and the code emission phase. With retargetability as one of the main thrusts of MESCAL, the compiler is automatically driven by the MAD specification described in Section 6. Minimal compiler knowledge is needed to retarget the back-end.

Embedded processors such as DSPs often contain non-orthogonal instruction sets and irregular data-paths like multiple register banks to reduce code size; to optimize area/power; to increase ILP; and to offer a wide set of addressing modes. These features pose a variety of problems to the compiler such as selecting the optimal addressing mode by the code generator; supporting diverse register banks efficiently during register allocation; handling irregular ILP in the scheduler, etc. Retargetable solutions to many of the problems are still being worked on.

To support architectures with irregular constraints within an algorithmic framework, we seek low-cost retargetable solutions rather than architecture (family) specific optimizations [33]. Here we briefly describe one such method that enables the use of resource based VLIW schedulers for processors with irregular ILP where the ISA restricts the sets of operations that can be issued in parallel, even though the physical resources may not impose them. We have developed the Artificial Resource Allocation (ARA) [28] algorithm which takes the set of all possible combinations of operations that can be issued in parallel from the machine description and assigns artificial resource (AR) usages to each operation such that, an AR is assigned to every pair of operations that cannot be issued in parallel; an AR is not assigned to every pair of operations that can be issued in parallel; and the total number of ARs is minimum. This is achieved by constructing a compatibility graph that has the operations in the ISA as vertices and an edge is drawn between every pair of vertices that can be issued in parallel. The ARA problem then translates to labeling the complement of the compatibility graph with the minimum number of labels (ARs) such that each pair of vertices (operations) connected by an edge in the complement graph is assigned at least one label (AR). For further details, we refer the readers to [28].

8   Conclusion

We are seeing a significant move from application development in dedicated hardware on ASICs, to programmable solutions on Application Specific Embedded Processors. However, these processors must achieve high power and performance efficiency in order to replace ASICs. This is accomplished through application specific customization in the form of specialized hardware resources. This customization places significant requirements on the software development environment needed for both processor development, as well as application deployment. We have described a set of tools used for simulation and compilation with the following key characteristics:

- ability to handle a wide range of architecture customization
- fully retargetable, starting from a unified architectural specification
- ability to handle on-chip communication architectures in addition to processing element architectures
- ability to model and simulate power consumption for both PEs and OCAs

We believe that the above infrastructure will significantly enable this transition from ASICs to Application Specific Embedded Processors.

References

1. Paulin, P.: What is the next EDA driver? Design Automation Conference Panel (2002)
2. Pai, V.S., Ranganathan, P., Adve, S.V.: RSIM reference manual, version 1.0. Technical Report 9705, Department of Electrical and Computer Engineering, Rice University (1997)
3. Vachharajani, M., Vachharajani, N., Penry, D., Blome, J., August, D.: Architectural exploration with Liberty. Technical Report Liberty-02-01, Liberty Research Group, Princeton University (2002)
4. The Liberty Research Group: http://liberty.princeton.edu/ (2002)
5. Kiczales, G., Lamping, J., Menhdhekar, A., Maeda, C., Lopes, C., Loingtier, J.M., Irwin, J.: Aspect-oriented programming. In: Proceedings of the 11th European Conference on Object-Oriented Programming. (1997) 220–242
6. SystemC Community: http://www.systemc.org (2002)
7. IBM Corp.: The CoreConnect™ bus architecture. Technical White Paper (1999)
8. ARM Holdings PLC: Advanced microcontroller bus architecture (AMBA) specification rev 2.0. http://www.arm.com/Documentation/UserMans/AMBA (2001)
9. Dally, W.J., Towles, B.: Route packet, not wires: On-chip interconnection networks. In: Proceedings of Design Automation Conference. (2001)
10. Sgroi, M., Sheets, M., Mihal, A., Keutzer, K., Malik, S., Rabaey, J., Sangiovanni-Vincentelli, A.: Addressing the system-on-a-chip interconnect woes through communication-based design. In: Proceedings of Design Automation Conference. (2001)
11. Taylor, M.B., et. al.: The Raw microprocessor: A computational fabric for software circuits and general-purpose programs. IEEE Micro **22** (2002)
12. Rumbaugh, J., Blaha, M., Premerlani, W., Eddy, F., Lorensen, W.: Object-Oriented Modeling and Design. Prentice-Hall, New York, NY (1991)
13. Davis, J., et. al.: Ptolemy II - heterogeneous concurrent modeling and design in Java. Technical Report UCB/ERL M01/12, Dep. of EECS, Univ. of California at Berkeley (2001)
14. Zhu, X., Malik, S.: A hierarchical modeling framework for on-chip communication architectures. In: Proceedings of International Conference on Computer-Aided Design. (2002)
15. Katevenis, M., Vatsolaki, P., Efthymiou, A.: Pipelined memory shared buffer for VLSI switches. In: Proceedings of Conference on Applications, Technologies, Architectures, and Protocols for Computer Communication. (1995)
16. Yang, X., Lee, R.B.: Fast subword permutation instructions using omega and flip network stages. In: Proceedings of International Conference on Computer Design. (2000)
17. Wang, H.S., Zhu, X.P., Peh, L.S., Malik, S.: Orion: A dynamic power simulator for interconnection networks – enabling power-performance tradeoffs for emerging microprocessor systems. Technical Report PU-02-06, Department of Electrical Engineering, Princeton University (2002)
18. Peh, L.S., Dally, W.J.: A delay model and speculative architecture for pipelined routers. In: Proceedings of International Symposium on High-Performance Computer Architecture. (2001)

19. Wang, H.S., Peh, L.S., Malik, S.: A power model for routers: Modeling Alpha 21364 and InfiniBand routers. In: Proceedings of Hot Interconnects 10. (2002)
20. Qin, W.: Mescal architecture description. http://www.ee.princeton.edu/~mescal/mad.html (2002)
21. Zimmerman, G.: The MIMOLA design system: a computer aided processor design method. In: Proceedings of Design Automation Conference. (1979) 53–58
22. Freericks, M.: The nML machine description formalism. Technical Report 1991/15, Technische Universität Berlin, Fachbereich Informatik, Berlin, DE (1991)
23. Hadjiyiannis, G., Hanono, S., Devadas, S.: ISDL: An instruction set description language for retargetability. In: Proceedings of Design Automation Conference. (1997) 299–302
24. Pees, S., Hoffmann, A., Zivojnovic, V., Meyr, H.: LISA – machine description language for cycle-accurate models of programmable DSP architectures. In: Proceedings of Design Automation Conference. (1999) 933–938
25. Halambi, A., Grun, P., Ganesh, V., Khare, A., Dutt, N., Nicolau, A.: EXPRESSION: A language for architecture exploration through compiler/simulator retargetability. In: Proceedings of Conference on Design Automation and Test in Europe. (1999) 485–490
26. Paakki, J.: Attribute grammar paradigms – a high-level methodology in language implementation. ACM Computing Surveys **27** (1995) 196–255
27. ARM Ltd.: ARM architecture reference manual. http://www.arm.com/arm/documentation (1996)
28. Rajagopalan, S., Vachharajani, M., Malik, S.: Handling irregular ILP within conventional VLIW schedulers using artificial resource constraints. In: Proceedings of International Conference on Compilers, Architectures and Synthesis for Embedded Systems. (2000)
29. Bradlee, D.G., Henry, R.R., Eggers, S.J.: The marion system for retargetable instruction scheduling. In: Proceedings of Conference on Programming Language Design and Implementation. (1991) 229–240
30. Chen, K., Malik, S., August, D.I.: Retargetable static timing analysis for embedded software. In: Proceedings of International Symposium on System Synthesis. (2001)
31. Fraser, C.W., Hanson, D.R.: A Retargetable C Compiler : Design and Implementation. Addison-Wesley, Menlo Park, CA (1995)
32. Triantafyllis, S., Vachharajani, M., August, D.: The Liberty Compiler intermediate representation. Technical Report Liberty-02-02, Liberty Research Group, Princeton University (2002)
33. Marwedel, P., Goossens, G.: Code Generation for Embedded Processors. Kluwer Academic Publishers (1995)

Processor Pipelines and Their Properties
for Static WCET Analysis*

Jakob Engblom and Bengt Jonsson

Dept. of Information Technology
Uppsala University
P.O. Box 337
SE-751 05 Uppsala, Sweden
www.it.uu.se

Abstract. When developing real-time systems, the worst-case execution time
(WCET) is a commonly used measure for predicting and analyzing program and
system timing behavior. Such estimates should preferrably be provided by static
WCET analysis tools. Their analysis is made difficult by features of common
processors, such as pipelines and caches.

This paper examines the properties of single-issue in-order pipelines, based on
a mathematical model of temporal constraints. The key problem addressed is
to determine the distance (measured in number of subsequent instructions) over
which an instruction can affect the timing behavior of other instructions, and when
this effect must be considered in static WCET analysis. We characterize classes
of pipelines for which static analysis can safely ignore effects longer than some
arbitrary threshold. For other classes of pipelines, pipeline effects can propagate
across arbitrary numbers of instructions, making it harder to design safe and precise
analysis methods.

Based on our results, we discuss how to construct safe WCET analysis methods.
We also prove when it is correct to use local worst-case approximations to construct
an overall WCET estimate.

1 Introduction

The purpose of *Worst-Case Execution Time* (WCET) analysis is to provide a priori information about the worst possible execution time of a program before using the program in
a system. Reliable WCET estimates are necessary when designing and verifying embedded real-time systems, especially when used in safety-critical systems like vehicles and
industrial plants. WCET estimates can be used to perform scheduling and schedulability
analysis, to determine whether performance goals are met for periodic tasks, to check
that interrupts have sufficiently short reaction times, to find performance bottlenecks,
and for many other purposes.

---

*   This work is performed within the Advanced Software Technology (ASTEC,
    http://www.astec.uu.se/wcet) competence center, supported by the Swedish National In-
    novation Systems' Administration (VINNOVA, http://www.vinnova.se) and IAR Systems
    (http://www.iar.com).

A. Sangiovanni-Vincentelli and J. Sifakis (Eds.): EMSOFT 2002, LNCS 2491, pp. 334–348, 2002.
© Springer-Verlag Berlin Heidelberg 2002

WCET estimates must be *safe*, i.e. guaranteed not to underestimate the execution time, and *tight*, i.e provide acceptable overestimations. The safeness of an estimate is critical when the estimate is used in the construction of a safety-critical system. The purpose of *static WCET analysis* is to generate safe and tight estimates by analyzing the source code and object code of the program without executing it.

The introduction of hardware features like caches and pipelines in the processors used for embedded real-time systems complicates static WCET analysis (and the measuring of execution times) by increasing the variability in execution time and by requiring more complex analysis methods.

A variety of concrete analysis methods for pipelines have been proposed, ranging over cycle-accurate simulators [6,7,22], special-purpose models using reservation tables [4,9,14,21], dependence graphs [15], abstract interpretation of pipeline behavior [8,20], and tables of instruction execution times and inter-instruction effects [2,3].

The timing benefit (effect) of pipelines is to a large extent due to the overlapping of pairs of adjacent instructions. This has motivated techniques that use the speedup for pairs of instructions to model the effect of pipelining [2,3,4,19,21]. The WCET is then calculated by summing execution times of instructions and subtracting the speedups.

For many pipelines, there are also timing effects that only occur for sequences of three or more instructions; in this case the entire sequence has to be considered in a precise and safe timing analysis that involves the first instruction. Such *long timing effects* (LTEs) are introduced in [7].

In this paper, we investigate general properties of pipelines relevant for static WCET analysis, in particular the issue of how far away a single instruction in a program can affect the pipeline behavior of other instructions. Sometimes, it is enough to consider pairs of adjacent instructions, while other pipelines require that instructions quite far apart are handled in the same analysis unit. To our knowledge, this is the first work that explores the theoretical limitations of pipeline analysis. Previous WCET research has been more focussed on actually building concrete and useable WCET analysis methods than exploring the limits of analyzability.

The concrete contributions of this paper are the following:

- We define a mathematical model of pipeline behavior, as a basis for investigating the occurrence of LTEs.
- We give general conditions under which no LTEs occur.
- A central theorem shows that for a class of pipelines, all LTEs are time savings. This implies that a safe (but not necessarily precise) analysis can be performed by considering only time savings for short sequences of instructions (typically pairs).
- We demonstrate that in many pipeline structures, there are cases where LTEs may occur for arbitrarily long sequences, i.e., disturbances can propagate over arbitrary distances. If such LTEs may add time, then it is hard to construct a safe and precise analysis.
- We prove that in-order pipelines are not subject to the kind of timing anomalies described by Lundqvist and Stenström [16]. This indicates that local worst-case assumptions for each instruction can be used to construct the overall worst case.

We do not address the issues raised by out-of-order processors, so this should only be considered a first step in our understanding of processor pipelines.

Paper outline: Section 2 presents the model of execution times, pairwise timing effects, and long timing effects. Section 3 presents the pipeline model built on constraints. Section 4 proves and demonstrates properties of pipelines. Section 5 discusses the implications of the properties for static WCET analysis.

2   Timing Model

For the discussion in this paper, we assume that a program is represented by a set of *nodes*, each containing one or more instructions. Nodes are connected by *edges*, and *sequences* of nodes can be formed by following the edges. For simplicity, this presentation will assume that each node contains just a single instruction (however, the same model applies where each node is a basic block).

Our goal is to statically calculate the execution time for a sequence of instructions $I_1 \ldots I_m$, which is denoted by $T(I_1 \ldots I_m)$. We define $T(I_1 \ldots I_m)$ as the time from which I_1 enters the first pipeline stage in a state where the pipeline is empty (cold pipeline) until I_m leaves its last pipeline stage. An important assumption is that the same sequence of instructions always yields the same execution time. This requires that the hardware is deterministic, and that effects outside the pipeline (like cache hits and misses, variable-length instructions, etc.) are fixed by extra information in the program graph. If such information is not known, several nodes might be used to represent the same code, with different information about its execution. Techniques for such transformations are described in, for example, [6,8].

The execution time $T(I)$ of a single instruction I is denoted t_I. To capture the timing effect of pipelines, we introduce *timing effects* $\delta_{I_1 \ldots I_m}$ for sequences $I_1 \ldots I_m$, defined as follows.

$$t_I = T(I) \tag{1}$$

$$\delta_{I_1 \ldots I_m} = T(I_1 \ldots I_m) - T(I_2 \ldots I_m) - T(I_1 \ldots I_{m-1}) + T(I_2 \ldots I_{m-1}) \quad m \geq 2 \tag{2}$$

We can then calculate the execution time $T(I_1 \ldots I_m)$ for a sequence $I_1 \ldots I_m$ in terms of times and timing effects:

$$T(I_1 \ldots I_m) = \sum_{j=1}^{m} t_{I_j} + \sum_{1 \leq i < k \leq m} \delta_{I_i \ldots I_k} \tag{3}$$

Equation (3) expresses that the execution time for a sequence $I_1 \ldots I_m$ be obtained by adding the node times t_{I_j} for all nodes in the sequence, and the timing effects $\delta_{I_i \ldots I_k}$ of all subsequences (of length ≥ 2) of the sequence.

Intuitively, the timing effects concisely capture the effect of pipelines on the timing of a sequence of instructions. For pairs of instructions, the *pairwise timing effects* correspond to the speedup obtained by the pipeline overlap between adjacent instructions, as illustrated in Figure 1. In general, pairwise effects are negative. For longer sequences of instructions, we could get *long timing effects* (LTE). Whenever $\delta_{I_1 \ldots I_m} \neq 0$, this is due to instruction I_1 having some effect that disturbs the execution of instruction I_m (across the sequence $I_2 \ldots I_{m-1}$). Precisely, the execution of nodes $I_2 \ldots I_m$ in the sequence $I_1 \ldots I_m$ is different from the execution of the nodes $I_2 \ldots I_m$ starting with node I_2 (see Section 4.1 for more details).

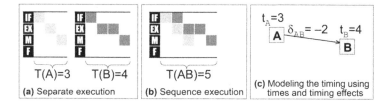

Fig. 1. Pipelining of instruction execution

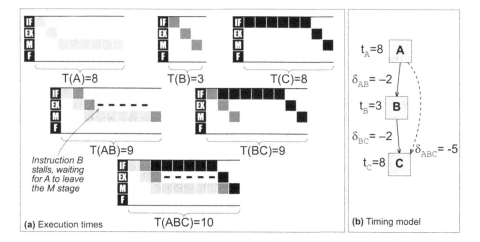

Fig. 2. Example long timing effect

Figure 2 shows an example of a LTE, where the execution profile of BC is different when executed in isolation and when executed as part of the sequence ABC. Note that we illustrate pipeline execution using *pipeline diagrams*, similar to the *reservation tables* commonly used to describe the behavior of pipelined processors. Time runs horizontally, with each tick of time corresponding to a processor clock cycle. The pipeline stages are shown on the vertical axis. Instructions progress from upper left to lower right, and each cycle of execution is shown as a square.

LTEs can in general be both negative and positive, and must be accounted for by a static WCET analysis method that wants to be safe and tight. *Positive timing effects* add execution time to a program, and are critical to consider since otherwise an underestimate of the WCET could result. *Negative timing effects* indicate potential savings in execution time, and ignoring them only makes the WCET estimate less tight.

Positive LTEs comprise a central problem for WCET analysis, since they make it necessary to consider effects across more than just adjacent instructions assumption in order to create a safe analysis. To prove a particular WCET analysis method safe, it is necessary to address the question of whether all positive LTEs have been accounted for. A central issue in this paper is therefore to give sufficient conditions for when LTEs are guaranteed not to be positive.

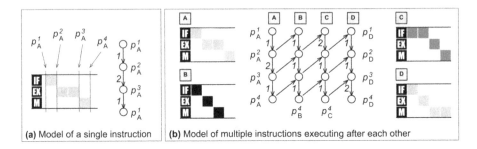

(a) Model of a single instruction | (b) Model of multiple instructions executing after each other

Fig. 3. Constraint model of pipeline execution

3 Pipeline Model

We model the timing behavior of pipelined execution by simple temporal constraints. This model is only used to describe execution timing, and is not intended as a basis for building pipeline simulators. It can be used to model all in-order pipelines that do not use dynamic dispatch, including VLIW processors [6].

For in-order pipelines with a single pipeline, we consider the pipeline to consist of n *pipeline stages*. Each *instruction* I_i is considered as a sequence $r_i^1 \ldots r_i^n$ of resource requirements, where r_i^j corresponds to the time the execution of the instruction requires in stage j. Only one instruction can occupy a pipeline stage at any particular point in time. Instructions are numbered from 1 to m, all instructions use all pipeline stages, and use them in the same order. Instructions proceed to the next stage as soon as possible. Time is discrete and expressed in clock cycles.

Consider the execution of a sequence $I_1 \ldots I_m$ of instructions. For an instruction I_i, we let p_i^j be the point in time at which I_i enters the pipeline stage j. By convention, p_i^{n+1} is the time at which instruction I_i leaves the last stage of the pipeline. The pipelined execution of $I_1 \ldots I_m$ is model by the following constraints:

$$p_i^{j+1} \geq p_i^j + r_i^j \qquad (1 \leq i \leq m, 1 \leq j \leq n) \qquad (4)$$

$$p_{i+1}^j \geq p_i^{j+1} \qquad (1 \leq i < m, 1 \leq j \leq n) \qquad (5)$$

Equation (4) models the fact that an instruction cannot enter its next stage before the current stage is completed, and Equation (5) models the fact that the next instruction cannot enter a certain pipeline stage before the current instruction has started its next stage.

We can graphically represent this constraint system as a weighted directed acyclic graph where the nodes correspond to the points p_i^j and the arrows correspond to the constraints between the points. Each instruction I_i is drawn as a column of points $p_i^1 \ldots p_i^{n+1}$, with the constraints from Equation (4) shown as vertical arrows. The weight between p_i^j and p_i^{j+1} corresponds to r_i^j. For example, Figure 3(a) shows the points for the instruction A in a three-stage pipeline. p_A^1 is the point where A enters the pipeline, and p_A^4 is the point at which it leaves the pipeline. The constraints from Equation (5) are drawn as diagonal arrows with no weight, since they have weight zero. An example is shown in Figure 3(b) (we only show some of the p_i^n variables to reduce the clutter).

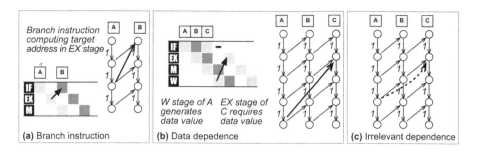

Fig. 4. Constraints for branches and data dependences

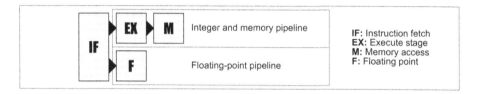

Fig. 5. Example in-order pipeline with parallel units

Additional dependences between instructions are represented by adding constraints to Equations (4) and (5).

– *Branch instructions* generate dependences between the end of the stage where the branch is decided (and the target address of the branch computed) and the fetch of the next instruction. A branch decided in stage j of instruction I_i generates the constraint

$$p_{i+1}^1 \geq p_i^{j+1} \qquad (6)$$

– *Data dependences* between instructions, which imply that instruction I_i can enter stage j, only after some previous instruction I_k has completed stage l, generate the constraints

$$p_i^j \geq p_k^{l+1} \qquad (7)$$

Examples of constraints for branches and data dependences are shown in Figure 4(a) and Figure 4(b). Note that these forms of constraints have effect only if they connect points that are not otherwise transitively connected via the basic constraints from Equations (4) and (5). Figure 4(c) shows some (irrelevant) data dependences that are subsumed by the basic constraints.

In a processor with multiple parallel pipelines, like the one shown in Figure 5, not all instructions will use all stages. In the constraint system, each instruction will then only have points corresponding to its entry into the pipeline (p_i^1), and points corresponding to the entry into each stage of the pipeline that it actually uses. The constraints Equations (4) and (5) are then reformulated using the functions $\texttt{previ}(i, j)$ and $\texttt{nexti}(i, j)$ which report for instruction I_i the previous and next instruction using pipeline stage j, and the functions $\texttt{prevs}(i, j)$ and $\texttt{nexts}(i, j)$ which report for a certain instruction I_i and

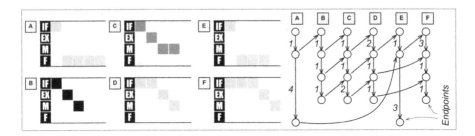

Fig. 6. Constraints for multiple pipelines

pipeline stage j reports the previous and next pipeline stage used by I_i. The reformulated constraints are:

$$p_i^{\texttt{nexts}(i,j)} \geq p_i^j + r_i^j \tag{8}$$

$$p_{\texttt{nexti}(i,\texttt{prevs}(i,j))}^{\texttt{prevs}(i,j)} \geq p_i^j \tag{9}$$

Equation (8) corresponds to Equation (4) and Equation (9) corresponds to Equation (5).

Rrom these constraints we can calculate the execution time $T(I_1 \ldots I_m)$ of the sequence $I_1 \ldots I_m$ as follows. Define a *path* from p_i^j to p_k^l as a sequence of arrows from p_i^j to p_k^l in the constraint graph. The length of a path P, denoted $length(P)$, is the sum of the weights on the arrows in P. The *distance* $D(p_i^j, p_k^l)$ between two points p_i^j and p_k^l is defined as the maximal length of all possible paths from p_i^j to p_k^l (note that the distance can only be constructed if p_k^l can be reached from p_i^j):

$$D(p_i^j, p_k^l) = \max_{P \in (\text{all paths from } p_i^j \text{ to } p_k^l)} (length(P)) \tag{10}$$

We say that a path P from p_i^j to p_k^l is a *critical path* if $length(P) = D(p_i^j, p_k^l)$. In general, there may be more than one critical path between two points. The central proposition of this model is the following:

Proposition 1. *The execution time $T(I_1 \ldots I_m)$ of a sequence of instructions $I_1 \ldots I_m$ is the maximal distance from p_1^1 to some point in the constraint system.*

$$T(I_1 \ldots I_m) = \max_{1 \leq i \leq m, 1 \leq j \leq n+1} D(p_1^1, p_i^j))$$

The proof is straight-forward, see [6], and depends on the fact that the constraint graph is acyclic. Proposition 1 is analogous to a result in scheduling theory, saying that an ASAP (as-soon-as-possible) schedule always gives an optimal schedule in an acyclic graph of dependences. It is also analogous to the distance calculations used with simple temporal constraints [5].

4   Properties of Pipelines

Using the model introduced in Section 3, we can make general characterizations of when LTEs occur and whether they are positive and negative.

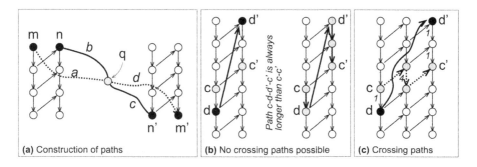

(a) Construction of paths **(b)** No crossing paths possible **(c)** Crossing paths

Fig. 7. Illustrating the principles of Theorem 2 and Theorem 3

4.1 Source of LTEs

Given a sequence $I_1 \ldots I_m$ of instructions, we say that I_1 *stalls* I_i if $D(p_1^1, p_i^j)) > D(p_2^1, p_i^j)) + r_1^1$. Intuitively, this means that some stage j of some successor instruction I_i is delayed due to waiting for some corresponding stage of I_1 (we assume that the first stage occurs in all instructions). Note that due to data dependences and parallel pipelines, such stalls can occur between non-adjacent instructions.

Theorem 1. *For a single in-order pipeline, a timing effect $\delta_{I_1 \ldots I_m} \neq 0$ can occur for a sequence of instructions $I_1 \ldots I_m, m \geq 3$ only if I_1 stalls the execution of some instruction in $I_2 \ldots I_m$.*

Proof. (Sketch) Intuitively, if I_1 does not disturb any of its successor instructions, the execution of $I_2 \ldots I_m$ will be identical to the case when they are executed starting with I_2. The theorem can be proven by a straight-forward calculation, using the definition of stalling. A full proof is given in [6, Section 5.2.5]   □

Note that for pipelines that fork, an LTE over $I_1 \ldots I_m$ can occur if I_1 uses some resource that is not used by $I_2 \ldots I_{m-1}$, as shown by example in Section 4.3.

4.2 Pipelines without Positive LTEs

The central result of this section is a characterization of pipeline structures that have no positive LTEs. We say that a pipeline has the *crossing critical path* (CCP) property if for any constraint system model of a sequence $I_1 \ldots I_m$ of instructions with $m \geq 3$, there is a critical path P_1 between p_1^1 and p_m^{n+1}, and a critical path P_2 between p_2^1 and p_{m-1}^{n+1} such that P_1 and P_2 have a common point. We assume that there is a common last step $n + 1$ in the pipeline (thus, we do not consider forking pipelines here).

We will later give classes of pipelines that have the CCP property. The importance of CCP is that it guarantees the absence of positive LTEs.

Theorem 2. *For a sequence of instructions $I_1 \ldots I_m, m \geq 2$, executing on a pipeline with the CCP property, $\delta_{I_1 \ldots I_m} \leq 0$.*

Proof. (Sketch) Consider the sequence $I_1 \ldots I_m$ and its corresponding constraint system. We shall prove that $\delta_{I_1 \ldots I_m} \leq 0$. Introduce the following names for points in the constraint system (see Figure 7(a)):

- m, corresponding to the start of instruction I_1
- n, corresponding to the start of I_2
- n', corresponding to the end of I_{m-1}
- m', corresponding to the end of I_m

The distances between these points form the execution times involved in the $\delta_{I_1 \ldots I_m}$ calculation as follows:

$$T(I_1 \ldots I_m) = D(m, m')$$
$$T(I_2 \ldots I_{m-1}) = D(n, n')$$
$$T(I_1 \ldots I_{m-1}) = D(m, n')$$
$$T(I_2 \ldots I_m) = D(n', m)$$
$$\delta_{I_1 \ldots I_m} = D(m, m') + D(n, n') - D(m, n') - D(n, m')$$

To prove that $\delta_{I_1 \ldots I_m} \leq 0$, we must show that $D(m, m') + D(n, n') \leq D(m, n') + D(n, m')$. Select a critical path P_1 from m to m', shown as a dashed line in Figure 7(a), and a critical path from n to n', shown as a solid line in Figure 7(a). By the CCP property, we can choose P_1 and P_2 so that they cross at some point q, dividing each of the two paths into two parts. Label the path segments by a, b, c, and d as in Figure Figure 7(a). Using the fact that the distance between two points is at least as long as any path between the points, we get the following inequalities:

$$D(m, m') = a + d$$
$$D(n, n') = b + c$$
$$D(m, n') \geq a + c$$
$$D(n, m') \geq b + d$$

We infer that $D(m, m') + D(n, n') \leq D(m, n') + D(n, m')$, from which we conclude $\delta_{I_1 \ldots I_m} \leq 0$. $\square$

We can now proceed to characterize pipelines with the CCP property.

Theorem 3. *A single in-order pipeline has the CCP property if each constraint introduced by branches (Equation (6)) and data dependences (Equation (7)) either*

- *occurs between adjacent instructions, or*
- *is subsumed by the basic constraints from Equations (4) and (5), as explained in Section 3*

Proof. (Sketch) For single in-order pipelines without any branch or data dependency, the CCP property follows from the observation that the corresponding constraint graph is planar, and hence that critical paths cannot overtake each other without intersecting at some point. When adding constraints that represent branches and data dependences, the

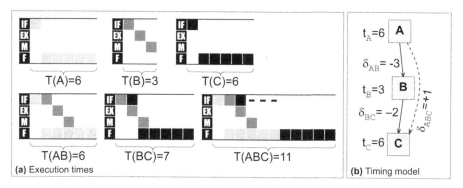

Fig. 8. Long timing effect in parallel pipelines

critical issue is whether they may allow critical paths to overtake without intersecting. As illustrated in Figure 7(b), this is not the case for constraints between adjacent instructions, since such constraints will always be included in the critical path if they make it longer.

□

Note that if we have data dependences across more than two instructions, the case in Figure 7(c) can occur, and the two paths can cross without sharing a node.

All branch dependences are between adjacent instructions, so the critical issue for the applicability of Theorem 3 is whether data dependences appear between non-adjacent instructions. No such dependences can appear if all data dependences in a pipeline only reach from a stage j to its predecessor stage $j-1$. This is thanks to the fact that since the dependence goes at most two points back in the pipeline, and all dependences beyond the non-adjacent instructions will be subsumed by the regular constraints (as illustrated in Figure 4(c)).

In practice, data dependences only between adjacent instructions is a common case, thanks to data forwarding paths [11] that avoid most data dependences. Examples of processors with pipelines exhibiting this nice behavior are the ARM9 [1], NEC V850 [17] (not the V850E), Hitachi SH7700 [12], and Infineon C167 [13].

4.3 Parallel Pipelines Cause Positive LTEs

A pipeline that forks into parallel pipelines can exhibit positive long timing effects due to interference between instructions being sent into one pipeline, if some intervening instructions are sent to some other pipeline. An example is shown in Figure 8.

There might be pipelines where such effects never actually materialize, but in most real-life forking pipelines, this type of positive timing effects do occur and have to be accounted for in WCET analysis. Examples of such processors are the NEC V850E [18], MIPS R4000 [10], MicroSPARC I [9], and basically any processor employing a separate floating point pipeline.

4.4 LTEs Across Unbounded Number of Instructions

It is not in general possible to provide a bound on the length of the sequences of instructions that can exhibit long timing effects.

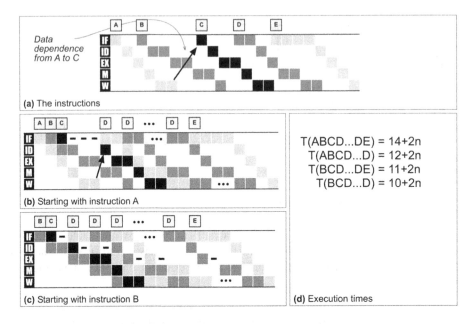

Fig. 9. Example of an unbounded positive timing effect

The example in Figure 9 demonstrates that we can get a positive LTE after an unbounded number of instructions. There is a data dependence between instructions A and C, which causes the execution of BCD . . . E to be different depending on whether A is executed before B or not. After an arbitary number of instructions D, we get a positive timing effect when instruction E is added, since:

$$\delta_{\text{A...E}} = 14 + 2n - 12 - 2n - 11 - 2n + 10 + 2n = +1$$

Thus, we can have LTEs across an arbitrary number of instructions. Note that there is a timing effect $\delta_{\text{ABC}} = -1$, but no other timing effect until the effect across A . . . E appears. One should also note that it is possible that several positive timing effects occur from the same disturbance [6].

4.5   Absence of Timing Anomalies

Using the model in Section 3, we can also establish a different but important property of in-order pipelines, the absence of *timing anomalies*, as introduced by Lundqvist and Stenström [16]. Given a sequence of instructions $I_1 \ldots I_m$, when we change the execution time of the first instruction by adding n cycles, we will get a new execution time for the sequence. If this time is less than the previous time, or the new time is more than n cycles longer than the previous time, we have a timing anomaly. We translate this property into our model by assuming that precisely one pipeline stage for I_1 is extended to take more cycles.

By example, Lundqvist and Stenström demonstrated that out-of-order processors can suffer from timing anomalies. Here, we show that for pipelines that can be modeled by our constraint systems (in-order pipelines), such effects cannot occur. Note that branch prediction coupled with speculative cache fetches can cause timing anomalies, regardless of the simplicity of the pipeline, as demonstrated for the Coldfire 5307 [8]. To avoid timing anomalies, we require that a processor is free from all kinds of dynamic scheduling and speculative processing.

The important consequence of timing anomalies is that if anomalies occur, we cannot use the simplifying assumption that the worst-case execution time for the program can be derived by assuming worst-case execution times for each individual instruction. Otherwise, every possible pipeline and/or cache state has to be considered, which is very complex [8].

Theorem 4. *For in-order pipelines, no timing anomalies can appear when we increase the execution time of an instruction.*

Proof. The original execution time for $I_1 \ldots I_m$ corresponds to the critical path in a constraint system C_1. We increase the execution time by increasing the time for I_1 to complete one of its stages, obtaining a new constraint system C_2, where some r_1^j is bigger than in C_1.

The new execution time for $I_1 \ldots I_m$ corresponds to some critical path in constraint system C_2. If the arrow with r_1^j was on the critical path before, the execution time will increase by k cycles, $d = k$. If it was not, and now is included, the time will increase by at most k. If it is not on the critical path of either C_1 and C_2, $d = 0$. Thus, $0 \leq d \leq k$, and no timing anomaly can appear. □

Theorem 5. *For in-order pipelines, no timing anomalies can appear when we decrease the execution time of an instruction.*

Proof. Analogous to the proof of Theorem 4 [6]. □

5   The Safety of WCET Analysis

To perform safe WCET analysis for pipelines, we need to make sure that no positive LTEs are missed. If no positive LTEs can occur at all, as is the case for the processors with the CCP property, any timing model that considers instructions, pairs of instructions, etc. is safe, since there are no positive LTEs that can be missed. However, for many types of processors, positive LTEs can occur, and there are several ways of handling them.

For approaches only analyzing adjacent pairs of instructions, the presence of positive LTEs makes it necessary to use conservative approximations. Such an approximate model would overestimate the execution time over shorter sequences, in order to make sure that the total execution time when LTEs are taken into account is not underestimated.

One way to construct such a model is to use reservation tables and consider their pairwise concatenation, but not allow the instruction profiles to change their shape when concatenated. This means that stalls will not materialize, as each instruction will execute as it would in isolation. Thus no long effects can occur within a pipeline, according to Theorem 1. To avoid the potential of LTEs resulting from parallel pipelines, it is necessary

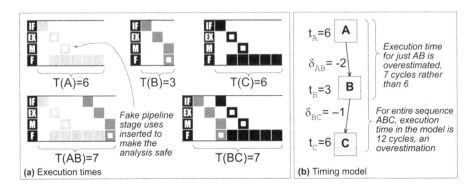

Fig. 10. Pairwise conservative model for Figure 8

that each instruction (or basic block) use every pipeline stage, as proposed in [19] [1].
Also, if there are data dependences between non-adjacent instructions it is necessary to
account for the worst possible delay due to data waits, in each pair of instructions. Note
that just concatenating instructions pairwise without stalls [4,21] is not necessarily safe
for parallel pipelines.

Figure 10 shows how the case in Figure 8 would be modeled with this type of
approximation: node A would not be allowed to completely overlap node B (as shown
for the sequence AB), which makes the timing effect between the nodes −2 instead
of −3. Thus, the positive timing effect of the interference between A and C is taken
early, on the edge between A and B, which is safe but pessimistic. If a processor has
instructions that can execute for quite a long time in parallel to other instructions, this
type of approximation is likely to give very high overestimations.

In our WCET analysis method based on examining sequences of nodes [6,7], it is
critical to define correct criteria for the termination of the search that finds all (positive)
LTEs. If those criteria are wrong, we might get an underestimated WCET. In practice,
this type of analysis works very well for simple processors.

Another approach maintains multiple pipeline states for each basic block, and in
each step tries to prune the states that cannot result in the longest execution time [14].
This pruning operator has to consider the potential of LTEs to be correct.

There are some analysis approaches where the pipeline behavior is modeled along
paths consisting of many basic blocks [9,22] (usually, this means that several different
paths between two points in the code are analyzed). Inside each path, LTEs are absorbed
with perfect precision, but where paths are concatenated, approximations that cover all
possible LTEs have to be used.

A different philosophy is to maintain all possible states of the pipeline for each node
in the analysis, without attempting to prune the set of pipeline states [8,20]. In such
approaches, the presence of LTEs will mean an increased analysis complexity (as each
instruction will be subject to more different states). This approach is not dependent on
the absence of timing anomalies and should find all LTEs. The resulting analysis is very
expensive, however [8].

---

[1] The placement of such extra pipeline stages is qiute important to achievable precision, and has
to be carefully considered for each pipeline

6   Conclusions

In this paper, we have presented a mathematical model of instruction execution on in-order single-issue pipelined processors. We have used this model to examine the timing of instructions from the perspective of static worst-case execution time (WCET) analysis, especially considering timing effects between non-adjacent instructions (long timing effects, LTEs). There are negative LTEs, which can be safely ignored, and positive LTEs that add instruction time to a sequence of instructions, and that have to be accounted for in a safe analysis.

Even simple pipelines can exhibit LTEs across arbitrary numbers of instructions, which makes it necessary for static WCET analysis to consider more than pairs of instructions. For many pipelines, all LTEs are negative, which means that they can be ignored safely, at the cost of lower precision. Measurements indicate that (we have experimented with the NEC V850E processor) ignoring all negative LTEs can give overestimations of up to 20% of the execution time of a program [6]. For processors with parallel floating point pipelines, the effect could be much greater.

Another result obtained using our pipeline model is that in-order single-issue processors are not subject to timing anomalies, which indicates that it is possible to use local worst-case assumptions to derive a global worst-case execution time. This allows for efficient static analysis, since we do not have to consider all possible execution times for each instruction in order to find the WCET.

The results in this paper indicates that certain processors are better suited for use in predictable systems. For example, the timing of a processor without timing anomalies and only negative LTEs is very easy to analyze compared to a processor with positive LTEs and timing anomalies. It would be interesting to try to design a high-performance high-predictability processor for embedded real-time systems.

In conclusion, we reached a better understanding of how to construct safe static WCET analysis methods for pipelined processors, and have identified some non-trivial problems related to the achievable safety and precision of WCET analysis. This provides static WCET analysis with a firmer theoretical background, which will help us build better analysis methods. We hope to continue this work by extending the pipeline model to more classes of pipelines and continue the investigation into pipeline properties.

References

1. ARM Ltd. *ARM 9TDMI Technical Reference Manual*, 3rd edition, March 2000. Document no. DDI 0180A.
2. P. Atanassov, R. Kirner, and P. Puschner. Using Real Hardware to Create an Accurate Timing Model for Execution-Time Analysis. In *Proc. IEEE Real-Time Embedded Systems Workshop, held in conjunction with RTSS 2001*, December 2001.
3. I. Bate, G. Bernat, G. Murphy, and P. Puschner. Low-level Analysis of a Portable Java Byte Code WCET Analysis Framework. In *Proc. 7th International Conference on Real-Time Computing Systems and Applications (RTCSA'00)*, pages 39–48. IEEE Computer Society Press, December 2000.
4. A. Colin and I. Puaut. A Modular and Retargetable Framework for Tree-Based WCET Analysis. In *Proc. 13th Euromicro Conference on Real-Time Systems, (ECRTS'01)*. IEEE Computer Society Press, June 2001.

5. Rina Dechter, Itay Meiri, and Judea Pearl. Temporal constraint networks. *Artifical Intelligence*, 49:61–95, 1991.
6. J. Engblom. *Processor Pipelines and Static Worst-Case Execution Time Analysis*. PhD thesis, Dept. of Information Technology, Uppsala University, April 2002. Acta Universitatis Upsaliensis, Dissertations from the Faculty of Science and Technology 36, http://publications.uu.se/theses/91-554-5228-0/.
7. J. Engblom and A. Ermedahl. Pipeline Timing Analysis Using a Trace-Driven Simulator. In *Proc. 6th International Conference on Real-Time Computing Systems and Applications (RTCSA'99)*. IEEE Computer Society Press, December 1999.
8. C. Ferdinand, R. Heckmann, M. Langenbach, F. Martin, M. Schmidt, H. Theiling, S. Thesing, and R. Wilhelm. Reliable and Precise WCET Determination for a Real-Life Processor. In *Proc. First International Workshop on Embedded Software (EMSOFT 2001), LNCS 2211*. Springer-Verlag, October 2001.
9. C. Healy, R. Arnold, F. Mueller, D. Whalley, and M. Harmon. Bounding pipeline and instruction cache performance. *IEEE Transactions on Computers*, 48(1), January 1999.
10. J. Heinrich. *MIPS R4000 Microprocessor User's Manual*. MIPS Technologies Inc., 2nd edition, 1994.
11. J. L. Hennessy and D. A. Patterson. *Computer Architecture A Quantitative Approach*. Morgan Kaufmann Publishers Inc., 2nd edition, 1996. ISBN 1-55860-329-8.
12. Hitachi Europe Ltd. *SH7700 Series Programming Manual*, September 1995.
13. Infineon. *Instruction Set Manual for the C166 Family*, 2nd edition, March 2001.
14. S.-S. Lim, Y. H. Bae, C. T. Jang, B.-D. Rhee, S. L. Min, C. Y. Park, H. Shin, K. Park, and C. S. Ki. An Accurate Worst-Case Timing Analysis for RISC Processors. *IEEE Transactions on Software Engineering*, 21(7):593–604, July 1995.
15. S.-S. Lim, J. H. Han, J. Kim, and S. L. Min. A Worst Case Timing Analysis Technique for Multiple-Issue Machines. In *Proc. 19th IEEE Real-Time Systems Symposium (RTSS'98)*, December 1998.
16. T. Lundqvist and P. Stenström. Timing Anomalies in Dynamically Scheduled Microprocessors. In *Proc. 20th IEEE Real-Time Systems Symposium (RTSS'99)*, December 1999.
17. NEC Corporation. *V850 Family 32/16-bit Single Chip Microcontroller User's Manual: Architecture*, 4th edition, 1995. Document no. U10243EJ4V0UM00.
18. NEC Corporation. *V850E/MS1 32/16-bit Single Chip Microcontroller: Architecture*, 3rd edition, January 1999. Document no. U12197EJ3V0UM00.
19. G. Ottosson and M. Sjödin. Worst-Case Execution Time Analysis for Modern Hardware Architectures. In *Proc. ACM SIGPLAN Workshop on Languages, Compilers and Tools for Real-Time Systems (LCT-RTS'97)*, June 1997.
20. Jörn Schneider and Christian Ferdinand. Pipeline Behaviour Prediction for Superscalar Processors by Abstract Interpretation. In *Proc. ACM SIGPLAN Workshop on Languages, Compilers and Tools for Embedded Systems (LCTES'99)*, May 1999.
21. Friedhelm Stappert. Predicting pipelining and caching behaviour of hard real-time programs. In *Proc. of the 9th Euromicro Workshop on Real-Time Systems*. IEEE Computer Society Press, June 1997.
22. D. Ziegenbein, F. Wolf, K. Richter, M. Jersak, and R. Ernst. Interval-Based Analysis of Software Processes. In *Proc. ACM SIGPLAN Workshop on Languages, Compilers and Tools for Embedded Systems (LCTES'2001)*, June 2001.

ILP-Based Interprocedural Path Analysis

Henrik Theiling

Universität des Saarlandes and AbsInt Angewandte Informatik GmbH
Saarbrücken, Germany

Abstract. Program analysis usually works on control flow graphs (CFGs) and on a call graph (CG). The standard CGs contain one node for each function, but for precise analyses, it may be desirable to distinguish function invocations by their execution history.

This distinction is useful, e.g., to improve the precision of worst-case execution time (WCET) analysis for real-time systems. Our WCET analysis supports these advanced techniques for interprocedural analysis. The first part of the WCET analysis, i.e, the prediction of microarchitecture behaviour, uses Abstract Interpretation, for which tools already support the methods for function distinction by execution history.

The second part of WCET prediction is the worst-case path analysis, which can be performed using the well-established technique of Implicit Path Enumeration using Integer Linear Programming.

So far, support for arbitrary interprocedural analysis techniques in one framework was not discussed in literature. This paper closes this gap.

1 Introduction

Worst-case execution time (WCET) analysis can be split into two steps. The first step is the microarchitecture analysis. Like most program analyses, it works on control flow graphs, containing basic blocks as nodes, and on call graphs. The result of the first step is a worst-case execution time for each basic block of the program under examination.

The microarchitecture analysis often consist of a chain of sub-analyses for different parts of the hardware, like cache and pipeline analyses.

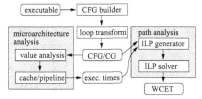

In our research project[1], we analyse the WCET of real-time systems. For all the microarchitecture sub-analyses, Abstract Interpretation (AI) (*see* [2]) is used.

The second part of a WCET analysis is the worst-case path analysis. Based on the results of the microarchitecture analysis, it computes the predicted WCET of the program.

---

[1] Transferbereich 14 'Runtime Guarantees for Real-Time Systems', supported by Deutsche Forschungsgesellschaft

A. Sangiovanni-Vincentelli and J. Sifakis (Eds.): EMSOFT 2002, LNCS 2491, pp. 349–363, 2002.

Path analyses can be implemented in several ways. Because of good precision and speed, we use Implicit Path Enumeration (IPE) (*see* [11]), which uses Integer Linear Programming (ILP) to find the WCET.

For improving the precision of program analysis, function invocations and loops can be distinguished by their execution history, e.g., by the *call stack* as distinctive features, which we call execution *contexts*.

To make use of the contexts in analyses, nodes of the analysis graphs are pairs of original nodes and assigned contexts, so nodes in the original graph are potentially transformed into several nodes in the analysis graphs, due to the context distinction.

Our tool PAG (*see* [14]) for writing analyses using AI comes with interprocedural analysis methods, so these advanced techniques are directly usable by our microarchitecture analysis.

Previous work extended IPE to interprocedural analysis techniques (*see* [26, 27]), showing that the combination is possible in principle. It was shown to work for one context computation method (which was sufficient for showing the principle).

This paper shows how *arbitrary context computation techniques* can be combined with IPE as long as the contexts are computed statically. This makes our WCET tool open to other approaches not yet programmed or thought of, and to other distinction methods, e.g., those used by other work groups, contributing a lot to genericity of our tool.

ILP-based path analysis (*see* [11]) generates an *objective function* and a set of constraints.

Loops in the call graph pose a problem, because the structure of the original call graph without contexts and the call graph the analysis works on (with context) is different w.r.t. to the structure of loops: entry and back edges of loops in the original call graph are not necessarily entry and back edges of loops in the call graph with context.

The biggest problem is that contexts at the entry edge and at the back edges of some loop are usually different, because back edges have a longer execution history (because they are traversed after the entry edges).

This paper will deal with the trade-off between analysis precision and speed. High precision by using contexts is desired, but a distinction by the whole execution history usually is too expensive. For best results, context computation should be most flexible and should be limitable and adjustable for differents programs under examination. We will outline an ILP-based path analyses for arbitrary static context computations.

The paper is structured as follows. Section 2 will give technical definitions, Section 3 shows how ILPs are generated. Section 4 gives an overview of the experimental results, Section 5 compares this work to related work, and finally Section 6 draws conclusions.

2 Basics

Program analyses usually work on two graphs: the Control Flow Graph (CFG), containing nodes for each basic block and edges for intraprocedural control flow, and on the

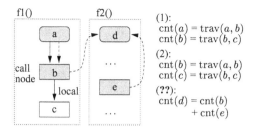

Fig. 1. CFG and CG of a call of a recursive function. All nodes are part of CFG, shaded ones are part of CG. Rounded boxes identify function start nodes. Solid edges are in the CFG, dashed edges in the CG.

Call Graph (CG), containing nodes for each function and function call and edges for all function invocations.

Our CFGs contain a *local* edge after each call node, because the call graphs will not contain flow information about function returns, but it is needed for the generation of correct constraints (*see* Section 3). This is shown in Figure 1.

Definition 1. *Let* $\mathcal{P}$ *be the **program** under examination.*

Let F *be the set of **functions** of* $\mathcal{P}$*. Let* $V_f, f \in F$ *be the **basic blocks** of each function* f *(the* V_f *are pairwise disjoint).* $V = \bigcup_{f \in F} V_f$ *then is the set of all basic blocks of* $\mathcal{P}$*.*

Let $\mathsf{CFG}_f = (V_f, E_f), f \in F$ *be the **control flow graph** of function* f*.*

Let $\mathrm{Calls} \subseteq V$ *be the set of nodes containing **function calls** of* $\mathcal{P}$ *and let* $\mathrm{Starts} \subseteq V$ *be the set of function **start nodes**.* $\forall c \in \mathrm{Calls}$ *let* $\mathrm{target}(c) \in \mathrm{Starts}$ *be the **target** of the function call* c*.* $\mathrm{target}(c)$ *defines the interprocedural call edges of the call graph. Note that our call graphs do not contain return edges.*

For a path in graph G from node v_1 to v_2, we will write $v_1 \rightarrow^*_G v_2$.

Definition 2. *Let* $\mathsf{CG} = (\hat{V}, \hat{E}), \hat{V} = \mathrm{Calls} \cup \mathrm{Starts}, \hat{E} \subseteq \hat{V} \times \hat{V}$ *be the **call graph** of* $\mathcal{P}$*, where* $\hat{E}$ *is defined as follows.* $\hat{E} :=$

$$\{(c, s) : c \in \mathrm{Calls}, s = \mathrm{target}(c)\} \cup \bigcup_{f \in F} \{(s, c) : s \in \mathrm{Starts}, c \in \mathrm{Calls} : \exists s \rightarrow^*_{\mathsf{CFG}_f} c\}$$

The first set in the definition of $\hat{E}$ consists of *call edges*, the second set consists of edges from the start node to all reachable call nodes in the same function.

It is required that call nodes have exactly one incoming edge in the CFG. (This can be ensured by inserting additional empty nodes for the call nodes that contradict this requirement.) This way, together with the above definitions, each call node c also has exactly one outgoing edge in the CFG, namely the local edge. In the CG, c also has exactly one incoming edge (from the the start node) and one outgoing edge (defined by $\mathrm{target}(c)$) in the CG. By this, each traversal of these edges corresponds to exactly one execution of c.

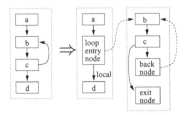

Fig. 2. CFG modifications by loop transformation. Dotted rectangles show functions. The loop transformation introduces a new function and new call nodes for each loop and transforms the loop into a recursive function. Dashed lines represent edges in the call graph, that are introduced by the transformation.

Example in C:
```
void a() {
    ...    // basic block b1
}
void b() {
    a();   // invocation c3
}
int main() {
    a();   // invocation c1
    b();   // invocation c2
}
```

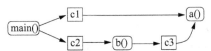

CG (without context). Start nodes are labelled with the name of the function and a pair of parentheses, call nodes are labelled as shown in the comment in the C source code. Note that our CGs contain no return edges, only call edges.

Loops: We handle loops and recursion uniformly in our approach. This is done by transforming all loops into recursive functions by making the loop body a function on its own and inserting interprocedural edges accordingly. Figure 2 depicts this and also clarifies the node names that we will use in the following text:

loop entry nodes are call nodes that invoke a recursive function from outside of that loop.

back nodes are call nodes that invoke a recursive function from inside of that loop.

Definition 3. *Let L be the set of **loops**, and $\forall l \in L$: let $\mathrm{Entries}(l) \subset \mathrm{Calls}$ be the set of **loop entry calls** (the sources of each loop entry edges of l), and let $\mathrm{Backs}(l) \subset \mathrm{Calls}$ be the set of **back calls** (the sources of each back edge of l)*

Contexts: Our framework provides the possibility to statically categorise different executions of basic blocks in different classes. These classes are called contexts and are usually computed by considering the execution history of a function.

Contexts are computed in different ways, depending on the desired level of precision and the acceptable computation effort for the specific analysis problem. The computation depends on the execution history by which the basic block is reached. The computation of contexts will be called a *mapping*. Each basic block must only be assigned a finite number of contexts.

Mappings that depend on the history of calls (often represented by a call stack), i.e., on the invocation history of a function, are said to follow the *call graph approach*. CallString(k) is a mapping that uses a suffix of length k of the call history. The most simple mapping method is CallString(0), which assigns the same, empty context to every basic block, thus making no distinction by execution history. k, the context length bound, is used to make the context mapping computable and to limit the complexity of the mapping to make the analyses perform well.

In Example 2, basic block b1 in function a() is executed with two different call stacks: c1 and c2 ∘ c3 depending on the control flow that led to the invocation of function a. Starting from CallString(2), we thus get two contexts for basic block b1.

A mapping will be seen more or less as a black box that computes graphs we use for analysis based in the original CFGs and CG.

Nodes in these CFGs and CGs with contexts are pairs of basic blocks and contexts. We show the presence of context information by writing these graphs with a suffixed '$\star$':

Control flow graph: CFG$^\star = (V_f{}^\star, E_f{}^\star)$
Set of all nodes: $V^\star = \bigcup_{f \in F} V_f{}^\star$
Call Graph: CG$^\star = (\hat{V}^\star, \hat{E}^\star)$

The sets Calls* and Starts* are defined for nodes in CG in all contexts:

$$\text{Calls}^\star = \{(v, c) : (v, c) \in \hat{V}^\star, v \in \text{Calls}\}$$
$$\text{Starts}^\star = \{(v, c) : (v, c) \in \hat{V}^\star, v \in \text{Starts}\}$$

The graphs the mapping computes are not totally arbitrary. Nodes and edges in CG* always have corresponding nodes and edges in CG.

$$(v, c) \in \hat{V}^\star \Rightarrow v \in \hat{V}$$
$$(v_1, c_1) \rightarrow_{\text{CG}^\star} (v_2, c_2) \Rightarrow v_1 \rightarrow_{\text{CG}} v_2$$

Further, edges inside functions do not change context:

$$\forall f \in F, v_1, v_2 \in V_f : (v_1, c_1) \rightarrow_{\text{CG}^\star} (v_2, c_2) \Rightarrow c_1 = c_2$$

Figure 3 depicts the Example 2's CG*. It can be seen from the figure that the CallString(2) CG* is maximally precise w.r.t. control flow, i.e., no control flow from two different calls ever joins in deeper calls. In contrast to this, in the CallString(0) CG* on the right, control flow from the calls c1 and c2 joins when a() is invoked from c3.

Consider the following program:

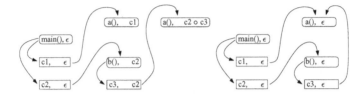

Fig. 3. CG*: each node is a pair of basic block and context. a) left: CallString(2), b) right: Call-String(0). b) is isomorphic to the CG of this program.

```
void a (int x)
{   ...
    a(x-1);    // c2
    ...
}

int main (int, char**)
{
    ...
    a(5);      // c1
    ...
}
```

The contexts for CallString(2) and CallString(1) are as follows:

	CallString(2)	CallString(1)
for main()	ε	ε
for a()	c1	c1
	c1 ∘ c2	c2
	c2 ∘ c2	

As can be seen, the 'older' parts of the execution history are chopped off. This is the main reason that causes problems for the loop bound computation as will be seen later.

Recursive Example: This section will clarify how different mappings make different CGs*. Consider the following program:

```
void a(int i) {
    ...
        a(...); // c3
    ...
}
int main() {
    a (10);        // c1
    a (20);        // c2
}
```

Figure 4 shows the CG and some CGs* for different context mappings.

VIVU(n, k): For better precision of loop analysis, we have developed a mapping technique that distinguishes the first few iterations from all other iterations, which are joined in one context. By this, we *virtually unroll* loops. To do this, the CallString(k) approach is modified to add a *saturated counter* to each context element in order to count how often the corresponding call occurs on the call stack via which a basic block is reached. Saturation of the counter is indicated by the symbol ⊤. Loop back nodes do not occur in contexts anymore, but instead, the corresponding counter is incremented. VIVU(n, k) is the mapping where n distinctions are the maximum, i.e., the counter may have the values $1, \ldots, n - 1, \top$, and where the contexts may not be longer than k elements.

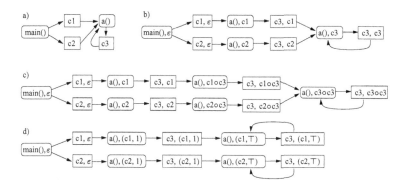

Fig. 4. a) CG of Example 2. b) CG* with CallString(1) mapping: the distinction by the two calls from main() is always lost in a(), because of the recursion. c) CG* with CallString(2): regardless of the maximum length, a() is never distinguished by the call from main(). d) CG* with VIVU(2, 1) mapping: the two calls in main remain distinguished in spite of the recursion.

Figure 4 also shows a VIVU(n, k) mapping for the example recursion to show how the mapping works.

Most significantly, the counter element of VIVU(n, k) prevents that the CG* contains joints for every recursion, because the contexts are not shifted, but simply a counter is incremented. This yields better precision w.r.t. execution history.

Times and Execution Counts: In the following we will use the following symbols.

Definition 4. *The **execution time** per execution of a node in a graph $G = (V, E)$ will be written* $t(v), v \in V$. *In the ILP, these symbols are constants provided by previous analyses.*

*The **execution count** of a node in G will be written* $cnt(v), v \in V$. *The traversal count of an edge in G will be written* $trav(e), e \in E$. *In the ILP, these symbols are variables and will be derived from a solution of the ILP.*

*The **minimum loop execution count** per entrance of that loop from a call node $v \in V$ will be written* $m(v)$. *The **maximum loop execution count** per entrance will be written* $M(v)$. *In the ILP, these symbols are constants provided either by previous analyses or by the user.*

All these symbols can be used for all kinds of graphs, i.e., with or without context information.

3   ILP

This section briefly describes how an ILP is generated for worst case path analysis. The techniques are described in detail in previous work, e.g. in [11, ?].

In the following, the generation of ILPs on graphs with context information is outlined.

Objective Function: The objective function sums up execution cycles of the program. Each basic block's total execution time contributes to this sum. The total execution time per block is the product of the time of one execution and the number of times it is executed. The sum is to be maximised to compute the WCET of the program:

$\max : \sum\limits_{v \in V^\star} \text{cnt}(v) \cdot \text{t}(v)$.

Our framework also allows the user to weigh edges of the program for more flexibility and higher precision. This is especially interesting for the pipeline analysis.

Program Start Constraint: Let v_0 be the start node of the program. Since the WCET for *one* execution of the program is to be derived, its execution count must be 1 (we do not permit recursion back to the program entry): $\text{cnt}(v_0) = 1$.

Structural Constraints: For all nodes, we sum up the outgoing and incoming control flow. The following constraints are generated from the CFGs*.

$$\forall f \in F, v \in V_f^\star, \{(v, v') \in E_f^\star\} \neq \{\,\} : \text{cnt}(v) = \sum\limits_{(v,v') \in E_f^\star} \text{trav}(v, v') \quad (1)$$

$$\forall f \in F, v \in V_f^\star, \{(v', v) \in E_f^\star\} \neq \{\,\} : \text{cnt}(v) = \sum\limits_{(v',v) \in E_f^\star} \text{trav}(v', v) \quad (2)$$

Call nodes are also handled correctly by these constraints (*see* Figure 1).

Care has to be taken at nodes with no incoming edges (e.g. start nodes of functions) or no outgoing edges (e.g. exit nodes of functions), since it is usually wrong to generate constraints of the form $\text{cnt}(v) = 0$, as these nodes are really potentially executed. Therefore, these constraints are excluded in the description above.

For each unreachable node $v \in V^\star$, we generate constraints of the form $\text{cnt}(v) = 0$.

From the CG* we have to generate the following equations that state that start nodes are executed as often as the sum of their call nodes.

$$\forall v \in \text{Starts}^\star : \text{cnt}(v) = \sum\limits_{(v',v) \in \hat{E}^\star} \text{cnt}(v')$$

Loop Constraints: Loop constraints bound the number of iterations of a loop. They are specified as the minimum and maximum number of iterations for each invocation of the loop. Because the ILP-based approach adds up the execution counts on the loop entry nodes, the most precise measure is the *ratio between the number of executions of the loop entry node and the number of executions of the start node of the loop*. As defined before, for a loop entry node n_0, the minimum and maximum ratios are called $m(v_0)$ and $M(v_0)$, resp. (*see* Definition 4).

Note that there may be more than one loop entry node for recursive loops (but not for transformed iterative loops). Therefore, the minimum and maximum loop counts are given for each loop entry node, not for each loop.

In the case of graphs without context, loop bound constraints are generated as follows. For each loop l:

$$a := \sum_{v \in \text{entries}(l)} \text{cnt}(v), \quad b := \sum_{v \in \text{back}(l)} \text{cnt}(v)$$

$$\sum_{v \in \text{entries}(l)} \text{cnt}(v) \cdot m(v) \leq a + b \leq \sum_{v \in \text{entries}(l)} \text{cnt}(v) \cdot M(v)$$

(Note that $a + b$ is the number of times the start node of the recursive function is executed.)

Here, we add all the minimum and maximum loop counts to generate constraints. This method has poor precision. Consider Example 2 together with Figure 4d. The two loop entries c1 and c2 from main() are fully distinguished by this mapping. Lets assume that we know that the loop is executed 11 times when entered from c1 and 21 times when entered from c2. Lets further assume that a() is much slower (e.g. because of pipeline effects) when entered from c1.

If we combined the two loop bounds in one constraint, because we didn't want to distinguish the two loop entries, we could only state that the total is 32 iterations for the two calls together. And because in the first invocation, a() is slower, the worst-case solution for the ILP would be that the first iteration had 31 iterations, the second only 1. So this is much less precise than having an own loop bound constraint for each of the two invocations.

This is the reason why we want to keep the distinction for loop bound constraints as precise as the mapping allows.

Generating constraints for loop bounds in call-graphs with contexts is complicated. The reason is that the edges that contribute to the loop bound constraints might occur in *different* contexts which depend on each other in non-trivial ways, depending on the used mapping.

The major problem is the *context length bound* that most mappings use to ensure computability and to reduce complexity. This bound leads to collapses of context distinctions in the control flow from different loop entry edges. This then leads to the fact that edge traversal counts e.g. for the back edges sum up for different loop entries. Our previous work presented in [26] and [27] handled a simpler case, because no length bound was involved in mapping computation.

To generate correct loop bound constraints, it is necessary to consider all loop entries that join in a later part of the CG^*. This will require a graph algorithm that collects the appropriate edge contexts.

Idea: The loop bound constraints that have to be generated are very similar to the ones shown for graphs without context. One difference is that the nodes are now pairs of basic block and context. Because the constraints compare non-adjacent nodes in the CG^*, it is quite unclear which contexts to use for the nodes. Let us neglect this problem for now and assume these contexts are known.

For each loop l and each loop entry node $v_0 \in V^\star$, we need the correct set of back nodes with the precise contexts $\mathcal{B}(v_0) \subseteq V^\star$ and the correct set of entry nodes with the precise contexts $\mathcal{V}(v_0) \subseteq V^\star$ to generate the loop bound constraints as before:

$$a := \sum_{v \in \mathcal{V}(v_0)} \mathrm{cnt}(v), \quad b := \sum_{v \in \mathcal{B}(v_0)} \mathrm{cnt}(v)$$

$$\sum_{v \in \mathcal{V}(v_0)} \mathrm{cnt}(v) \cdot m(v) \leq a + b \leq \sum_{v \in \mathcal{V}(v_0)} \mathrm{cnt}(v) \cdot M(v)$$

The problem of the algorithm is thus reduced to finding $\mathcal{V}$ and $\mathcal{B}$. The most simplistic approach would be to ignore the contexts and sum up *all* loop entry calls in all their contexts and all back nodes in all their contexts. However, we lose a lot of precision in doing so, therefore, we want to search for those $\mathcal{V}$ and $\mathcal{B}$ that are most precise for the given mapping, i.e., those that allow the maximal number of distinctions between loop invocations.

Consider Figure 4 again. There is only one loop l (in the CG in 4a), for which $\mathrm{Entries}(l) = \{\texttt{c1}, \texttt{c2}\}$ and $\mathrm{Backs}(l) = \{\texttt{c3}\}$.

If in $CG^\star$, l is still distinguished by the invocation in $\texttt{main}$, then finding the back nodes that correspond to, e.g. $\texttt{c1}$, is easy, since $\texttt{c1}$ must be part of the context. In Figure 4d, these are the back node $(\texttt{c3}, (\texttt{c1}, 1))$ (back node of the first iteration) and $(\texttt{c3}, (\texttt{c1}, \top))$ (back node of all other iterations). This was the basis of the computations performed in previous work (*see* [27]).

It becomes more complicated when the distinction is lost as in Figure 4b. If we want to generate loop bound constraints for the loop entry node $(\texttt{c1}, \varepsilon)$, we will have to compute the correct set of back nodes for this entry node. The nodes $(\texttt{c3}, \texttt{c1})$ and $(\texttt{c3}, \texttt{c3})$ are clearly back nodes for this call, as they are reachable from that loop entry node.

Unfortunately, $(\texttt{c3}, \texttt{c3})$ also belongs to the set of back nodes that is reachable from $(\texttt{c2}, \varepsilon)$, so we cannot handle the two loop entry nodes separately, since the execution count of the back node $(\texttt{c3}, \texttt{c3})$ contributes to both invocations. This must, therefore, be accounted for by summing up *in one constraint* the execution counts of *all corresponding loop entry calls* for the back nodes that we have found.

For the set of found back nodes for the call $\texttt{c1}$, we have to search for all the other call nodes whose corresponding set of back nodes intersects with the one we just found. If we do this in the above example, we end up with both initial loop entry nodes to the loop, $(\texttt{c1}, \varepsilon)$ and $(\texttt{c2}, \varepsilon)$. To find these, we simply search backward in $CG^\star$ for a path from the back nodes to the loop entry node.

Finally, we need to extend the set of back nodes to those reachable from all the newly found loop entry nodes. In the example, we find the additional back node $(\texttt{c3}, \texttt{c2})$.

Intuitively, for nested loops, care has to be taken. Indeed, reachability of nodes must be computed *without regarding return edges* (from the called function back to the caller). Otherwise, the loop we are searching back nodes for might be reachable in a different context by first using the return edge and then re-entering the loop in a different context.

Our call graphs do not contain return edges, so this does not give rise to any problems (*see* Definition 2).

Algorithm: The algorithm for finding $\mathcal{V}$ and $\mathcal{B}$ is defined as follows. Let l be a loop and v_0 be a loop entry call for which we want to generate a loop bound constraint. First we define the preliminary set of back nodes $\mathcal{B}'(v_0)$, then we define $\mathcal{V}(v_0)$ and $\mathcal{B}(v_0)$.

$$\mathcal{B}'(v_0) := \{(b,c) \in \hat{V}^\star : b \in \text{Backs}(l), v_0 \rightarrow^*_{\text{CG}^\star} (b,c)\}$$

$$\mathcal{V}(v_0) := \{(b,c) \in \hat{V}^\star : b \in \text{Entries}(l), \exists v \in \mathcal{B}'(v_0) : (b,c) \rightarrow^*_{\text{CG}^\star} v\}$$

$$\mathcal{B}(v_0) := \{(b,c) \in \hat{V}^\star : b \in \text{Backs}(l), \exists v \in \mathcal{V}(v_0) : v \rightarrow^*_{\text{CG}^\star} (b,c)\}$$

4   Experimental Results

We use a very efficient implementation based on hash tables for storage of the graphs and the sets that are involved. By this, it is no problem to generate $\mathcal{B}$ and $\mathcal{V}$ in just a few seconds even for large graphs with thousands of nodes in the CG*. Usually, loops are very local, so the algorithm does not need to search long paths to find the desired nodes. Furthermore, only a fraction of the nodes in the call graph are loop nodes, so the scope of reachability search is limited. Moreover, back nodes are very often located in the same function as the loop header, so reachability search can be performed very locally.

In order to measure only the path analysis, programs were considered without microarchitecture analysis. Of cause, for real-life examples, we use the microarchitecture analysis of our framework (*see* [6]).

Further, for comparing a wide range of mappings, from simple ones to very complex ones, in the first step of experiments, we used a small program for an embedded controller (which operates and updates a liquid crystal display) and analysed it with very different mappings. The structure of the program involves 4 loops and the nesting level is maximally 3. By using different, complex mappings, the biggest ILPs became much larger than those of our real-life applications' ILPs with some thousand constraints. (Due to the loop nesting level of 3 and the expected solving time being quadratic for nice ILPs, the number of contexts is expected to increase cubically when increasing the unroll count, and the run-time of the solve by the power of 6. So this is a good way to increase complexity without using large programs.)

Figure 5 compares mappings and their sizes (number of contexts) with the generation and solving times of the corresponding ILP. The tests were done on an AMD Athlon XP1900+ machine with 1,600 MHz clock and 512 MB main memory running SuSE Linux 7.2 (kernel 2.4.10). The largest example, VIVU(5, 16) had 45,000 nodes and 58,000 edges in the CFG* which yielded over 100,000 variables in the ILP before the ILP simplification.

The figure is organised as follows: first, the loop unrolling level is increased to generate ILPs of considerable size. Then, the context length limitation is used in order to limit the number of contexts. Long unroll counts meaning good loop analysis precision can then be analysed in a reasonable amount of time. In the third part of the table, it is shown that call string approaches are also analysable with IPE.

mapping	#ctxts	#constr.	gen.time[s]	solv.time[s]	mapping	#ctxts	#constr.	gen.time[s]	solv.time[s]
VIVU(∞, 1)	8	49	< 1	< 1	VIVU(3, 14)	506	1,637	4	1
VIVU(∞, 5)	176	773	1.5	< 1	VIVU(3, 15)	572	1,843	4	3
VIVU(∞, 10)	1,151	4,783	9	7	VIVU(3, 16)	642	2,061	5	1.5
VIVU(∞, 12)	1,933	7,969	16	39	VIVU(2, 16)	356	1,450	3	1
VIVU(∞, 13)	2,432	9,997	22	69	VIVU(1, 16)	68	233	< 1	< 1
VIVU(∞, 14)	3,011	12,347	28	111	CallString(0)	0	49	< 1	< 1
VIVU(∞, 15)	3,676	15,043	36	176	CallString(5)	119	281	< 1	< 1
VIVU(∞, 16)	4,483	18,109	45	409	CallString(10)	594	1,081	2	< 1
VIVU(3, 12)	386	1,261	2.5	< 1	CallString(15)	1,794	2,781	6	2
VIVU(3, 13)	444	1,443	3.5	< 1	CallString(20)	4,094	6,031	12	18

Fig. 5. For a fixed embedded controller program, the mappings, the number of contexts, number of non-trivial constraint, and the time to generate and solve the ILP are shown. Of course, large unrolling counts result in a lot of contexts due to the nested loops. (Note that a constraint simplification reduces the ILP to non-trivial constraints only.)

Our approach was implemented in order to improve the analysis time of large executables. W.r.t. the path analysis, the standard examples that are widely used for experiments (e.g. FFT, Bubblesort, Matrix Multiplication, Circle Drawing Algorithm, Prime Test) all resulted in an optimal 100%.

In a second step, we ran tests of real-life programs from safety critical embedded hard real-time systems for the Motorola ColdFire MCF 5307 (*see* [17]) architecture. Due to the complex nature of these programs, the real WCET is not known.

So the most interesting measure is the analysis speed for real-life executables.

The framework (*see* [6]) we used for finding the run-time of the path analysis comes with microarchitecture analyses for value analysis (*see* [22, 7]), (instruction and data) cache analysis (*see* [5, 27]), and pipeline and memory bus analysis (*see* [21]). These can be parameterised (at least) with a specific mapping. Loops are transformed at the beginning of the analysis suite, just after the ELF executable's CFG has been reconstructed (*see* [24, 25]). The loop transformation also computes the sets Entries(l) and Backs(l) for each loop l.

The pipeline and memory bus analysis, which runs just before the path analysis, yields execution times for each basic block/context pair. The path analysis then reads these results and also the loop-transformed control flow graph, has the needed CG* computed by the given mapping and then generates constraints. In the last step of this generation, loop bound constraints are generated using the algorithm described above. After the ILP has been generated, lp_solve[2] is used to solve the ILP.

For us, it was most interesting to see how fast the ILP-generator is, and also how long the ILP takes to be solved. The solving step has quite a high theoretical worst-case run-time, namely exponential, due to the used branch-and-bound technique (which can be reduced to polynomial run-time, if the ILP was relaxed to an LP). With respect to this theoretical worst case run-time, an ILP with some thousand variables and constraints is quite threatening. Relievingly, the generated ILPs will be very similar to network flow structures and are, therefore, quickly solvable.

---

[2] lp_solve was written by Michel Berkelaar and is freely available at ftp://ftp.es.ele.tue.nl/pub/lp_solve.

For further speed tests, we used twelve test programs from a real-life hard real-time application that all had a size in the order of about 50kB. The target architecture was the Motorola ColdFire MCF 5307 processor (*see* [17]). We used several mappings for testing, including our most precise mapping, namely VIVU without context length restriction, which resulted in the largest ILPs.

The largest CFG* had over 15,000 nodes (basic blocks) and over 20,000 edges. The largest CG* had over 2,300 nodes (function starts and calls) and over 4,500 edges. The ILP generation for any of these executables never took longer than 30 seconds on an Athlon processor with 700 MHz and 768 MB main memory, so the algorithm can be said to perform very well.

The resulting ILPs had some thousand non-trivial variables (more than 8000 plus over 28000 pairs of variables that were removed due to constraints of the form $x = y$) and also some thousand constraints (more than 6800). Still, solving took less than a minute even for our most precise mappings. So this also shows very good performance.

5 Related Work

Work about ILP-based path analysis was first published by Li et.al. in [9, 10, 8] who extended his work to include non-direct-mapped cache analysis in [11]. For caches with high associativity, a pure ILP-approach is not feasible using that technique due to complexity problems. In [26] an alternative approach was presented that split off the microarchitecture modelling from the path analysis by ILP. The method is usable for simple mappings. In contrast to this, this new paper presents how ILPs can be computed for all statically computed mappings. Analysis techniques using contexts are described in detail in [16, 15].

Ottoson and Sjödin also used ILP-based path analysis with a different objective function weighing the edges instead of the nodes (*see* [19]). In total, the basic technique can be said to be well-established. However, to our best knowledge, no other work group yet published the use of basic block contexts for precision improvement of ILP-based path analysis.

Lim et. al. have proposed a method of WCET computation called extended timing schema (*see* [12, 13]). The approach also does not handle contexts.

In [4], Engblom and Ermedahl present a technique of constructing an ILP from a scope graph and a flow graph in order to generate structural and loop constraints. Their approach handles a simpler case of constraint generation than this paper, since their scope graphs are rather trees, so they do not have any joints in the graph resulting from collapsed scope distinction inside a loop that is entered from different scopes (their scope graph is a perfect hierarchy, which we do not have in the general case). Since our context computation algorithms provide the method of bounding complexity, and therefore producing complex relationships between contexts, handling this was an important design goal of our algorithm.

Another technique of path search has been proposed by Stappert et.al. (*see* [23]) where instead of extensive path search or implicit path enumeration by ILP, an approach based on acyclic directed graphs (DAGs) is proposed. The result is a fast way of computing the WCET using a well-known graph algorithm (Dijkstra). The techniques for context distinction are the same as in [4], so the differences mentioned in the previous paragraph are true for this approach, too.

Further, the paper uses simulation to predict microarchitecture behaviour, which is not applicable to architectures like the ColdFire MCF 5307 whose execution depends very much in execution history. Using safe techniques of microarchitecure modelling with provably correct result, however, seems to be possible for their approach as well, since the analysis phases for microarchitecture behaviour prediction and for path analysis are decoupled as in our approach.

6   Conclusion

In this paper, we have presented an extension to the established technique of implicit path enumeration using ILP for WCET prediction. Our approach makes it possible to add a very fine-grained tuning mechanism for analysis precision and speed by arbitrary static execution context distinction. This method of basic block distinction was used already for our microarchitecture behaviour predictions as these use the PAG framework for analysis where the methods are integrated. This paper contributes by providing this for ILP-based path analysis as well.

Acknowledgements

I would like to thank Reinhard Wilhelm, Florian Martin and Christian Ferdinand for their support and for fruitful discussions. Thanks are also due to Reinhold Heckmann for proof-reading and for giving many valuable hints.

References

1. R. Arnold, F. Mueller, and D. Whalley. Bounding Worst-Case Instruction Cache Performance. In *Proceedings of the 15th IEEE Real-Time Systems Symposium (RTSS)*, Dec. 1994.
2. P. Cousot and R. Cousot. Abstract Interpretation: A Unified Lattice Model for Static Analysis of Programs by Construction or Approximation of Fixpoints. In *Proceedings of the 4th ACM Symposium on Principles of Programming Languages*, 1977.
3. J. Engblom. Processor Pipelines and Static Worst-Case Execution Time Analysis. PhD Thesis, Acta Universitatis Upsaliensis, 2002.
4. J. Engblom and A. Ermedahl. Modeling Complex Flows for Worst-Case Execution Time Analysis. In *Proceedings of the 21st IEEE Real-Time Systems Symposium*, Dec. 2000.
5. C. Ferdinand. Cache Behavior Prediction for Real-Time Systems. PhD Thesis, Universität des Saarlandes, 1997.
6. C. Ferdinand, R. Heckmann, M. Langenbach, F. Martin, M. Schmidt, H. Theiling, S. Thesing, and R. Wilhelm. Reliable and Precise WCET Determination for a Real-Life Processor. In *Proceedings of EMSOFT 2001, First Workshop on Embedded Software*, volume 2211 of *Lecture Notes in Computer Science*, 2001.

7. C. Ferdinand, D. Kästner, M. Langenbach, F. Martin, M. Schmidt, J. Schneider, H. Theiling, S. Thesing, and R. Wilhelm. Run-Time Guarantees for Real-Time Systems — The USES Approach. In *Proceedings of Informatik '99 – Arbeitstagung Programmiersprachen*, Paderborn, 1999.
8. Y.-T. S. Li and S. Malik. Performance Analysis of Embedded Software Using Implicit Path Enumeration. In *Proceedings of the 32nd ACM/IEEE Design Automation Conference*, 1995.
9. Y.-T. S. Li, S. Malik, and A. Wolfe. Efficient Microarchitecture Modeling and Path Analysis for Real-Time Software. In *Proceedings of the 16th IEEE Real-Time Systems Symposium (RTSS)*, 1995.
10. Y.-T. S. Li, S. Malik, and A. Wolfe. Performance Estimation of Embedded Software with Instruction Cache Modeling. In *Proceedings of the IEEE/ACM International Conference on Computer-Aided Design*, 1995.
11. Y.-T. S. Li, S. Malik, and A. Wolfe. Cache Modeling for Real-Time Software: Beyond Direct Mapped Instruction Caches. In *Proceedings of the 17th IEEE Real-Time Systems Symposium (RTSS)*, 1996.
12. S.-S. Lim, Y. H. Bae, G. T. Jang, B.-D. Rhee, S. L. Min, C. Y. Park, H. Shin, K. Park, S.-M. Moon, and C. S. Kim. An Accurate Worst Case Timing Analysis for RISC Processors. *IEEE Transactions on Software Engineering*, 21(7), 1995.
13. S.-S. Lim, J. Hee Han, J. Kim, and S. Lyul Min. A Worst Case Timing Analysis Technique for Multiple Issue Machines. In *Proceedings of the 19th IEEE Real-Time Systems Symposium (RTSS)*, 1998.
14. F. Martin. *PAG Reference Manual*. Universität des Saarlandes, 1995.
15. F. Martin. *Generation of Program Analyzers*. PhD thesis, Universität des Saarlandes, 1999.
16. F. Martin, M. Alt, R. Wilhelm, and C. Ferdinand. Analysis of Loops. In *Proceedings of the International Conference on Compiler Construction (CC'98)*. Springer-Verlag, 1998.
17. Motorola. *Coldfire Microprocessor Family Programmer's Reference Manual*, 1997.
18. F. Mueller, D. B. Whalley, and M. Harmon. Predicting Instruction Cache Behavior. In *Proceedings of the ACM SIGPLAN Workshop on Language, Compiler and Tool Support for Real-Time Systems*, 1994.
19. G. Ottoson and M. Sjödin. Worst-Case Execution Time Analysis for Modern Hardware Architectures. In *Proceedings of the ACM SIGPLAN Workshop on Language, Compiler and Tool Support for Real-Time Systems*, 1997.
20. P. Puschner and C. Koza. Calculating the Maximum Execution Time of Real-Time Programs. *Real-Time Systems*, 1, 1989.
21. J. Schneider and C. Ferdinand. Pipeline Behaviour Prediction for Superscalar Processors by Abstract Interpretation. In *In Proceedings of the ACM SIGPLAN Workshop on Languages, Compilers, and Tools for Embedded Systems*, 1999.
22. M. Sicks. Adreßbestimmung zur Vorhersage des Verhaltens von Daten-Caches. Diploma Thesis, Universität des Saarlandes, 1997.
23. F. Stappert, A. Ermedahl, and J. Engblom. Efficient Longest Executable Path Search for Programs with Complex Flows and Pipeline Effects. In *Proceedings of the 4th International Conference on Compilers, Architectures, and Synthesis for Embedded Systems (CASES 2001)*, Atlanta, Georgia, USA, November 2001.
24. H. Theiling. Extracting Safe and Precise Control Flow from Binaries. In *Proceedings of the 7th International Conference on Real-Time Computing Systems and Applications (RTCSA)*, Cheju Island, South Korea, 2000.
25. H. Theiling. Generating Decision Trees for Decoding Binaries. In *Proceedings of the ACM SIGPLAN Workshop on Language, Compiler and Tools for Embedded Systems*, Snowbird, Utah, USA, June 2001.
26. H. Theiling and C. Ferdinand. Combining Abstract Interpretation and ILP for Microarchitecture Modelling and Program Path Analysis. In *Proceedings of the 19th IEEE Real-Time Systems Symposium (RTSS)*, Madrid, Spain, 1998.
27. H. Theiling, C. Ferdinand, and R. Wilhelm. Fast and Precise WCET Prediction by Seperate Cache and Path Analyses. *Real-Time Systems*, 18(2/3), May 2000.

Enhancing Compiler Techniques
for Memory Energy Optimizations

Joseph Zambreno[1], Mahmut Taylan Kandemir[2], and Alok Choudhary[1]

[1] Department of Electrical and Computer Engineering
Northwestern University
Evanston IL 60208, USA
{zambro1,choudhar}@ece.northwestern.edu
[2] Microsystems Design Lab
Pennsylvania State University
University Park PA 16802, USA
kandemir@cse.psu.edu

Abstract. As both chip densities and clock frequencies steadily rise in modern microprocessors, energy consumption is quickly joining performance as a key design constraint. Power issues are increasingly important in embedded systems, especially those found in portable devices. Much research has focused on the memory subsystems of these devices since they are a leading energy consumer. Compiler optimizations that are traditionally used to increase performance have shown much promise in also reducing cache energy consumption. In this paper we study the interaction between performance-oriented compiler optimizations and memory energy consumption and demonstrate that the best performance optimizations do not necessarily generate the best energy behavior in memory. We also show a simple metric that a power-optimizing compiler can utilize in order to capture the energy impact of potential optimizations. Next, we present heuristic algorithms that determine a suitable optimization strategy given a memory energy upper bound. Finally, we demonstrate that our strategies will gain even more importance in the future when leakage energy is expected to play an even larger role in the total energy consumption equation.

1 Introduction

As the market for embedded systems continues to grow, power consumption issues are becoming increasingly important. In fact, as new cell phones, PDAs, and e-mail devices are being developed, the metric of performance / battery hours is considered crucial [24]. Much research has been done on developing low-power systems and techniques, ranging from circuit-level to architecture to compiler and operating system support. Our research concentrates on the memory subsystem mainly because it is a significant contributor of power consumption in embedded systems [19] and high-performance processors [8].

Current optimizing compilers perform various optimizations for increasing instruction-level parallelism and improving data locality. Many of these compiler optimizations, such as loop unrolling, loop tiling, and function inlining

A. Sangiovanni-Vincentelli and J. Sifakis (Eds.): EMSOFT 2002, LNCS 2491, pp. 364–381, 2002.

tend to increase code size. This increased code size is an important drawback in embedded systems, as many of these systems execute a single or a small set of applications, and application code sizes (executable sizes) are the primary factor that determines instruction memory size. An increase in instruction memory size, in turn, increases both per access dynamic energy consumption and leakage energy. Therefore, in an energy-conscious environment, the aggressiveness of compiler optimizations must be tuned carefully to keep instruction memory energy consumption under control.

In this paper, we investigate the effect of performance-oriented compiler optimizations on the memory energy consumption. We first analyze the tradeoffs between code size and performance by compiling several benchmark programs with different performance-oriented optimizations. Using analytical SRAM energy dissipation models, we investigate how an increased code size increases the memory energy consumption due to instruction accesses. In doing so, we also illustrate that a simple metric can be used as a first-degree estimate of instruction and data memory energy. Our second contribution is a compiler algorithm that determines a suitable optimization strategy for a given memory energy constraint. We study the effectiveness of our strategy in reducing memory energy for both loop unrolling and function inlining, and examine a futuristic scenario where leakage energy constitutes a sizeable portion of the overall memory energy budget. Note that the leakage energy consumption is particularly important in large SRAM memories that are active throughout execution and all trends [5] indicate that it will be much more important in upcoming process technologies.

Our experimental results emphasize the importance of taking into account the energy impact of optimizations early in the design process, and show that an energy-conscious function inlining algorithm can reduce energy consumed in memory by as much as 30% as compared to an aggressive performance-oriented inlining strategy, with comparable results for our loop unrolling strategy. Based on our results, we conclude that loop unrolling and function inlining are two optimizations that illustrate the tradeoff between performance and energy.

The remainder of this paper is organized as follows. Section 2 discusses related work in low-power research and the contribution of this paper within that framework. Section 3 presents results detailing the effects of some standard compiler optimizations on performance and resulting code size. Section 4 presents and analyzes energy-conscious heuristics for loop unrolling and function inlining. Section 5 reports on the energy impact of our approach when leakage energy is taken into account. Finally, Sect. 6 concludes the paper by summarizing our contributions and giving an outline of the planned future research on this topic.

2   Related Work

We discuss the related research in the field of low-power computing as it fits into three categories. At the *circuit-level*, there have been numerous optimizations proposed for minimizing energy consumption. Powell et al. [22] present a gated supply voltage design that interacts with a dynamically resizable instruction cache. By turning off the supply voltage to unused sections of the cache, their method effectively eliminates the leakage power consumption in those sections. Ye et al. [30] developed a method of transistor stacking in order to reduce leakage energy consumption while maintaining high performance. Chandrakasan and Brodersen [5] present several techniques on low-power circuit design.

At the *architectural-level*, much work that has been done to improve memory and CPU performance with the added expectation that power consumption will also improve. Also in this area several techniques have been proposed to reduce switching and leakage energy consumption at the cost of small performance losses. Hajj et al. [9] present instruction cache energy reduction by using an intermediate cache between the instruction cache and main memory. Their research shows that this smaller intermediate cache allows the main instruction cache to remain disabled most of the time. Delaluz, Kandemir, et al. [7] discuss using low-power operating modes for DRAMs to conserve energy consumption by effectively shutting off the DRAM when not in use. They present compilation techniques to analyze and exploit memory idleness and also a method by which the memory system can use self-detection to switch to a lower-power operating mode. In [1], Balasubramonian et al. suggest a cache and TLB layout that significantly decreases energy consumption while increasing performance. Their suggested layout allows for a dynamic memory configuration that analyzes size and speed tradeoffs on a per-application basis. Kaxiras, Hu, and Martonosi [13] present a method to reduce cache leakage energy consumption by turning off cache lines that likely will not be used again. By realizing that most cache lines typically have a flurry of frequent use when first introduced and then a period of "dead time" before they are evicted, Kaxiras et al. were able to reduce L1 cache leakage energy by $5\times$ for certain benchmarks with only a negligible performance decrease.

At the *software-level*, many preliminary investigations have been conducted into compiler techniques, more specifically to analyze how optimizations developed to increase performance can also improve energy consumption. In [4], Catthoor et al. offer a methodology for analyzing the effect of compiler optimizations on memory power consumption. Mehta et al. [17] investigate the effect of loop unrolling, software pipelining and recursion elimination on CPU energy consumption. They also present an algorithm for register relabeling that attempts to minimize the energy consumption of the register file decoder and instruction register by reducing the amount of switching in those structures. An introductory look into other high-level optimizations such as loop fusion, loop distribution and scalar replacement is performed with SimplePower in [26]. Hajj et al. examine function inlining in [9], but only in the context of its effectiveness with custom cache architectural modifications. In [14], Ellis et al. propose an integrated hardware/software approach for exploiting a power-aware memory hierarchy. Ramanujam et al. [23] present an algorithm to estimate the actual memory requirement for data transfers in embedded systems. They also present loop transformations that attempt to minimize the amount of memory required. In [10], Halambi et al. investigate a novel compiler technique to reduce the bit-width of instructions to reduce code size. Muchnick [21], Morgan [20], and Leupers [16] propose techniques for limiting the aggressiveness of function inlining. Our work is different from theirs in a number of ways: first, we focus on energy consumption; second, we present a metric that captures the energy behavior of the applications being optimized; and third, in addition to inlining, we also study other classical performance-oriented techniques.

Before developing a low-power technique, a predetermined method of estimating its effectiveness is required. Most research in this field leverages cycle-level simulators. Much work has been done on extending the popular SimpleScalar simulator [3] to include power-estimation models. As an example, both the Wattch simulator [2] and the SimplePower simulator [26] leverage the SimpleScalar framework to model power consumption in a standard 5-stage pipelined RISC datapath. The SimplePower simulator uses a table-lookup system based on power models for memory and functional units, while Wattch relies on more detailed parameterized models. Although these simulators provide detailed analysis of the energy consumption in the major system components, they are not primarily meant for investigating compiler optimizations. Also in this category are tools and methods that give run-time energy estimates. For example, the Castle tool [11] profiles hardware performance counters and feeds that data into energy models to estimate the overall consumption in the main CPU components. Kamble and Ghose [12] derive analytical cache energy dissipation models and verify them against a low-level simulator. The models in [12] are used to investigate architectural-level cache changes. In contrast, in this work, we exclusively study the impact of code optimizations on energy and performance.

3   Analyzing Performance and Energy Tradeoffs

We focus on a System-on-Chip (SoC) design where we have both an instruction memory and data memory. We also assume the existence of a data cache and a larger off-chip data memory. Consequently, data locality optimizations [29] are vital to take advantage of the small on-chip data memory structures. As with other architectures, it is also important to increase instruction level parallelism (ILP) as much as possible. This is particularly important in environments that process digital signal processing applications as many DSP codes have high ILP requirements.

The dynamic energy consumption in instruction memory during the execution of an application depends on two factors: the size of the instruction memory and the number of accesses to the instruction memory [4]. Applying aggressive performance oriented optimizations can increase both these factors. The size of the instruction memory can increase due to the fact that many compiler optimizations such as function inlining, procedure cloning, iteration space tiling, and loop unrolling increase code size. The number of instruction memory accesses can increase due to the fact that instruction reuse is decreased after most performance-oriented compiler optimizations for data locality [21]. In this section, we investigate the effect of various standard compiler optimizations on performance, executable size, and energy consumption.

3.1   Estimating Energy Consumption

In order to obtain the energy consumption results when compiler optimizations are applied, we have enhanced the analytical models for cache energy dissipation found in [12] to model energy consumption in instruction and data memories. These models use the run-time data from the cache such as hit/miss counts, data and address bit widths, and switching probabilities in order to estimate the energy consumption in its major components. The overall cache energy consumption is determined by this run-time data and also by the specifics of its organization, such as cache size, block size, and associativity.

We have changed these models to reflect an on-chip memory hierarchy such as would be found in an embedded SoC architecture, with an instruction memory, a data cache, and a data memory. In many embedded devices, the memory is of a preset size that is determined by the fixed applications that run on it. That is, the memory size is chosen by taking the executable size into account, plus a small amount of space for temporary variables. For our experiments, we set the memory size equal to the code size of a given benchmark. There are numerous capacitive coefficients that need to be evaluated in order to use our model. These values come from the data for the 0.8μ transistor implementation found in [27]. A memory power supply of 3.3 V is assumed, although for relative energy calculations its value is unimportant.

3.2   Methodology

We measured the effect of compiler optimizations using benchmarks from the SPEC CPU2000 [25] and MediaBench [15] suites. The chosen benchmarks from the MediaBench suite perform audio/video encoding and decoding and are similar to the tasks performed by typical embedded processors in multimedia devices. The SPEC benchmarks, while not normally considered to be indicative of an embedded workload, nonetheless have interesting locality characteristics and make for a good comparison to their MediaBench brethren.

To perform our experiments we decided to leverage a pre-existing optimizing compiler, the MIPSPro compiler from Silicon Graphics, Inc. The MIPSPro compiler allows us to pick and apply both loop nest optimizations and interprocedural optimizations by using compiler directives and/or setting runtime parameters. There are four major modes [18] of the MIPSPro compiler that perform different performance optimizations:

−**O0:** No code optimization is done.

−**O1:** Performs copy propagation, dead code elimination, and other local optimizations.

−**O2:** Performs non-loop if conversion, with some cross-iteration optimizations (no write/write elimination on loops without trip counts). This mode also performs loop unrolling and recurrence fixing. Basic blocks are reordered to minimize the number of taken branches.

−**O3:** Performs more if conversion and software pipelining. This mode also activates the Loop Nest Optimizer (LNO) that attempts locality-enhancing optimizations such as tiling, fission/fusion, and loop interchange [21,29].

Used in conjunction with these four optimization modes is the **–IPA** flag that turns on the interprocedural analysis optimizations, which include function inlining, interprocedural constant propagation, and dead function elimination. More details on these optimizations can be found in [18,28,29,21].

We also needed an accurate way to estimate the values of the run-time data for our target embedded architecture. The MIPS R10000 we were compiling on contains several relevant hardware counters that we were able to sample by using the SGI performance counter profiler tool, *perfex* [18]. Of course the R10000 is a general-purpose processor, with several advanced features that would most likely not be present in an embedded CPU core (L2 cache, out-of-order execution, multi-instruction issuing, etc.). We were able to overcome this obstacle by carefully choosing which hardware counters to profile, ignoring some statistics all together (L2 cache hit/miss rates), and using other data (percentage of speculated instructions) to mask the modern features of the R10000. In the end, we plugged the run-time data and memory size data into our analytical energy equations and estimated the energy output for a given code optimization.

3.3   Code Size/Performance Analysis

Figure 1 shows the resultant code size and dynamic instruction count for three of our benchmarks compiled using the various MIPSPro options. These results are normalized with respect to –O0. From these results, we can observe several trends. First, with the interprocedural analyzer turned off, each optimization mode from –O1 to –O2 shows (in general) both a smaller code size and a smaller dynamic instruction count. This is due to the fact that these levels perform many optimizations that either remove unnecessary code or optimize for performance without adding code. The largest benchmark, *mesa*, shows the least change in code size for all of the optimization modes. Even though it executes billions of instructions, the *equake* benchmark has a relatively small unoptimized code size, and the optimizations are very successful at decreasing the code size. For these benchmarks, there is a trend that shows that the larger the original (unoptimized) code size, the less effect these optimizations have on decreasing that code size. The –O2 optimization level leads to the smallest code size, on average a 10% improvement over no optimizations at all.

Second, at the –O3 optimization level, the loop nest optimizer performs more aggressive loop unrolling along with other trade-offing optimizations, and the results are mixed. For the benchmark codes in our experimental suite, running the LNO at the –O3 level leads to on average a 1% performance increase over the –O2 level across all benchmarks used, at the cost of a 11% increase in code size. This small performance improvement is due to the fact that some of our benchmarks do not contain too many regular nested loop structures to take full advantage of the aggressive optimizations in the LNO option. The –O3 optimization level leads to the best overall performance, the average benchmark running in 52% of the time of its unoptimized counterpart. On average, the optimizations have more of an effect on instruction count than they do on code size. However, there

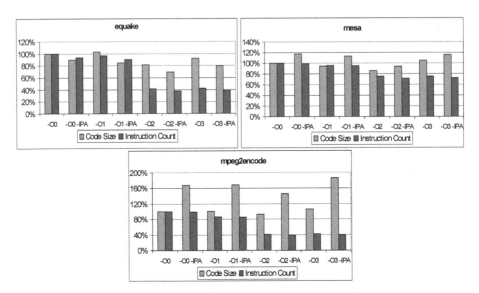

Fig. 1. Normalized code size and instruction count for MIPSPro optimization settings. These results show that the –O2 optimization level leads to the smallest code size on average, while the –O3 –IPA optimization level leads to the best performance on average. These results clearly show the tradeoff between code size and performance

does not appear to be a trend between the number of unoptimized instructions executed and the effect of the optimizations on that instruction count.

Third, we see that adding the –IPA option leads to more interesting results. Many of the optimizations in this group, most notably function inlining, generally increase the code (executable) size. On average, compiling with the –IPA flag leads to a code size that is 19% larger as compared to the same level of optimization without interprocedural analysis. With this penalty comes on average a 7% improvement in performance. The MediaBench benchmarks, which have a lower unoptimized instruction count than their SPEC counterparts, show a much smaller effect of the interprocedural analysis on performance. For example, compiling with the –IPA flag on the *mpeg2encode* benchmark leads to on average a 1% performance increase. We also observe that the most sophisticated optimization level (that is, –O3 –IPA) generates an average performance improvement of 55% and increases the executable size by 25% as compared to the original unoptimized code. Since the instruction memory energy consumption is proportional to the executable size, these results clearly show the tradeoff between memory energy and performance.

Therefore, an important question now is to determine an optimization strategy that gives an acceptable performance without too much of an increase in energy consumption. Later in Sect. 4, we present a heuristic approach for addressing this problem. In the following, we present a simple metric that allows an optimizing compiler to estimate instruction memory energy consumption without actually using an energy estimation tool.

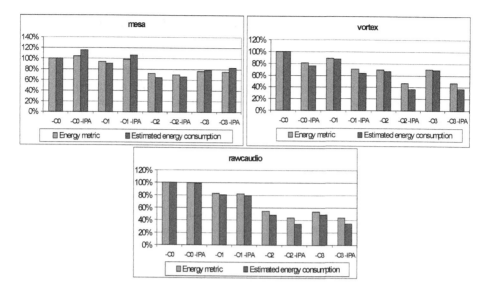

Fig. 2. Normalized energy metric values compared to normalized calculated energy consumption. These results show that the −O2 −IPA optimization level leads to the lowest energy on average, and that the energy metric shows similar trends to the analytically determined values (within 9% on average)

3.4   Analyzing Energy Consumption

In general, the per-access energy cost is directly related to the memory size, which in embedded devices is determined by the number of bytes required to store its code or data. Also, the total number of instructions executed is an accurate measure of the number of times that an instruction memory would need to be accessed. For this reason, we explored using the product of the code size and the instruction count as an early estimate to how much energy a given benchmark would be consuming in instruction memory. Similarly, for data memory, the energy consumption would be dependent on the number of accesses and the data size. In practice profiling can be utilized to find values for the instructions executed and number of data accesses. We used profiling to find the instruction count, but for simplification purposes we estimated the data access count by assuming a constant ratio (30% is a common choice) of data accesses to total instructions.

Figure 2 depicts the effect of the MIPSPro optimizations on the sum of these two metrics and compares the observed trends with those obtained through actual energy calculations. We see from these graphs that both our metric and actual energy calculations indicate that the −O2 −IPA option is the most energy-efficient one. In other words, using the most aggressive optimization strategy (−O3 −IPA) may not be the best choice from the energy perspective. We also observe that turning on the −IPA option appears to help the −O2 optimization mode more than others.

The results shown in Fig. 2 clearly indicate that the energy trends estimated when our metric is employed are similar to those obtained when actual energy calculations are carried out. For example, both approaches indicate that the $-$O2 optimization level with the interprocedural analysis turned on leads to the best energy conservation, consuming on average only 46% of the energy of the unoptimized benchmarks. More importantly, the relative estimated energy consumption shows very similar trends to our metric of $IC \cdot (CS + 0.3 \cdot DS)$. The metric is a good predictor of the relative energy consumed, on average being within 9% of the energy estimate.

Based on these observations, we conclude that a compiler optimization technique that minimizes the metric of $IC \cdot (CS + 0.3 \cdot DS)$ will also minimize the memory energy consumption in most cases. That is, the $IC \cdot (CS + 0.3 \cdot DS)$ metric can be utilized to rank the memory energy consumptions of different optimized versions of a given embedded code. This is an important conclusion as it indicates that, instead of using complex energy calculations, a compiler can adopt an energy estimation strategy based on the estimation of dynamic instruction count along with executable and data size. Also, previous work [28] shows that accurately estimating static and dynamic instruction count at compile time is possible even for sophisticated superscalar processors such as the MIPS R10000. Therefore, such estimates can be used for obtaining an idea about instruction and data memory energy consumption of a given code under a set of optimizations.

However, in many cases, instead of trying to reduce energy consumption as much as possible (at the expense of performance), it might be more important to compile a given application under a memory energy constraint. The following section addresses this issue, and proposes a heuristic technique that can easily be employed by an embedded compiler that targets both energy and performance.

4   Energy-Constrained Compiling

Since overly aggressive loop restructuring and interprocedural optimizations can lead to an undesirable tradeoff between energy consumption and performance, it is of interest to investigate tailoring these optimizations to fit to energy constraints. In this section we present and analyze heuristics that provide a systematic way of choosing a suitable loop unrolling strategy that attempts to improve performance while keeping in mind energy consumption. We then provide the same treatment to a heuristic for function inlining.

4.1   Energy-Aware Loop Unrolling Heuristic

Loop unrolling is a commonly used optimization whereby the loop body is replaced by several copies of the loop body [21]. The main performance benefit of loop unrolling is the removal of the execution of many of the branches found in the loop iteration limit test code. Unrolling code also has the potential to improve the effectiveness of other optimizations such as software pipelining. For

```
ENERGY_UNROLL(C, E_limit) {
        C_new = C;
        unroll_factor = 1;
        repeat {
                C_old = C_new;
                l_unroll = ∅;
                L = loop_list(C_old);
                for each loop l ∈ L do {
                        if (loop_size(l) < unroll_factor) then {
                                l_unroll = l;
                                break;
                        }
                }
                if (l_unroll ≠ ∅) then {
                        C_new = perform_unrolling(C_old, l_unroll, unroll_factor);
                        E = estimate_energy(C_new);
                }
                else {
                        unroll_factor = unroll_factor * 2;
                }
        }
        until (E > E_limit);
        return(C_old);
}
```

Fig. 3. Energy-aware loop unrolling heuristic

these reasons it is generally expected that applying loop unrolling will lead to both performance and energy improvements. However, the unrolled version of a code is in general larger than the original version. Consequently, loop unrolling may increase the per-access energy cost of instruction memory, and it would be important for an embedded compiler to be careful in applying unrolling to leverage the performance gains while limiting the increase in energy consumption.

Figure 3 shows our energy-aware unrolling heuristic. Our approach to the problem is as follows. We start with an unoptimized program and a set of loops inside the function that we are interested in unrolling. The value of the unrolling factor n is set to 1 in the initial iteration. At each step, we choose the first loop that has not been unrolled yet by a factor of n, and then unroll it by that amount. After the unrolling, we estimate the resultant energy consumption and compare it with the upper bound. If the upper bound has not been reached, we select the next loop to unroll. If all the desirable loops have already been unrolled by a factor of n or more, we increment n and repeat the process. Once the energy consumption after an unrolling becomes larger than the upper bound, we undo the last optimization and return the resulting code as the output.

Figure 4 shows the performance (in terms of graduated instruction count) for the *mesa* benchmark when our unrolling heuristic is applied under different

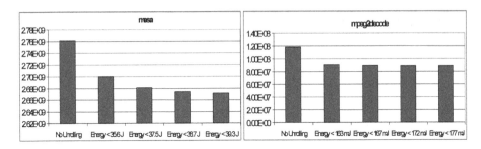

Fig. 4. Instruction count for the *mesa* and *mpeg2decode* benchmarks as a function of the energy upper-bound of our loop unrolling heuristic algorithm. These results show that by carefully choosing our energy upper bound, we are able to leverage the performance gains of unrolling while saving energy consumption when compared to the more aggressive unrolling strategies

memory energy upper bounds. The benchmark is compiled at the –O2 MIPSPro optimization mode with unrolling turned off as the base case. It can be observed that we achieve a performance improvement of 14% on the average across all energy bounds used. As seen in the second bar in each subgraph in Fig. 4, in the most restrictive case our heuristic algorithm is able on average to provide a 10% energy consumption savings while keeping performance to within 2% of the more aggressive unrolling strategies.

4.2   Energy-Aware Function Inlining Heuristic

Function inlining is an interprocedural compiler optimization whereby a copy of the code for a procedure call is replicated at a call site [29]. There are two major reasons that an optimizing compiler might apply inlining. First, applying inlining eliminates the overhead associated with a procedure call (saving and restoring register values, passing parameters, etc.). Second, inlining exposes the function code to the calling environment enabling subsequent code/data optimizations. For this reason, function inlining tends to increase performance and is employed by many commercial compilers. The main disadvantage to function inlining is that it generally increases code size, which, as we showed in Sect. 3, can lead to an undesirable instruction memory energy increase in embedded systems. Also, aggressive inlining can increase the number of local variables, potentially creating more register spills and increasing data memory energy. Therefore, an optimizing compiler designed for embedded environments should be careful in applying inlining and should try to strike a balance between increased performance and increased energy consumption. In particular, it is important to maximize the performance (through inlining) while keeping the increase in instruction memory energy under control.

Figure 5 shows our energy-aware inlining heuristic. Our approach to this problem is as follows. We start with the unoptimized program and, at each step, try to select the most appropriate (function, call-site) pair and perform

```
ENERGY_INLINE(C, E_limit) {
      C_new = C;
      repeat {
            C_old = C_new;
            F = function_list(C_old);
            if |F| < 2 then {
                  return (C_old);
            }
            else {
                  [f_inline, cs_inline] = best inlinable candidate ∈ F;
                  C_new = perform_inlining(C_old, f_inline, cs_inline);
            }
      }
      until (E > E_limit);
      return(C_old);
}
```

Fig. 5. Energy-aware function inlining heuristic

inlining. After an inlining is performed, we estimate or measure the resulting energy consumption and compare it with the energy upper bound. If we are still under the upper bound, we select the next (function, call-site) pair, and so on. The process stops when the energy consumption after the inlining becomes larger than the upper bound. When this occurs, we undo the last inlining, and return the resulting code as the output. This algorithm does not attempt to find an optimal inlining strategy in terms of energy consumption; it just guarantees that a specified upper-limit is not exceeded.

Note that our heuristic is not specific about how the most appropriate (function, call-site) pairs are chosen and in practice, there are several methods that can be used in order to select these pairs. The simplest approach is by brute force. An optimizing compiler can iterate through every possible function call to choose the one that gives the most performance benefit when inlined. This approach, while not very efficient, works well for applications with relatively small numbers of (function, call-site) pairs. A more advanced approach involves using an execution-profiling tool such as the SpeedShop tool on SGI machines [18]. By measuring hardware counters such as the number of graduated instructions, a profiling tool can provide hints to an optimizing compiler about call-sites where a large percentage of total instructions are executed. Many of these tools can also generate basic-block profiling runs, where the exact number of times that a function is called from a particular call-site can be exposed to the compiler. In practice, any of these methods can be used separately or in some combination to find appropriate (function, call-site) pairs for our inlining heuristic algorithm. For our experiments, we used the SpeedShop tool to generate lists of functions where inlining was potentially beneficial, and then we applied the brute force approach to select the most appropriate (function, call-site) pairs.

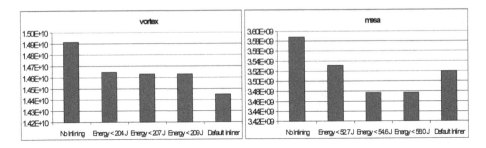

Fig. 6. Instruction count for the *vortex* and *mesa* benchmarks as a function of the energy upper bound of our function inlining heuristic algorithm. These results show that as we relax the energy upper bound, we see a diminishing benefit in terms of performance improvements. Also, these results show that our heuristic will produce very competitive code when compared to the MIPSPro default inliner

Figure 6 shows the energy consumption and performance (execution time) in terms of graduated instruction count for the *vortex* and *mesa* benchmarks compiled with the –O2 MIPSPro optimization mode when our inlining heuristic is applied under different memory energy upper bounds. It can be observed that we achieve a performance improvement of 10% on the average across all energy bounds used. It can also be seen that as we increase our energy upper bound (i.e., allow more energy consumption in memory), our function inlining strategy produces better-performing code, demonstrating the tradeoff between energy and performance. Comparing our heurstic to the default inliner of the MIPSPro compiler, it can be noted that our heuristic reduces the overall memory energy consumption while producing code that is within a few percent of the performance. For the *mesa* benchmark, the default inliner leads to a code that consumes over 83 J while our heuristic chooses an inlining strategy that consumes just under 58 J and performs slightly better. For the *vortex* benchmark, our heuristic consumes 70 J less than the default inliner, with a performance that manages to stay within 2%. The results given in Fig. 4 and 6 indicate that our heuristics improve performance while keeping the energy consumption in memory below a pre-set limit.

5   Leakage Energy

Energy consumption has two major components: dynamic energy and static (leakage) energy. While in CMOS circuits dynamic energy is the dominant part, the current trends indicate that the contribution of leakage energy to the overall energy budget will increase exponentially in upcoming circuit generations [5]. For example, recent energy estimates for 0.13μ process indicate that leakage energy accounts for 30% of L1 cache and as much as 80% of L2 cache energy [22]. Note that leakage energy is consumed as long as the circuit is powered on independent of whether it is actually accessed or not. This is in contrast to dynamic energy,

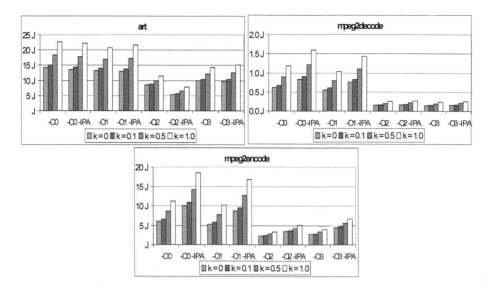

Fig. 7. Total energy consumption (as the sum of both dynamic and leakage energy) for the MIPSPro optimization modes. The value of k refers to the relative weight of the per-cycle leakage energy to the per-access dynamic energy. These results show that as leakage energy begins to dominate the total energy consumption equation, optimizations that lead to code growth lead to an even greater overall energy increase

which is spent only when there is an access. The leakage energy consumption of large SRAM memories is expected to be particularly problematic due to the fact that it increases with the size of memory.

In this section, we first show the impact of taking leakage into account on the tradeoff between memory energy and performance of loop restructuring and interprocedural optimizations. After that, we show how our energy-sensitive compilation approach in Sect. 4 performs when leakage is accounted for. Due to the fact that absolute values for leakage and dynamic energy consumption are closely tied to fabrication processes, in this work, we concentrate on the relative weight of leakage energy to dynamic energy. A common approximation is to take the per-cycle leakage energy consumption to be a ratio of the per-access dynamic energy consumption. We represent that ratio as a nonnegative value k where a smaller k value ($0.1 \leq k \leq 0.2$) represents current fabrication technologies and larger k values ($0.5 < k \leq 1.0$) represent a futuristic scenario where the effect of leakage energy will begin to outpace that of switching energy. Note that similar approaches have been used by previous research as well (e.g., [6]).

Figure 7 shows our results when we compile three of our benchmarks using the major optimization modes of the MIPSPro compiler when considering leakage energy. These results show an increasingly pronounced tradeoff between performance and energy. For example, compiling with the −O0 −IPA optimization mode leads to a performance/energy tradeoff when compared to un-optimized

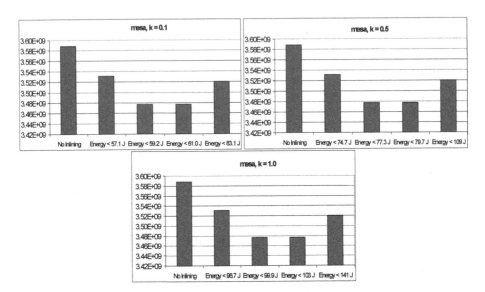

Fig. 8. Graduated instruction count versus memory energy upper bound for different values of k for the *mesa* benchmark. These results show that as we increase the relative weight of leakage energy, we require a greater upper energy bound to achieve the same performance via function inlining

code. For the *mpeg2encode* benchmark, when $k = 0.1$, there is a 1.5% performance improvement that is offset by a 4.3 J energy consumption increase. When $k = 1.0$, there is an equal performance boost that is now offset by a 7.3 J energy consumption increase. This can be explained by the fact that as we increase the relative weight of leakage energy, optimizations that lead to code growth lead to an even greater overall energy increase.

Figure 8 shows our results when we apply our function inlining algorithm to the *mesa* benchmark with an energy upper bound that takes leakage energy into account. For this experiment, we plotted the minimum energy upper bound that would be required for certain performance improvements. The results in Fig. 8 show that as we increase k, we require a greater upper energy bound to achieve the same performance via function inlining. For example, to achieve a performance improvement of 3.1% (as represented by the middle bar of each subgraph of Fig. 8), there is an almost 40 J difference between energy upper bounds when $k = 0.1$ and $k = 1.0$. Clearly, as leakage energy becomes more of a factor in future design fabrication methodologies, it will become increasingly important to limit code and energy growth at the expense of performance gains.

6   Conclusions and Future Work

Power consumption is an important design focus for embedded and portable systems. In this work, we have provided a systematic methodology for analyzing the effect of compiler optimizations on memory energy consumption. Realizing that many performance-oriented optimizations lead to a tradeoff between increased performance and larger code sizes, we have shown that the product of instruction count and code size is a fairly accurate energy measurement. We have also presented heuristics that attempt to tailor the aggressiveness of both loop unrolling and function inlining, and have analyzed their effectiveness. Finally, we have clearly demonstrated that our techniques will gain greater importance in future design generations, where leakage energy will constitute a larger percentage of the overall memory energy budget, and consequently optimizations that increase code size will increase instruction memory energy consumption by a greater factor.

The results in this work can be exploited in several ways. First, since embedded systems can tolerate much larger compilation times than their general purpose counterparts (as many of them run a single application for which a large number of processor cycles can be spent in compilation), we can run different optimized versions of the code and select the one with the best energy efficiency. Our results presented in this paper indicate that the compiler should attempt to minimize the product of the code size and dynamic instruction count since it is a very good first level approximation for instruction memory energy consumption. Second, systems with strict energy requirements can utilize our function inlining and loop unrolling heuristics to improve performance without violating design constraints. We have shown that the interprocedural optimizations such as function inlining can often lead to dramatic energy consumption increases, while the loop transforming optimizations, if applied intelligently, can lead to energy decreases alongside performance gains. Since interprocedural optimizations are often applied before their loop transforming counterparts, in order to maximize performance it would make sense to allow for the interprocedural optimizations to increase energy a certain percentage past the desired maximum, as the application of the loop transformations will be able to bring the energy consumption level back down to the limit.

In this paper, we introduced concepts and techniques that deal with embedded processor and more specifically Systems-on-Chip (SoCs). In the future we plan on extending our analysis to more generic SoCs, where perhaps embedded CPU cores, FPGAs, and ASICs are incorporated along with numerous memory devices. These heterogeneous SoCs require complicated interconnection protocols, an example being the AMBA bus standard. Optimizations that are meant to improve cache performance gain greater importance in an AMBA configuration, as a cache miss from the CPU can lead to lengthy latencies due to contention on the bus from other on-chip resources. Consequently our future work will include adapting our energy model to reflect the AMBA bus and analyzing how our loop restructuring and interprocedural optimizations effect the energy consumption of different SoC configurations.

Acknowledgement

This work was supported by a National Science Foundation Graduate Research Fellowship.

References

1. R. Balasubramonian, D. H. Albonesi, A. Buyuktosunoglu, and S. Dwarkadas. Memory hierarchy reconfiguration for energy and performance in general-purpose architectures. In *Proc. of the 33rd Int'l Symposium on Microarchitecture (MICRO)*, 2000.
2. D. Brooks, V. Tiwari, and M. Martonosi. Wattch: A framework for architectural-level power analysis and optimizations. In *Proc. of the 27th Int'l Symposium on Computer Architecture (ISCA)*, 2000.
3. D. Burger and T. Austin The SimpleScalar tool set, version 2.0. Techincal Report CS-TR-97-1342. University of Wisconsin-Madison, 1997.
4. F. Catthoor, S. Wuytack, E. De Greef, F. Balasa, L. Nachtergaele, and A. Vandecappelle. *Custom Memory Management Methodology: Exploration of Memory Organisation for Embedded Multimedia System Design*, Kluwer Academic Publishers, 1995.
5. Chandrakasan and R. Brodersen. *Low Power Digital CMOS Design*, Kluwer Academic Publishers, 1995.
6. G. Chen, R. Shetty, M. Kandemir, N. Vijaykrishnan, M. J. Irwin, and M. Wolczko. Tuning Garbage Collection in an embedded Java environment. In *Proc. of the 8th Int'l Symposium on High Performance Computer Architecture (HPCA)*, 2002.
7. V. Delaluz, M. Kandemir, N. Vijaykrishnan, A. Sivasubramaniam, and M. J. Irwin. DRAM energy management using software and hardware directed power mode control. In *Proc. of the 7th Int'l Symposium on High Performance Computer Architecture (HPCA)*, 2001.
8. J. Edmondon et al. Internal organization of the Alpha 21164, a 300-MHz 64-bit quad-issue CMOS RISC microprocessor. *Digital Technical Journal*, 1995.
9. N. B. I. Hajj, C. Polychronopoulos, and G. Stamoulis. Architectural and compiler support for energy reduction in the memory hierarchy of high performance microprocessors. In *Proc. of Int'l Symposium on Low-Power Electronics and Design (ISLPED)*, 1998.
10. A. Halambi, A. Shrivastava, P. Biswas, N. Dutt, and A. Nicolau. An efficient compiler technique for code size reduction using reduced bit-width ISAs. In *Proc. of Design, Automation, and Test in Europe (DATE)*, 2001.
11. R. Joseph and M. Martonosi. Run-time power estimation in high-performance micrprocessors. In *Proc. of Int'l Symposium on Low-Power Electronics and Design (ISLPED)*, 2001.
12. M. B. Kamble and K. Ghose. Analytical energy dissipation models for low-power caches. In *Proc. of Int'l Symposium on Low-Power Electronics and Design (ISLPED)*, 1995.
13. S. Kaxiras, Z. Hu, and M. Martonosi. Cache decay: exploiting generational behavior to reduce cache leakage power. In *Proc. of the 28th Int'l Symposium on Computer Architecture (ISCA)*, 2001.
14. A. R. Lebeck, X. Fan, H. Zeng, and C. S. Ellis. Power-aware page allocation. In *Proc. of the 9th Int'l Conference on Architectural Support for Programming Languages and Operating Systems (ASPLOS-IX)*, 2000.

15. C. Lee, M. Potkonjak, and W. H. Mangione-Smith. MediaBench: a tool for evaluating and synthesizing multimedia and communication systems. In *Proc. of the 30th Int'l Symposium on Microarchitecture (MICRO)*, 1997.

16. R. Leupers. *Code Optimization Techniques for Embedded Processors*, Kluwer Academic Publishers, 2000.

17. H. Mehta, R. M. Owens, M. J. Irwin, R. Chen, and D. Ghosh. Techniques for low-energy software. In *Proc. of the 25th Int'l Symposium on Computer Architecture (ISCA)*, 1998.

18. *MIPSpro compiling and performance tuning guide*. Silicon Graphics, Inc., 1999.

19. J. Montanaro et al. A 160-MHz, 32-b, 0.5W CMOS RISC microprocessor. *Digital Technical Journal*, 1996.

20. R. Morgan. *Building an Optimizing Compiler*, Butterworth-Heinemann, 1998.

21. S. Muchnick. *Advanced Compiler Design and Implementation*, Morgan Kaufmann Publishers, 1997.

22. M. D. Powell, S-H. Yang, B. Falsafi, K. Roy, and T. N. Vijaykumar. Gated-Vdd: A circuit technique to reduce leakage in deep-submicron cache memories. In *Proc. of Int'l Symposium on Low-Power Electronics and Design (ISLPED)*, 2001.

23. J. Ramanujam, J. Hong, M. Kandemir, and A. Narayan. Reducing memory requirements of nested loops for embedded systems. In *Proc. of the 38th Design Automation Conference (DAC)*, 2001.

24. D. Singh and V. Tiwari. Power challenges in the Internet world. In *Cool Chips Tutorial: An Industrial Perspective on Low-Power Processor Desgin* (held in conjunction with *The 32nd Int'l Symposium on Microarchitecture (MICRO)*), 1999.

25. The Standard Performance Evaluation Corporation. http://www.spec.org.

26. N. Vijaykrishnan, M. Kandemir, M. H. Irwin, H. S. Kim, and W. Ye. Energy-driven integrated hardware-software optimizations using SimplePower. In *Proc. of the 27th Int'l Symposium on Computer Architecture (ISCA)*, 2000.

27. S. E. Wilton and N. Jouppi. An enhanced access and cycle time model for on-chip caches. In *DEC WRL Research Report 93/5*, 1994.

28. M. Wolf, D. Maydan, and D. Chen. Combining loop transformations considering caches and scheduling. In *Proc. of the 30th Int'l Symposium on Microarchitecture (MICRO)*, 1997.

29. M. Wolfe. *High Performance Compilers for Parallel Computing*, Addison-Wesley Publishing Company, 1996.

30. Y. Ye, S. Borkar, and V. De. A new technique for standby leakage reduction in high-performance circuits. In *IEEE Symposium on VLSI Circuits*, 1998.

FlexCC2: An Optimizing Retargetable
C Compiler for DSP Processors

Valérie Bertin*, Jean-Marc Daveau*, Philippe Guillaume*, Thierry Lepley*,
Denis Pilat*, Claire Richard*, Miguel Santana*, and Thomas Thery*

STMicroelectronics, Central R&D
Embedded System Technology,
850 Rue Jean Monnet,
F-38926 Crolles cedex, France
{valerie.bertin,jean-marc.daveau,thierry.lepley,denis.pilat,
claire.richard,miguel.santana,thomas.thery}@st.com

Abstract. The design of efficient compilers for embedded processors has
emerged with the growing importance of embedded application-specific
processors and DSPs in consumer, multimedia and communication applications. We present in this paper the FlexCC2 compiler. FlexCC2 is
a retargetable compiler for embedded processors, part of the FlexWare
embedded software development environment. Application specific processors often contain specific and dedicated features like specific instructions that traditional compilers hardly accommodate. In this context,
compilers able to produce high quality code, both in size and performance while being easily retargetable and able to use processor specific
instructions represent a particular competitive differentiation. FlexCC2
offers such a differentiation to its users.

1 Introduction

Embedded processors are increasingly used in today's complex Systems-on-Chip
(SoC) as a good compromise between flexibility, performance, power and competitive cost. While RISC based embedded processors are still widely used, an
emerging alternative is the application-specific processor approach. This approach attempts to combine the flexibility of general-purpose programmable
processors with the performance achieved through domain-specific architecture
optimizations. This approach has been used for both μcontroller and DSP processors.

ST has numerous examples of SoC products that have benefited from the
application-specific processor approach. Areas where these processors are being adopted is in constant growth, resulting in a strong demand for embedded
software development environments and tools [12]. Embedded programming is
naturally evolving from assembler to high-level C and compilers for application-
specific processors have become very desirable [8,10]. This trend raises the need

---

* Authors listed in alphabetical order.

A. Sangiovanni-Vincentelli and J. Sifakis (Eds.): EMSOFT 2002, LNCS 2491, pp. 382–398, 2002.

for powerful C compilers capable of producing hand-coded quality assembler code on both standard and application specific processors. However, due to the specialized architecture and instruction set of ASIPs, fully exploiting their capabilities requires dedicated code generation and optimization techniques [9]. Many issues need to be addressed by a compiler for embedded applications:

- Compiler development time is essential for time-to-market of embedded processors and their applications.
- Traditional optimizations are required to achieve good performance but are usually not sufficient to achieve performances equivalent to hand-coded assembly code.
- Application-specific processors[1] provide many interesting features that are not covered by traditional compilers: hardware-do loops, irregular datapath, specific instructions, etc. Exploiting such features is fundamental to achieve higher performances.
- Some machine related optimizations must be addressed on a per-machine basis, requiring compiler support at machine instruction-level for rapidly developing them.

The FlexCC2 compiler, presented in this paper, addresses all these issues: it is flexible, easily and quickly retargetable, and it includes standard and DSP-oriented optimizations.

The paper is organized as follow: in section 2, we give an overview of FlexCC2. Section 3 presents the architecture of FlexCC2, including the CoSy[2] compiler framework and our EliXir back-end infrastructure. Sections 4 and 5 present respectively our high and low-level optimizations. The retargeting process is described in section 6. We show some results in section 7 before presenting some perspectives, related work and concluding respectively in sections 8, 9 and 10.

2   FlexCC2 Overview

FlexCC2 is a retargetable compiler for embedded processors, especially tailored to cope with application-specific processors and in particular AS-DSPs[3]. It aims at providing state-of-the-art optimizations for these processors, addressing in particular the issues defined above. FlexCC2 has been designed as a modular framework allowing the development and integration of new optimizers both at the high and low levels.

Several advanced optimizations techniques presented in literature [4,6,14,17] have been redesigned for embedded processors, solving many related issues often ignored by research, and mainly due to the irregular architecture of application-specific processors. Moreover they have been integrated into a very complete framework, providing a large choice of compiler analysis and optimizations. Several of those techniques were not in the end applicable in our context because

---

[1] Frequently called ASIP, standing for Application-Specific Instruction-Set Processor
[2] CoSy is an international trademark of ACE Associated Computer Experts bv.
[3] Standing for Application-Specific DSP

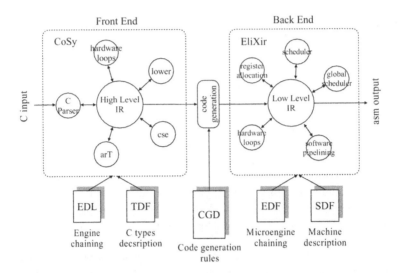

Fig. 1. FlexCC2 architecture

they were inadapted, too restrictive, or making assumptions that did not hold in real contexts.

Side effects between optimizations, which can be magnified by the irregularity of an architecture, have been considered and solved by changing the phase ordering of optimizations or developing specific heuristics.

Furthermore, several DSP-oriented optimizers have been integrated in the framework, composing a powerful retargetable DSP compiler. Moreover many target specific optimizers have been easily developed and added to this framework to deal with some peculiar processor features. Finally, the achieved results show that we have reached our goals, especially for code quality.

3   Architecture of FlexCC2

3.1   Overview

The architecture of FlexCC2 is depicted in figure 1. It is built around the CoSy compiler development suite [1] with an in-house back-end called EliXir. Our approach is to build ST specific high-level optimizations modules on top of the CoSy technology and to complete it with a powerful back-end infrastructure and the corresponding low-level optimizations modules.

3.2   CoSy

The CoSy framework (figure 2) is a compiler construction environment designed to build optimizing compilers. It provides an ANSI C front-end, a set of pre-built generic optimizations and a code generator generator. The framework is architectured around the concept of *engine*. An engine is a module performing

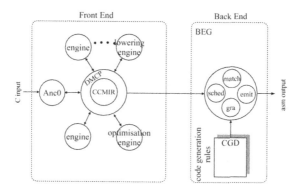

Fig. 2. CoSy compiler architecture

optimizations, transformations or analysis on an internal form called CCMIR (Common CoSy Medium Intermediate Representation). The compiler is a sequence of engines, called one after the other. CoSy provides a full set of engines needed to build a compiler.

Access to the intermediate representation is ruled by the fSDL (Full Structure Definition Language). An important feature of the CoSy intermediate representation is its extensibility. fSDL allows user nodes and fields to be added to the intermediate form and manipulated through automatically generated functions and macros.

CoSy optimizers. CoSy provides a set of standard optimization engines such as: common subexpression elimination, copy propagation, constant folding, strength reduction, loop unrolling, tail recursion, switch optimization, ...

CoSy also provides a set of lowering engines that are used to transform the intermediate representation and adapt it to the features supported by the processor, making easier the retargeting process: bitfield, structure, array and union access lowering, calling conventions and argument passing, fixed/floating point conversion to library calls.

Engine chaining determines the order in which optimizations are applied. CoSy allows loop or conditional execution of a sequence of engines based on command-line options or the result of an optimization or analysis engine. Engine chaining order can greatly influence the performances of a compiler.

BEG: the back-end generator. BEG is a back-end generator. From a set of Code Generator Description (CGD) targeting files describing CCMIR tree covering rules, it generates the necessary set of engines to perform code generation, scheduling and register allocation. In our compiler infrastructure, BEG is also used to connect CoSy to EliXir.

3.3   EliXir

EliXir is a STMicroelectronics proprietary back-end designed to replace CoSy back-end optimizers (i.e. the scheduler and register allocator) by a more modular

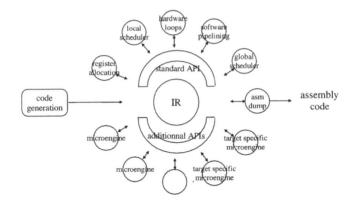

Fig. 3. EliXir structure

infrastructure allowing powerful low-level optimizations. The structure of EliXir is represented on figure 3. It is based on a low-level intermediate representation built around the notion of machine instruction. Moreover EliXir relies on the concept of micro-engines, a concept similar to Cosy engines. A micro-engine can be generic or designed for a specific processor.

The goal of EliXir is to perform analysis and optimizations that require detailed information about the target processor. Main optimizations at this level are register allocation, scheduling and peephole optimization. The goal of the low-level IR itself is to hold the program information. Because of the wide range of optimizations that can be run on it, the structure of the IR has been intentionally chosen simple and generic enough to support any kind of low-level optimizations.

EliXir is targeted by a machine description file that describes relevant processor information for low-level optimizations: register structure, memory banks, computational hardware resources and a variety of operation features, such as output syntax, control semantics, resource usage, dataflow. An example of machine description is given on figure 7.

Compared to other similar frameworks [15], the processor model handled by EliXir has been extended to offer better support for irregular AS-DSPs or ASIPs architectures. Examples are composite register files, hardware loops, multiple memory spaces.

An important part of low-level optimizations in modern compilers is scheduling and code compaction. Schedulers use the parallelism model of the processor to reorganize and compact instructions. Two main properties drive scheduling: instruction encoding properties and processor hardware resource usage. Low-level infrastructures are generally based on reservation tables that are relatively flexible and simple enough to avoid too large compilation times and engineering complexity. Nevertheless, reservation tables are not sufficient to entirely deal with irregularities and parallelism of AS-DSPs. EliXir is based on a resource usage extended in two major directions:

1. The VLIW slot notion proposed in [4]. This technique, which relies on standard reservation tables, avoids binding an operation to a computational resource or an encoding slot too early in the scheduling process.
2. The concept of stimulated resource. Stimuli are used to allow non-conflicting concurrent access to functional units. Two concurrent access to a resource with the same stimulus do not conflict. Stimulated resources allow to handle operand dependent parallelism at scheduling time, instead of enforcing it earlier in the compiler flow. This concept is particularly interesting to manage at scheduling time complex post-operation such as post-incremented addressing modes.

4   High-Level Optimizations

FlexCC2 offers a complete set of standard and advanced high-level optimizations. Standard optimizations rely exclusively on CoSy optimizations engines. Advanced optimizations have been developed by the FlexCC2 team. Our approach consists in focusing our effort exclusively on optimizations having a high added-value for embedded applications, while relying on CoSy for new general optimizations. The modular aspect of CoSy and the ability to support user nodes in the intermediate representation allowed us to specialize easily the compiler for embedded applications. Up today, our advanced developments have been focused on DSP optimizations:

1. Array to pointer transformation.
2. Efficient use of DSP addressing resources and modes.
3. Support for zero-overhead hardware-do loops.

4.1   ArT

ArT [6] is an ARray Transformation module replacing array references by pointers, making efficient use of complex addressing modes. The arT flow applied to each loop is represented on figure 4. In a first step, arT extracts induction variables and analyzes based induction expressions of the loop. A based induction expression is an expression of the form $¡base + \sum_k \alpha_k \times i_k + cte¿$ where $base$ is a base address, i_k are induction variables and α_k and cte are loop invariants. Connivance sets[4] are then built and used to assign induction expressions to pointers.

When connivance sets are formed, a single pointer variable is associated to each set and all based induction expressions in it can be obtained using a loop invariant displacement from that pointer, using at best pre or post modification addressing schemes. Pre-modification initializes the pointer to the base address and uses $base+displacement$ addressing mode to access the data.

---

[4] A connivance set groups induction expressions which are associated to the same base address and belong to the same induction variable family.

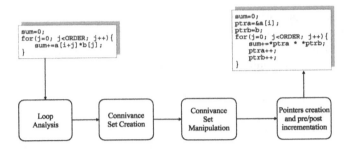

Fig. 4. ArT transformation flow

Post-modification initializes the pointer to the first data address and use *post-incremented/decremented* addressing mode to update the pointer all along the loop body. ArT handle any loop nest level and multi-dimensional array although multi-dimensional accesses are not always optimal.

4.2 Support for Hardware-Do Loops

Hardware-do loops are a DSP oriented feature, rarely found in general purpose processors. In these loops, the loop counter and jumps are managed by the hardware providing a significant performance improvement in the execution of the loop (zero overhead). To be transformed into hardware loops, software loops have to fit several criteria, among which some are known at high-level (iteration count for instance) and some others only after code generation (like loop code size). In FlexCC2, hardware loop candidates are detected at high-level, when information on loops is easily available, and transformed in the back-end, after code generation, when the final loop size and other acceptance criteria are known. The selected loops are transformed using the special hardware loop instruction and suppressing any now redundant instruction (tests and jumps). On the other hand, if a given loop is rejected, we keep its standard form, suppressing any specific information added at high-level.

The interest of this approach is that it can totally be undone when a loop does not match any hardware-do loop criteria, eliminating the need for any recovery mechanism.

4.3 GarT

GarT is an extension of arT to handle more efficiently multi-dimensional arrays inside nested loops. ArT processes each loop level independently and multi-dimensional array accesses in a loops nest are transformed using several pointers whereas the memory representation of multi-dimensional arrays would allow to use only one.

The scope of array transformations, restricted by arT to one loop level, is widened to nested loops. Induction expression analysis and array references replacement by pointers are applied globally by GarT to nested loops. In particular,

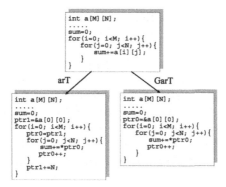

Fig. 5. GarT

a single pointer is used to access elements of a multi-dimensional array, counterbalancing its value at the end of each nested loop in order to start next iteration of the outer loop with the right value. Figure 5 illustrates the transformations done by GarT.

5   Back-End Optimizations

Back-end optimizations are implemented as microengines in EliXir. Low-level optimizations include: advanced register allocation, support for hardware-do loops, software pipelining, global and local scheduling, peephole optimization.

Currently, early register assignment is performed in FlexCC2 for different reasons. First, AS-DSPs are often constrained by their small number of registers and maximum allowed register pressure is easily reached even using register pressure sensitive heuristics scheduling approaches. Second, the irregularity of execution distribution in DSP algorithms, spending most of their time in loops, makes that any small mistake in the shape of badly placed spill code can end up into non neglectable performance loss. As a consequence, software pipelining and global scheduling are done as a classical postpass scheduler, after register allocation.

5.1   Register Allocation

Register allocation deeply impacts the performance result of the compiled application, not only by the amount of spill code introduced but also by enabling, limiting or even preventing the application of other optimizations such as scheduling and software pipelining. Our primary concern for register allocation has been loops. In the context of DSP code, spill in loop must be avoided at all costs. Spill reduction is mainly achieved through a combination of live range splitting and hierarchical allocation. Live range splitting is performed using an SSA[5]

---
[5] Static Single Assignment

form. Embedded processors are characterized by irregular and constrained register sets. Therefore efficient coalescing is necessary to limit *move* between register classes.

The FlexCC2 register allocation API provides a retargetable register allocation framework designed to cope with irregular and composite register sets. It currently implements the Briggs coloring heuristic with iterated coalescing [5] as well as spill optimizations (spill in unused register sets, spill location coalescing) and support for code in SSA form.

The standard allocator of FlexCC2, built on top of the register allocation API, implements the Callahan and Koblenz's hierarchical algorithm [3] where the hierarchy concern loops. Unfortunately, results of this algorithm have not met all our expectations and different improvements as well as other hierarchical approaches are being considered.

5.2   Software Pipelining

Software pipelining is a scheduling technique that overlaps successive iterations of a loop in order to increase loop's throughput. This is a fundamental optimization for DSP processors, since signal processing applications spend most of their execution time in loops.

A large range of software pipelining techniques exist in literature but not all are applicable to our context. FlexCC2 implements the modulo scheduler described in [14] on top of the EliXir scheduling API. It is based on a modified list scheduling algorithm, with limited backtracking, that allows to efficiently pipeline a large variety of loops. Today, software pipelining is performed on hardware loops only.

Early software pipelining techniques and scheduling were not satisfying in our context even using register pressure sensitive heuristics approaches. The main problem came from the difficulty to accurately evaluate register pressure in the context of composite register files. We are investigating now a cooperative *register allocation/scheduling* approach that will perform register allocation on the data dependence graph to maximize parallelism and loop pipelining opportunities.

5.3   Scheduling

Global scheduling techniques have been designed to efficiently exploit deeply pipelined and VLIW processors. Even if application-specific DSPs have generally a small pipeline, they unveil a certain amount of instruction level parallelism that is not entirely used by local schedulers. Moreover embedded processors generally do not provide support for speculative execution and spend most of their execution time in already software pipelined loops. These two points reduce the impact of global scheduling on embedded programs compared to general purpose processors. Nevertheless, we decided to implement a global scheduler in FlexCC2, essentially to improve code density, expecting however minor performance improvements. Surprisingly we achieved very good results.

Code density being a fundamental criterion in embedded processors, as memory is limited and area consuming, general techniques such as trace scheduling did not catch our attention. We preferred to use global scheduling techniques that do not require compensation code, such as superblock scheduling [7]. Nevertheless, we found in the dominator path scheduling [17] the most promising technique, since it generalizes superblock scheduling.

5.4 Peephole Optimizer

Peephole optimizations improve the assembly code by replacing sequences of consecutive instructions with equivalent but more efficient sequences. These optimizations are based on a pattern-matching engine that looks for user-defined patterns (consecutive instructions) in a given program. Such optimizations allow to clean the final code simply and at very low cost such as fine-grain common sub-expression elimination, generally difficult to perform at high-level.

In FlexCC2, we have extended the concept of peephole to patterns based on dataflow relationships (e.g. def, use, kill), extending considerably their capabilities with respect to strictly consecutive sequences. Nevertheless, the heavy cost of def-use recomputation enforces to carefully limit the pattern description space and the scope of the pattern in the recognition phase.

6   Retargeting

Concurrent development of the architecture and the C compiler for a new processor has proven essential, especially when considered in the context of a high-level language driven embedded software development process. Early availability of the compiler allows to design carefully the ISA (Instruction Set Architecture) from a compilation perspective and remove compiler unexploitable instructions to achieve the best *combined* compiler-processor performance.

Consequently fast compiler retargeting is fundamental and so it was considered as a major objective for FlexCC2. We achieved it by automating as much as possible lowering and target file description. FlexCC2 retargeting is divided in three phases:

- Lowering. The intermediate representation is transformed to match target processor capabilities. CoSy provides a set of lowering engines for this task. Moreover, we have contributed to the design of new lowering tools for CoSy, now available in ACE commercial releases.
- Code generation rules and machine description. These files are used as input by respectively BEG and EliXir. The former needs to be written by a targeting expert as it requires CCMIR and target processor instructions knowledge.
- Engines and microengines chaining description file.

We use code generation to produce EliXir intermediate form through calls to an EliXir generated API. This API is automatically generated by EliXir from

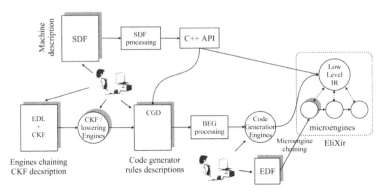

Fig. 6. FlexCC2 retargeting flow

```
// General purpose data registers
regset rl[7] syntax "r##l";
regset rh[7] syntax "r##h";
regclass rlh = rl,rh;            // short
regset r = rl:rh;               // long
regset ext[7];                  // extensions
regset xr = rl:rh:ext syntax "r##"; // long long

// Multiplier register
regclass ml = rl[0], rh[0];
regclass mr = rh[0], rh[1], rl[1];

// Non scratch registers
non_scratch = xr[0..1], xr[6], r[0..1], r[6];

// Slots (XBUS and ALU "move")
slot SALU, SXBUS;

/Functional units
unit MULT;      // DCU
unit ACU;       // ACU
unit ACU_SAR;   // ACU
unit Y_BUS;     // BUS
unit CST_BUS;   // BUS
```

```
operation lea_ACU(register base, int offset,
register ax){
    syntax="lea\t#{offset}+{base},{ax}";
    reserv_table = [
        read base (1),
        write ax (1),
        use CST_BUS,
        use ACU,
        use ACU_SAR[ax]
    ];
}

operation mv (register rs, register rd){
    syntax = "dmv\t{rs}, {rd}";
    slot SALU = "dmv\t{rs}, {rd}";
    slot SXBUS = "xmv\t{rs}, {rd}";
    reserv_table = [
        read rs(1),
        write rd(1)
    ];
    semantic = {
        type = MOVE;
    }
}
```

(a) Architecture description   (b) Instruction description

Fig. 7. EliXir processor description (SDF)

the machine description file. Figure 6 describes the retargeting flow of FlexCC2, targeting files appear in shadow. A machine description example is given on figure 7.

Processor Specific Instructions and Features

Specific instructions are handled today in FlexCC2 by lowering engines, in charge of recognizing and replacing the corresponding subtrees in the high-level IR by a specific user node. Covering rules for these nodes are then added to the code generator description (CGD) to produce the appropriate instructions. Processor specific features are exploited through target specific microengines. Code generation can generate virtual instructions that are transformed to real instructions by specific (e.g. non-orthogonal post-operations) or generic (scheduler exploiting the *slot* notion) microengines.

```
(a) Assembly code before addressing mode optimization

...
ldx_f   ax1,r41
add     r01,#1,r21
xmv     axx1,ax1
...

(b) Optimized code using non-orthogonal post-operation

...
ldx_f   ax1,r41 || xmv_ACU  axx1,ax1 || add   r01,#1,r21
...
```

Fig. 8. Specific instruction optimization

Intrinsics. Intrinsics are function calls directly mapped onto processor instructions. They are used as mean to easily use processor specific features at C language level. This feature is commonly used in DSP applications. Intrinsics are described in CoSy in a specific file and automatically detected by the front-end. The user is in charge of transforming them into standard or user CCMIR nodes through a lowering engine, and to map them to the required instructions during code generation.

Virtual Instructions. Non orthogonal post-operations on addressing modes are a feature frequently found on application-specific processors, generally because of encoding constraints. For instance:

- Transferring a value between two different register banks as a post-operation, but using the same register number for both banks: $A_i = R_i$.
- Post decrementing an address register with the value of an index register, but using the same register number for both register banks: $A_i \mathrel{-}= I_i$.

These operations are essential for performance, but difficult to exploit at code generation time. The FlexCC2 approach consists in generating virtual instructions that will be detected and replaced later by EliXir microengines. This is also applied to orthogonal addressing post-operations. Figure 8 shows an example of this kind of optimizations, where a non-orthogonal post-operation is introduced in the form of a *xmv_ACU* instruction by an addressing mode optimization microengine.

7   Results

FlexCC2 has been retargeted to the STMicroelectronics MMDSP+ single-MAC audio processor. Several large applications as well as test[6] and benchmarking[7] suites have been compiled with the resulting compiler. Figure 9 shows an example of C code and the assembly code produced by the compiler.

---

[6] PlumHall, SuperTest
[7] NullStone

```
for (i = 0; i < lg; i++){
    s = L_mult (x[i], a[0]);
    for (j = 1; j <= m; j++){
        s += L_mult(a[j], x[i-j]);
    }
    s = L_shl (s, 3);
    y[i] = round (s);
}
```

```
L1:
     cmp r5h,#0
     ble L17
L5:
     rep L17,r5h
L6:
     xmv     ax1,axx1
     ldx_f   ax2--,r01
     xmv     ax2,axx2
     mea     axx1,++#1
     ldx_f   ax1,r0h
     L_fmul r01,r0h,r2 || ldx_f axx1++,r01
; Loop pipelined with II=2
     ldx_f   axx2--,r0h || repi  PIPEL14,#9
L10:
     L_fmul r01,r0h,r3 || ldx_f axx1++,r01
     L_addsat  r2,r3,r2 || ldx_f    axx2--,r0h
PIPEL14:
     L_fmul r01,r0h,r3 || mea   ax2,++#2
     L_addsat  r2,r3,r2
     L_msl  r2,#3,r2
     round_L   r2,r21
     stx_f  r21,ax3++
L17:
```

(a) C source   (b) Assembly code

Fig. 9. Source and assembly code

The retargeting effort for this compiler is difficult to evaluate, because
FlexCC2 developments were done in parallel. However we consider that four
months were necessary to achieve a first prototype.

Retargetability is essential for time-to-market, but performance is still more
important for DSP compilers. Table 1 shows comparative results for FlexCC1
and FlexCC2 technologies for various DSP applications. The FlexCC1 compilation technology is a retargetable C compiler based on the rule-driven approach
described in [11]. This approach is very effective at mapping onto irregular architectures with very limited resources, since the compiler developer has good
control over the optimization and code generation process [12].

A representative benchmark for FlexCC technologies is the ETSI C specification of the Enhanced Full Rate (EFR) codec of the GSM wireless communication
standard. This is a complex DSP application of approximately 15000 lines of C
code. Its source code compiled *without any modification* with FlexCC2 requires
21.4 MIPS[8] to run the application in real-time, i.e. *within 7%* of the performance of hand-coded assembly code (table 1, on top). Adding some directives
for Y memory placement and some pragmas (a total of 5), a performance of 18.7
MIPS is reached, i.e. *7% better* than hand-coded assembly. Furthermore, we anticipate additional savings with our new register allocator and global scheduling
microengines[9]. For comparison, we obtain a value of 52,8 MIPS with a pure
CoSy compiler, while the theoretical limit of the EFR benchmark is estimated
to about 16 MIPS for such a class of processors.

---

[8] Performance metric frequently used for embedded processors. It is equivalent to the
processor clock frequency (in Mhz) necessary to run the application in real-time. In
this case, we need a 21.4 Mhz MMDSP+ to run the EFR. The lowest is this value,
the better is the compiler.

[9] Our latest result for the original EFR code (without pragmas or source code modifications) is 18.6 MIPS.

Table 1. FlexCC2 compiler performance results

	FlexCC1	FlexCC1 low level C	FlexCC2	FlexCC2 + directives
Mips	52,8	25,5	21,4	18,7
Instructions	6366	6322	6312	6345

	FlexCC1		FlexCC2	
	Mips	Instructions	Mips	Instructions
AMR	56,0	20127	25,9	19324
MP3 encoder	54,4	12850	43,6	12902
Prologic	29,0	1683	21,57	1692
G723.1	98,0	5879	36,6	6464
Shectl (control code)	110,0	3518	99,5	2075

8   Perspectives

Improved versions of FlexCC2 are already planned. They will include new optimizers that are currently being designed or under development. These optimizers will tackle some new problems as well as still not addressed topics:

1. Exploitation of multimedia instructions. Such instructions have been added to traditional instruction-sets to improve multimedia application performance. However they are rarely exploited by compilers except through builtin functions. An optimizer allowing to recognize sets of expressions or statements that can be favorably replaced by multimedia instructions is currently under development. It is based on sophisticated pattern-matching techniques [13].

2. Automatic use of special instructions. Today most special instructions are accessible at C level only through intrinsic functions. As a consequence, embedded programmers need to adapt their applications to these functions to achieve better performances, but with a serious impact on productivity and portability. Pattern-matching techniques developed for multimedia instructions will be used to automatically detect and replace expressions equivalent to such instructions.

3. Interprocedural analysis. This will enable our technology to perform global optimizations by getting across procedures calls boundaries.

4. Alias analysis. FlexCC2 provides today a restrict pragma to relax aliasing constraints into the compiler for program variables. However, we have developed in parallel an alias analysis component based on a highly compact data structure that automatically computes alias information and provides it to high and low level optimizers. Such a component will be integrated to FlexCC2 as soon as the interprocedural infrastructure will be available.

5. Automatic memory placement. Multiple memory banks is a feature commonly found on DSPs and ASIPs. Memory placement aims at efficiently distributing variables across multiple memory banks to exploit data access parallelism. Such an optimization will naturally rely on alias and interprocedural analysis as well as in heuristic techniques to do the distribution.

We are also working on an architectural database that will allow to generate part of the retargeting files, and to reduce or eliminate inconsistencies due to multiple descriptions needed at high and low level in the compiler.

9   Related Work

FlexCC2 is a general compiler infrastructure providing a modular framework for developing new optimizations and experimenting with compiler flow. FlexCC2 differentiates from other compilers at several levels:

- Modular optimization framework covering both high and low levels. Machine-Suif [16] and Zephyr [2] also provide a complete infrastructure, while Suif [18] is restricted to high-level optimizations. All them have been intensively used in research projects, to develop new algorithms and to explore new compiler topics. FlexCC2 provides however much more flexibility, especially for compiler flow definition and construction. Moreover FlexCC2 has been led upto an industrial stage. Last but not least, FlexCC2 allows multi-level optimizations, i.e. optimizations starting at high level and being completed at low level.
- Support for specific instructions, irregular architectures and instruction sets. This was already addressed by FlexCC1 [11], but has been enhanced in FlexCC2. This allows to fully exploit the processor capabilities without requiring hand coded assembly code, a key point for embedded processors. Many optimizers in FlexCC2 (register allocation, scheduling, software pipelining) have been developed to cope with application-specific processor architectures. Several efforts in this area have been described in the literature [9,10], however FlexCC2 covers many more aspects, integrating them into a global and consistent framework.
- DSP-oriented optimizations. As we have seen in previous paragraphs, FlexCC2 offers a strong support for DSP processors. General purpose compilers have been used for embedded DSP processors with poor results. No other specific DSP compilers exist at our knowledge.
- Generic hardware loop system. DSP applications are generally composed of some intensive computing loops operating on arrays, monopolizing most of the execution time. Therefore DSP processors provide special mechanisms to improve the implementation of such loops. Unfortunately most compilers are not able to exploit conveniently such mechanisms. To our knowledge, only CoSy [1] provides a generic retargetable hardware loop system.
- Retargetability. Results achieved in this area by FlexCC2 are very good [10] and are a key factor for the success of our processors and of early products that use them.

Moreover, using general purpose compilers for ASIPs has rarely been successful, due to a bad or a lack of support for specific processor features. This has been the case in particular for bitstream, multimedia and now network processors. Furthermore, generic optimizations tend to become processor dependent when reaching a certain level of optimization. An example of this is scheduling for code compaction, as it needs to deal with features such as instruction encoding constraints, parallelism, data path irregularities and so on, to be really efficient. Flexibility of FlexCC2 combined to previous points turn our infrastructure into an excellent solution for ASIPs and more generally for embedded processors.

Finally, several FlexCC2 components are based on original ideas, resulting of advanced in-house research done on different topics: array to pointer transformation, dataflow peephole optimizer, support for irregular architectures, etc.

10 Conclusion

We have presented here the FlexCC2 compiler for embedded processors. The growing place of ASIPs and AS-DSPs in Systems-on-Chip (SoC) design has brought the need for a new category of compilers capable of dealing with embedded processors specificities. The FlexCC2 compiler tries to meet the challenge of being easily retargetable while offering performances rivaling that of hand-coded assembly. These results are achieved by developing a modular compiler infrastructure relying on CoSy and adding specific DSP optimizations modules. Irregular architectures can be accurately modeled in our back-end machine description format and target specific microengine can be written to cope with it. Finally, our benchmarks have shown that performance results achieved make of FlexCC2 a highly competitive compiler for DSPs.

Acknowledgment

The authors wish to thank Jean-Marc Gentit and Sebastien Leduc of TPA/DMD ST division for their contribution to MMDSP+ C compiler based on FlexCC2.

References

1. ACE Associated Compiler Expert bv. The CoSy Framework, a Compiler Construction System. *Ref. CoSy-8006-fw, 2000.*
2. A. Appel, J. Davidson, and N. Ramsey. The Zephyr compiler infrastructure. *Internal Report, http://www.RCS.virginia.edu/zephyr, 1998.*
3. D. Callahan, B. Koblenz. Register Allocation via Hierarchical Graph Coloring. *Proceedings of the ACM SIGPLAN'91 Conference on Programming Languages Design and Implementation, Volume 26, June 1991, Pages 192-202.*
4. Z. Chamski, C. Eisenbeis, E. Rohou. Flexible Issue Slot Assignment for VLIW Architectures. *Proceedings of the Software and Compilers for Embedded Systems Symposium, SCOPES'99, September 1999.*

5. L. George, A. Appel. Iterated Register Coalescing. *ACM Transactions on Programming Languages and Systems, Vol 18, No 3, May 1996, Pages 300-324.*

6. P. Guillaume. Contribution aux Aspects Dorsaux de la Synthèse de Systèmes Monopuces. *Ph.D thesis. University of Grenoble, June 1999.*

7. W-M. Hwu & all. The Superblock: An effective Technique for VLIW and Superscalar Compilation. *Journal of supercomputing A:229-248, 1993.*

8. R. Leupers. Code Optimization Techniques for Embedded Processors, Methods, Algorithms and Tools. *Kluwer Academic Publishers, 2000.*

9. S. Liao, Code Generation and Optimization for Embedded Digital Signal Processors. *Ph.D. thesis, Massachusetts Institute of Technology, 1996*

10. C. Liem. Retargetable Compilers for Embedded Core Processors. *Kluwer Academic Publishers, 1997.*

11. C. Liem, P. Paulin. "Compilation Techniques and Tools for Embedded Processor Architectures", in *"Hardware/Software Co-Design: Principles and Practice," J. Staunstrup, W. Wolf (editors), Kluwer Academic Publishers, 1997.*

12. P. Paulin, M. Santana. FlexWare: A Retargetable Embedded Software Development Environment for Application-Specific Instruction-set Processors. *IEEE Design & Test Magazine, Special Issue on Embedded Processors, Summer 2002.*

13. G. Pokam, F. Bodin. A Retargetable Preprocessor for Multimedia Instructions. *Proceedings of the 9th workshop on Compilers for Parallel Computers (CPC'2001), June 2001.*

14. B. Ramakrishna Rau. Iterative Modulo Scheduling. *Hewlett Packard HP:-94-115 research report, November 1995.*

15. E. Rohou, F. Bodin, A. Seznec. SALTO: System for assembly language transformation and optimization. *Technical report 1032, IRISA, September 1996.*

16. M.D. Smith and G. Holloway. The Machine-SUIF Documentation Set. *Technical report, Harvard University, 2000.*

17. P.H. Sweany. Inter-Block Code Motion Without Copies. *Ph.D thesis, Colorado State University, 1992.*

18. R. Wilson & all. SUIF: An Infrastructure for Research on Parallelizing and Optimizing Compilers. *ACM SIGPLAN Notices, 29(12), Dec. 1996.*

Physical Programming: Beyond Mere Logic

Bran Selic

Rational Software Canada
770 Palladium Drive, Kanata, Ontario, Canada K2V 1C8
bselic@rational.com

Abstract. Conventional wisdom encourages software designers to take a Platonic approach to design; they are instructed to focus on ensuring the correctness of the logic of their software while playing down or even ignoring the generally unpleasant characteristics of the underlying computing platform. However, as software systems become increasingly more integrated into our everyday activities, this approach can be highly counterproductive. For example, when a software system is distributed over multiple physically distinct platforms, seemingly mundane things such as transmission delays or component failures can have a critical impact on program logic. The widely-held view that physical concerns only matter in highly specialized domains, such as real-time or fault-tolerant systems, leaves us singularly unprepared for the coming generation of Internet-based software. In this talk, we first examine the different ways in which software logic can be affected by its physical context. We then outline a conceptual framework for extending traditional software engineering concepts to deal with these issues.

1 Introduction

The mind knows no limits other than those imposed by the imagination. On a whim, in our thoughts we can make time run backwards, reverse gravity, and exceed the speed of light many times over. The unbounded nature of the world of ideas is so enticing that Plato postulated it to be the true reality, claiming that our physical experience was merely its anomalous and flawed reflection, corrupted by the imperfections and sluggishness of matter. In this ideal world, for example, perfect triangles – formed out of perfectly straight lines possessing no thickness – always have angles that add up to exactly 180 degrees. Physical triangles, on the other hand, being constructed out of imperfect physical fabric using imperfect physical tools, invariably deviate from this ideal, no matter how carefully crafted.

It is the unfortunate lot of engineers to have to cope with the idiosyncrasies, intricacies, and impediments of the physical world. A good engineer learns very quickly not only that form must follow function but also that it must respect the inherent properties and limitations of the construction materials used: a skyscraper must be capable of carrying its own weight, the shape of an automobile is limited by the plasticity characteristics of steel. In fact, the choice of construction materials is a primary issue in most engineering design.

How does software engineering fit in this picture? Software is certainly unique in that, of all engineering media, it allows the most direct realization of human design

A. Sangiovanni-Vincentelli and J. Sifakis (Eds.): EMSOFT 2002, LNCS 2491, pp. 399–406, 2002.

ideas. There is no metal to bend, concrete to pour, or material to cut and shape. It almost sounds like the perfect construction material, the stuff of pure ideas, unhampered by the recalcitrant nature of physical matter. This widely held view is succinctly expressed in the following quote from a recent article on the nature of software engineering:

> *"Because [programs] are put together in the context of a set of information requirements, they observe no natural limits other than those imposed by those requirements. Unlike the world of engineering, there are no immutable laws to violate."* [9]

The thesis put forward in this paper is that this is not the case, that despite its unique nature, most software is very much susceptible to the laws of physics and that these laws can often have a profound effect on the design of our program logic. Furthermore, we argue that we need to adjust our basic programming technologies and methods of software design to accommodate this – an approach that we call, somewhat whimsically, *physical programming*.

2   Software and Its Platforms

All software, of course, executes on some computing *platform*. A platform consists of the computing hardware and, usually, some supporting software such as an operating system and, in many cases, an application programming framework such as .NET [5] or EJB [4]. In a very real sense, the platform represents the construction material out of which we fashion software. In this section, we illustrate how and why a platform can affect the design of software.

2.1   Real-Time Systems

The most obvious effect that a platform has on software is that it controls its speed of execution. In principle, a slower processor will execute the same software more slowly than a faster one. If we care about the speed of execution (i.e., response times) than this effect may be important, even crucial. In real-time programming for example, getting a response out before a deadline expires may be the difference between a correct and an incorrect program, or to put it more dramatically, the difference between safe operation and a catastrophe.

Consequently, in such applications, we must be aware of the capabilities of the platform on which our software is intended to execute. If our processor does not have the throughput that we would prefer, we will have to adjust our algorithms accordingly – for instance, we may decide to use a faster but less precise calculation instead of a slower but more accurate one. This is the type of trade-off that is common in all forms of engineering.

Another frequent design issue in real-time and embedded software development is the partitioning of software into concurrent tasks. Ideally, we would like to dedicate a separate task to each concurrent activity. Unfortunately, it often happens that the context switching time from one operating system task to another is so high that we are forced into a partitioning scheme that minimizes this overhead rather than one that is logically most appropriate. In this case, the top-level design is driven by the constraints of the underlying operating system platform.

2.2   Distributed Systems

The impact of platforms is even more serious when it comes to distributed software systems. This is because physically distributed computing environments introduce a whole spectrum of complex physical phenomena that cannot be hidden from our software, no matter how hard we try. (The theory that, by virtue of remote procedure call mechanisms, distributed programming can be made the same as "regular", non-distributed programming, is mostly a marketing myth promulgated by vendors with vested interests.)

One of these phenomena is the possibility of partial failure, that is, a situation where some part of our platform is no longer operating properly due to an underlying hardware or a software failure. Because there is typically no single point of failure in a distributed environment, it is often expected or even required that the software should be able to recover from such partial failures (in fact, this may be the primary reason why a distributed solution is being used). A common technique in these situations is to keep some kind of back-up component that takes over the lost functionality when the primary component fails. This is a rather tricky business involving many complex mechanisms. First, there is the very difficult issue of maintaining the stand-by in a state such that it can take over the function of the failed part with minimal impact on the rest of the application (e.g., by minimizing recovery time or minimizing the amount of recovery code in the remainder of the application). There is also is the problem of detecting that a component has failed. Usually, the only mechanism available is some kind of time out, whereby we determine that a failure has occurred because an expected response has not been received within some pre-defined period. Determining how long to wait is a difficult design decision. Waiting too long may lead to unacceptable response times while not waiting long enough may lead to false conclusions about failures, which, of course, can result in even more complex failure and recovery scenarios. Note that the time-out interval is dependent on the specific needs of the application, indicating that it may not always be possible to solve this problem in a general way by some underlying shared failure detection facility.

Another notoriously difficult category of problems in distributed systems stem from communication delays. Very long delays can result in status information that is out of date. This can greatly complicate decision-making. (Just imagine how we would change our driving style if the visual feedback that we get about our car's position on the road has a delay of, say, 2 seconds.) Furthermore, if different parts of a distributed application experience different transmission delays, the possibility of relativistic effects in the Einsteinian sense opens up. Some parts of the application will learn about changes of state before others, resulting in different and possibly inconsistent views of the state of a system. If each part of the system reacts according to its view of the system state then it becomes very difficult to devise a system that acts in a coherent and consistent manner. (For a summary discussion of this complex issue and some proposed solutions to the problem the reader should start with the paper by Lamport [3]).

The essential problems of distribution are nicely captured in a set of so-called "impossibility results". These are (unfortunately) little-known but extremely important theorems about certain fundamental limitations inherent in distributed computing. One of these results, proven by Fischer, Lynch, and Patterson in 1985 [1], states that, in a distributed system it is not possible to guarantee that agreement can be reached in finite time over an asynchronous communication medium, if that medium can lose messages or if one of the distributed sites can fail. As we noted above, if the various distributed sites cannot agree on what needs to be done, then there is no guarantee that the distributed program will behave consistently. Hence, if there are strict reliability requirements for our distributed software, we will likely need to design our software to deal with it in some way.

Another important impossibility result (proven by Halpern and Moses [2]) asserts that, even when communication is fully reliable (i.e., there no messages are lost or re-ordered by the communication medium), it is not possible to guarantee distributed agreement if communication delays are unbounded. This result does not even mention the possibility of site failure!

Perhaps the most important thing to note about these impossibility results is that they stem from the underlying physics of the platform and, like all physical laws, they cannot be eliminated by technological means.

In particular, this means that it is not possible to hide these undesirable features by wrapping a layer of "virtual machine" software around the distributed platform. Yet, this is the approach that usually offered as the "solution" to the problem, often by those who are ignorant of its inherent limitations (trying to devise a foolproof distributed agreement protocol is the modern-day equivalent of attempts to square the circle). The best that such a virtual machine layer can achieve is to reduce the likelihood that these unpleasant effects will occur, but it can never remove them altogether.

It is, of course, theoretically possible to create a virtual machine such that the probability of these events happening is so small that it is negligible for practical purposes. But, the more we strive to improve the reliability of such a layer, the greater its complexity and cost and the higher its performance and memory overheads. (In a seminal paper on this topic Saltzer and his colleagues argue that providing reliability-improving services in lower software levels is often of little or no value [7] – the so-called *end-to-end* argument. Unfortunately, as with the impossibility results, many practitioners are unaware of these conclusions.)

Thus, it becomes a question of engineering: balancing the cost of constructing the virtual machine and its overheads against the simplicity of the application. It is difficult to do this in practice though, since vendors generally do not provide hard data about the reliability levels of their software. Part of the reason for this is that there is no standard framework for describing such information. One of the objectives of this paper is to initiate a campaign to change this unsatisfactory state of affairs.

2.3   Platform-Independent Design?

These examples all demonstrate that program logic may have to bend itself to deal with platform issues. Yet many of our fundamental computing technologies are designed as if these issues do not exist (revealing the batch processing origins of most "modern" technologies). Much of today's software is part of larger on-line systems that are fully integrated into and interoperate with the physical world. Consequently, the need to address platform issues in the design of our software is even more pressing now than it ever was.

In that light, it is interesting to examine the latest discussions on so-called "platform independent" software – a term that is in much in vogue these days [1]. The intent here is to be able to target a software system to a variety of different, possibly mixed, platforms, without having to adapt it separately for each specific platform.

This is a perfectly reasonable objective that yields significant benefits, such as portability and separation of concerns. However, far too often, it is interpreted naively to mean that platform issues should simply be ignored when writing software. This is a head-in-the-sand approach that ignores the kinds of platform dependencies that we just discussed. In fact, as argued later in this paper, the only practical way that platform independence can be achieved is to be explicit about computing platforms and their properties.

3   Physical Programming

We conclude that, just like their colleagues in other engineering disciplines, software engineers must also take into account the properties of their construction materials in their designs. We now briefly outline an approach to software engineering that is based on that premise. For want of a better name, we call this approach *physical programming*.

3.1   Resources and Quality of Service (QoS)

Many of the platform effects described in the previous section stem from the finite nature of the physical world. There is always a finite amount of memory, information propagation speeds are finite, the reliability of hardware is finite, and so on. When we have a finite supply of something, we often refer to it as a *resource* – an element or fabric whose capacity is limited in some way by its underlying physical nature.

Hence, resources play an important role in physical programming. For convenience, in our approach we shall model resources as servers, that is, elements that provide some kind of service (storage service for memory, processing service for CPUs, communications services for hardware busses and operating systems, etc.). Since these services are limited in some way, it is appropriate to talk about their *quality of service* (or *QoS* for short). By this we mean a specification of how well the service can be performed. Usually, this is a quantitative measure of some kind: bits per second, kilobytes of memory, number and size of buffer blocks, availability level of the hardware, and so on. Therefore, a resource can be represented as a server whose services can be characterized by explicit quality of service attributes.

When talking about QoS, it is useful to differentiate between *offered QoS* and *required QoS*. Offered QoS is a characteristic possessed by a resource, while required QoS is a characteristic associated with its clients. For example, a client may require from a database that a read operation should be performed within some deadline (required QoS), while the database may provide a guarantee that a reply to a read request will occur within some maximum interval (offered QoS).

A fundamental problem of all engineering is to determine whether the offered QoS will meet the required QoS; i.e., is the construction material capable of sustaining the loads that we intend to impose on it? If the offered QoS is adequate (i.e., better or equal than the required QoS), we will say that such a system is *quantitatively consistent*.

Determining the quantitative consistency of a system is typically a difficult question to answer in any engineering discipline, but it is particularly difficult in the case of software. This is because in software so many resources, such as CPU and memory, are shared between otherwise independent elements. Two or more software tasks will share a physical processor and contend for its resources, thereby interfering with each other in complex ways. The patterns of interference are difficult to establish since they depend on the specific dynamics of the competing software entities. Since there is so much variety in software logic, this is very hard to generalize and, therefore, it is very hard to devise a general analytical approach to solving these problems. In this respect, software lags significantly behind other engineering disciplines and, until we come up with generic solutions, we will likely remain dissatisfied with the level of dependability of software engineering. (It is worth reminding ourselves that no other engineering discipline has failure rates that are even comparable to those of software engineering.)

Nonetheless, some analytical techniques for determining quantitative consistency of software systems have emerged. Perhaps the most prominent and most generally useful ones are performance analysis techniques, mostly based on queuing theory. Another very useful set of techniques, unfortunately limited primarily to real-time systems, is schedulability theory.

With such techniques are often able to model our software systems and predict their key QoS characteristics *before* we actually construct the final systems. This, of course, is the standard way of doing things in engineering, but is quite rare in software development. The much more common scenario is to construct the complete system, find out whether and where it is deficient, and then try to fix it by using various ad hoc techniques such as caching critical code and data or applying compiler and code optimizations. All too often, these attempts are unsuccessful.

3.2   Physical Types

In programming languages, a type is essentially a predicate that defines the qualities required to perform a particular function or role. They are primarily used to determine and ensure logical consistency of programs without actually having to execute them. Traditionally, programming language types are restricted to specifying only qualitative aspects such as the ability to perform specific operations. To exploit the benefits of this technique for something like physical programming, we need to add quantitative aspects (QoS characteristics) to the notion of types. For instance, we may add to the signature of an operation of a type its QoS characteristics, such as its average and maximum response times (for a given platform, of course). This allows us to determine if a particular software system is quantitatively consistent: if a client accesses that operation with a specific response requirement, we can match directly it against the type of the server. We will refer to these expanded type definitions with QoS characteristics as *physical types*.

Can such physical types be statically checked the way that standard programming language types are checked? The answer is "yes" in most cases. This is the good news. The bad news is that it may require very complex analysis methods, due to the extreme level of coupling of software described earlier. Thus, decisions on type compatibility in most cases cannot be determined locally, but may require analysis of the complete system.

This raises the specter of scalability limits of physical type checking. This is indeed a problem that requires further research. However, it is not a new problem and is, in essence, no more complicated than the problem of trying to prove the qualitative consistency of a system using techniques such as model checking and theorem proving. In fact, it may be simpler, since quantitative techniques are much more amenable to simplification based on approximations (e.g., by linearization).

3.3   Specifying Platform-Independent Software

So, how can these concepts help us achieve meaningful platform-independent software? As noted previously, the answer is not to ignore platform issues. Instead, *platform-independent software needs to be defined with an explicit statement of the QoS properties that it expects of its underlying platform in order to function correctly.* Since QoS specifications are technology neutral, such a statement, in effect, defines the full range of platforms that are capable of supporting that software application without being explicit about any single one them. It also allows us to formally verify whether a specific candidate platform has the capacity to support that software or not.

In fact, this is based on the same resource-client model described for physical types. The client in this case is the entire software application, with explicit required QoS characteristics (so many buffers, so much communications bandwidth, so much CPU speed, etc.) while the resource is the underlying platform with its offered QoS characteristics.

The job of verifying whether a particular platform can support a particular software application can be greatly simplified if the application incorporates a *canonical platform model* and a *targeting specification* that describes how the various parts of the software are mapped to elements of the canonical platform model. The semantics of this mapping are that the source (software) elements are realized by the corresponding target (platform) elements. For example, we may decide to map a whole set of application objects to a single canonical "task" entity (which is a generalization of the concept of an operating system task) with a defined maximum context switching overhead. The implication is that all of these objects would exist in the shared address space provided by an actual operating system task or equivalent.

In this way, each element of the canonical platform model summarizes the QoS requirements of all the software elements that it realizes. (Typically, multiple software elements are mapped onto a single canonical platform model element, although other combinations are possible.)

One major advantage of this approach is that it allows us to verify if the software application is internally quantitatively consistent without reference to any specific platform – which is precisely what platform-independence is about.

The second advantage is that it simplifies the task of deploying the software to a specific target. Since we have already mapped the software to the canonical platform model, targeting the software to an actual platform now involves the much simpler mapping of one platform model to another.

Last and not least, the canonical platform model can greatly simplify quantitative consistency verification, since we only need to verify the quantitative consistency between two platform models rather than between the software and a platform (which requires much more complicated analyses).

4   Conclusion and Summary

The influence of computing platforms and the physical world on the design of software will not go away. If anything, as software becomes more pervasive in our everyday lives, platform issues will become a more critical issue in the design of most software. Ignoring these aspects can and will lead to major failures of software systems (and projects) resulting in potentially severe economic and social breakdowns as our dependency on software increases. Consequently, it is high time for us to start adapting our basic programming and related technologies to make them more capable of addressing these critical issues.

In this paper, we outlined one potential approach to the problem. At its core, it is based on two very simple concepts: resources and quality of service. However, these concepts are rich enough to be extended to cover most quantitative issues that occur in software and can serve as a basis for constructing predictive models of software. Such models can then be analyzed to ensure that proposed designs will meet their basic quantitative requirements before the systems are actually constructed. This, in turn, should increase the reliability of software engineering and software systems to be more in line with the levels of reliability that we have come to expect of more traditional engineering disciplines.

Note that this or any similar approach to the problem can only be effective if we define standards for the specification of resources and their QoS characteristics. This allows platform providers and software application developers to have a common language, which is the prerequisite for platform independence. At least one such standard already exists: the OMG standard UML profile for schedulability, performance, and time [7]. Although this standard is intended primarily for real-time applications, it provides a general conceptual framework for modeling QoS and resources that can be easily extended to other application domains.

References

1. Fischer, M., Lynch, N., and Paterson, M.: Impossibility of Distributed Consensus with One Faulty Process, Journal of the ACM, (**32, 2**)(1985) 374–382
2. Halpern, J. and Moses, Y.: Knowledge and Common Knowledge in a Distributed Environment, Proceedings. of the 3rd ACM Symposium on Principles of Distributed Systems, (1984) 50–61.
3. Lamport, L.: Time, Clocks, and the Ordering of Events, Communications of the ACM, (**21, 7**) (1978) 558–565
4. Matena, V. and Stearns, B.: Applying Enterprise JavaBeans – Component-Based Development for the J2EE Platform, Addison Wesley, New York (2001)
5. Microsoft Corporation: What is Microsoft .NET? (http://msdn.microsoft.com/netframework/productinfo/overview.asp) (2002).
6. Object Management Group (OMG): Model Driven Architecture – A Technical Perspective, OMG document ormsc/01-07-01, (http://www.omg.org/cgi-bin/doc?ormsc/2001-07-01) (2001)
7. Object Management Group (OMG): UML Profile for Schedulability, Performance, and Time, OMG document ptc/02-03-02 (http://www.omg.org/cgi-bin/doc?ptc/2002-03-02) (2002)
8. Saltzer, J., Reed, D., and Clark, D.: End-to-end Arguments in System Design, ACM Transactions in Computer Systems, (**2, 4**) (1984) 277–288
9. Wang, W-L.: Beware the Engineering Metaphor, Communications of the ACM, (**45, 5**) (2002) 27–29

Processes, Interfaces and Platforms.
Embedded Software Modeling in Metropolis

F. Balarin[1], L. Lavagno[1,2], C. Passerone[2], and Y. Watanabe[1]

[1] Cadence Berkeley Labs, 2001 Addison St. 3rd Floor, Berkeley CA 94704, USA
[2] Politecnico di Torino, C. Duca degli Abruzzi 24, 10129 Torino, Italy

Abstract. The goal of the Metropolis project is to provide a framework for modeling embedded systems across several levels of abstraction, from functional (untimed) to RTL, for various implementation choices, from dedicated hardware to programmable hardware and processors. Emphasis is placed on formal specification and refinement, in order to allow one to apply both synthesis, analysis and verification algorithms at all steps of design. The framework itself provides some such algorithms, as well as allowing one to "plug in" new ones.
In this paper we focus on the embedded software design problem, starting from abstract specifications, then decomposing them into networks of processes and communication media, and finally mapping them onto a platform including a processor, a Real Time Operating System and communication components. We illustrate how a clean separation of concerns between functionality and interfaces, as well as between computation and communication, leads to better re-use and a more optimized implementation. We also discuss how the problem of efficiently mapping a process network to a software platform can be formulated and solved.

1 Introduction

The complexity of embedded software design is increasing exponentially, because programmable platforms are seen as the only economically viable way to use a growing number of transistors, in the face of rising costs of silicon design and mask fabrication. Such programmability can take the form of both traditional software, on multiple interconnected micro-processors and Digital Signal Processors, and reconfigurable logic, as embedded FPGAs. Thus the number of embedded software designers, according to recent industry surveys, is growing much faster than that of hardware designers. This shifting of functionality from hardware to software obviously implies that many problems that were traditionally tackled by digital electronic design automation, will now extend into the more traditional software design domain.

While software programmability may reduce the number of silicon re-spins, due to easier ways of fixing bugs and upgrading designs, the increasing complexity of the software components, and the real-time and safety requirements of most embedded systems, mean that traditional methods of software design are no longer adequate. In particular, informal natural language specifications, poorly architected Application Programmer Interfaces, haphazard communication and synchronization mechanisms among concurrent tasks, and implementation flows based on the common compile-load-debug cycle, are becoming less and less suitable to tackle the demands outlined above. It is thus not surprising that a number of approaches that were traditionally reserved to hardware design, such as executable specifications, synthesis flows, standardized APIs, and formal

A. Sangiovanni-Vincentelli and J. Sifakis (Eds.): EMSOFT 2002, LNCS 2491, pp. 407–421, 2002.
© Springer-Verlag Berlin Heidelberg 2002

verification, are gaining acceptance in many embedded software design areas. The first domain where formal specification and software synthesis have become widespread is telecommunications, where the need for international standards, to interface equipment from different producers, is obvious. Similar interfacing and interconnection factors are at play in automotive electronics, where the cost of mistakes can also be prohibitive, due to the potential damage to people and property, and the resulting liabilities.

This paper focuses on the software content of embedded systems, which are defined as electronic systems that use computers and electronics to perform some task, usually to control some physical system or to communicate information, without being explicitly perceived as a computer. A key characteristic of such systems is the *heterogeneity* both of specification models, because of the habits and needs of designers from very different application fields, and of implementation mechanisms, because of the variety of tasks and environmental conditions.

This heterogeneity has so far caused a huge fragmentation of the field, resulting in very diverse design methodologies with often scarce tool support. De facto standards in terms of specification models and tools have emerged only in a few areas, namely telecommunications and automotive, as discussed above. This is of course untenable in the long run, due to the growing gap between design needs, i.e. available transistors and potential applications, and design capabilities, since the number of lines of code per designer per day has remained approximately constant for a number of years. This gap can be tackled only, analogously to what happened to digital hardware through the physical and logic design automation revolutions, by automating the design process from higher and higher levels of abstraction.

We claim that sequential programming languages, even with the use of object-oriented design methods, are insufficient to tackle the needs outlined above. This is because they are not specifically suitable to any application area, i.e. they do not provide the abstractions that a control algorithm designer or a protocol designer needs (a transfer function or a finite state machine, e.g.). Moreover, they do not satisfy the requirement to represent concurrency explicitly, in order to exploit the availability of a large number of computing resources (CPUs, DSPs and FPGA cells). Finally, they poorly document design intent and interfacing requirements, thus resulting in limited re-usability and extensibility across multiple designs.

While the general-purpose computing world is dominated by the Intel Instruction Set architecture, the IBM PC architecture, and the Windows and UNIX operating systems, embedded platforms are much more diversified. This is mostly due to the different needs of each application area, from the huge number crunching requirements of modern multi-media standards such as MPEG, to the ultra-high speed data movement and analysis needs of networking, to the sensor and actuator interfacing aspects of automotive. This means that designing some functionality without keeping the hardware requirements in mind, in terms of both platform selection and platform configuration (e.g. by sizing bus widths and choosing peripherals) is absolutely unthinkable. Design once, run anywhere is not for embedded computing, or at least is limited to some non-real-time areas (e.g. user interfaces) and requires significant attention whenever the platform configuration changes.

1.1   The Metropolis Approach to Embedded Software Design

In this paper we propose a design methodology for embedded software, while paying close attention to the selection and configuration of the platform (both hardware and software) on which the application software runs. The methodology is based on the following key aspects.

First of all, it leaves the designer relatively free to use the specification mechanism (graphical or textual language) of choice, as long as it has a sound semantic foundation (Model Of Computation). Secondly, it uses a single formalism to represent both the embedded system and some abstract relevant characteristics of its environment and implementation platform. Finally, it separates orthogonal aspects, such as:

1. Computation and communication. This separation is important because:
   - refinement of computation is generally done by hand, by compilation, by scheduling, or by other complex techniques,
   - refinement of communication is generally done by use of patterns (such as circular buffers for FIFOs, polling or interrupt for hardware to software data transfers, and so on).
2. Functionality and architecture, or "functional specification" and "implementation platform", because they are often defined independently, by different groups (e.g., video encoding and decoding experts versus hardware/software designers in multimedia applications). Functionality (both computation and communication) is "mapped" to architecture in order to specify a given refinement for automated or manual implementation.
3. Behavior and performance indices, such as latency, throughput, power, energy, and so on. These are kept separate because:
   - when performance indices represent constraints, they are often specified independent of the functionality, by different groups (e.g., control engineers versus system architects for automotive engine control applications),
   - when performance indices represent the result of implementation choices, they derive from a specific architectural mapping of the behavior.

All these separations result in better *re-use*, because they decouple independent aspects, that would otherwise tie, e.g., a given functional specification to low-level implementation details, or to a specific communication paradigm, or to a scheduling algorithm. It is very important to define only as many aspects as needed at every level of abstraction, in the interest of flexibility and rapid design space exploration. They also allow extensive use of synthesis, system-level simulation and formal verification techniques in order to speed up the design cycle.

Another fundamental aspect that we considered throughout this work is the ability to *specify* rather than implement, *execute* reasonably detailed but still fairly abstract specifications, and finally *use the best synthesis algorithms* for a given application domain and implementation architecture, as exemplified by the Quasi-Static Scheduling algorithm discussed in Section 3. For these reasons, we represent explicitly the concurrency available at the specification level, in the form of multiple communicating processes. We use an executable representation for the computation processes and the communication media, in order to allow simulation, formal and semi-formal verification techniques to be used. Finally, we restricted that representation, with respect to a full-fledged programming language such as C, C++ or Java, in order to improve both *analyzability* and *synthesizability*.

1.2 Platform-Based Design

Platform-based design has emerged as one of the key development approaches for complex systems, including embedded systems, in the last several years. In the discussion above we informally referred to the notion of a platform, by using the IBM PC as an example. In [7], a first attempt at a precise definition of platform-based design is given, where an architecture platform is defined as a specific "family" of micro-architectures, possibly oriented toward a particular class of problems, that can be modified (extended or reduced) by the system developer. A platform instance can be derived from a platform by choosing a set of components from the platform library and setting parameters of reconfigurable components. The choice of a platform is driven by cost and time-to-market considerations and is done after exploration of both the application and architecture design spaces. Further, as embedded software developers need a platform abstraction to hide architecture details and define the services that the platform offers, an API platform is defined as the Programmer's Model for the abstraction of a multiplicity of computational resources and available peripherals contained within the architectural platform; it is a unique abstract representation of the architecture platform via the software layer. This abstraction usually consists of a software layer that wraps the essential parts of the architecture platform and includes, among others, RTOS and device drivers.

A platform can be described in terms of the type and quality of the services it offers to its users, which can be developers of: other services of the same platform, platforms at higher abstraction levels, or applications. In fact, an embedded system application can be considered as a top-level platform, offering services to the controlled environment (e.g. an engine) or the end user (e.g. a person making a cellular phone call). Quality of Service (QoS) parameters, e.g. processing speed and I/O bandwidth, define platform performance and reliability and therefore are the essential distinguishing factors between platforms. The task of the designer is finding the platform that best supports the applications. This requires quantifying the performances of a set of candidate platforms and choosing the best match between the QoS requirements of the applications and the QoS offered by the platform.

In this paper, we consider two levels of platforms. One is the Model Of Computation platform, or Application Platform, which abstracts away aspects such as synchronization, communication, and mapping onto computation and communication resources, e.g. as hardware or software. It is used for functional modeling in Section 2.1, and for mapping to a single-processor software platform in Section 3.1. Another one is the RTOS platform, which abstracts implementation aspects such as register saving for context switching, and peripheral access via drivers. It is used to refine the MOC platform in Section 2.2.

The remainder of the paper is organized as follows. In Section 2 we describe a meta-model that satisfies the goals outlined in the previous section, and illustrate how it can be used to *refine* an abstract specification, by implementing its communication requirements with platform services. In Section 3 we show how, by judiciously applying powerful static scheduling and inlining techniques, the overheads due to our modular specification and refinement mechanism can be recovered.

2 Metropolis Meta-model

In Metropolis, behaviors, architectures, and environments are all specified using the formalism called the *meta-model* [1]. To specify any of these, one needs the capability of describing the following aspects: *actions*, *constraints*, and their *refinements*. The meta-model has this capability, as presented in the rest of this section.

A behavior can be defined as concurrent occurrences of sequences of actions. Some action may follow another action, which may take place concurrently with other actions. The occurrences of these actions constitute the behavior of a system to whom the actions belong. An architecture can be defined by the actions it can provide (at a cost). Some actions may realize arithmetic operations, while others may transfer data. Using these actions, one can implement the behavior of the system.

A description of actions can be made in terms of *computation*, *communication*, and *coordination*. The computation defines the input and output sets, a mapping from the former to the latter. The communication defines a state and methods. The state represents a snapshot of the communication. For example, the state of communication carried out by a stack may represent the number of elements in the stack and the contents of the elements. The communication methods are defined so that they can be used to transfer information. The methods may evaluate and possibly alter the communication state. For the example of the stack, methods called pop and push may be defined. Actions for computation and communication often need to be coordinated. For example, one may want to prohibit the use of the pop method, while an element is added to the stack by the push method.

In the meta-model, special types of objects called *process* and *medium* are used to describe computation and communication, respectively. For coordination, one can use the await statement illustrated below, write formulas in linear temporal logic [6], or use schedulers, not discussed here, to describe a particular algorithmic implementation of constraints.

When an action takes place, it incurs cost. Cost for a set of actions is often subject to certain constraints. For example, the time interval between two actions may have to be smaller than some bound, or the total power required by a sequence of actions may need to be lower than some amount. The meta-model provides a mechanism, illustrated in Section 2.3, allowing a design flow modeler to define a quantity such as time or power, and a platform modeler to constrain the amount of such quantity to be associated with actions, by means of predicate logic. In the rest of this section, we present more in detail these key points of the meta-model and illustrate them with examples.

2.1 Processes, Media, and Netlists

Figure 1 shows a network of meta-model objects, where rectangles represent processes and circles represent media. It consists of two independent data streams. In each stream, the two processes on the left send integers, and the process on the right receives them. The medium in the middle defines the semantics of this communication.

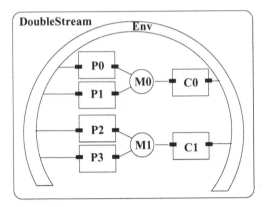

Fig. 1. A netlist of processes and media. The object around the processes is the environment, which is modeled by a medium in this example.

```
process IntX {
    port IntReader port0;
    port IntWriter port1;

    IntX() { }

    void thread() {
        int x;
        while (true) {
Rd:        x = port0.readInt();
Wr:        port1.writeInt(x);
} } }
```

```
interface IntReader extends Port {
    update int readInt();
    eval int n();
}

interface IntWriter extends Port {
    update void writeInt(int data);
    eval int space();
}
```

(a)   (b)

Fig. 2. (a) Process used in Figure 1 (b) Interfaces used for the ports of the process (a)

Processes are active objects in the sense that they take their own actions concurrently with those of other processes. The specifications of the processes in Figure 1 are given in Figure 2-(a). The syntax is similar to that of Java. A process always defines at least one constructor and exactly one function called thread, the top-level function to specify the behavior of the process. We call it *thread* because it is given as a sequential program to define a sequence of actions that the process takes. A process interacts with other objects through *ports*. A port is a special kind of field with the type being an interface. An interface declares a set of functions with the types of their inputs and outputs, without implementing them. A process may access its ports and call functions declared in the corresponding interfaces. The interfaces used in Figure 1 are shown in Figure 2-(b). The keyword update indicates that the corresponding function may change the state of a medium that implements the interface. Similarly, eval indicates that the function may only evaluate the state but not change it.

Figure 3 shows the specification of the media used in Figure 1. A medium implements interfaces by providing code for the functions of the interfaces. As with processes, a

```
medium IntM implements IntWriter,IntReader,IW,IR,IC,IS,IN {
    int storage, space, n;
    IntM() { space = 1; n = 0; }
    update void writeInt(int data) {
        await (space>0; this.IW, this.IS; this.IW)
            await (true; this.IC, this.IS, this.IN; this.IC) {
                space = 0; n = 1;
                storage = data;
            }
    }
    update int readInt() {
        await (n>0; this.IR, this.IN; this.IR)
            await (true; this.IC, this.IS, this.IN; this.IC) {
                space = 1; n = 0;
                return storage;
            }
    }
    eval int space() { await(true; this.IW, this.IC; this.IS) return space; }
    eval int n() { await(true; this.IR, this.IC; this.IN) return n; }
}
```

Fig. 3. Medium used in Figure 1

medium may define fields and functions, where some of the fields may be ports. They may not be accessed by objects other than itself. The only exception is that a function of an interface implemented by the medium object may be called by an object that has a port connected to the medium object. Such connections are specified in netlists, where a port may be connected to a single object of a medium type which implements the port's interface. With such a connection, a call of a function of the interface through the port will execute the code of the function provided in the medium.

Instances of the await statement often appear in functions of both processes and media. This is one of the most important constructs, since it is the only one in the meta-model to specify synchronization among processes in the execution code (in addition to the logic formulas described in [1]). It is used in situations where a process needs to wait until a certain condition holds, and once the condition becomes true, the process takes a sequence of actions. We call such a sequence *critical section*. Further, it is possible to specify actions that should not be taken by other processes while the process is in the critical section.

Consider the code of the process shown in Figure 4. Inside the keyword await, the parentheses specify a condition to be checked and actions to be excluded. This is followed by a specification of the critical section, inside the braces in the example. The parentheses consist of three sections separated by semicolons, which are called the *guard*, *test list*, and *set list* respectively.

The guard, a Boolean expression, specifies the condition that must hold when the execution of the critical section begins. In Figure 4, an interface function n() is called in the guard. Suppose that this function returns the number of data elements available in the storage of the corresponding medium object. Then the guard becomes true when both of the media connected to the ports of the process have at least one data element

```
process Y {
    port IntReader port0;
    port IntReader port1;
    port IntWriter port2;
    ...
    void thread() {
        int z;
        while (true) {
            await { (port0.n()>0 && port1.n()>0;
                port0.IntReader, port1.IntReader; port0.IntReader, port1.IntReader) {
                    z = foo(port0.readInt(),port1.readInt());
            } }
            port2.writeInt(z);
        } }
    int foo(int x, int y) { ... }
}
```

Fig. 4. Process using an await statement

respectively. This is the semantics used in dataflow and Kahn process networks, as exemplified in Section 3. In general, await is capable of modeling different semantics by using different guards. For example, if the conjunction used in the guard in Figure 4 is replaced by disjunction, then the guard becomes true if at least one of the media has data, which is the semantics employed in discrete event systems.

The test list specifies actions that must not be executing when the critical section starts. The set list specifies actions that should not start while the critical section is executed. For example, in Figure 4, both test list and set list contain an element specifying the IntReader interface of the medium connected to port0, indicating that the critical section is mutually exclusive to the set of actions that contains all function calls made by other processes to that medium through the IntReader interface (e.g. calls readInt() of that medium).

Multiple critical sections can be specified in a single await statement. If there are more than one critical sections that can be entered because their pre-conditions are satisfied, the process non-deterministically chooses exactly one of them to execute, and exits the entire await statement when the execution of the chosen section is completed.

2.2 Refinement

Once objects are instantiated and connected, some of them may be refined further to provide details of the behavior. Such details are often necessary when particular architecture platforms are considered for implementation. For example, the specification of Figure 1 assumes communication with integers, and each medium has a storage of the integer size. However, the chosen architecture may have only a storage of the byte size, and thus the original communication needs to be implemented in terms of byte-size communication. In the refinement, the semantics of the communication must remain the same as the original when observed from the processes, i.e. the processes can issue functions of reading and writing integers under the exclusion specified in the original medium.

Figure 5-(a) illustrates a refinement of the medium of Figure 3. In general, a refinement of an object is specified as a netlist of objects, and a refinement relation between the netlist and the original object is specified using the refine statement. Such a netlist is often specified by a designer who defines the architecture platform, and is stored in a library together with the original object being refined. Since this designer is in general different from a system designer who instantiates the platform objects to specify his system, it is usually unknown how the original object is used in a particular system. The system designer, who first instantiates the original object to constitute his system behavior, then chooses a particular refinement netlist for the object to meet cost/performance goals.

In Figure 5-(a), the refinement netlist RefIntM contains three types of media.

1. ByteM is the medium with a byte storage. It implements interfaces called ByteWriter and ByteReader, which are identical to IntWriter and IntReader except that the size of data is byte. One object of this type is used in the refinement, which may be provided externally.
2. ByteW implements the IntWriter interface so that each of its objects is connected from a port of an object (such as $P0$ in Figure 1) that originally accesses IntM with the interface. The function writeInt(), which is implemented by ByteW different from the higher-level version shown in Figure 3, is a very simple example of what in embedded software is known as a device driver. In the refinement illustrated graphically in Figure 5, it must be implemented so that it divides the integer into bytes and iteratively calls the write function writeByte() of ByteWriter while ensuring the exclusion specified originally (that no other process can execute the bodies of the functions of IntWriter implemented by the media in this refinement netlist during this period).
3. ByteR implements the IntReader interface and is connected from a port of an object (such as $C0$ in Figure 1) that originally accesses IntM with the interface. As with ByteW, in the implementation of readInt(), the read function readByte() of ByteReader (another example of simple driver) is called iteratively to compose an integer.

This refinement netlist is instantiated for each one of the original medium objects. The resulting netlist is depicted in Figure 5-(b). Note that both refinement netlists (RefM0 and RefM0) are instantiated with the same byte storage BM in place of ByteM. In this way, the byte storage is shared between the refinement netlists. This is possible for this particular refinement, because it allows the object of ByteM to be provided externally.

While hierarchical refinements are excellent for modularity and re-use, they may be inefficient when it comes to implementation. We will discuss in Section 3 how optimization techniques can be used to reduce the resulting overhead in the context of embedded software synthesis.

2.3   Quantity Constraints

To specify performance and cost constraints in the meta-model, a quantity, such as time, power, or Quality of Service, must be defined first, in terms of its domain (e.g. real numbers for time) and axioms that it must satisfy.

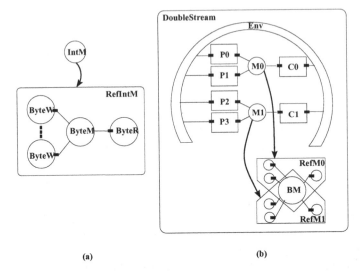

(a)   (b)

Fig. 5. (a) A Refinement of the Medium IntM (b) A Refinement of the netlist of Figure 1 using the refinement netlist given in (a). The objects shown with names are instantiated in the netlist DoubleStream,while those without names are created inside the refinement netlists of (a).

Then the amount of each quantity can be associated with the occurrence of each *event*, i.e. the beginning and ending of actions, in the behavior of the modeled system. For example, in the DoubleStream netlist, if we consider as an action the execution of the statement labeled with Wr in Figure 2 by the process $P0$, the beginning and the end of the execution are the events of this action. We then consider the i-th occurrence of an event e in a given execution of the behavior specified in a netlist. We denote it by $e[i]$, where i is a natural number. For example, beg(P0, P0.Wr)$[i]$ denotes the beginning of the i-th execution of the statement Wr by $P0$ that takes place in executing the behavior of the DoubleStream netlist.

The correspondence between the quantity and actions is established by defining a function $f(e[i])$, called *annotation function*, that designates the quantity associated with $e[i]$. This function is *computed* by the meta-model semantics (e.g., a simulator based on the meta-model, or a worst-case execution time analysis tool) based on *constraints* provided by the platform modeler. For example, a given piece of code in the behavior of a process requires to take at least some amount of units of processor time. All such amounts required during an execution by processes mapped to the same processor are accumulated by the quantity manager, thus providing an annotation of execution time to each action executed on that processor.

3   Software Synthesis for Concurrent Specifications

3.1   Models Of Computation as Metropolis Platforms

Concurrent specifications are interesting because they expose the inherent parallelism in the application, which is much harder to recover a posteriori by optimizing compilers. They arise quite naturally in data processing applications, which often employ particular

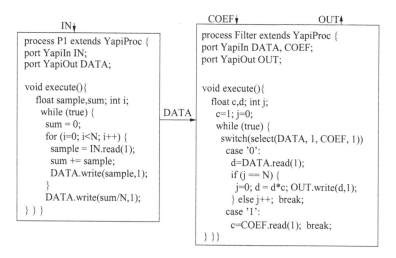

Fig. 6. Metropolis YAPI Platform

communication and computation semantics and are represented by Models Of Computation such as dataflow networks [5] or Kahn process networks [3]. Such models are provided as platforms in Metropolis [1]. One of the Metropolis platforms models an extended Kahn process network called YAPI [3]. It provides two interface types, a process type, and a netlist type for the user to capture designs. The interfaces include write and read methods, which are implemented in media to realize unbounded FIFO communication. They also provide a select method, which waits for possibly several ports to be enabled to read or write a given number of tokens, and non-deterministically chooses one of the enabled ports. The thread method of the process type iteratively calls a method called execute(), which is specified by the user to define the body of the process computation. The netlist type connects instances of the process type as specified by the user, while internally instantiating media to guarantee point-to-point connections. With this platform, the user specifies only the core algorithms of the specification and the resulting behavior is guaranteed to obey the intended semantics. Figure 6 depicts a meta-model specification made with this platform, where media are drawn by directed arcs to indicate that they are transparent to the user and the directed point-to-point communication is ensured by the platform.

Thus by inheriting from the YAPI process and media types, one can write process behaviors that are syntactically almost identical (and semantically identical) to those written using the C++ API described in [3].

3.2 Software Synthesis

Software implementation of concurrent specifications requires to solve a fundamental scheduling problem. *Static scheduling* techniques do most of the work at compile-time,

---

[1] Metropolis platforms are more general than just providing semantics of communication or computation, since the platform services are in general annotated with quantities and constraints to define cost to be charged when the services are used.

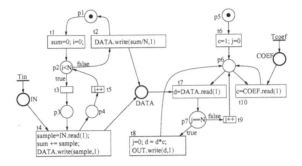

Fig. 7. Petri net for the specification of Figure 6

thus the resulting behavior is highly predictable [4] and the overhead due to task context switching is minimized. They may also achieve very high CPU utilization if the rate of arrival of inputs to be processed from the environment has *predictable regular rates* that are reasonably known at compile time. Static scheduling, however, is limited to specifications without run-time choice (called Marked Graphs or Static Dataflow [5]). Thus researchers have recently started looking into ways of computing a static execution order for operations as much as possible, while leaving data-dependent choices at run-time. This body of work is known as *Quasi-Static Scheduling* (QSS) [2].

We have developed a synthesis procedure to automate this step, where a quasi-static schedule of a specification captured in the YAPI Metropolis meta-model platform is computed, and the resulting implementation is generated (again using the meta-model) to refine the original specification. To use this procedure, the original specification must be represented by a Petri net, which is the model for computing a schedule. This can be done easily by a back-end tool of Metropolis, where the primitives of the YAPI platform are translated to Petri net fragments, while a syntax-driven translation is applied to abstract the user code to create the complete Petri net. Figure 7 shows a Petri net generated for the specification given in Figure 6.

The scheduling transformation can be represented as a *refinement*, as illustrated in Section 2.2, applied at the netlist level rather than at the medium level. One can write constraints, using the Linear Temporal Logic described in [1], to impose that the QSS procedure is correct, i.e. that the sequences of values observed on the outputs of the scheduled netlist are the same as those of the original netlist, if the input value sequences are the same.

3.3   Example: MPEG Decoder

We applied the QSS technique to an MPEG-2 video decoder developed by Philips [8]. The system is composed of 11 processes modeled in the YAPI platform with 51 communication arcs, as shown in Figure 8. The original specification was made of approximately 7700 lines, with 16 calls of communication primitives per process on average.

We focused our attention on five processes: Tisiq, Tidct, TdecMV, Tpredict and Tadd. They consist of about 3000 lines of code and account for more than half of all communications occurring in the system. The Petri net generated from the meta-model specification has 115 places, 106 transitions and 309 arcs. An example of the resulting

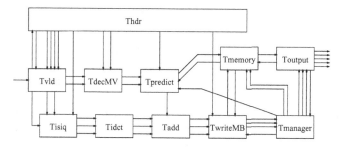

Fig. 8. MPEG-2 video decoder block diagram

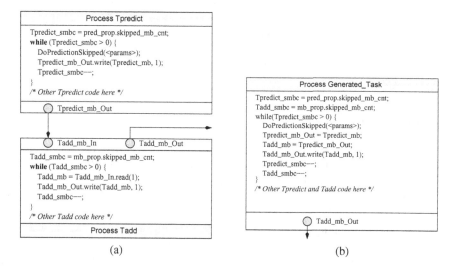

(a)   (b)

Fig. 9. (a) Example of meta-model specification, (b) Portion of the generated code for the MPEG-2 decoder.

code is shown in Figure 9. Figure 9(a) shows a small fragment of code taken from processes Tpredict and Tadd. They both implement a while loop during which they exchange some data. Figure 9(b) shows the same fragment of code in the synthesized process, which contains a single loop interleaving statements from the original processes. Note that the write and read calls in processes Tpredict and Tadd occurring on the medium connecting them have been transformed into assignments through a temporary variable, which can be easily eliminated by an optimizing compiler. The write call in Tadd on the output medium is instead preserved as is, which communicates with the rest of the system.

We compared the performance of the original concurrent specification of the MPEG-2 decoder with that of the same system where a single statically scheduled process is used in place of the five initial ones. In both cases, each process is treated as a single thread and multiple threads are managed by a run-time operating system. Both systems received as input a video stream composed of 4 images (1 intra, 1 predicted, 2 bidirectional predicted). Table 1 summarizes the total execution time on a Sun Ultra Enterprise 450 with 512 MBytes of main memory for simulating the two implementations. It also shows

Table 1. CPU time, in seconds, of the MPEG-2 example

	Total	MPEG2			Test	OS	Code
		Total	Parser	5Procs	bench		Size
Orig.	7.5	4.66	0.94	3.72	0.27	2.58	18K
QSS	4.1	2.51	0.94	1.57	0.28	1.31	24K

the individual contributions due to the processes implementing the MPEG-2 decoder, the test-bench and the operating system. The improvement in performance is around 45%, which is concentrated in the statically scheduled processes. The overhead due to communication between merged processes is drastically improved, because after scheduling we can statically determine that all media connecting the five considered processes never contain more than one element at a time. Therefore, communication is performed by assignment rather than by FIFOs. The table also reports the object code size, which increases in the generated single task with respect to the 5 separated process: this is due to the presence of control structures representing the static schedule in the synthesized code.

4   Conclusions

In this paper we argued that a formal design methodology is required for embedded software, just as it has become the standard for digital hardware. We also described some elements of such a methodology, by outlining how a model of computation, called the Metropolis meta-model, can be used to specify embedded software, as well as the platform on which it will run. This meta-model has a formally defined semantics, in order to define a precise meaning for refinement and optimization techniques. We showed how refinement can be used to identify implementation choices that are dependent on the chosen platform, such as for example the selection of drivers for a given bus protocol. We also illustrated how synthesis techniques can be used to recover part of the efficiency that is lost when using modular refinement-based specifications.

Acknowledgments

We would like to thank the whole Metropolis team for their work on the definition and implementation of the meta-model semantics and of the QSS algorithm. In particular, we acknowledge the contribution of: Rong Cheng, Jordi Cortadella, Robert Clariso, Gregor Goessler, Alex Kondratyev, Grant Martin, Marc Massot, Marco Pinello, Alessandro Pinto, Alberto Sangiovanni-Vincentelli, Marco Sgroi, Guang Yang. We also thank Jean-Yves Brunel, Erwin de Kock, Wido Kruijtzer for their help with YAPI and the MPEG example.

References

1. F. Balarin, L. Lavagno, C. Passerone, A. Sangiovanni-Vincentelli, M. Sgroi, and Y. Watanabe. Modeling and designing heterogeneous systems. Technical Report 2002/01, Cadence Berkeley Laboratories, January 2002.

2. J. Cortadella, A. Kondratyev, L. Lavagno, M. Massot, S. Moral, C. Passerone, Y. Watanabe, and A. Sangiovanni-Vincentelli. Task Generation and Compile-Time Scheduling for Mixed Data-Control Embedded Software. In *Proceedings of the 37th Design Automation Conference*, June 2000.

3. E.A. de Kock, G. Essink, W.J.M. Smits, P. van der Wolf, J.-Y. Brunel, W.M. Kruijtzer, P. Lieverse, and K.A. Vissers. YAPI: Application Modeling for Singal Processing Systems. In *Proceedings of the 37th Design Automation Conference*, June 2000.

4. H. Kopetz and G. Grunsteidl. TTP – A protocol for fault-tolerant real-time systems. *IEEE Computer*, 27(1), January 1994.

5. E. A. Lee and D. G. Messerschmitt. Static scheduling of synchronous data flow graphs for digital signal processing. *IEEE Transactions on Computers*, January 1987.

6. A. Pnueli. The temporal logic of programs. In *Proc. 18th Annual IEEE Symposium on Foundations of Computer Sciences*, pages 46–57, 1977.

7. A. Sangiovanni-Vincentelli and A. Ferrari. System design - traditional concepts and new paradigms. In *International COnference on Computer Design, ICCD '99*, October 1999.

8. P. van der Wolf, P. Lieverse, M. Goel, D.L. Hei, and K. Vissers. An MPEG-2 Decoder Case Study as a Driver for a System Level Design Methodology. In *Proceedings of the 7th International Workshop on Hardware/Software Codesign*, May 1999.

Author Index

Lecture Notes in Computer Science

For information about Vols. 1–2414
please contact your bookseller or Springer-Verlag